Cannae
Studies of Envelopment

Alfred von Schlieffen in 1906

Cannae
Studies of Envelopment

by

Alfred von Schlieffen

Foreword by
Robert B. Marks

Legacy Books Press
Military Classics

Published by Legacy Books Press
RPO Princess, Box 21031
445 Princess Street
Kingston, Ontario, K7L 5P5
Canada

www.legacybookspress.com

The scanning, uploading, and/or distribution of this book via the Internet or any other means without the permission of the publisher is illegal and punishable by law.

This edition first published in 2021 by Legacy Books Press
1

This edition © 2024 Legacy Books Press, all rights reserved.

Foreword © 2024 Robert B. Marks, all rights reserved.

ISBN: 978-1-927537-89-3

First published in the VI and X annual volumes of the "Vierteljarshifte für Truppenführung und Heereskunde" (1907-1913) E. S. Mittler and Son, Berlin.

This translation first published in English as *Cannae (Authorized Translation)* in 1931 by The Command and General Staff School Press, Fort Leavenworth, Kansas.

This book is typeset in a Times New Roman 11-point font.

Table of Contents

Foreword: Schlieffen – The Myth and the Man iii

Introduction. xxxvii

Chapter I – The Battle of Cannae 1

Chapter II – Frederick the Great and Napoleon 7

Chapter III – The Campaign of 1866 94
    The Prussian and Austrian Concentration 95
    The Campaign of 1866 in Germany 102
    The Campaign in Bohemia of 1866 until the Evening of 30
        June 135
    Koniggratz 201

Chapter IV – The Campaign of 1870-71 264
    From the Concentration of the Armies to the Retreat of the
        French across the Moselle 264
    The Advance of the Germans to and across the Moselle
    290
    The Battles of Colombey-Nouilly and Mars la Tour
    290
    The Battle of Gravelotte—St. Privat 332
    The Battles of Beaumont and Sedan 383

About the Author 470

Foreword: Schlieffen – The Myth and the Man
By Robert B. Marks

One might find it difficult to imagine a military theorist as mythologized as Count Alfred von Schlieffen (1833-1913). The creator of the "Schlieffen Plan," he is remembered in the general conception of the Great War as either a visionary mastermind who created a blueprint for the conquest of France that accounted for every detail, or a fool so obsessed with the Battle of Cannae and encirclement that he missed the obvious, plunging the world into war as a result. As is so often the case when men become myth, neither is true.

But, the myth remains, and the Schlieffen Plan and its failure in 1914 looms large over everything Schlieffen actually wrote or planned. Trying to part the mists and reveal the real Schlieffen brings one into conflict with decades of received wisdom. Part of this was due to historical mythmaking, while part was due to the fact that until the late 1990s, almost nobody working on Schlieffen's war planning had access to the original documents, either through obfuscation or (in some cases, perceived) destruction. For almost 90 years, all that anybody had to go on was the received wisdom, which they accepted or rejected based on the results of August and September 1914. Indeed, work on the

Schlieffen Plan up to the 1990s may be aptly described by misquoting Churchill: "Never has so much been written by so many who had read so little."

But, how did this come to pass, and what are we to make of the real Count Alfred von Schlieffen? To part the veil and made sense of the man, we first have to explore the making of the myth.

The Rise and Fall of the Schlieffen Myth

The end of the opening campaign of the Great War left many German generals with a conundrum: how had they gotten so far, only to lose at the Marne? To many, it appeared that victory had been within their grasp and snatched away. Many who had led troops in the campaign sought answers for a different reason: a desire to rehabilitate their reputation after losing a campaign they should have won.

As such, the mythmaking began almost as soon as the guns had fallen silent. Looking for somebody to blame, the fault for the defeat on the shoulders of Schlieffen's successor on the Great German General Staff, Helmuth von Moltke the Younger. But, in bringing Moltke down, they elevated Schlieffen and his war planning to legendary levels.

Hermann von Kuhl, the chief of staff serving under von Kluck in the First Army at the Marne, was one of the first to pick up his pen and declare that the fault lay with Moltke's modifications to Schlieffen's plan in his book on the Marne Campaign in 1920:

> Under General von Moltke, the successor of Count Schlieffen, a change was gradually made in the relation of forces between the right and left wings. General von Moltke had been loath to leave Alsace unprotected in the face of a probably successful French attack. The country was not to be vacated at once in case of a war and abandoned to every enemy operation. Initially, the XIV Corps was assigned to the protection of upper Alsace, and later a total of eight corps, in addition to the war garrisons of Metz and Strassburg and a large number of Landwehr brigades, were stationed in Alsace-Lorraine. The tasks of the Sixth and Seventh Armies were accordingly much extended.

> The Schlieffen plan was preferable. It was a very simple one. The main thought was brought out with the greatest clarity, and all other considerations were subordinated to it. The course of events in August and September, 1914, has demonstrated the correctness of Count Schlieffen's view.[1]

He further stated:

> Count Schlieffen had shown us the only correct way: only in movement was the victory for us to be won, only by victory was a decision of the war to be attained. An exhaustion strategy necessarily led to a war of position. As soon as we had thus lost freedom of movement, technique took the place of the art of leadership, the materiel battle the place of Cannae. In technique and materiel we were doomed to be just as inferior to our enemies as in food supplies after the establishment of the blockade. Germany became a besieged fortress, our battles were reduced to sallies on the part of the garrison to hold back the advance of the siege, until in 1918 we attempted once more to burst the ring by force. When this failed, the war was lost.[2]

It should be noted that when von Kuhl was writing in 1920, the supremacy of the Schlieffen Plan was far from accepted. An entire section of von Kuhl's first chapter was dedicated to a discussion of Schlieffen Plan detractors such as Hans Delbruck, Erich Falkenhayn, and Erich Ludendorff, and von Kuhl actively engages with the arguments of the Schlieffen Plan's critics. However, his conclusion in the end was unequivocal:

> If our concentration had been effected logically, according to the Schlieffen plan, the success, in so far as the human understanding can judge, could not have failed to be ours. Our advance to the north of the Marne completely surprised the French and upset their campaign plan. The great August battles might already have brought the decision; the battle of the Marne or of the Seine could certainly have

---

[1] Herman von Kuhl, *The Marne Campaign of 1914*. Kingston: Legacy Books Press, 2021, p. 26.

[2] Ibid., p. 33-34.

brought it in September when Joffre's measures presented us with the brilliant opportunity of throwing the French back toward the southeast.

The plan of Count Schlieffen was not outmoded; it was instinct with life, not "the recipe of the deceased Schlieffen." But we did not follow it.[3]

Von Kuhl's work was convincing, and that is not surprising. He had a clear understanding of the strategic principles behind the formation of the plan, and was less engaged with myth making than he was with arguing his interpretation of events. That Schlieffen would become mythologized at this time was not a foregone conclusion – the German official history of the war, whose first volume released in 1925, took a balanced approach to Schlieffen's war planning. This too, is not a surprise – the authors had full access to Schlieffen's war planning documents in the Berlin archives (known as the Reichsarchiv), and in the official history provided a summary of the strategic concerns that Schlieffen had considered, as well as his solutions leading to underpinning of the German strategy of 1914. They correctly identified his 1905 document laying out how an invasion of France could play out as a "memorandum," and not a war plan or deployment orders.[4] Their ultimate description of the document was both definitive and succinct:

> Schlieffen's December 1905 memorandum was based on that year's Deployment Plan I, in which the entire German field army would be sent to the West. But, it also called for the use of more forces than were actually available at the time. In this respect, the memorandum amounted to an argument for the expansion of the army as well as for improvements in its plan of mobilization.[5]

---

[3] Ibid., p. 316

[4] Mark Osborne Humphries and John Maker, eds. *Germany's Western Front: Translations from the German Official History of the Great War, 1914, Part 1.* Waterloo: Wilfred Laurier University Press, 2013, p. 65-68.

[5] Ibid., p. 68.

Foreword: Schlieffen – The Myth and the Man

It was clear from the German official history that the Schlieffen Plan had not been a document containing a master plan with timetables to be followed to the letter – instead, it was a set of strategic principles that Schlieffen had worked out during his time as the Chief of the General Staff which became the basis for German war planning to follow. This distinction would not last, and the December 1905 memorandum would soon displace Schlieffen's final operational orders as the "Schlieffen Plan."

Much of the fault for this lies with the Reichsarchiv itself. Having allowed access to the war planning documents to those writing the official history, it then restricted them to everybody else. Part of this was due to the impact they would have on the question of Germany's war guilt, and part of this was due to the fact that by 1934 they were being used once again for German war planning, turning them into military secrets.[6] It did not help that during World War II the German army archive in Potsdam was bombed, destroying everything within, including most of Schlieffen's war planning documents.[7] What this meant for historians was that they were now left with Schlieffen's 1913 book *Cannae*, what little the official history had quoted of Schlieffen's writing, and the confidence of generals like von Kuhl in their superiority.

By 1930, the Schlieffen myth had displaced reality. Basil Liddell Hart, who would wield an overpowering influence over World War I scholarship until his death in 1970, wrote about Schlieffen as a mastermind who had accounted for everything in his 1930 book *The Real War 1914-1918*:

> Schlieffen's plan allowed ten divisions to hold the Russians in check while the French were being crushed. It is a testimony to the vision of this remarkable man that he counted on the intervention of Britain, and allowed for an expeditionary force of 100,000 'operating in

---

[6] Hans Ehlert, Micahel Epkenhans, and Gerhard P. Gross, eds., *The Schlieffen Plan: International Perspectives on the German Strategy for World War I*. Kentucky: The University Press of Kentucky, 2014, p. 5-6.

[7] Humphries and Maker, p. 2.

conjunction with the French'. To him also was due the scheme for using the Landwehr and Ersatz troops in active operations and fusing the resources of the nation into the army. His dying words are reported to have been: 'It must come to a fight. Only make the right wing strong,'[8]

In 1930, when Churchill abridged and revised his account of the Great War into a single-volume addition published in 1931, he added his own commentary to the myth:

> The Schlieffen plan staked everything upon the invasion of France and the destruction of the French armies by means of an enormous turning march through Belgium. In order to strengthen this movement by every means, General von Schlieffen was resolved to run all risks and make all sacrifices in every other quarter. He was prepared to let the Austrians bear the brunt of the Russian attack from the east, and to let all East Prussia be overrun by the Russian armies, even if need be to the Vistula. He was ready to have Alsace and Lorraine successfully invaded by the French. The violation and trampling down of Belgium, even if it forced England to declare war, was to him only a corollary of his main theme. In his conception nothing could resist the advance of Germany from the north into the heart of France, and the consequent destruction of the French armies, together with the incidental capture of Paris and the final total defeat of France within six weeks. Nothing, as he saw it, would happen anywhere else in those six weeks to prevent this supreme event from dominating the problem and ending the war in victory.
>
> To this day no one can say that the Schlieffen plan was wrong. However, Schlieffen was dead. His successors on the German General Staff applied his plan faithfully, resolutely, solidly, — but with certain reservations enjoined by prudence. These reservations were fatal. Moltke, the nephew of the great Commander, assigned 20 per cent more troops to the defence of the German western frontier and 20 per cent less troops to the invasion of northern France than Schlieffen had prescribed. Confronted with the Russian invasion of East Prussia he still further weakened the Great Right Wheel into France. Thus as will be seen the Schlieffen plan applied at four-fifths of its intensity just

---

[8] Basil Liddell Hart, *The Real War 1914-1918*. London: Faber & Faber Limited, 1930, p. 61-62.

failed, and we survive to this day.⁹

The end of the Second World War, however, started the process of re-evaluating Schlieffen. Around 1950 Walter Görlitz published *The History of the German General Staff, 1657-1945*, which was translated and published in English in 1953. Görlitz still treated the Schlieffen plan as a master plan, but he also approached it as a gradual transition from earlier war planning, created as a reaction to Germany's strategic situation.[10] Like everybody else, however, Görlitz was hampered by not being able to read the document – his analysis was good, but only able to present the broadest of strokes.

The next major development in the understanding of Schlieffen and his war planning came in 1956 in Germany. Gerhard Ritter, a German historian, managed to locate Schlieffen's 1905 memo, a number of its drafts, as well as some surviving planning documents that had been captured by the American army and placed in the National Archives in Washington (and were later returned to Germany).[11] He published them in *The Schlieffen Plan: Critique of a Myth*, which was translated and published in English in 1958, with a Foreword by Basil Liddell Hart. For the very first time, scholars who were studying the war could actually read the famous document, as well as its drafts, along with Ritter's summary of Schlieffen's road to the famous memorandum.

Ritter had also made some important discoveries, one of which was that the final draft of the memo had been written in January 1906 and then back-dated to December 31, 1905 – Schlieffen's final day in office.[12] This meant that the December 1905 memorandum had not been part of Schlieffen's official duties, but something he

---

[9] Winston Churchill, *The World Crisis 1911-1918*. London: Thorton Butterworth, Limited, 1931, p. 155.

[10] Walter Goerlitz, *The History of the German General Staff, 1657-1945*. London: Hollis & Carter, 1953, p. 132-133.

[11] Gerhard Ritter, *The Schlieffen Plan: Critique of a Myth*. London: Oswald Wolff (Publishers) Limited, 1958, p. 14

[12] Ibid., p. 133.

had drafted on his own time as he left his position. This did not mean that his analysis was without issues – while he had seen more of Schlieffen's writings than anybody else since the publication of the German official history, he was still hampered by the fact that much of Schlieffen's work had not been captured by the American army, but instead stored in the Reichsarchiv in Potsdam, which had been destroyed.

Even despite its unavoidable shortcomings, Ritter's book was a major shift in the discourse. Scholars were now able to read the December 1905 memorandum and its drafts and realize that Schlieffen had not written a master plan for the invasion of France, but instead explored the strategic principles and challenges of such a campaign through a hypothetical that could never have been carried out in real life with the army Germany had at the time. There was no timetable involved in the memo, Russia was mentioned only in terms of the French not being able to depend on Russian support,[13] and it even concluded with a statement that even more divisions would be needed for a siege of Paris.[14] It is a testimony to the power of the growing Schlieffen myth that instead of being brought back to reality, Ritter's work initially helped it snowball.

Barbara Tuchman presented an updated version of the Schlieffen myth in her 1964 book *the Guns of August*. While she did reference Ritter's book (as well as the 1905) in her citations, her description of Schlieffen's plan bore little resemblance to the actual memorandum or the description by the German official history:

> Schlieffen's completed plan for 1906, the year he retired, allocated six weeks and seven-eighths of Germany's forces to smash France while one-eight was to hold the eastern frontier against Russia until the bulk of her army could be brought back to face the second enemy.[15]

---

[13] Ibid., p. 134-135.

[14] Ibid., p. 143-144.

[15] Barbara Tuchman, *The Guns of August*. Ballantine Books, 1984, p. 19.

Foreword: Schlieffen – The Myth and the Man

This was not the only misrepresentation of primary source documents in Tuchman's book – she also misrepresented the French doctrine, relocating the famous statement "The French Army, returning unto its traditions, no longer knows any law other than the offensive" to the beginning of the French Decree of October 1913,[16] when in reality it appeared in the appendix in a discussion about the importance of concentrating forces to ensure success before launching an attack[17] – but at least she knew that Ritter's book existed. The same cannot be said for Alistair Horne, who in his 1962 book *The Price of Glory* compared the Schlieffen plan to a blitzkrieg to knock out France before Germany turned its attention and forces to the east (which was true of how it developed), but added that, "Fortunately for France and unfortunately for Germany, Schlieffen's successor, Moltke, tampered with the master plan."[18]

A correction had begun in professional academic circles, however. Colonel T.N. Dupuy wrote in his 1979 book *A Genius for War: The German Army and General Staff, 1807-1945* that Schlieffen had been neither politically irresponsible nor militarily reckless, but was making the best decisions he could with what he had available.[19] Gunther E. Rothenberg's essay in the 1986 edition of *Makers of Modern Strategy from Machiavelli to the Nuclear Age* provided a reasonable and nuanced assessment based on Ritter's book and other available German sources. But with this correction came the beginnings of an over-correction, as writers began to shift the blame for the failure of the Schlieffen plan from Moltke to Schlieffen himself, specifically his study of the battle of Cannae and the lessons he learned from it.

---

[16] Ibid., p. 33.

[17] Ministère de la Guerre. *Service des Armées en Campagne: Conduite Des Grandes Unités, Volume arrêté à la date du 28 octobre 1913.* Paris: Henri Charles-Lavauzelle, 1913, p. 50.

[18] Alistair Horne, *The Price of Glory: Verdun 1916.* London: Penguin, 1993.

[19] T.N. Dupuy, *A Genius for War: The German Army and General Staff, 1807-1945.* Eaglewood Cliffs: Prentice Hall, Inc., 1977.

Foreword: Schlieffen – The Myth and the Man

In the Preface of the Command and General Staff College Press edition of *Cannae*, published in the early 1990s, Richard M. Swain, the Director of the Combat Studies Institute, closed his introduction to Schlieffen's "Cannae Studies," by stating:

> ...it is probably not remiss to caution readers that Hannibal's victory at Cannae still did not produce a strategic success, even though it was a tactical masterpiece. Hannibal lost the war with Rome. Likewise, Schlieffen's operational concept collapsed in World War I in the face of logistic and time-space realities he had chosen to discount because he believed they were inconvenient to his needs. The lesson to be learned from Schlieffen's experience is that history misapplied is worse than no history at all.[20]

Holger Herwig went even further. In his essay for the 1992 book *The Making of Strategy: Rulers, States, and Wars*, he declared that:

> Driven by a fanatical belief in a Cannae miracle, Schlieffen blithely ignored anticipated British forces on the continent, overestimated the combat-readiness of German reserves, rejected Clausewitz's principle of the "diminishing force of attack," and contemplated a siege of Paris requiring seven or eight army corps – forces that as yet existed neither in reality or on paper. Had the chief of the general staff conveniently overlooked the fact that in 1870 the elder Moltke had enjoyed a numerical advantage of seven infantry divisions over the French? Grandiose visions of German troops marching through the Arc de Triomphe with brass bands playing the "Paris Entrance March" substituted for Bismarckian Realpolitik.
>
> Schlieffen, in short, possessed no eye for broad strategic and political issues. He allowed no room for Clausewitz's notion of the "genius of war"; his rigid operation studies permitted no free scope for command; his widely acknowledged operational expertise had evolved only in war games, staff rides, and theoretical exercises without a battlefield test. The plan bearing his name was a pipe dream from the beginning. It was criminal to commit the nation to a two-front operation gamble with the full knowledge that the requisite

---

[20] Alfred von Schlieffen, *Cannae (Authorized Translation)*. Fort Leavenworth: U.S. Army Command and General Staff College Press, 1992, p. i.

Foreword: Schlieffen – The Myth and the Man

forces did not exist and that, given the mood of the Reichstag and War Ministry, they were not likely to materialize in the near future.[21]

Herwig, too, took aim at Schlieffen's analysis of the Battle of Cannae, declaring that Schlieffen had apparently failed to notice that, "while winning the battle, Hannibal lost the war, or drew the deeper lesson that Carthaginian land power eventually succumbed to Roman sea power!"[22] In 2000 Geoffrey P. Megargee also represented Schlieffen as an inflexible military thinker who discounted basic principles of war, repeating the idea that Schlieffen had required armies to move according to strict timetables and that he had attempted to remove "any opportunity for flexibility or initiative."[23]

This was nothing compared to what was to come. An American historian named Terence Zuber, a former U.S. Army who received his Ph.D. from the University of Wuerzburg, made a remarkable discovery – a number of the German war planning documents, including material written by Schlieffen, had survived the Second World War. Prior to the bombing of the Reichsarchiv building in Potsdam, they had been moved to a different location for research purposes, where they had been captured by the Soviets.[24] In a 1999 article published in *War in History*, he astounded the Anglophone academic community with the revelation that between Schlieffen's surviving writing and Wilhelm Dieckmann's unfinished historical survey *Der Schlieffenplan*, it was now possible to reconstruct much of German war planning prior to the Great War, and it was not what it had first appeared.[25] In fact, Zuber concluded:

---

[21] Holger H. Herwig, "Strategic uncertainties of a nation-state: Prussia-Germany, 1871-1918." Published in Williamson Murray, MacGregor Knox, and Alvin Bernstein, eds., *The Making of Strategy: Rulers, States, and War*. Cambridge: Cambridge University Press, 1994, p. 260-261.

[22] Ibid., p. 274.

[23] Geoffrey P. Megargee, *Inside Hitler's High Command*. Lawrence: University Press of Kansas, 2000, p. 11.

[24] Zuber, "The Schlieffen Plan Reconsidered". *War in History* 1999 6 (3), p. 270.

[25] Ibid., p. 270 onwards.

It is therefore clear that at no time, under either Schlieffen or the younger Moltke, did the German army plan to swing the right wing to the west of Paris. The German left wing was never weak; rather it was always very strong – indeed, the left wing, not the right, might well conduct the decisive battle. The war in the west would begin with a French, not a German attack. The first campaign would end with the elimination of the French fortress line, not the total annihilation of the French army. It would involve several great conventional battles, not one battle of encirclement. If the Germans did win a decisive victory, it would be the result of a counter-offensive in Lorraine or Belgium, not through an invasion of France. There was no intent to destroy the French army in one immense Cannae-battle.

There never was a 'Schlieffen plan'.[26]

Zuber was not the first to analyze Dieckmann's *Der Schlieffenplan* – that honour probably goes to Stig Förster, who published an analysis of it in German in 1995[27] – but he was the first to publish anything about it in English. To call the paper a bombshell is an understatement – in a single article, Zuber had upended everything known about German war planning in English-language scholarship.

Terence Zuber's place in the understanding of Schlieffen and German war planning is both significant and controversial. On one hand, Zuber single-handedly did more to bring previously unknown sources into English than any other scholar – he followed up his article with a 2002 book titled *Inventing the Schlieffen Plan: German War Planning 1871-1914*, in which he summarized the documents he was working from and further developed his argument that the entire idea of the Schlieffen Plan had been a myth. In 2004 he published *German War Planning 1891-1914*, which translated many of these documents into English, including Dieckmann's *Der Schlieffenplan*, and followed that up in 2011 with *The Real German War Plan 1904-1914*, in which he summarized additional and newly discovered war planning documents. His work also started what could be described as a scrum through various archives by scholars to locate and analyze

---

[26] Ibid., p. 305

[27] Gerhard P. Gross, "There Was a Schlieffen Plan." Published in *The Schlieffen Plan: International Perspectives on the German Strategy for World War I*, p. 93.

Foreword: Schlieffen – The Myth and the Man

as many of the surviving documents as could be found. Robert T. Foley published his own translation of a number of Schlieffen's documents in 2003 under the title *Alfred von Schlieffen's Military Writings*, including a number of post-1906 documents demonstrating Schlieffen's views of military developments after his retirement. In 2014 the papers from a 2004 German conference on Schlieffen in Potsdam were translated and published into English as *The Schlieffen Plan: International Perspectives on the German Strategy for World War I*, and included in its appendix translations of the surviving deployment plans from 1893-1914. Arguably, without Zuber's article in *War in History*, this either would have happened much more slowly or not at all.

Zuber's thesis, however, set off a firestorm and a running war of words lasting until around 2014 between Zuber, Robert T. Foley, Annika Mombauer, and Terence Holmes. The unfortunate result was a polarization of the debate that made it at least as much about Zuber's thesis as it was about the widening picture of German war planning. The 2004 conference on Schlieffen was telling – sold to Zuber as a two day opportunity for debate on the meaning of the documents with the documents present for examination, he arrived to discover that there were no documents present, the conference would be a single day with no session for debate at all, and the press present to report on it.[28] The introduction published in the English edition of *The Schlieffen Plan: International Perspectives on the German Strategy for World War I* described the purpose of the conference entirely in terms of Terence Zuber:

> Since Zuber's provocative thesis caused such a stir, it seems reasonable to bring together all sides of the debate to the Military History Research Institute in Potsdam in the autumn of 2004. The object of such a meeting was to discuss Zuber's pertinent theses and perhaps convince him to modify them if necessary, in order to establish a basis for debate.[29]

---

[28] Terence Zuber, *Inventing the Schlieffen Plan: German War Planning 1871-1914*. Oxford: Oxford University Press, 2014, p. xiv-xv.

[29] *The Schlieffen Plan: International Perspectives on the German Strategy for World War I*, p. 9.

It would be safe to say that the discussion was not dispassionate. While only the participants of the conference and the media who were there can speak with any certainty as to its true tone, one cannot help but raise an eyebrow at Robert T. Foley quoting von Kuhl explicitly stating the Schlieffen was using his staff rides to work out operational ideas and then declaring that they were mainly training tools for officers, followed by declaring that Zuber stood in a "long line of apologists" arguing against German war guilt.[30] One also cannot blame Terence Zuber for refusing permission to publish his paper in the English edition of the conference proceedings.[31]

But between the mythmaking and over-corrections, the revelations and controversies, one also cannot help but feel that the real Schlieffen has become somewhat lost in the debate. So, what do we make of Alfred von Schlieffen, his book *Cannae*, and his famous (or perhaps better put, infamous) Schlieffen Plan?

The Real Schlieffen

When one looks at Schlieffen through his biography, one finds a brilliant and accomplished mind peering back. It is quite possible that he never originally intended to make the military his career – his enlistment in the 2nd Guard Uhlans was as a one-year volunteer. His family background was not that of Prussian military family with a long history of service; instead, he was from a line of "Kolberg burgesses who had been mayors and aldermen," whose "great successor had the habit of attributing his own industry to the traditions of these simple, dutiful folk."[32] The rise of the Prussian

---

[30] Robert T. Foley, "The Schlieffen Plan – A War Plan". Published in *The Schlieffen Plan: International Perspectives on the German Strategy for World War I*, p. 72 and 79

[31] *The Schlieffen Plan: International Perspectives on the German Strategy for World War I*, p. 14.

[32] Goerlitz, p. 127.

kings brought the Schlieffens their title and lands, but Schlieffen himself would always be proud of his commoner heritage.[33] Schlieffen's father had been a Major in the 2nd Foot Guards, however, but this didn't inspire Schlieffen to follow his example – instead, Schlieffen went to university to study law.[34] Once in the 2nd Guard Uhlans he discovered that the military life suited him, and he transferred to the regular service before his enlistment was up, being commissioned as an officer in 1854.[35]

The Prussian army must have found that Schlieffen suited them just as well – they quickly put him into a fast-track position. He gained early admission into the War Academy and was appointed into the General Staff in 1865, just in time for the Prussian war against Austria. This brought him into action on the battlefields of Munchengratz, Gitschen, and Koniggratz. This would not be the only war in which he saw action on the battlefield – he served in the field during the Franco-Prussian War as well, seeing action at Noisseville, Toul, Soissons, and the Loire.[36]

But, while the start of his military career suggested that a meteoric rise through the ranks into prominence might have started, combat experience soon brought Schlieffen's suitability for the General Staff into doubt. He had the misfortune to be assigned to work as a staff officer under the Grand Duke of Mecklenburg, whose performance was poor enough to raise doubts about everybody who had served under him. When, Moltke the Elder determined that Schlieffen was otherwise an excellent officer, he lacked the initiative and decision making abilities that were

---

[33] Dupuy, p. 128.

[34] Ibid.

[35] Gunther E. Rothenberg, "Moltke, Schlieffen, and the Doctrine of Strategic Envelopment". Published in Peter Paret, ed., *Makers of Modern Strategy from Machiavelli to the Nuclear Age*. Princeton: Princeton University Press, 1986, p. 311.

[36] Rothenberg, p. 311; V.J. Curtis, "Understanding Schlieffen", *The Army Doctrine and Training Bulletin* 6, no. 3 (2003), p. 56.

required for an officer of the General Staff.[37]

How much this bothered Schlieffen was difficult to say – the military was only one part of a full and happy life. The young officer who entered his military career was enough of a hell-raiser to be nicknamed "Crazy Schlieffen." In 1868, however, he settled down into wedded bliss with his cousin, Countess Anna Schlieffen. This bliss only lasted four years – in the wake of the birth of their second daughter, Anna died, leaving Schlieffen bereft and heartbroken. He never remarried, and his military career (and children) became his life.[38]

This refocusing on military matters was enough to change Moltke's mind about him, and in 1875 Moltke decided that he was proper General Staff material after all.[39] In 1876 he left the General Staff to command the 1st Guard Uhlans, a position he held until 1884. At this point, he returned to the General Staff to head their military history section. This would not be the only section he would head, and the experience had clearly made him an ideal candidate for greater things – in 1889, he was appointed to be the first deputy of Count Alfred von Waldersee, the Chief of the Great General Staff. Two years later Waldersee had been sacked and the position went to Schlieffen.[40]

It would be difficult to find a more ideal candidate for the position in 1891 than Alfred von Schlieffen. He had a keen mind, had led troops on a battlefield, and decades of experience both working in and leading departments in the General Staff, capped off with two years learning the job of Chief of the General Staff under Waldersee. It is little surprise then, that despite his retirement at the end of 1905 he cast so long a shadow over the war planning that would follow.

---

[37] Daniel J. Hughes and Richard L. Dinardo, *Imperial Germany and War*, 1871-1918. Kansas: University Press of Kansas, 2018, p. 132

[38] Goerlitz, p. 128; Dupuy, p. 128.

[39] Hughes and Dinardo, p. 132-133

[40] Rothenberg, p. 311.

Foreword: Schlieffen – The Myth and the Man

But to understand how the Great General Staff conducted its war planning, one first has to understand the role of the Great General Staff. When one compares it to the general staffs of other countries, it can appear strangely limited in its scope. As Annika Mombauer wrote, it "created Germany's strategy, it devised the annual mobilization plan and had to ensure that the army was ready for war at all times."[41] The war planning was covered by the "Concentration Section," also known as Section 2, with the department head being the Chief of the Great General Staff, and its mandates were:

1. The military affairs of Germany.
2. Home defence.
3. Mobilization and concentration.
4. Troop exercises, with the exception of Kaiser Manoeuvres.
5. Exercises with signalling units, exercises in reconnaissance, technical artillery and engineering questions, so far as these are concerned with operations against fortresses, in conjunction with Section 4.
6. Results of Kaiser Manoeuvres, in conjunction with Section 6.
7. Observing and working out the technical development of Transport, both at home and abroad.[42]

The General Staff did not create or revise doctrine, which was the responsibility of the Minister of War and unit commanders, nor did it determine the structure of the army, which fell to the Minister of War and the Reichstag, nor did it get to determine appointments to high positions, which fell to the Kaiser's Military Cabinet.[43] This left any Chief of the Great General Staff in the odd position of having to determine where the German army would

---

[41] Annika Mombauer, *Helmuth von Moltke and the Origins of the First World War*. Cambridge: Cambridge University Press, 2001, p. 14.

[42] General Ludendorff, *The General Staff and its Problems: The History of the relations between the High Command and the German Imperial Government as revealed by Official Documents, Vol. 1*. London: Hutchinson & Co., 1920, p. 1.

[43] Mombauer, p. 14.

fight with relatively little say in how it would fight, or what it would fight with. Chiefs could make requests for changes, such as an increase in the number of divisions, but requests were all they could make.

The Great General Staff, and particularly its chief, was also limited in what they could do in the political sphere. The relationship between the German General Staff and the German politicians was very one sided – those in the political sphere could exercise influence on the Great General Staff to ensure that war planning would support foreign policy goals, but the General Staff could not exercise influence on policy. Attempting to do so was a career-ending mistake for any Chief of the General Staff, as Schlieffen had witnessed first-hand when Waldersee had attempted to convince the Kaiser to stop the naval buildup and lost his job as a result.[44]

This placed Schlieffen in a bind. He was well informed of German foreign policy through weekly meetings with Freidrich von Holstein, the Privy Councillor in charge of German foreign policy.[45] He was therefore able to make changes and alterations to each year's deployment orders to meet the requirements of foreign policy. But, he could not directly state that something was a bad idea on a military level and suggest that policy be changed to avoid it, and getting the men he would need to carry out the requirements of the German government required him to first sell the Minister of War on the idea, who would then have to convince the Reichstag. This left him often having to take an indirect approach, such as describing a scenario in which the German army does not have enough units to finish an invasion of France to make the point that the German army needed to be expanded.

Schlieffen's writing upon taking up the mantle of Chief of the Great General Staff can be divided into two broad categories:

---

[44] Rothenberg, p. 315.

[45] Gross, p. 112.

Foreword: Schlieffen – The Myth and the Man   xxi

1. Deployment orders (*Aufmarsch*). These were the actual German war plans that the army was expected to carry out in the case of war, issued each April 1st and covering the next twelve months. There were often at least two, if not three variants, covering a war against France, a war against Russia, or a war against both. They were based on a combination of the German foreign policy requirements for that year, intelligence estimates of enemy intentions and capabilities from the "Language Section," and the capabilities of the German army. At the end of each mobilization year, the new deployment orders would be issued and the old ones gathered up and burned.[46]

2. Hypotheticals. These can be further divided into three sub-categories, the staff rides (*Generalstabreisen*), annual winter war games (of which only one write-up survives), and memorandums (*Denkschrift*). While some of these did become the basis for deployment orders, a number did not. These explored either what would happen if the German army attempted a thing, or what it would take for the German army to accomplish a thing. As such, these often assigned to the German army units it did not have, and had no way of raising at that time.

It is arguably the hypotheticals that cause historians the most difficulties in understanding the development of Schlieffen's strategic thought. While the assumption that an individual will develop their ideas in a relatively linear fashion – moving from the initial premise to refinements and variations of it – Schlieffen's intellectual methodology as Chief of the General Staff could be best described as a series of shotgun blasts, with anywhere from no ideas to a few ideas to all ideas from any given part of each blast later being incorporated into his strategic thought. This has left scholars like Zuber and others in a situation of attempting to find an end point representing the culmination of Schlieffen's doctrine,

---

[46] Mombauer, p. 34-41. It is a minor miracle that any copies survived.

and then figuring out what to do with all of the unused and unrelated threads. Many of the ideas from Schlieffen's first 1904 staff ride became incorporated into the deployment orders for 1905/1906, while few of the ideas from his annual winter war game in 1905 were used in the deployment orders for 1906/1907.

But while this methodology may have been confounding to historians and undoubtably infuriating to those officers who had to put up with it (who in 1904 rebelled and forced Schlieffen to redo the staff ride, but this time with the actual army units they would have to command in a war),[47] it worked for Schlieffen. The staff rides, which were a sort of outdoor manouevre in which only the commanding officers were involved, had a purpose in training officers for command in the field – but, as von Kuhl wrote, they also served as one of Schlieffen's primary laboratories for working out operational concepts:

> It is no lie that Graf Schlieffen usually altered now and then the course of General Staff rides and war games. For him, it was less about the free play of the two parties against one another than the carrying out of a particular operational idea. He tested how an operation would take place under particular circumstances, which courses of action a commander could find against the actions of an enemy. To this goal, he often deliberately put difficulties before one commander, while he made the situation easier for the other.[48]

How then, do we trace the development of Schlieffen's ideas, and of his focus on the Battle of Cannae? While the short answer may be "with difficulty," common threads can be found in his analyses. But, these threads must be considered within the context of the job he had to do and the strategic situation in which he had to do it.

Schlieffen took office in 1891 around the same time that Bismarck had been replaced by Wilhelm II, the secret alliance with

---

[47] Terence Zuber, *The Real German War Plan 1904-1914*. Stroud: The History Press, 2011, p. 22.

[48] Quoted and translated in Foley, p. 72.

Russia had been repudiated, and only a year before Russia would form an alliance with France. This meant that rather than facing a likely single front war with France in which he would be able to bring to bear superior numbers, he now had to figure out how to win a war on two fronts, one in which Germany would be outnumbered and outgunned.[49]

This would be the defining strategic problem for the entirety of Schlieffen's time as the Chief of the Great General Staff. He summed it up in 1891:

> Our past victories were gained with superior numbers. [...] [The] essential element of the art of strategy [is] to bring superior numbers into action. This is relatively easy when one is stronger from the outset, more difficult when one is weaker, and probably impossible when the numerical imbalance is very great.[50]

The first part of this problem rested in dealing with the French. Attempts to get the Reichstag to approve increases to the size of the army had just failed, and this left Germany in a situation where the French army was growing while the German army remained stagnant.[51] In 1891, however, it looked like between the strength of the French border fortifications and the fact that the French would probably wait for a German attack on those fortifications before counter-attacking, the question of what would happen in the West wasn't up to Germany at all, and main effort would have to be in the East to bolster the Austrians.[52] France still represented the greater threat, and Schlieffen wrote in April 1891 that "However

---

[49] Eric Born Brose, *The Kaiser's Army: The Politics of Miliary Technology in Germany during the Machine Age, 1870-1918*. Oxford: Oxford University Press, 2001, p. 76-77.

[50] Quoted in Rothenberg, p. 312.

[51] Wilhelm Dieckmann, *Der Schlieffenplan*, p. 11-12, translated and quoted in Terence Zuber, *German War Planning 1891-1914: Sources and Interpretations*. Woodbridge: The Boydell Press, 2004, p. 53.

[52] Ritter, p. 22.

much it goes against our tradition to build fortifications, we cannot, as the weaker side, reject the means used by our opponent to paralyse our military plans." However, if the Austrians could ever be properly integrated into the German war effort, "the French fortifications – since they could be by-passed through Belgium – would not form a great enough obstacle to rule out an offensive."[53]

When Schlieffen wrote this 1891 memorandum, the idea of bypassing the French fortifications by going through Belgium was not new, nor was Schlieffen its originator. It was also not an idea that would have been hard to come by – in the case of a war, the French border was lined by border forts on one side and a theoretical German military build-up on the other. The only way to bypass either was to go through another country – this left it as a choice between a heavily armed Switzerland to the south, and a far more lightly armed Belgium and Holland to the north. The choice of which would be preferable was not a hard one.

It was also one that was not missed by anybody who could read a map in the military, political apparatus, or press. Bismarck had asked Waldersee if going through Belgium was practical in the late 1880s, and Schlieffen had taken an earlier stand against a proposed string of German forts across Lorraine on the grounds that it would force the French army in an offensive to attempt to bypass the German army by going through Belgium. The press in multiple countries had also picked up on the idea, and frequently discussed the potential march through Belgium of either the Germans or the French. It was true that Britain would declare war on whoever violated Belgian neutrality, but they would also be slow enough to mobilize that by the time they could land in Antwerp, the march would be a *fait accompli*. The only way to go avoid the grind of attritional warfare at the French and German border was to march through Belgium, and everybody in the world seemed to know it.[54]

But, despite the speculations by the press and the discussions by politicians and military planners in the Great General Staff, a

---

[53] Ibid., p. 23.

[54] Dieckmann, p. 56-61, translated in Zuber, p. 71-73.

move through Belgium was not an option for Germany. While Russia had gone from a potential enemy to an almost certain one as Schlieffen took up his office, Britain was still considered a friend. As such, the German government, and therefore the General Staff, treated the neutrality of Belgium as sacrosanct.[55] The 1891 memo may represent Schlieffen flirting for the first time with the idea in his capacity as Chief of the General Staff, but flirting was all it was. It was wishful thinking that an easier option was not viable, rather than an actual intent.

Schlieffen therefore took the stance of keep the main effort in the East and letting the French wait for a German attack on the West while Germany and Austria dealt with Russia.(Ritter, p. 22) However, events the next year would render this approach near-impossible. As Schlieffen wrote in 1892, the challenge with Russia was that between the Russians re-orienting their own defences to deal with their new relationship with Germany, the massive size of their territory, and the signs that the Russian ability to mobilize had reached parity with Germany, a breakthrough in the East had become almost impossible:

> Even if [the intended breakthrough against Russia on the Narew line] should succeed, the enemy would not withdraw to the south, in order to run straight into the Austrians, but rather to the East, where he will find the railheads that he used to conduct his deployment. We will therefore not succeed in fighting a decisive battle and destroying the Russian army, but rather engage in frontal battles against an enemy who could withdraw into the interior of an immense Empire, while our lines of communications would be the least favorable that we could imagine and endangered to the highest degree.[56]

The German strategy of holding in the West while seeking a decision in the East was no longer workable. To make matters worse, any attempt to engage in offensive warfare in the East would reduce the troops available in the West to the point where

---

[55] Dieckmann, p. 61, translated in Zuber, p. 73.

[56] Dieckmann, p. 9-11, translated in Zuber, p. 52.

Germany would be unable to deal with French action.[57]

At this time, Schlieffen made the decision that would forever mark German war planning – on the grounds that it was necessary to first deal with the most dangerous enemy (France) with the greatest possible force, he abandoned anything but holding to the defensive in the East. As of the 1893/1894 deployment orders, three quarters of the German army would go to the West, where they would defeat the French. The problem was how this was to be done – a frontal assault on the French border forts would be inadvisable at best, and all indications were that any offensive by the French army, which would outnumber the Germans would not be so foolish as to attack where the German line was strongest, but instead go around, meaning that waiting for a French attack would simply mean waiting to be flanked by a superior force. There was one possible option, however: the town of Nancy was not fortified, and if the Germans attacked before the French were ready for their own offensive with enough artillery, it could be taken and used to break through the French lines to the Meuse river.[58]

Unfortunately, as this was happening yet another attempt to convince the War Minster to increase the capabilities of the army had failed.[59] The attack on Nancy was already a gamble, and a bad one. It was unlikely to succeed for some very simple reasons, as Schlieffen wrote in a July 1894 memorandum:

> The French mobilization is compressed to the highest degree. It will be difficult to surpass our opponent. The French deployment has also become just as fast as ours.[60]

Schlieffen's options coming out of 1894 were all bad, and this would continue to be the trend. Any frontal attack on the French

---

[57] Deickmann, p. 11, translated in Zuber, p. 53.

[58] Dieckmann, p. 11-21, translated in Zuber, p. 53-57.

[59] Dieckmann, p. 38-40, translated in Zuber, p. 62-63.

[60] Dieckmann, p. 50, translated in Zuber, p. 68.

Foreword: Schlieffen – The Myth and the Man   xxvii

fortresses would almost certainly land the German army in, as Dieckmann noted as he discussed Schlieffen's fears about the situation, a "laborious and costly struggle, trench warfare of indeterminate length and yet to an uncertain conclusion."[61] Schlieffen had noted in his 1894 memorandum that there was one solution – bypass the French forts by going north around Verdun while supported by a frontal attack on the fortresses.[62] Unfortunately, the only way to accomplish this was to take the army through Belgium, which Schlieffen was forbidden from doing. Part of the foreign policy situation was changing, however. Due to a number of factors, including clumsy German policy, the relationship between Germany and Britain was degrading, and it began to look like Britain would be taking arms against Germany anyway.[63] In a probable bid to forestall this emerging delicate situation, the German deployment orders for 1897-1898 included an instruction to the First army that "The Belgian border must not be crossed."[64] But, this situation also meant that it might be possible to take troops through Belgium after all.

Schlieffen promptly worked out a hypothetical to see just viable an outflanking manoeuvre to the north of Verdun would be. In his memorandum of August 2, 1897, he ran through a scenario in which Germany not only would outflank the French border forts but succeed in doing so. Having first established that the territory between Verdun and the Belgian border was too small for the manoeuvre, he ran through the scenario in which Germany marched through Belgium.

The results were decisive. The problems began to emerge almost immediately. The two manoeuvring armies would require a third army to provide cover. As soon as they passed Verdun, they

---

[61] Dieckmann, p. 56, translated in Zuber, p. 71.

[62] Dieckmann, p. 57, translated in Zuber, p. 71.

[63] Dieckmann, p. 61-62, translated in Zuber, p. 73.

[64] Aufmarsch 1897-1898, translated in *The Schlieffen Plan: International Perspectives...*, p. 356

would find themselves alone against most of the French army. The only way to alleviate that would be to attack the French border forts with three additional armies. A seventh army would be required to protect Alsace. Just to succeed would not only require the entire German field army, but the raising of dozens of additional units and reserve divisions.[65]

There could be no question – a march through Belgium would not work. The deployment orders of 1898-1899 not only once again included instructions to the First Army that the Belgian border was not to be crossed, but provided instructions for the defence of the armies various lines.[66] If the German army was going to get a decision against France, it would have to start with a defensive battle and a counter-attack.

For the next four years, winning a defensive battle before taking the war to France became the cornerstone of Schlieffen's strategy. It wasn't as though Schlieffen had any choice in the matter – a defensive stance in the West was the only hope of engaging the French in such a way as to ensure the destruction of the French army. As he wrote as part of his staff ride write-up in 1901,

> A German advance against the French fortresses does not appear wise in a two-front war. We must wait for the enemy, who will eventually advance out of his protective walls.
> [...]
>   We must hold firmly to one principle. We must conduct enveloping attacks against the enemy's line of retreat, for in a two front war we require complete victories![67]

Schlieffen also recognized the problem of Germany's interior lines of communication. Although many would see these as a strength in a two-front war, Schlieffen correctly realized that for

---

[65] Dieckmann, p. 64-67, translated in Zuber, p. 74-76.

[66] Aufmarsch 1898-1899, translated in *The Schlieffen Plan: International Perspectives...*, p. 360-365.

[67] Translated in Zuber, *German War Planning 1891-1914*, p. 142.

Germany it was an exploitable weakness, one so severe that failure to win a decisive victory at the beginning would make any war unwinnable. He noted in his write up of a 1903 staff ride,

> The question is, what was Germany to do? If it acted in the east as it had done in the west, and driven the enemy behind the Narew, the Vistula, or some other line, it would have soon seen itself forced to send at least some of the corps back to the west to oppose the renewed French advance. The Russians would have used this to renew their advance. After a time, we would have again needed to send troops from the west of the east. This back-and-forth movement of German troops, pushing the enemy back here and there, then a renewed enemy advance, is the sort of strategy which must lead eventually to the complete exhaustion of the German army.
>
> Such a war on two fronts can only be brought to an end by the most complete annihilation of one enemy, then the other, and not by throwing back one enemy or the other.[68]

Schlieffen's strategy was not a good solution to the problem, but at least it appeared to be one that could work. But then, in 1904 in the fields of Manchuria, everything changed.

It is impossible to overestimate the importance of the Russo-Japanese War (1904-1905) when it comes to the war planning in the years prior to the Great War. In many ways, one cannot understand how the opening strategies played out without the Russo-Japanese War. On the battlefields of Manchuria and the siege of Port Arthur, military observers got a proper preview of a modern trench war in all of its horror. The impact it had on the 3rd Section of the Great General Staff was to conclude that the French army would shift wholly to defensive warfare and wait behind their border forts for the Germans to come to them.[69] The impact it had on Schlieffen was to destroy any hope that the German army's strategy of winning a defensive strategy could succeed, even if the French did come to them. It was under these circumstances that

---

[68] Translated in Zuber, p. 153-154.

[69] Hellmuth Greiner, *The German Intelligence Estimate in the West*, p. 95, translated in Zuber, *German War Planning 1891-1914*, p. 22.

Schlieffen dusted off the possibility of a march through Belgium and gamed it out in his 1904 staff ride. If the 1897 memorandum had been on the level of a feasibility study, this brought it into the stage of operational planning. The irony that this probably made the German General Staff the *last* organization to give full consideration to a march through Belgium was not lost on Schlieffen:

> Given this situation, Britons and Americans who have studied the problem, as practical people with few scruples, have assumed that it is self-evident that the Germans will attack the French through Belgium. The Swiss have happily agreed in the hopes that in this way they will avoid damage to their own country. The Belgians have drawn a practical conclusion from the question. Earlier, so long as they only felt threatened by the French, they limited themselves to Antwerp. They would withdraw there and wait until the British or the Germans liberated them. In the current state of affairs they have fortified Liege-Namur, naturally against both neighbours, for the most part the Germans.
>
> The French have not considered the matter with the same enthusiasm as the less involved nations. They credit us with such a high offensive spirit that we will attack straight at their fortresses. They hope that the offensive will fail, and then they will attack us in the flank. Since this will hardly be possible except through Belgium and Luxembourg it can therefore be said that all the nations that have anything to do with the question expect the violation of Belgian neutrality to be a given fact. We would therefore be permitted at least to examine the matter more closely and academically.[70]

The exercise went well, and went on to become the basis of the deployment orders for 1905-1906.[71] The German strategy now included a march through Belgium. Schlieffen's mixed feelings and reservations about it, however, along with the degree to which the Russo-Japanese War loomed over his decision making, was clear in his 1904 staff ride write-up:

---

[70] Translated in Zuber, *German War Planning, 1891-1914*, p. 157.

[71] Aufmarsch 1905-1906, translated in *The Schlieffen Plan: International Perspectives...*, p. 416-423.

The defensive is the stronger form of war. Therefore it is usual for the party which perceives itself to be the weaker to take refuge in a defensive position. This is the beginning of the end, unless there are forces outside the defensive position which can effect a relief. If this is not the case, in the end even the best position will be made untenable by being outflanked or enveloped. If the envelopment is to succeed, it must be conducted in conjunction with a frontal attack. The Frontal attack must not wait for the envelopment. Rather, the flank attack must meet an enemy who has been fixed in place to the front.

[...] A few weeks ago a massed Russian rifle regiment was shot down by encircling Japanese troops. Nevertheless, one commander wanted to commit a closed-up mass of 32 battalions against the concentrate fire of enemy batteries and infantry.[72]

In the wake of this, Schlieffen's 1905 winter war game – perhaps the last thing he did before his retirement at the end of the year – seems almost to be driven by wishful thinking. It was huge, pitting Germany against France in the East and Russia in the West. The scenario was the opposite of the deployment plans – Germany defended against a French attack, while Britain joined Germany's side due to French violation of Belgian neutrality. The key to victory for Germany was to figure out which side to engage first:

To conduct an offensive against both and march with one army on Moscow and another on Paris would in the best case very quickly put us in a situation that Clausewitz characterized as "strategic emaciation". Even an offensive against one enemy alone, whether into the swamps and forests of Poland and Lithuania or into the maze of French fortresses, would require so many forces and so much time that too little would be left over for a defensive against the other. It is advisable to wait for our enemies to advance, and attack the first to cross our borders, then turn on the other. The enemy can thwart this plan by crossing our borders in the east and west simultaneously. The question then is, should we concentrate the strongest possible forces and first engage the stronger or the weaker enemy? There are many points for and against both courses of action.[73]

---

[72] Translated in Zuber, p. 164-165.

[73] Translated in Zuber, p. 168.

But, if there was one thing hanging over Schlieffen it was the problem of Manchuria and what it meant to the war to come. As Schlieffen wrote in his analysis:

> We could not conduct war in the Manchurian manner, pushing the enemy slowly from position to position, sitting for months inactively opposite each other, until both adversaries were exhausted and decided to make peace. Rather, we need to eliminate one enemy in the shortest possible time in order to be free to turn on the other.[74]

He further stated that:

> In a future war we will have to contend with long positions reinforced with field fortifications. The ability of a few troops in a more or less dug-in position to resist far superior enemy forces will easily lead to an increase in the incidence of positional warfare. The Russo-Japanese war has demonstrated that. Over in Manchuria it may be possible for the opposing sides to sit for months in invulnerable positions. In western Europe we cannot allow ourselves the luxury of waging war in this manner. The machine, with its thousand wheels which provides the livelihood for millions, cannot be brought to a halt for long. We cannot fight twelve-day battles, moving from position to position, for one or two years, until both sides, completely fought out and exhausted, sue for peace and accept the other's conditions. We must seek to quickly defeat and destroy the enemy.[75]

Schlieffen's method and hypotheticals suggest a mind that could not leave a sleeping problem lie, and this probably best explains why after his retirement, Schlieffen kept working on the problem – it would be the primary preoccupation of his retirement and remaining years. In January 1906, he finished what would become back dated and known as the December 1905 memorandum, and later "The Schlieffen Plan." It was a hypothetical trying to figure out what would be necessary to succeed in carrying out the strategic concepts he had adopted in his

---

[74] Ibid.

[75] Translated in Zuber, p. 174.

Foreword: Schlieffen – The Myth and the Man   xxxiii

final war plans and deployment orders. And, as he had concluded before, the German army just did not have the manpower needed to carry the campaign to a conclusion:

> Even more troops must be obtained. We have just as many ersatz battalions as infantry regiments. Form these battalions and the remaining troops from the reserve, if necessary from the Landwehr too, we must form forth battalions as we did in 1866, and from these and ersatz batteries create divisions and corps, as we did in 1866. It is possible to create eight corps in this fashion. We cannot wait to raise these new formations until the need for them has become painfully evident, when the operation has been brought to a halt, but rather immediately after the mobilization of the other units.[76]

Even with these additional units, the end to the campaign – the siege of Paris – remained its own problem, and his description of it would be familiar to any student of the Great War's Western Front:

> All along the line the corps will advance from position to position according to the principles of formal siege warfare. They will seek to close with the enemy by day and by night, moving forward, digging in, moving forward again, digging in again. They will use all the means of modern technology that are available to weaken the enemy in his field fortifications. The attack can never be allowed to come to a halt as it did in East Asia.[77]

It was in this context that Schlieffen came to publish his Cannae studies. Schlieffen spent his entire time in office as the Chief of the Great General Staff attempting to find a solution to an impossible situation, and never with any success. His writing reveals a keen mind that missed nothing. He knew what would be required for the German army to stand any chance in a two front war – he also knew from his hypotheticals and the calculations therein that it was not able to do it. He had been placed in the

---

[76] Translated in Zuber, p. 196.

[77] Translated in Zuber, p. 197.

position of knowingly issuing deployment orders that the army did not have the manpower to carry to a successful conclusion. Like just about all of the war planners in the years prior to the Great War, he was left having to implement a terrible solution, but it was the best option he had available.

However, the essential problem of the German position was the sort of conundrum that Schlieffen's mind could not put down. Germany was in a position where it had to win a war in which it needed to be able to strike an annihilating blow against an enemy who had superior numbers. There was a historical precedent for this on the battlefield, however: Hannibal at the Battle of Cannae.

As Schlieffen noted in his first chapter:

> A battle of complete extermination had been fought, most wonderfully through the fact that in spite of all theories, it had been won by a numerical inferiority. Clausewitz said "concentric action against the enemy behooves not the weaker" and Napoleon taught "the weaker must not turn both wings simultaneously." The weaker Hannibal had, however, acted concentrically, though in an unseemly way, and turned not only both wings, but even the rear of the enemy.

Schlieffen's *Cannae* occupies its own remarkable place in canon of military arts and sciences. While it never reached the prestige (or publication figures) of Clausewitz's *On War* or Jomini's *The Art of War*, it survived in the public consciousness of military history far longer than most of its contemporaries. It was well enough known that an episode of the alternate history Japanese animated series *The Saga of Tanya the Evil* had a library scene in which its titular protagonist struggled to reach a copy of *Cannae* from a high shelf.

Cannae also has a remarkable parallel with Clausewitz's *On War*: while *Cannae* was intended to be eventually published as a book, it too was never completed by Schlieffen within his lifetime. Instead, it was compiled together from the *Cannae Studies* he published in the General Staff's *Quarterly* between 1909 and 1913[78] and some of his collected writings by an editor after his death in

---

[78] Antulio J. Echevarria II, *After Clausewitz: German Military Thinkers Before the Great War*. Kansas: University Press of Kansas, 2000, p. 189.

1913. The text has multiple footnotes talking about battles that Schlieffen had intended to include, along with references of where to find discussions of them in his other writings.

Despite giving its name to the title, the Battle of Cannae receives a tiny number of pages. It is a miniscule slip of a first chapter, but one that sets the scene for the rest of the book. In Cannae was a perfect envelopment against a superior force. The following chapters would compare the campaigns of modern warfare against it, looking at where a result like Cannae was possible, but also where it was not and why the attempt at a battle of annihilation either succeeded or failed. The second chapter examines both the campaigns of Frederick the Great and Napoleon. However, the bulk of the book lies in chapters III and IV, covering the German wars of 1866 and the Franco-Prussian War of 1870-1871. These close with a brief discussion of the conditions that are required for a Cannae to take place.

Schlieffen has often been criticized for forgetting that Hannibal lost the war in the end. But this is at the least unfair – Schlieffen understood quite well that one can win a battle and still lose the war. He also understood that one cannot win a war without winning at least one battle, even if it is the final one. What Schlieffen was trying to figure out in the end was how to best win that battle. *Cannae* represents Schlieffen's final answer to the question that dogged him while he was the Chief of the General Staff: how does a smaller force defeat a larger one on the battlefield? The Battle of Cannae provided an answer, but it was a also a very unsatisfying one: you need a brilliant commander, skilled subordinates and an opponent who, through incompetent command, will help you do it. As Schlieffen ultimately concludes,

> All these desirable conditions will not be found combined on either side. A few of Hannibal's qualities and some of the means at his disposal were possessed by other generals. Terentius Varro, on the other side, was always the product of the school. Thus it happened, that, though no real Cannae, with the exception of Sedan, has been fought, there has been a whole series of nearly annihilating battles, and these have always been found at the turning points of history.

xxxvi   *Foreword: Schlieffen – The Myth and the Man*

Robert B. Marks has a Master of Arts Degree from the Royal Military College of Canada, and is the owner and publisher of Legacy Books Press. He is also the translator (with the aid of translation software) of Grandmaison's Training of the Infantry for Offensive Combat, The French Doctrine of 1913, *Joffre's* Memoirs *(Vol. 1), and Moltke the Younger's* Memories, Letters, and Documents. *His primary research focus is the rise of the Cult of the Offensive in the years prior to the Great War.*

Publisher's note: Schlieffen's *Cannae* relied upon over a hundred maps to illustrate his analysis and guide the reader. For this edition, the maps have been integrated into the text for ease of understanding. As much as possible, they have also been restored. Additionally, the text has been reformatted for ease of reading.

Introduction

The work of General Field Marshal Count von Schlieffen, as Chief of the General Staff of the German army, took place remote from publicity. Since the World War, however, his name is mentioned by all. It came to be known that it was his spiritual heritage which, at the beginning of the war, brought to the German arms their great successes. Even where his doctrines were misapplied, his schooling of the General Staff remained, nevertheless, a priceless possession.

Strictly, the Cannae studies of Count Schlieffen are not presentations from Military History. They comprise, rather, a conversational document of instruction. Just as the Field Marshal, in his activity as Chief of the General Staff of the Army, always endeavored, during the long period of peace, to keep alive in the General Staff, and thus in the army at large, the idea of a war of annihilation, so, likewise, is this expressed in his writings. Germany's situation demanded a quick decision. Though the Count set great store on the efficiency of the German army, he was, nevertheless, always preoccupied with thoughts of how our leaders would acquit themselves when the time came. Hence. in his writings he often attributes his own ideas to the leaders of the Past—among them Moltke—when he wishes to prove that to achieve a decisive victory of annihilation outflanking—preferably from two or three sides—-must be resorted to, as Hannibal did at Cannae. In everything which Count Schlieffen wrote the two-front war which threatened Germany hovered before him. In such a war we would be victorious only if soon after its outbreak we succeeded in obtaining an annihilating defeat of France. Modern battles Count Schlieffen characterizes even more than earlier battles as a "struggle for the flanks." Therefore he stresses the necessity, in case parts of an army have made frontal contact with the enemy, that the neighboring columns be allowed to march further so that they may be able to turn against flank and rear. In this method of presentation the Count is not always just to the actors of war history, especially the subordinate leaders of our own army of 1866 and 1870-71. However, he explains their conduct as born of the Napoleonic traditions in the absence of war experience by their own generation. Notwithstanding the severity of his judgement, the writings of the Field Marshal show a real appreciation of true military art, for within him there abided an incomparable military fire. The reckless urge to the offensive of our Infantry he emphasizes as the pre-requisite to victory.

Notwithstanding the sharp delineation of the Cannae doctrines Count Schlieffen was no schematist. He knew that in war many means lead to the goal. However broad his knowledge of the achievements of modern war technique and however constantly he had furthered its development in our army, his opinions remained steadfastly tentative in this domain, because the possibility of testing the technique of new weapons on a large scale was wanting in peace time. Before the war we all could only surmise their actions on the ground and in the air. Reconnaissance, Victory, and Pursuit, the paving of the way for a Cannae, as well as the penetration, all evinced more than ever before, and in a much higher degree, that they depended on the effect of the weapons of the enemy. This explains partly why, except for Tannenberg, a real Cannae did not occur in the World War. That one did not occur in the west at the beginning of the war is the fault, in the first instance, of the Supreme Command. Indeed it was the Schlieffen plan on which our operations were based, yet in their actual execution it was departed from. His constant exhortation to make the right army flank as strong as possible was not heeded.

As in this respect, so also the apprehensive foreboding of the Field Marshal in his composition, "The War of the Present Time," came true. The long dragged out war ruined world industry. The frontal juxtaposition of the forces excluded a complete decision. The appeal for a stronger war establishment for Germany made by Schlieffen in his "About the Armies of Millions" was heeded too late. Count Schlieffen resembles in this respect the other great counsellor of his day, Prince Bismarck. In the work: "Benedeck's leadership of the army from the newest researches" Count Schlieffen's purpose is to point out where an unlucky selection of a Commander-in-Chief may lead. This is another exhortation.

The Field Marshal shows in his writings that he always aspired to the ideal, well knowing that one must set up a demand for this to attain anything of high standard. In this, at least, we were successful in the World War. From the publications of our enemies we know now how near we were, several times, to final success, in spite of our numerical inferiority; and that is not a trifle. The annihilation doctrine has not died in the German Army. Count Schlieffen was the one best fitted to further Moltke's art of war. He drew the most pertinent deductions from the constant growth of armies and the enlarged conditions of the present. The fear of mass armies we have overcome, thanks to him, and in the handling of the weapons we have shown ourselves to the last superior to our opponents. If the World War constitutes a high title of honor for us, General Field Marshal Count Schlieffen has a rich share therein.

BARON VON FREYTAG—LORINGHAVEN,
General of Infantry, Retired,
German Army.

NOTE: The translation of the body of this English edition has been made from part of the 1918 edition of the "Collected Writings." The maps and the list of same are likewise from that edition. The introduction and some of the footnotes have been taken from part of the 1925 Edition of "Cannae." .

Chapter I – The Battle of Cannae

The army of Hannibal, fronting west, stood on 2 August, 216 B.C., in the Apulian plain to the left of Aufidus (Ofanto) in the vicinity of the village Cannae,* situated near the mouth of the river, and opposite the troops of Consul Terentius Varro. The latter, to whom had been transferred by the other Consul Aemilius Paulus the daily alternating commandership, had

        55,000   heavily armed men,
          8,000   lightly armed men,
          6,000   mounted men,

on hand and, in the two fortified camps,

          2,600   heavily armed men,
          7,400   lightly armed men.
        10,000   men.

---

* Hans Delbrück, "Geschichte der Kriegskunst" (History of the Art of War) I.

at his further disposition, so that the total strength of the Roman army amounted to 79,000 men.

Hannibal had at his disposition only

32,000	heavily armed men,
8,000	lightly armed men,
10,000	mounted men.
50,000	men.

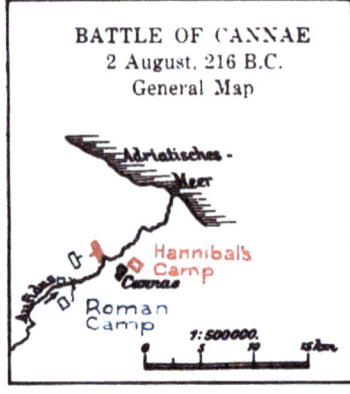

BATTLE OF CANNAE
2 August, 216 B.C.
General Map

His position, with a considerably superior enemy in his front and the sea in his rear, was by no means a favorable one. Nevertheless, Consul Aemilius Paulus, in concurrence with Proconsul Servius, wished to avoid a battle. Both feared the superior Carthaginian cavalry to which Hannibal particularly owed his victories on the Ticinus, on the Trebia and at the Tresimene lake. Terentius Varro, nevertheless, wished to seek a decision and avenge the defeats suffered. He counted on the superiority of his 65,000 heavily armed men as against the 32,000 hostile ones, consisting of only 12,000 Carthaginians and of 20,000 Iberians and Gauls who, in equipment and training, could not be considered as auxiliaries of full value. In order to give increased energy to the attack, Terentius gave his army a new battle formation.* The cavalry was placed on

---

* The heavily armed men (templates) would have been formed, according to regulations, in three lines, in close formation, the two foremost lines in equal strength (hastati and principes) with 4000 men in the front, and a total of 12 files, the third line (triarii) only half the strength in 160 equally distributed columns of 60 men (10 in the front. and 6 in depth) immediately in the rear. This formation of 18 files, appearing too broad to the commander, was deepened into 36 files with a front of 1600 men.

BATTLE OF CANNAE
2 August, 216 B.C.
Position before the Battle, and Cavalry Engagement

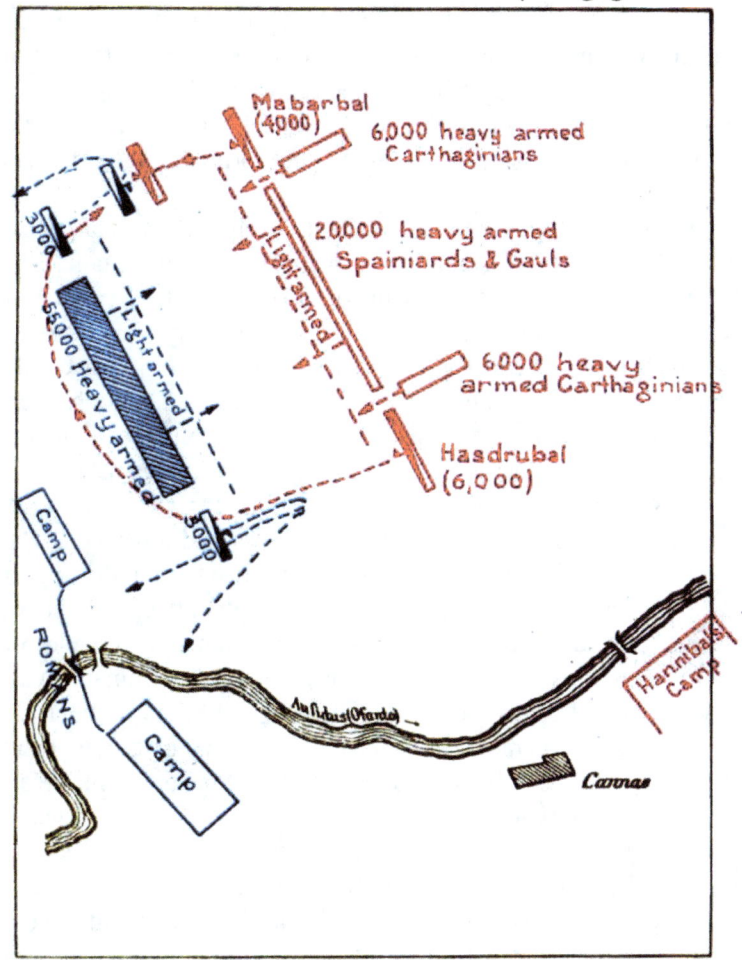

The heavily armed men (hoplites) were generally equipped with helmet, breastplate, legplates, round shield, spear and short sword. The Iberians and Gauls had, as defensive equipment, only the helmet and a large shield.

The formation into lines was not made in one connected line, but in six-file manipel columns with short intervals.

Both formations, the broad as well as the deep, required 57,600 men. There lacked, consequently, 2,600 men of the regulation strength.

the wings. The lightly armed troops, destined to begin the combat, to envelop the enemy and to support the cavalry, were not much considered by either side.

Hannibal opposed to the enemy's frort only his 20,000 Iberians and Gauls, which were probably 12 files deep. The greater part of his cavalry under Hasdrubal was placed on the left wing and the light Numidian on the right. In rear of this cavalry the 12,000 heavily armed Carthaginian infantry were formed equally divided between the two wings.

Both armies advanced against each other. Hasdrubal overpowered the weaker hostile cavalry on the right flank. The Roman knights were overwhelmed, thrown into the Aufidus or scattered. The conqueror turned the hostile infantry and advanced against the Roman cavalry on the wing which, until then, had only skirmished with the Numidian light horse. Attacked on both sides, the Romans were here also completely routed. Upon the destruction of the hostile cavalry, Hasdrubal turned against the rear of the Roman phalanx.

In the meanwhile, both infantry masses had advanced. The Iberian and Gallic auxiliary forces were thrown back at the impact not so much on account of the strength of the attack of the 86 Roman files as on account of the inferior armament and the lesser training in close combat. The advance of the Romans was, however, checked, as soon as the Carthaginian flanking echelons, kept back so far, came up and attacked the enemy on the right and left, and as soon as Hascrubal's cavalry threatened the Roman rear. The triarii turned back, the maniples of both wings moved outward. A long, entire square had been forced to halt, fronting all sides and was attacked on all sides by the infantry with short swords ard by the cavalry with javelins, arrows, and slingshots, never missing in the compact mass. The Romans were constantly pushed back and crowded together. Without weapons and without aid, they expected death. Hannibal, his heart full of hatred, circled the arena of the bloody work, encouraging the zeslous, lashing on the sluggish. His soldiers desisted only hours later. Weary of slaughter, they took the remaining 3000 men prisoners. On a narrow area 48,000 corpses lay in heaps. Both Aemilius Paulus and Servilius had fallen, Varro had escaped with a few cavalrymen, a few of the heavily armed

BATTLE OF CANNAE
2 August, 216 B.C.
Collision of the Two Armies

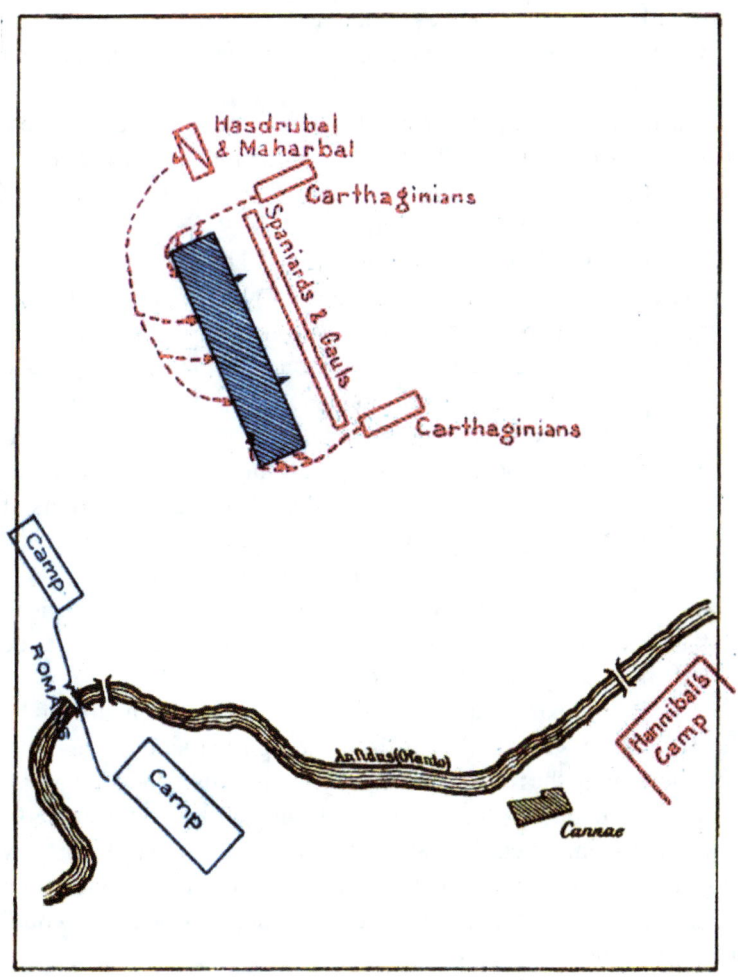

and the greater part of the lightly armed men. Thousands fell into the hands of the victors in the village of Cannae and in both camps. The conquerors had lost about 6,000 men. These were mostly Tberians and Gauls.

A battle of complete extermination had been fought, most wonderfully through the fact that in spite of all theories, it had been won by a numerical inferiority. Clausewitz said "concentric action against the enemy behooves not the weaker" and Napoleon taught "the weaker must not turn both wings simultaneously." The weaker Hannibal had, however, acted concentrically, though in an unseemly way, and turned not only both wings, but even the rear of the enemy.

Arms and the mode of combat have undergone a complete change during these 2000 years. No attack takes place at close quarters with short swords, but firing is used at thousands of meters range; the bow has been replaced by the recoil gun, the slingshot by machine guns. Capitulations have taken the place of slaughter. Still the greater conditions of warfare have remained unchanged. The battle of extermination may be fought today according to the same plan as elaborated by Hannibal in long forgotten times. The hostile front is not the aim of the principal attack. It is not against that point that the troops should be massed and the reserves disposed; the essential thing is to crush the flanks. The wings ought not to be sought at the advanced flank points of the front, but along the entire depth and extension of the hostile formation. The extermination is completed by an attack against the rear of the enemy. The cavalry plays here the principal role. It need not attack "intact infantry," but may wreak havoc among the hostile masses by long range fire.

A condition of success lies, it is true, in a deep formation of the hostile forces with shortened front through massing of reserves, thus deepening the flanks and increasing the number of combatants forced to remain in inactivity. It was Hannibal's good luck to have opposed to him Terentius Varro, who eliminated his superiority by disposing his infantry 36 men deep. At all times there have been generals of his school, but not during the period when they would have been most desirable for Prussia.

Chapter II – Frederick the Great and Napoleon

None more than Frederick the Great was so apt to fight a battle of extermination with a numerically inferior strength. He was, however, unable to attack at Leuthen with his "unequal force" of 35,000 men, however thin he might have made it, the wide front of Prince Charles of Lorraine with his 65,000 warriors. He would not have had any troops left for the surrounding of the overpowering superiority of the enemy. He directed the main attack against one flank, as had already been attempted at Soor and executed at Prague. He succeeded in deceiving the enemy, turning him and bringing up the Prussian army perpendicularly to the lengthened front against the hostile left flank. The extreme left wing, thus placed in a precarious position, was broken.

The Austrians turned their masses towards the threatened flank; however, they were unable to reform, in their haste, their original long front in the new direction, but fell unintentionally into a formation 40 men deep, quite similar to the one assumed by Terentius Varro. The position, in general, corresponded to that of Cannae. The narrow Austrian front was attacked by the not much wider Prussian. Cavalry was assembled on both wings. There

BATTLE OF LEUTHEN
5 December, 1757

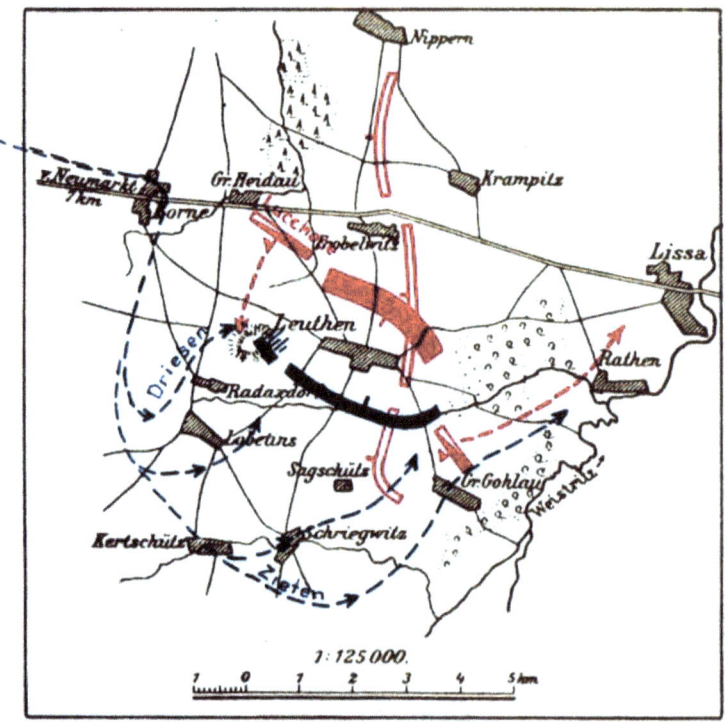

lacked, however, the two echelons of Carthaginian Infantry of 6000 men each. The numbers on hand did not suffice for their formation. The little that was left was not sufficient to turn in to the right and left. The entire deep envelopment had to be replaced; on the right—by an oblique drawing up of a few battalions against the hostile left wing, on the left—by placing a battery acting in a similar way. The preponderance of cavalry was likewise lacking. It is true that Zieten had thrown back the hostile cavalry on the right. He was, however, prevented from advancing against the infantry by the difficulties of the terrain. On the left, Driesen was too weak to advance at once and had to await a favorable moment in order to overthrow Lucches' cavalry and to strike a decisive blow by attacking the right infantry flank and force the enemy to retreat shaken by a long frontal combat. The retreat, starting in confusion on the left flank toward Lissa, was changed into rout by pursuit. The disproportion of strength was too great, the forces too unequal. Leuthen could be only a mutilated Cannae. The problem of fighting a battle of extermination with a strength half that of the enemy was, however, solved to a certain degree. What was lacking during the combat for extermination in turning, enveloping, and surrounding was, at least, partially compensated for by the forced retreat to the left flank. If, during the further pursuit by Zieten and Fouqué, they could have acted "with more vivacité," and sat "closer on the heels of the enemy," the results would have been greater but were still considerable. "Of the proud Imperial army which crossed the Queiss at Lauban with 90,000 men, scarcely one fourth left the soil of Silesia and returned over the frontier of Bohemia in the greatest dejection and discouragement." This came pretty close to extermination.

The turning movement at Zorndorf was to be executed in a still more effective way. Fermor, with 40,000 Russians, invested Küstrin in August, 1758, on the right from the Warthe and the Oder. Frederick the Great had formed, on the other bank of the Oder, at Manschnow and Gorgast, an army of 36,000 men with the troops brought from Bohemia and those which advanced with Count Dohna from East Prussia and Pomerania. To lead these troops through the fortress against the Russians did not promise much success. The King marched downstream and on 23 August, crossed the Oder at Güstebiese, for the purpose of pushing the enemy against the river and the fortress and thus to surround him entirely. Fermor met this turning movement and took up position in rear of the Mietzel, at Quartschen.

It was impossible for the Prussians to deliver an attack against the Russians over the marshy little river, difficult to cross. A new turning movement was to be made and a crossing sought further up. The left bank of the Mietzel was won on 25 August, at the Neudamm mill and Kerstenbrügge. It was found too difficult to immediately attack the eastern flank of the Russian army, assembled at Quartschen, over a row of ponds situated between Wilkersdorf and Grutzberg as well as over the Langengrund. The turning movement was continued over Batzlow and Wilkersdorf

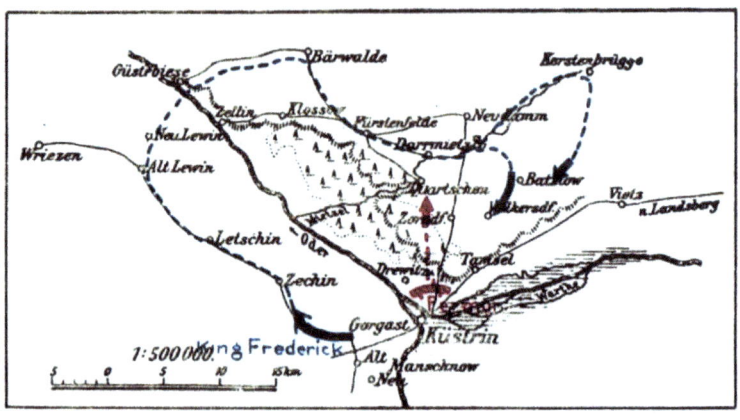

BATTLE OF ZORNDORF
Movements from 23 to 25 August, 1758

against Zorndorf, and when the head of the columns reached the Zaberngrund, they marched to the right. The advance was directed against the rear of the enemy and not against his flank. According to this, Fermor made a countermarch within the regiments, making them turn back, placing the second line in the line and the first line in the second. The width of the front was not narrowed but maintained the same as before. The attack, was, consequently, not rendered less difficult. Only after a victory would it be seen that an obstacle, situated in the rear of the Russian army and difficult to surmount, would prove of great advantage. Should the Russians be vanquished, they would likewise be destroyed. Fortunately, the battlefield was divided. The Russians were drawn up near Quartschen, fronting Zorndorf, their right wing between the Zabern and the Galgengrund, the center and left wing between the Galgen and Langengrund, the mass of cavalry under Demiku, to the left and in the rear near Zicher.

The flanks of this position were securely protected; the wings could not be surrounded. The King decided to press upon the right wing, separated from the rest of the army, with superior forces, then to attack the center and left wing from the west. For this purpose, the advance guard (8 battalions) under Manteuffel and, following at 800 paces, the left flank (nine battalions of the first and six battalions of the second line) under Kanitz advanced

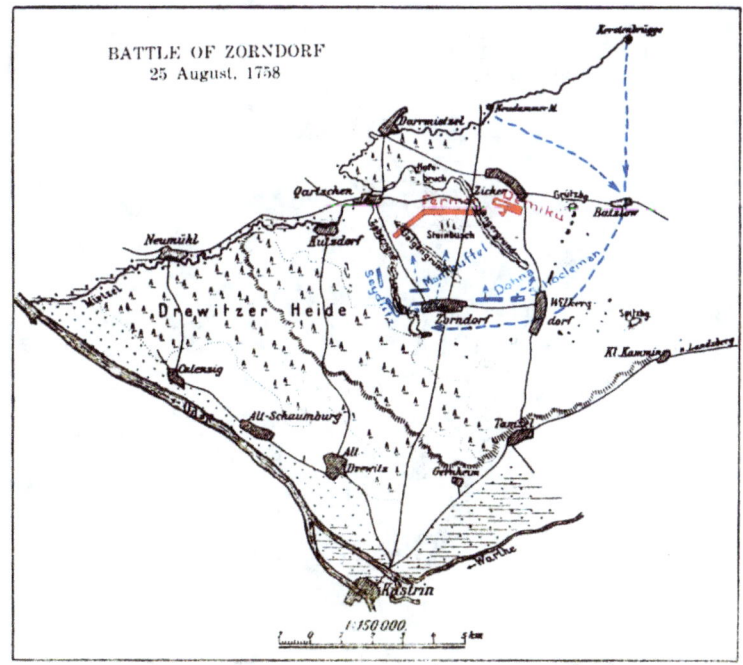

between the Zabern and Galgengrund, the right wing (eleven battalions of the _ first and four battalions of the second line) under Dohna, kept back to the east of the Galgengrund, were to cover the right flank; Seydlitz with 36 squadrons on the left, Schorlemer with 20 squadrons on the right were to secure the advance march and take part in the combat, if necessary, while 20 squadrons of dragoons followed as reserve. Sixty heavy guns opened the battle.

Their effect on the close and deep formation of the 16 Russian battalions on the right wing was annihilating. After two hours, the attack seemed sufficiently prepared to allow the advance of the vanguard. The Russian artillery, however, was not yet dead. Their canister fire was likewise murderous. The thinned battalions of Manteuffel closed and relinquished the position on the Zaberngrund. There were no reserves to fill the gaps in their ranks. Kanitz, accustomed to maintain touch and communication with the lines, before all things, moved up to Dohna on the right and advanced, east of the Galgengrund, against the Russian center

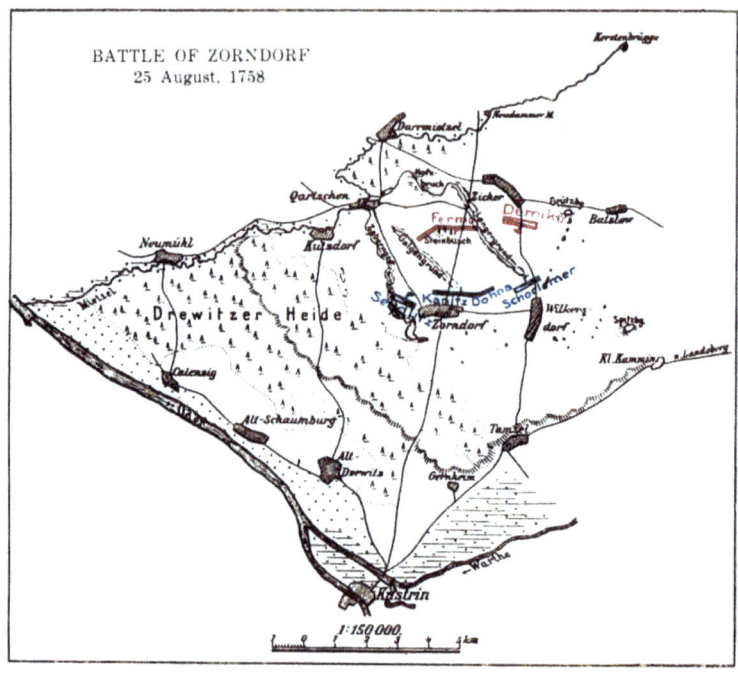

Battle of Zorndorf, 25 August, 1758

which was still unshaken and 24 battalions strong. When he and Manteuffel approached the enemy, they saw themselves enveloped on both sides by the hostile line.

The advance of the 14 battalions of the Russian left wing against Kanitz, stopped Dohna's energetically firing artillery which had been kept behind. The right wing rushed with 16 battalions and 14 squadrons against the left flank and the front of Manteuffel. The Prussians were thrown back with great losses. The pursuing Russians, however, left their flank uncovered and Seydlitz succeeded in crossing in three places the Zaberngrund which until then was deemed unpassable. At the same time, the dragoons of the reserve advanced. Twenty squadrons attacked the front, and the flank and rear were attacked by 18 squadrons each. The Russians, shaken by the artillery fire, and scattered during the heat of pursuit, defended themselves obstinately. After a long and bloody hand to hand fight, the remaining men fled over the Galgengrund to Quartschen or to the Drewitzer Heide. In spite of the initial victory, the Russian right wing, attacked on three sides was entirely annihilated. It was, however, impossible for Seydlitz to follow up his victory, to advance over the Galgengrund, support the frontal attack of the infantry by a flanking attack. The attack of Kanitz was repulsed by superior numbers and the Russian center was well able to hinder any movement over the Galgengrund.

The entire army had to be assembled again near Zorndorf for a second battle. The advance guard, however, was unfit for further use. It was, consequently, withdrawn. Of the remaining 30 battalions, 15 battalions of the right wing, under Dohna, were to advance along the Langengrund and, with the aid of Schorlemer, rout the Russian left wing, if possible, after which they were to turn left to attack the center which was to be simultaneously pressed by Kanitz from the south and Seydlitz from the west. The plan seemed doomed. While ninety-seven guns were preparing the combat and Dohna advanced to the half right towards the Langengrund, Demiku rushed unexpectedly with his cavalry against the great battery of the right wing, against the right flank of the infantry and against Schorlemer's cavalry. The battery was lost, one battalion was surrounded and put down its arms, others were confused for the moment, but the Russian cavalry was finally repulsed by the fire of the infantry and retreated before Schorlemer's cavalry towards Zicher. This enemy was eliminated.

In spite of his defeat he succeeded in gaining considerable advantages. The Prussian left flank, though not touched by Demiku's attack, was so shaken by the previous unfortunate combat and so discouraged by the expectancy of a new catastrophe, that it was seized with panic and fled, being arrested only at Wilkersdorf in its flight and brought to a standstill. Seydlitz marched with his 56 squadrons to the evacuated place and advanced principally left of the Steinbusch, while Dohna advanced with his right wing, along the Langengrund, against the closely massed 38 Russian battalions. After a hot hand to hand fight, the Russian left flank retreated first. In order to avoid being pushed into the Hofebruch, it attempted to escape towards Quartschen. This left the left wing of the Russian center unprotected. Dohna turned to the left. Attacked on two sides, hemmed in on the third by an insurmountable obstacle, the center was gradually pushed back over the Galgengrund. It took up position on the hills on the other side.

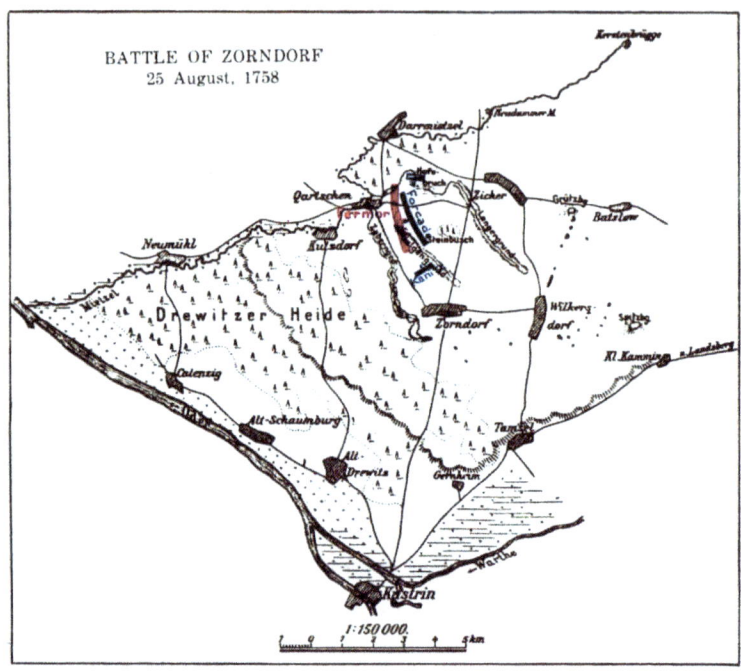

It was absolutely necessary to annihilate the enemy up to his last man. The King wanted to fight another battle in the evening. The cavalry, however, after two most excellent feats in the morning and in the afternoon, was unfit for further action. Forcade, taking the place of the wounded Dohna, was to attack the Russians in front, while Kanitz, who had again brought up his battalions, was to strike at their right flank. These troops, however again went to pieces. Forcade alone could not possibly execute the attack. The Russians held their position. Their condition was nevertheless quite critical. They had only 19,000 men left out of the 44,000 with which they went into battle. The Warthe, the Oder and the Mietzel formed, in rear of this remnant of troops which had escaped annihilation, a how of rivers, the only passage over which was hemmed in by the fortress of Küstrin. An army, which had suffered greatly and appeared incapable of attack, was standing in front of them.

The Russians could move neither forward nor backward. They could not remain in position as they lacked ammunition and food.

BATTLE OF KUNERSDORF
12 August, 1759

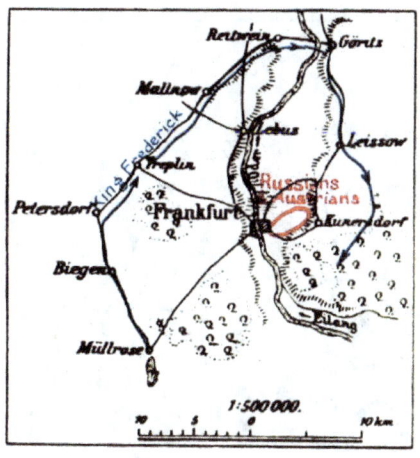

The primary intention of the King—to surround and bottle up the enemy, had been attained. The victorious Prussians were, however, unable to continue the attack immediately. They would now rally, however, as their losses were much smaller than those of the enemy. They were now superior in numbers by some 23,000 men, and would soon be able to engage in a new battle. The latter would doubtlessly be crowned with complete success. Yet considering the obstinate capacity for resistance of the Russians, the victory would have to be bought at the cost of greater sacrifices than the King could for the moment afford. It was necessary for him to go back, without loss of time, to Silesia or Saxony in order to check the advance of the Austrians. He decided to build a golden bridge for the enemy and marched off late in the afternoon of the 26th, beyond the Langengrund towards Zicher. The enemy took advantage of the outlet left him and marched early in the morning of the 27th, going around the south of Zorndorf and Wilkersdorf, to Klein-Kammin, in order to occupy a fortified position there. The King went into camp at Tamsel. With natural communications in their rear, the two adversaries remained opposite each other until 30 August. On the 31st, Fermor marched towards Landsberg. Followed by Dohna, he began the gradual retreat beyond the Vistula. He had saved one third of his strength. He had not been annihilated, but eliminated. The King turned to other problems.

Leuthen had freed the King from the Austrians, like Zorndorf from the Russians. His enemies had to form new armies for the continuation of the war. The difficulties encountered in the mode of procedure, chosen by Frederick the Great, came clearly to light.

BATTLE OF KUNERSDORF
12 August, 1759

It was proven in these battles, and still more in others, that it is not easy to even partially annihilate one's enemies with numerically inferior strength. At Prague,* the enveloped enemy had had time to form a new front almost on a similar extension as the old front. At Kolin, the Austrians had only to move a little to the right in order to frustrate the turning movement.

The intended flank attack was transformed into a frontal attack, an attack which was opposed at Kolin by greatly superior numbers

---

* It was the Fieldmarshal's intention to include the "Battle of Prague" in the book edition of "Cannae." The description of this battle may be found in the second volume of "Collected Writings" in the study entitled "Frederick the Great."

(20,000 against 85,000 infantry) and by a much more extended line. In the first battle it was possible to execute a surrounding movement, while in the second, Zieten was not able to cope with the difficult problem. Should it be impossible to succeed in deceiving the enemy to a certain extent, to conceal the turning movement, the outcome would be more than doubtful. A certain surprise was necessary, at least where the Austrians were concerned. The stolid Russians could be treated with less caution. They could help themselves in another way. The 70,000 Austro-Russians who defended themselves at Kunnersdorf against 40,000 Prussians, had transformed their strong position into a fortress by means of entrenchments and ditches. They would be, however, entirely cut off by a turning movement via Goritz. A victory was still necessary for annihilation. This could not be attained with 40,000 men against 70,000 well entrenched enemies. The Leuthen program was executed insofar that Mühlberg, the supporting point of the left wing, was captured. In a further attempt to throw back the enemy from the left to right, the Prussian infantry failed before a too strong artillery and against ever newly forming flanks, and finally broke before the powerful position of the Spitzberg. Even Seydlitz could do nothing with his cavalry against ditches and entrenchments.

It may be seen from all the battles, won or lost by Frederick the Great, that his aim was to attack from the very beginning a flank or even the rear of the enemy, to push him, if possible against an insurmountable obstacle and then to annihilate him by enveloping one or both of his flanks.

A similar intention will be found in Napoleon. Turning movements, executed by the King in the immediate vicinity of the battlefield within a few hours, were begun by the Corsican days and weeks in advance and extended over vast areas. A surprise could not be thus attained. This was not necessary, however. The mass of troops at the disposition of Napoleon assured victory and eliminated from his battles, with similar fronts, the venturesomeness of Frederick's combats.

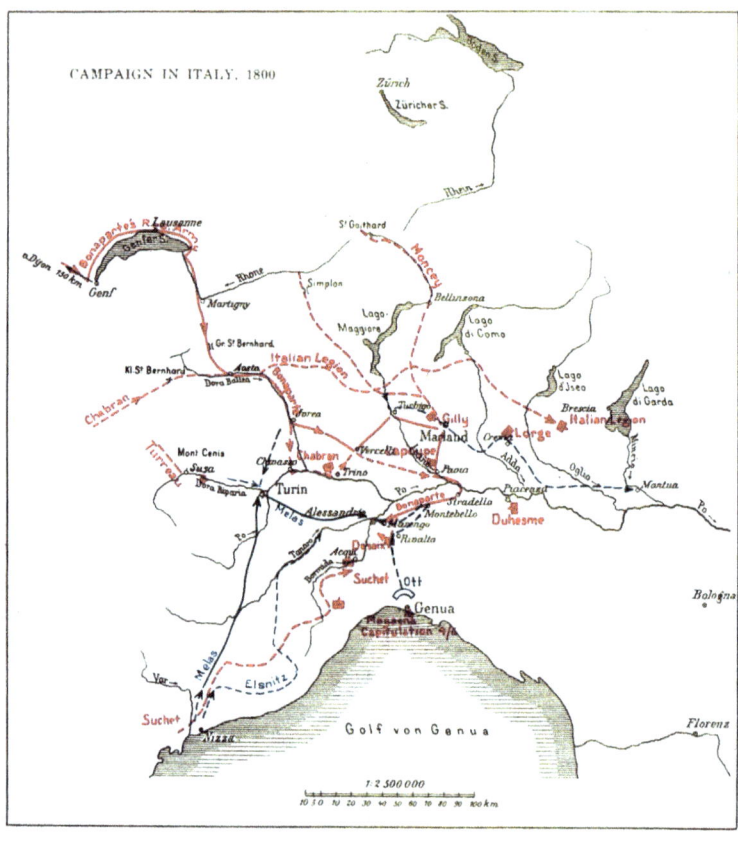

We find the first example in the campaign of 1800. Melas, the Austrian commander-in-chief in Italy, let Massena be besieged in Genoa by Ott with 24,000 men and opposed on the Var 28,000 men to Suchet's 12,000. A force of 35,000 men, divided into numerous small detachments, was to secure the passes of the Alps in a wide semicircle between Nice and Bellinzona. General Bonaparte made Suchet detain Melas as long as possible, caused Turreau with 6300 men to make a demonstration over the Mont Cenis and Susa down in the valley of the Dora Riparia and the division of Chabran to cross the lesser St. Bernard in the direction of Aosta; while he himself led the reserve army from Dijon via Geneva, Lausanne, and Martigny over the great St. Bernard and reached at Ivrea the North Italian lowland with 36,000 men. Indescribable obstacles were overcome by the energy of the commander and the zeal of his officersandmen. Melas did the same thing as Prince Charles of Lorraine and Fermor had done in their time: He turned against the enemy who was turning him, left Elsnitz with 17,000 men opposite Suchet and marched with about 11,000 men to Turin.

A French attack in this direction would not have achieved a complete decision. Melas would probably have escaped east. Bonaparte continued, under protection of a flanking detachment marching by Chivasso, Trino, Vercelli, and Pavia, the turning movement by Vercelli and Turbigo to Milan in order to unite, at this point, with 15,000 men under Moncey who had crossed the St. Gothard, a portion of them having also crossed via the Simplon. After Suchet had routed Eignitz, he pushed the enemy, stationed along the Po, to the Mincio, pursued him as far as Brescia, Crema, and Piacenza, barred the communication with the rear over the St. Gothard to Zurich and occupied the crossings over the Po, the right bank of the latter was won at Stradella. In the meantime, Melas endeavored to unite his forces at Allessandria.

The opponents confronted each other with a totally changed front. Neither one nor the other had succeeded in assembling an army corresponding to the total strength. Melas had only 28,500 men, while Bonaparte had only 22,000 men out of 69,000 on account of numerous flank and rear detachments. He was, however, forced to advance if he wished to prevent the enemy from crossing the Po in a northerly direction and cutting the French line of communications over the St. Gothard, or from rushing south to Genoa which had just been evacuated by Massena. An advanced Austrian detachment was thrown back at Montebello. Melas himself did not seem as yet to want to leave Allesandria. The French troops extended to the right towards the Bormida. Melas crossed the river early on 14 June.

The Frenchmen, surprised at Marengo, could not hold out long. The Consular Guard was vainly sent into action as a reserve. All lost ground. The retreat, almost a flight, was in full swing. The Austrians followed in two long columns. Desaix, sent with 5,000 men to Rivalta to protect the flank, arrived there and threw himself on the nearest column. The surprised enemy, in unfavorable position, could not easily advance. Kellerman rushed in with his

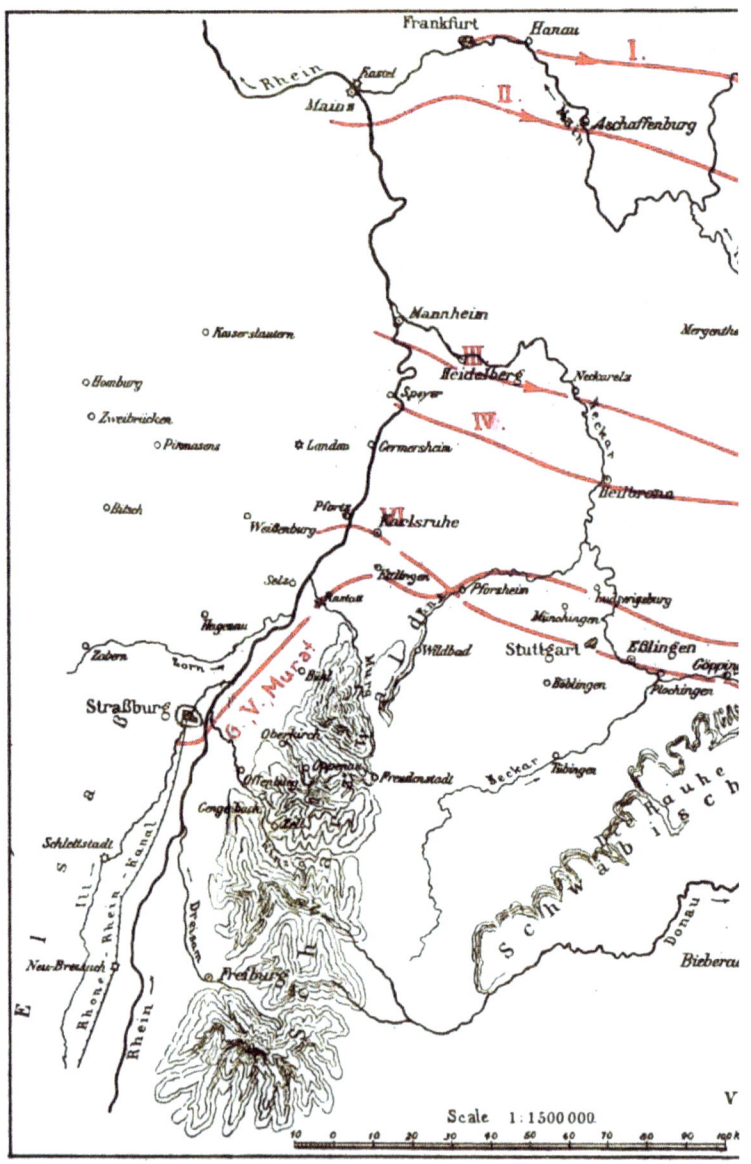

GERMANY 1805

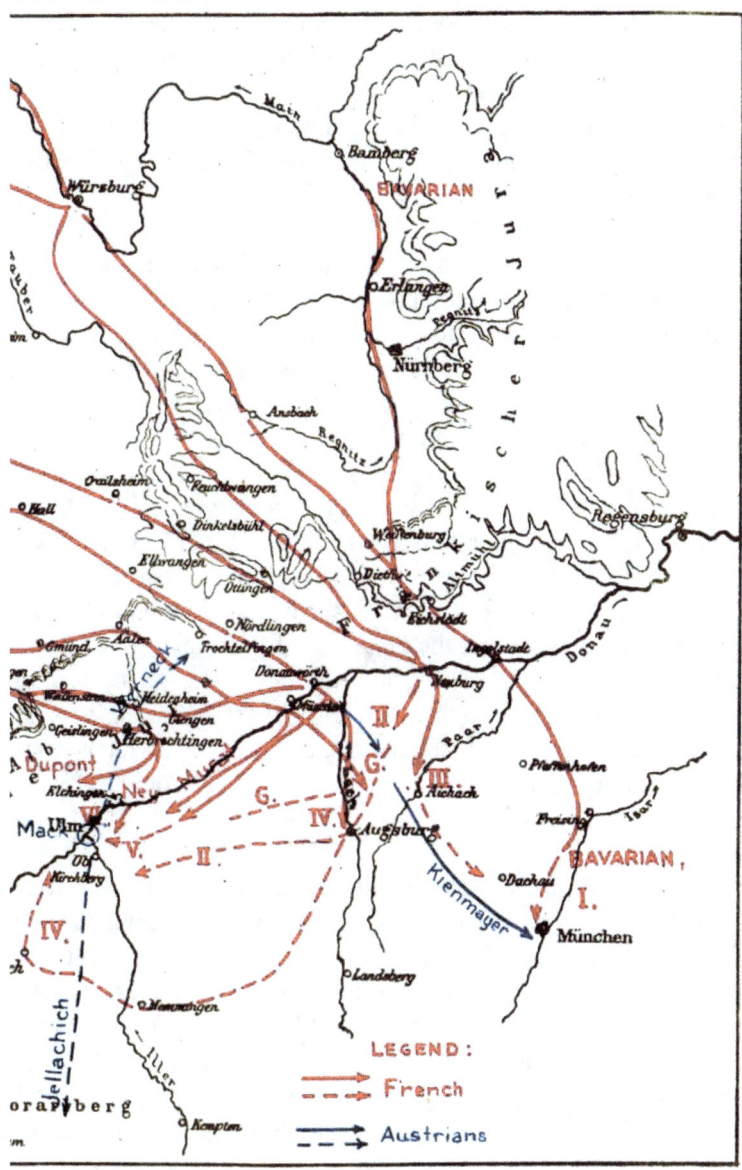

brigade of dragoons and decided the combat. The head of the column was thrown back upon its center and rear. The Austrians retreated in confusion.

Still the victory was not a decisive one. While the fronts were being changed, Melas could have gone downstream along the Po, assembled reinforcements, and offered new resistance. This would have brought about an endless campaign. Leaning against the Alps with his rear, surrounded by Suchet at Acquie, by Turreau below Susa, by Chabran at Trino, and Lapoye near Pavia, the Austrian general was in a desperate condition. Only a complete victory could relieve him. But he could not hope for the latter, as Bonaparte could count upon considerable reinforcements, while he could get none. An agreement was concluded by which Melas was allowed to lead his troops beyond the Mincio on condition that they would not take part in further military operations in this war and of giving up Northern Italy.

Bonaparte did not annihilate his enemy, but eliminated him and made him harmless, and attained, at the same time, the aim of the campaign——the conquest of Northern Italy. He owed this success not so much to a battle which had been almost lost, but to the turning of the flank, the winning of the hostile line of retreat; in a like manner as Frederick the Great owed the retaking of Silesia, and the freeing of the left bank of the Vistula, to the turning movements at Leuthen and at Zorndorf. It is true that this was not solely due to the turning movements. A battle and a victory were also necessary. But a decisive victory is possible only when the rear or at least one flank of the enemy is made the aim of the attack.

In 1805 Napoleon was at war with England. Albion was to be vanquished not only on the high seas but also on land. The threatened insular realm attempted to escape the danger by entering into an alliance with other European Powers. Naples, Austria, Bavaria, Russia, Prussia, Sweden, and Denmark were to advance concentrically and attack the enemy on his own territory. The plan was executed only in its smallest part. Prussia remained neutral, Bavaria took the side of the enemy. Naples, Sweden, and Denmark could not seriously be considered. Austria and Russia alone remained.

The principal army under Archduke Charles was to deploy into Italy behind the Adige. A secondary army under Archduke John in the Tyrol, while another secondary army, to which Bavaria had been originally counted, nominally under Archduke Ferdinand, in reality under General Mack, was to deploy on the Iller. They were to await at that point the Russians with whom they were to advance jointly. Napoleon anticipated the deployment and did not go against Archduke Charles, but sent against him a small army under Massena, while he advanced himself with 210,000 men against Mack who had only 60,000.

The movements and distribution of troops of the enemy were not immediately recognized by the Austrians. But had they been known, this circumstance would not and should not have caused a retreat, though the opposing forces were three times as strong as the Austrians. The position on the Iller, with its right resting on Ulm, was very strong. The crossings of the Danube below this point were secured by 16,000 men under Kienmayer. Should it be impossible to hold the Iller, Mack could have crossed the Lech, from position to position until he could join the Russians. This could have been executed if the attack had been a frontal one. The enemy would have grown weaker and weaker as he advanced, would have reached the decisive battlefield with greatly decreased numbers, encountering there not only the Russians, but the Austrian reserves and, possibly, also the armies of the Archdukes.

Napoleon, however, made only demonstrations against the front, advanced with four army corps and the Guard from the Rhine, crossed the Neckar between Stuttgart and Neckarelz, two corps advancing simultaneously from Mainz and Frankfort via Wurzburg, and the Bavarians from Bamberg, by Nuremberg. He wanted to cross the Danube with his left flank, depending on the position of the enemy, either at Ingolstadt, Regensburg, or still farther down. He counted on striking the Austrians, if not in the rear, then possibly in the right flank, push them to the west, or at least, to the south and force them to give battle.

Mack, relying on indefinite, conflicting, and improbable information about the advance of the enemy, did not wish to give up his position, destroy the wisely combined plan of action and expose the armies in Italy and in the Tyrol to a flank attack. He wanted to be clearly informed of the situation before abandoning the post entrusted to him. When, on 7 October, he deemed "that it was almost clear that the enemy wanted to repeat his play of Marengo, and attack the army in the rear," five French army corps, the Guard, Bavarians, and the cavalry reserves under Murat reached the Danube between Ingolstadt and Münster, while one corps (Ney) covered the right flank on the left of the Danube against Ulm. Kienmayer had abandoned the crossings in order to retreat beyond the Isar via Aichach and Munich. Mack was too weak for an attack against the powerful superiority of the enemy as the French columns were too close to each other and too well prepared for mutual support. Since Ingolstadt was closer to Munich than Ulm, there could be no thought of breaking through, no matter how far south the movement might be directed. The 210,000 French troops, advancing southward from the Danube, would have sooner or later surrounded Mack's 44,000 men and annihilated them.

After a weak attempt to attack the hostile columns one by one after they had crossed the Danube and after another attempt to escape via Augsburg, which was soon given up, Mack desisted from all operations on the right of the river and returned to Ulm on the 10th, fighting small battles on the way. A success might have been thought of only when the longingly expected Russian troops had arrived. But Napoleon had taken proper steps against this possibility also.

The French left wing (two corps and the Bavarians) had been pushed to the Isar for protection against the Russians. Two corps and the Guard took up a position on the Lech in the vicinity of Augsburg in order to block Mack's road to Vienna and to serve, simultaneously, as a reserve for the left wing. Murat, with the reserve cavalry and one division of infantry, went later towards Ulm. These troops were, however, gradually reinforced, until only Dupont's division remained on the left bank on 11 October. That division sufficed to frighten Mack sufficiently to make him desist from breaking through on that day. The attempt was to be repeated on the 13th, in several echelons. The foremost, (16,000 men under Werneck) succeeded in reaching Herbrechtingen, while Mack remained with the rest in Ulm, thinking that Napoleon, actuated by a supposed landing of the English at Boulogne and a threatened mobilization of Prussia, would determine upon a precipitate retreat. On the 14th, Ney gained in the face of only a weak Austrian detachment, the left bank of the Danube. The French troops penetrated from here against the northern side, others via Memmingen and Biberach, against the south side of Ulm, which was already invested on the east. On the 17th, 23,000 men were forced to capitulate. Jellachich had escaped earlier with 5,000 men west of the Iller to Vorarlberg. So as not to leave his commander-in-chief in the lurch, Werneck wanted to go back to Ulm, but returned by order of Archduke Ferdinand, and was caught at Trochtelfingen by Murat and Dupont. His troops were scattered and partly forced to lay down their arms. Archduke Ferdinand broke through with 2000 cavalry.

Of the 66,000 men, with which Mack had advanced to the Iller, more than half had been annihilated. Even this could have been avoided had Mack firmly resolved to break through on the left bank of the Danube on the 11th or 12th. The French had done enough to block the enemy on the right bank of the Danube, more than enough for protection against the Russians, but on the other hand, not enough for surrounding Mack. Certainty would have been attained best by a quick surrounding. With his great numerical superiority Napoleon could not leave to the enemy for days the possibility of breaking through. He ought not to have counted too much on Mack's indecision and on false reports.

One year later[*] the Prusso-Saxon army stood in position with about 100,000 men to the north of the Thuringian forest, principally between the Saale and the Werra on a parallel with Weimar and Erfurt. Napoleon crossed with 160,000 men in three columns, via Bayreuth and Bamberg, the Franconian forest and the Upper Saale with the intention of turning the left hostile flank and attacking it. This aim could be reached by turning the three marching columns according to the position of the enemy. Unfortunately no definite information concerning this position was at hand. Two combats had taken place on the upper Saale, but, without elucidating the situation.

---

[*] See "1806" and "Jena" in Vol. II of the "Collected Writings."

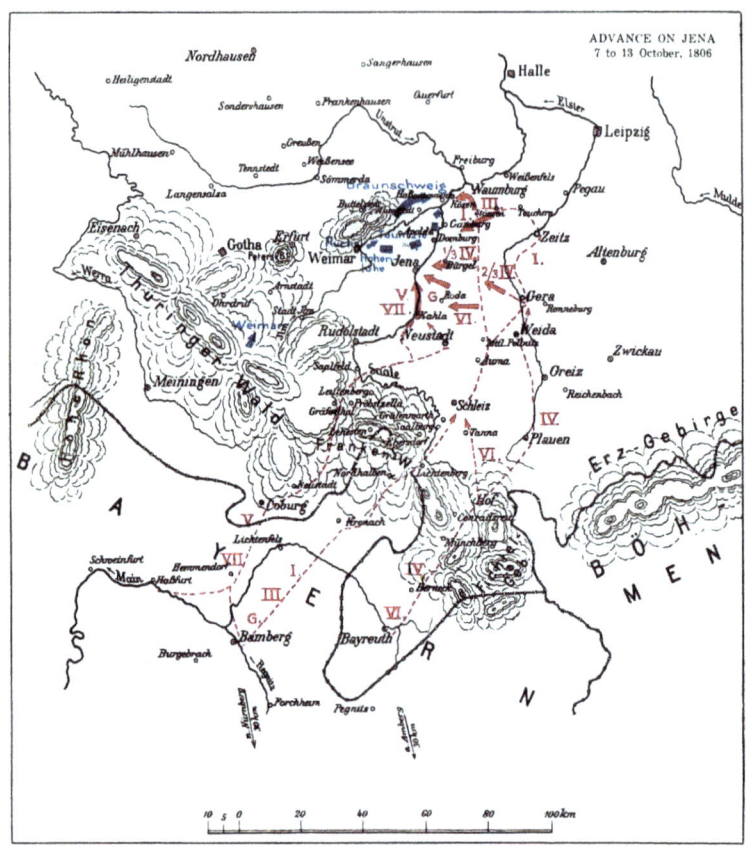

Napoleon thought at times to maintain the general direction of march to the north, at others, he deemed it necessary to turn eastward. One march column was halted, another was advanced. This caused some confusion to the battalion square formation in which the French army was marching and which was equally efficient for the march to the front as well as to the flank. When a flanking movement had to be executed on the Saale, it was found that at each of the crossings of Kosen and Dornburg was one corps, while the main forces were directed toward Jena, although according to the position then occupied by the enemy on the line: Jena—Weimar—Erfurt, the principal forces ought to have been directed to the crossings at Namburg, Kosen, and Freiburg. Napoleon thought that, corresponding to his own distribution of forces, the enemy had likewise assembled his army opposite Jena, leaving small detachments or no troops at all at Kosen and Dornburg. Consequently he wanted to attack the enemy at Jena and hold him in front until the corps had come up from Kosen and Dornburg in order to throw him into the Thuringian forest.

This plan did not correspond to the actual situation: the Prussian main forces were marching on Kosen and only a secondary corps under Hohenlohe, supported by Ruchel's army reserve, was to block the passes at Camburg and Dornburg, while the remaining forces were to stay in Jena without allowing themselves to be drawn into a serious combat, i.e, retreat when attacked. This problem could surely have been executed in one day, at least, insofar as the greatly superior enemy was gradually allowed to cross the Ilm at Apolda. This would give the Prussian main army time to strike an annihilating blow to the vastly weaker enemy at Kosen. Three French divisions could be held back by three Prussian divisions and thrown into the Saale by a large reserve still available.

That this did not happen was due to the fact that the Duke of Brunswick, the commander-in-chief, who was well informed of the battle conditions, had been severely wounded and that the King, on whom the leadership had devolved, had not the nerve to continue the battle, having been left in the lurch by all the assistants and advisers he had called together, and gave the order to retreat in order to join, on the following day, the army of Hohenlohe and resume the combat according to the order of the commander-in-chief. In the meanwhile, Hohenlohe did not fight any rearguard combat nor execute a gradual retreat, corresponding to the problem entrusted to him, but had been enticed into a combat with changed front against forces almost five times as strong as his own and was completely beaten, as was also Rüchel.

Napoleon's battle plan could not succeed, according to ordinary human calculations. He had turned too soon. His principal attack had been directed against a secondary army in a not very effective direction. Nevertheless he won an annihilating victory because the attack was still directed against the original flank, and hence, the retreat to the Oder could be executed only in a wide curve along the shorter radius of which the pursuer could reach, undisturbed and quickly, the same objective.

BATTLE OF AUSTERLITZ
2 December, 1805

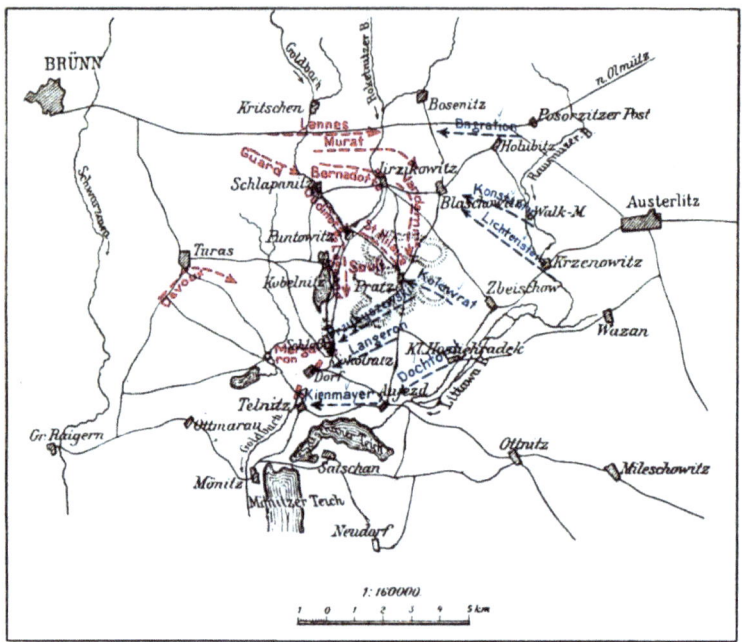

It would have been strange if Napoleon's and Frederick's turning movements, flank and rear attacks, had not been imitated by their opponents. Prince von Hildburghausen had received full recognition in 1757 for the battle of Prague. The commander-in-chief of 64,000 Imperial and French troops thought that he could easily turn and inflict a crushing victory upon the 21,600 Prussians at Rossback. The turning movement, however, encountered another turning movement and the planned attack met with a counterattack. Covered by a ridge, the Prussians came up close, surprised and threw themselves from all sides on the head of the narrow marching columns, while strong battery fire against the deep flank prevented deployment. Frederick himself had shown that his turning movements could best be parried by an attack. Napoleon acted in the same way.

The allied Russians and Austrians thought that they would find Napoleon with 75,000 men on 5 December, 1805, in a position difficult to attack, on the Brunn—Olmutz road in rear of the

Goldbach (Goldbrook) between Kritschen and Kobelnitz. They decided to keep the hostile front on the main road occupied by a demonstration by Bagration (11,500 men) from Holubitz, by the Russian reserve under Grand Duke Constantine (7000 men) from Walk—Muhle, and by 6000 cavalry under Prince Lichtenstein, 24,500 men in all, while the remaining troops were to cross the Goldbach between Kebelnitz and Telnitz, Kienmayer from Aujezd, Dochturcff from Little Hostiehradeck, Langeron from the south, Prybyshevsky from northeast, Kolovrat from east of Pratze, 60,000 men in all, and attack the hostile flank between Schlapanitz and Turas.

This turning movement might have been successful had Napoleon not left his position like Prince Charles of Lorraine at Leuthen or like Count Fermor at Zorndorf, and if the fords of the Goldbach could have been crossed without resistance. Neither the one nor the other condition was fulfilled. Napoleon had the crossings at Telnitz, Dorf, and Schloss-Sokolnitz occupied by Margaron with five battalions and twelve squadrons, and decided to attack with Soult (one half of Legrand's division at Kobelnitz, St. Hilaire at Puntowitz and Vandamme at Jirkowitz), Lannes (the divisions Caffarelli and Suchet on the Olmutz road), and Murat with the reserve cavalry, reinforced by Kellermann between Soult and Lannes in the first line, with the grenadier division (Oudinot) in rear of St. Hilaire, and Madotte's corps (division Drouet and Rivaud) in rear of Vandamme in the second line, and with the Guard, in the third line, striking the right hostile flank of the turning columns, after having routed the enemy immediately opposite them.

The plan was not executed entirely as he had thought it out. Kienmayer, Dochturoff, Langeron, and Prybyshevsky had already marched off and reached the Goldbach with the heads of their forces. Kolowrat, however, had been held hack by Kutusoff, the nominal commander-in-chief, and had just begun his march to Kobelnitz via Pratze when Soult ascended the commanding plateau north of the village and surprised him by an attack. Kolowrat's column was attacked in front by St. Hilaire, in the flank by Vandemme. In spite of the unfavorable position in which he was thus placed, the Austrian general succeeded in deploying his troops

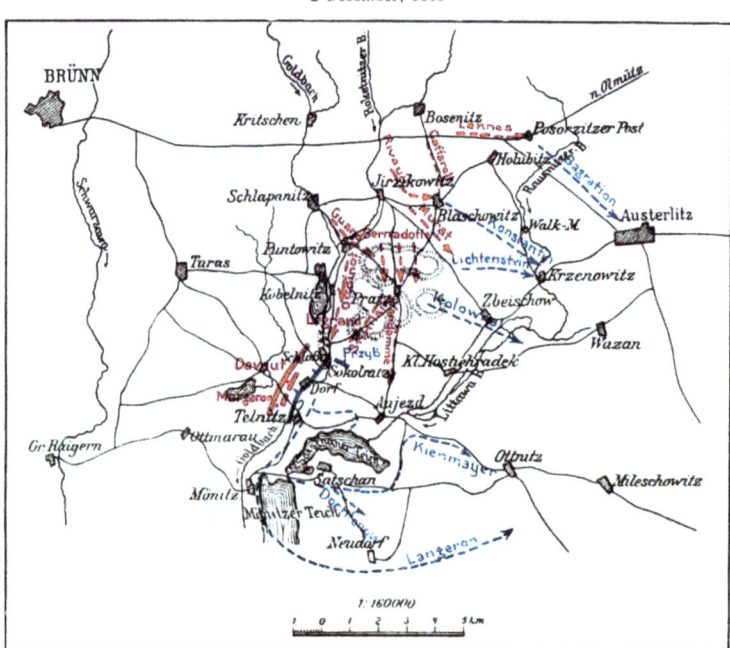

BATTLE OF AUSTERLITZ
2 December, 1805

and resisting the enemy for two hours. He was forced to retreat via Zbeischow to Wazan only when Bernadotte's Division Drouet attacked his right flank.

Threatened in the left flank, the following were forced to join this retreat: Prince Lichtenstein, who, supported by the Russian cavalry of the Guard had sustained a series of fluctuating combats against Murat, Kellermann, and the French cavalry of the Guard; further the Russian cavalry which had advanced to. Blaschowitz, was attacked by the Divisions Rivaud and Caffarelli; and lastly Bagration, who had opposed an obstinate resistance to the pursuing Lannes in the pass at the Posorwitz post, in order to move on unmolested to Austerlitz, while Lichtenstein and Grand Duke Constantine reached at Krzenowitz, the left bank of the Littawa creek.

Of the three turning columns, Kienmayer and Dochturoff had, in the meanwhile, forced a crossing, after a lengthy combat, over the Goldbach at Telnitz, Langeron at Dorf, and Prybyshevsky at

Schloss-Sokolnitz, and had accupied with part of their forces the height situated to the west. They were, however, prevented from advancing further by Davout, who had arrived to reinforce Margaron with the Division Friant and the dragoons of Bourcier from Great Raigern. Only a numerically inferior force of Frenchmen was opposed here to the mass of the allies, but it succeeded not only in maintaining its position, but even in gaining advantages. For this compressed mass could not gain ground to deploy and make use of its superiority.

The full disadvantage of their position came to light only when Napoleon had forced Kolowrat to retreat and sent Soult with two and one half divisions, followed by Oudinot, against the right flank of the turning columns, while himself occupying with the corps of Bernadotte and the Guard, the heights of Pratze. St. Hilaire and Legrand, who had been directed towards Sokolnitz, placed the right column under Prybyshevsky in the worst position. A few Russian battalions were thrown hastily against the flanking attack, but were annihilated by the superior forces, Others endeavored to escape to the west across the Goldback and came under the cross fire of Davout's and St. Hilaire's artillery. The entire column was either exterminated or taken captive. Langeron, however, obtained time, through these battles, to save, via Telnitz, the nine battalions which had remained east of the creek. Dochturoff and Kienmayer had turned back toward Aujezd, but when Vandamme advanced against this village, and after the bridge had broken down here, attempted to flee over the dam between the Monitz and Satschan ponds. Pursued by artillery fire, the remnants of the allies reached Mileschowitz, via Neudorf and Ottnitz.

Napoleon boasted that he had broken the enemy in two in the center at Austerlitz and scattered the foe in various directions. It is, however, difficult to recognize a breaking through or scattering of the enemy from the events of 2 December. The allies were assembled in the evening south of the Littawa. The French army, on the contrary, was divided into two parts. The main forces stood opposite the defeated enemy between Monitz and Krzenowitz, while a smaller force (Lannes and Murat) was stationed on the Olmutz road near the post office of Posorwitz. Napoleon had written to Soult early on the 3rd:

The Emperor will attach himself in person to the heels of the enemy. In his opinion nothing has been achieved in war as long as there remains something to be done. A victory is not complete where more can be achieved.

Napoleon did not pay much attention to this rule himself. Touch with the enemy was completely lost on the 2nd. It seemed that Napoleon had really remained in the belief that he had scattered the enemy in two directions. Accordingly, he let Soult and Bernadotte pursue on 8 December in a southern direction, and Lannes and Murat in the direction of Olmutz. The pursuit in the latter direction proved soon to be an airy notion. The combined pursuit thus lost its importance. This, however, was of no consequence. The defeated enemy was so intimidated that Emperor Francis arrived on the 4th, in person, in Napoleon's camp and sued for an armistice. The victory of Austerlitz would have sufficed, even without a pursuit, to throw out of the field, not only the allied Russo-Austrian troops, but also the advancing Archduke Charles, the Russian reinforcements, and the Prussian army.

A similar picture to the campaign of Austerlitz is offered us by that of Prussian-Eylau, although the result was different.[*]

In the beginning of the year 1807, the allied Russians and Prussians stood: L'Estocg at Angerburg; Bennigsen between Johannisburg and the Narew, behind the Pissa; Essen between the Narew and the Bug; while opposite them stood the French between the Narew and the Haff, in rear of the Omuleff and the Passarge. The positions were not yet occupied, the quarters not yet taken up, when Bennigsen, the commander-in-chief of the allies, broke camp. Leaving Essen on the Narew and a weak detachment under Sedmoratzky at Gonionds, he marched in two columns between the Mazurian lakes, accompanied on the right by the Prussians under L'Estocq, against the left wing of the enemy.

The French, standing in deep and extended formations, were surprised, but retreated in a southern direction without many losses. The allies followed and reached by 31 January, the line: Freystadt — Deutsch-Eylau — Osterode — Allenstein. They had

---

[*] See "Campaign of Prussian-Eylau," Vol. 2 of Schlieffen's works.

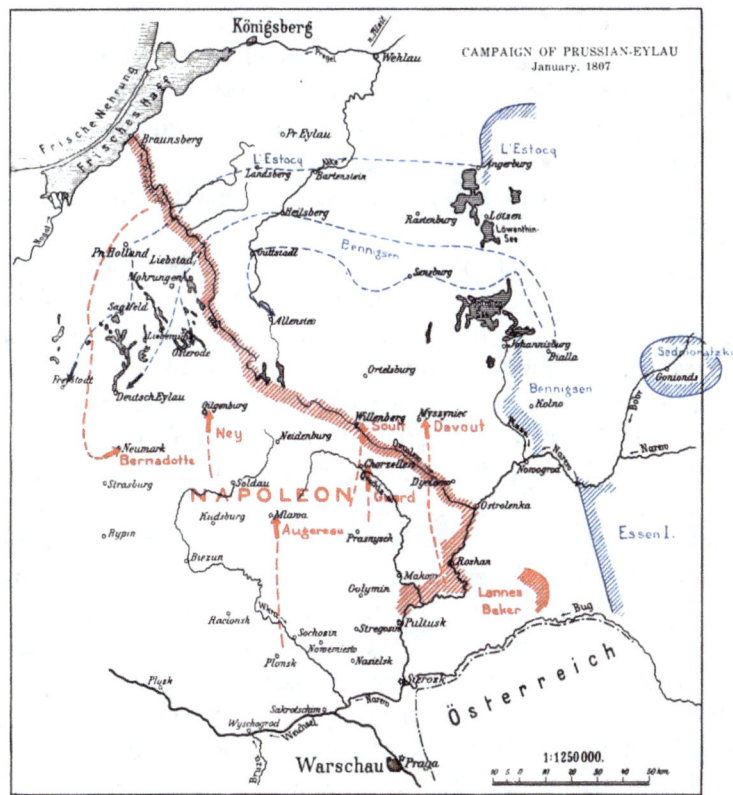

succeeded, as well as Napoleon on former occasions, in completely gaining one flank of the enemy. The position seemed most favorable. Should they be able to attack successfully, they would throw the enemy against the Vistula, the Bug, and the neutral Austrian territory. His complete annihilation could then be hoped for.

But Bennigsen was neither strong nor bold enough for such an enterprise. He hoped to be able to force the enemy to retreat beyond the Vistula by threatening his left wing himself and the hostile right wing by Essen. Napoleon, however, did not go back, but answered one turning movement by another, a threatened attack by a real attack. He covered himself with one corps (Lannes and Beker) against Essen, and turned with the rest against the principal enemy. This movement was greatly facilitated by the position and distribution of the troops in cantonments. In the beginning of January, the advanced French lines stood on the line: Myszyniec—Willenberg—Chorzellen—Gilgenburge—Neumark. The French had turned the enemy as well as he had turned them. Whichever attacked and conquered the other, would throw the enemy in the one case against the Vistula and the Bug, in the other, against the Haff.

Bennigsen would not permit this. His retreat had not yet been cut off. He could go back to Konigsberg or, via Wehlau, to Tilsit. He was, however, apprehensive of starting the retreat of his own accord. He wanted to be forced to do the inevitable. A favorable position on the left bank of the Alle near Allenstein made him place there his main forces. This improved Napoleon's position still more. It became similar to that of the previous October. The enemy stood, not left of the Saale, but left of the Alle. Napoleon could, by advancing on the right bank in his battalions-in-square formation, bring the enemy to a standstill at the first serious obstacle, even if the latter had succeeded in evacuating in time the recently occupied position on the Alle, could turn him and attack him under the most favorable circumstances. The enemy, however, did not seem desirous of abandoning his position on the Alle.

On 4 February, he was to be attacked in front and on the left flank as well as in the rear over the Alle crossings situated below him. Bennigsen did not await the attack, but started to retreat in the night. The road to the Alle was threatened too much. He therefore went a little to the west and wanted to reach the road to Wehlau by a slight curve via Wolfsdorf, Landsberg, and Friedland. Napoleon followed. Of his six corps commanders, Lannes had been left behind to cover the right flank against Essen; Bernadotte, who was to cover the left flank and secure Thorn, had remained behind too long. Ney, Augereau, and Soult pursued the retreating enemy on two sides and fell on his rear, though they had not intended to do so. Davout alone remained on the road which the entire army ought to have taken to "cut off," "outflank" the enemy and "press against his left flank." Ney was soon sent to the left also in pursuit of the Prussian corps under L'Estocq. All attempts to push Soult over to the other side to Davout remained unsuccessful. Augereau was not sufficiently strong to break the resistance of the Russian rear guard.

This would not have been important, according to Hannibal's point of view, if, Augereau, unable to advance, had even to recede a little. The flanking attacks of Davout and Soult would then have been more effective. Napoleon called Soult time and again to the main road for direct pursuit. The enemy, whom he wanted to "cut off" at all events, had to be driven back more rapidly.

The Russians had reached on the 7th, East Prussian-Eylau. Soult, then Augereau, Murat and the Guard, had followed them to this city. Ney stood on the left between Orschen and Landsberg, Davout on the right with two divisions at Beisleiden and one at Bartenstein. Bennigsen feared that, on account of the sharp turn to the east of the Friedland---Wehlau road, from Prussian-Eylau, he would be unable to ward off an attack against his left flank should he continue on his march. He decided to accept the inevitable attack not on the march but in a good position.

Napoleon did not intend to make use of the advantage offered him by the peculiarities of the road, but wished to continue the pursuit, as heretofore, with advance and rearguard combats. Ney was, consequently, sent again after the Prussians. Only the sight of the Russians who had come up to the heights east of Prussian-Elau, made the situation clear. The position was still very favorable. The enemy stood, like Terentius Varro, with a narrow front and deep formation. Had Napoleon assembled his forces, he would have been able to attack the enemy, who possessed almost equal strength to his own, with Augereau and the Guard in front, with Soult and perhaps also with Ney on the right, and with Davout on the left flank, while Murat would fall upon the rear. Chances for the annihilation of the enemy were as good as at Cannae.

Napoleon, however, intended differently. Augereau was to attack the front, Davout the left flank, while Soult was to cover his own flank, the Guard and Murat remaining behind as reserves. Only two corps were designated for the conquering of a very strong position. These forces were insufficient the more so as they did not attack simultaneously, but one corps after the other. The dense masses, led by Augereau, under cover of a snow storm, almost reached the Russian position, but were thrown back by a devastating canister fire and scattered by infantry and cavalry. Murat saved only remnants. A new advance against the front was

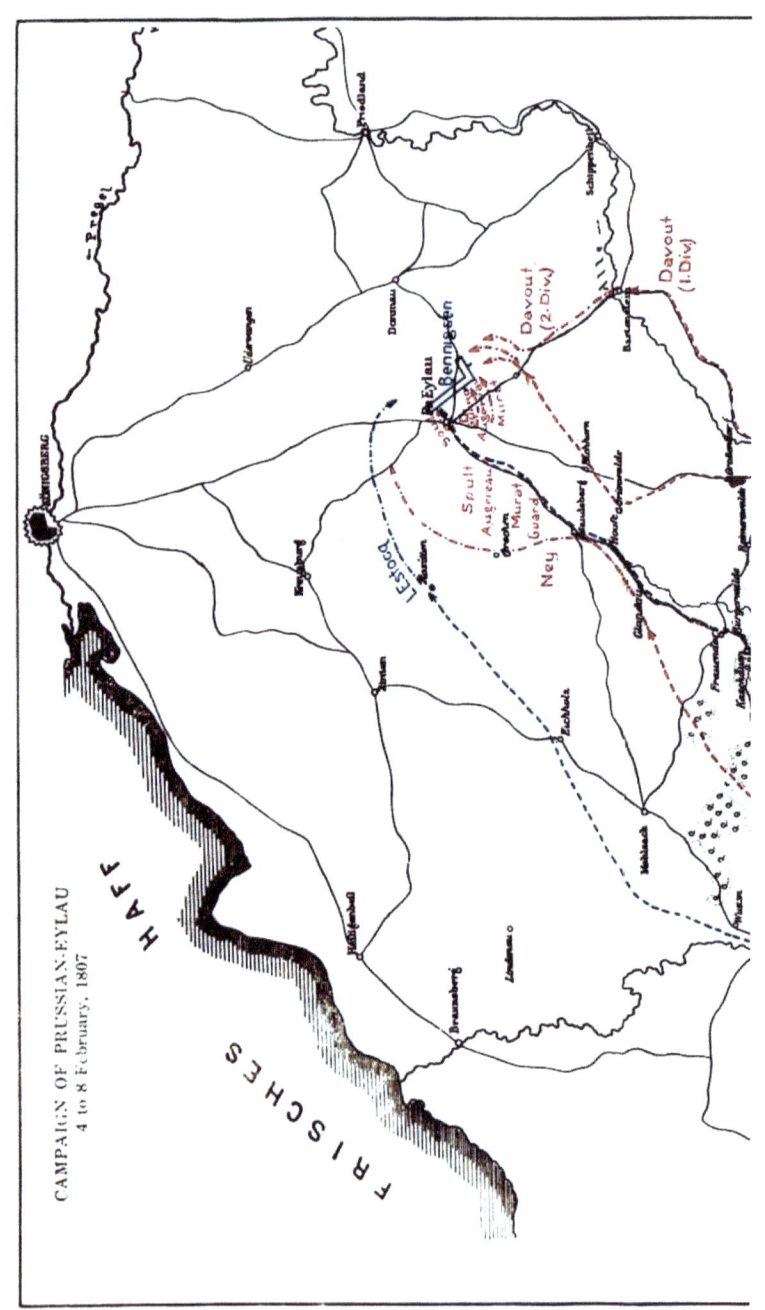

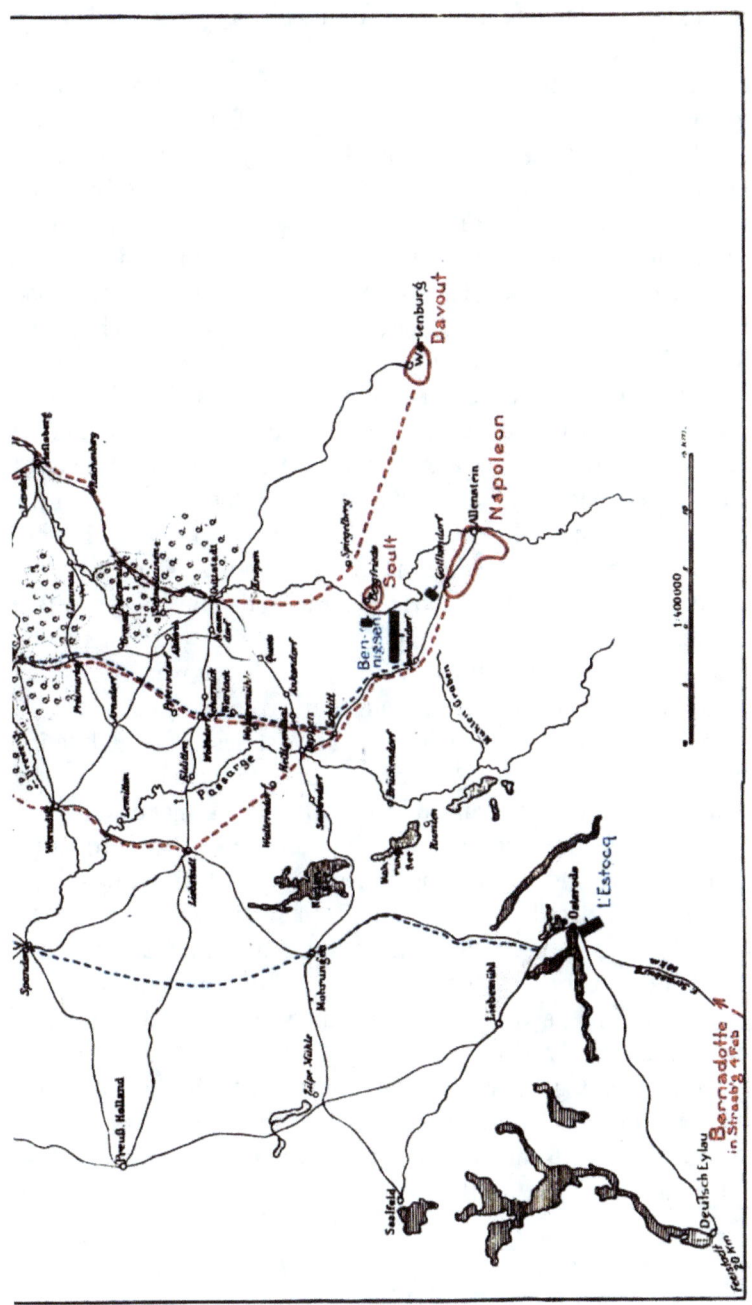

impossible. Napoleon had to limit himself to repulsing a counterattack.

Davout succeeded, however, in gaining some advantage after a lively and costly attack of the Russian left flank. The front was, in the meanwhile, not sufficiently occupied and the flank, consequently, was so difficult to surround that Davout's forces did not suffice to overpower it. The Russians stood at right angle with the front of Soult and the Guard facing towards Prussian-Eylau, their left flank opposite ~Davout. Neither of the two opponents had the strength or the desire to renew the attack. Napoleon had long ago called Ney; and Bennigsen had called L'Estoca with the Prussians. One of the two was to bring the decision to the one or the other side. Ney did not come up. L'Estoeq, though bringing but few troops, arrived at the eleventh hour. The right wing of Davout was thrown back, and later his center, with the assistance of the Russians. Both armies stood in the evening opposite each other almost in the same position as in the morning. There were no victors and no vanquished. On the following day Bennigsen started his retreat towards Konigsberg. Napoleon followed him slowly. However, unable to continue the campaign, he too went back soon.

The day of Prussian-Eylau marked a turning point in Napoleon's life as a general. The series of annihilating battles—Marengo, Ulm, Austerlitz, Jena—does not continue. The campaign of Pultusk, planned in a similar way as that of Jena, had miscarried completely. This could be explained by extraordinarily difficult circumstances. But PrussianEylau had likewise not succeeded. Nevertheless Friedland[*] (14 June, 1807) may still be considered as a successful battle of annihilation. But Napoleon himself could not attribute the victory in full to his own seif. The enemy had prepared the success too well. The Russians had crossed aimlessly, even blunderingly, inadvertently, the Alle at Friedland, took up a position with their rear to the river and thus accepted the attack of the enemy, twice as strong as they.

On account of numerical superiority of the enemy, a frontal attack developed of itself an attack against one of the flanks. An

---

[*] See "Campaign of Friedland." Vol. II "Collected Writings."

attack against the other flank might likewise have taken place, had not too great forces been placed in the reserve. Nevertheless the result was a powerful one. In addition to this, the Russians set on fire the suburb through which, and the bridge over which they had to pass to save themselves, not behind but in front of them. That Napoleon, on being informed that the enemy stood as yet at Friedland, paid no attention to the fatigue of his troops and hurried against him in quick decision, suffices to crown him with everlasting glory. The plan of the battle, however, was placed in his hand by the enemy himself.

Napoleon seems to strive to maintain in his later campaigns, the method to which he owed many brilliant successes. It was so in the Regensburg campaign of 1809.* The Austrians intended to surprise the hostile armies, consisting of Frenchmen and the troops of the Rhine Confederation, before their junction. On 10 April, Archduke Charles crossed, with 120,000 men in round numbers, the Inn at Brannau and below it; on the 16th, forced a crossing over the Isar at Landshut, against a Bavarian Division, and advanced in the direction of Kelheim in order to reach the right bank of the Danube, and unite there with two army corps (50,000 men) which were marching from Bohemia under Bellegarde, to defeat all the hostile detachments, situated to the north of the river, and by marching upstream to render untenable the position which the hostile main forces intended to occupy beyond the Lech. This was the answer to Napoleon's campaign against Mack. The French had to be driven to the south and, if possible, to the east.

When Napoleon arrived on the 17th, at the theater of war, he found the Bavarians, under Lefebvre, in retreat on the lower Abens. Behind them and further along the Danube the Division Demont was at Ingolstadt; the Cavalry Division Nansouty at Neuburg, the Wurttembergians under Vandamme at Donauworth; the Division Rouyer (the troops of the small Rhine states) at Nordlingen; Massena and Oudinot on the Lech, between Augsburg and Landsberg; and Davout north of Regensburg. The advance of

---

* See Mayerhoffer von Vedropolje. K. & K. Kriegsarchiv. Krieg 1809. Vienna 1907. Vol. I. Regensburg.

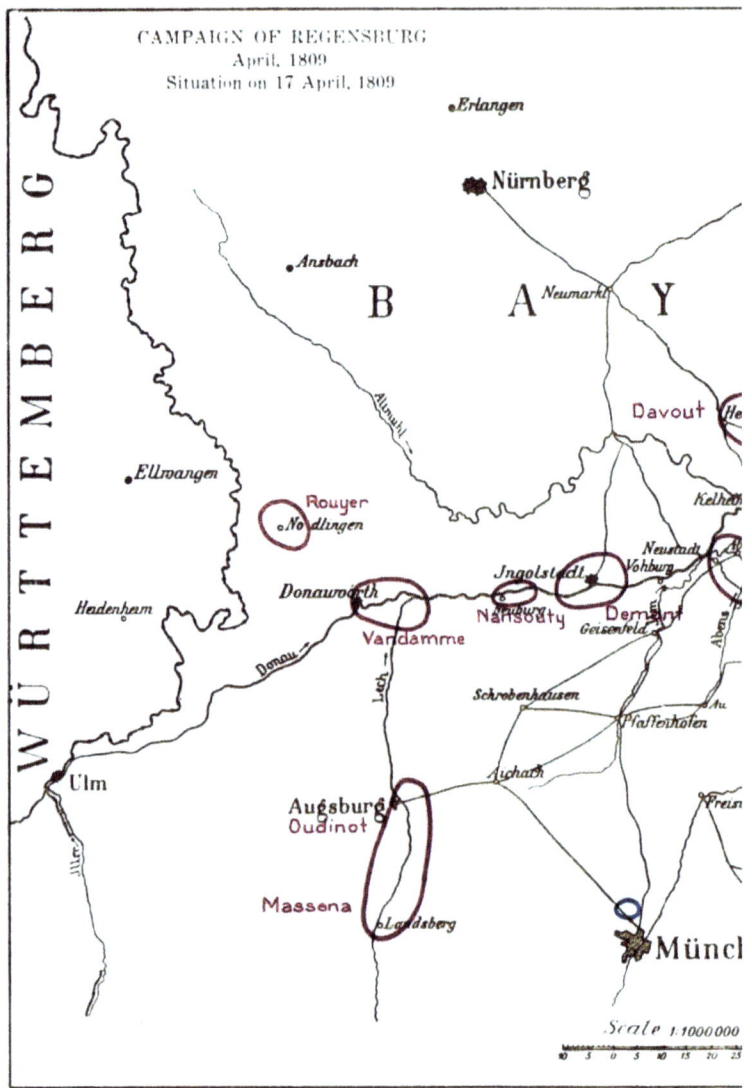

the Archduke did not give much promise, considering the condition of affairs. Ingolstadt and Regensburg were invested by the enemy, the bridge at Kelheim was destroyed; it was probable the construction of a new bridge somewhere between these two paints would be opposed by hostile troops on the left of the Danube. It was impossible to cross the river without one. Moreover, one

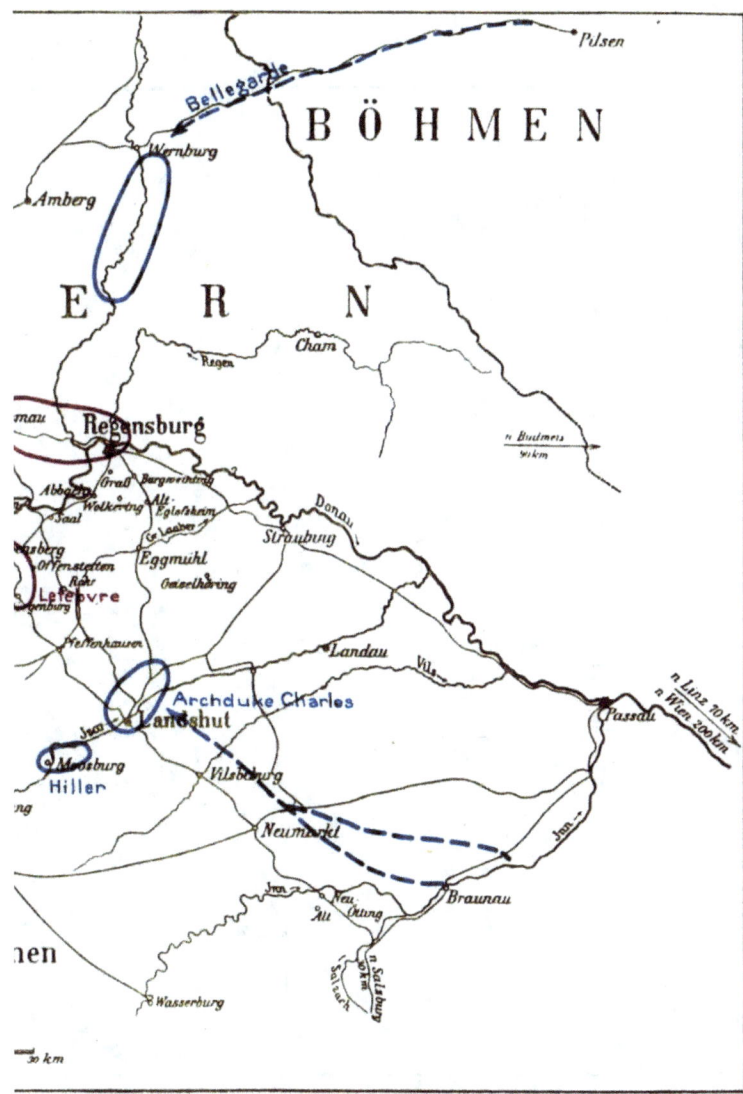

enemy was retreating across the Abens before them, another was on the right flank at Regensburg, while a third was marching toward the left wing from Augsburg. They were entering a cul-de-sac from which an outlet could be found only through a rapid retreat or the complete overpowering of one of the three enemies.

The Archduke saw the situation clearly when, marching slowly

42   *Frederick the Great and Napoleon*

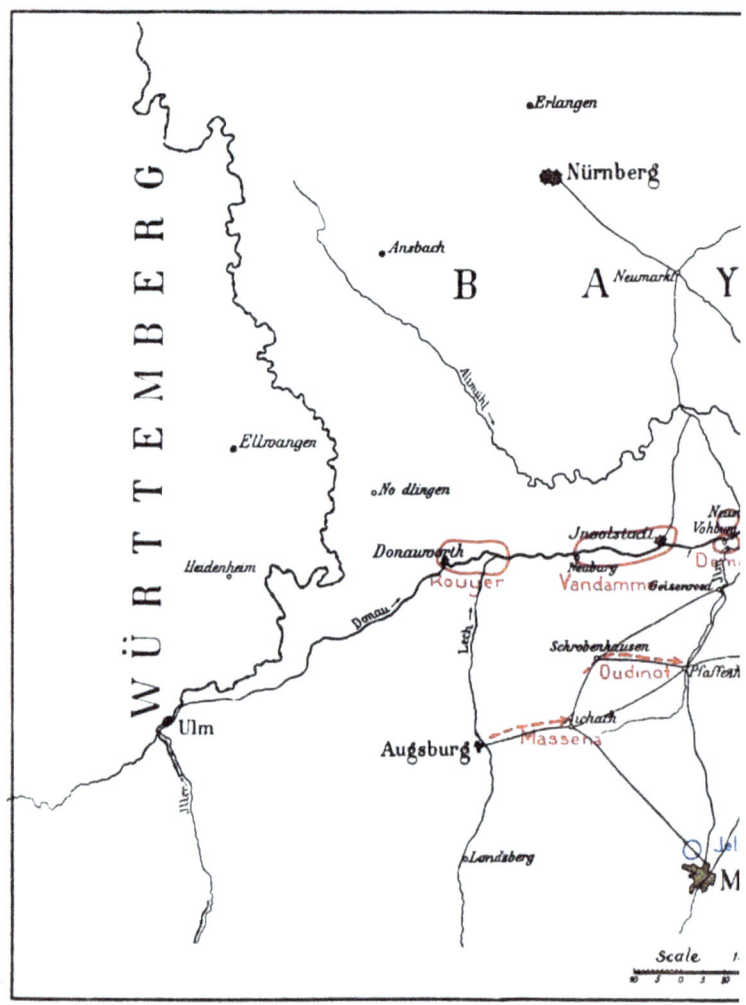

in two columns, he reached on the 18th, the locality of Rohr. Massena was still too distant for an attack against him. The Bavarians, advancing against the Abens and falling back on their reserves, would have rendered the position of the enemy still worse. The Archduke decided to move against Davout with his main forces and to annihilate him with the assistance of Bellegarde.

REGENSBURG
First Movements on 19 April

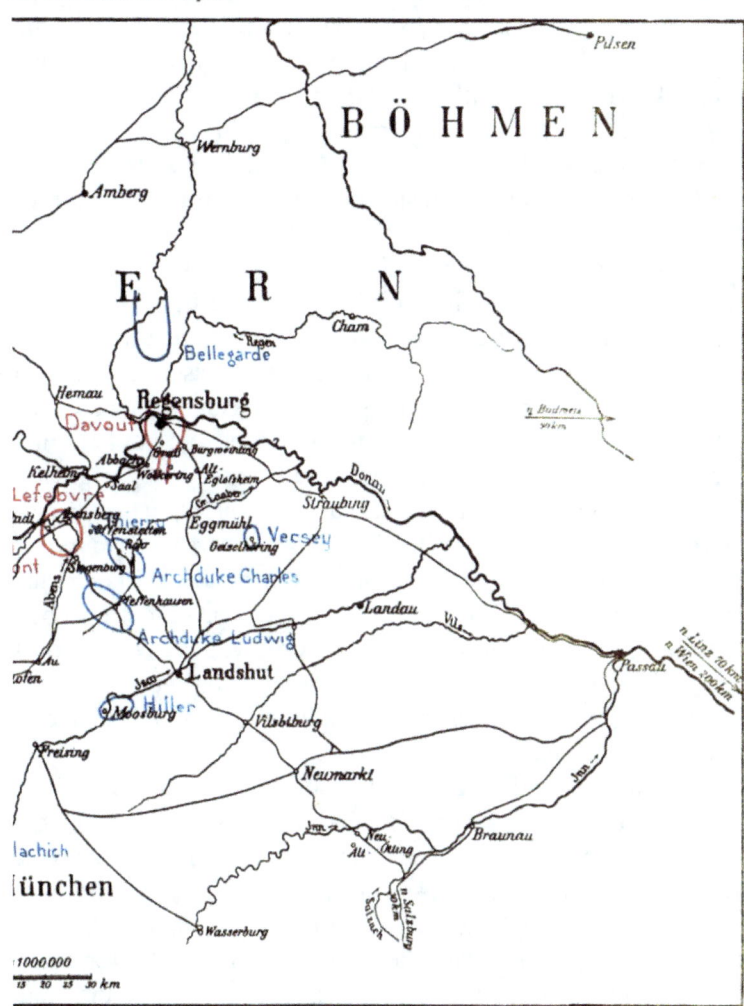

The plan would have been excellent if the bridge over the Danube at Regensburg had been accessible to Bellegarde. This necessary condition did not exist. Davout had crossed over to the right bank of the Danube and marched from Regensburg on the 19th, though holding the fortified city with a garrison. Bellegarde had to fight for his crossing. Until then the Archduke had to oppose

Davout with his own forces only. Only half of these were available, After the crossing of the Isar, Hiller was sent with 26,000 men to Moosburg to cover the left flank, and Vecsey with 6000 men to Geiselhoring for the protection of the right wing. Archduke Ludwig, with 18,700 men, was despatched to Siegenburg, and General Thierry with 5,800 via Offenstetten against the Abens. There remained 63,000 men to fight Davout's 57,000. This was a numerical superiority far from adequate for the solution of the problem.

It is apparent that the Archduke had greatly exceeded the necessary limits, by sending out the flank covering detachments and, in weighing the fighting power destined to beat the enemy, had fallen short just as much. It may serve him as an excuse that other generals in similar situations, and even Napoleon, had done scarcely better in 1813. This excuse, however, did not help him over the fatality of his action. He ought to have had a far greater force than 63,000 men to gain a decision. The problem here was to annihilate one of the best of the French Fieldmarshals and one of the best French corps or at least, eliminate them. Should the Archduke limit himself to hold back his opponent or to press upon him ever so little, the two other French corps would, in the shortest time, fall upon his rear and flank. His position was desperate. Fortunately, the enemy was not willing to take full advantage of this desperate situation.

Moltke has said: 'The junction of separate armies on the battlefield I consider the greatest feat which strategic leadership can achieve.'' Napoleon succumbed under this high demand on the leader four years later at Leipsig, and a second time, six years later at Waterloo. He ought to have felt the effectiveness of such a junction, yet he did not wish then to use this means. He remained faithful to his method of leading the entire army against the flank or the rear of the enemy. Supposing that the Archduke would turn against Davout at Regensburg, the central army was to deploy left of the Abens, Davout on the right of the Danube* advance from

---

* Bringing Davout on the left bank towards Ingolstadt, as had been planned, would have robbed Napoleon of all the advantages of his position and saved the Archduke from all his difficulties. The latter could have joined Bellegarde on the

Regensburg to Neustadt and Oudinot join the right wing from Augsburg, via Pfaffenhofen. Napoleon himself soon doubted the possibility of executing such a march to the front in the vicinity of the enemy, as well as its conforming to his purpose. Massena had reached with the head of his long column (Oudinot) Pfaffenhofen on the 18th, and dislodged from this point a hostile detachment. Would it be better to send him on the following day to Neustadt or would it not be more simple to push him straight via Au against the rear of the enemy? Napoleon decided on the recourse of letting Massena's column deploy on the 19th, near Pfaffenhofen, although the twisted skein had to be unravelled again on the following day in some direction or other.

The Archduke wanted likewise to advance on Regensburg on the 19th, in order to annihilate Davout with the assistance of Bellegarde. Davout, however, without coming in touch with the enemy, marched to Abensberg.* For this purpose he had the trains advance along the main road along Danube, two divisions marched via Teugn, and two via Saalhaupt towards Abensverg, while the cavalry went with some infantry detachments under Montbrun, via Dinzling. On the Austrian side the following were to march: Hohenzollern via Hausen and Teugn; Rosenberg with a flank detachment, via Schneidhart to Saalhaupt and with the main forces to Dinzling; Lichtenstein via Sanding; Veosey from Eggmiuhl to Regensburg.

The Archduke hoped to reach the position: Wolkering —Abbach, ahead of the enemy and to hold him at this point until the arrival of Bellegarde. But Davout was quicker, made the two columns turn to the right at the approach of the enemy so as to

---

right or left, according to his desire and gained secure communications. Davout's march along the right bank was absolutely necessary. However, he ought to have been directed straight against the enemy, whom Napoleon deemed weaker than he was in reality, and not ordered to turn his flank.

* It seems that Napoleon did not think that the Archduke had advanced quite so far on the 18th, but that he would march on the Eggmühl road against Davout. So much the more was it necessary for the latter to march against the enemy and bar the way to Regensburg. Should the offensive seem too hazardous to the Marshal, he could have awaited an attack in a position near Wolkering.

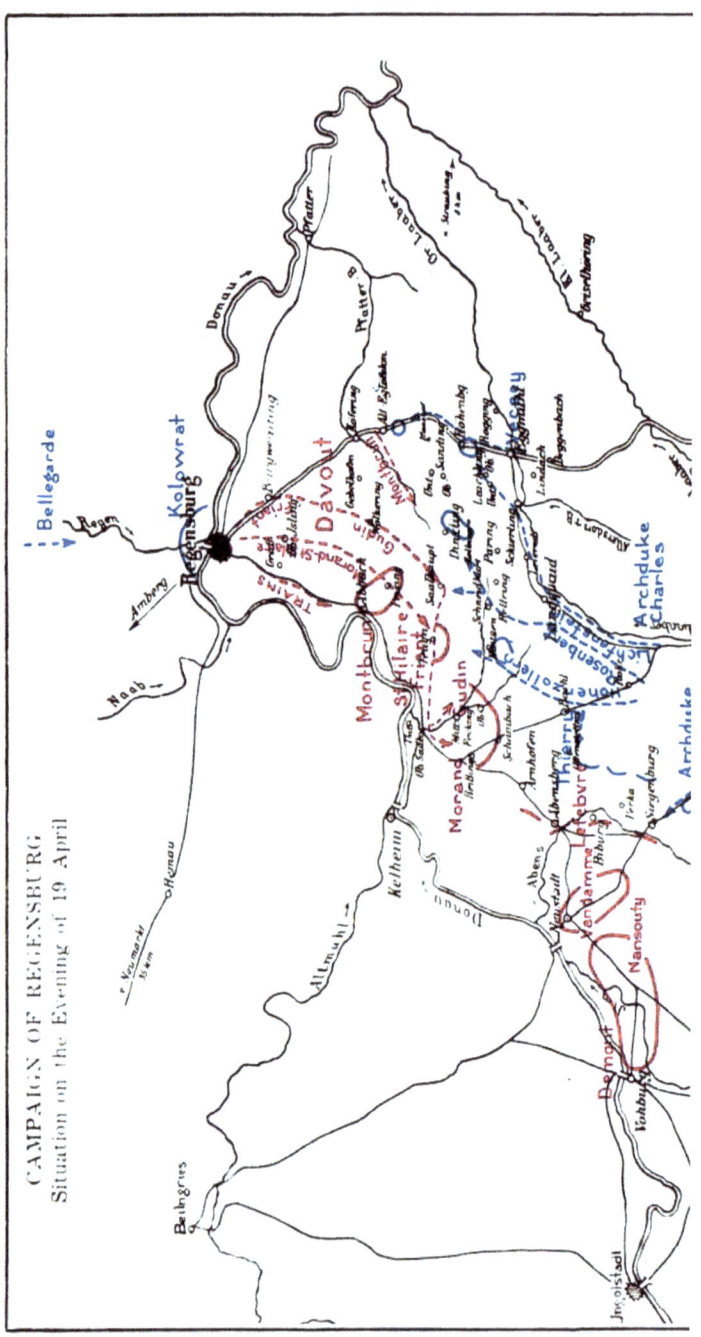

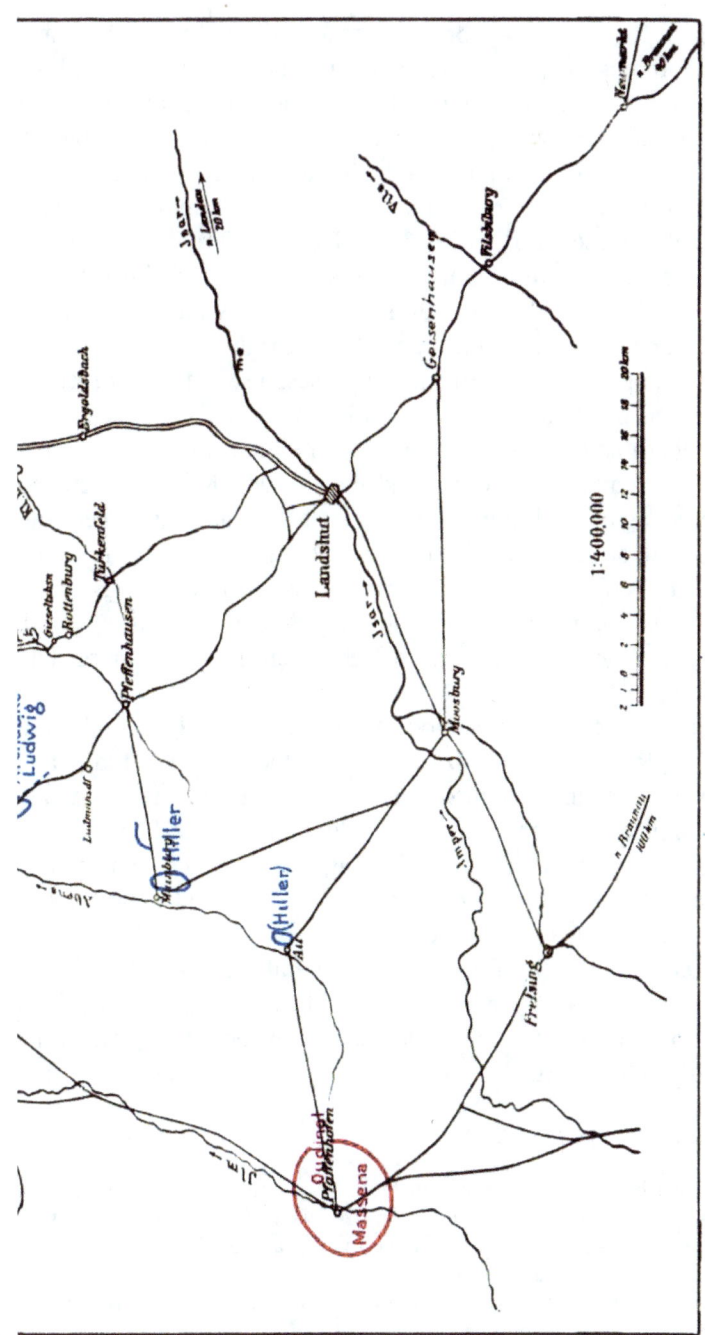

reach the Regensburg—Abensberg road via Teugn and Lower Saal. The foremost division (Morand) reached this road without molestation. The second (Gudin) reached the goal only after flanking combats, though not severe ones. The third (St. Hilaire,), however, was forced to turn to the left at Teugn, as Hohenzollern was advancing via Hausen. The French general immediately sent his entire force into battle, while Hohenzollern used only his advance guard, reinforcing it gradually by regiments and battalions, but could do nothing against the wider front of the enemy and was, in the end, attacked on the right wing by the fourth division, of Friant. Suffering heavy losses, he was forced to retreat to Hausen, pursued as far as the southern edge of the wooded ridge. Rosenberg had to sustain with his two columns tedious, but not decisive combats in the wooded terrain, which was difficult to observe, against Montbrun and against the flank guard sent out from Saalhaupt, allowed himself to be deceived and kept his main forces back. Lichtenstein, marching in rear of Rosenberg, did not reach Sanding in the evening but only Schierling; and retreated, without combat, in the dark, to Vecsey on the Regensburg road toward Héhenberg.

In the evening there stood: on the one side, Hohenzollern at Hausen, Rosenberg at Dinzling; on the other side, St. Hilaire and Friant at Teugn, Montbrun at Peising—Abbach, Morand and Gudin, placed from that time on under command of Lannes, with their leading troops at Ober-Fecking, Reissig, and Schambach. Beilegarde's army had remained on the left of the Danube after a vain attack against Regensberg.

Davout had skilfully avoided a general victory, but could not get out of the way of a partial one. Had he not obeyed the artificial order of the Emperor,[*] but followed the instinct of the soldier, he would not have turned his two columns from Teugn and Saalhaupt

---

[*] Napoleon had brought his army, with the assistance of Davout's flanking march, to a strength of 76,000 men. Since he attacked with this mass, on the following day, only the 24,500 men of Archduke Ludwig and of General Thierry, the advantage obtained was of no great importance. It was far more important that Archduke Charles had been delivered from the threatened attack of his flank and obtained the possibility of joining Bellegarde.

to the right towards Lower Saal, but would have gone straight at the enemy and defeated Rosenberg with two divisions just as he had thrown back Hohenzollern with the same. Since the latter had to retreat to Hausen, the other would have had to go at least as far as Hellring and Paring. Davout and Lannes would have resumed the attack on the following day, while Napoleon with Lefebvre, Vandamme, Demont, and Nansouty would have advanced via Siegenburg, Biburg, and Abensburge against Archduke Ludwig and Thierry, while Massena would have marched from Pfaffenhofen or, if possible, from Au (which he could have easily reached in the morning of the 19th) to Pfeffenhaugen. The campaign could have been ended in the evening and, at the latest on the 21st.

Through pushing Davout to the side and holding back Massena, the danger to the Austrians of being surrounded was eliminated. The two opponents stood facing each other though in widely separated groups. Surrounding could no longer be thought of. Only Hohenzollern's corps was threatened between Davout and Lannes in a rather critical position. An Austrian attack of this wing, which was later urgently recommended, promised no success. It is true that Davout could have been kept busy by Rosenberg. But an attack against Lannes by the recently defeated corps under Hohenzollern could he so much the less successful as the French center, marching towards the Abens, would have come upon its rear.

It is almost impossible to admit that Archduke Charles could have reviewed the entire situation in the evening of the 19th. He knew, however, that only under the condition of concentrating all his fighting strength would he be able to defeat an opponent who, as the previous battles had shown, had troops superior in numbers and in training. The most urgent thing was to open a crossing at Regensburg and bring over Bellegarde with his 50,000 men. Until then the Archduke intended to be on the defensive. Rosenberg was to hold back Davout at first, Hohenzollern was to go back to Leierndorf over the Great Laaber, Thierry and Archduke Ludwig join them in the night, and Hiller more to the left, having reached Mainburg, come up to cover the flank via Pfeffenhausen.

Archduke Charles thought that on the 20th, he would be able to withstand, in a good position, an attack by the left hostile flank. Lichtenstein was sent to Regensburg to open access to the Danube

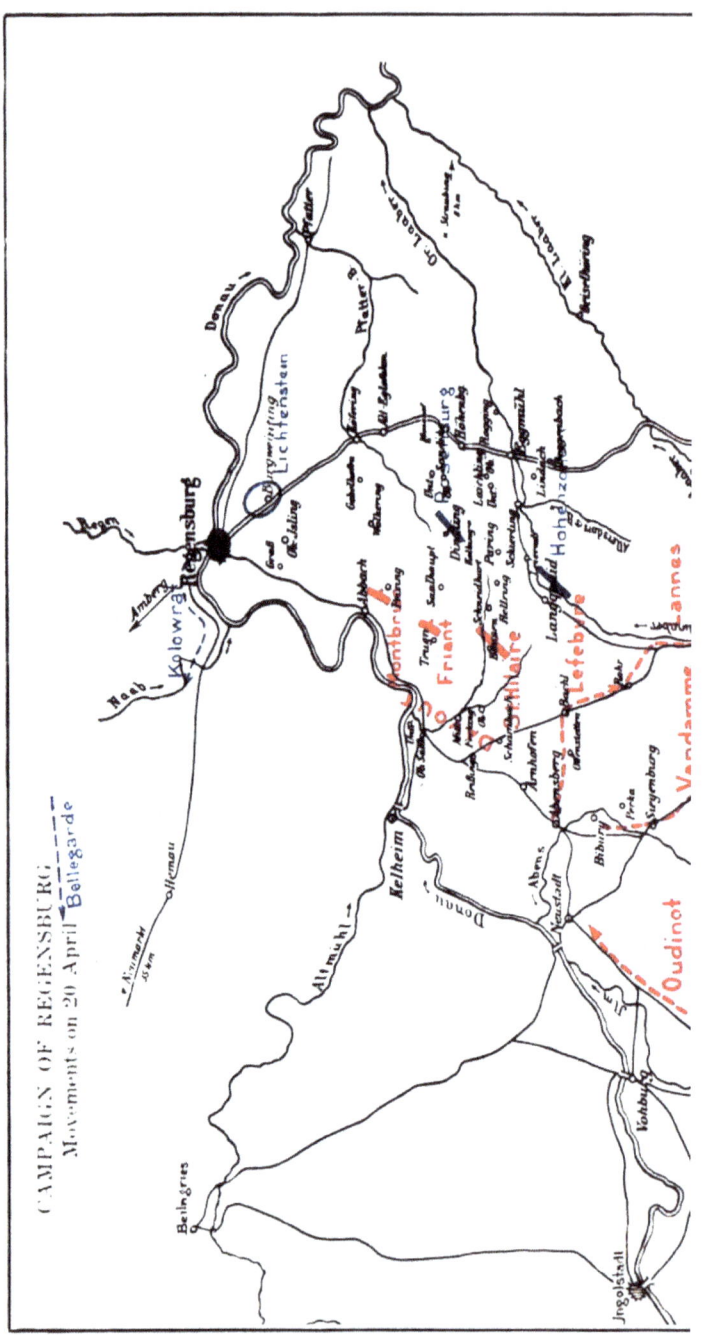

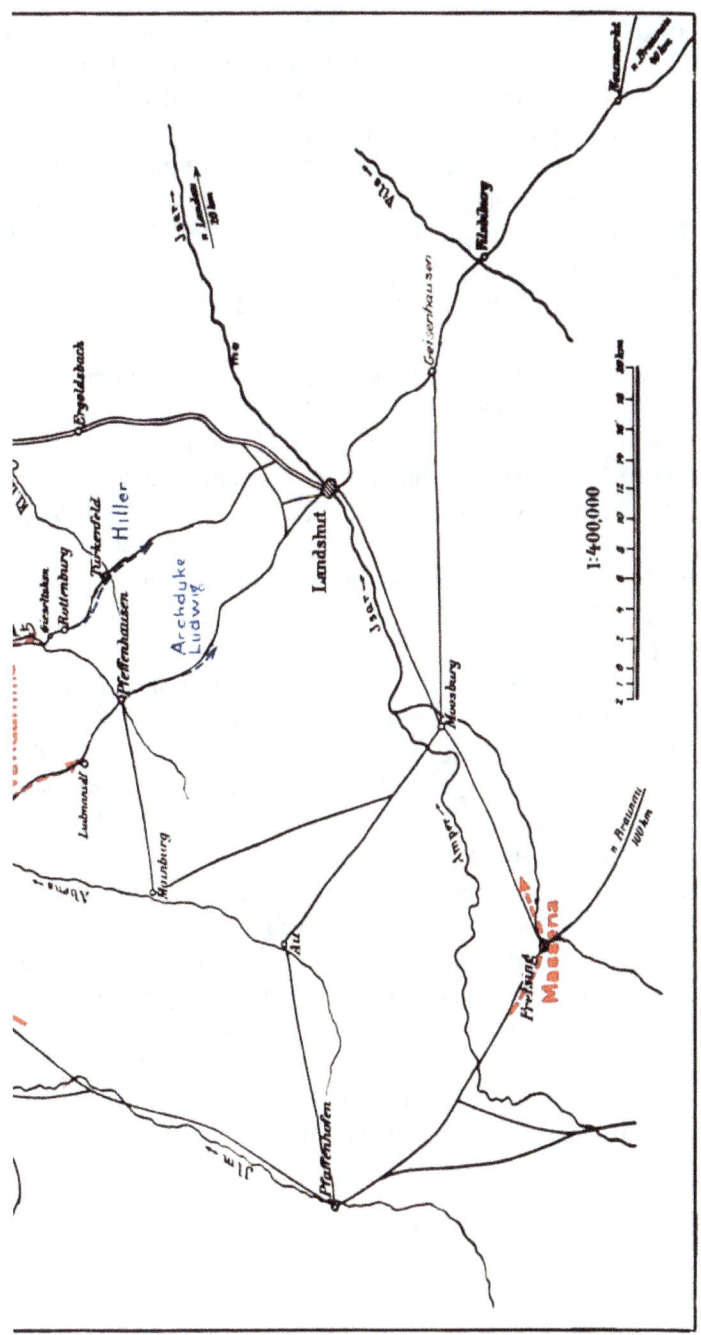

to Bellegarde. The latter was to attack the left hostile flank with 50,000 men on the 21st. The plan was surely not without hope of success and the position not unfavorable. It shaped itself still more favorably on account of the measures taken by Napoleon. He had translated Davout's message of the 19th: "I have maintained the field of battle after severe fighting," into "*l'ennemi bat en retraire à toutes jambes*."* The Archduke, being in full flight, was to be pursued not only "*l'épée dans les reins*,"† but cut off. Should this not be possible any more on the Isar, it should surely take place on the Inn.

Massena received the order to march to Freising on the 20th, in order to reach Braunau, by a shorter route, before the Austrians. Not quite in conformity with the purpose of pursuit Oudinot, who stood with Massena at Pfaffenhofen, was simultaneously sent in an opposite direction to Neustadt. The initial plan of assembling there the entire army was to be carried out, at least in part, in spite of the seemingly altered situation. Massena and Oudinot were thus, with one third of the French forces, placed out of the scope of activity for at least two days.

The Archduke would encounter on the 20th, in rear of the Great Laaber only equally strong hostile forces and on the 21st, after the junction with Bellegarde, he could have attacked the enemy with numerically greater forces. This beautiful outlook was frustrated by the Austrian corps commanders. Archduke Ludwig, insisting upon his better knowledge of the situation and on the right of a corps commander to make independent decisions, did not want to give up the protection of the Landshut road and leave his position on the Abens. Contrary to the order received, he remained there during the night and also during the following morning.

When he began to understand in the forenoon of the 20th the difficulties of his position and was on the point of retreating, Lannes with the divisions of Morand and Gudin was already starting from Schamback, Lefebvre with two Bavarian Divisions

---

* "The enemy is in full retreat."

† "Sword in the kidneys."

and Nansouty, was starting from Abensberg, Vandamme with Wrede, the Wurtembergers and Dumont were marching from Biburg, in all, 75,000 men against the 24,500 Austrians deployed as a cordon to the right of the Abens. Many of the small detachments were cut off and annihilated. The remainder retreated towards Pfeffenhausen. Hiller, intending to restore the combat by a counter blow, marched by this point to Rottenburg, came here upon Lannes, and returned to Turkenfeld. The enemy followed by both roads up to Gieseltschausen and Ludmansdorf.

Napoleon still believed that the hostile main forces, past whose left wing he had just marched, were still retreating towards Landshut and thought that he had scattered a rearguard covering this retreat. He hoped that, by taking up an immediate pursuit on the 21st, he would force the entire hostile army to halt at the Landshut bridge. Massena was to advance from Freising on the right bank of the Isar and complete the annihilation. Lefebvre, with the Divisions of Demont and Deroi, was placed at Bachl to reinforce Davout and to protect the left flank against a possible attack by Bellegarde.

In order to escape the threatened doom, Hiller and Archduke Ludwig continued their retreat during the night. They found at Landshut the roads and the entrances to the town completely blocked by trains. Only with great difficulty and loss of time could the task be overcome. Before this could be done and before the troops could pass through the town, the pursuers came up on the 21st. Fighting took place northwest of the town and in the town itself. The pursuers were, however, forced to halt by the deployment of the pursued on the right bank of the Isar. Massena arrived only after further retreat had started in orderly manner and the rear guard had left the heights situated on the right side. The Austrians succeeded, though with great losses, in continuing their march unmolested towards the Inn.

Napoleon, seeing the enemy before him, and from the messages sent him by Davout, was now convinced that he had followed for two days with the greater part of his troops only a secondary army and that the hostile main forces stood in his left rear. He decided to entrust the pursuit of Hiller and Archduke Ludwig to Bessieres with 15,000 infantry and 3000 cavalry, to

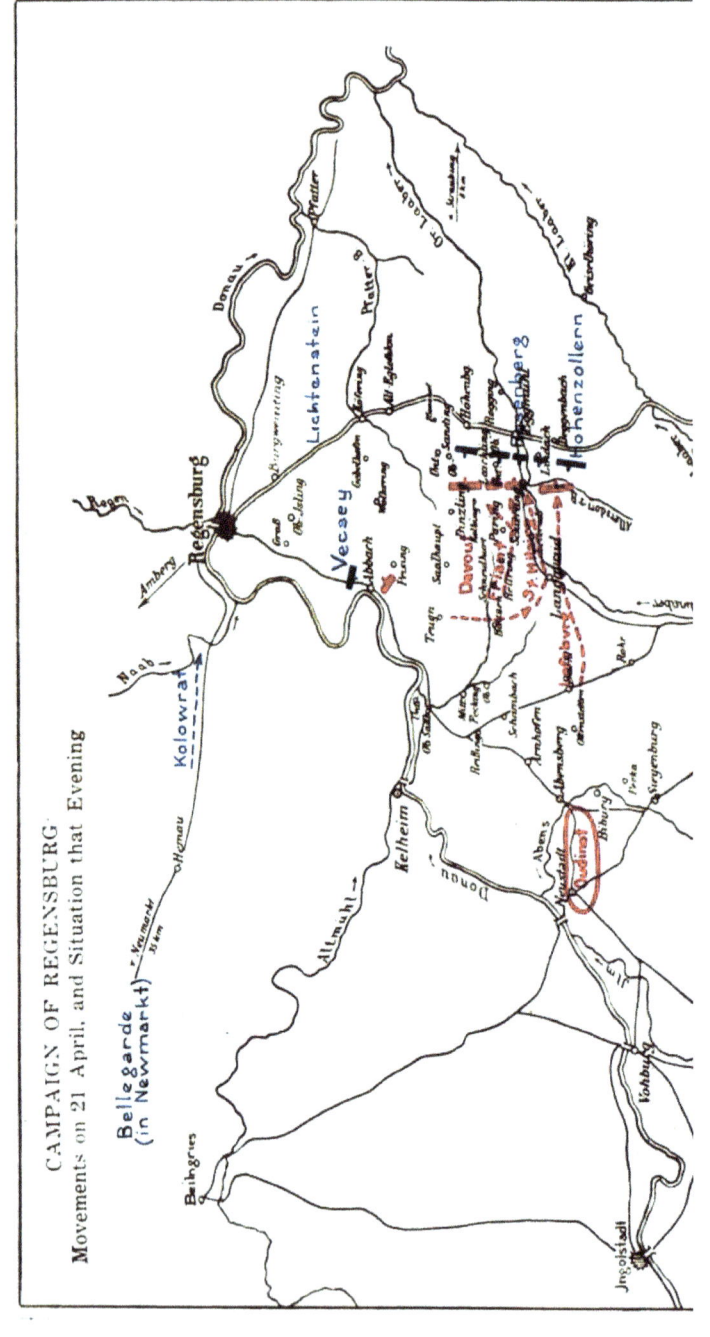

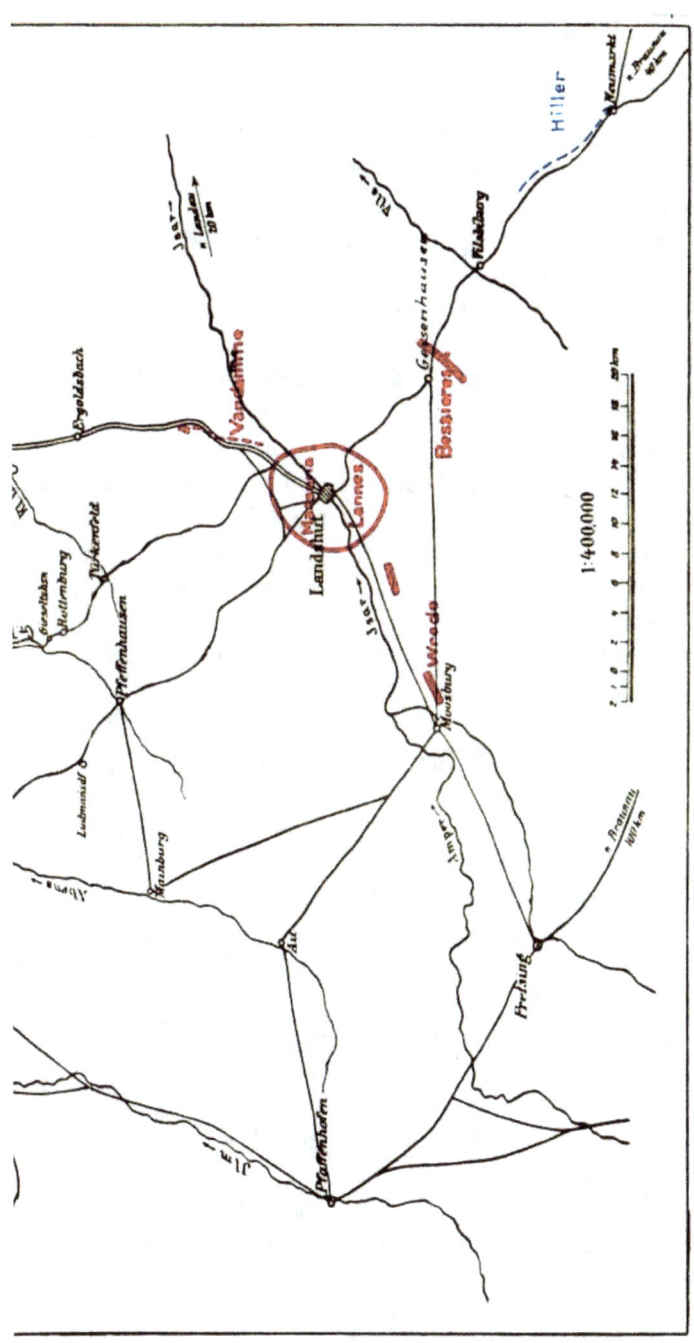

leave Wrede in Landshut, and to march with 60,000 men on Eggmühl in order to surround Archduke Charles and annihilate him.

On the 20th, the latter had taken the III Corps (Hohenzollern) beyond the Great Laaber without being molested by the enemy. Lichtenstein had succeeded in bringing about the capitulation of the weak garrison holding Regensburg, which was threatened from both banks. Communication with the left bank was thus restored. It might be supposed that Bellegarde would now cross the river and on the 21st, attack with 50,000 men the left flank, while Archduke Charles with 60,000 men would attack Davout and Lefebvre in front. In a most surprising manner only the II Corps under Kolowrat was on the spot while the I Corps was far distant, marching toward Neumarkt. Even this one corps did not cross the river, but started on the march to Hemau. The order, given days before, to cross over to the right bank of the Danube, is said to have been lost. Bellegarde, not favorably impressed by recent events, was still executing the original plan of operations; he wanted to join the Archduke on the left of the Danube in order to attack the enemy behind the Lech. Should it be impossible for him to cross, he could do nothing better than force the enemy to retreat by a diversion on the left bank. The operation against Regensburg was considered a secondary event. When the mistake or misunderstanding was recognized and the two corps called back, Kolowrat coming up in the evening of the 21st, before Regensburg, the favorable moment had passed.

According to an order received the evening of the 20th, Davout was to march wherever there were any enemies, in order to annihilate or capture them. The following letter was sent, at the same time, to Lefebvre: "Pursue the enemy, the sword against their ribs." In conformity with the above, Davout marched on the 21st, from Teugn to Hausen, and thence with Friant, via Hellring, to Paring and with St. Hilaire to Lanquaid. Lefebvre directed his march to the same point from Bachl. Hohenzollern retreated, fighting rearguard combats, beyond the Allersdorf creek south towards Schierling. Rosenberg marched from Dinzling to Laichling. At the positions of Lindach, Upper Laichling, Upper Sanding, on the one hand, and Allersdorf creek, Schierling,

Frederick the Great and Napoleon 57

Kolbing, the edge of the woods, on the other, serious fighting took place until dark with thrust and counter thrust.

Archduke Charles knew nothing on the evening of the 21st, of the retreat of Archduke Ludwig and Hiller, nor of Napoleon's advance to Landshut. He was still counting on the reinforcement of his left wing by the corps of the two generals and wanted to attack Napoleon with them and Kolowrat, expecting the advance of the enemy from Abensberg downstream along the Danube. Upon receiving information in the night of Archduke Ludwig's and Hiller's fate, he did not deem his position greatly damaged since a great part of the French troops would be hampered by the two generals. Rosenberg was to maintain, on the 22nd, his position opposite Davout and Lefebvre, Vucassovich to cover with his brigade the left flank south of the Great Laaber, the Grenadiers to remain in reserve at Mooshof, Hohenzollern to advance from Alt-Eglofsheim to Dinzling, Lichtenstein from Gebelkofen to Peising, Kolowrat from Upper Isling to Abbach where there was only a small hostile detachment and carry the latter off by frontal attack. A success could be hoped for if the projected movements had been begun in the morning.

But, since it was necessary to await Kolowrat, it was possible to break up simultaneously only in the afternoon at the time when Napoleon with 60,000 men, marching from Landshut, surprised Eggmühl by appearing there, and when Davout and Lefebvre advanced for attack. According to theory, the impending flanking attack would be harmless, as the Great Laaber, a deep and wide stream, could be crossed only at an easily defended point near Eggmühl. However, there existed other crossings. Vueassovich could not resist the attack made by Lefebvre from Schierling, by Vandamme from Deggenbach, by Lannes via Rogging and by the reserve cavalry which forded the stream at several points. He had to cross the Laaber and then recross it. Rosenberg, attacked on two sides by greatly superior numbers, could escape from the throttling embrace only through heavy fighting and great losses. Hohenzollern, as well as Lichtenstein, had to be called in, cavalry had to be opposed to the pressure, until it was possible to assemble the entire army in the dark of night on the heights of Grass and at Burgweinting. There was no staying at that point either. A retreat

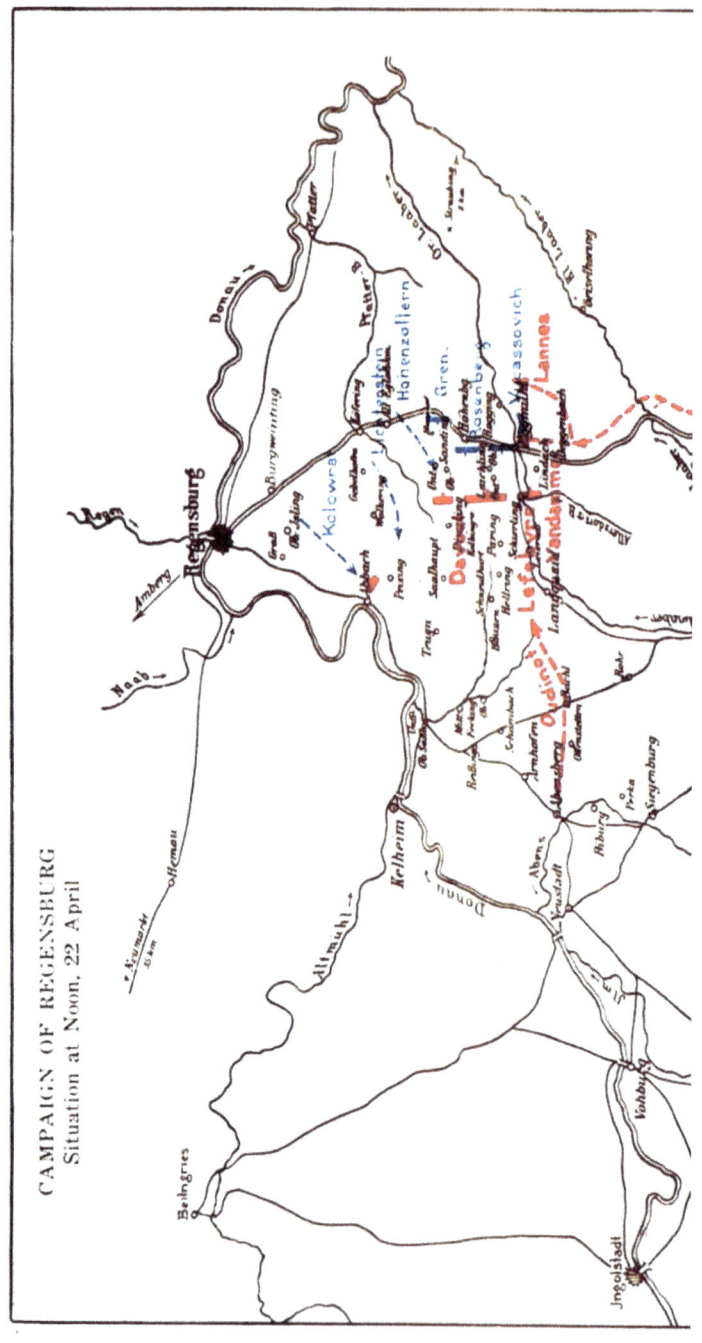

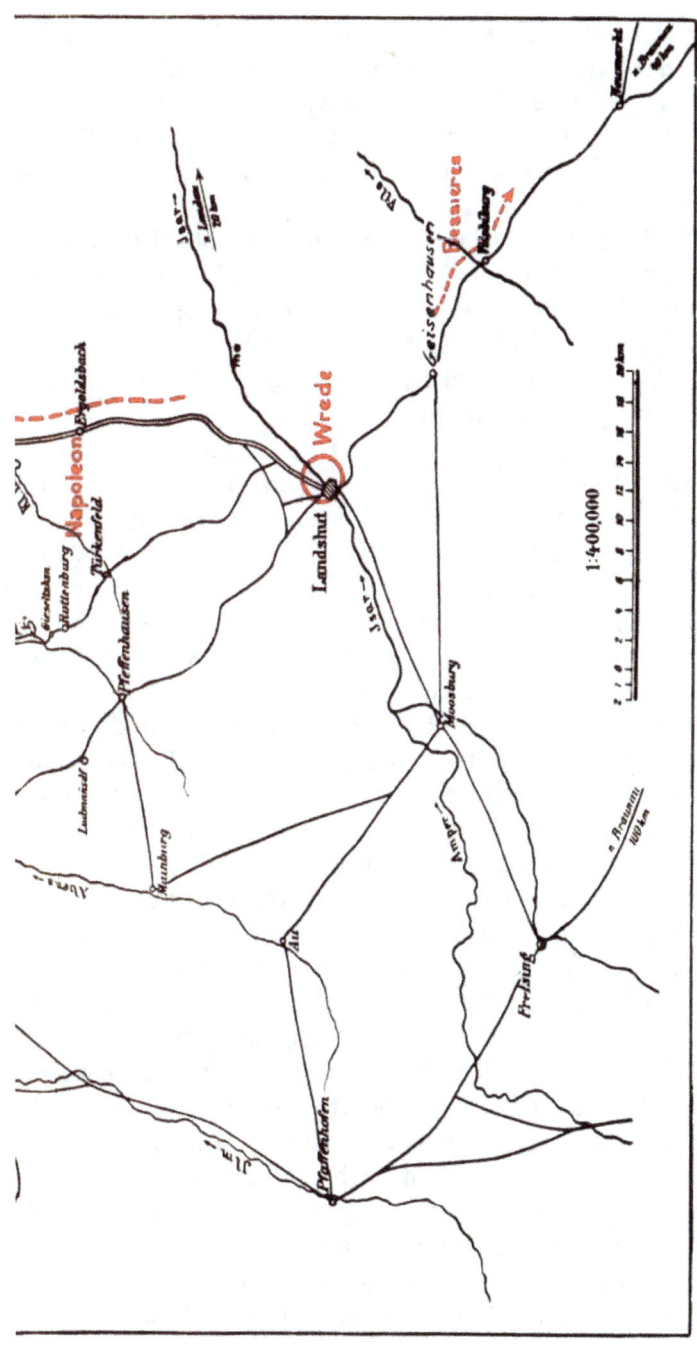

to the left bank of the Danube had to be effected in the night of the 23rd, and with the aid of an emergency bridge. The retreat was not yet completed when the morning dawned and the enemy moved again. The Austrian cavalry, which had fought gloriously the day before, was again forced to do its utmost in order to keep the enemy from the ponton bridge.

On the 25th, Archduke Charles has assembled Bellegarde, Kolowrat, Hohenzollern, Rosenberg, and Lichtenstein at Cham behind the Regen. Hiller and Archduke Ludwig were at Alt-Otting behind the Inn. Napoleon turned against this part of the enemy. During the seven days fighting the Austrians had lost 40,000 men, while their opponent had lost only 16,000.

To cause losses of one third of its strength to an army of 120,000 men and to scatter them in two parts from one point to the other, by an army of 180,000 men, would have been an enviable thing for any general. For Napoleon, who had in his hands the means of completely annihilating this army and "to close the matter with Germany within from two to three days," this was hardly sufficient. The Emperor stood on the 17th with three armies of about 60,000 men each near Augsburg, along the Danube with the heads at Neustadt and Regensburg. All he had to do was to advance against the Archduke who, after leaving 26,000 men on the Isar, marched into the river bend Abens—Danube with 94,000 men, to attack him from three sides and to execute what Moltke deemed the highest that strategic leadership could achieve.

On 18 April, Massena reached Pfaffenhofen, Lefebvre assembled his troops on the Abens. Davout erossed the Danube at Regensburg. Massena could have reached Au on the 19th, Lefebvre could have closed up more, Davout could at least have occupied the position: Abbach— Wolkering, on the right bank of the Danube, and on the 20th all three could have advanced against the enemy wherever he might be. The Archduke was, it is true, in the position to turn against any one of the three opponents with his entire force. Yet it would have been impossible for him to assemble a greatly numerically superior force since part of his army was held back by the Bavarians posted on the Abens. He would have succeeded, at any rate, in throwing back one of his opponents. This would have aided him as little as it helped

Terentius Varro at Cannae to throw back the Iberians and Gauls. If it were impossible for him to annihilate one of his opponents or to put him at least out of the field, even a victory would not have saved him from being completely surrounded.

Napoleon rejected the simple measure of a concentric advance. He wished to adhere to the tried method of assembling his entire army in the rear or on the flank of the enemy. This method which brought him brilliant success at Marengo, Ulm, and Jena, which could have achieved it at Prussian-Eylau, failed him here. The enemy had already advanced too far to allow a complete execution of the difficult advance. Hampered in his plans, Napoleon was forced to make new plans day by day, because of the false information received by him and the misleading ideas he formed about the enemy. The Archduke acted in a similar way.

Napoleon finally won in this contest. And this is no wonder. He had a force greatly superior in numbers in his favor. His troops were extraordinarily fit for marching, superior to all others in battle, in covered and broken terrain. His marshals executed his orders, putting all their power into their execution, while the Austrian commanders lacked in general training and discipline for effective action. Above all, Napoleon made his decisions quickly and, whatever might be their outcome, put them into immediate execution with determination and energy, while the Archduke awaited the clearing up of the situation, remained stationary and allowed matters to develop against him. He owed the fact of escaping the threatened annihilation to the measures of Napoleon himself who not only cut off the exit via Landshut too late, but opened a new one via Regensburg.

The final results of the April campaign were: the Austrians had suffered severe losses, but were not annihilated. Four weeks later they opposed Napoleon again and threw him over the Danube at Aspern. Since Napoleon had disdained to wage the offered annihilation battle, he could not "complete the matter in Germany within two to three days." It required a campaign of several months, a war, not limited only to the valley of the Danube, but extending over Tyrol, Italy, Poland, North Germany, and Holland, to reach an end, through the exhaustion of all forces, which could have been attained with one blow.

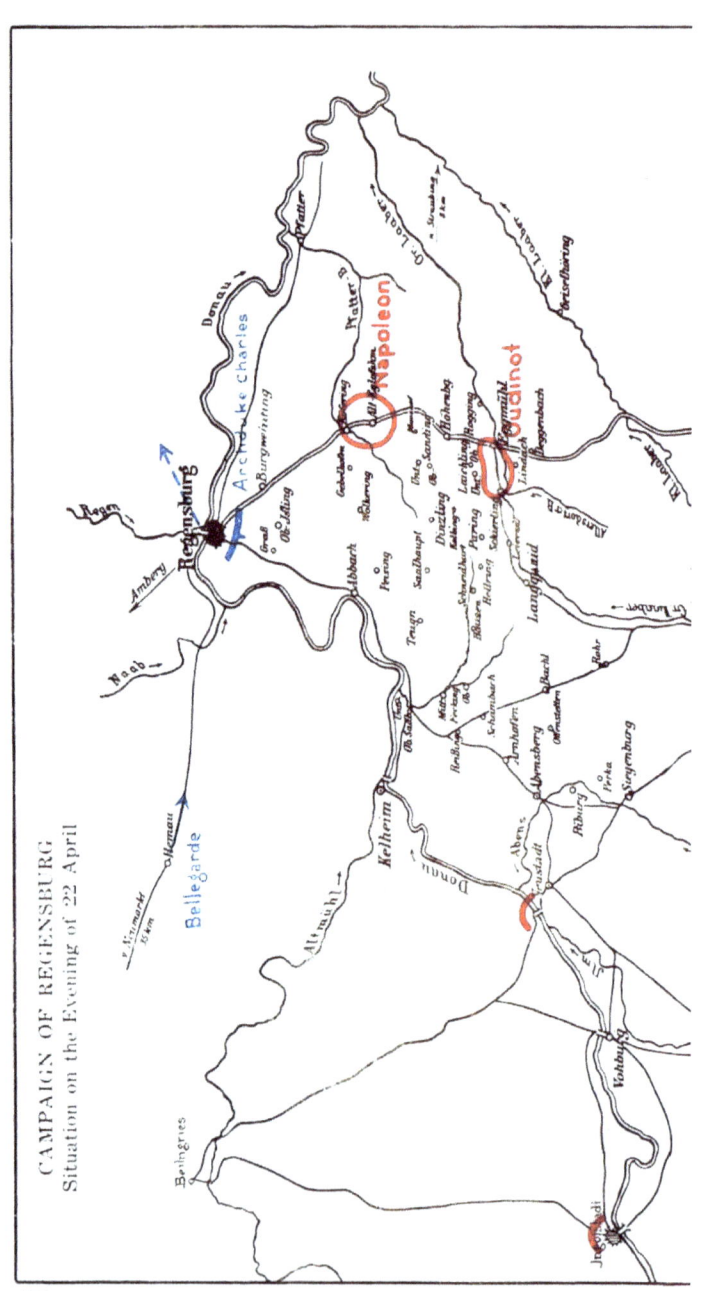

CAMPAIGN OF REGENSBURG
Situation on the Evening of 22 April

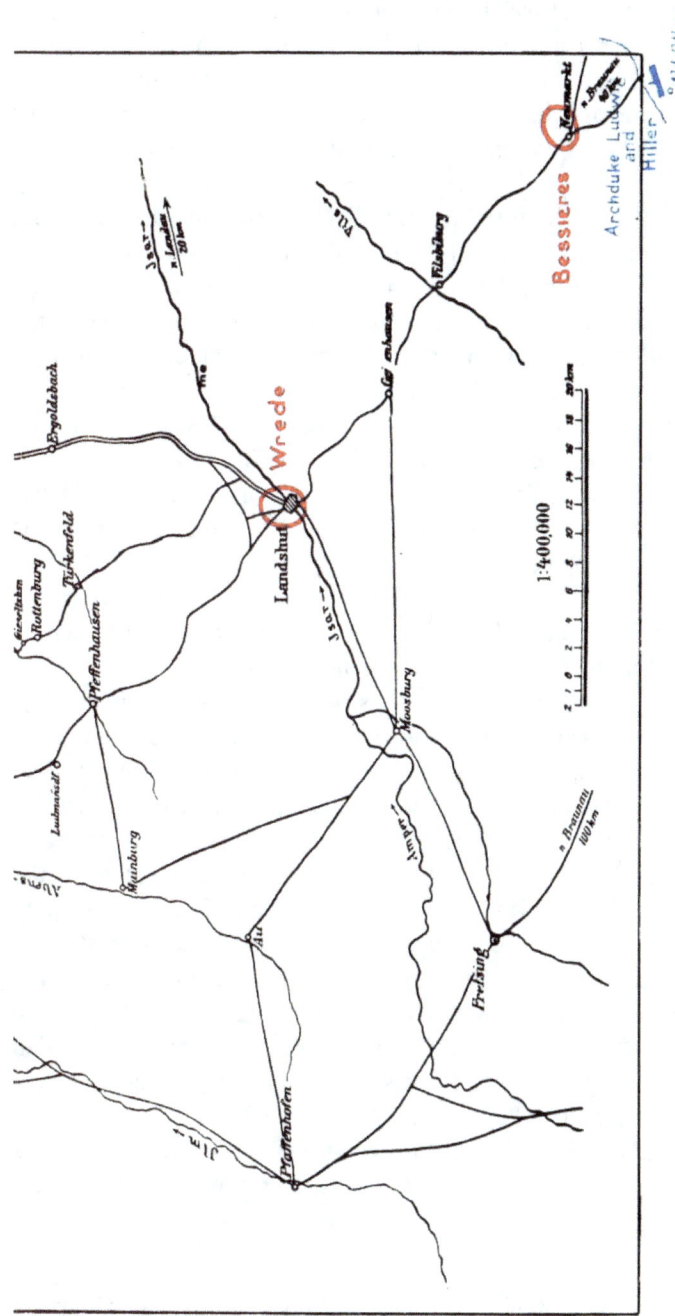

Napoleon several times more had the occasion to fight an annihilation battle. The attempt failed before Smolensk because of the length of his marching column, the development and deployment of which took up too much time. During the days before Dresden he gave up timidly a plan which had been elaborated with genius. Once more did the spirit of the victor of Marengo awaken before Montmirail, Napoleon gave up the turning of one flank, the cutting of the line of retreat and the combat with changed front. From that time on he went directly at his aim. This brought him to frontal attacks and attempts at piercing. Two of his battles, Borodino and Hanau, may be considered as victorious purely frontal battles. He owed it to his artillery that he was the victor in these combats. Notwithstanding the losses he suffered himself and inflicted on his opponent, only in Hanau did he reach actual success and furthering of the campaign. He succeeded here, though losing 19,000 men in saving 60,000 across the Rhine. At Borodino he pushed Kutusoff one kilometer backward. On the following day, however, the Russian general was able to continue an orderly retreat and Napoleon to continue an advance which brought him to disaster, both without molestation.

Not all Napoleon's later battles were pure frontal combats. The superior forces at the disposition of the Emperor, the consequently longer front, and the enveloping wings helped him at Wagram to surround the enemy and to achieve a success which could hardly have been obtained by attacks in masses against the Austrian front. The same thing would have happened at Gross-Gorschen if the allied armies had awaited the 3rd of May, left of the Elster. Such successes, however were too small. At Wagram, the exhaustion of both sides, more than the victory, brought about the peace treaty. Striving after the best, Napoleon was forced to "assembling on the battle field the scattered detachments" a proceeding which he had scorned at Regensburg. This was nothing new. Frederick the Great had come upon this "expedient" as early as 1760.

On 2 November,[*] Daun had occupied, with 52,000 Austrians and a "formidable artillery," a position north of Stiptitz and west

---

[*] See Supplement to Militär-Wochenblatt 1897, book 4. The Battle of Torgau.

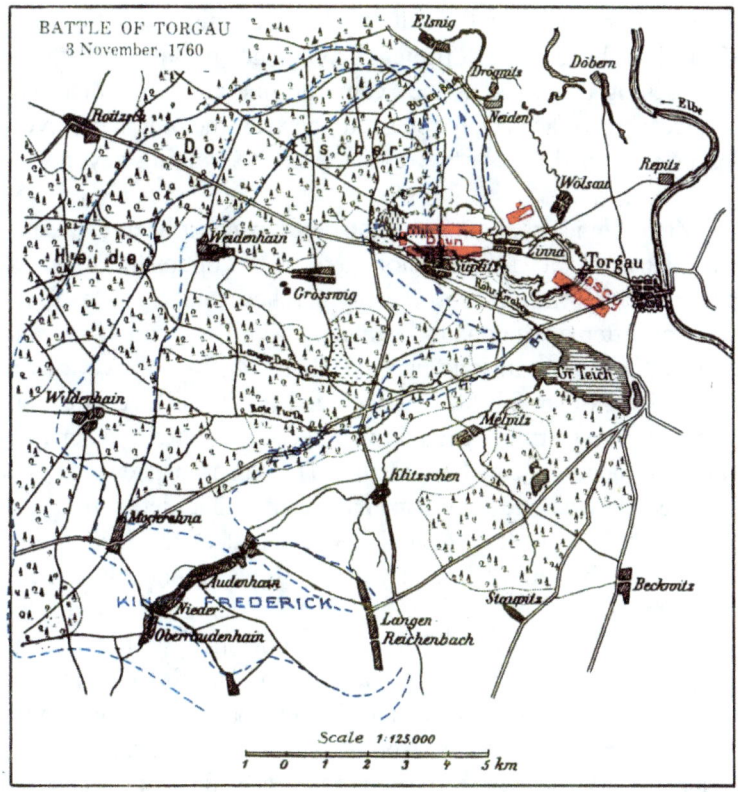

of Zinna. The ridge, only 800 meters broad, sloping gently southward to Rohr-Graben, northward to the Dommitzscher Heide and to the plain of the Elbe, was considered impregnable in front, according to previous experiences. A special corps under Lascy was stationed southwest of Torgau to cover the line of retreat, established on the left flank. The King, whose 44,000 men were encamped at Langen Reichenbach, intended on 3 November, to have Zieten attack the hostile front with 18,000 men, while he would turn the position in three columns across the Dommitzscher Heide and deliver a rear attack.

The march over the sandy heath, hampered by the artillery, was very slow. The afternoon of the short November day had already come when the advance guard debouched in the open near Neiden. It seemed too late for the columns marching on the left to continue toward Zinna over the difficult roads of the plain and to turn. The King thought to have sufficient time to go into attack with the brigades, in echelons, as they came up one after the other. The unsuccessful attacks were repulsed one after the other and severe losses sustained. The army retreated in the evening beyond the Strienbach.

Zieten, uneasy about his right flank, wanted to throw Lascy back. However, it was impossible to reach this opponent, stationed beyond the Rohr-Graben. Zieten marched under cover of his cavalry, after a cannonade lasting one and one half hours and attacked Suptitz with one brigade, then a hill northwest of the village by another. Suptitz was occupied and the hill ascended, but after this the storming brigade was forced to retreat under case shot. All success seemed impossible. The Austrians, however, had suffered likewise and were shaken by the fact that Zieten's artillery fire hit them from the north side while that of the King struck them: from the south side partly in rear. It was found advisable to draw the troops of the western flank, after dark, out of the encircling enemy towards Zinna. This movement was noticed by General Saldern and taken advantage of by him on his own responsibility for another attack. Zieten made the other troops follow. From the other front, generals and staff officers independently brought their troops against the flank and rear of the Austrians engaged in combat with Zieten. Twenty-five battalions, assembled at the last moment, pushed the enemy more and more against Zinna.

The following morning, Daun retreated from Torgau to Dresden. The Austrians were not annihilated, but put aside for a long time. The other enemies of the King, the Imperial army and the Russians, disappeared in a similar way. The field was open. The most important thing, however, was that the opinion began to prevail in Vienna that it was impossible to finish with this adversary. The King owed this brilliant success to the independent zeal of his officers, which no mishap could quench, their desire to conquer, to the fighting lust of the soldiers, and most of all, to the fire against rear and front, after an attack from two sides, which even the bravest cannot withstand for long.

Frederick the Great and Napoleon   67

The Russian General Bennigsen had likewise endeavored to assemble several separate army units on one battle field. In the first days of June, 1807, Napoleon stood with the corps of Bernadotte and Soult behind the Passarge, with Davout south of Allenstein—Osterode, with the remaining army in rear of the latter up to the Vistula and beyond it, with Ney's corps as advance guard in the region Guistadt, Altkirch, Scharnick, Queetz, Knopen. The French Emperor intended to deploy his army and attack the Russo-Prussians which were with the main corps under Bennigsen at Heilsberg (advance guard Launau), with the secondary corps under L'Estocgq at Heiligenbeil. Bennigsen wanted to ariticipate the attack of his adversary and annihilate the isolated Ney. On 5 June were sent forward: Remboff with one division of the secondary corps against the bridgehead of Spaden to keep back Bernadotte, and Dochtorew with two divisions against the bridgehead of Lemitten against Soult. The former was repulsed, the second took the bridgehead of Lemitten; both sustained great losses, but fulfilled their order to draw off the two marshals.

Since Davout was too far away to join in the combat, the annihilating attack against Ney could be undertaken. For this purpose, the advance on 5 June was to be as follows: Sacken with three divisions and strong cavalry, followed by the Guard to Wolfsdorf via Arnsdorf; Bagration with the advance guard from Launau via Gronau to Altkirch; Gortschakow with half a division to Guttstadt along the right bank of the Alle; Platow with his Cossacks and half a division to Heiligenthal via Bergfriede. When Bagration reached Altkirch, nothing was to be seen of the other columns. He decided to await them before beginning the attack. This gave Ney time to assemble his scattered detachments and, when Sacken appeared two hours later at Wolfsdorf, he had started on an orderly retreat. It would still have been possible to cut off the Marshal if Sacken had led his column, greatly superior in numbers to that of the enemy, via Warlack to Deppen or Heiligenthal. Sacken however, joined Bagration. The guard had been withdrawn some time before to Neuendorf via Petersdorf; the entire army was then assembled and the advance to Queetz begun. Platow had, in the meanwhile, broken into the retreating French trains. This, however, did not deceive Ney. He halted at Ankendorf and awaited the attack which the adversary, exhausted by long marches, had no longer the strength to deliver.

"Slowly and unbelievably cautiously" did the Russians advance toward Ankendorf on the 6th. When they threatened both flanks with their superior numbers, Ney began his retreat. Although three bridges had been built at Deppen, the passage could be effected only with "quite considerable losses." The Passarge stopped the pursuit.

The carefully elaborated plan had miscarried because Bagration had hesitated to hold the front of the enemy by an attack and because Sacken had been afraid to advance independently against his flank or rear and had turned toward the center, thus arriving likewise before his front. The latter was considered as the

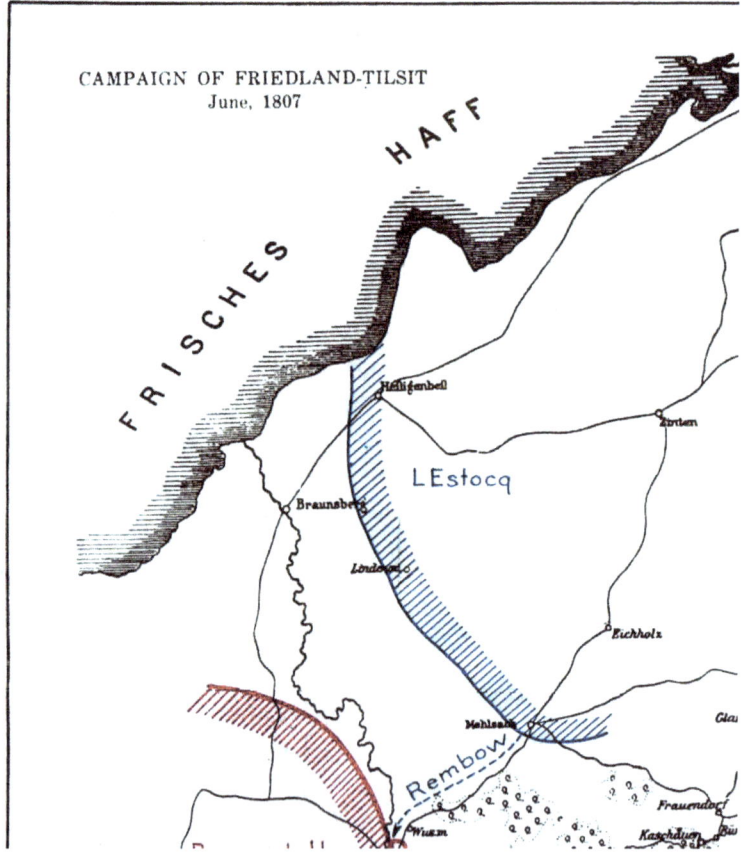

most guilty, was tried by a court-martial and sentenced to dismissal, but was soon pardoned and reinstated. This measure had not much effect. Later too many generals were not afraid to commit the same mistakes as Bregration and Sacken. Even now separated army detachments have the beloved habit of pressing together before the enemy's front before starting the attack. In order to counteract this, it behooves the superior leader to see that the inevitable disparity in time between the arrival of one unit before the front and of the other in flank or rear, be as short as possible and give orders adequate to the purpose.

Even Napoleon had never solved this problem entirely. He endeavored to assemble his forces on the battle field by only threatening the enemy on his front, while a detached unit was

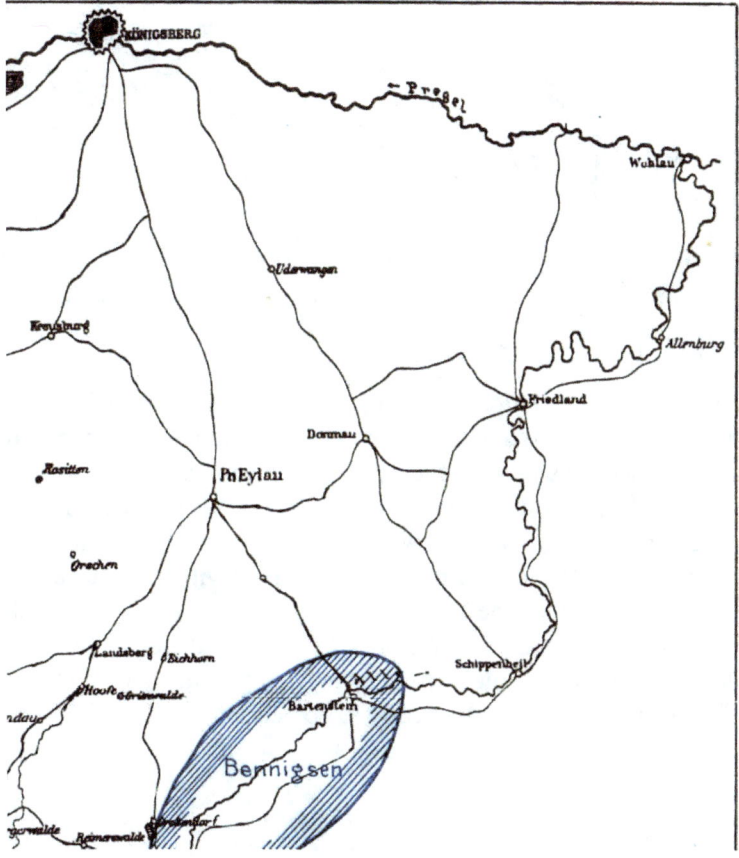

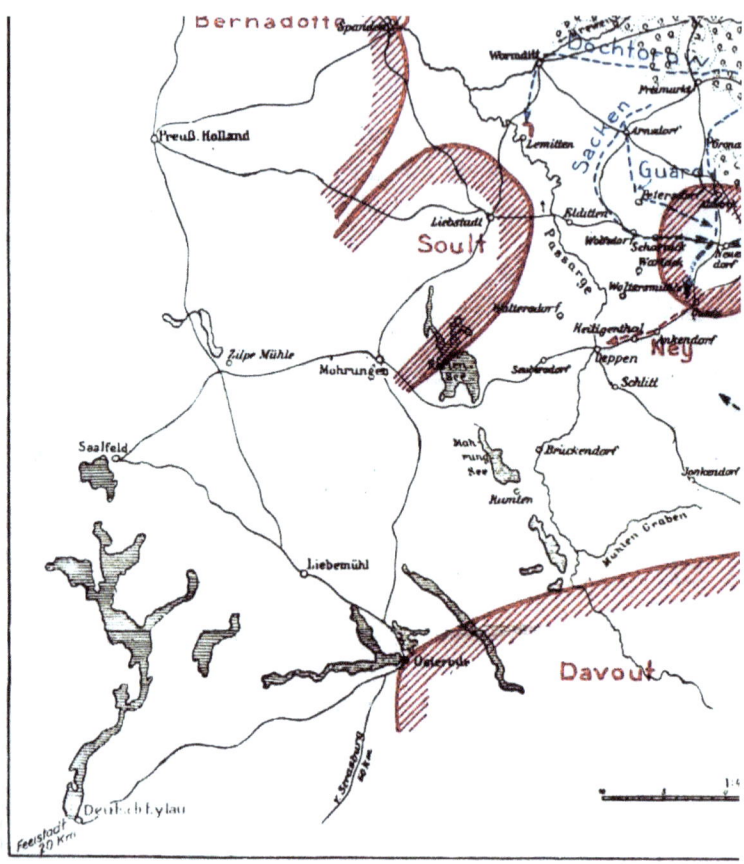

advancing from afar for a flanking attack. This could succeed when the enemy attacked and the detached army unit arrived rapidly. It did not succeed when the enemy preferred to await the attack and the detached unit was held back by a hostile detachment. It was necessary then to overthrow without much ado the checking enemy. But if the latter did not yield to that "without much ado," much time was lost, the entire plan of junction and flanking attack speedily recognized, the decision not awaited and the retreat of the doomed enemy took place, before the noose could be drawn tight. This happened almost identically at Lowenberg and Dresden with

Frederick the Great and Napoleon

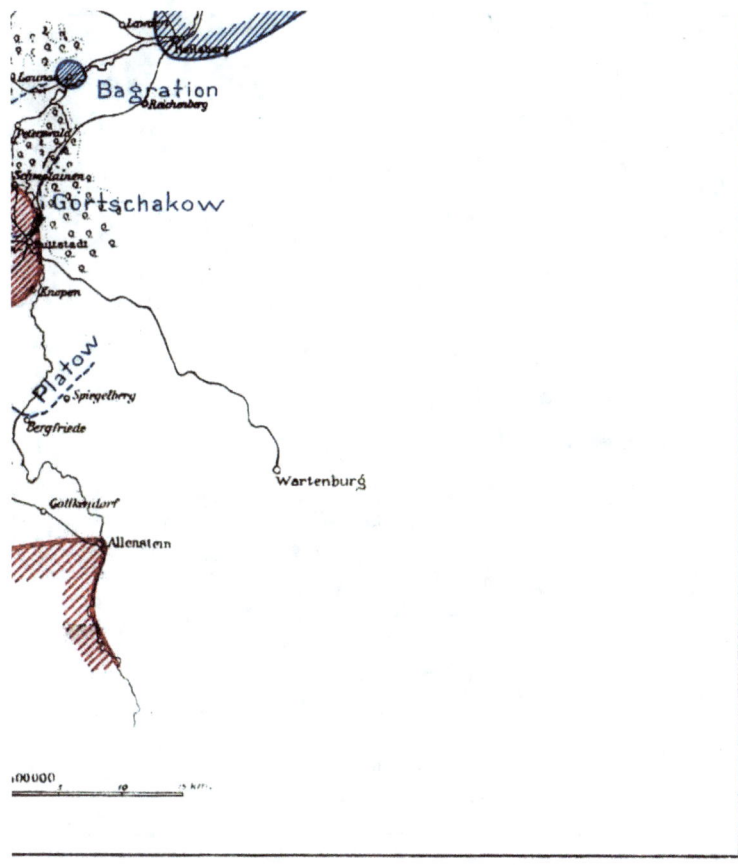

the intended flank attacks of Ney and Vandamme.*

When, however, at Bautzen Ney reached the battle field in time, he was not sent against the flank, but against the point of the right wing and Blucher, however great his wish to hold out, was able to escape the fatal blow and was obliged ta do so. Thus much has to be recognized: a frontal attack must take place simultaneously with a flank attack. The enemy must be fully occupied so as to be wholly unable to avoid the flank attack. If the attack is made by the enemy who is to be turned, like Melas at

---

* See "1813" in Vol. II of the "Collected Writings." The Marshal intended to include in the projected book edition of "Cannae," 1813, beginning with the armistice, as "this campaign represented a great Cannae."

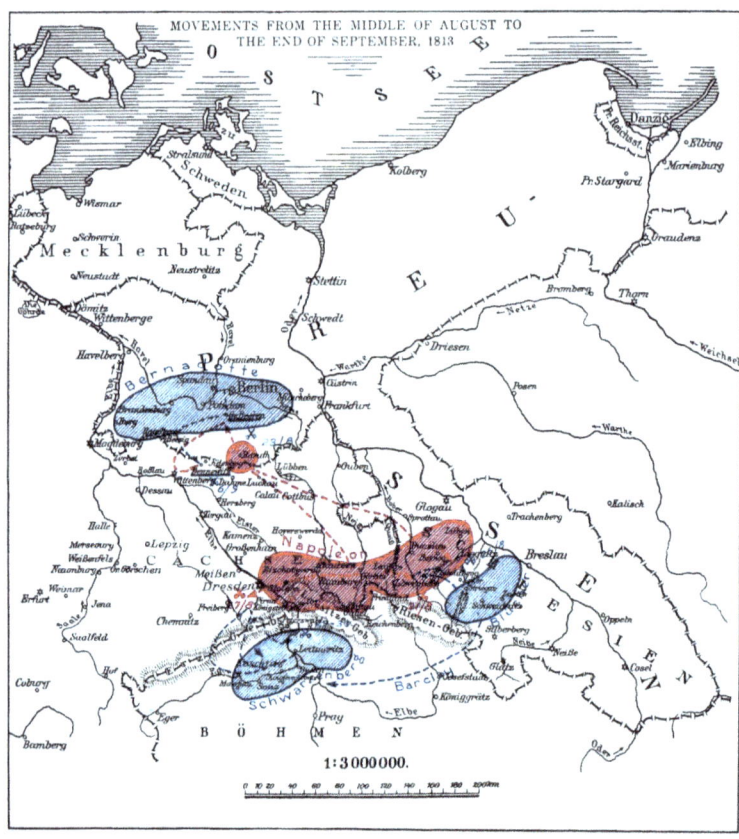

Marengo, Hohenlohe at Jena, Napoleon at Waterloo, so much the better; if not, the other side must decide to take the burden upon itself.

The manner of turning or surrounding at Bautzen, Lowenberg, and Dresden depended on the maneuvering of the enemy to the rear. If the throwing back of the enemy in the direction contrary to natural communications at Marengo, Ulm, and Jena was fatal, yea, annihilating for the vanquished, the maneuvering backward in the direction of natural communications was more injurious for the victor than for the defeated. The victories of Gross-Gorschen and Bautzen and the long drawn out retreat of the allies forced Napoleon to detach numerous units and flank guards, dissolved gradually the army of recruits and obliged him to make an

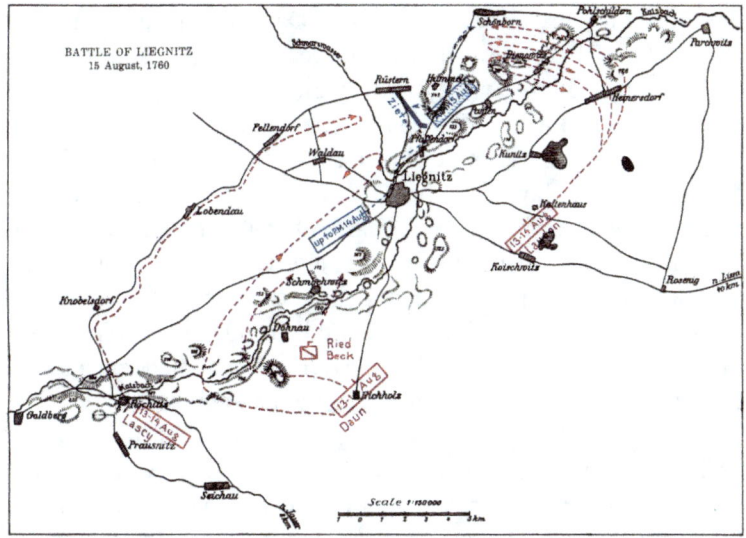

armistice which was just as welcome to the allies, but who could have done without it more easily than he who endeavored to take advantage of two victorious battles by an uninterrupted pursuit.

After the end of the armistice the situation had changed completely. The problem which devolved on Napoleon in the spring, or which he had chosen himself: i.e., the assembling of separated armies on the field of battle, devolved in August on the Allies. They had surrounded Napoleon, standing between Dresden and Liegnitz, with the Northern Army in Berlin, the main army in Silesia and the Austrian army in Bohemia, although they were at a respectful distance. It would have been a simple matter for the great war lord to draw out of the threatened surrounding and then to attack one of the hostile armies with numerical superiority of forces.

This is what Frederick the Great had done in 1760 in a much more dangerous situation. The King stood on 14 August,[*] with 30,000 men southwest of Liegnitz with Lascy, Daun, and Laudon opposite him, with 100,000 men. A Russian army had also crossed

---

[*] See "1818" of Vol. II of the "Collected Writings." See also Sup. to Militär-Wochenblatt 1906, No. 6, The Battle at Liegnitz.

the Oder and already reached Lissa. Daun intended to turn the enemy the night of the 15th, from three sides and to attack him in the morning with the main army against the right flank, Laudon against the left flank, Lascy against the rear and to hold him up in the front with the light troops of Generals Ried and Beck. In the very same night, however, the King marched off through Liegnitz and rested east of the city near Pfaffendorf and Panten in order to continue the march early im the morning. The approach of Laudon who was crossing the Katzbach in three columns in close vicinity of the Prussians, was suddenly reported during this rest. There was time, however, to occupy a hill—the Rehberg, situated opposite the hostile advance, to ward off the first impact and then to attack the Austrians while they were winding slowly through the difficult defiles of the Katzbach. Before they could deploy, they were thrown back across the river in spite of their numerical superiority (30,000 against 14,000). In the meanwhile, the main army under Daun, which was to come to the rescue, was held back at the Schwarzwasser by Zieten's small force. The force at his disposition did not suffice for the well deserved profiting by the victory. Enough was attained since the Russians recrossed the Oder and the threefold stronger Austrians forces modestly retreated permitting Frederick to march off and to join Prince Henry.

Napoleon was in a much more favorable position than Frederick. The ratio of his forces to those of the enemy was not less than 1:3, but more than 4:5. It would have been easy for him to execute an operation similar to that of the battle of Liegnitz. To retreat, even for the purpose of vanquishing, seemed below his dignity. He, consequently, remained between the three adversaries. Moreover, he could do it unhesitatingly. The allies had decided, it is true, to advance from three sides against the main enemy. That army, which was to attack Napoleon himself, was to fall back while the two others were to attack so much the more forcefully. Napoleon must ultimately fall before this plan, having only one object.

However good the intentions had been, two of the army commanders firmly resolved not to fulfil them. The Crown Prince of Sweden wanted to remain stationary as long as possible and retreat at the first danger threatening him. Schwarzenberg, considerably reinforced from Silesia, intended, not exactly to move against the enemy, but to turn him in a wide curve, to imitate to a certain degree the maneuvering at Marengo, Ulm, and Jena, certainly not with a determined intention to attack but with a modest one of threatening, of making a demonstration, a diversion. This would have placed the cautious general in great danger if the sun of Austerlitz were still shedding his rays. But he was already beginning to go down.

Napoleon did not keep the main part of his army in one assembled mass in order to strike a decisive and annihilating blow at a favorable point, but divided his strength pretty equally among his three opponents. All the mistakes of the allies, no matter how many, could not render this fatal move harmless. Whatever opportunities might have presented themselves to renew the days of Marengo, Ulm, and Austerlitz, forces were lacking which would have inspired the courage of decision and which would have allowed the execution of the ingenious plan. All attempts to wage a battle of extermination were abandoned. The combats on the part of the French were limited to what Napoleon called formerly an "ordinary battle," to frontal attacks and attempts at breaking through the enemy. The piercing detachments, hurled against the enemy, suffered reverses.

The allies advanced. Hesitatingly, timidly, it is true, but they advanced. Wherever the Emperor appeared in person, they retreated. His personality alone kept back every attack. Whenever he turned his back to attend to another side, the old state of affairs was resumed. Tired and exhausted, he returned to Dresden. He thought, in resignation, to await the coming storm. This show of weakness gave courage to the allies. Blucher crossed the Elbe to march with the Crown Prince to Leipzig for the junction with the main army. Exactly the thing which Marengo, Ulm, and Jena had prepared was going to take place. The allies wanted to place themselves squarely across the French line of retreat and then fight the decisive battle with reversed front.

The only deviation from the old program was that the advance march was to be executed from two directions and not from one alone. Napoleon could not possibly await the result of the march of concentration in Dresden. In the beginning he had the choice of

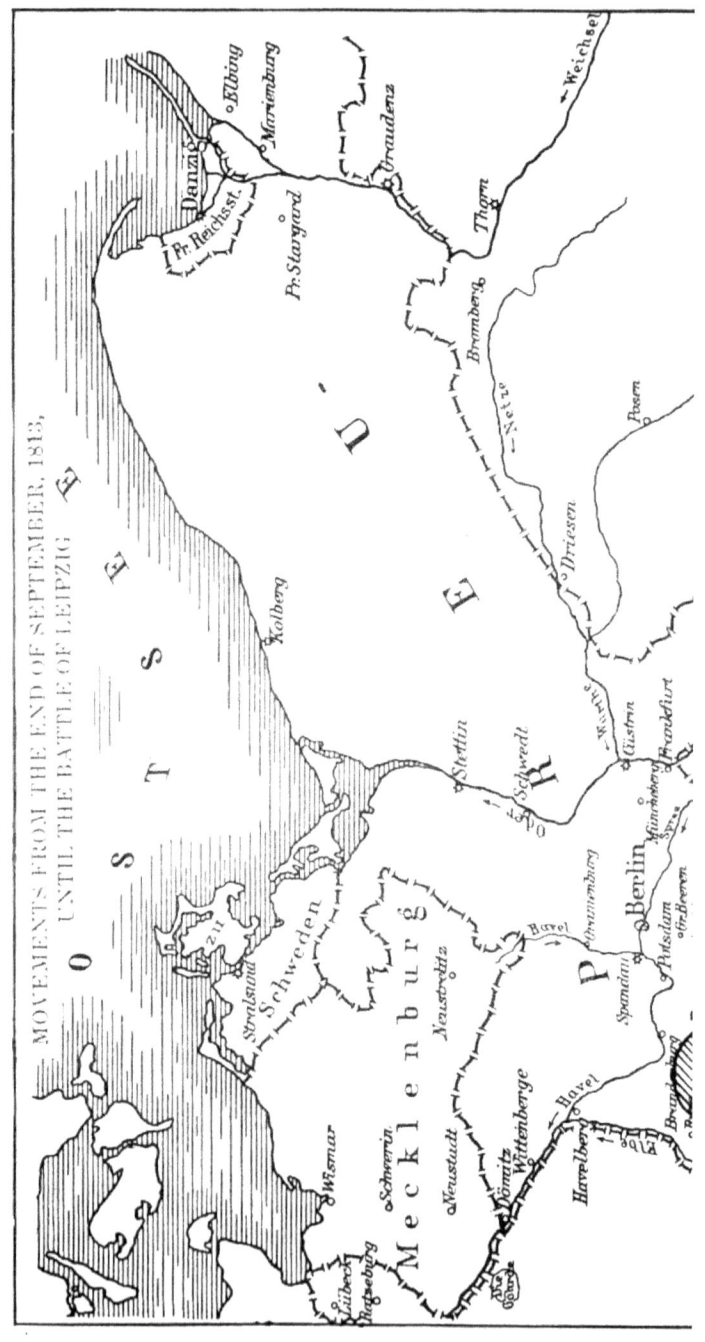

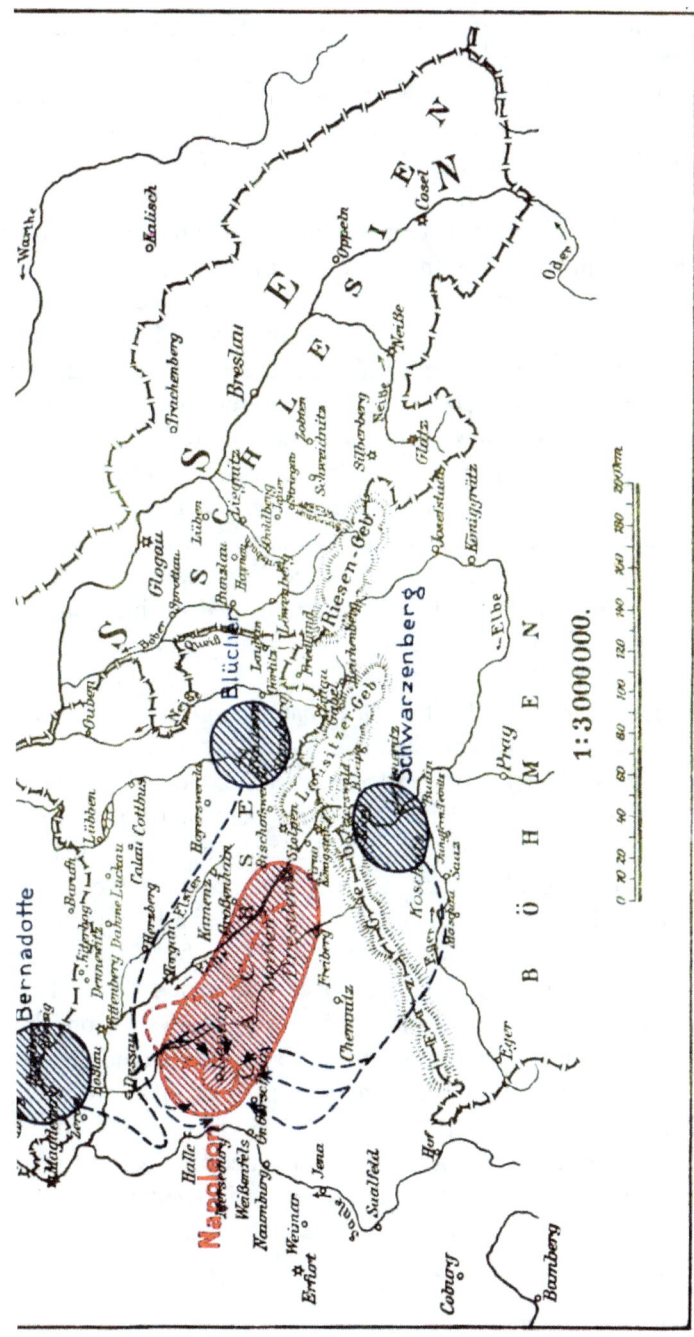

deciding upon the operation which has been observed in the battle of Liegnitz or upon another proceeding. Now he was forced to follow the example given by Frederick. He ought to have rushed between the two enemies, who were desirous of turning him on the right and the left, in order to repulse the one and to annihilate the other. He surely would have the time to withdraw in a brilliant manner, from the destruction threatening him, taking into consideration the slowness and indecision of the allies.

He, however, wanted to use another means. Like had to be opposed to like. Blucher and the Crown Prince wanted to cut off his line of communications to the rear. Well and good, he would do the same to them. The calculation had not entirely miscarried. The Crown Prince was immediately ready to escape the threatened surrounding by a hasty retreat. Blucher, however, stood by his decision, pulled the Crown Prince in against his will, achieved thus the junction with the main army and transformed the hostile turning movement into a blow in the air. When Napoleon realized his mistake, the mischief was done. There remained for him only to seek to break through the enemy at some point or other. A lucky chance and fluctuating resolutions of the enemy brought him to a point where a victory and with it *"le monde va tourner encore une fois,"** could be seized with the hand, as it seemed. All that was necessary was to defeat early on 16 October, 72,000 with 138,000.

This was a problem, the solution of which could surely have been entrusted to Napoleon. However, he failed, utterly. All that he achieved was the holding back of strong reserves which were used one by one where their need appeared, as well as a frontal attack which was undertaken only after the enemy had been reinforced and all hope of success had thus been eliminated. Instead of placing himself again by a brilliant action at the head of Europe, he made it possible for the allies to wage a battle of annihilation which might have been as complete as that of Cannae if pusillanimity had not opened a door to the vanquished through which he contrived to escape complete destruction. The first great catastrophe had overtaken him. The second followed in the short

---

* "The world will turn once more."

campaign of 1815 which shows up as none other the peculiarities of Napoleon's strategy of the later period.

The allied powers of Europe intended to penetrate into France with the right wing from the Netherlands, with the left from Basle in a concentric movement. Napoleon turned with 122,000 men and surprised the nearest and best prepared right wing of the enemy. Here stood in extensive positions the army of the Duke of Wellington with 93,000 men (26,000 Germans, 32,500 English, 24,500 Dutch) with the base in Antwerp to the right of the Scheldt up to Malines, Brussels and Binche (east of Mons), as well as the Prussian army under Blucher of 123,000 men with the corps of Zieten, Pirch, and Bulow along the Sambre and the Meuse from above Charleroi down to below Liege with the corps of Thielmann in the bend of the Meuse at Dinant, Namur, and Andenne.

The French army, assembled between Philippeville and Beaumont, crossed the Sambre at Chatelet, Charleroi, and Marchienne on 15 June. The advanced Prussian detachments retired to Fleurus. An advance guard followed them as far as Lambusart, while another went to Gosselies. The former saw the Prussians immediately before it. The latter had to wait to find the English on the road from Quatrebras to Brussels. With the available strength it was out of the question to defeat the two opponents. The problem could consist only in annihilating first one adversary, or at least defeating him decisively and cutting him off from the allies entirely, while remaining on the defensive in regard to the other opponent in order to deal with him in a similar manner after extermination of the former. A doubt as to whom to attack— the Prussians or the English—could not arise considering the nearness of the former. It was plausible that they could not come up in full strength on the following day.

According to Napoleon's principle of being as strong as possible in combat, it was imperative to send the greatest part of the French forces against the Prussians while directing a small one against the English. A French division commander had expressed the opinion in the evening of the 16th, that one division would be sufficient against Wellington, while all the remaining forces were to be used for defeating Blucher. Napoleon did not share on the 15th the opinion of his subordinate. On the 16th, Grouchy was to

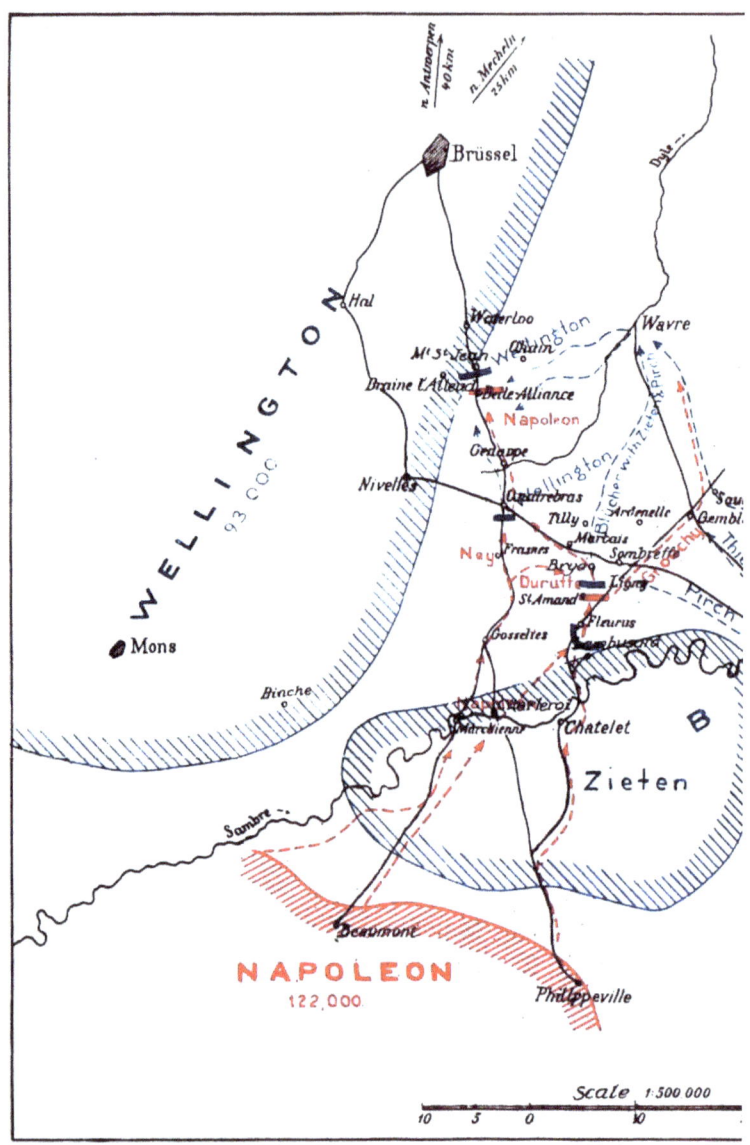

throw back the Prussians with the corps of Vandamme and Gerard, the cavalry of Pajol, Excelmann, and Milhaud, 41,600 men, while Ney was to march from Gosselies to Quatrebras with the corps of

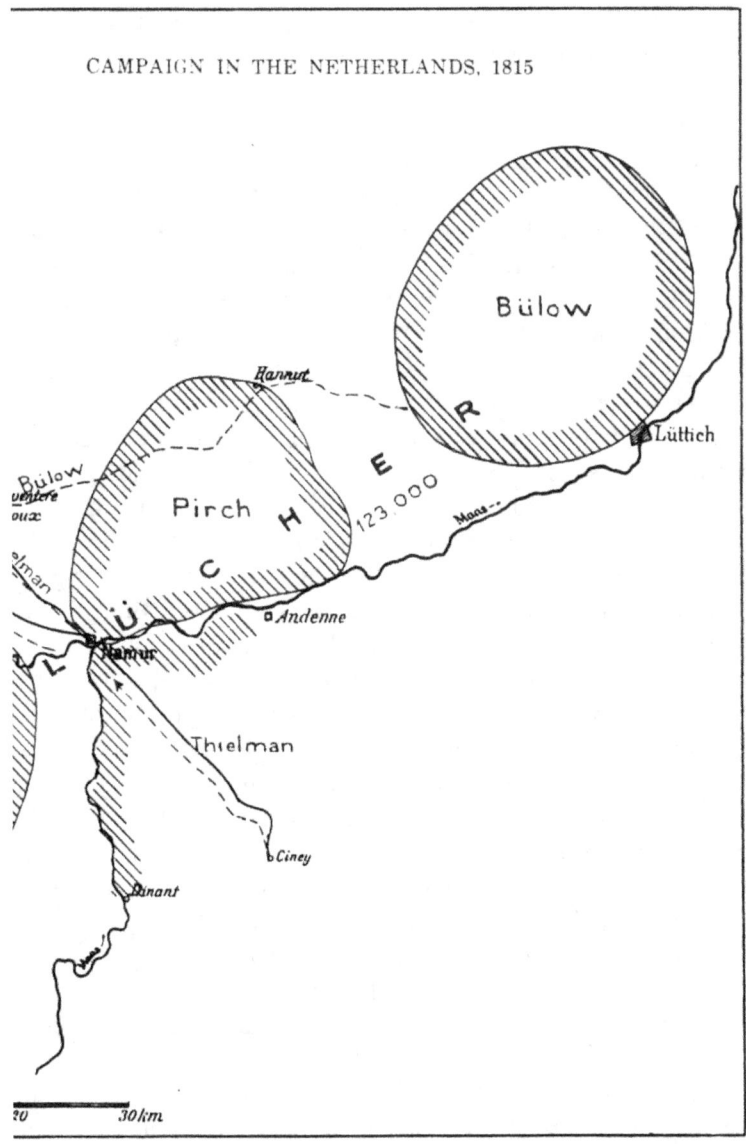

CAMPAIGN IN THE NETHERLANDS, 1815

Reille and Erlon, and the cavalry of Lefebvre and Kellermann, 58,000 men, in order to attack the English, should this be necessary.

The Emperor wanted to follow Grouchy with the guard—

16,500 men, Lobau with 10,000 being left at Charleroi until further order. He did not count on any stubborn resistance. Blucher might get together 40,000 men at the most. These he wanted to drive on the 16th, beyond Gembloux and leave them to Grouchy for complete destruction, while he would start in the night with the Guard, join Ney, and march to Brussels to which the English would flee at breakneck pace. He thought to enter the Belgian capital as early as the 17th. The proclamations to be issued there were already printed. These were beautiful thoughts, reminiscences of 1796, called forth by a vivid imagination, throwing into the background the seriousness of the moment.

At closer range, however, it seemed doubtful to him that Grouchy's 41,600 men, even if 16,500 of the Guard were added to them, would suffice for a decisive combat. The impending battle against the Prussians had to be considered as such. Were there no more than 40,000, all depended upon separating them from the English, delivering them an annihilating blow and enveloping the rest of the Prussian army in this defeat. Only when Blucher had been entirely eliminated, could Napoleon turn with all his strength against the English and toward Brussels. He would surely have encountered but little further resistance. According to this estimate, the Division Gerard of Reille's Corps—-5000 men—was added to Grouchy, whose forces were thus brought to 46,000 men. Moreover, the Corps Erlon was not to advance via Frasnes and a division was to be ready at Marbais for all eventualities. Ney, who was supposed to defeat the English with 53,000 men, found himself at the head of only 25,000. As compensation there was no lack of reserves: the Guard, Lobau, and Erlon—in all 46,000 men. The decision of two battles which were to begin in the afternoon was expected from these reserves, which were in rather extended positions.

The Prussians, left to themselves, would probably have done best to continue to retreat with their advanced troops until all their troops had been assembled on the battle field. But even a short retreat would have caused the English to take the road to Brussels and to their ships. The Prussians dared not retreat, even if Wellington had not promised his support and appearance on the hostile flank for the afternoon of the 16th, and even had the

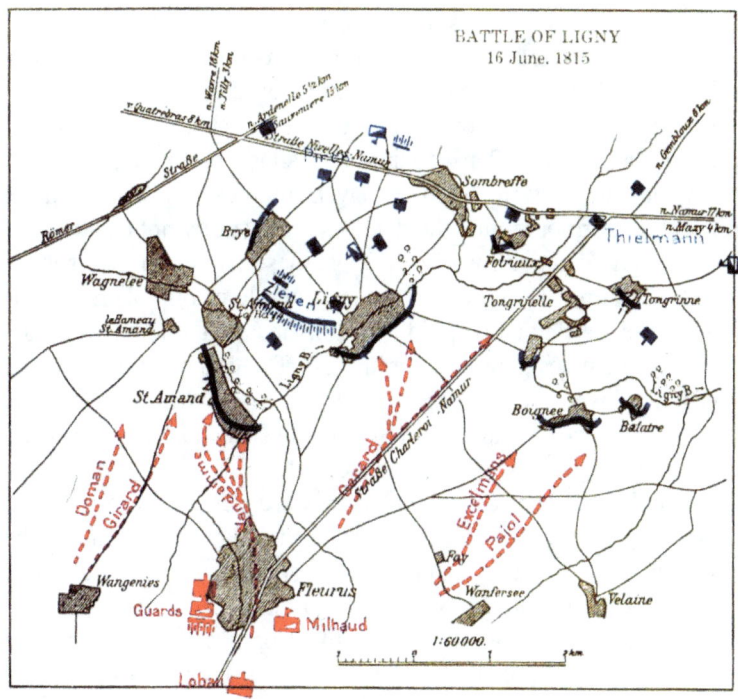

fulfillment of this promise been still more improbable. Gneisenau wanted, therefore, to halt at Fleurus. He consented, after urgent appeals, that the Corps of Zieten be taken to the hill between the villages of Lingy, St. Amand, and Brye. It was difficult to find a more unfavorable position. It is true that it allowed the use of artillery to advantage and counted in its zone four villages, large villages at that, indispensable for the battle tactics of the period. This, however, did not compensate for the disadvantage of a narrow front and a deep flank.

The position was worthy of a Terentius Varro. It was bound to be surrounded, whether the adversary wanted to or not. One flank he was forced to envelop, to envelop both was an easy matter. Should the latter take place, the defense was lost. Should there also be a Hasdrubal for attacking the rear, for which no less than three cavalry corps ought to have been made available, the highest aim would have been attained. On the eve of his fall, Napoleon was given an opportunity for a battle of annihilation such as had not arisen during the 19 years of his career.

Zieten occupied the position, Pirch was posted in the rear as a reserve. Thielmann was to secure the heights between Sombreffe and Tongrinne. He formed here a reserve echelon which seemed able to protect Zieten's left flank against any attack. Unfortunately, this strong position was protected by a swampy creek, a front obstacle so difficult to surmount, that the defense could surely not be attacked, but, though occupied by a few troops, these could not themselves, attack; Thielmann was forced to play the role of onlooker. He was out of the battle. Only Pajol, Excelmans and one of Gerard's divisions were designated to cut him off. The two other divisions of this general were to attack the left flank at Ligny, while Vandamme and Gerard attacked the front at St. Amand. The Guard and Milhaud remained, as reserves, at Fleurus, and still further in rear was Lobau.

For the battle itself 60,000 men were designated against an almost equal force of the enemy. The Prussians could indeed be beaten in that way, but not annihilated or separated from the English. In order to attain that, it was necessary, first of all, to attack the right flank. When Napoleon was forced to recognize this necessity, he ordered Ney to be called up. Soult was to write to the Marshal: "You are directed to envelop the enemy's right flank. That army is lost if you attack vigorously. The fate of France rests in your hands," and then: "take direction on the heights of St. Amand and Brye."

Ney was already fighting the English at Quatrebras. He could not break loose from them, even had he not received the ambiguous order to attack the opposing enemy with decision, rout him, and then hasten to give a decisive blow to the Prussians. The Marshal was not in a position to rout the enemy. On the contrary, one of his divisions had been forced to retreat. He attempted to bring the combat to a standstill by a desperate cavalry charge. However, he needed the support of fresh troops to attack again the stronger enemy and defeat him. The corps of Erlon was to come up. The latter had, however, by direct order of Napoleon, been. sent marching toward Brye. Ney sent him a strict order to return immediately. Erlon obeyed, let the Division Durutte continue the march toward the Emperor, and reached Ney when the latter had retreated to Frasnes at the advent of darkness. Durutte also reached the region of St. Amand when all was at an end at Ligny.

Frederick the Great and Napoleon

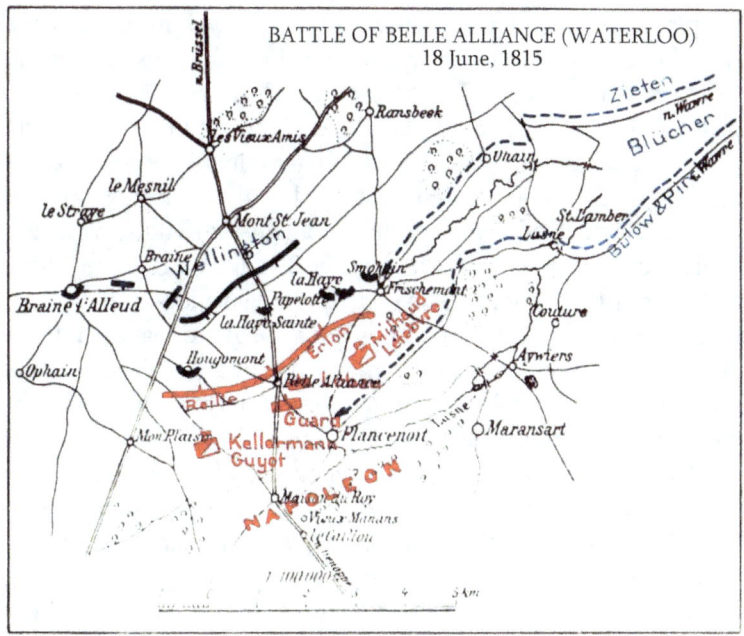

The battle had gone on there in the meanwhile. Vandamme had taken St. Amand, but could not do anything against the artillery. Gerard occupied St. Amand la Haye, but lost the village again to two Prussian brigades. Two other brigades were fighting at Ligny against Gerard's two divisions until, finally, the creek marked the frontier between friend and foe. Blucher hoped to decide the battle by an attack against the left flank of Vandamme. Two brigades of Pirch occupied Wagnelee and after a combat fluctuating back and forth, occupied Le Hameau. They could not penetrate farther, after Vandamme and Gerard had been reinforced by three brigades of the Guard. The cavalry of Jurgass and Marwitz was also checked by Domon and Subervie. When neither Ney, Erlon, nor Durutte appeared and the Prussians had sent their last reserves into battle and the evening came on, Napoleon led the rest of his Guard and Milhaud back to Ligny.

The two Prussian brigades, in disorder, could not withstand the fresh forces and the superior numbers. The village, enveloped from two sides, was taken. The entire position could no longer be held.

Desperate cavalry attacks could not save the day. Fortunately Brye was unoccupied. The troops could retreat through this village and past it in the direction of Tilly without much danger. The execution of the initial plan of halting here and renewing the battle of the following day, had to be abandoned on account of the condition of the troops. Zieten and Pirch continued in the night their retreat toward Wavre. They were protected against all attack by a rear guard which occupied Brye and by the Thielmann Brigade which took up position at Sombreffe in the evening. Bulow coming from Liege, reached Ardanelle with his advance guard, having left his main forces at Souveniere. Thielmann marched at 3:00 AM, on the following day to Gembloux. Both followed only the main body of the army on the next afternoon.

Ney was forced to retreat at Quatrebras before Wellington, while Napoleon had won a victory at Ligny. This was, however, what Napoleon himself deemed, only an "ordinary victory." A general, however, who desired to reconquer the lost dominion of the world, could not make anything of such a victory. It was necessary that he completely annihilate the two Prussian army corps opposing him at Ligny. Thielmann would then have hastily retreated. Bulow alone could not have opposed the pursuing victor. Wellington wanted to return, without Prussian support, to Brussels, i.e., to Antwerp and to his ships. The campaign would have come quickly to an end at this junction.

Everything centered upon a battle of annihilation at Ligny. Circumstances were as favorable as possible for it. For the purpose of being as close as possible to the promised English support, the Prussians had selected a position in which their destruction depended solely upon the judgment and pleasure of the enemy. If Napoleon could not or would not take advantage of the position in full, there remained to him the lesser, but urgent problem of separating the Prussians from the English and of attacking the former on the right flank. The Guard and Lobau would have sufficed here, had they been sent early enough in the decisive direction.

Orders and counter-orders did not prevent Napoleon from vanquishing at Ligny, but they did keep him from annihilating one half of the Prussian army and from entirely separating the

Prussians from the English. On the contrary, he forced the two separated armies to join each other. Until then, the one had its line of communications toward Brussels and Antwerp, the other toward Liege and the Rhine. Now both marched in the same direction toward Brussels. He had had before this two weak and divided enemies. At present he had to deal with a greatly superior and almost united adversary. Such was the actual situation. Another presented itself to Napoleon's mental view. According to the picture he saw in his mind's eye, not two, but four Prussian army corps had been beaten and had retreated either to Liege and thus disappeared entirely from the battle field, or marched to Brussels, beaten and greatly shaken, not to be taken into consideration for several days.

From this erroneous supposition, he drew the following extraordinary conclusion: "The enemy, who has completely disappeared or been rendered harmless, must be pursued by more than one third of my forces; the other opponent, who has just repulsed Ney's attack, must be beaten with the remaining insufficient minority."

One law prescribes: a beaten enemy must be pursued under any circumstances, while another reads: it is necessary to be as strong as possible in battle, at any rate numerically superior to the enemy. Both laws could have been fulfilled by Napoleon only by following Blucher with the greater part of his forces, beating him a second time or attempting to bring him to absolute dissolution and then by turning against Wellington who had been observed and kept busy by the lesser part of the troops. Should Napoleon have wished to go immediately against Wellington, he ought to have taken the greater number of his soldiers, detaching only a small part for the pursuit of Blucher.

The former move would have brought about a battle at Wavre, the latter a different battle of Waterloo. The outlook for the former was good since half of the Prussian'. army had been shaken. Napoleon could have used so much the greater preponderance of troops, as Wellington employed disproportionately large bodies of troops for unjustifiable secondary aims. Here too the prospect was good. The circumstances grew worse both at Wavre and at Waterloo, when Blucher arrived at the one point and Wellington at the other for the support of the threatened comrade. Blucher showed that he was fit for the problem. It is doubtful if Wellington would have given up his line of communications and the immediate protection of Brussels and Antwerp, had these been threatened ever so little, which was doubted, at the time, by Gneisenau. A march on Wavre promised quickest success.

Napoleon had placed before himself a difficult problem when he crossed the Sambre at Charleroi on 15 June, in order to beat Blucher and Wellington. His victory at Ligny on the 16th, did not lessen his difficulties, on the contrary it increased them. By making Grouchy follow Blucher on the 17th with a good third of his fighting contingent, by leaving 5000 men aimlessly at Fleurus and seeking a decision against Wellington with less than half of his army, he jeopardized the chances of success.

Wellington had assembled in the course of the 16th, first a few, then gradually sufficient forces for the repulse of Ney's attacks and stood with the greater part of his troops at Quatrebras in the evening. Upon receiving information of the retreat of the Prussians, he likewise started the retreat on the 17th, but halted at Mont St. Jean upon receiving the promise of at least one Prussian army corps for his support. After sending off 16,000 men to Hal and other detaching of units, he remained there in the evening with 62,000 men, thus voluntarily affording the 70,000 men of his adversary an unmerited superiority. The latter had advanced with his vanguard, while his main body was echeloned in great depth beyond Genappe.

The position south of Mont St. Jean, selected in advance, along the Braine L'Allend—Chain road, had a sufficient field of fire. The narrow crest of the hill afforded cover to the forces keptin rear. Several farm buildings of massive construction reinforced the front. Wellington wanted to offer here a defensive battle. Napoleon who had gained all his victories, Borodino and Hanau excepted, by the turning of a flank or by pushing his opponents away from the natural line of retreat or by both, wanted to make at this point a purely frontal attack. The enemy, standing perpendicularly to his line of retreat, was to be vanquished not through a maneuver. but through the force of the impact, the superiority of the French soldier. The obstinate will was to decide.

Frederick the Great and Napoleon

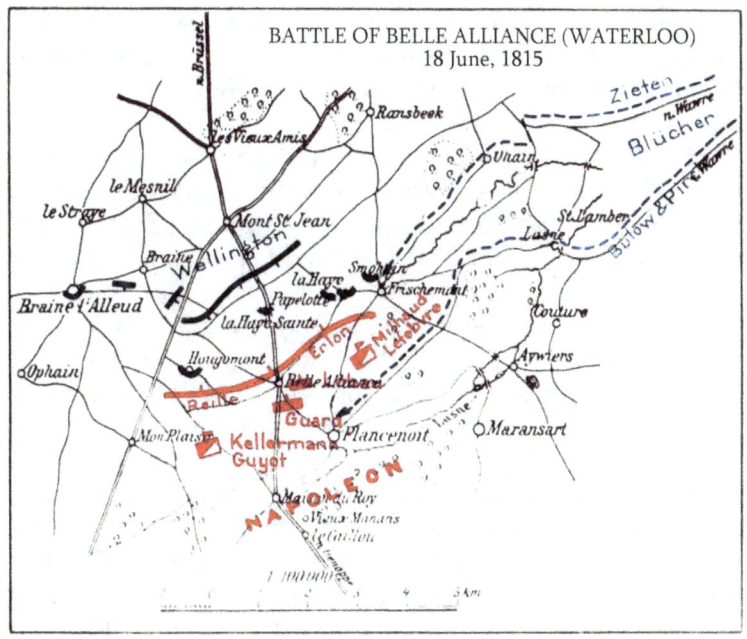

Napoleon had but one fear—the despised enemy might not oppose any resistance. The army had to be brought, moreover, for the advance march from the deep echelon formation over the soft ground along the road. This took up the forenoon of the 18th. Only at about 11:00 AM, did Erlon's four divisions take up a position on the right and Reille's three divisions on the left of the Brussels road; in rear of these— Lohau; while the Guard and the reserve cavalry formed the reserve in position of readiness. The start was to be made by taking Hougomont. The left wing division of Jerome was designated for this operation. It could not fulfill its task even with the aid of a large part of the neighboring division of Foy. At the end of the battle a remnant of the defenders had remained in the burning farmhouse. The end of this hopeless combat could not be awaited as the advance of the Prussians against the right flank, though as yet at a great distance had already been reported.

After an insufficient artillery preparation, Erlon was to attack with four divisions formed in mass, one battalion at the front, seven or eight battalions following in echelons from the left wing east of the Brussels road. The right echelon (Durutte) was stopped by

Smohain, La Haye, Papelotte, half of the left (Brigade Quiot) by La Haye-Sainte. Only two and a half echelons reached the main position. Decimated by artillery fire, they were received by the English infantry with well aimed volleys.

In vain was the ponderous endeavor to deploy so as to bring more rifles and more combatants to the front. They were attacked with sabre and bayonet in the flank and were forced back. An attempt was made in a deep valley offering cover to bring order into these fragments. Durutte fought on and, after a combat fluctuating back and forth, occupied Pappelotte, La Haye, and Smohain. Quiot, likewise, did not vive up his fight for La Haye-Sainte. But time was pressing. The Prussians were approaching. First Domon and Subervie, with their cavalry, then Lobau with his corps were sent against the threatening flank attack.

In the meanwhile the enemy at the front had to be thrown back. The cavalry was to achieve what the infantry could not do. Milhaud, Lefebvre, Guyot, Kellermann, rushed one after the other against the hostile center. Squares were dispersed, the cavalry thrown back. Yet in spite of the greatest heroism, the 9000 cavalrymen could neither throw back the entire English army nor resist it for a lengthy period. Ney came too late on the idea of letting the infantry take advantage of the first success. The only available division, Bacheln of Neille's Corps, of the seven divisions of the first line, was brought up. It succeeded in taking La Haye-Sainte in joint action with Quiot. Nothing, however, could be changed in the fate of the French cavalry. It was forced to retreat as the infantry had previously been obliged to do.

Bulow's Corps of Blucher's army had come up in the meanwhile, encountering the resistance of Lobau's Corps at Plancenoit. The fight for the village wavered back and forth. After having been lost by Lobau it was retaken by the Young Guard, again lost by the latter and retaken by three battalions of the Old Guard. This unconquerable troop seemed to insure the lasting hold of this disputed village and Napoleon thought that he could direct his last reserves against the English. He left only three battalions behind. The rest of the Old Guard was again to be led forth by Ney.

What 14,000 infantry, 9000 cavalry could not achieve, 5000 men of the Old Guard would be able to attain. Since we are acquainted with the battle of Cannae, we know that even the success of these attacks could not help Napoleon and that everything hinged on the elimination of Bulow and Blucher, or at least on repulsing them. According to some, one column was formed and to others,—two mighty, deep columns which all had joined that could be found of Erlon's and Reille's corps in the swales of the battlefield. The attack was bound to break under the case shot of the artillery and the volleys of the infantry, as all such attacks had done for the past six years. The enemy's hasty retreat and flight, however, was brought about by Zieten who had come up from Chain with at least one brigade, taken Smohain, La Haye, and Papelotte and now swept the battle field with his artillery. Even the Old Guard could not withstand this fire in their rear.

The fortune of the day had been decided. The last reserves rolled back. It was not possible to pass Plancenoit in safety. The Fifth Prussian Brigade, the first of the Corps of Pirch, following Bulow had retaken the village. Bulow's batteries commanded Napoleon's line of retreat. The dissolution caused by their fire could not have been greater. Nevertheless, Wellington, who had followed the fleeing enemy, desired to give a worthy finish to the battle and demanded that the presumably strong position of Belle-Alliance be stormed, requesting that firing be ceased. Many were thus able to escape destruction, even though the Fifth Brigade further stormed from Plancenoit to Maison du Roy and Vieux Manans. After the Duke had occupied the former French position he returned to his camp and left the pursuit to Blucher.

Of the Prussian army only Bulow's Corps and one brigade each of Zieten's and Pirch's Corps had taken part in the battle. This was surely not due to lack of zeal and good will, but to inadequate marching orders. According to Napoleon's principles, attempt was made to keep as many troops as possible on one road and when it had been decided to use several roads, the advantage of this move was frustrated by the various columns crossing each other at will. A prompt movement of great masses could not be attained in this way. The crossing of the Lasne brook necessitated a halt, the deployment caused another. No wonder then that Thielmann was still to be found in the vicinity of Wavre in the evening whence Bulow had marched early in the morning.

Thielmann was on the point of marching off along the left bank of the Dyele when Grouchy appeared on the right. The French Marshal had started in the afternoon of the 17th from the battlefield of Ligny and reached Gembloux in the night. After wavering us to the direction of the hostile line of retreat, he took the road to Wavre, strengthened by the order of the Emperor. When the thundering of Waterloo's guns was heard, Gerard, one of his corps commanders, advised him to leave Blucher alone and to hasten at once to the battle field and to join the decision. Grouchy refused. What he could have done of his own free will and, maybe, at the right time, he was ordered to do most urgently by an officer who arrived too late. He was to stop Bulow and cover the main army from a flank attack.

Attempting to fulfill this order as far as possible and then to cross the Dyele, he encountered the resistance of Thielmann. He succeeded, however, in crossing the river higher upstream. Night came on before he had been able to repulse the enemy on his right flank. This much had been shown by the events: the Marshal, even with the expenditure of greater energy, could never have stopped by a pursuit on the right of the Dyele, Blucher's entire army coming to the support of Wellington. He might have operated more effectively had he accompanied the French army along the Dyele and forced Blucher and Bulow on their march to Plancenoit, to face him and give up the proposed flank attack. That this was the only adequate employment of Grouchy was shown by Napoleon's order to this marshal to come up rapidly and ward off Bulow.

How the battle was to be conducted later may be seen from the Emperor's admitting at St. Helena, that it had been his intention to attack the left flank simultaneously with the front. He had sufficient cavalry and reserves to achieve this. It is true that, in order to escape being molested too early, he ought to have advanced so far on the 17th, and in the night of the 17th, that the attack might take place at the opportune moment. Then Grouchy might have been sufficient to halt that part of the Prussian army, which could have come up, long enough to allow a victory over Wellington. The attacks, following one upon the other, of two and one half infantry divisions, three cavalry corps and 5000 men of the Guard in the most unfavorable and ineffective formation against the hostile center, could not possibly be crowned with success.

It is impossible to recognize the Napoleon of 1800, 1805, and 1807, in the Napoleon of the June days of 1815. The general who wavered on the 15th and 16th, if a corps had to be sent hither or thither, right or left, was not the man with the eagle eye, who, after a long march, started in the evening in order to rush at Friedland like a tiger on his prey. The Emperor who, in the forenoon of the 18th, slowly restored the order of battle and found time to hold a review was not the man of will power and energy who called out to his marshals "*activite, activite, vitesse*"[*] and in the night of 14 October, 1807, torch in hand made his artillery climb the steep Landgrafen-Hill! The master of warfare, who sent first the infantry, then the cavalry, and lastly the Guard against Wellington's front, was not the God of battles, who, at Austerlitz, swept down with his entire army against the flank of the enemy. Assuredly not. For he himself had said in 1797: "One ages rapidly on battle fields." And at the time he said it, he was in the second year of his career as a fieldmarshal.

Since then, in the course of 17 years, many things had happened, bound to shake the solid structure of this colossus. A mass of indebtedness had accumulated, gnawing at the marrow of this Titan. Halting or turning back was impossible. He was driven forward, ever forward, against ever increasing forces. And to oppose them he lacked the strength. His fall was imminent, if not on 18 June, then later. It was inevitable. His mother had foreseen this when she said to her son in bidding him goodbye on the Isle of Elba: 'Heaven will not permit that thou shouldst die by poison[†] or in unworthy degree, but with the sword in thy hand." To find such an end ought to have been the aim of the battle of Waterloo.

---

[*] "Action, action, speed."

[†] He had made an attempt at Elba to poison himself.

Chapter III – The Campaign of 1866

Napoleon had gradually turned from the battle of annihilation, had left the road which brought him to his great victories. His opponents took hold of the abandoned weapon hesitatingly and cautiously. The roles were changed. The Katzbach, Dennewitz, and Kulm do not reach the scope of extermination battles. The advance in the rear of the enemy, his surrounding on all sides would have made a complete Cannae from Leipzig, had not the terror inspired by the formidable man counselled them to leave a loophole open. With Waterloo we returned again to Marengo after the lapse of 15 years. Doubtful, yes, more than doubtful, was the combat at the front. Then came the deadly blow against the flank. A part of Cannae, not a full Cannae, but still a very successful part. One battlefield served as "the anteroom through which Ceasar entered the coronation hall." The other led to St. Helena. The assembling of the separated armies on the field of battle was the problem, often vainly striven after, fortunately solved in both battles. What had been forgotten was taken up again half a century later. The thread spun in Blucher's headquarters was again picked up.

The Prussian and Austrian Concentration

From the very first months of 1866, Prussia saw herself facing a war with Austria alone for the present. It was still doubtful whether the German Central States would take sides with the one or the other or whether they would remain entirely out of the struggle. The frontier line: Gorlitz—-Oderberg, formed by a mountain ridge, separated the two opponents which were preparing for war. The two armies had to advance toward this line from the north and south.

Strategic authorities insisted upon the assembling of the Prussian army in Upper Silesia. From this point only a short blow was necessary to strike at the heart of the dual monarchy, thus putting with one stroke an end to the war. The road from the Prussian realm to Vienna was, in truth, shortest through Silesia. Yet in order to reach this extreme point of the country, to make it the point of issue whence the short blow would be struck, it was necessary for the assembling armies to take the longest possible roads. No Prussian advance demanded a longer time than the one through Silesia and none required so short a time as the advance march of the Austrians through Moravia. The enemy, at all events, had the chance to bar the way and parry the blow against his heart.

The attacking army would have come upon the entire hostile force latest at Olmutz. Mass would then oppose mass. Should the Prussians be defeated, they would be in danger of being "thrown back on Poland." Should they win the battle, the Austrians would, probably be free to retreat on Vienna and beyond the Danube, assemble reinforcements and even up the losses suffered. The victors could hope for a Wagram, but should be prepared for an Aspern. The campaign was apparently leading that way, affording the powers, which had remained outside the conflict, the opportunity and time to enter it and rob the victor of the fruit of his success. The problem was, evidently, not a short blow against Vienna, but the throwing back of the hostile army on Vienna and beyond the Danube.

Such calculations and views proved objectless. The foundation of the entire plan was faulty, an advance into Upper Silesia was not only tedious, but hardly possible. The VI and part of the V Army

Corps might reach by marching the region of the Upper Oder. The remaining seven or eight corps, which had to be transported by rail, would have been limited, in the end, to one line: Breslau——-Ratiber, were they coming from Konigsberg or Wesel or Trier. The single track branch line, Liegnitz—Frankenstein, would not have materially aided the overburdened main tine. The enemy would scarcely have awaited the concentration necessitating more than two months, but would have scattered the half-completed concentration. Moltke wished the advance to be made into Upper Silesia only in case Prussia could get there more quickly and stronger than the enemy. However, no one could promise him the fulfillment of this condition. Concentration of combined railway transportation and marching in Silesia, could at best take place at Breslau. Thence the road through Upper Silesia to Vienna is the shortest. Even Napoleon had not always chosen the shortest way to get at his enemy, but made considerable detours.

These, however, led him to the flank or rear of the enemy. This could have happened there only if the Austrians had done the improbable, the impossible, ie., directed their march to Bohemia. Should they remain in Moravia, the turning movement through Silesia would have been brought up exactly against their front.

Another route of advance had to be chosen. Since the Prussians wanted to ascribe the "burden of the aggression" to the enemy, it was necessary to prepare for the defensive. It was easiest to oppose from the Lausitz the attack of the Austrians, should they advance against Berlin through Bohemia or through Silesia. Should, however, favorable circumstances give the initiative into the hands of the cautious and reserved policy, it would be easiest to penetrate to Vienna by Gorlitz with the view of cutting off the enemy, marching from Bohemia or Moravia, from the capital, and the Danube.

All the advantages, however, were unavailable. An advance in the Lausitz was connected with no less difficulties than that in Upper Silesia. To carry nine army corps over one railway line to the region of Gorlitz, would take a longer time than the enemy would concede. It would have been impossible to feed the assembled masses, about 250,000 men, in the sterile heathland, and the forcing of these numbers through the narrow passage via

Gorlitz, Seidenberg, Friedland, and Reichenbach, into Bohemia, would be impossible. It was clear that the entire army could not be assembled in a mass and by means of one railway line, also that the mountain ridge could not be crossed on one road. All available railway lines were to be used for the transportation of the troops. Of these there were only two: Kreuz—Posen— Lissa—Breslau and Frankfurt—Kohlfurt—Gorlitz with branch lines from the rear and to the front. Having a mass of troops in the Lausitz, another in Silesia, with the mountain ridge in front, not much had been gained.

An improvement in the situation took place when it was found out that Saxony would join with Austria. The following new lines opened against these allies: Berlin—Juterbog—Herzberg, Magdeburg — Halle, and Hisenach — Weissenfels — Zeitz. Since the corps located nearest to the frontier could reach their goal at least partly on foot, there were about five corps to transport by each of the five available lines, and the advance could take place proportionately quickly until 5 June. The army stood now in a long line from Zeitz to Wakenburg—Schweidnitz.

The attack could not be awaited in this cordon formation. It was, consequently, Moitke's intention to cross the frontier immediately after the arrival of the last transport train, and to seek junction in Bohemia, not at one point, but in such manner that the corps could, upon encountering the enemy, give mutual support to each other. It was, first of all, necessary to penetrate into Saxony, win the passes of the Lausitz and Erzgebirge with the right army wing and to advance into Bohemia from two directions—-from Saxony and Silesia, thus effecting their junction. The concentration was thus to be made in Bohemia. The road to Vienna thence was not farther than from Upper Silesia. Berlin was in the rear and it was not possible for the Prussians to be pushed toward Poland.

At the same time, there was the possibility of cutting off the enemy, who had selected his central point at Olmutz, from Vienna and the Danube. This march could have been effected easily at the time. Scarcely an appreciable obstacle. was to be expected. The army could have effected a junction before coming to battle or even to appreciable encounters. Political reasons forbade the crossing of the frontier and forced a situation which was thought to be an easily surmountable transition.

In order to shorten somewhat the long line, the corps detraining at Zeitz and Halle (half of the VII and VIII), were sent to Torgau, those between the Elbe and the Lausitz Neisse, assembled by rail or by marching (II, III, and IV Corps) to Hoyer-swerda, Spreeberg, Muskau; the Guard Corps, in rear of these, to Kottbus; the I Corps from Gorlitz to Hirschberg, and the V and VI Corps to Landeshut. They could advance into Bohemia from these positions as follows: the right wing (Army of the Elbe) along the left bank of the Elbe; the center (First Army) via Bautzen and Gorlitz; the I Corps, via Warmbrunn and Schreiberhau, the V and VI (Second Army) from Landeshut. Without appreciably prejudicing the offensive, limiting too much the number of march routes and losing the direction of the right wing toward Vienna, the army could not be more closely concentrated. Pressing upon the Saxon army from the south was already essentially jeopardized by giving up Zeitz.

In a similar way, as the experts on the subject advised the Prussians to assemble in Upper Silesia, they demanded that the Austrians advance through Bohemia. Here too the advantages of a short blow on Berlin could be reached by being quicker and stronger than the enemy. This condition was as impossible to fulfill for the Austrians in Bohemia as for the Prussians in Upper Silesia. For the latter because seven to eight corps could not be transported by one railway line, Breslau—Ratiber, for the former because six army corps were too much for the single-track railway defile, Bohmisch—-Trubau—Pardubitz. It would have been possible to reinforce the troops, stationed in Bohemia during peace time, and the expected Saxon corps from the rear. The region for the massing of troops, however, was determined by the railway lines running from the south via Vienna, Ganserdorf, Lundenburg, Brunn, from Hungary likewise, but over separate tracks, via Ganserdorf and Lundenburg and further via Olmutz to Bohmisch—Trubau, from Galicia the line joining at Prerau.

Moltke designated in 1870, exactly where the French army would concentrate. In order to do this, he had not paid numerous spies nor bribed high officials. In order to fathom the state secret he limited himself to the cost of a passable railway map, In the age of railways, the advance of each army is dependent on and determined by the railway lines. It may be laid a little forward or a little backward. But in the main it is immutable. Even today this is so wherever a thick network of railway lines covers the country and it was all the more the case in 1866, when but a few lines led to the frontier.

Criticism, hence, of the Prussian and Austrian advance was unduly excited, ranting against the scattering of the one and the holding back of the other. Both were virtually determined. The concentration, forced upon the Prussians, was favorable to them, in spite of some inevitable obstacles. The concentration in Moravia with one or two advance corps in Bohemia corresponded to the idea which the Austrians had of their problem. They were sure that "the Prussian army, considering its rapid mobilization, could be at the frontier prepared for combat before the home army would have finished its concentration, possibly even before the war formations had been completed."

If they did not wish to be hindered and surprised, they had to lay their concentration toward the rear, as was done by the Germans four years later in directing their advance beyond the Rhine. Should the hesitancy and irresolution of the enemy place the initiative in their hands, in an unforeseen way, an offensive movement on their part would be more successful in Moravia than in Bohemia. In the latter place, they were threatened from the beginning with being surrounded and forced to go through separate mountain roads in the face of the enemy, while in Moravia they could make an attack against the left flank of the long drawn out Prussian deployment. The Austrians were far from taking advantage of the favorable situation. In the knowledge of being the weaker in numbers and organization, they deemed themselves obliged to adhere to the defensive which they accepted as "a regrettable, but settled fact." They preferred to await the enemy, should he come up from Upper Silesia, in a position at Olmutz—Mahrisch—-Trubau. Should no enemy appear there, they would march to Bohemia and occupy a position at Josefstadt—Koniginhof—Miletin.

The intentions of the Austrians were understood differently by the inhabitants of the neighboring Prussian province of Silesia. The advance posts placed in the vicinity of the frontier of Upper Silesia and the County of Glatz, left no doubt in their minds that the invasion of the province and the burning of Breslau were imminent. The commander-in-chief of the Second Army thought these apprehensions, confirmed by numerous reports, had to be taken into consideration and decided, for the salvation of the threatened country, to advance to a position in rear of the Neisse between Patschkau and Grottkau, which had been reconnoitered in advance.

Since two army corps did not suffice for such a long front, the support of the I Corps and of one other was requested. The request was approved by the King. The I, V, and VI Corps were started toward the Neisse and the Guard Corps, standing in reserve in rear of the First Army, was transported by rail to Brieg. The rest of the army advanced as follows: the III Corps to Lowenberg, Friedeberg, and Wiegandsthal; the IV to Laubau and Greiggenberg; the II to Niesky, Reichenbach, Gorlitz, and Seidenberg; the Cavalry Corps to the region of Lowenberg. If anything could threaten Silesia, these were thus the measures taken for her safety. The Austrians were firmly decided to remain on the defensive, but such a separation of the enemy—one half between Torgau and Gorlitz, the other more than 120 km. from that point on the Neisse—was sure to shake the firmest resolution.

If the Austrians did not think themselves strong enough to deal with the entire Prussian army, they were surely capable of encountering the smaller half. The attack of the isolated Second Army, however, would not have been so easy and simple as it looked at first. The chosen position was pretty strong, the numerical superiority of the attack not overpowering, a turning movement rendered difficult through the mountains and by the fortress of Glatz. Should the position prove untenable, it was proposed to draw back the Second Army without serious damage so far that it could be received by the First.

The danger, to which the Second Army had exposed itself by advancing to the Neisse, was not to be considered too great. It was far worse that the general offensive, so well planned, had become doubtful. The execution of the plan: advance of the right wing through Saxony up to the Austrian frontier, penetration into Bohemia from there and from Silesia, seeking the enemy with a united army of nine army corps with the intention of cutting him off from Vienna, would have protected Silesia and Breslau better than any position and would have given the possibility of a battle of annihilation. At present not fully five corps were available for the advance into Bohemia. The possibility and the manner of a joint operation of the two halves of the army depended upon the measures which the easily assembled Austrians would take against the seemingly irretrievably divided Prussians.

The unfavorable situation could not be averted by Moltke. The safeguarding of Silesia was represented to the King as a duty devolving upon the father of his country. The proving by Moltke that this duty could be fulfilled very well by an offensive in Bohemia and very badly by a defensive in Silesia, was not convincing. The authority of the Chief of the General Staff was still small at the time and personal influence as well as political considerations were so much the more effective. More than once, in this war, a carefully elaborated plan by Moltke was spoiled in preparation, mobilization, and concentration. It was left to him to assemble the fragments and construct something new.

In spite of all difficulties placed in his way, he adhered to the offensive. He was decided to enter Bohemia with the First Army and the Army of the Elbe. As soon as this had taken place, the Austrians would, notwithstanding any plans they might have made, turn to that point, at least with their main forces, sending a smaller part against the Second Army. A victory over this weaker enemy would be rendered easy to the Second Army and a possibility given for the joint action of the two units. The Prussians hesitated and waited so long to do this that the Austrians prevented this movement by an offensive in Silesia. The resolution of the Austrian Commander-in-Chief, Benedek, could be counted upon not to allow himself to be enticed back by a later counteroffensive into Bohemia. All that would then be left to do would be to go with the First Army to the assistance of the Second or to receive it and advance in the direction of the Neisse. The hope, not of victory, but of an annihilating victory, would have to be given up. The defeated Austrians might, without considerable molestation, retreat to Vienna —Olmutz, behind the Danube

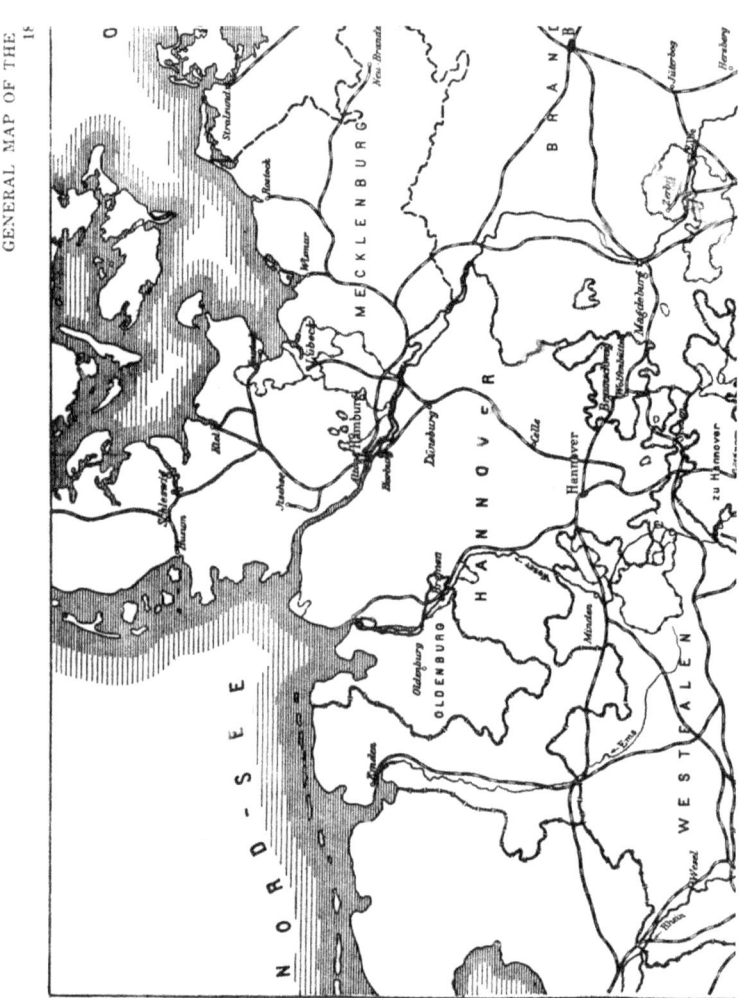

The Campaign of 1866 in Germany

It was lucky that Austria made a break earlier, before the circumstances in Silesia had been elucidated and the advantages of an offensive movement there had become known. As she knew herself to be inferior to the enemy, she desired to assure herself of the support of the German Central States. At the voting of the Federal Diet on 14 June, the majority of the States declared against Prussia. To have the declaration followed by action, neither

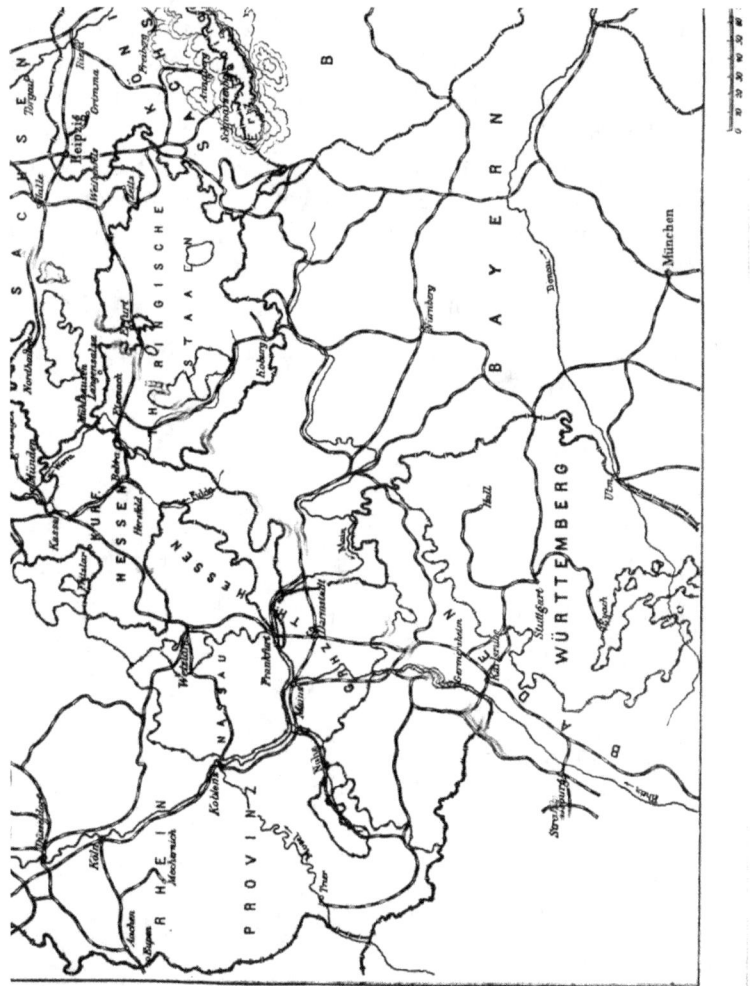

Austria nor the Central States were sufficiently prepared; both had hoped either to intimidate by the number of her enemies, thus determining her to desist from her demands, or to obtain, through negotiations, the necessary time for mobilization and completion of the equipment of their armies. This, however, proved to be an illusion.

Prussia saw that it was the highest time to leave the cautious reserve behind. An ultimatum was sent as early as 15 June, to Saxony, Hanover, and The Hesse Electorate, followed on the same day, upon its rejection, by a declaration of war and on the next day by the beginning of hostilities against the three powers. This forced Austria's decision. In the Federal Diet on the 16th, the Vienna cabinet declared that "on account of Prussia's advance against Saxony, Hanover, and the Hesse Electorate, His Majesty the Emperor would assist those powers with all his strength and, accordingly immediately begin operations with all his military forces."

This immediate action could not consist in a stay in Moravia

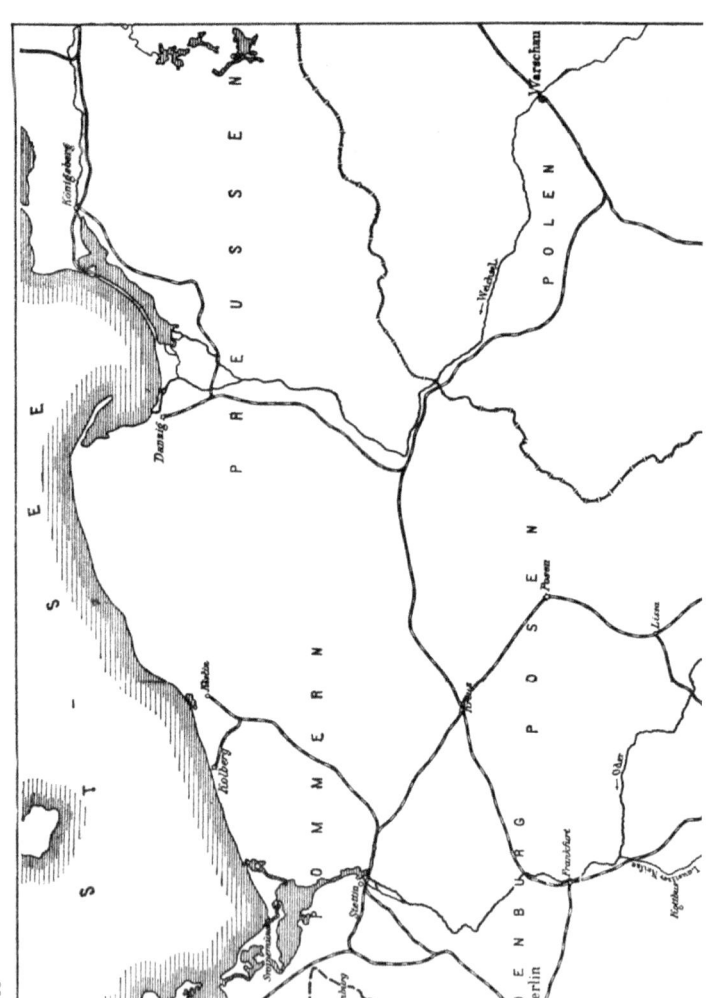

or a penetration into Silesia, but only in an advance into Bohemia, if troth should be kept with the trustiest of the allies—Saxony, and assurance of the support of the next powerful ally—-Bavaria, maybe also Wurttemberg and Hesse obtained. Only with the 40,000, or 50,000, Bavarians could Austria hope for superiority over Prussia. This advantage weighed enough in the balance to allow overlooking the disadvantage of a continuous threatening of the right flank in the march of the army from Moravia to Bohemia. It was not known how great was the number of the hostile troops

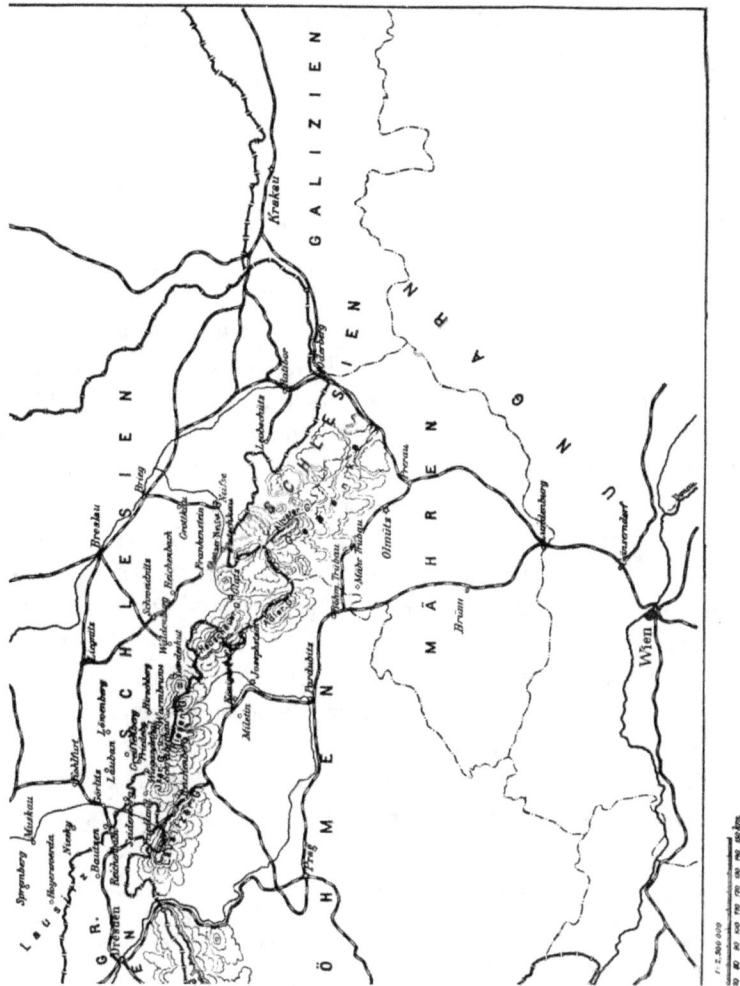

in Silesia. The Austrians were informed for quite a long time in regard to the positions and movements of the enemy. They could not, however, be cognizant on the 16th, of the marches and transportation of troops taking place in Silesia up to the 18th. Vienna knew of the two corps which were to be in the vicinity of the Neisse and Glatz. But it was known surely that the Prussian main army was still between Torgau and Landeshut. They could not allow themselves to be misled by the "demonstrations" of these two corps. The order for the advance into Bohemia was issued on the 16th.

It was imperative for Prussia to move first against Hanover and Hesse Electorate. These two powers, whose territory was situated between the eastern and western halves of the monarchy, could not be left in rear in going to war against Austria and the South Germans. A sudden attack against the rear might be expected, once engaged in combat against the Austrians. The Hanoverian and Hessian contingents must likewise not be allowed to march to the south and increase the already superior forces of the enemy. It was necessary that they should, while still within the Prussian zone of power, "be placed out of activity by disarmament or attack."

A further problem of Prussia consisted in drawing the fighting strength of the South German powers, especially of Bavaria, from Bohemia. Austria desired to fight at the head of all the German Central States against an isolated Prussia. Prussia wished to isolate Austria at the price of three divisions. In order to solve these two problems the following troops were available: Beyer's Division (18 battalions, 5 squadrons, 18 guns)* at Wetzlar, the 13th Division under Goeben (12 battalions, 9 squadrons, 41 guns) at Minden, Manteuffel's Division (12 battalions, 8 squadrons, 24 guns) at Altona, the two last named ones under command of General von Falckenstein. These three divisions crossed on 16 June, the hostile frontiers in the direction of Kassel and Hanover and already on the following day this city was occupied by the 18th Division. The Hanoverians as well as the Hessians had withdrawn before the

---

* Formed by detaching the ninth regiments of eight Army Corps and two more regiments from the IV and V Corps.

sudden attack. The former were transported by rail to Gottingen, the latter to Hersfeld. From this terminal, the Hessians, some 4000 men strong, continued their retreat to Frankfort and escaped.

The Hanoverians remained first at Gottingen in order te somewhat prepare for combat after a hurried retreat. As Goeben's Division followed on the 19th, there was little time to retrieve what had been lost. Though reservists streamed from all sides and trains with war materiel followed during the 17th from Hanover, the condition of the troops remained completely "unprepared." The ammunition on hand might last, perhaps, for two fighting days in all. Should the Hanoverians, while left to themselves, start on a campaign in North Germany, they might have won a single success against the yet widely scattered enemy, but would have gone under in the end through lack of ammunition and the numerical superiority of the enemy.

Views wavered at the headquarters between "a battle at Gottingen," "opening of negotiations" and the possibilities lying between the two. The difficulties of a campaign without hope of success, reserves, or reinforcements pressed. The necessity of seeking reserves, paid for by the loss of the capital and the greater part of the country, led them to the resolution of "an immediate departure toward the Bavarians and to an avoidance of serious encounters." The danger of being attacked by Goeben in the front and Beyer in the rear hastened the execution of the plan. The road via Kassel was already occupied, that via Eschwege threatened.

It was decided to take a third route via Heiligenstadt, Wanfried, and Treffurt to Eisenach. With 20 battalions, 24 squadrons, 42 guns, about 17,000 armed and 3000 unarmed men, the march was begun on the 2ist. This retreat was too well founded on the existing circumstances not to have been foreseen in Berlin. The pursuit had to be started. According to Napoleonic principles, part of the troops had to follow the enemy *"l'épée dans les reins,"*[*] another head them off on the shortest line. Goeben had reached on the 20th, Alfeld—Bodenburg. Manteuffel stood with a brigade near Hanover, with another at Celle, Beyer had entered Kassel with

---

[*] "The sword in the kidneys."

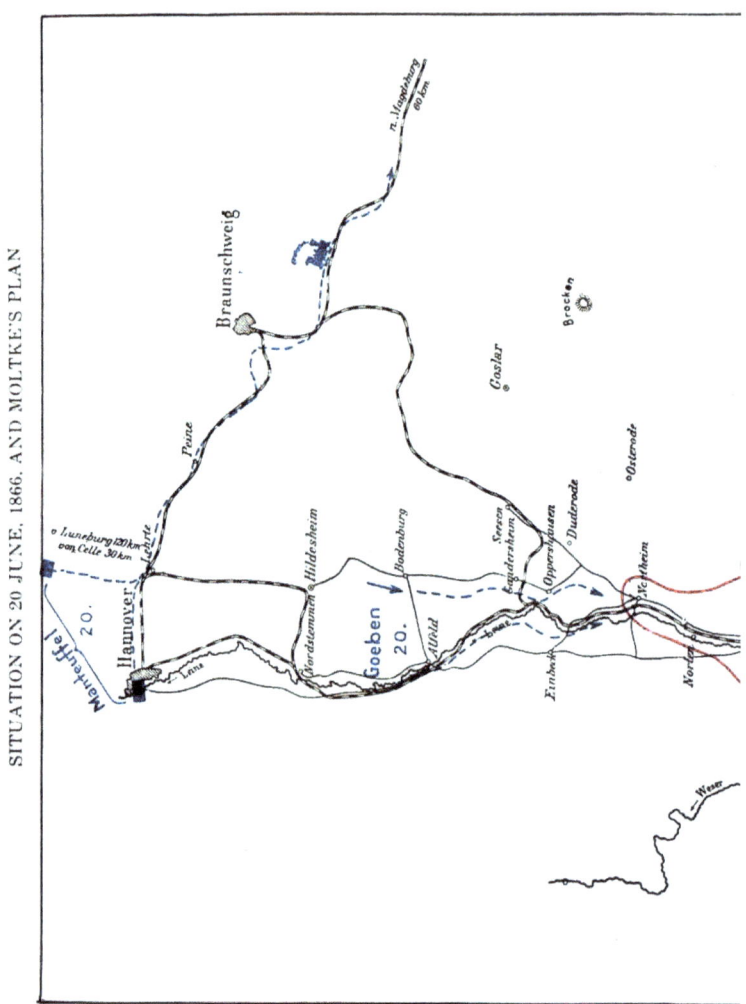

the main forces and thence had taken a short road to Eisenach when the enemy left Gottingen. Another still shorter road was by rail via Braunschweig, Magdeburg, and Halle.

Moltke's simple plan was as follows: Beyer to march via Otmannshausen to Eisenach; Manteuffel's Division to be transported to the same point by rail, both to march against the enemy wherever he might be. Goeben would follow as before and attack him in the rear. The plan, however, was executed only in so

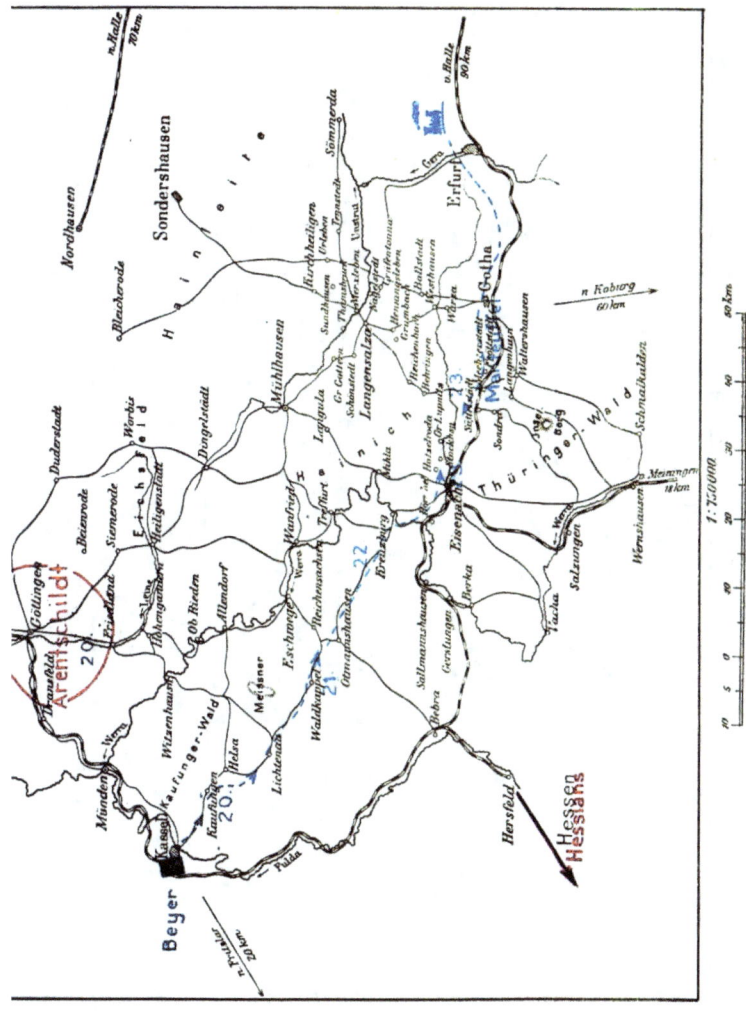

far that Beyer, after garrisoning Kassel and occupying Munden, went on the 20th in the direction of Otmannshausen toward Waldkappel and Goeben continued the march to Gottingen. Falkenstein rejected the transportation of Manteuffel's Division to Magdeburg. He wanted "to avoid a division of his fighting strength, which seemed inexpedient to him, and not to let part of it get entirely out of his hands."

It was, however, impossible to avoid a division of forces. For

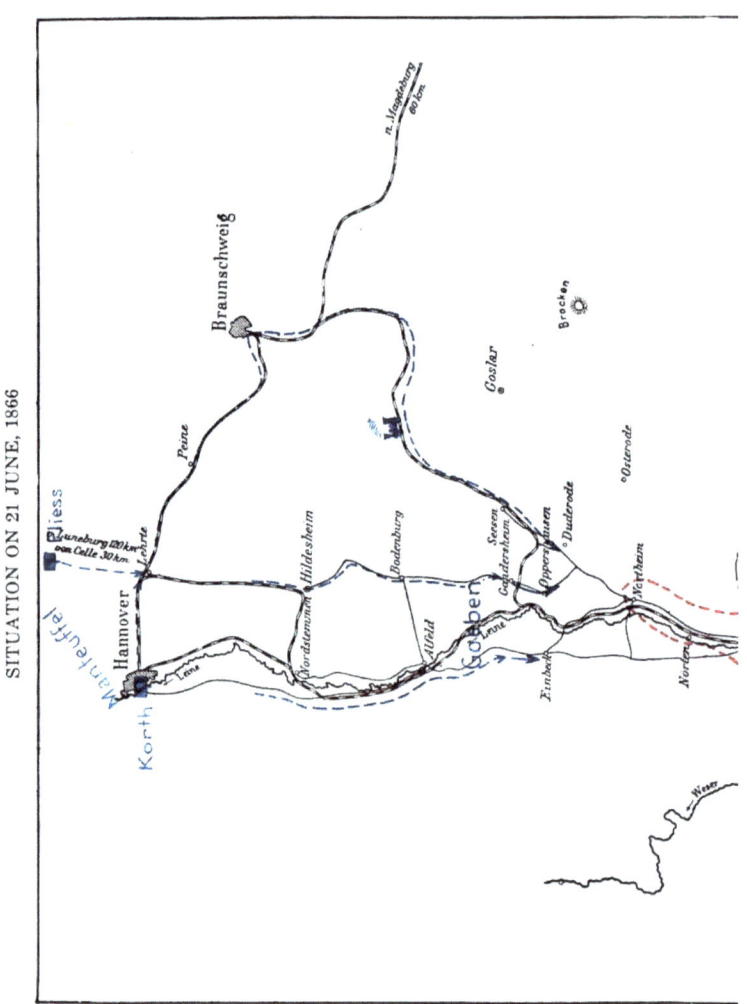

SITUATION ON 21 JUNE, 1866

it existed already in the highest degree: Beyer's last battalion was on the 20th still at Fritzlar, Manteuffel at Luneburg. The Prussian troops, separated by the Hanoverians, lay in a long line between these two points. The problem was not to avoid such a division, but to remedy it. This could not be effected in a quicker or simpler way than by Moltke's plan. The surrounding of the Hanoverians and the junction of the three divisions would have taken place at one stroke. Before the 24th, one campaign might have been ended and

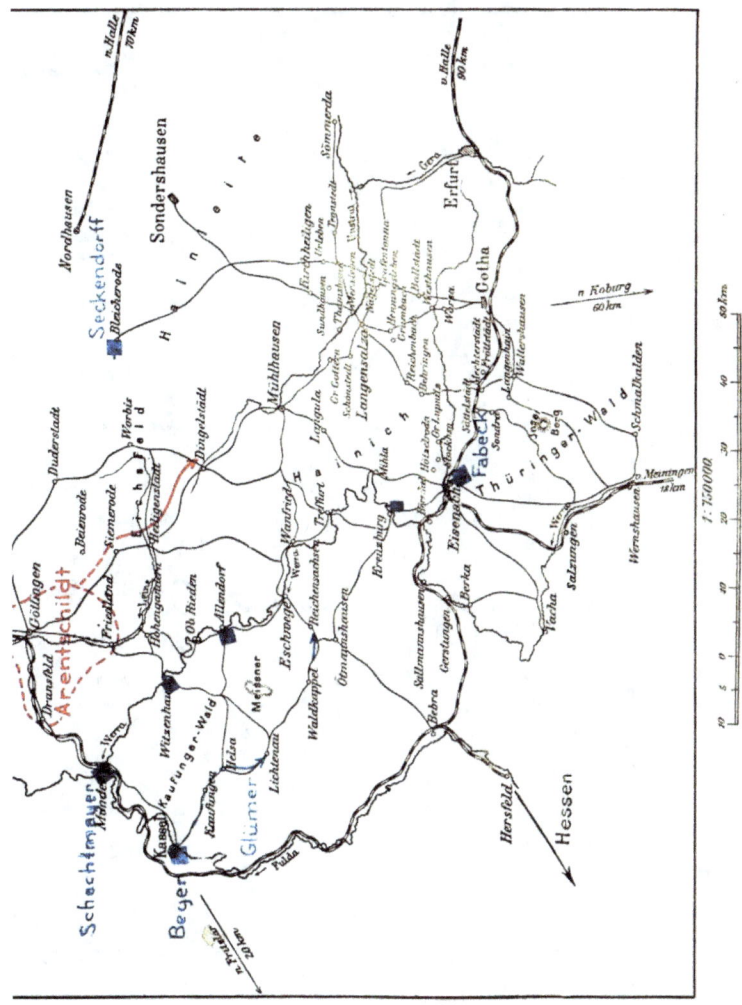

the army assembled to begin another. Since, however, Falkenstein ordered that Manteuffel's Division should not go from Hanover and Celle via Magdeburg to oppose the enemy, but via Braunschweig and Seesen, should fellow the 18th Division, battalion by battalion, the scattering of forces remained, Manteuffel's Division removed from the scope of activity for a time and the surrounding of the Hanoverjans was rendered doubtful.

The Campaign of 1866

Moltke had taken pains to replace the falling out of one division. The Coburg-Gotha regiment, three battalions, some cavalry, two sortie guns from Erfurt, were placed under the command of Colonel von Fabeck and transported to Eisenach. If Beyer continued his march from Waldkappel to that point and Goeben followed the Hanoverians, it would be possible to do without Manteuffel.

All began well on the 21st. Fabeck had reached Hisenach, Beyer, subordinate to Falkenstein, held Kassel, sent out detachments to Munden and Allendorf, and reached Reichensachsen and Lichtenau with his main body, Goeben reached Hinbeck—Oppershausen and two Landwehr battalions from Magdeburg under General von Seckendorff reached Bleicherode. Within this wide circle, the Hanoverian marching column pushed into the space between Dingelstadt and Siemrode. All would have taken place as per orders, if Falkenstein had not assumed against all contrary reports and information, that the Hanoverians would oppose resistance in a good position on the road halfway between Norten and Gottingen, and had he not decided to attack them at that point on the 23rd. That Goeben received an order to turn toward the front for the impending battle did not bring about any disadvantage; it rather spurred on the 138th Division to greater rapidity of march toward Gottingen. More doubtful was the order sent to Beyer to cut off the retreat of the enemy.

After all kinds of reports and information, this general had to assume that the departure of the Hanoverians from Gottingen was, at least, highly probable and he could therefore fulfill his task in the simplest way by continuing his march to Eisenach. The wording of the order, however, seemed to indicate clearly an attack against the rear of the "Hanoverians, standing between Gottingen and Norten." Beyer, consequently, held Kassel and Allendorf and sent the advance guard from Munden to Dransfeld, the main body from Reichensachsen and Lichtenau to Witzenhausen, the reserve to Kaufungen. A march direction contrary to the preceding was assumed. The enemy, freed from all threatening flank attack, seemed to be able to continue unmolested his march to the South of Germany.

The appearance of Beyer's troops on the 21st, at Allendorf, of patrols on the right of the Werra, the possibility of the Prussians occupying the crossing over the Hainich east of Wanfried, Treffurt, and Miehla on the 22nd, decided the Hanoverian General von Arentschildt to desist from the march from Heiligenstadt to Wanfried, then from the one from Muhlhausen via Langula to Eisenach and to march via Langensalza. With this detour Eisenach would be reached by the Hanoverians, who stood on the evening of the 22nd between Dinge1stadt and south of Muhlhausen, not much earlier than by Goeben, who stood at the time in Gottingen, and by Beyer, standing with the main body and reserve at Allendorf, Witzenhausen, and Kaufungen. Should some resistance be shown in the defiles of Eisenach, Beyer might come up in time via Otmannshausen and Goeben via Eschwege to render an escape impossible, But should Goeben follow the enemy via Muhthausen, the start won by him would not be great. At the hour when Goeben entered Gottingen on the 22nd, the Hanoverian rear guard left Heiligenstadt in order to halt at Dinge1stadt. If the enemy should remain there for one day, the pursuit would be able to reach him. Moltke's zealous endeavor lay in procuring that one day.

Since by the Hanoverians' march to Muhlhausen, Gotha was likewise threatened, the five battalions, thus far disposable at Eisenach, could not suffice. More troops had to be called. Seckendorf was ordered with his two Landwehr battalions from Bleicherode to Gotha, by immediate Royal command two battalions of the 4th Regiment of the Guard were placed in a train, two batteries from Dresden, two to three reserve and Landwehr battalions were ordered from Dresden, and Fabeck with his five battalions was sent to Gotha. On the 23rd, when the Hanoverians reached Behringen with Bulow's Brigade, Reichenbach with the reserve cavalry; with the terrain north and south of Langensalza, Knesebeck's and de Vaux's Brigades, Bothmer's Brigade—Gross-Gottern, the rear guard—Muhlhausen, they found Fabeck in front of them near Gotha, Seckendorf on their left flank near Urleben, and had to consider Eisenach occupied, according to all information received. They could not go on without a combat, although against inconsiderable forces. They seemed also decided to give battle. Early on the 24th, the troops were prepared for attack against Gotha. Fabeck was lost.

The attack was not executed, however. Moltke had contrived to

The Campaign of 1866

SITUATION ON 23 JUNE. 1866

have a parliamentary sent with the categorical request that the entirely surrounded enemy lay down arms. The Hanoverians were surrounded, it is true, but by weak detachments at long distances. They were also cognizant of the condition of affairs, knowing the small numbers of Fabeck's troops. But the demand, made with such firmness and calm assurance, did not fail to produce its effect. The Hanoverians entered upon negotiations in the hope of obtaining free departure in exchange for a promise not to take part in the war for a certain length of time.

The coming and going of the parliamentaries, demands in Berlin, answers thence taking up a long time, the troops were allowed to disband and go to their quarters. Scarce had they reached these, when a resolute aide-de-camp decided the King to order the occupation of Eisenach now free of troops. Bulow's Brigade was to make a reconnaissance, occupy the city if it were free of the enemy and thus assist in breaking through the entire army.

In the meanwhile, Colonel von der Osten-Sacken[*] had arrived with five companies of the 4th Regiment of the Guard at the threatened point and left no doubt to the parliamentary sent to him, that he would defend to the utmost with his small unit, the post entrusted to him. The uncertainty of success against an infantry armed with needleguns, though scarcely one third their own strength, the fear of firing against a peaceful, wholly unconcerned city, the knowledge of being left to themselves alone, lastly the uncalled for mixing in of a Hanoverian parliamentary, who did not wish to have his negotiations disturbed, persuaded the council of war and the brigade commander to desist from an attack and to conclude an armistice until the next morning. This rendered all attempt at breaking through impossible, and more than one day had been won. The pursuit ought to be quite close. The disarmament could be started on the following day.

The pursuit, which, according to Napoleon ought to have been executed toward Gneisenau "*l'épée dans les reins*" and "until the last gasp of man and horse," was interrupted by Goeben after four

---

[*] Three companies had occupied the crossing at Mechterstadt.

days of march on the 23rd, by one day's rest. Only a weak advance guard under Wrangel was sent to Siemerode and brought the not surprising report that the enemy had continued the retreat. Beyer had, it is true, received orders to march to Otmannshausen. But he alone reached it with a weak reserve. The main army and the advance guard, left without sufficient orders and elucidation of the situation, wanted to give a decisive blow in the "battle of Gottingen,' marched to Friedland and arrived in the evening, after elimination of all misunderstandings, in Hohengandern, Witzenhausen, and Allendorf.

Since the Hanoverians did not give battle where he wanted it and did not allow themselves to be overtaken, Falkenstein decided to leave them to their fate, march off to Frankfort, scatter the VIII Federal Corps and cover the threatened Province of the Rhine. On the 24th, Goeben was to reach Munden, Manteuffel, Gortingen, and Beyer assemble at Otmannshausen. Falkenstein left thus the Hanoverians unmolested in his rear, gave free hand to the Bavarians to take part in the impending decisive action in Bohemia, and turned against an enemy who was far from being prepared for war and who could have been left unnoticed. As Silesia could have been best protected by an invasion of Bohemia, thus could the Rhine Province best be guarded by the disarmament of the Hanoverians. After such a success no South German would have dared to cross the Nahe. The Hessians and Nassauers would have known that they could not then invade the countries of others, but would have to protect their own skins.

The march to Frankfort could not be permitted. If it were desired not to give up everything, or to open the war with a fatal disaster, it was necessary that the King take the matter personally in hand. His first order to transport as many troops as possible via Kassel to Kosenach was answered by a curt "Impracticable." The railway track at Munden was destroyed. A second order received early on the 24th, to bring one of Manteuffel's brigades, via Seesen and Magdeburg, to Gotha, showed the seriousness of the King's will. The impossible became possible.

Goeben made a forced march to Kassel and entrained there six battalions with corresponding cavalry and artillery. Beyer received orders to march to this point. One of Manteuffel's brigades went

120 The Campaign of 1866

The Campaign of 1866

SITUATION ON 25 JUNE, 1866

under General Fliess by rail, via Magdeburg to Gotha. Part of the troops reached their goal as early as the night of the 25th. The rest were expected in the course of the day at Eisenach and Gotha. In spite of the loss of two days, Moltke's original plan was still to be put into execution to a certain extent. In addition to Fabeck's and Sacken's troops, two mixed divisions were ready to oppose the enemy at Eisenach—Gotha.

The 3rd Division, which was to follow via Gottingen, was lacking. Of the brigades, which might have formed it, one (Goeben's) was in Kassel, the other (Manteuffel's) was echeloned between Munden and Gottingen. It was clear that it was impossible to effect the concentration of all fighting forces against the Hanoverians. One third had to be kept in readiness for the hoped for campaign against the VIII Federal Corps. Goeben, to whom the command over the troops assembled at Eisenach and Gotha had been entrusted, was not ready for attack on the 25th. Only part of the battalions were on hand. Many of Beyer's division were still at a distance on the march. The last of Fliess' unit were to be expected early on the 26th, and those that had arrived were exhausted by the long march.

An armistice of 24 hours, which Adjutant General von Alvensleben, sent to the Hanoverian headquarters, had concluded, was most welcome. It was of still greater advantage to the Hanoverians. After the latter had desisted from breaking through the enemy and the hope of marching off in peace had dwindled, their principal faith lay in their liberation through the Bavarians. In order to secure it, they had to win time. It happened that the beginning and end of the armistice had not been fixed and that the time of making known the latter had not been settled. Only with much trouble had it been possible to settle the state of affairs, make known the armistice, and set the Prussian attack for 10:00 AM on the 26th.

The Hanoverians still occupied on the 25th, the quarters taken up two days earlier along the road: Gross-Lupnitz—Behringen—Langensalza—Gross-Gottern— Muhlhausen. Since the localities occupied could not offer much after two days, it was hoped to have the possibility of extending the occupied locality beyond Muhlhausen, trusting to the concluded armistice. This brought about movements of troops which would have been impossible had Mantueffel, instead of remaining in Kassel and Gottingen, advanced on the 24th and 25th via Heiligenstadt to Muhlhausen. These movements were interpreted by the population: "Hanoverian troops are marching against Muhlhausen,"—followed by "The Hanoverian army is marching through Muhthausen," arriving in Berlin as "The Hanoverian army has marched through Muhlhausen."

At the opposite end of the long Hanoverian deployment, Goeben saw troops at Gross-Lupnitz and Stockhausen, a detachment at Mechterstadt and heard about stronger troops at Behringen where he supposed that the entire Hanoverian army had assembled. He thought of attacking it on the following day. He did not wish to advance against the enemy like Hannibal, keep him occupied on the front and then turn against his flanks with echelons that had been kept back for this purpose. He did not intend like Frederick or Napoleon to turn a hostile flank with his entire army. He placed in the evening of the 25th, the brigade of the 13th Division under Kummer at Waltershausen, Langenhain, and Sondra ready for a flanking attack, while Beyer was to advance for a frontal attack from Hotzelroda.

It is easily understood that the enemy did not await for the artfully laid noose to be drawn tight. Bulow took his advance troops from Gross-Lupnitz and Mechterstadt before midnight and prepared to retreat further before the advance of the enemy. The report of the retreat of the Hanoverian advance troops arrived in the night of the 26th simultaneously with a message from Berlin in which Councilor of the State Wintzigerode announced the passage of the Hanoverian army through Muhlhausen. The disparity of these reports was apparent. Nevertheless none doubted them. None deemed it necessary to ascertain their correctness by the sending out of a patrol.

Moltke might have believed or not. At any rate he saw a liberation from the binding agreement of the armistice. It was possible now to attack immediately and to pursue. He telegraphed, consequently, to Falkenstein who had arrived, in the meanwhile, at Eisenach: "follow immediately and instruct Manteuffel in Gottingen to start at the same time. Part of the troops in Gotha

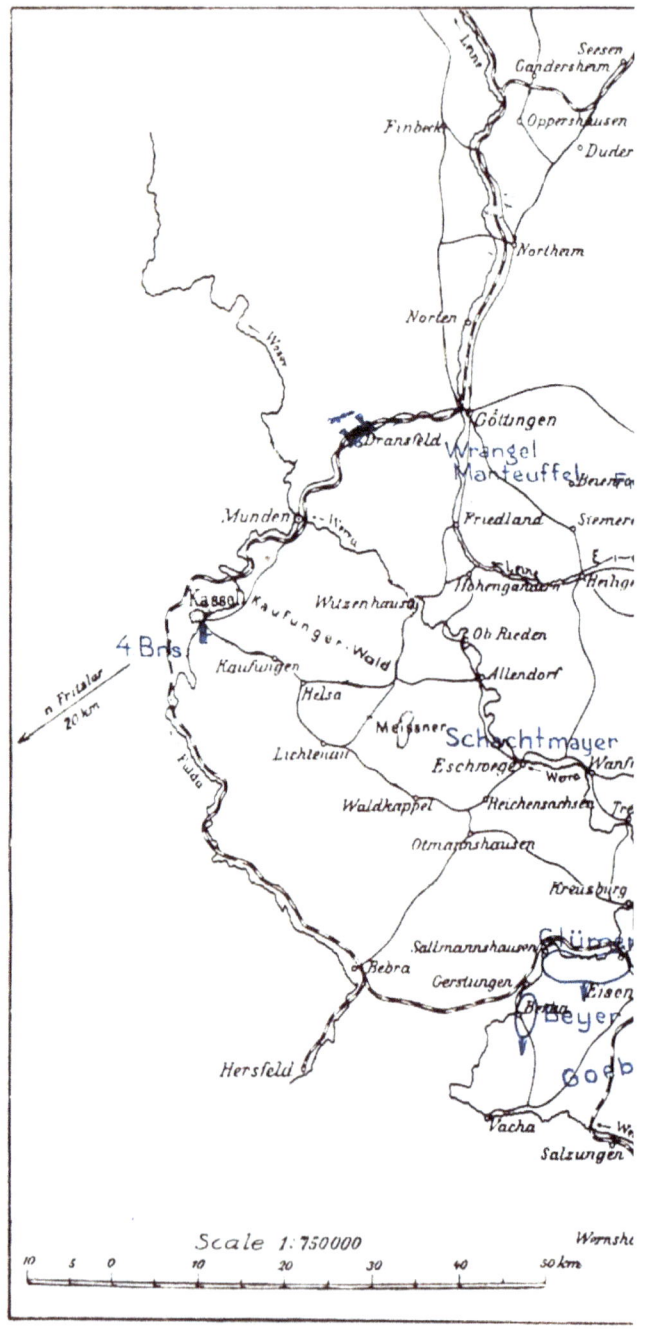

may, perhaps, be transported by rail to Nordhausen. General Fliess shall receive a copy of this telegram. It would be advisable, considering your superiority, to leave the necessary troops for the observation of Bavaria, etc., and in consideration of operations to come." The last sentence was not understood as it was meant. Moltke wanted to leave only a small detachment in Eisenach.

Falkenstein, having heard the rumor that the Bavarians had already reached Vacha, considered that half of his forces would be sufficient against the Hanoverians, using the other against the Bavarians. Beyer with his reserve was sent to Berka—Gerstungen, Glummer to Sallmanshausen—Horschel, Kummer to Hisenach. Schachtmeyer was to stay in Eschwege and occupy Allendorf. The attack of the Bavarians was awaited in an extended position: Berka—Eisenach. Only on the 26th would twelve battalions be assembled for Manteuffel. Fliess alone received orders for "immediate pursuit."

Moltke had intended the joint action of all forces at one point. Falkenstein held fast to the division into three parts. Thus measures were adopted to attain no success at any point and perhaps defeats at many. The movements ordered were in full swing when the following information arrived in the afternoon: from Berlin—the Hanoverians were still at Langensalza: from Vacha—nothing was to be seen of the Bavarians. The movements ordered proved aimless. But nothing could be changed on the 26th. Manteuffel alone had, acting independently, sent the north detachment from Gottingen to Duderstadt and the troops arriving gradually by rail from Munden, Kassel, and Eisenach[*] to Beienrode and Siemerode.

The Hanoverians, as a matter of course, were far from making a retreat via Muhlhausen to "the Kingdom." At the conclusion of the armistice, an attack from Gotha, Waltershausen, and Eisenach seemed impending. They did not wish to await it at Langensalza in a position exposed to a turning movement. The commanding general von Arentschildt ordered consequently: "The Prussian troops are advancing. Resistance will be offered them. Each brigade shall retreat fighting in the direction of Sondershausen."

---

[*] 2 battalions of the 4th Regiment, of the Guard.

There should concentrate for this purpose: the Brigades of Bothmer at Grafentonna; that of de Vaux south of Langensalza; that of Bulow at Schonstadt; Knesbeck and the reserve cavalry between Sundshausen and Thamsbruck. The movements of these two latter units from Langensalza to the heights on the left bank of the Unstrut were observed by one of the many Prussian parliamentaries, going to and fro between Gotha and Langensalza, and interpreted as a retreat to Kirchheiligen. The "retreat to Kirchheiligen" reached Falkenstein as a "retreat to Sondershausen" and was accepted by him as such until a report from the President of the Regency in Erfurt: "retreat over Tennstedt to Sommerda" appeared still more probable. Falkenstein held on to the retreat to Sommerda, based merely on rumors, although Fliess, who had advanced as far as Henningsleben, reported that the Hanoverians were as before at Langensalza. Falkenstein maintained just as firmly that the Bavarians were advancing in the valley of the Werra, though rumors alone reported that they were first at Meiningen, then at Wernshausen.

On the basis of this pretended condition of affairs: retreat of the Hanoverians to Sommerda, and advance of the Bavarians through the valley of the Werra, Falkenstein decided to await, with Goeben, the Bavarians in the position: Berka—Gerstungen—Eisenach, which was over 20 km. long. Fliess did not have to attack the Hanoverian "rear guard" at Langensalza, but remain at its heels, in case it should return. Manteuffel had to stay in Gottingen in case of emergency. The general adhered to this resolution although the King had commanded by telegraph in the evening to bring the Hanoverian matter to an end, cost what it may. It is certain that Falkenstein had the right and the duty to change orders, given by the King from a distance, according to the state of affairs on the spot. However, it must be supposed that the despised order should: be replaced by something better. In view of two real or supposed enemies, to remain standing with three separate troop units could by no means be something better.

Since Falkenstein disregarded the orders of the King, it was logical and clear for the division commanders to disregard the orders of Falkenstein. They received from Berlin copies of the King's order and judged of the state of affairs not from afar, but like their commander-in-chief, on the spot. Manteuffel, who had already advanced on the 26th, at his own initiative, to Duderstadt and Beienrode, wanted to advance again on the 27th, independently, to Worbis and Dinge1stedt, and Fliess resolved, according to the Royal order, to bring the affair to a close, cost what it might, and to attack the Hanoverians in spite of their forces being twice as strong as his. He could surmise that Falkenstein, according to the same order, would come to his support.

On the other side, deliberations took place in the evening of the 26th, as to whether it were expedient to attack the isolated Fliess on the morrow. The intention, expressed in the beginning as a principle to escape, without serious encounter, to South Germany, as well as the unshakable hope of the Bavarian support, kept them from adopting the only measure which could bring the matter to a tolerable end. It was decided to await, beyond the Unstrut, on both sides of the road leading from Langensalza to Sondershausen, the attack of the Prussians and the arrival of the Bavarians. The following positions had to be occupied: Bulow and the reserve artillery at Thamsbruck, de Vaux at Merxleben, Knesebeck, in his rear; Bothmer at Nage1stedt; the reserve cavalry at Sundhausen.

Fliess, who had fallen back for the night to Westhausen—Warza, could attack this position occupied by a numerically superior enemy, only by crossing the Unstrut, perhaps at Grafentonna and then turning against the hostile left flank. He advanced, however, on the 27th against the center of the line and drove out the advanced troops left at Langensalza. Two of Knesebeck's battalions, sent out for support by way of Merxleben, were likewise driven back and the Judenhugel was occupied.

This success did not give any special advantage for further attack. The Prussians found themselves before a long defile—the Kirchberg—and a river, bordered by dams. All was strongly occupied. The crest of the Judenhugel commanded, it is true, the Kirchberg, situated opposite, but it was so narrow in the direction of the enemy that the few available batteries could be placed only in echelon formation. It seemed quite impossible to fight down the superior hostile artillery, to penetrate then through the narrow passage and maybe across the river. To hold fast at this point and seek a crossing at another place, the force was too small. The defensive was assumed unintentionally. Six rifled 4-pounders and

ENGAGEMENT AT LANGENSALZA
27 June, 1866

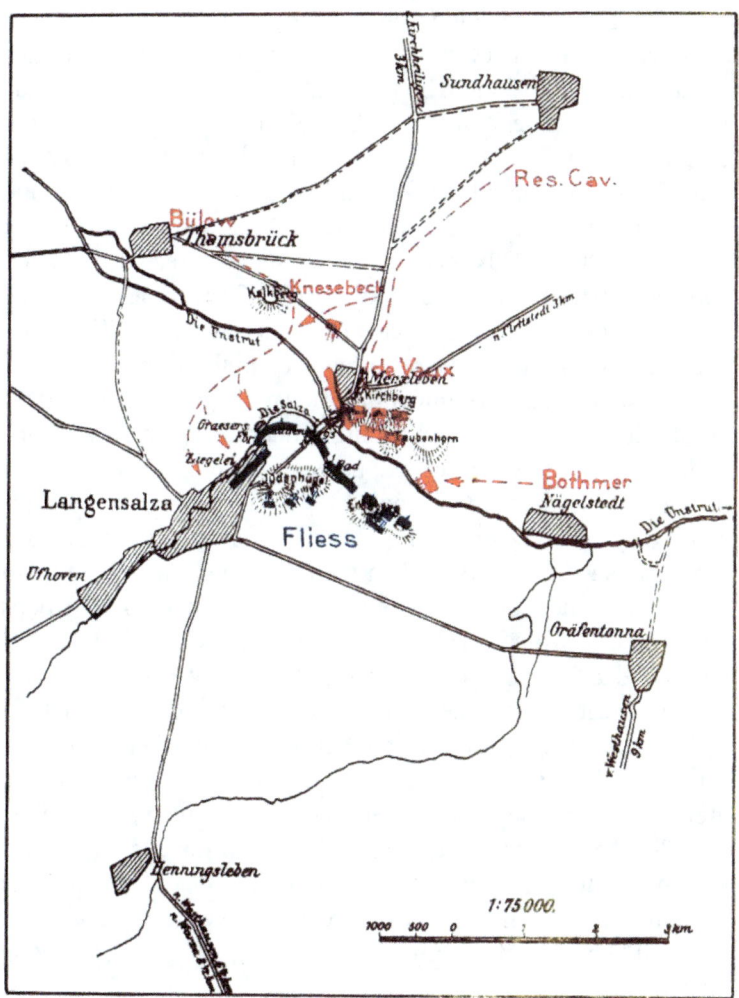

fourteen smooth bore guns, the range of which was not entirely sufficient, on the Prussian side, opposed twelve rifled six-pounders and three smooth bore guns on the Kirchberg, six rifled 6-pounders in rear of Merxleben and four similar guns south of Taubenhorn near the Unstrut, which took the position on the Judenhugel in flank and rear.

In order to fight this formidable enemy, the rifled battery was taken from the Judenhugel to the Erbsberg, so that only fourteen smooth bore guns remained on the former, In spite of the great numerical superiority of the enemy, the Prussian artillery was able to maintain its positions. The Prussian infantry occupied first the Baths, the Kallenberg Mill and the right bank of the Salza from Graesers factory as far as the Ziegelei and later on, the Erbsberg also. Thus there stood two defenders, a weaker south of and stronger north of the Unstrut. The stronger was constrained against his will, to attack. This seemed very simple to execute. De Vaux would attack from Merxleben, Bulow from Thamsbruck, followed by Knesebeck and the reserve cavalry from Nagelstedt. The battle of Cannae would thus have been repeated in the simplest way.

Bulow, as well as Bothmer had, however, gone from the right and the left toward Merxleben and rendered thus their advance difficult. The former succeeded, however, in crossing the river at the Kalkberg. Knesebeck foliowed. Their attack against the Salza up to Ziegelei did not need to be successful, in spite of their numerical superiority. But when their right wing penetrated into Langensalza, the Judenhugel could no longer be held. Since troops advanced also from Merxleben, the defense, especially the units who had decided upon obstinate resistance in various localities, were in great stress. The defeat would have been complete if Bothmer had likewise crossed the Unstrut and attacked the enemy in the rear. He had, however, desisted from all crossing after an attempt at Taubenhorn had failed. The reserve cavalry, assembled according to Napoleonic principle, in rear of the center, crossed with difficulty over bridge and dam in order to pursue the retreating enemy. The attacks undertaken broke, however, against the good behavior of the Line and the Landwehr and were soon abandoned.

The victor was content with the occupation of the hostile position. The road via Henningsleben remained open and in the evening Fliess was able to occupy his camp near Westhausen and Warza which he had left in the morning. The situation, with the exception of losses suffered by both sides, had altered but little during the 24 hours. The Hanoverians stood near Langensalza, Fliess at Westhausen. Manteuffel had advanced a little closer though not close enough to assume immediate action.

It was more important that Goeben, after the defeat of Fliess, could no longer remain idle at Hisenach. He had been made commander-in-chief for the 27th (Falkenstein had gone to Kassel on administrative business) and had remained immobile all day long at Eisenach—-Gerstungen in expectation of an attack by the Bavarians. The thundering of the guns at Langensalza did not trouble him much since be thought it an insignificant rear guard combat. The real enemy occupied his mind less than the imaginary one. He telegraphed in the evening to Beyer, stationed at Gerstungen: "I let the alarm be given. Hostile columns are marching towards the heights opposite, they are descending. I shall defend Eisenach if the enemy is strong."

The hostile columns were only phantoms. Had these phantoms been of flesh and blood and had the Hanoverians had a Napoleon at their head, Fliess would have been annihilated on the 27th, and, on the 28th, Goeben, for whom a Cannae would have been prepared by a frontal attack by the Bavarians and in rear by the Hanoverians. It would have been shown that it was wrong to offer defensive battle to one opponent, while another was in the rear.

Goeben was first awakened from his trance in the night by a royal telegram directed to Falkenstein, saying: "I order you to go immediately and directly against the Hanoverians. No attention shall be given so far to the Bavarians and the South Germans, but, according to my will and my opinion, the Hanoverians shall be entirely disarmed."

Battalions were now sent by rail to Gotha, to the immediate support of Fliess; Beyer was called from Gerstungen and, finally, in the afternoon of the 28th, at 3:00 PM the march to Langensalza was begun. Goeben had not advanced far when a parliamentary reached him with the information that the Hanoverians desired to capitulate.

A council of war was held early in the morning at the headquarters in Langensalza. In front was the enemy who had been defeated the day before. A second was advancing against Muhlhausen. A third stood at Hisenach. It was just as improbable that any one of these should come up before late in the evening, as that the support of the Bavarians might reach them before that

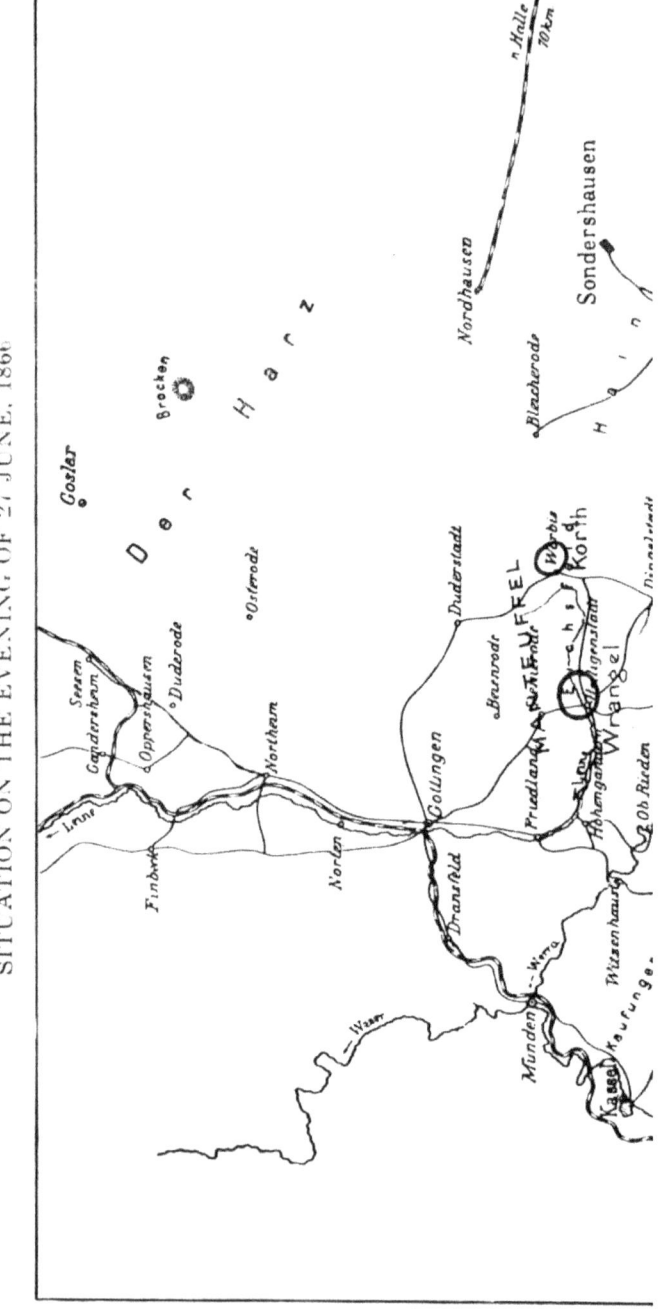

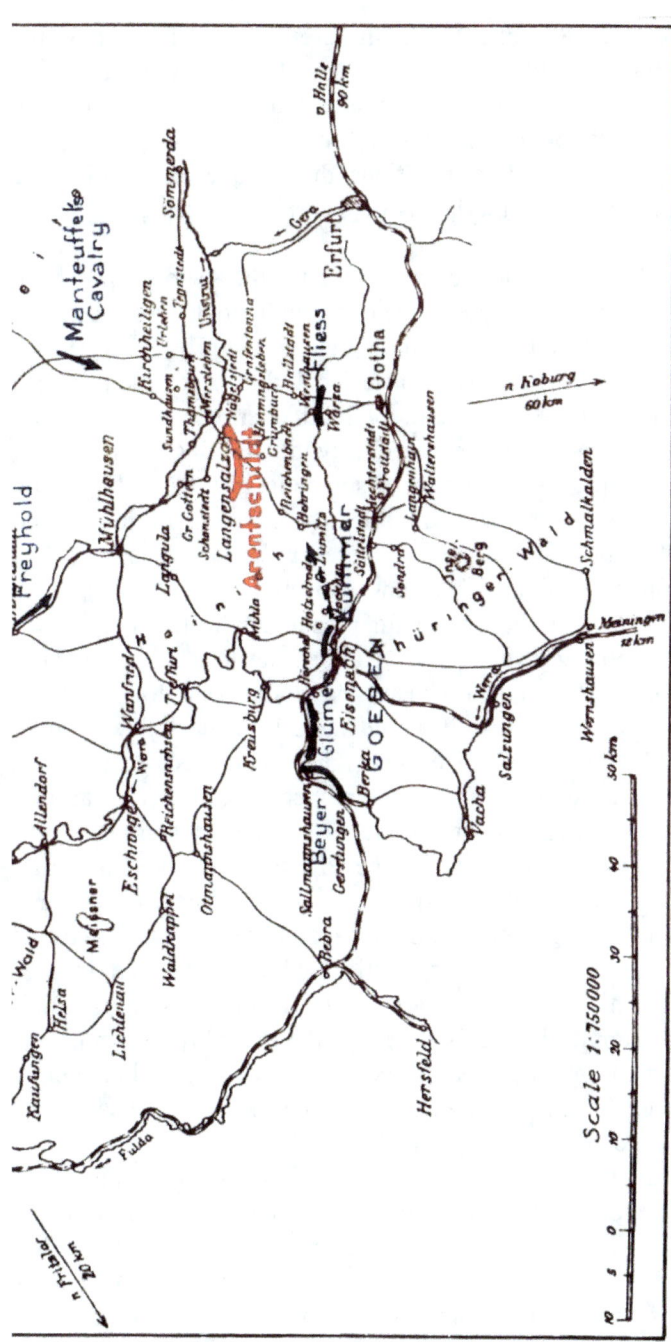

time. For the 28th, at least for the greater part of that day, the Hanoverians would have only the defeated enemy to deal with. Should they attack him immediately they might drive him, probably, as far as Gotha. But little would be gained by this. After using up the rest of their munitions, the Hanoverians would have fallen unarmed into the hands of the enemies advancing on all sides.

In order for them to escape such a fate, Fliess should have been annihilated. They had let slip the opportunity to do so on the 27th. It was improbable that they would be able to retrieve on the 28th what they had lost the day before. Should they be able to do so, they would win free retreat to South Germany. But without ammunition, without the possibility of fighting, armed with weapons a little better than sticks and cudgels, they could give no aid to their allies, but would burden them with provisioning and caring for their 20,000 men. Wherever they might come, they would find unfamiliar rifles, guns, and ammunition. It would take a longer time than the war would, presumably last, to prepare for combat. Nothing would have remained, but to place the men in other contingents and to disband the Hanoverian army. From a soldier's point of view, it would have been desirable to fight another battle on the 28th. The King demanded it also. The generals opposed him. They evidently considered a last battle of desperation not consistent with the lost political situation.

The success, obtained by the Prussians on the 28th, after overcoming numberless difficulties, committing mistakes and misunderstandings, after numerous marches and countermarches and after the loss of a bloody battle, could have been attained on the 24th smoothly, unhesitatingly, and without bloodshed, if Moltke's simple plans had been adopted. But the Prussian generals, notwithstanding their prominence and excellence, could not enter into the cycle of ideas of the gray-haired theorist who had never commanded even a company. They held to the views they had absorbed from Napoleonic principles, which they had misunderstood, and from experience gleaned in time of peace on maneuver grounds. These did not teach them annihilation battles, pursuits, turning movements, and similar phantasies. An enemy occupies a position, the other, having one or two battalions more than the former, attacks. The defeated retreats. The victor allows him to go his way and turns to the problem of the following maneuver day. Moltke endeavored calmly and indefatigably to rebuild the broken cycle. In the beginning he limited himself to kindly persuasion. He was forced in the end to resort to royal commands of the most peremptory character. It is not the least of his achievements that he carried out his will, and brought everything to a fortunate conclusion.

A battle of Cannae was fought on the 28th or rather initiated and planned. Initiation and planning were sufficient to convince the enemy of the futility of resistance and to place him out of the sphere of activity. Corresponding to the ancient program of the battle of the Aufidus, a victory of Arendtschildt over Fliess similar to that gained by Terentius Varro over the Iberians and Gauls, had preceded the turning and surrounding. Only through this victory was the victor placed in the fatal position bringing about his destruction.

The next result of the modern battle of Cannae was the constitution of a North German Confederation, of a united Germany, at least as far as the Main, to which the Kings of Saxony and Hanover and the Elector of Hesse had disdained to belong. The other princes of North Germany declared themselves ready to place their contingents at the disposition of the new commander of the Confederation.

The Campaign in Bohemia of 1866 until the Evening of 30 June

On 14 June, 1866, Saxony had voted with the other German Central States at the Federal Diet against Prussia, and on the 15th, the latter declared war on Saxony and Hanover.[*] On the 16th,

---

[*] War organization:
  Prussia:
   Army of the Elbe: VIII Army Corps, 14th Division, Guard-Landwehr Division;
   First Army: II, III, IV Army Corps, Cavalry Corps, Division

Herwarth advanced with the Army of the Elbe (14th, 15th, and 16th Divisions) from Torgau along the left bank of the Elbe into Saxony. On that same day, Austria promised, at the Federal Diet, her support to the Central States. She had thus entered into war against Prussia and had to shoulder the onus of aggression. Prussia could consider herself as attacked and forced against her will to a counterattack. Even the most cautious of policies had to be abandoned, in regard to Austria and action had to be taken.

The armies were still engaged in concentration.

The Army of the Elbe reached Dresden on the 18th, also Kesselsdorf and Tannesberg. The Saxon army had gone before it to Teplitz over the Erzgebirge, not hurriedly like the Hessian and Hanoverian armies, but well prepared and equipped with all that was necessary for a campaign. To the left of the Army of the Elbe, the First Army had entered Saxony with its right wing and stood between the Spree near Bautzen and the Bober near Lowenberg. A mixed brigade of the 1st Corps had been left at Landeshut—-Waldenburg. The rest of the Second Army came up on the 18th, on the Glatzer Neisse. The position, through which Silesia could be saved, had, before it could be reached and occupied, become objectless.

Austria would not invade Silesia. She wanted to support Saxony, whose army had advanced into Bohemia, and be supported by her, seeking likewise the support of Bavaria, whose troops were assembled on the frontier of Bohemia. On the other frontiers of Bohemia, the hostile main armies were ready to invade the country. Whatever might have been Austria's plans and intentions and whatever plans and intentions she should have had, after what had taken place on the 14th, 15th, and 16th on the one and the other

---

    Alvensleben's, Division Hann's;
    Second Army: Guard Corps, I, V, VI Army Corps, Hartmann's Cavalry
     Division.
  Austria:
    Austrian Army of the North: I, H, III, IV, VI, VIII, X Army Corps, 1st
     & 2nd Light Cavalry Divisions, 1st, 2nd, 3rd Reserve Cavalry
     Divisions.
  Saxon Army.

The Campaign of 1866

side, there remained for a general, who was not exactly a Napoleon, nothing but to lead the army assembled in Moravia to Bohemia. Prussia was to go against this army. On the 19th, it was decided in Berlin to invade Bohemia.

It would have seemed adequate to assemble first the three armies, to have the Second Army join the First north of the mountain ridge, in order to penetrate into the hostile territory in one irresistible mass. But this mass had not found sufficient roads to cross the mountains rapidly. The few leading elements that fortunately reached the other side would have become an easy prey of a resolute and skillful enemy. The mass, coming slowly and gradually, unmolested, through the mountains, would have found nothing more than the enemy, opposing it in a better and more favorable condition. In spite of the distance separating the First Army from the Second, Moltke held to his plan of junction at the front of the enemy's country. In addition to other advantages, he obtained a greater number of routes, though not too many. The roads were all heavily burdened; the only considerable passage was closed by the Riesan and Iser Mountains.

No doubt could remain as to the mode of advance of the First Army. It had to march from Bautzen, Gorlitz, Lauban, via the Lausitz ridge towards the Iser. The route for the Army of the Elbe had been planned first from Dresden along the left bank of the Elbe, crossing over the river at Tetschen and marching further via Bohmisch-Leipa to the Iser. This march, however, was threatened by a flank attack, the Saxons being at Teplitz, the Austrians having joined them at that point and the Bavarians being expected to advance at any moment. It was preferred to have the Army of the Elbe join the First Army via Stolpen.

After the Guard Landwehr Division had been added to the Army of the Elbe, both armies had reached the strength of five army corps and one cavalry corps. The space available for the advance march of these 150,000 men was narrowed on the right by the Elbsandstein mountains, on the left by the Iser ridge and barred in front by the Lausitz Mountains. Nevertheless five passable roads were found:

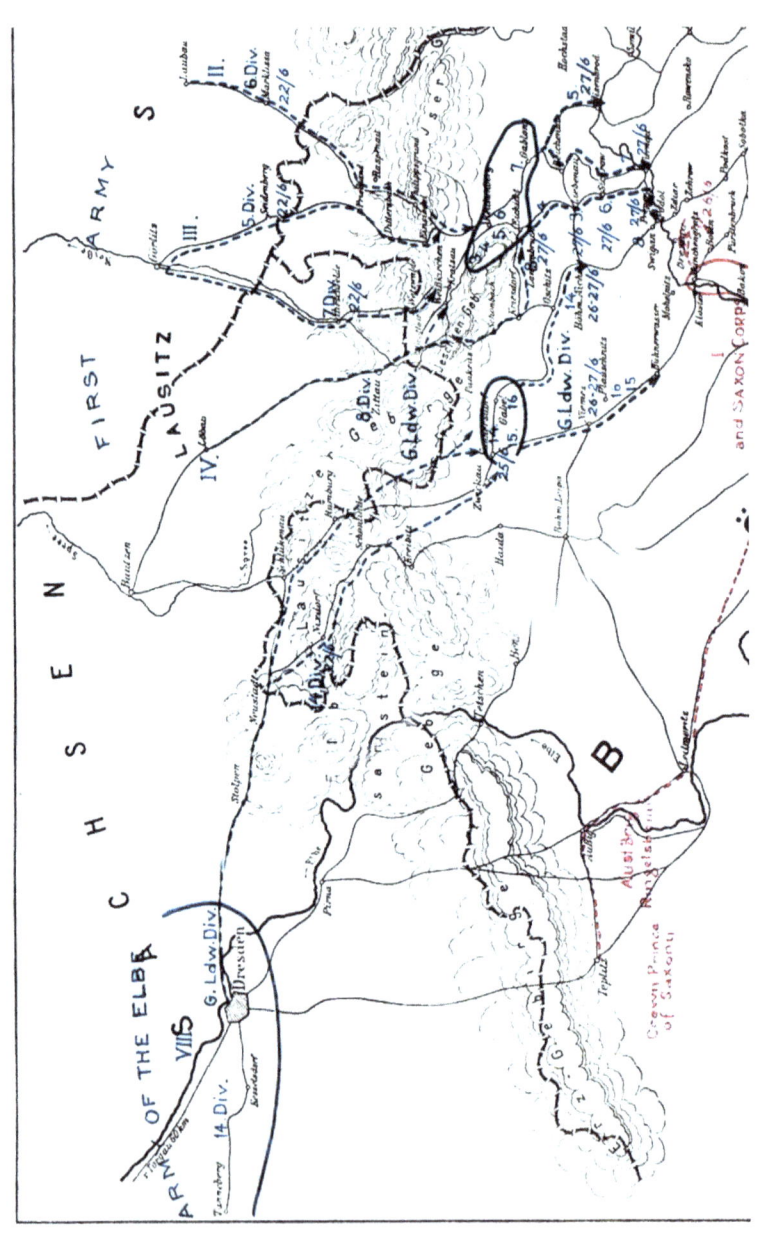

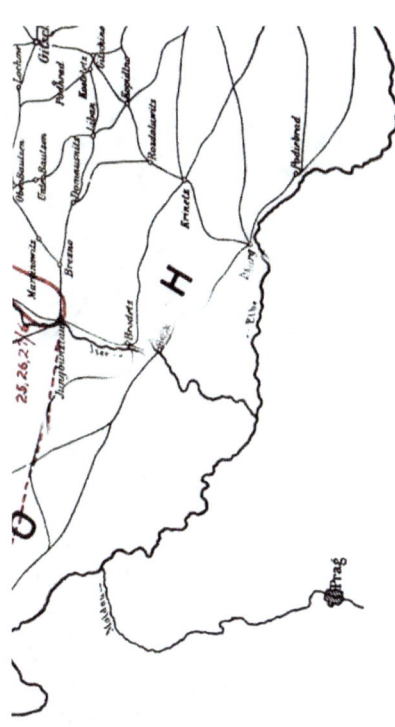

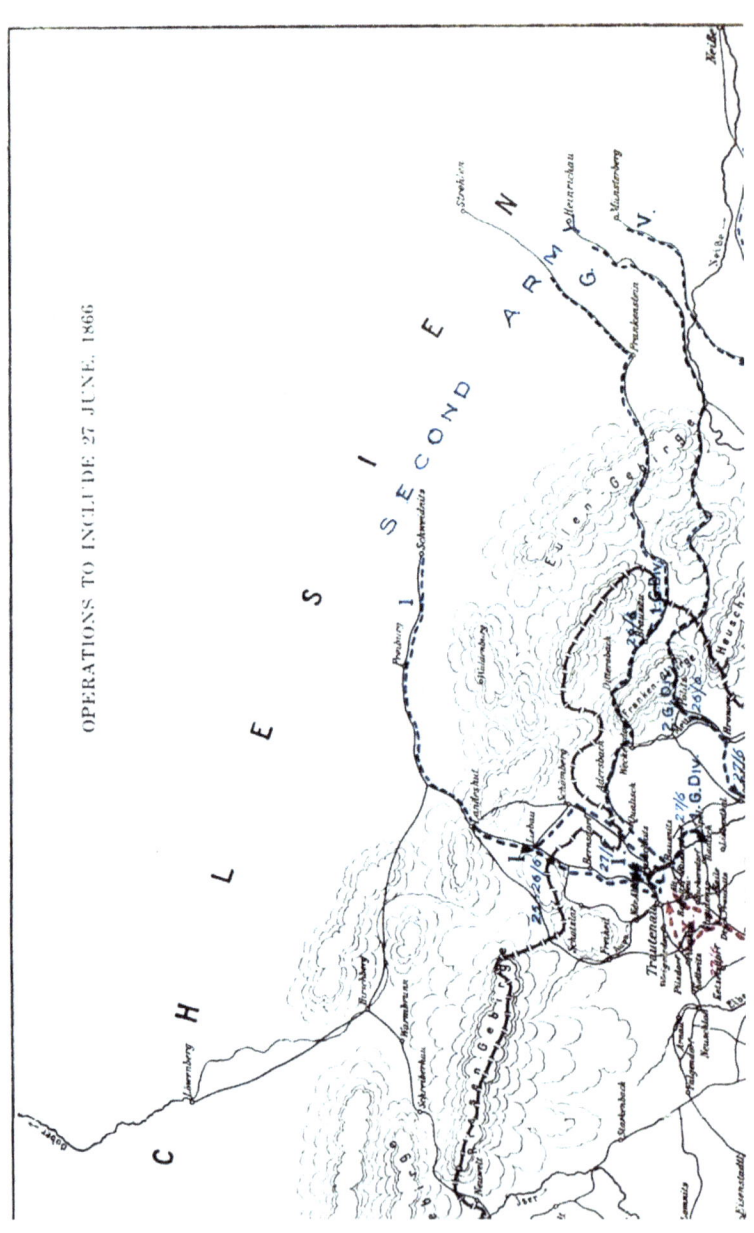

The Campaign of 1866

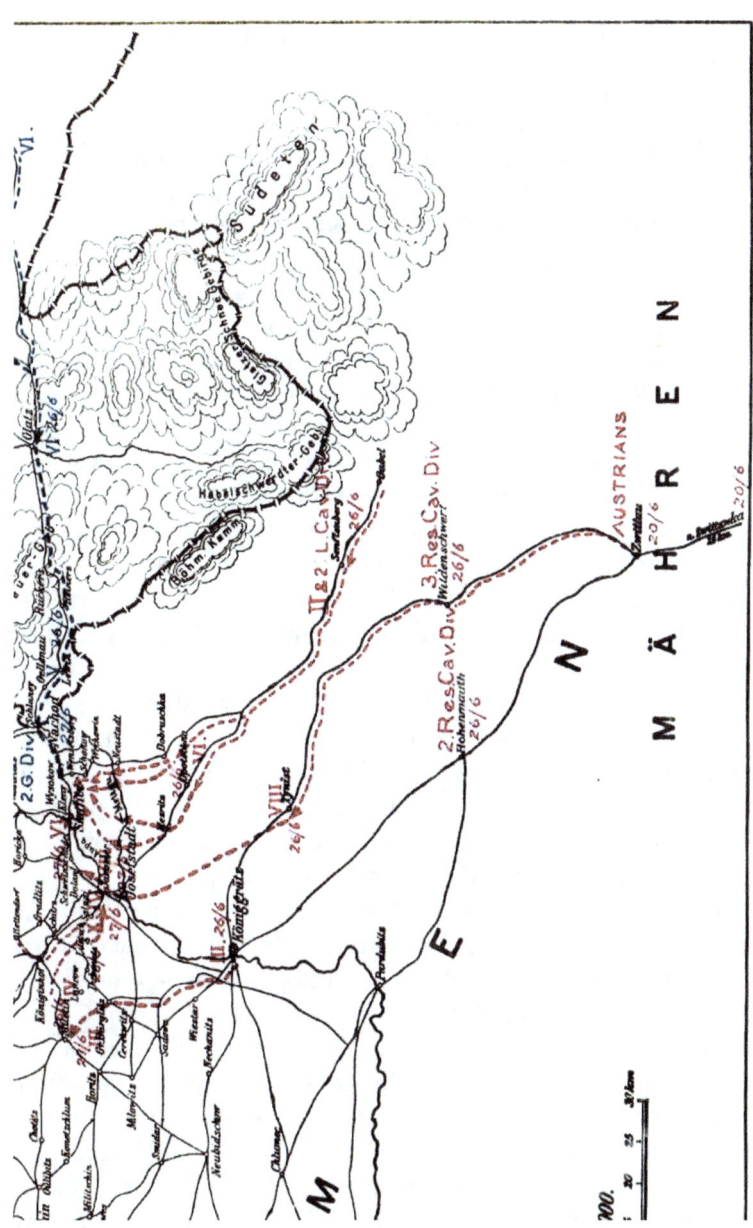

1. Neustadt—Schonlinde—Kreibitz—Haida—Bohmisch-Leipa—Jungbunzlau;
2. Neustadt—Rumburg—Zwickau—Neimes— Munchengratz;
3. Lobau—Zittau—Grottau—Pankraz—Oschlitz— Bohmisch-Aicha—Podol;
4. Gorlitz (left bank of the Neisse)—Hirschgelde—Wetzwalde—Kratzau—Reichenberg (west)—Liebenau—Turnau;
5. Gorlitz (right bank of the Neisse)—-Seidenberg—Friedland, Hinsiedel—Marklissa—Raspenau—Reichenberg (east)—Gablons—Hisenbrod.

These five routes, to which might be added a sixth, via Hirschberg—Warmbrunn—Schreiberhau—Neuwelt—Hochstadt to Semil, were very close to each other; but they must and could be sufficient since the expected enemy could not be very strong, not strong enough, at any rate, to bar all five roads. Did he oppose one of the columns, the others would soon come up to its assistance. It was disadvantageous only that the Army of the Elbe was several days' march in rear of the First Army and that only one road was available for it from Dresden to Neustadt. The First Army was thus forced to stand still several days until the neighboring army had come up with it.

The I Corps of the Second Army was immediately sent via Schweidnitz to Landeshut in order to join the First Army from this point or, if possible, from Hirschberg. The VI Corps was to "demonstrate" south of the Neisse towards Moravia, in order to hold part of the Austrian main forces and prevent them from marching to Bohemia. The two remaining corps (the V and the Guard) were to go so close to the First Army that they could be echeloned on the roads via Frankenstein and Glatz. Their employment would depend on the development of the situation. It was expected that the First Army would start early from Gorlitz —Bautzen, drive back the as yet weak forces in Bohemia and march further. Expecting a simultaneous start of the Austrians from Moravia and the Prussians from Gorlitz, an encounter with the hostile main army could take place soon after the latter had crossed the Elbe. The Second Army would then be in readiness with the V, VI, and the Guard Corps to attack the flank and rear of the enemy while he was occupied with the First Army.

The Campaign of 1866   143

This plan had to be abandoned because the First Army could not advance, awaiting the Army of the Elbe. Instead of it a junction of the three armies was ordered on 22 June, to take place on the road to Gitschin. This, under the most favorable conditions, would bring about an attack against the main forces of the enemy, which would have penetrated as far as Gitschin, by the First Army from the Iser, by the Second Army from the Upper Elbe, and, in less favorable circumstances, an attack against the enemy who would have come up only as far as Josefstadt—Koniggratz, by one army over the Elbe, by the other over the Aupa and Mettau, maybe also from Glatz, at all events an attack from three sides—a battle of annihilation.

The Second Army, to which the I Corps had again been attached, advanced first along the designated route. On the 25th, the I Corps reached without molestation Liebau; on the 26th, the Guard Corps reached Braunau and Politz; and the V Corps, Lewin. The latter was followed from Glatz by the VI for covering the left flank.

On the 22nd, the First Army had advanced with the 8th, 7th, 5th, and 6th Divisions to Zittau, Hirschfelde, Seidenberg, and Marklissa, while the Army of the Elbe after three days' march had reached, with one column each, Nixdorf and Schluckenau. From this point the march could be continued first over six then over five roads to Jungbunzlau—Eisenbrod. The commander-in-chief of the First Army, however, intended to open the campaign with a brilliant success. With this object, an enemy, who had decided upon obstinate resistance, at Reichenberg was selected. In order to attack him on the 24th, the 8th Division marched on the 23rd from Zittau to Grottau over the Jeschken ridge to Pankraz and Schombach, with its extreme head as far as Kriesdorf, the 7th went from Hirschfelde to Kratzau, the 5th, from Seidenberg via Friedland to Dittersbach and Hinsiedel, the 6th, from Marklissa to Raspenau and Phillippsgrund. The II Corps followed via Zittau and Hirschfelde on the heels of the 7th Division.

On the following day, the 7th and 5th Divisions were to attack the front and the 8th, after a second ascent of the Jeschken ridge, the rear of the Reichenberg position. However, before this could be done, the enemy (8 squadrons) had marched off. Two belated

Radetzky hussars could be brought before the victor. The entire First Army, 93,000 men, was assembled in a narrow space in front of Reichenberg. The "calamity of concentration" of which Moltke had warned, made itself felt. These masses could not be quartered, fed and, most of all, moved. Of the two outlets, leading via Liebenau and Gablonz, from the mountain valley, the first was barred by the enemy, the second could be easily closed. It seemed desirable to await the arrival of the Army of the Elbe to extricate itself from this point. The latter assembled only on the 25th at Gabel and Kummersdorf.

After the two armies had reached the same line, the following advance began on the 26th: the 15th and 16th Divisions from Kummersdorf to Niemes, the 14th from Gabel to Oschitz, the 8th from Kichicht to Liebenau, the 7th from Gablonz via Reichenau to Turnau. The road to Jungbunzlau had been given up and both armies were crowded into the narrow Iser strip: Munchengratz—Turnau. The advance guard of the first column drove back a weak hostile force at Hunnerwasser and followed the main army to Plauschnitz. The second reached Oschitz. South of Liebenau and Sichnow the third encountered Edelsheim's Cavalry which was driven, after two lengthy artillery combats, via Preper to Podol beyond the Iser. The 4th column reached Turnau and repaired the destroyed, though not occupied bridge. The 8th Division was followed by the 6th as far as Liebenau, the 7th was followed by the 5th as far as Gablonz. On the same day, the First Army reached the line of the Iser and the Second the mountain passes between Liebau and Nachod. The further problems of both were plain.

The Second Army was confined, on its march to Gitschin, by the mountain ridge on the right and the fortress Josefstadt on the left. There should consequently advance: the I, V, and Guard Corps from Liebau via Trautenau to Neuschloss (Arnau), from Dittersbach and Politz, via Eipel and Kosteletz to Koniginhof and from Nachod via Skalitz to Schurz and the Elbe; the VI Corps was to follow the V in echelons for the cover of the left flank.

The further march of the Army of the Elbe and of the First Army had to take place, according to Moltke's program, from Gitschin as a general objective and the orders for the left wing to halt, in the mountains were all sufficient. The northernmost road leading to Gitschin close to the mountains went from Eisenbrod via Lomnitz to Eisenstadt. The left column had to take it. The further marching routes were: Turnau—-Gitschin, Podol—Sobotka—Kosteletz—Munchengratz—Unter-Bautzen—Liben—Kopidlno, Jungbunzlau--Domausnitz—Rossdalawitz. Five columns, of two divisions each, on these five roads could hardly expect to meet any resistance from the I Austrian, or Saxon Corps, taking their numerical superiority into consideration. The enemy, who attempted to bar the one or the other column, would soon have been turned and surrounded by the others.

This could have been executed more successfully by taking the cavalry along. At that time it was hardly possible to think of using the cavalry corps attached to the First Army and the cavalry division attached to the Second, outside the battlefield. The masses of cavalry were taken along by the trains as *articles de luxe*.* They were, it is true, of little use at the front for reconnoitering the mountainous regions. The first defile occupied by the enemy would have put a stop to their advance. A weaker cavalry was sufficient here for the support of the infantry. On the right wing of the Army of the Elbe the cavalry had reconnoitered the terrain south of the Lausitz ridge via Bemsen and Bohmisch-Leipa, as far as the Elbe and endeavored in vain to reassure the commander as to a threatened attack of the right flank.

Reports in war, however, always give way to rumors. The place of the Cavalry Corps was where the cavalry of the Army of the Elbe had done its work, to which no attention had been paid. As soon as the invasion of Saxony had been ordered, it ought to have gone close to the Army of the Elbe, follow it in its advance and, as soon as the mountain passes had been won, taken up position close to its right column. While the latter was marching to Jungbunzlau, the cavalry corps ought to have taken the direction of Brodetz and Benatek and accompanied it on its march via Krinetz to Nimberg and Chlumec. It would thus have prolonged the front of the First Army and the Army of the Elbe which would have reached Gitschin—Neubidschow—Chlumec almost at the time that the Second Army reached the Upper Elbe.

---

* "Luxury goods."

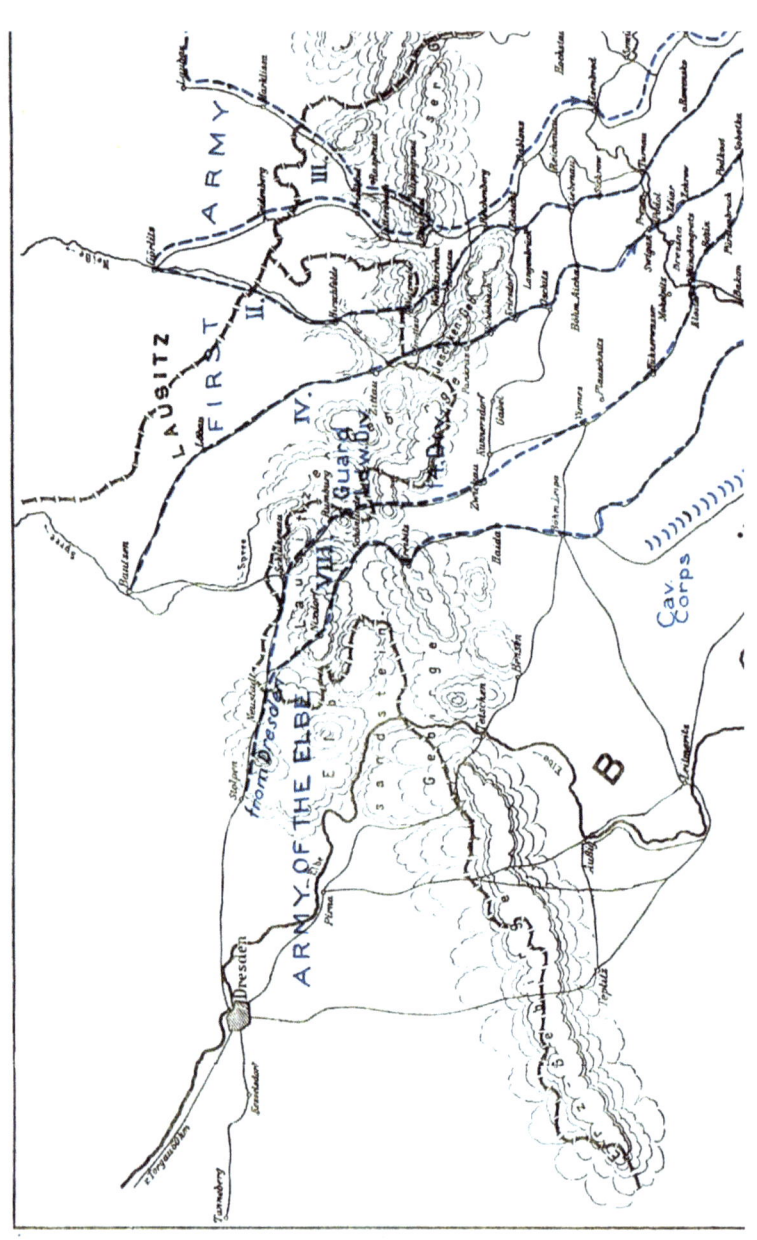

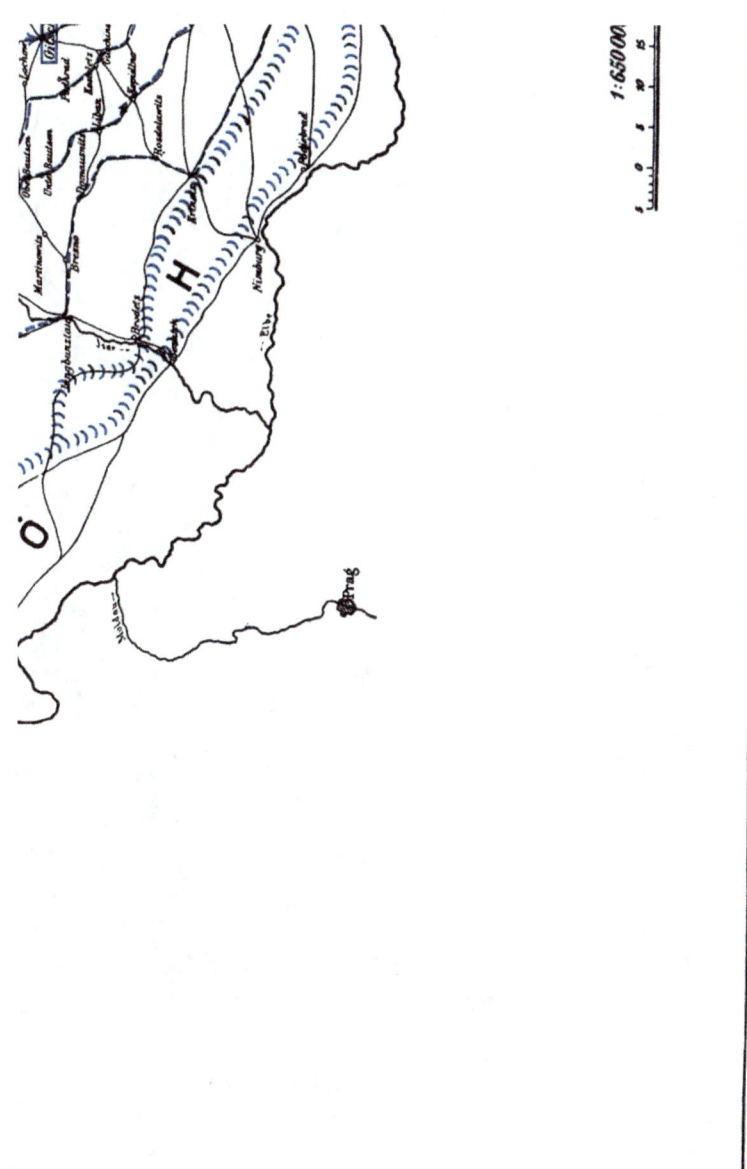

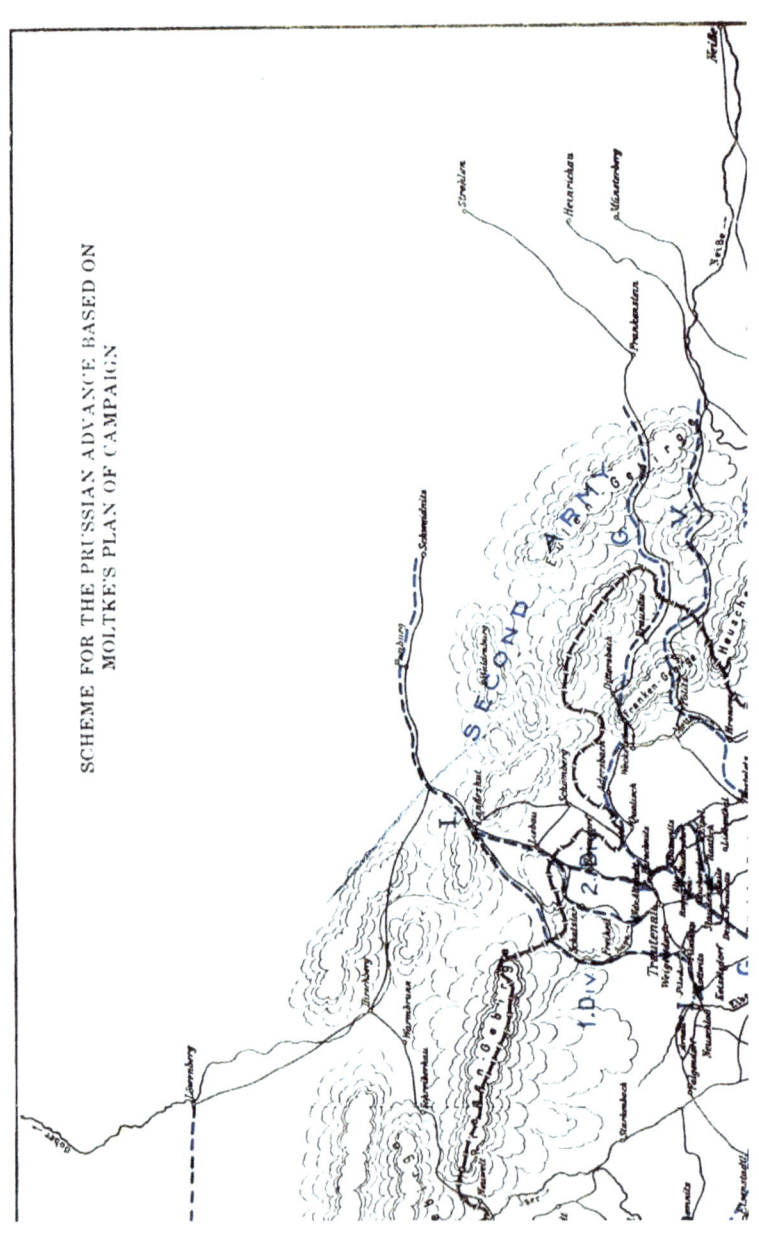

SCHEME FOR THE PRUSSIAN ADVANCE BASED ON MOLTKE'S PLAN OF CAMPAIGN

The Campaign of 1866

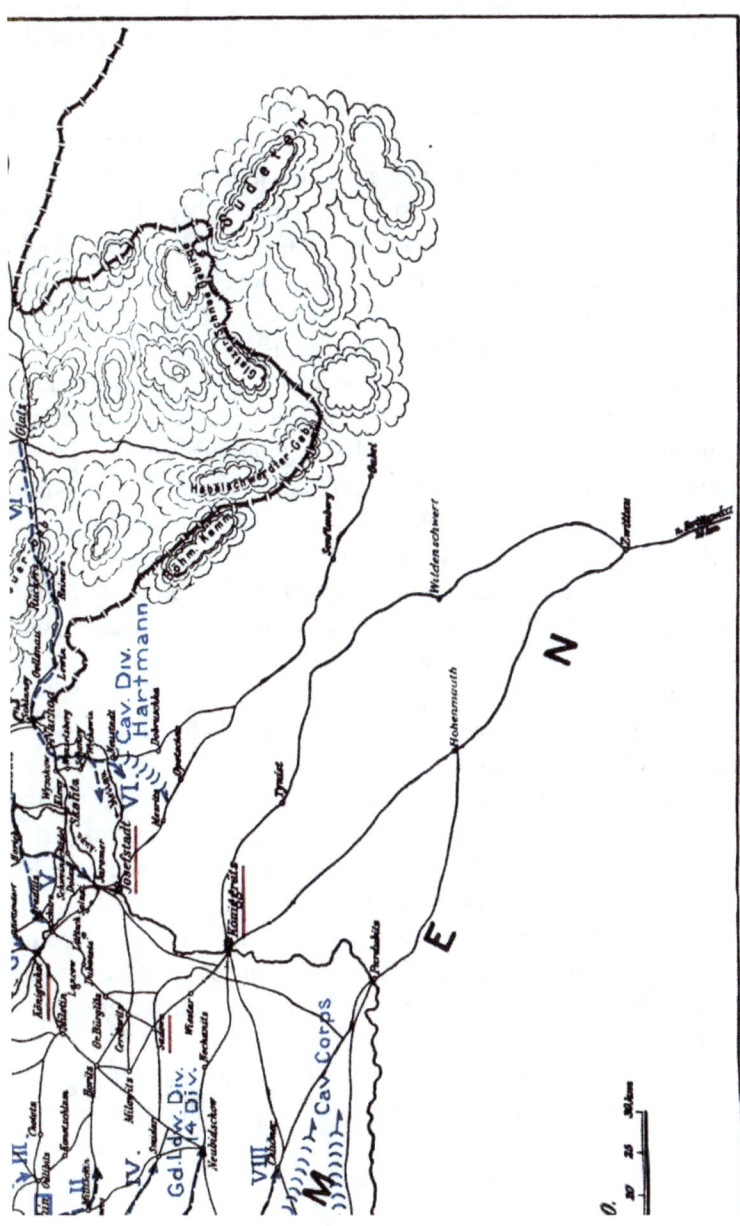

Had the enemy, as expected and supposed by Moltke, marched over the Elbe sector between Josefstadt and Koniggratz, he would have had to turn sooner or later part of his forces against the Second Army, threatening his flank, in order to throw it back or at least to check it. It was a question whether there would be a sufficient number of corps left to master the First Army and the Army of the Elbe. It was to be expected that the First Army would suffice for the attack of the hostile front, the Army of the Elbe and, possibly the cavalry corps, turning against the left hostile flank, would win the road: Gitschin—Koniggratz, while the cavalry division of the Second Army, supported by the VI Corps, would endeavor to cut off Josefstadt from the east.

The Austrian Army had hardly begun its advance fo Bohemia, when on the 18th, word came that the Bavarians could not effect a junction with it, but were forced to defend their country on the Main in the north against the enemy advancing from the north. Falkenstein's three divisions though still at a distance, had apparently not missed their effect. This report was disturbing, but no changes could be made in the intention to go against the enemy who was known to be at Gorlitz and in Saxony, to advance beyond the Elbe "near Josefstadt, Koniginhof, and Miletin," and then to act according to circumstances.

It was ascertained on the 20th through reliable information,[*] that not only the V and VI Corps, but also the I and the Guard Corps were in Silesia, that these four corps had been drawn to the Neisse, but that they had already retreated. One Prussian corps, according to information, had been sent to Hirschberg for immediate junction with the main army, which had to await its arrival in the vicinity of Gorlitz. The Guard and V Corps were said to be on the march to Landeshut, the VI between the Neisse and Glatz. The former disposition had to be reassumed with a few changes; one corps at Glatz—Neisse, two at Landeshut, one at Hirschberg, the main army at Gorlitz—Bautzen, the Army of the Elbe no longer at Torgau but at Dresden. Should all these positions

---

[*] An exchange of telegrams between the Prussian First and Second Armies was intercepted on the wire.

be won, the invasion of Bohemia could be expected. The enemy, however, was not yet concentrated and this fact could be taken advantage of.

Since the head of the Austrian right column had reached Zwittau on the 20th, and that of the center column, Zwittawka, an advance against the enemy, reported to be on a flanking march from the Neisse to Landeshut and Hirschberg, could scarcely be thought of. It was dubious if he could be reached in time at the mountain pass near Liebau, south of Landeshut. But the Upper Elbe, between Josefstadt and Arnau, formed a strong barrier which, if occupied by a sufficient force, would check the advance of the enemy from Landeshut and Glatz. The march was directed on that point. It was accelerated to the utmost. The 1st Reserve Cavalry at the head of the right column, formerly destined to Gross-Burglitz, turned on the 25th from Jaromer to Dolan and Skalitz, sent out detachments to Dobruschka, Neustadt, Nachod, Kosteletz, and came in touch with the Dragoon Regiment, for a long time on fronteir duty, at Trautenau. The X Corps advanced then to Josefstadt—Schurs. On the following day a brigade of this corps advanced to Kaile and Deutsch-Prausnitz, while the IV Corps marched past it to Koniginhof. The position on the Upper Elbe was thus occupied.

The occupation was to be completed on the 27th, by sending one brigade each to Arnau and Falgendorf. Cavalry in the first line, one infantry brigade at Prausnitz—Kaile, six brigades in rear of the Elbe resting with their right on Josefstadt, one at the defile at Falgendorf for the security of the left flank: everything was organized in the best way. Farther in rear there arrived on the 26th: the VI Corps at Opochno, II Corps and 2nd Light Cavalry Division at Senftenberg, the III Corps at Koniggratz, the VIII at Tynist, the 3rd and 2nd Reserve Cavalry Divisions at Wildenschwert and Hehenmauth. Information was brought in the evening of the 26th: enemy at Liebau, enemy at Politz advancing via Hronow to Nachod and enemy at Lewin. These were probably the two corps expected from Landeshut.

Only one had marched thither. The other crossed the mountains more to the south in two columns and intended to join the other at Nachod. Should these advance farther, as might be expected, an attack on the Upper Elbe with two corps at the front and one coming via Hirschberg and Starkenbach on the left flank, might be expected as early as the 29th. At the same time, the hostile main army, advancing from Saxony and the Lausitz, might already be not far distant. A battle might occur with the latter on the 30th, after completed concentration in the locality: Horitz—Miletin, while the battle on the Upper Elbe would be in its second day.

How would it be possible to fight for victory with one enemy when another, close by, directly threatened the rear and flank? It was impossible to allow 'them to come so close. The forces at hand did not suffice to attack both and drive them back. A success might be hoped for if one enemy were held with the weakest possible force while the other were attacked with the greatest possible strength. It was enticing to attack the enemy, advancing from Silesia, with the II, VI, X, and IV Corps, then at hand. A protracted defense against the other enemy seemed possible only on the Iser. The corps at that point, however, were not sufficiently strong and there was no time to reinforce them.

The attack had to be made against the Iser, the defense against the other side, the Silesian. However, it was not on the Elbe, but at the mountain passes that the enemy should have been stopped so as to have elbow room. Gablenz, was to advance toward the enemy, reported at Liebau, as far as Trautenau, Rammig with the VI Corps was to take a position, against the other, at Skalitz, sending out an advance guard to Nachod. It was left to the discretion of the two generals to await the enemy in a position or, according to circumstances, "go at him," though not to pursue the defeated enemy too far. If the "reliable information" concerning only two corps at Landeshut and vicinity, were correct, Gablenz and Rammig would likewise be sufficient.

In war there is, however, nothing more dangerous than reliable information. It is overtaken by events. What was adequate yesterday, would be wrong tomorrow. Here likewise, not two, but three and, taking into consideration the VI which was soon to come up, four corps were to be expected. Had greater caution been exercised, the IV Corps could have been sent from Koniginhof to Trautenau and the V to Eipel and Kostelnitz. It was quite comprehensible, however, why it was feared to weaken the intended offensive against the enemy on the Iser, by using three corps. It was sufficiently threatened. The enemy might come up in that direction, before the advance on the right of the Elbe had been completed. This slow advance and deployment from endless depths of march was the principal evil which rendered all bold undertakings impossible. Under this stress a telegram was sent to the Crown Prince of Saxony, commander-in-chief of the I and the Saxon Corps, on the 26th "to hold Munchengratz and Turnau at any price." Two corps, the VI and the X, were to throw the hostile army back into the Silesian mountain passes or keep them from debouching from them while two others, the I and the Saxon, were to hold the enemy on the Iser, the rest executing their deployment on the right bank of the Elbe.

The Saxon corps and the Austrian Brigade Ringelsheim had been called from Teplitz—Aussig via Leitmeritz to the Iser, had effected there a junction with the Austrian I Corps under Clam-Gallas and jointly occupied a position at Jungbunzlau—-Munchengratz, while the Cavalry Division Edelscheim guarded the road from Reichenbach to Podol and Turnau. The directions received from the Army commander wavered between "retreating without combat at the approach of the enemy" and "retreating with licht fighting." When the order of "holding Munchengratz and Turnau at any cost," now arrived, the latter point had already been lost and Podol was threatened.

Supposing that only small advance guards were at these two points, the Crown Prince resolved to retake Turnau and gain from Podol the heights of Swigan, situated in front of it, late in the evening of the 26th, advance further on the morrow, occupy the narrow passes and prevent the enemy from debouching from the mountains. The plan would have succeeded 24 hours earlier, now it was too late. The Prussians had meanwhile reinforced their weak advance guards. A few Austrian battalions, advancing hastily from Podol, were after initial success thrown back over the Iser by Bose's Brigade of the 8th Division and were forced to abandon the bridge to the enemy.

After this failure, the operation against Turnau was likewise abandoned and it was decided to limit the defensive to

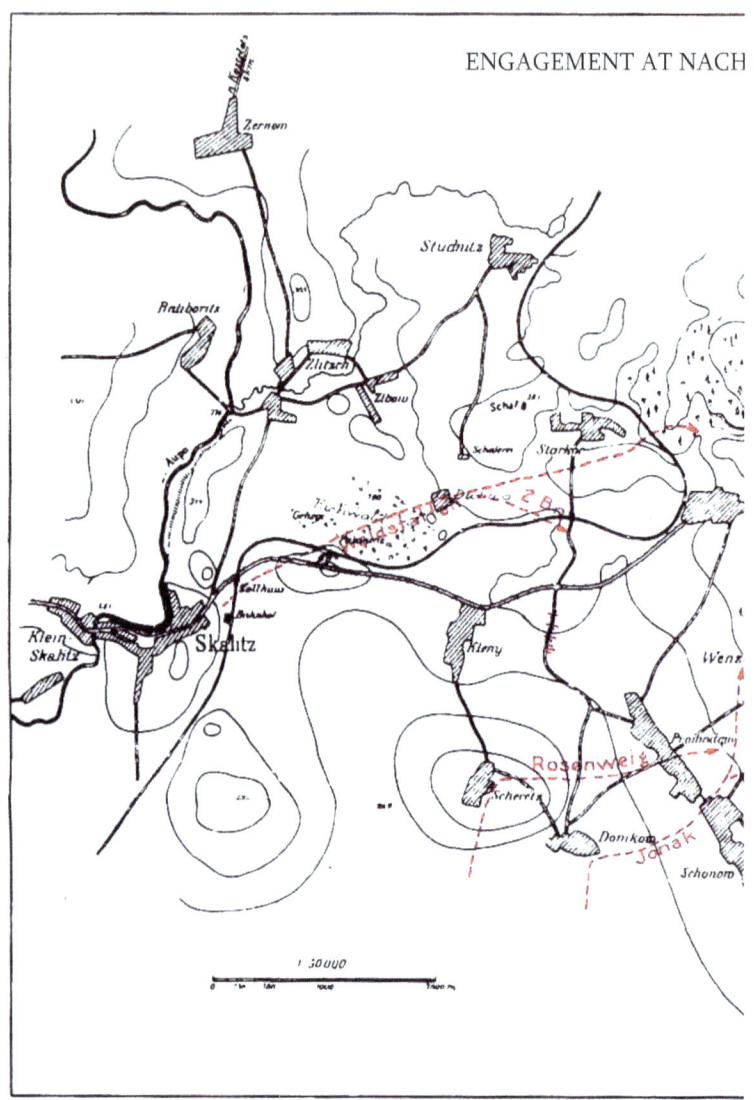

ENGAGEMENT AT NACH

Munchengratz. This decision might have brought on a catastrophe if the Prussian armies had crossed the Iser in five columns between Jungbunzlau and Eisenbrod. It was, however, executed within 24 hours, because the Army of the Elbe had taken advantage of this time for a day of rest and the First Army for preparations and

dispositions for the attack which had been postponed to the 28th. Not these preparations decided the Crown Prince to retreat on the following morning (the 28th), but the rumor that the enemy was on the march from Turnau to Gitsehin, which decision was confirmed by an order from Benedek.

While a relative rest and inactivity was enjoyed here on the 27th, sharp fighting took place on the other front at two points. On the 26th, the V Prussian Corps under General von Steinmetz had reached Cellenau with the van-, Lewin with the advance guard, the main army was at Reinerz and the reserve at Ruckers. Steinmetz's problem for the next day was to gain and hold the pass at Nachod. Since this point had been reported occupied by the enemy, General von Loewenfeld went forward with the advance guard, drove back the weak enemy, occupied Nachod and the nearest heights with his leading troops under Colonel von Below and had the advance guard follow as far as Schlaney. The depth of the corps was thus about 25 k.m.

Still it was necessary to be prepared for an encounter with the enemy, for a battle, a decisive battle, not only be prepared for it but seek it in order to begin the war in a promising manner. Napoleon, such as we know him at Jena, would have taken not only the vanguard, but the entire advance guard through the Nachod defile in the evening or in the night, occupied a position on the other side and taken care that early the following day the rest of the corps had begun to cross over the Mettau bridge. Steinmetz made the various echelons, maintaining their intervals, break camp at the usual hour of 6:00 AM and after having made half of the march, halted for one half hour, according to custom. Consequently it was not surprising that both van- and advance guards were opposed during several hours by a numerically superior enemy and exposed to a complete defeat.

The VI Austrian Corps under Lieutenant Fieldmarshal v. Rammig was posted on the 26th north of Opochno between Dobruschka and Metzritz. The four brigades had to march thence by four different roads to Wysokow, Kleny, and Stalitz in order to occupy there a position facing east. They had not yet reached their goal when the enemy was reported on the hills northeast of Wenzelsberg. The right wing brigade, which had taken the road from Wrchowin to Schonow, turned to the right at this village and deployed for attack. Four battalions in three echelons, the first in division,[*] the others in battalion columns, a few skirmishers in front,

---

[*] One division—two of the six companies forming a battalion.

a battery coming up on the side, went against the 2nd Battalion of the 37th Regiment, half a company of rifles and a battery of the Prussian advance guard which had taken up a position northeast of the Wenzelsberg half way up the slope between the Waltchen (little wood) and a thicket, situated much more south. The Austrian battery was soon silenced. The five battalions marched on, the bands playing. They were brought to a halt by the rapid fire of the rifles; the volleys of the deployed line forced them to retreat and the pursuing fire changed the retreat into a rout.

It was a battle of deep against wide formation; a battle of one opponent feeding the combat against the other opponent throwing in his full strength; a battle column against line; "of the entire man, the bayonet" against "the fool, the bullet"; of the muzzle loader against the breech loader; of the target against the sharpshooter. Once again the two battalions of the third line were sent against the front and one battalion, advanced to the vicinity of the Neustadt road, against the left flank of the enemy. The failure was identical.

The Hertwek brigade disappeared. Only two battalions had taken up position in Wenzelsberg and in the church of that village. Battalions of the Prussian advance guard, coming up over the Branca hill, took part in the last fights. In pursuing the enemy, they penetrated on the right into the Waldchen, on the left to Sochors and the assistant forester's lodge. There now stood in an extended line: three and one half companies in Wyschow, four and one half in the western part of the Waldchen, the 2nd Battalion of the 87th Regiment between the woods and the thicket, situated more to the south, two batteries and four squadrons to the left of the thicket, ten companies at Sochors and the assistant forester's lodge, two companies in reserve at Altstadt and two on the Neustadt road. All could advance for a concentric attack against Wenzelsberg.

But the Brigade Jonak was now advancing. It had interrupted its march to Kleny at Domkow, deployed and advanced in three lines through the northern end of Schonow on Wenzelsberg. Fire from the left out of the Waldchen, fire from the right out of the assistant forester's lodge forced it to divide. Four battalions turned to the right against the forester's lodge, three to the left against the western edge of the Waldchen. A battalion of rifles attacked simultaneously from the Skalitz road.

The Brigade Rosenzweig entered into the open space between the two parts of the Brigade Jonak. Two of its battalions were sent into the woods, into which the greater part of Wenzelsberg's garrison had turned, so that seven to eight battalions fought against the four and one half Prussian companies. Attacked on three sides with such superiority of numbers, they were forced to retreat from the wood. The Prussians could not hold out either at the forester's lodge or at Sochors. One battalion of Rosenzweig was left with the battery. Three advanced past the Wenzelsberg church. The 2nd Battalion repulsed their attack, but its right flank being threatened from the wood, it was forced to retreat. The twelve guns, which resisted a long time against the 24 Austrian guns were forced to follow it. After the five battalions of the Prussian advance guard had escaped the double surrounding of the sixteen Austrian battalions, they halted with their two batteries on the hill on the Neustadt road, their right wing at the Branca defile and the left in the vicinity of Bracetz.

The Austrians followed on the right as far as the forester's lodge and Sochors, in the center as far as the former position of the 2nd Battalion of the 37th Regiment, on the left as far as the eastern edge of the wood. Further to the left went the Solms Cavalry Brigade between the wood and Wysokow, but retreated towards Kleny, after a skirmish with the Wunck Cavalry Brigade. All attempts of the Austrian infantry to advance from the wood against the Prussian position were repulsed by a hot, rapid fire, as well as by flanking attacks of the infantry and cavalry. The Austrians however, held the gained positions until the main forces of the VI Corps reached the battlefield. Two battalions of its leading Brigade, the 19th, were sent to Wysokow and four against the wood. They sufficed to drive the enemy, greatly shaken by many repulsed attacks and unable to deploy on account of lack of space, not only out of the wood, but also out of Wenzelsberg and forced him to retreat as far as Prowodow and Schonow. The Austrian right wing at the forester's lodge and Sochors' joined this movement, although it had not been attacked. An advance of the Prussians from the west end of the wood and through Wenzelsberg stopped the fire of the Austrian artillery reserve which had arrived from Skalitz and taken position on the heights east of Kleny.

Waldstatten's Brigade came likewise up from Skalitz. It was to re-establish the battle by turning the right flank of the enemy and attacking Wysokow from the hill to the north. This flank attack could succeed only in joint action with the three Brigades Hertwek, Jonak, and Rosenzweig against the weak hostile front from the line: Schonow— Prowodow, and the Skalitz highroad. The three brigades, were, however, unfit for such action or, at least, considered so. The two battalions of Waldstatten's Brigade, sent to the western end of the wood, could not re-establish the frontal attack of the three brigades, and brought about only a new failure, weakening the flank attack. The fact that three batteries of the corps artillery reserve were attached to Waldstatten's command, was of no advantage to the situation as a whole. Until then the powerful artillery reserve held the entire field under its fire. After it had been weakened by 24 guns, the Prussian artillery began to get the upper hand; stationed as it was between the wood and Wysokow as well as in Wenzelsberg, it could prepare an attack south of Wysokow for the execution of which the 20th Brigade, at least, had to be awaited.

Waldstatten reached the Wysokow plateau with 4 battalions, 4 squadrons, and 1 battery, soon reinforced by one and one half batteries. The rest of his artillery remained west or northwest of the village without going into action. The attack against the center of the long extended village took place first with two battalions. As the two and one half battalions, designated for the defense of the village, were extended along its entire length and as the terrain and buildings favored the attack, the Austrians succeeded in occupying a portion of the houses.

This success was, however, of short duration. The occupied buildings, as well as the coming reinforcements, were attacked not only in the front, but also on the left flank by two battalions of the 20th Brigade, led by General von Wittich, and on the right flank by the garrison of the western part of the village. The enemy, surrounded on three sides, retreated in confusion through the wood in rear of the railroad. The artillery which had suffered much from infantry fire was attacked, when about to drive off, by several squadrons of General Wunck's Brigade, which came up under cover, and lost a few guns. The complete defeat of Waldstatten's

Brigade decided Rammig to commence the retreat with the entire corps and to continue it to Skalitz, on receiving information that the enemy was marching from Kosteletz.

The victor limited himself to the occupation of the heights on either side of Wysokow. The troops were considered too exhausted and tired for pursuit, as if each victorious army were not exhausted and tired at the end of a victorious battle and as if, notwithstanding its condition, pursuit were not required as the only thing to make the victory complete.

The pursuit, desisted from, may be excused by the fact that the Prussian army had only two thirds of its strength at the end of the combat on hand and that these two thirds were entirely scattered. The responsibility for this unfavorable situation lies entirely at the door of the Prussian commander. The commanding general found himself at Nachod in a similar situation to that of Napoleon at Jena. However, he did not follow the example of the master who caused our greatest defeat.

Here as well as there, a defile had to be traversed in order to give battle on the following day at the other end. Napoleon shunned no effort, no obstacle, no difficulty to bring over in the evening, in the night, sufficient troops to take a firm stand on the heights beyond the defile. Here as well as there, the enemy wore himself out by vain frontal attacks. Napoleon let him do so, did not waste his strength in the pursuit of small successes, did not divide his forces into numberless small detachments. The deployment of the hurriedly advancing troops had to be completed first. The enemy might fill in the time by slowly losing blood. He then went forward with a wide front and extended encircling wings in an annihilating attack against the enemy, tired, exhausted, and almost incapable of resistance. Pursuit came of itself. The needle gun and the firing tactics of the one, the shock tactics of the other at Nachod, had improved the condition of things to a certain degree. But a real victory had not been won.

The I Army Corps reached south of Landeshut as early as 25 June. After one day's rest, it was to continue its march on the 27th and 28th via Trautenau to Arnau. Should it take the main road leading through Trautenau and Liebau, it would be sure to encounter resistance at the defile near Trautenau and to expose

The Campaign of 1866

itself to defeat should the enemy be sufficiently strong. It was, consequently, advisable to go around Trautenau with at least part of the troops and to endeavor, at the same time, to take the enemy in flank.

For this purpose the 1st Division and the reserve cavalry was to go via Freheit to Pilsdorf, the 2nd Division from Liebau with a brigade via Schatzlar, with the other via Bernsdorf to Trautenau. This march was completed by the 1st Division of the Guard which had received the order to march on the 27th, from Dittersbach via Weckelsdorf, Adersbach, Qualisch, and Parschnitz and thence to Eipel, also by the 2nd Division of the Guard which was to advance from Kosteletz to Korika. Should the I Corps encounter the enemy at Trautenau, the latter would be attacked by the 2nd Division in the front, by the 1st on the left and by the 1st Guard Division on the right flank. Should the enemy be farther south, the march would be continued, under cover of the reserve cavalry, in three columns—from Pilsdorf to Deutsch-Prausnitz, from Trautenau to Kaile, from Parschnitz to Eipel. Should one of the columns meet the enemy, the others would be ready to turn the threatened point. Should no enemy be found, the I Corps would take up position in echelon between Pilnika and Trautenau for the continuation of the march on the following day to Arnau, while the 1st Division of the Guard went with one brigade to Hipel—Raatsch, with the other, by the shortest road, to Koniginhof via Bausnitz to Alt-Rognitz.

All this could be seen several days ahead and could have been arranged by giving proper march direction and cantonments on the 25th, or in case of need by a short march the afternoon of the 26th. However, the commanding general would have nothing to do with such combinations. He went with the 1st Division from Liebau and the 2nd from Schomberg, that is, on two roads, but on two roads joining at Parschnitz, immediately at the defile of Trautenau. Bonin intended to advance from there in one column up the narrow valley of the Aupa, on the high southern edge of which the enemy was to be expected.

Chance brought it about that the 2nd Division, contrary to the intention of the commanding general, reached Parschnitz much earlier than the 1st Division. It was thus obliged to take upon itself the role of advance guard, while it was intended to play the role of

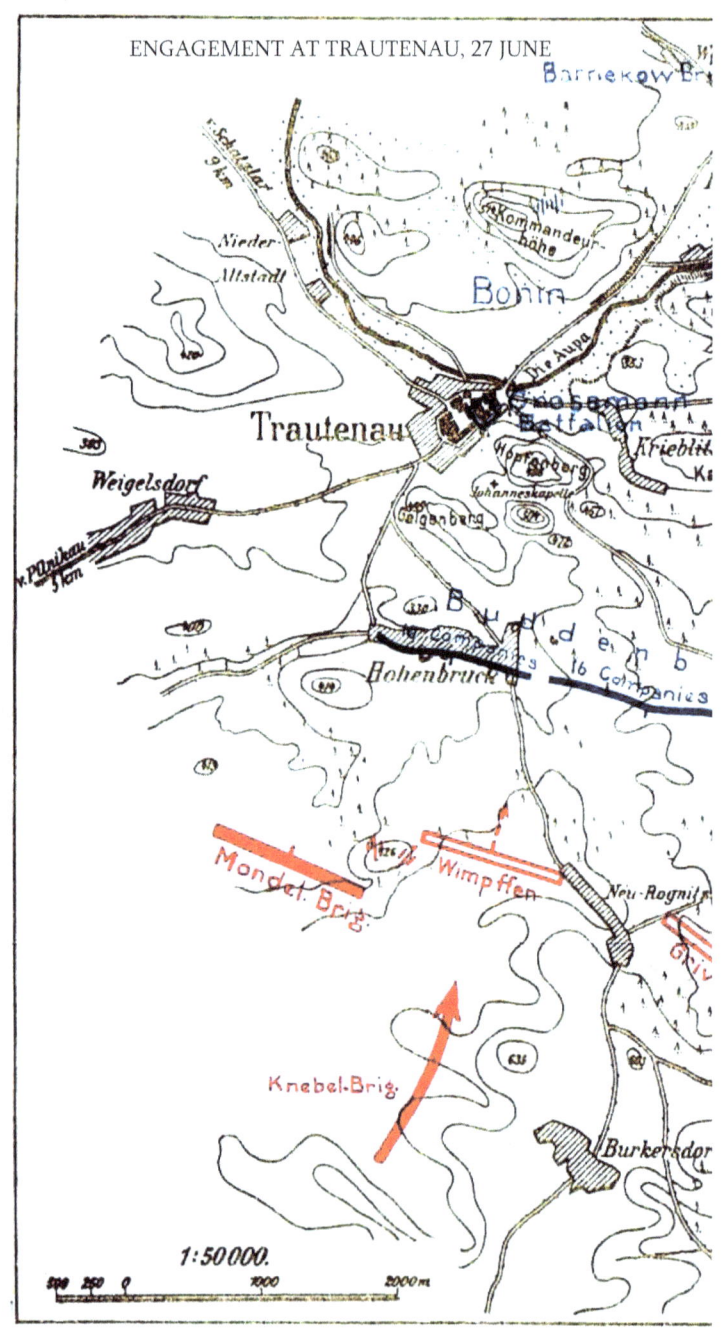

The Campaign of 1866

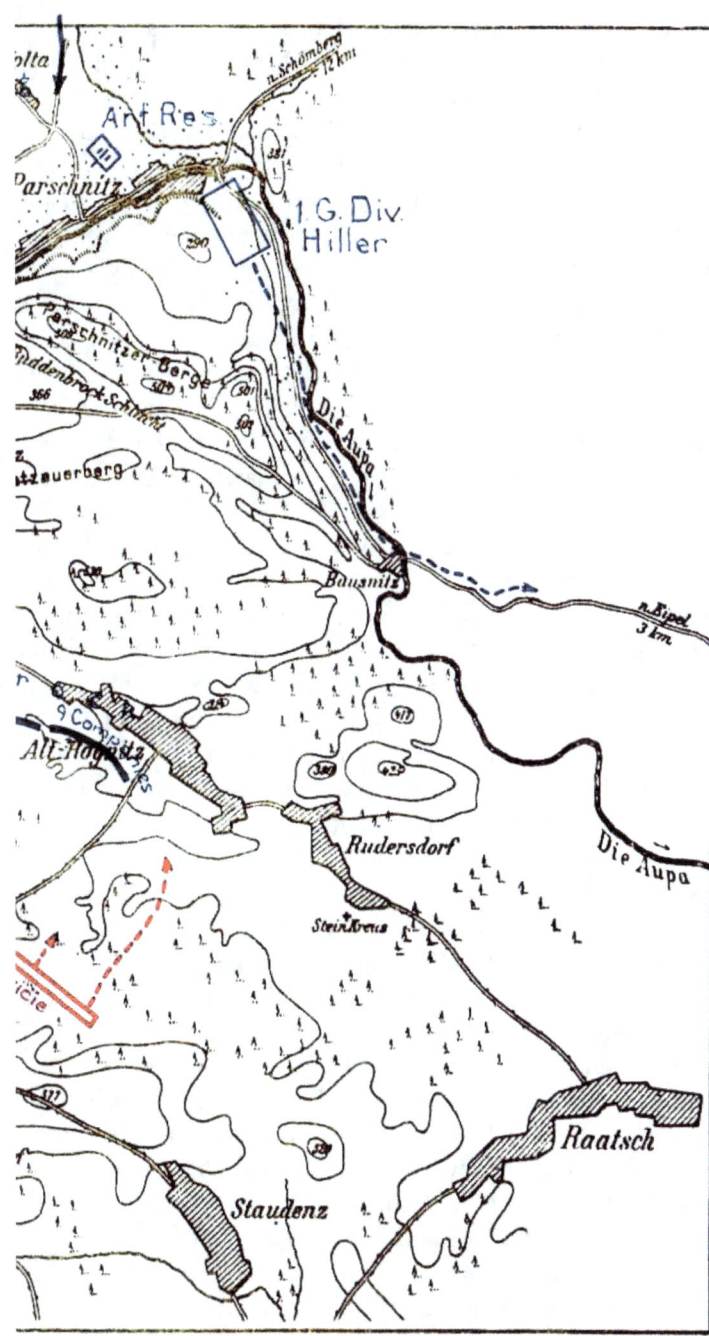

main body. The reconnaissance undertaken by it was limited to finding out that the bridge over the Aupa at Trautenau was occupied by a few dismounted dragoons. These were not driven back, the march through and beyond Trautenau was not continued and no steps were taken to find out whether more of the enemy was to be encountered beyond this handful of cavalry. The division commander, von Clausewitz, let the matter alone and did not receive the information that Mondel's Brigade had already reached the locality south of Trautenau as an advance guard of the X Austrian Corps and occupied the Hopfen and Kapellen hills. Bonin reached Parschnitz two hours later than Clausewitz. Upon learning that the bridge over the Aupa was occupied by the enemy, he sent the advance guard (1st Brigade) to drive the dragoons from the bridge over the Aupa and to continue the march via Trautenau to Pilnikau.

Hardly had the advance detachments left the town on the road to Pilnikau, when the troops which followed received a hot fire from the southern heights. The long marching column had only to turn left and close the ranks a little in order to be quickly ready for the attack of the front and flank of the hostile position. But the surprise, the lack of knowledge, the invisible enemy, the contradictory orders confused the five battalions. Considerable time elapsed before action was taken according to some kind of a plan. But the attack was difficult and no cover was at hand. The hostile skirmishers were well posted. Two battalions, one and a half squadrons, and two guns, marching as a right flank guard via Schatzlar and from Nieder-Altstadt via eastern Weigelsdorf against the left flank of the enemy, hurried to Trautenau, the focus of the combat, and increased there the confusion and the mass of troops not taking part in the battle.

We should think that the artillery would have effectively prepared, by fire, the attack against the heights. But it had not succeeded or at least it had not sufficiently tried to bring the many batteries from the narrow road into a favorable position. An Austrian battery, placed in position at Hohenbruck, succeeded, on the other hand, in supporting the defense most effectively and in forcing the Prussians to evacuate the Galgenberg which they had ascended. The greatest losses were caused to the defense by the

Jagers who sped their well aimed bullets from the upper stories and the roofs of the Trautenau houses.

The Austrians might have held out a long time if eight battalions of the Prussian main body under General von Buddenbrock had not come up, partly crossing the Aupa, in the west and climbing through Parschnitz, partly through the Buddenbrock defile, partly over the roadless, steep, wooded, and rocky Parschnitz ridge in the direction of Hopfenberg—Katzauerberg. Two battalions of Mondel's Brigade were thrown against the enveloping troops. The other five evacuated the position in time. All fell back gradually. One regiment of the Prussian advance guard remained in Trautenau, the other followed slowly in order to first wait for the battalions of the main body, but later, at the signal of "Assembly" given in Trautenau, decided to retreat. Only a few companies, the commander of which did not wish to obey the signal of retreat in the face of the enemy, continued the advance. Thus, ten companies of the advance guard and the main body under Buddenbrock, reached Hohenbruck, sixteen gained the wooded heights between this village and Alt-Rognitz and nine, the flat area west of this point.

The exhausted troops could not advance further. On the heights commanding Neu-Rognitz, they met a strong artillery which the one Prussian battery, coming up under untold efforts, did not dare to attack. All that could be done was to hold the occupied positions until the mass of the corps, which had stayed behind, could come up and then to go on to victory. The movements, effected by von Buddenbruck's eight battalions toward Hohenbruck—Alt-Rognitz, were still under way when General von Hiller reported the arrival of the 1st Guard Division east of Parschnitz and offered to use these troops. Bonin declined the offer. He had deployed only eight battalions. The enemy seemed to withdraw. Seventeen battalions, the entire cavalry and artillery were still at his disposition. Bonin did not lack troops, but he lacked the chance of making use of them. To throw twelve more battalions and four batteries into the narrow valley would not have been a support, but an added difficulty. Moreover, Hiller wanted to let his division rest for two hours east of Parschnitz. Consequently it remained there, for some time as a reserve.

Since the enemy seemed to have retreated via Hohenbruck, Bonin intended to draw his troops out of the defile and let the head advance as far as Pilnikau. The orders were being prepared when it was reported that the enemy was advancing from Neu-Rognitz. General von Grossmann was then instructed to support Buddenbrock with the advance guard, reinforced by three battalions from the main body. This could be executed only by bringing the ten available battalions from Trautenau in a westerly direction and then sending them to attack the enemy's left flank. The attack against the right flank fell, of itself, to the lot of the 1st Division of the Guard. It could not march down the narrow valley of the Aupa unconcerned, when the battle was raging on the heights on its immediate right flank. Hiller was forced to ascend the edge of the valley with all his troops or, at least with part of them, at Bausnitz, not for the purpose of forcing the refused support upon Bonin, but for his own security and in conformity with the most elementary rules of warfare. Should this take place, then the attack of the hostile right flank would result as a matter of course. The battle seemed to be best arranged as follows: Buddenbrock to halt at Hohenbruck—Alt-Rognitz, and even to retreat if necessary until Hiller should attack from the one side and Grossmann from the other with superior numbers. At all events Barnekow's Brigade, stationed at Wolta, ought to have crossed the Aupa below Trautenau and occupied the hills in the south as a reserve.

Only this one disposition was carried out. The order sent to General Grossmann never reached its destination, was never repeated, and was not replaced by the initiative of the advance guard commander. Ten battalions were kept out of the combat. General Hiller supposed he had no other task than to march to Eipel and considered it an unwarranted intrusion to mix into the battle of another corps.

That marching to the sound of cannon cannot be considered as a rule without exceptions, has been pointed out by criticism on this occasion. It might be so. But here the question was of marching away from the sound of cannonading and of a peaceful march along the edge of a battlefield. Both can hardly be justified. Buddenbrock's eight battalions were placed in a precarious situation by the defection of Grossmann and Hiller. The battalions and companies were completely mixed up by a march over mountains, wooded and very difficult terrain. The mounted officers had to leave their horses behind and, being on foot, could not overlook the terrain or control their troops by orders. One battery of the main body was the only artillery. Two more batteries went into position on the Kapellenberg later on. Of these, one was soon withdrawn, followed by the other after it had expended all the ammunition in its limbers. The eight battalions with no artillery whatever, were thus exposed, to the fire of at least 36 guns.

The situation seemed not favorable when Gablenz gave the order to Grivicie's Brigade, which had just arrived, to attack Alt-Rognitz, about the same time as Hiller started on his march from Parschnitz to Eipel. The attack, directed against the front of the nine Prussian companies west of Alt-Rognitz, by seven battalions formed into three echelons, took place as similar attacks at Nachod. The nine companies, however, retreated when the attack was renewed simultaneously with an attack against the extended left flank.

This uncovered the left flank of the two other groups. The right wing in the low-lying Hohenbruck did not oppose any considerable resistance to the attack of Wimpffen's Brigade which followed shortly, and started to retreat as the center had done. It was continued by all the eight battalions without serious encounters as far as the Aupa and beyond it. The advance guard and main body were thus as good as eliminated. There remained the reserve—four and one half battalions under General von Barnekow. Of these, two battalions of the 48d Regiment were placed in position from the Galgenberg via Johanneskapelle and hill 504 to the edge of the wood at 457, while two and one half battalions of the 3rd Grenadier Regiment were left west of Parschnitz to the right of the Aupa.

Wimpffen's Brigade marched against the position of the 43rd. Its attack was repulsed. Hill 472 was taken during the pursuit and three more attacks were repulsed. Knebel's Brigade, arriving in support, would have suffered the fate of Wimpffen's Brigade if Grivicic's Brigade, advancing via Katzauerberg and Krieblitz, had not threatened the flank and rear of the 438d and forced its retreat through the northern part of Krieblitz, across the Aupa in the direction of Wolta. Grivicic now encountered the 3rd Grenadiers, who had occupied Hill 853, the wood north of Krieblitz, and the slopes of the Parschnitz Berge and held their ground until Trautenau and the valley above Parschnitz had been evacuated by the Prussians, and the troops who held the Kommandeur Hill, had also begun to retreat. Then they began to withdraw through the Buddenbrock ravine and across the Aupa, where they joined the 1st Rifle Regiment.

Thus the occupation of the principal position north of the river was of no value whatever. It had long since been prepared on the Kommandeur Hill. At least 24 of the guns, so painfully missed in front, were drawn up here. Three battalions and four squadrons, which could easily have been reinforced, were ready to defend this almost impregnable position. It seemed during the course of the day that the real battle would be waged at this point. It was impossible to foresee how the enemy could take this bulwark with exhausted troops. Still the last position was evacuated before the more advanced ones had been abandoned. Seemingly too exhausted to make a stand the troops streamed back as darkness set in, in order to reach the quarters left that morning, and that after a march of no less than eight miles.

The outlook for the I Corps the evening before, was as good as one could wish. If the enemy were at Trautenau or advanced thither, he exposed himself to annihilation as completely as could be desired, especially if the 1st and 2nd Guard Divisions were not entirely held back. The advance via Liebau and Schomberg wrecked the advantages which a lucky chance had placed in the hands of Bonin. Not through a ruse of the enemy but through his own deliberation he was led into a defile, whence it was difficult to withdraw. Unusually broken terrain increased the difficulties. All this could-be overcome only by the stern purpose of defeating the enemy. Bonin would have been satisfied if he were not beaten. Such contentment with little was bad in the face of an enemy who was resolved to stop at no sacrifice to obtain victory.

To defeat such an enemy every nerve must be strained and not small detachments sent out for attack. In the series of combats, constituting the battle of Trautenau, the troops were sent into the fray in driblets. Three, at the most four, battalions fought around the Kappelienberg, and Hopfenberg. Only two were in a serious encounter at Hohenbruck and Alt-Rognitz. Two repulsed the attack of Wimpffen's Brigade. Two and one half held the position at Aupa. Out of the 96 guns only a few went into action for a short time. During the second part of the battle, positions were taken up which, though well defended, must sooner or later fall a prey to a surrounding movement, on account of their very narrow fronts. The only possible end of such a course of action was a general retreat. The commanding general could not or would not utilize his forces to obtain a victory; all that was left for him to do was to withdraw from the battlefield.

The results of the 27th appeared in no way to be unfavorable to Austria. At Trautenau, a decisive victory was won, at Nachod it must be admitted an attack had been repulsed, but the position of Skalitz on the possession of which Benedek had laid the greatest stress, had been held. The enemy had made no progress whatever on the Iser. Nevertheless the day had brought a great disillusionment. The shock tactics, on which Austria had built such hopes, had not verified in the least their expectations. Attacks by three times greater hostile forces were repulsed in a short time. The superiority of the needle gun had been proved beyond all refutation. Not only the vanquished of Nachod, but also the victor of Trautenau was discouraged. The losses were disproportionately great and so much the more felt as the efforts of the last ten days were quite exhausting.

The march had been made in one long column, first of one corps, then of four and finally of five, one behind the other. In order to reach the distant goal of the day, camp was broken early. A few hours later, the advance was hampered by the vehicles of the preceding corps. Forced halts alternated with short marches. The troops crawled on slowly to reach after dark the desired encampment, but found there scarcely any water or food. The marching demands were soon increased. Finally the march continued day and night with short halts for rest, little food and water, in the hope of soon reaching the battlefield and crushing the enemy with a weighty blow. Discouragement followed so much the greater upon the frustrated hope, as the latter had been so exalted.

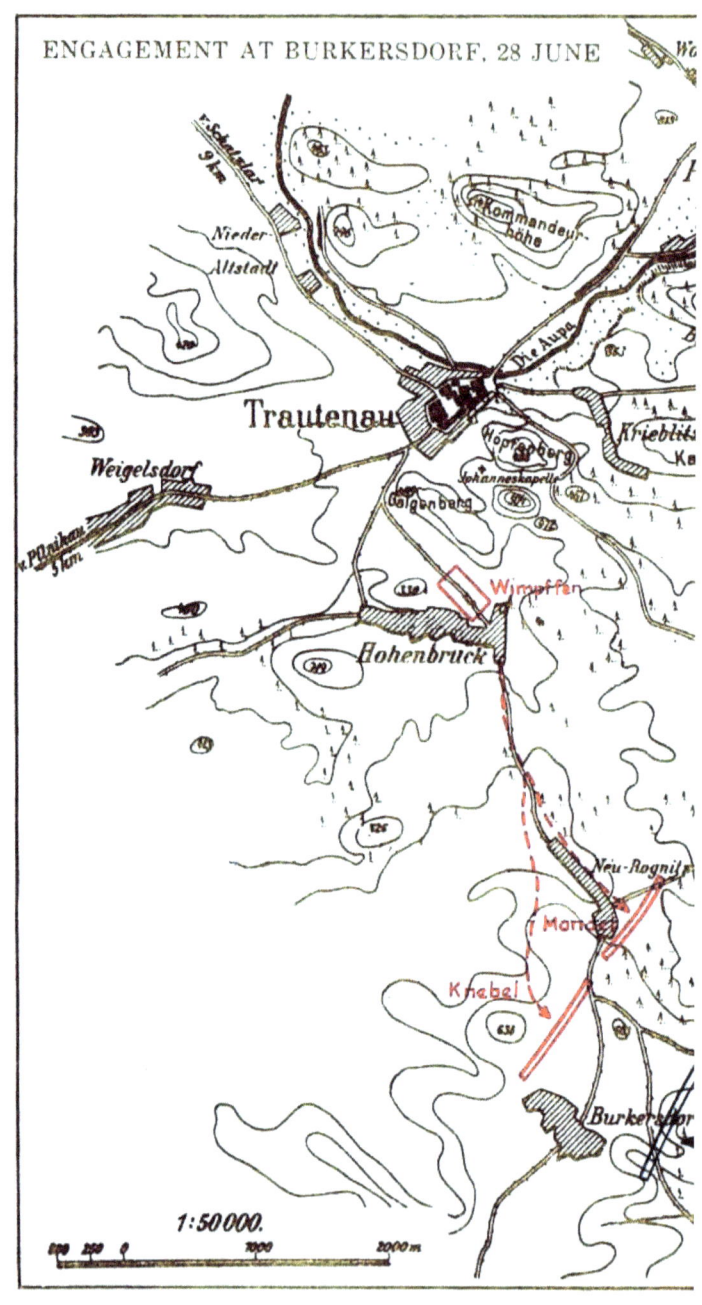

ENGAGEMENT AT BURKERSDORF, 28 JUNE

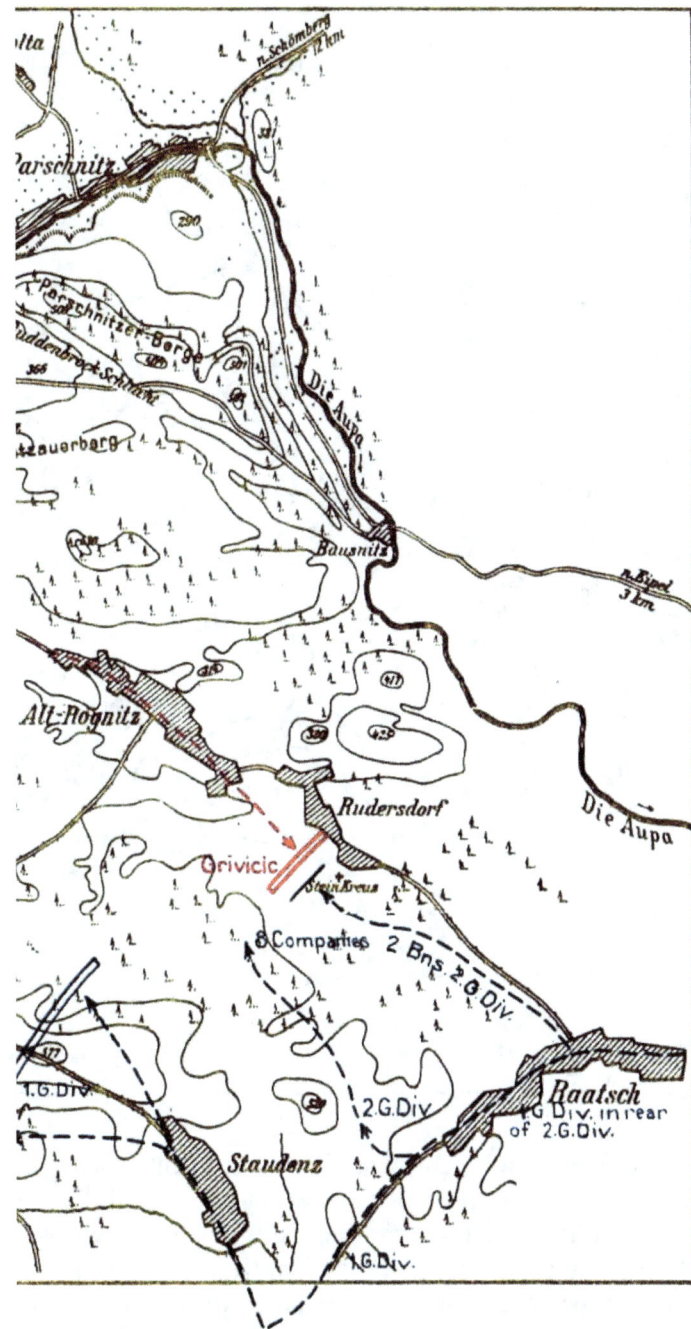

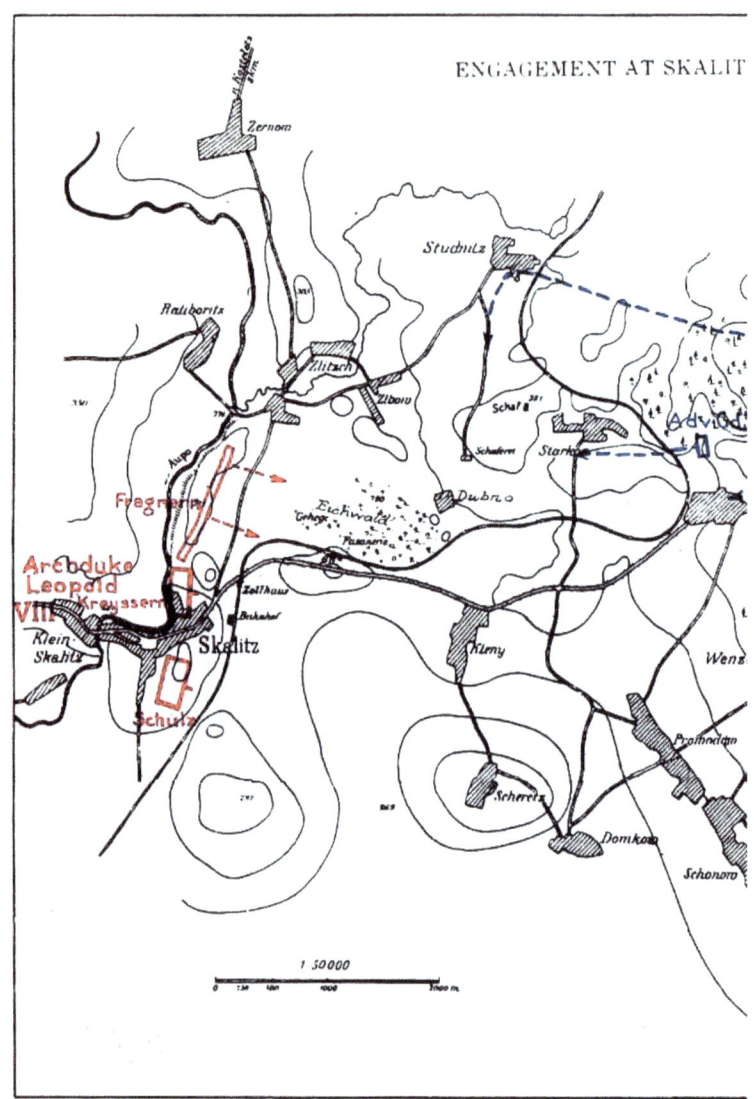

ENGAGEMENT AT SKALIT

Rammig declared that his corps was incapable of either attack or defense. Even the victorious X Corps was in a depressed state.

The Austrian condition of affairs was not bad, however. Benedek had called the VIII Corps to Skalitz, the IV to Dolan. It would have been better to have placed these two corps not in rear

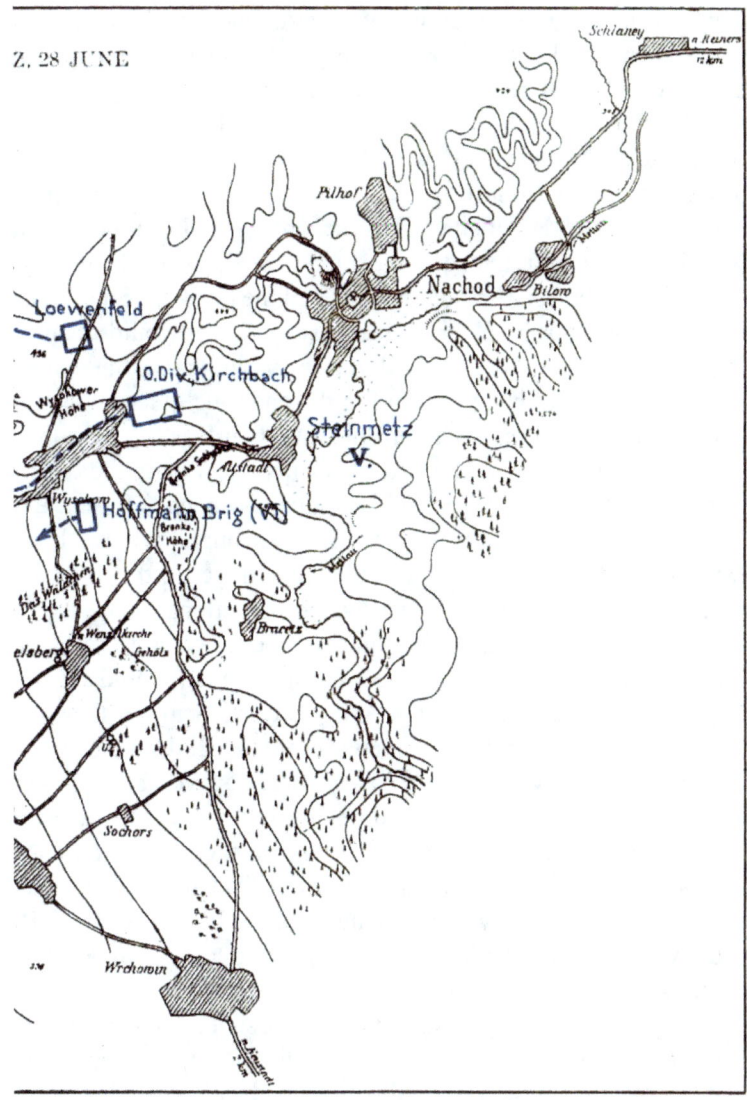

of the VI, but the one on its right, the other on its left. Nevertheless, three Austrian Corps, stood near Skalitz the morning of the 28th. Opposite these, as already said, there stood only one Prussian Corps—the V. The VI was marching further east and it was doubtful if it would arrive on the 28th. There was no doubt that Austria would be numerically the stronger here. It is true that a new enemy had been reported at Eipel. But he could have been held in check by the X Corps for one day at least.

Though no great feats could be expected from the VI Corps, it still could withstand an attack in the strong position at Skalitz left of the Aupa, at least until the VIII Corps could be brought up on the left and the IV on the right, according to Hannibal's and Napoleon's method, in order to encircle the flanks of the enemy, slowly losing his heart blood in attacks of the position. Should the Prussian Corps not attack, the three Austrian Corps would advance together in order to annihilate, by a deadly embrace, the enemy wherever he might have to stand in the end. Such victory would have brought decision on this front. It was, at least, to be hoped that, after the repulse of the I and V Corps, the VI and the Guard Corps would likewise retreat. This would have been of little use if the First Army and Army of the Elbe, as ought to have been expected earlier, had advanced rapidly and attacked the pursuing enemy in the rear. But considering the operations of these two armies, no surprise or quick action could be expected from them.

It seemed, on the contrary, not improbable that, should the 2nd Army begin to retreat, the First Army and the Army of the Elbe would not cross the Iser. An attack on the 28th, against the Prussian V Corps with his three corps, offered a favorable prospect to Benedek. The Austrian army commander did not wish, however, to drop his former plan; defensive with two corps to the east, offensive with six corps to the west. He had no wish to take advantage of the victory won at Trautenau. He had drawn the VIII and IV Corps to Skalitz only in order to delay, under any circumstances, the enemy advancing with great force from Nachod.

When no attack was made during the forenoon of the 28th, two corps were more than enough for the defense. It is commendable that a commander does not easily abandon the plan decided upon, but it is still more laudable if he utilizes the lucky chance of the moment to strike a crushing blow. On the eastern front, the IV Corps was to remain at Dolan, the X to march to Deutsch-Prausnitz in order to get ahead of the Guard Corps, both to cross the Elbe on the following day. The VI and VIII Corps received orders to start, should no attack take place before 2:00 PM. A second order, issued

The Campaign of 1866 175

at 11:00 AM, commanded their immediate departure. The VIII Corps had relieved the VI in the position near Skalitz. The latter was thus the first to march. When the VIII Corps was on the point of following, the enemy attacked. The corps had now to hold its position. After ten forced marches and the occupation of a position, it dared not turn back as soon as the enemy advanced and, moreover, it dared not pass through the one defile of Skalitz without apprehending a decisive defeat from the pursuing enemy.

The position on the heights of the left bank of the Aupa, north and south of Skalitz, was very strong, almost impregnable in front, although the Eichwald and the Fasanerie offered a covered approach. Only a turning movement from the north on the right bank of the Aupa seemed dangerous. But this would be met, as might be expected, by the flanking movement of the IV Corps from Dolan.

The V Prussian Corps, reinforced by a brigade of the VI, stood, early on the 28th, in expectation of an attack, with the advance guard north, Hoffman's Brigade south, the main body and the right flank detachment under Loewenfeld east of Wysokow. In this position, Steinmetz wanted to await the support of the 2nd Guard Division which he had asked, in order to attack with the advance guard the front, with the Guard and Loewenfeld, who had been sent to Studnitz, the left flank of the hostile position. Hoffmann was to remain in reserve and cover the left flank of the corps.

Upon receiving information that the 2nd Guard Division had to be utilized at another point, Steinmetz decided to attack even without this support. The advance guard was to advance south of Starkoc in a westerly direction, the main body to follow north of the Wysokow—Kleny road, then debouching to the left to support the attack, while Loewenfeld was to turn to the left toward the Schafberg and thence surround the left flank of the enemy, Hoffman, with the reserve, to act according to his own judgement. It was impossible to see how the intended envelopment of the well secured left flank could succeed. The whole affair ended in a frontal attack on a very strong position. It would have been more to the purpose to direct the principal attack against the left flank, advancing with two brigades on the right bank of the Aupa, with one brigade via Zlbow and the southern Zlitsch on the left bank, while one brigade went through the Eichwald and another one south of the railroad against the front.

Even the slimmest hope of success of a flanking attack was eliminated by the right flank detachment marching from the Schaferie not in a westerly direction, but via Dubno and through the Eichwald, by the advance via Starkoc taking the same road and by Hoffmann also going west, sending at least two of his battalions into the wood and to the Fasanerie. Thus nine battalions streamed into this thicket while the remainder belonging to the detachments of Loewenfeld and Hoffmann, as well as to the advance guard, remained as reserves, partly outside the wood and partly occupied villages like Studnitz, the Schaferei, Starkoc, Dubno, and Kleny.

It was impossible to tell how the jumbled up half-battalions, companies, and platoons were to be led in a joint attack out of the wood against the hostile position. The enemy, however, removed all difficulty. One of his battalions was sent into the oak wood. It was forced to retreat before the Prussian numerical superiority. General von Fragnern, commanding the left wing, sent one battalion for support and later led forward the remaining six of his brigade. Since the enemy could not be seen and could be recognized only by his fire, the brigade, turning slightly to the right from the north, reached the locality next to the wood—Gehege. Hostile detachments, which had come thither earlier, were repulsed. Further south, the brigade came upon the locality of the railway guard's house where it met two of Loewenfeld's half-battalions which had taken up a position behind the railroad embankment. To the rapid fire against the front was soon added rapid fire against the flank from the Tananerie and finally against the rear from the Gehege. After losing its commander and several officers, the brigade retreated partly to Skalitz, the lesser part going to its former position.

In order to pick up the remnants, Kreyssern's Brigade in position north of Skalitz, advanced against the railway track and the Gehege. Its fate was very similar to that of its predecessor. It streamed back to Skalitz also. There remained nothing for the corps commander, Archduke Leopold, but to order the retreat, which was started by Schulz's Brigade which stood untouched south of the town. The two other brigades followed under the protection of several battalions, posted near the railway, in the custom house,. and in the railway depot, as well as of a strong artillery position east of the city. A few Prussian companies, which rushed against this position, met with a bloody repulse.

A united, to a certain degree orderly, pursuit by the mixed up leaderless troops in the wood could not be thought of, therefore the retreat could be started in fairly good order. The Prussian main forces had deployed west of Wysokow in the meanwhile. General von Kirchbach recognized that the directed "debouching" to the left would bring about a hopeless attack over an open field against the Austrian artillery position. He preferred, after leaving one regiment at Starkoc, to advance with the right wing, via Zlbow, and with the left through the Eichwald. The right wing, advancing southward from the north, gradually drove back the few troops still in position. The left wing, which was joined by the troops in the wood, arrived, after crossing the railway line, under a most effective fire of the hostile artillery, against which only a few batteries had been directed. The Austrian rear guard, however, was forced to retreat when battalions of the Prussian right wing penetrated into the town near the Aupa, while some even crossed the river and threatened Klein-Skalitz. The pursuit was scarcely extended across the Aupa. Steinmetz was satisfied with the occupation of the heights on the left bank.

It might have been expected from Gablenz that he would take advantage of the victory of the 27th and 28th. But should he follow the defeated opponent, the enemy, reported at Kipel, would attack him in the rear. Should he advance against the latter, he would have to take into account the advancing troops of Bonin and new ones coming up from the south. A continuation of the offensive movement in the one or the other direction was fraught with risk which could be undertaken and was advisable only for a general who, like Napoleon, knew himself to be master of the battlefield. The victor of Trautenau, who had tested the superiority of the enemy's arms, could not have this consciousness. Even did he possess it, it would have been impossible for him to continue the offensive, if it were not joined in simultaneously from Skalitz. For the retreat, which Gablenz had to start, the surest road would have been via Kottwitz. Thence he could have barred the enemy in time at Koniginhof on the right or left bank of the Elbe. But in that case he would have left the road to Skalitz open to the Guard Corps for the annihilation of the detachment probably fighting at that point. The order of the commander to go back to Deutsch-Prausnitz and to halt there, was consequently justified. The mode of execution, however, must be considered.

The trains and ammunition park were to march first to Rettendorf, then Knebel's Brigade was to occupy the heights at Burkersdorf, Wimpffen's Brigade to advance to the heights of Kaile, Mondel's Brigade as rear guard, follow at the proper distance, lastly Grivicie's Brigade to advance from the Katzauerberg via Alt-Rognitz and Rudersdorf as far as Raatsch in order to occupy there a position as advance guard facing Eipel. As the army order was received at 7:30 AM, and the trains could start only later, the orders could be executed only if the enemy halted at Eipel. The wish to do so existed at least.

On receiving the false report that hostile columns were advancing from Deutsch-Prausnitz to Trautenau, the 1st Guard Division wanted to await the cooperation of the I Corps in a position behind the Aupa. Correct reports that the enemy was marching in an opposite direction decided the commanding general to give the 1st Guard Division orders to advance via Staudenz. This advance could have been supported effectively if on the day before the 2nd Division of the Guard, instead of halting at Kosteletz, had gone to Horicka and had advanced to Kaile in time on the 28th. To make a detour, via Horicka, at the time was not considered advisable. Another road via Liebenthal was found impracticable. The 2nd Guard Division was thus condemned to follow the first and play a secondary role. When the advance guard of the 1st Guard Division came in touch with Staudenz, Gablenz ordered the trains, which had not yet passed Burkersdorf, to turn to Pilnikau and Knehel's Brigade as well as a few batteries of the artillery reserve to deploy between Neu-Rognitz and Burkersdorf.

The deployed Prussian advance guard went against this position, drove off a far advanced battalion, but halted after this in order to await the main body which had remained behind. When the latter came on a line with the advance guard, Mondel's Brigade had also reached Neu-Rognitz. Thus two almost equally strong

The Campaign of 1866   179

forces opposed each other and the Austrian troops had no reason to avoid a combat. But the false report that the Prussians had penetrated into Kaile (thus executing what the 2nd Guard Division ought to have done) induced Gablenz to start the retreat—Wimpffen's Brigade from Hohenbruck, and Mondel's Brigade from NeuRognitz to Pilnikau under cover of Knebel's Brigade. The latter had to withstand an attack of the 1st Guard Division before it could follow the two others. It suffered quite considerable losses. The Prussians would have achieved a real success only if they had pursued the enemy as far as the road to Pilnikau. But the commander as well as the troops were kept back from such an operation by firmly rooted maneuver considerations. The enemy was retreating. The signal "Halt all!" was given. Even under serious war conditions these peace customs were maintained, although all manuals taught that pursuit in war was one of the principal operations.

Long before the question arose as to whether or not pursuit should take place, Grivicic's Brigade, according to orders received, had reached Alt-Rognitz. One battalion of the 2nd Guard Division, following the 1st Division via Raatsch, was directed against the enemy appearing on the flank. It fought a very bloody battle south of Rudersdorf near the Stein Krenz. A second battalion brought the combat to a standstill. A pause took place in the fighting. Grivicic hesitated to advance and awaited the order to retreat, which the other brigades had already received. The two Prussian battalions were too weak to attack. The commanding general did not deem it necessary to support them.

The commander-in-chief held the opinion, "we will see them (Grivicie's Brigade) all captives this evening at Trautenau and all the more surely, if we have greater success at the front." This was quite right. But success at the front must first be achieved by advancing as far as the Pilnikau road. It could not be obtained by a bivouack at Burkersdorf. The commanding general was at last prevailed upon to send eight companies forward to Alt-Rognitz.

This flanking attack forced the Austrian brigades to retreat. After the wounding of their leader, the cohesion of the troops was lost. A few severe encounters between separate detachments still took place. Then the Austrians endeavored to reach the road to Pilnikau via Neu-Rognitz, Hohenbruck, and Trautenau. They fell

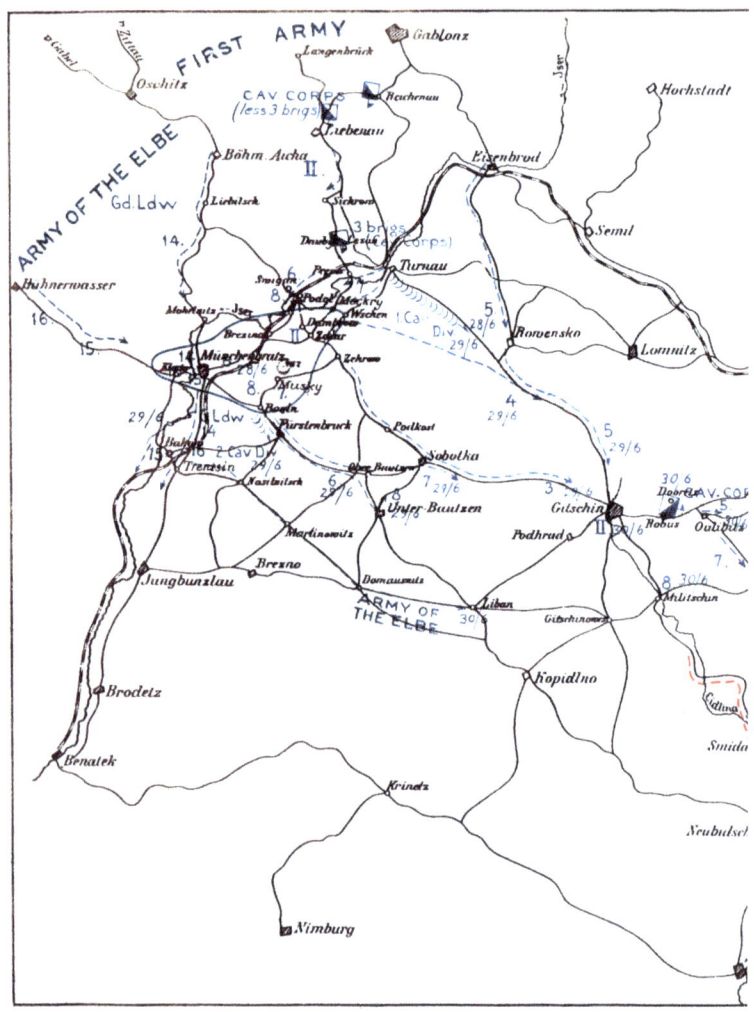

mostly into the hands of the main body of the 2nd Guard Division advancing on Trautenau. This success over a brigade shows what advantages could have been attained over the entire corps if the 2nd Guard Division had been directed at once to Kaile and if both divisions had advanced, without loss of time, by the Trautenau—Prausnitz road up to the Trautenau—Pilnikau road.

The following troops of the First Army and of the Army of the Elbe were to advance on the 28th for the attack of the position at

The Campaign of 1866

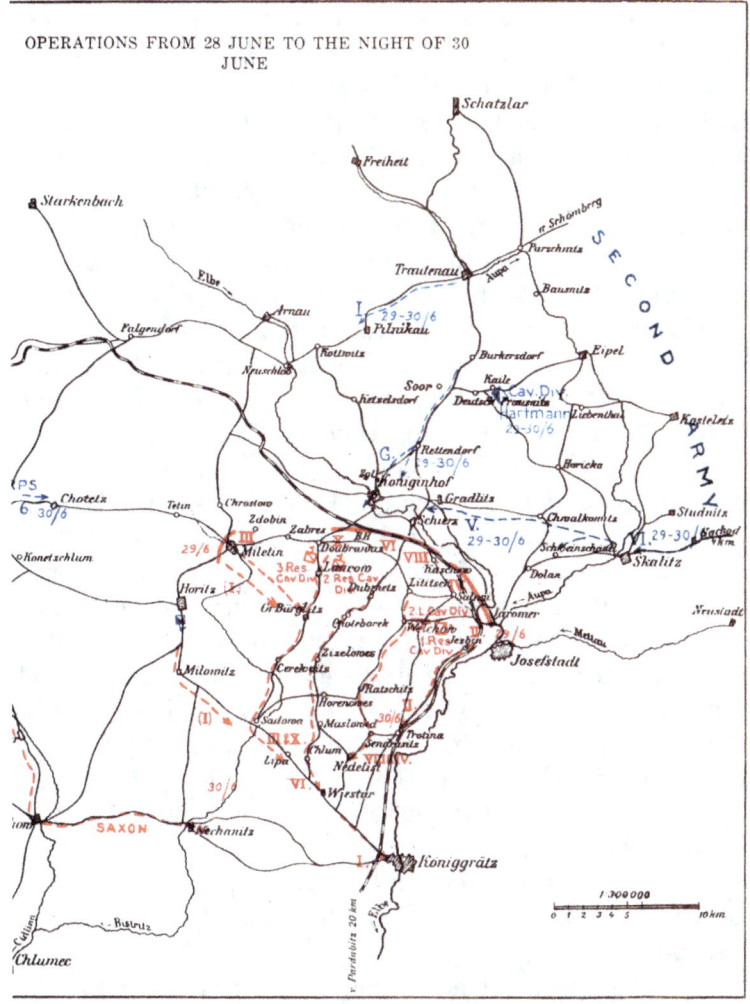

OPERATIONS FROM 28 JUNE TO THE NIGHT OF 30 JUNE

Munchengratz: the 15th and 16th Divisions from Huhnerwasser to Munchengratz, the 14th via Liebitsch to Mohelnitz, the Landwehr Division of the Guard to Huhnerwasser, Horn's Division (8th) and that of Manstein (6th) from Podol to Brezina, Fransecky (7th) from Mockry—Wschen to Zider, the Cavalry Corps with three brigades to Dauby and Lozan, the II Corps to Sichrow, the rest of the Cavalry Corps to Liebenau—-Reichenau, and Tumpling's Division (5th) to Rowensko.

Without awaiting this attack the Crown Prince of Saxony ordered a retreat as follows: Ringelsheim's Brigade via Podkost, Poschacher's, Pirte's, and Abele's Brigades via Furstenbruck and Sobotka to Gitschin, the Saxon Corps via Trentsin, Nasilnitsch, and Brezno to Domausnitz, the Saxon cavalry to Unter-Bautzen, the Saxon heavy artillery and the trains to Jungbunzlau and east thereof. Since the Army of the Elbe had to cover considerable distances and the attack therefore could not begin until 9:00 AM, the Austrians and Saxons could have withdrawn without any loss if Leiningen's Brigade, left as rear guard near Kloster, the other side of the Iser, had not awaited the attack of the 15th Division and if two horse batteries and some infantry had not been placed on the Musky Hill north of Musky to receive that brigade.

Hence ensued combats between Leiningen's Brigade and the advance guards of the 15th and 14th Divisions, as well as between Fransecky's Division and the troops posted on the Musky hill. After some not inconsiderable losses and the capture of prisoners from the Italian reserves, the Austrians retreated on Abele's Brigade via Furstenbruck. On the Prussian side almost all their forces had been concentrated in the narrow space of the battlefield. Only the Landwehr Division of the Guard had remained at Huhnerwasser, Alvensleben's Division of the Cavalry Corps at Liebenau-Langenbruck and Tumpling's Division at Rowensko. The mass, consisting of one cavalry and eight infantry divisions, about 120,000 men, was united immediately under the eye of its commander, but suffered under "the calamity of concentration," lacked the most needful things, and could be employed only with difficulty.

Although there was no pursuit, army headquarters was well informed by the cavalry as to the location of the enemy. The march of a long column from Sobotka to Gitschin had been observed, strong Austrian cavalry had been found near this town as well as a rear guard near Podkost in the evening. It was not difficult to guess where the Austrian corps would be in the evening. Reports concerning the Saxons were less satisfactory. The patrols had met outposts not far from Jungbunzlau. Nothing, however, had been observed of a departure from Bakow to Unter-Bautzen. Army headquarters deduced from all this that, if not the entire hostile army, then at least the Saxon Corps had taken up again a position at Jungbunzlau and would have to be attacked there. For this purpose, in the afternoon of the 29th, the following should be in readiness: the 15th Division on the right and the 16th on the left bank of the Iser near Bakow, the 14th and the Landwehr Division of the Guard in their rear at Munchengratz. The II Corps was to march from Dambrow via Zehrow to Martinowitz by the road Jungbunzlau—Ober Bautzen, Tumpling's Division to Sobotka, the remaining troop units to remain where they were. On the 30th the attack was to take place against an unoccupied position.

Benedek's situation thanks to the victory at Trautenau, and in spite of the unfortunate combats of Nachod, Skalitz, and Burkersdorf, was not very unfavorable on the evening of the 28th. The IV and X Corps were undoubtedly capable of preventing the Prussian Second Army from crossing the Upper Elbe for two, even three days. Although the VI and VIII Corps of the six remaining ones had suffered considerably, there were still sufficient forces available for an offensive against the Prussian First Army with good prospect of success, as it could not deploy in full force in any direction.

It was the highest time that action be taken. The encounter in which, on the Prussian side, the Army of the Elbe and probably more troops would have been lacking, had to take place on the 30th at the latest. An annihilating victory was by all means necessary to the Austrians. A simple retreat of the enemy or an undecided battle would have brought from the one side the Second Army, from the other the Army of the Elbe and a doubtful victory would have been transformed into a sure defeat. However, it was problematic if the Austrian army leadership was capable of fighting a battle of annihilation, taking into consideration the proofs given so far.

There was no inclination to make that attempt. The unfortunate messages from Skalitz and Burkersdorf, as well as the false report that the enemy had penetrated into Gitschin, affected Benedek's confidence in himself and his troops so deeply that he abandoned the intended offensive and wanted to seek salvation in the position —Josefstadt (II), Jaromer (IV), Salnai (VIII), Lititsch (X), Lancow (VI), Miletin (III), Horitz (I), Milowitz (Saxon Corps). Benedek gave up the possibility of a victory by adopting this decision. The naturally strong position: Josefstadt—Miletin, was so strongly occupied by six corps that the Prussian Second Army had little chances of taking it soon. But so much the weaker was the flank in the locality: Horitz—Milowitz, facing west, for the defense of which against the First Army and Army of the Elbe, the I and the Saxon Corps were not sufficient. The narrow flank had to be pushed back against the Elbe by the much wider Prussian armies, while the cavalry corps crossed the Elbe below this point, Hartmann's Cavalry Division crossing the Mettau in order to complete the impending "Cannae" by the occupation of the fords between Koniggratz and Josefstadt.

The question was not: will the Austrians be thrown back, as was the highest aim of army headquarters, but will they be surrounded on the left bank of the Elbe, as Moltke had wished. In other words, shall the campaign be continued step by step, i.e., from the Elbe and the Main to the Danube and, maybe, across the Danube; will the powers, onlookers at present, join the fray from right and left, or shall Prussia's war against Austria, against the German Central States and, as she would have to show her hand, against France, be ended like the war of Italy against Austria, in one. day and on one battlefield?

What the Second Army could do for the solution of these questions had already taken place, or might be made up for in the next few days. The most essential thing to be done, however, fell to the lot of the two other armies. Had these started originally in five columns, without caring about the enemies, who either did not exist or were too weak for serious resistance, they might have reached Jungbunzlau—Eisenbrod on the 27th, at the latest on the 29th, could have reached Gitschin with the left wing, and Neubidschow or Chlumec with the right as actually happened. After this a short pressure only was necessary to put into execution Moltke's plan on the 30th. This could no longer be done since the 28th had been spent in a "Sham Battle" in which "everything had worked well together," and could no more be thought of when on the 29th a storming of Jungbunzlau had been prepared, to be executed only on the 30th.

It was high time that Moltke should urge early on the 29th, by a telegram that the great aim could be partially attained. The

The Campaign of 1866 185

Second Army needed no other instructions. It wanted to proceed on the 29th with the I Corps to Pilnikau, the Guard Corps of Rettendorf, the advance guard to Koniginhof, with the V Corps to Gradlitz, the VI Corps to Skalitz. This intention led to new combats.

General von Steinmetz. at Skalitz had opposite him on the road from Josefstadt to the Walowski valley the outposts of the Austrian IV Corps. He did not want to let this enemy "lure him to Jaromer," but planned to turn his left wing by marching off via Westetz, Wetrnik, and Chwaltkowitz without having much to do with him. But when the advance guard ascended the plateau southwest of Wetrnik between Chwalkowitz and Miskoles, it encountered the enemy who had occupied an advantageous position near Schweinschadel and Sebuc between the Aupa and Schwarzwasser. The march could not be continued unless it were expected that the flank or rear should be exposed to attack.

The advance guard jointly with a left flank detachment which had marched up from Trebeschow by the Walowski valley, formed for attack on the height of Miskoles. Count Festetics, the Austrian commander, had received instructions to avoid combat with superior forces. However, "not to demoralize his troops by an early retreat," he wanted to repulse the first onset of the enemy and then only start the retreat. A combat took place with the usual Austrian counter thrusts of individual troop units, repulses of such attacks by rapid fire, around Schweinschadel, the thicket near the Schaferei and the Ziegelei and near Sobuc, finally a breaking off of the fight on the part of the Prussians and a retreat to Jaromer on the part of the Austrians. Since the fight began in the afternoon, the first troops of the V Corps reached Gradlitz only in the night.

The X Corps and Fleischhacker's Brigade of the Austrian IV Corps were to march on the 29th from Neuschloss via Koniginhof to Dubenetz. Wimpfiten's Brigade alone was sent over the nearest and best, but also the most threatened road via Ketzelsdorf. It reached Koniginhof without having come into touch with the enemy and continued its march to Dubenetz. The remaining brigades, the artillery reserve, the ammunition park and the trains had to make a detour on the right bank of the Elbe, cross the river immediately in front of Koniginhof and thence return to the right bank.

To cover the march through the town, ten companies of the

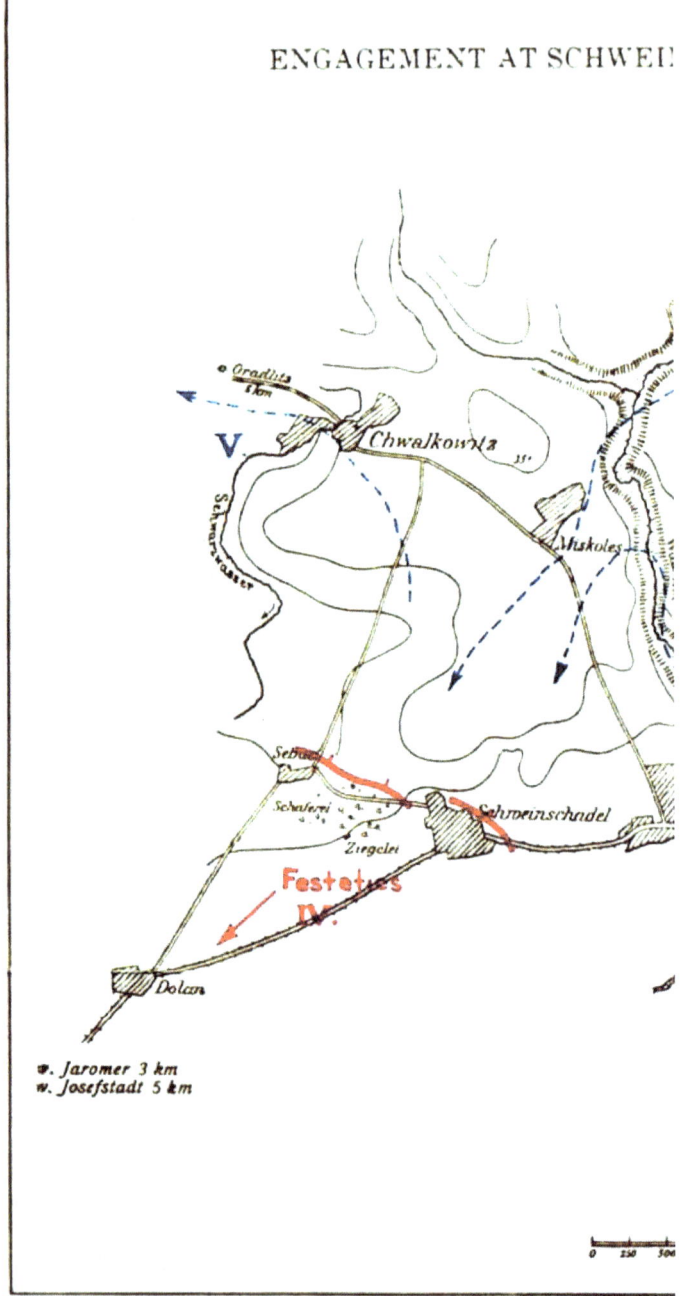

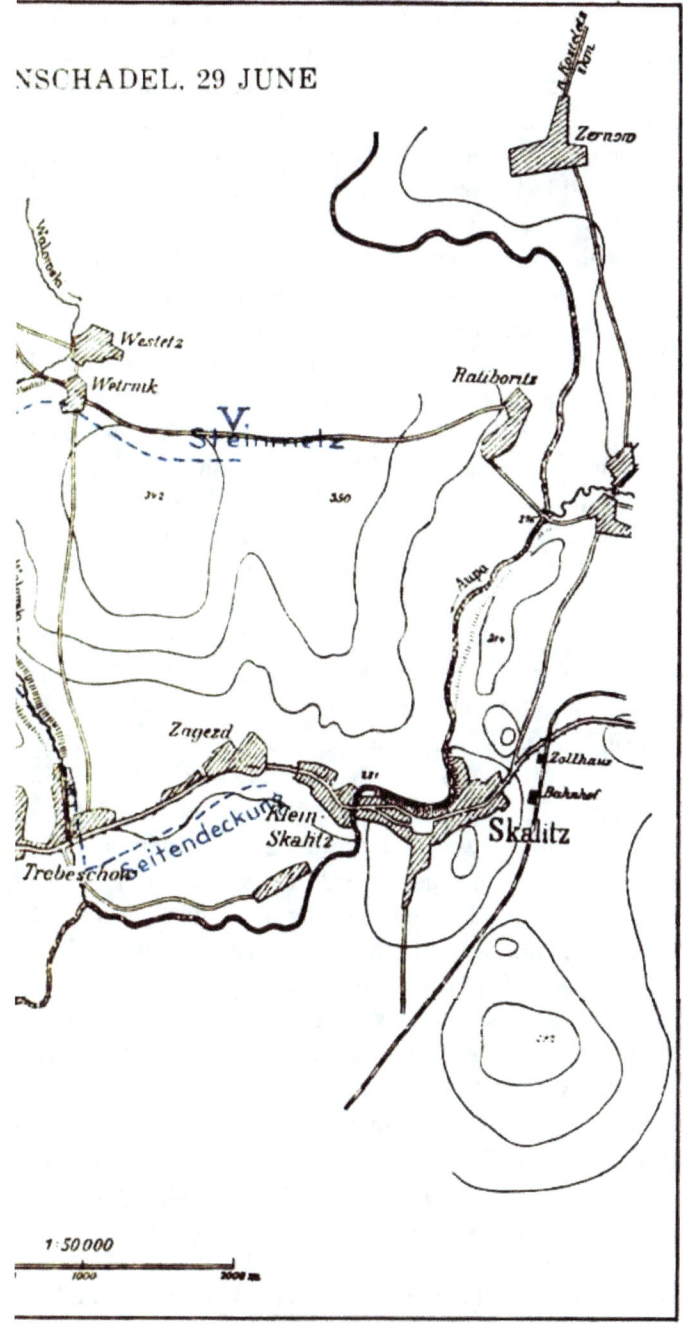

Coronini regiment were sent to the eastern exit, three of them occupying the brick kiln. The trains, the ammunition park, the artillery reserve and Knebel's Brigade had crossed the southern bridge, two battalions (the remnants of Grivicic's Brigade) rested on the market place when the advance guard of the Guard Corps appeared at 2:00 PM, from Burkersdorf. The three companies in the brick kiln were reinforced by three companies of the reserve. The six companies could not long resist the two batteries and two and one half battalions of the advance guard. They found, on retreating, the northern bridge barred by a Prussian company. The two Grivicic battalions, two battalions of Mondel's Brigade covered by the ten Coronini companies, were forced to retreat over the southern bridge after street fighting and serious losses in casualties and prisoners. The Mondel battalions, which had remained behind, as well as Fleischhacker's Brigade marched obliquely over the field to opposite the railway depot where a numerous artillery had arrived and checked all pursuit over the Elbe.

In the evening of the 29th, the left bank of the Elbe above Jaromer was evacuated by the Austrians and won by the Prussians. Of these there stood the Guard and the V Corps with Hoffman's Brigade near Rettendorf, Koniginhof, and Gradlitz, the I Corps near Pilnikau, the VI near Skalitz, the Cavalry Division near Kaile. On the other bank, in a very strong position formed by the edge of the valley of the Elbe between Kaschow and Doubrawitz, stood the VI, VIII, and X Corps, the 2nd and 3rd Reserve Cavalry Divisions in readiness. The right flank between Jaromer and Kaschow was covered by the II and IV Corps, the 1st Reserve and the 2nd Light Cavalry Divisions while the left was covered by the III Corps in the region: Miletin—Zabres—Zdobin—Chrostow—Tetin. The Second Army did not deem it possible to attack this numerically superior army in so strong a position.

An attack by the Austrians, on the contrary, seemed to have a good chance. In their hands were several crossings above and below over which they could make a flank attack against the concentrated Prussian position. But since four of his corps had been defeated with severe losses, Benedek abandoned all thought of attack. All his hopes lay in repulsing an attack against the long known and celebrated position. In order to be as strong as possible for this combat, an order had been prepared early on the 29th for the Crown Prince of Saxony to effect a junction with the main army without becoming engaged in any obstinate combats. The defensive battle against the Second Army was to take place before the First Army and the Army of the Elbe should have time to come up. The Second Army, however, had not given its consent to this plan. It did not wish to attack, but to rest on the 30th.

The Austrian and the Second Armies both decided to wait. It was so much the more urgent to call the First Army. It was, however, impossible to advance rapidly against the enemy out of the "calamity of concentration" in the direction of Horitz—Koniggratz and strike at his flank and rear. The divisions could be taken only one by one out of the thick mass formation. It was also impossible to leave Jungbunzlau out of consideration. Orders were, consequently given: Under General von Schmidt, commanding the II Corps, will march: Tumpling's Division (5th) from Rowensko, Werder (3rd Division) from Zehrow to Gitschin, Herwarth (4th Division) from Zidar and Alvensleben's Cavalry Division will follow the former, Fransecky (7th Division) from Bosin via Sobotka, following the latter. After these divisions there should start in the evening, Horn (8th Division), Manstein (6th Division), and Hann's Cavalry Division to Lower and Upper Bautzen to serve as a reserve for the divisions marching to Gitschin as well as for the Army of the Elbe remaining opposite Jungbunzlau. Not in spite of but because the commanders always endeavored to keep all their forces firmly and resolutely together, they could send against the enemy only two divisions instead of ten. The two divisions of Herwarth and Fransecky, following in second line were at too great a distance from Tumpling and Werder to be able to take part in a combat on the same day. And yet a decision had to be reached on that very day.

Poschacher's Brigade and Edelsheim's Cavalry Division had reached Gitschin already on the 28th. Piret's, Leiningen's, and Abele's Brigades followed to that point in the afternoon of the next day. Ringelsheim's Brigade reached Lochow, Stieglitz's Saxon Division reached Podhrad, while Schimpff's Division arrived at Gitschinowes only towards evening. Through these marches the

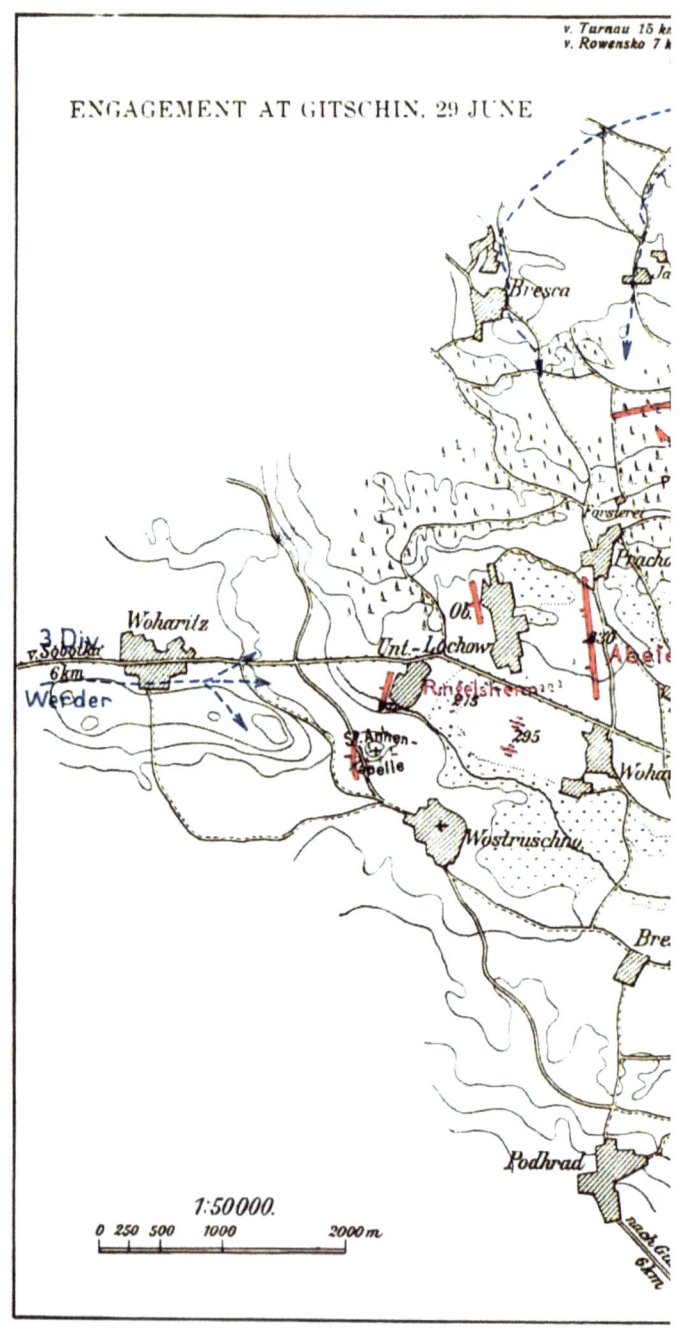

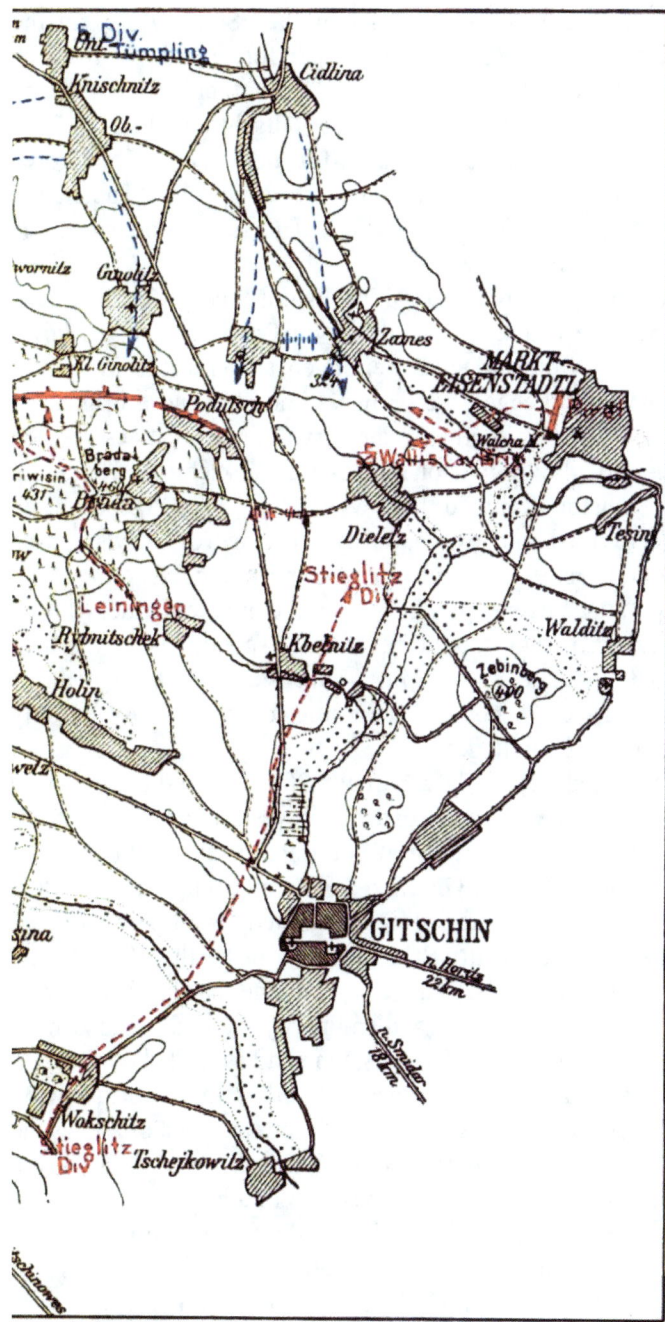

intention, given in the army order of the 28th, "to prevent the enemy from penetrating between the main forces and your troops," seemed to have been fulfilled. By another report "Army Headquarters at Miletin on the 29th, at Gitschin on the 30th," the prompt advance of the army seemed to be in view. The Crown Prince decided, consequently, to remain at Gitschin. The enemy had not followed. Only Tumpling's Division stood since the evening before, near Rowensko.

In order to secure the position against these, Count Clam-Gallas had the Bradaberg occupied by Poschacher and Markt-Hisenstadtl by Piret, placing Leiningen as a reserve in rear of Poschacher, and begged the Crown Prince to send a brigade to Dieletz, followed by another as a reserve. Since no attack seemed imminent, Stieglitz's Division remained at Wokschitz and Podhrad. Abele's Division occupied the lowland steep near Prachow. The position, divided into two parts by the ridge of Priwisin, was unfortunately chesen. Should one of the defenders retreat, the victorious attack came upon the rear ot the other defender. If both parts advanced, they would be entirely separated. It was also unfortunate that Dieletz and Markt-Hisenstadt] were situated in a lowland and were occupied, according to ancient custom, only because they were villages.

Unexpectedly came the report at 3:30 PM, that the enemy was advancing on the Turnau road. The western edge of Markt-Eisenstadtl, the northern edge of South Podulsch and the edge of the wood south of Klein-Ginolitz, were now occupied, Stieglitz's Division was called up, the place designated for it being occupied temporarily by the Cavalry Brigade of Wallis north of Dieletz, the artillery east of Brada. The enemy came partly from Ober-Knischnitz along the main road and partly via Cidlina to Zames. Thence he forced Wallis' Hussars, who had ascended on foot and occupied hill 324 west of Zames, as well as the two right wing batteries between Brada and Dieletz, to retreat. West of Zames the enemy occupied the northern Podulsch, Ginolitz, and the hill south of Jawornitz and advanced via Bresca to Prachow.

The enemy halted on the edge of the wood and at southern Podulsch and marched against Dieletz. Two skirmish lines had already penetrated into the village when the Saxon Brigade came up and won back what had been lost. The Prussian artillery, which had come in a southern and southwestern direction from Ober Knischnitz, advanced west as far as Zames and forced part of the Austrian and Saxon batteries to go from east of Brada to north of Kobelnitz. Such was the situation when at 7:00 PM Benedek issued the order to continue the movement for the junction with the army, avoiding the more serious encounters. In spite of that the Crown Prince would have maintained his position until dark if Ringelsheim had not sent the exaggerated report that he had been attacked with forces four times superior to his.

Retreat was ordered. Piret was to hold Markt-Hisenstadtl, Stieglitz was to go to Zebimberg, Leiningen and Poschacher to Gitschin. The Saxons were on the point of evacuating Dieletz when a general, encircling attack was made on this village. Part of the still fighting defenders were cut off. Piret wanted to tear from the enemy the advantages obtained and crossed the Cidlina back at the Walcha mill with three battalions each against the northern exit of Dieletz and against Zames. The attack in column formation, executed with band playing, broke at both points against a scathing rapid fire. After losing one sixth of its strength, the brigade abandoned Markt-Hisenstadtl and went back to Gitschin.

Poschacher had also undertaken a successful attack against Klein-Ginolitz with a few battalions shortly before retreating. The retreat through the wood and out of the villages was rendered more difficult by this success. Several companies were cut off when Tumpling took Podulsch and Brada by an encircling attack at 8:30 PM. The wounding of the General brought the advance to a standstill. Before General Kaminsky had taken over the command at 10:00 PM, and ordered the continuation of the advance, Piret, Stieglitz, and Wallis had departed to the east and Leiningen, Poschacher and the mass of the artillery and cavalry through Gitschin.

Ringelsheim's Brigade had taken up position west of Wohawetz, that of Abele north of Prachow. Detachments had been sent forward to Lower and Upper Lochow, also on the road and into the wood toward Bresca. Werder marched against these positions from Sobotka. The advanced detachments of the enemy were driven back by his advance guard, Lower Lochow, the wood to its north and St. Annenkapelle were taken. Upper Lochow, however, was strongly garrisoned, the meadow strip east of Lower Lochow was hard to cross and the Austrian artillery on height 330 was very effective. General Januschevsky was entrusted with turning the difficult position via Wostruschno with four battalions and one battery.

The goal had not yet been reached when the Austrians made a counterattack from Upper Lochow with two, and from Wohawetz with four battalions, while three battalions occupied the southern edge of hill 295. The attack on Upper Lochow succeeded. Two companies were forced to evacuate the wood north of Lower Lochow. The attack from Wohawetz was repulsed, however, by the rapid fire of the Prussian infantry which had come up in the meanwhile over the meadow strip east of Lower Lochow. The order to retreat arrived at this junction and was executed without much disturbance as two roads, via Holin and Wohawetz, were available and no pursuit took place. Only the flank detachment near Prachow was pushed back in part.

As there was not sufficient water at Wohawetz, General Schmidt decided to march further, although darkness had already set in. He rode at the head of the troops with his staff before the infantry could follow. Close to Gitschin he was met by fire. A battalion which followed him, found one of the gates unoccupied and entered the town. Ringelsheim's Brigade, designated in the beginning as rear guard for holding the town, was no longer in a condition to execute this task, and had retreated through the streets. A Saxon Brigade, called as a substitute, arrived almost at the same. time, (10:30 PM), from the northeast as the Prussian battalion came up from the west into the town. The battalion had to go back. Another attempt to penetrate into the town was repulsed. The Saxons occupied the town. Werder's Division went into bivouac west of and close to the town. Shortly before midnight the advance guard battalion of the 5th Division arrived in front of the town. Its attack was likewise repulsed. The Saxon Brigade evacuated the town and retreated to Smidar, only when Lieutenant Colonel von Gaudy advanced with three and one half battalions from Dicletz east of Kbelnitz, crossing the Cidlina and coming up from the north. Gitschin was then occupied by the Prussians.

The Campaign of 1866 195

Desisting from the time honored procedure, pursuits were undertaken on that day. The effect was not slow to show itself. Count Clam-Gallas in Gitschin was on the point of giving orders for further retreat when the foremost Prussians penetrated into the town. He was forced to ride away in a hurry. The orders could not be carried out. His troops, partly also the Saxons, mixed up together, found themselves on the following morning far dispersed between Miletin, Horitz, Smidar, Neubischow, and even Josefstadt.

First Army Headquarters demanded after this several days of rest, later on the reserves were drawn from Upper and Lower Bautzen to Gitschin and, after the destruction of the phantom of Jungbunzlau, the Army of the Elbe was brought to Liban. Thus the First Army was assembled at Gitschin. The pursuit was begun from there in the afternoon in the direction of Miletin: by Manstein (6th Division) as far as Chotez, Tumpling (5th) as far as Quilbitz; in the direction of Horitz: by Fransecky (7th) as far as Konetschlum in the direction of Smidar: by Horn (8th) as far as Miletin. The II Corps remained at Gitschin and Podhrad. The Cavalry Corps, which had asked permission to go in pursuit of the enemy, was refused its request presented at an inopportune moment, and sent to Dvoretz and Robus. How much would it not have been able to do when the appearance alone of a cavalry regiment before Horitz decided Clam-Gallas to continue his retreat from Horitz to Sadowa, from Miletin via Gross-Burglitz and Maslowed to Koniggratz.

The left flank of the Austrian army was now entirely uncovered. An insignificant cannonade took place on the Elbe, but on the morrow an attack must follow against the front and, via Horitz and Miletin, against the rear. The result of this could not be awaited. At dark the retreat was begun in silence: by the III and X Corps via Lancow, GrossBurglitz, Cerekwitz, Sadowa, to Lipa; by the V Corps via Dubenetz, Choteborek, Zizelowes, Horenowes, to Wiestar; by the VI Corps via Dubunetz, Choteborek, Welchow, Ratschitz, Sendrasitz, to Nedelitst; by the II Corps via Salnai and Jezbin to Trotina; the Saxon Corps in Smidar was asked to join via Neubidschow and Nechanitz.

This was a success, but not the success Moltke had intended it to be, as he had thought it out. His plan of operations was simple enough. He let the widely scattered armies march to the point to which, according to his calculations, the Austrians must decide to go. To friend and enemy the same rendezvous had been assigned. From Saxony, from the Lausitz and Silesia, as well as from Moravia, the Prussians and the Austrians were to stream to the locality between the Elbe and the Iser, the former for the purpose of unitedly fighting two separated enemies, the latter for the purpose of fighting the united enemy from two different sides, the former to take advantage of the interior, the latter of the outer lines.

By exerting their utmost efforts, the Austrians were the first to come to the rendezvous. The length of their marching columns extended their advance over five days. Five long days must they wait before the intended offensive could be undertaken against the hostile main army advancing against the Iser. Was it not possible for this main army, which was to be attacked, to make an attack before the end of this period, and was it not possible that the Silesian army, which had arrived as far as the mountain passes, might appear earlier on the upper Elbe? The Austrian army would then have been forced, before or possibly immediately after the completed concentration, to struggle with the Prussian army in the vicinity of Miletin for the decision, while, close by, two corps had already begun to ward off attacks against flank and rear. The position on the upper Elbe was strong. But sooner or later its left wing must be turned. Then the flood would break over the left flank and rear of the Austrian army. No matter how many attacks might have been repulsed, had the enemy not been annihilated, the Austrian army faced destruction. .

Such a situation must be avoided, the two hostile armies must be kept farther apart. The Crown Prince of Saxony received the order to prevent the enemy at any cost from crossing the Iser. Gablenz was sent to Trautenau and Rammig to Skalitz and Nachod to hold back the two corps, expected from Silesia, near the exits of the mountain passes. Both measures were inadequate, considering the two forces opposing each other. Nevertheless, they were not unsuccessful. The enemy was not held back at the Iser, it is true, but he stopped of his own accord. Gablenz threw his opponent out of the field. Rammig, at least, maintained his position at Skalitz, and was reinforced by two corps.

The situation was entirely changed. The Austrians were in

The Campaign of 1866   197

superior numbers on the eastern front. Four corps opposed two, three opposed one. They had only to attack. No surprise was to be expected on the western front for several days. Benedek, however, did not utilize the advantage which was already in his hands. He wanted to abide by his old plan and leave two corps at the Upper Elbe while preparing with the remaining forces at his disposition for an offensive on the Iser. He thus jeopardized all hope of success. Four corps might have achieved a great success on the eastern front on the 28th. Two corps were not sufficient to ward off a defeat, which they would have suffered as early as the 27th without the great mistakes made by Bonin and Hiller. The Prussians had advanced in four columns. The Austrians had been able to oppose only one corps to each pair of these columns. Had these conquered or opposed successful resistance in one position, they were still exposed to a turning of the rear by one of the other Prussian columns.

The advantages which thus accrued to the enemy and the disadvantages which fell to their own lot, were soon recognized by the Austrians, but were not comprehended by the Prussian generals, or at any rate they were not utilized. Steinmetz was not able to accomplish much more at Nachod than to repulse the attacks of the enemy. Still Rammig went back as far as Skalitz because he took it for granted that the 2nd Guard Division would not remain at Kosteletz, but would attack him in the rear. Hiller had only to cross the Aupa at Bausnitz to defeat Gablenz most decisively.

Recognizing this danger, the Austrian Fieldmarshal left Trautenau on the day following his victory. At Burkersdorf, however, he might have opposed successful resistance to Hiller had he not believed that the only reasonable operation for the 2nd Guard Division was to advance against his rear. The retreat from Munchengratz was ordered because the advance towards Gitschin of the Prussian corps which had arrived at Turnau, appeared imminent on account of the situation. A Prussian attack at Skalitz was not necessary. Archduke Leopold would have retreated without it. But he should have been directed against the enemy who was advancing in the rear from the Iser. The Crown Prince of Saxony was to break off the engagement at Gitschin because the

Second Army threatened to cross the Elbe. Always threatened by a turning or enveloping movement, the Austrians were forced to concentrate toward their center and would have been surrounded, had the Prussian army and corps commanders known their business better.

The idea of annihilating the enemy, which completely absorbed Moltke, was not fathomed by the subordinate commanders. They understood the problem before them to lie in the junction of the separated armies. In this they agreed with Moltke. But he wished to see the opponent within the circle of the united armies, while they were willing to leave it to the enemy to concentrate his forces where he desired. Once the armies were concentrated, no matter where, it could then be decided whether to accept battle or not. For the commanding generals, the principal aim was to assemble 250,000 men at Gitschin or Miletin in a single mass. The enemy who sought to oppose the concentration must by all means be pushed aside, unless one were willing to continue the march on the designated point without considering the nearby adversary, as was attempted by Bonin at Trautenau and Steinmetz at Schweinschadel, and actually accomplished by Hiller at Parschnitz.

This was easily accounted for. The commanding generals of the Second Army, as they considered, had not received the order to fight the enemy, but to reach Arna, Koniginhof, and Schurz on 28 June. From this task they were permitted to deviate as little as possible. Moreover, an attack of considerable importance could not be easily executed, as the troop units were separated from the very beginning. Steinmetz could repulse the enemy at Nachod, but could not attack him, because his corps, though it was on the ground, was scattered in small units all over the field. At Trautenau, General Grossmann was ordered to carry forward with him into the attack, along with his own ten battalions, the eight of Buddenbrock. It is said that he never received the order. But even had he received it, it would have been impossible to lead into the attack the ten battalions, scattered as they were into small detachments. At Skalitz the greater part of the Prussian infantry was thrown into the Hichwald and the Fasanerie. Single companies might rush thence against the hostile position, but it was beyond human power to undertake an attack with mixed half-battalions, companies, and platoons. The united attack of Kirchbach at Skalitz encountered only a weakly occupied position and that of Hiller at Burkersdorf an already retreating enemy.

The First Army at least started orderly attacks. However, instead of letting the corps which encountered the enemy, attack him, and the remaining corps march on until they had reached the hostile flank or rear, a halt was first ordered, then everything prepared for an attack against front and flank. Before these movements were executed, the enemy, if there was any, had already retreated. The preparations were too thorough and took too much time. That the advance and deployment must go hand in hand was seen to be necessary. But the longer the marching columns, the greater were the difficulties encountered. The corps of that time had not yet been brought to the strength of the present corps in artillery and transportation, but they endeavored to replace their lack, on the march at least, by great intervals between the van-, the advance guard, the main body, the reserve infantry, the reserve artillery, and the reserve cavalry.

These overlong columns advanced but slowly. At Nachod the last reserves reached the battlefield at 11:00 PM. Bonin might have reached Trautenau ahead of the enemy, had he not required the infantry, according to Regulations, to reconnoiter carefully the slopes along the road, behind houses, bushes, and mounds, to see if concealed enemies were not lurking there. To cross the Iser from the dense concentration at Reichenberg, the infantry of the First Army needed four whole days. The chief of staff, General von Voigts-Rhetz, complained of the terrain being too narrow for the deployment of all the troops. It lay in his hands to widen the narrow terrain right and left in order to give breathing space to the compressed masses.

There surely could not be found in the movements of the First Army, the restlessness and impetus with which Napoleon rushed his columns onward. The battles were decided by strong artillery. This much was known of the wars of the beginning of the century. In order not to exhaust this costly means too early, the reserve artillery was given a place far down the marching column. It was also well for the commander to be placed as late as possible into the embarrassment of using this strange arm. When an attack had at last to be made, the infantry stood perplexed and powerless in front of the long Austrian battery lines.

It might be supposed that the Austrians should have had easy work under the circumstances. But their mode of fighting did not lack considerable peculiarities. The eternal dispute over the problem whether soldiers armed with rifles should be deployed in line, where they may be able to use their weapons, or extended in depth where they will not be able to use them had been settled by the Austrians in the extreme latter sense. There stood at Nachod four brigades, one behind another, each in three lines, twelve in all.

The columns of the two foremost battalions were not able to contend against one battalion deployed in one line. The fact that this battalion was armed with the needle gun was of no importance; the fight of the attacking column against the standing line had long been decided at Preussich-Eylau, Waterloo and recently, on the Alma, in favor of the latter. It is true that the devastating fire of the needle gun transformed the repulsed attack into a bloody defeat. The attack in deep columns, feeding the combat by their rifles, in conjunction with the invention of the locksmith's Journeyman Dreyse, had shaken the defeated corps of Rammig and Archduke Leopold to their very foundations, just as much as had the victorious corps of Gablenz.

The decision, however, rested in the turning movements, advocated in Moltke's plan, which were not executed though they still threatened the enemy. The battles of the 27th and 28th of June, should have, in total, brought about the annihilation of the enemy on the part of the Second Army. They at least effected a victory. The many mistakes and sins of omission of the commanders could not, however, remain without result. It was well that the company commanders and platoon leaders were imbued with initiative and the capability of coming 10 a decision and that the rank and file were inspired with the highest spirit and a readiness to accomplish anything. It was, however, impossible to gain decisive victories with a disorganized crowd. The Prussians had to be thankful that the enemy had Jet himself be induced to retreat not because of what had been done, but because of what he supposed had been done.

The troop leadership of the other army, too formal as a rule, appeared sufficient, as at Gitschin there was no time for lengthy preparations. A success was there won with inferior numbers which was converted into a real victory by pursuit. A column encountered a stronger enemy and fought indecisively. The neighboring column met a weaker opponent, threw him back and advanced against the rear of the stronger, doing what the Second Army ought to have done in every battle. This brought about the decision. The Austrian position became untenable, the intended defensive battle could not be fought. However, an immediate second attack by the Second Army against the hostile front and an advance of the First Army against Horitz—Koniggratz was not made so as to take advantage of the victory. This could not be executed with two divisions. The First Army and the Army of the Elbe, instead of having reached Chlumee with the right wing, stood with eight divisions far in the background. The enemy had time to escape from the surrounding movement. The battle of annihilation, planned by Moltke, was transformed into an "ordinary victory."

Koniggratz

On 27 June, 1866, one Austrian corps at Nachod and on the 28th two others at Skalitz and Burkersdorf were so crippled that their further use for either attack or defense seemed doubtful. Consequently, Benedek formed a plan for defensive with two corps against the enemy who was coming from the east, and for an attack with six corps against an opponent marching from the west, which was impossible of execution. The forces at his disposition were no longer sufficient for the simultaneous solution of two quite difficult problems. However, since the enemy from the west was advancing very slowly, he could be left alone for a short time during which all the forces should be employed against the other enemy who, it seemed was impetuously advancing. Had the latter been defeated, there would have been sufficient time to turn with the victorious army against the other opponent.

The Crown Prince of Saxony was immediately called up. Eight corps were to be thrown against the four corps of the Prussian

Second Army. Even though the possibility of utilizing three of the eight corps was doubtful, much could be said in favor of the success of the new plan. The Prussian First Army was, in reality, intending to allow itself to be held up two or three days at the Iser by an enemy existing only in its imagination and it seemed needless to consider it. The last corps of the day-long marching column of the Austrians had arrived on 29 June. Two others came up on the same day, having remained on the 28th on the left bank of the Elbe, though not without suffering losses and having encounters in rear of the protecting river. Six corps were assembled there in the evening. They seemed sufficient, in a strong position, for the successful repulse of an attack by the Second Prussian Army on the 30th. The Crown Prince of Saxony could come up on the same day and on 1 July, it would have been possible to pass to an overwhelming attack on the repulsed enemy.

But this plan had hardly been adopted when one condition after another, necessary for its success, disappeared. Early on the 29th the Prussian First Army was ordered by Moltke to leave alone the self-created enemy and to go immediately to the assistance of the Second Army. It obeyed the orders as well and promptly as it was possible from the narrow area to which it was confined. The Crown Prince of Saxony, who had remained in Gitschin according to a previously received order, was ordered to come up immediately at a time when he had already been drawn into a serious combat. The Prussian Second Army did not attack on the 30th, and, consequently, could not be repulsed. The two opponents were occupied by an aimless cannonading. Instead of the desired attack, the following was learned during the day: The Crown Prince of Saxony had been defeated the evening of the 29th at Gitschin, the 1st Light Cavalry Division and the Saxon Corps had retreated to Smidar, the I Corps to Miletin and Horitz, while many detachments of the two corps had scattered in several directions. Hostile cavalry appeared in front of Horitz by noon. Count Clam-Gallas had, consequently, retreated immediately to Koniggratz. Once more two corps appeared to have been beaten.

Thus Benedek had only the six corps assembled between Jaromer and Miletin. With these he had to face on the following day, not only the hoped for attack of four corps against the front,

The Campaign of 1866 203

but a very undesirable one of five against flank and rear. He then probably considered the recipe given by Clausewitz "what was left him of the masses which might still be called available, i.e., which had not burnt out like extinct volcanoes." He must have also considered "how stood it with the security of his rear" and must have found that he had about five extinct volcanoes on his hands, while three corps were still available and that the security of his rear was quite defective. From the results of these considerations, then arose the decision to abandon the battlefield.

The III Corps was brought in the afternoon from Miletin to Lancow, the trains sent out in advance in the evening; at 1:00 AM, of 1 July, six corps, four cavalry divisions, and the army artillery reserve started the march. The execution of the retreat was not easy. The enemy, whose cavalry had caught up with I Corps about noon of the 30th, could be expected any moment from the line: Horitz—Neubidschow. If it were desired to avoid a flanking attack from that direction by crossing the Elbe, it must be expected that the Second Army would attack from the direction from the Mettau.

The march was resumed in the night in four columns on a narrow strip between the Lancow road, Gross-Burglitz, Sadowa, and the Elbe. As the numerous trains often blocked the road, the march columns were very long and friction could not be avoided, and it is not to be wondered at that at 10:00 AM, the III Corps was still at Lancow, that a rearguard with some artillery was seen at Liebthal (3 km. south of Koniginhof) and that only late at night, about 2:00 AM, the last troops reached their designated bivouacks in the region: Sadowa—Koniggratz—Elbe—-Trotina. The Saxon Corns and the 1st Light Cavalry Division had been drawn via Neubidschow and Nechanitz to Lubno and Nieder-Prim (2 and 5 kms. east of Nechanitz).

The army, brought back by Benedek, was a speinlekely defeated one. What had been left it of spirit up to the 30th, had been lost entirely through the night march. The sights, coming under the eyes of the commander-in-chief during this retreat, robbed him of the rest of his confidence in his army and in himself. He telegraphed in despair about noon on the 1st, upon his arrival at Koniggratz: "I urgently implore Your Majesty to conclude peace at any price; a catastrophe to the army is unavoidable."

PROBABLE SITUATION ON THE EVENING OF 1 JULY,
IF MOLTKE'S DIRECTIONS (TELEGRAM IN THE
NIGHT OF 30 JUNE-1 JULY, OCCASIONED BY
THE CHANGES IN THE SITUATION THAT
DAY), HAD BEEN FOLLOWED.

The Campaign of 1866

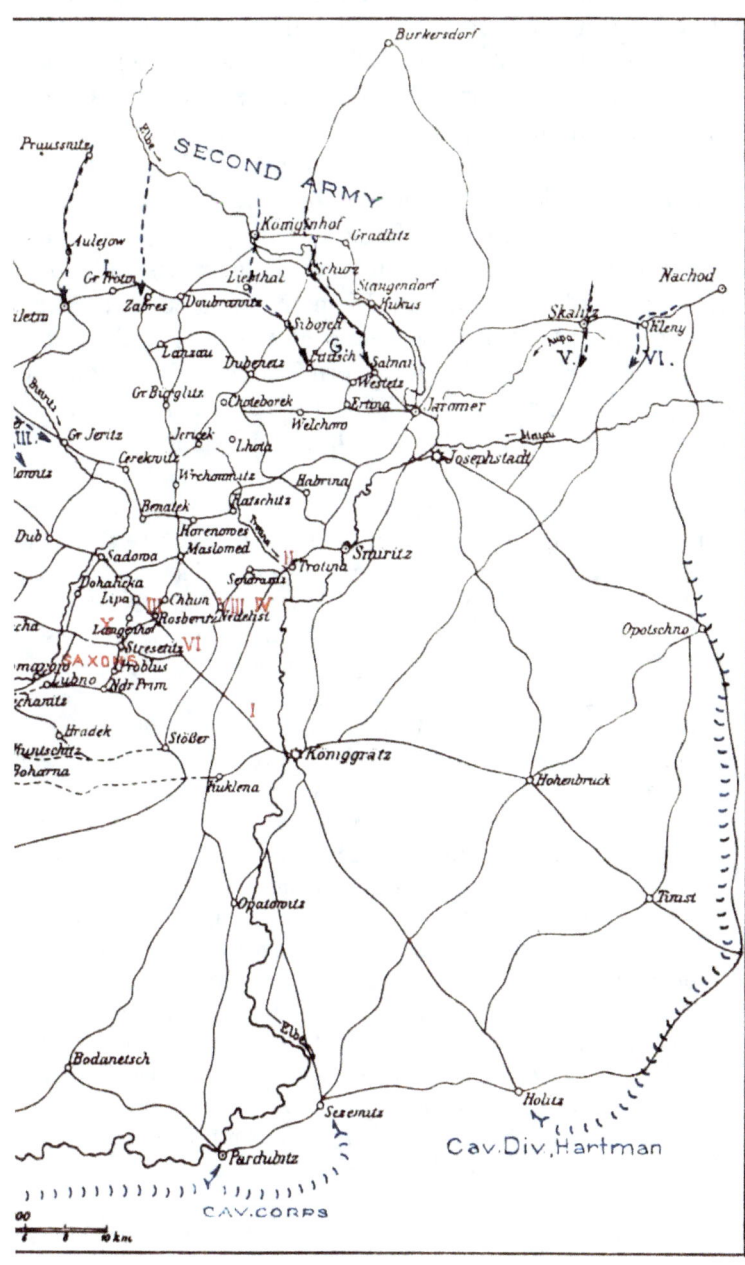

A catastrophe would surely have taken place, had the enemy followed even with cavalry alone, if the retreat had been transformed into flight and dissolution. But since no enemy was to be seen, since no encounter had taken place at any point, some hope arose again in the heart of the unfortunate general. Patrols were sent out in various directions in order to bring information about the inexplicable absence of the enemy. The telegram, arriving from Vienna in the afternoon: "Impossible to conclude peace. If unfavorable, I order you to retreat in the best order. Has there been a battle?", found Benedek more composed. He prepared the positions of the troops, was greeted by them heartily, spoke words of encouragement, ordered fortifications to be built on the side facing the enemy between Nedelist and Lipa and expressed his impressions and intentions in the following telegram:

> VI and X Corps have suffered terribly, the VIII very much, the I and the Saxon Corps have likewise suffered and need several days to assemble, the IV Corps also had some losses. Of eight corps, without a battle, and only with partial encounters, but two are intact, and these, as well as the cavalry, are greatly fatigued. The great losses were mostly caused by the needle gun fire, all who have even been in battle being greatly impressed by its murderous effect. All this forced me to retreat to this point. I found on the road the massed trains of the army, which could not be sent to the rear and if, under such circumstances, the enemy had delivered an energetic attack, before the I and Saxon Corps were again in order and the army somewhat rested, a catastrophe would have been unavoidable. Fortunately the enemy up to the present moment has not pressed forward; consequently, I will let the army rest tomorrow and send the trains to the rear, but can not remain here any longer, because by day after tomorrow there will be a lack of drinking water in camp so that I shall continue the retreat on the 3rd to Pardubitz. If the enemy does not intercept me, I shall be able to count again on the troops. Should occasion for an offensive movement arise, I shall deliver the blow, otherwise I shall endeavor to bring the army, as well as possible, back to Olmutz and to obey Your Majesty's order in so far as it lies in my power, yet always with unhesitating readiness for sacrifice.

Had this telegram reached, in some way or other, hostile headquarters, it would have been considered as a precious possession. And still, it did not contain anything that had not been known so far. The Second Army boasted of having defeated four hostile corps, and the First of having destroyed two. What could have become of these ruins after a night march undertaken hastily over a narrow strip? Although the cavalry, in spite of its urgent request, had been placed in security in rear of the infantry, Hartmann's Cavalry Division sent in a direction opposite to that of the enemy, and although the Prussians had cut off themselves wilfully from all information about the enemy, yet this much was known: the defeated enemy had retreated hastily and should have been pursued without delay. One part of the army should have marched behind him along the Elbe. Two other parts should have accompanied him on the right and left, turning towards his flanks as soon as he halted and took up the defensive. A fourth part, especially the cavalry, should have tried to intercept him, to bar his road, to hold him until the other parts arrived. Thus had Hannibal acted at Cannae, thus Napoleon at Jena, thus could it have been done here since the enemy could move or rest only in dense masses.

An order from Moltke, received during the night of 1 July, gave moreover, information concerning the method and direction of the pursuit. It read as follows

> The Second Army must remain on the left bank of the Elbe, its right wing ready to join the left of the advancing First Army via Koniginhof. The First Army must march without halting to Koniggratz. General von Herwarth will attack larger hostile units on the right flank of the advance march, cutting them off from the main forces.

This order was issued at the time when the Austrian main army was as yet on the right of the upper Elbe between Jaromer and Miletin, when Gitschin had been evacuated and the Second Army was awaiting an attack by Benedek. After the Austrian army had withdrawn, Moltke's instructions ought to have been adapted to the changed situation. The left bank of the Elbe should no longer have been occupied between Koniginhof and Jaromer, but wherever the enemy might have taken up a position on the other bank. Since the enemy had withdrawn to the south, the advance of the First Army should have been in a more southerly direction, the Army of the Elbe should have been shifted toward the right.

From this it is deduced: the Army of the Elbe should march in the direction of Chlumetz and Pardubitz on 1 July, about as far as Konigstadtl and Gross-Hluschitz (west of Neubidschow), the First Army, awaiting the neighboring army, advancing only as far as Neubidschow, Milowitz, Gross-Jeritz. The right wing of the Second Army should join the left of the First Army, the I Corps, already ordered to Aulejow, march on Miletin and Zabres, the Guard to Lititsch and Salnai. The left wing of the same army should go to Skalitz and Kleny. In the evening of the 1st, before the last hostile troops had entered the narrow strip at Koniggratz between the Elbe and Bistritz, the three Prussian armies would have stood on the line: Konigstadt—Kleny.

The Prussian Royal headquarters could not foresee whether the Austrians would make a stand on the 2nd or again withdraw before the attack; therefore, all measures should have been taken for a continuation of the pursuit. On the left bank of the Elbe, the Koniggratz—Hohenbruck—Tinist road could have been reached on the 2nd, on the right bank the right wing of the Army of the Elbe could almost have reached Bodanetsch (northwest of Pardubitz).

Only the road leading from Koniggratz via Pardubitz, Sezemitz, and Holitz would have been available for the retreat of the Austrians. For the retreat from the Upper Elbe to Sadowa, Koniggratz, and Tratina six corps needed 24 hours on the 1st, marching on four roads. Eight corps on three roads would have needed much more time. Before the rearguard could have gained room for the march, it would have been overtaken by the I and the Guard Corps, coming via Horenowes and Smiritz, and at the same time the flanks of the miles-long columns would have been attacked by the corps of the First Army and the Army of the Elbe, marching on parallel roads. The Austrians would have had to halt and take the defensive. Even the leading columns might have been prevented from escaping if the Prussian cavalry had been utilized correctly and, of course, had been armed for the purpose. Had the cavalry corps taken from the start a place on or in front of the right wing of the Army of the Elbe, had Hartmann's Cavalry Division accompanied the left wing of the Second Army, the former would have been able to block in good time the crossing at Pardubitz and Sezemitz, the latter the road from Holitz. The Austrian army would have been surrounded in the evening of the 2nd, no matter whether it went forward, backward, or remained stationary.

It was quite out of the question for Moltke's order to be executed in this manner or any other. Both army headquarters did not think of pursuing the enemy, still less of surrounding or annihilating him. All that had transpired so far was considered by them as an introduction to the war. The battles waged so far were not to be ascribed to the one or other side as considerable gain or loss. Strength had been tested and weighed on both sides. The troops would now have to be assembled into one mass and a decisive battle fought. But the "decisive battle" had already been fought on the 27th, 28th, and 29th. During these three days, the right wing and the center of the Austrian army had been thrown beyond the Elbe, after hot fights. Moltke had succeeded during the last day in bringing forward at least part of the numerous reserves, in throwing back entirely the hostile left wing and thus forcing the remainder of the Austrian army to retreat. The battle had not come out as had been desired and expected. It was not a battle of annihilation, but it was, at least, a battle rendering the greater part of the hostile army unavailable for further fighting. Nothing could be changed in the incomplete results obtained by preparation for a newly planned battle. An attempt should have been made by immediate pursuit to recover what had been lost.

Though Moltke's plan had been badly disfigured, the armies were placed not unfavorably for such a pursuit. The fact that the Second Army remained on the left bank of the Elbe especially allowed of itself the cutting off of the retreat, as was attained with difficulty in similar campaigns of 1757, 1800, and 1870. But army headquarters opposed strenuous objections to this remaining on the left bank of the Elbe. Separated by the river from the First Army, it thought itself exposed to "isolation and defeat." This apprehension was in great contrast to the existing condition of the Austrian army, defeated in six encounters and combats. Had the latter been on the left bank of the Elbe, it would have been

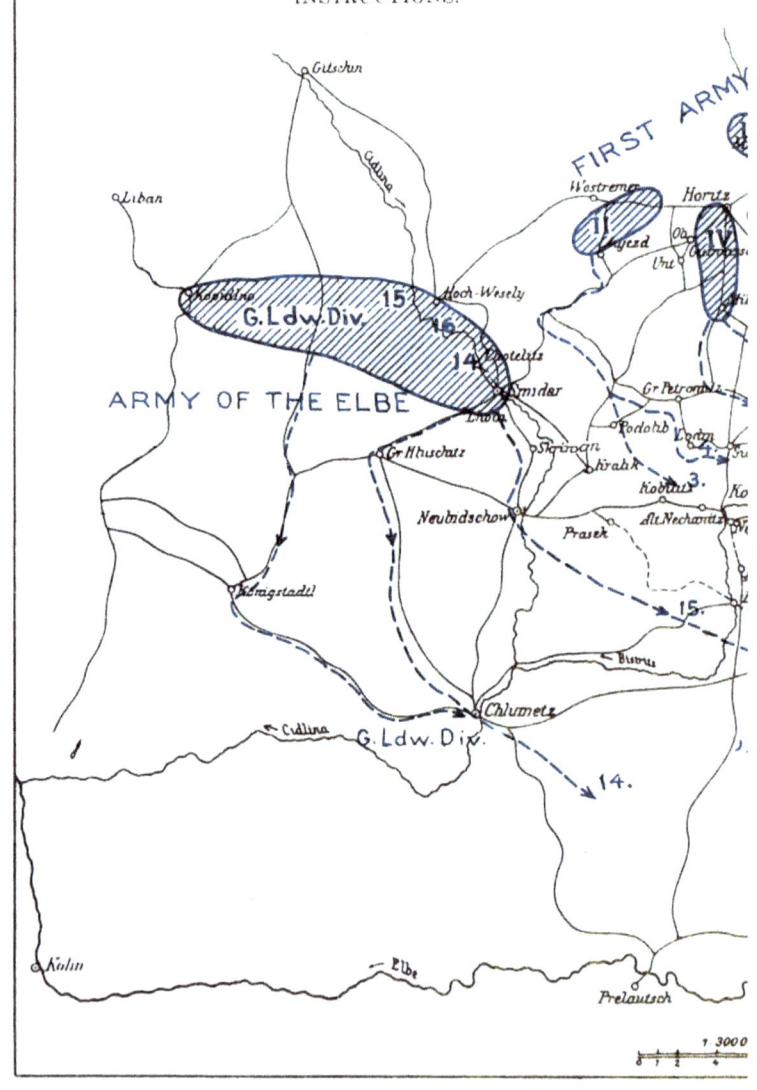

The Campaign of 1866

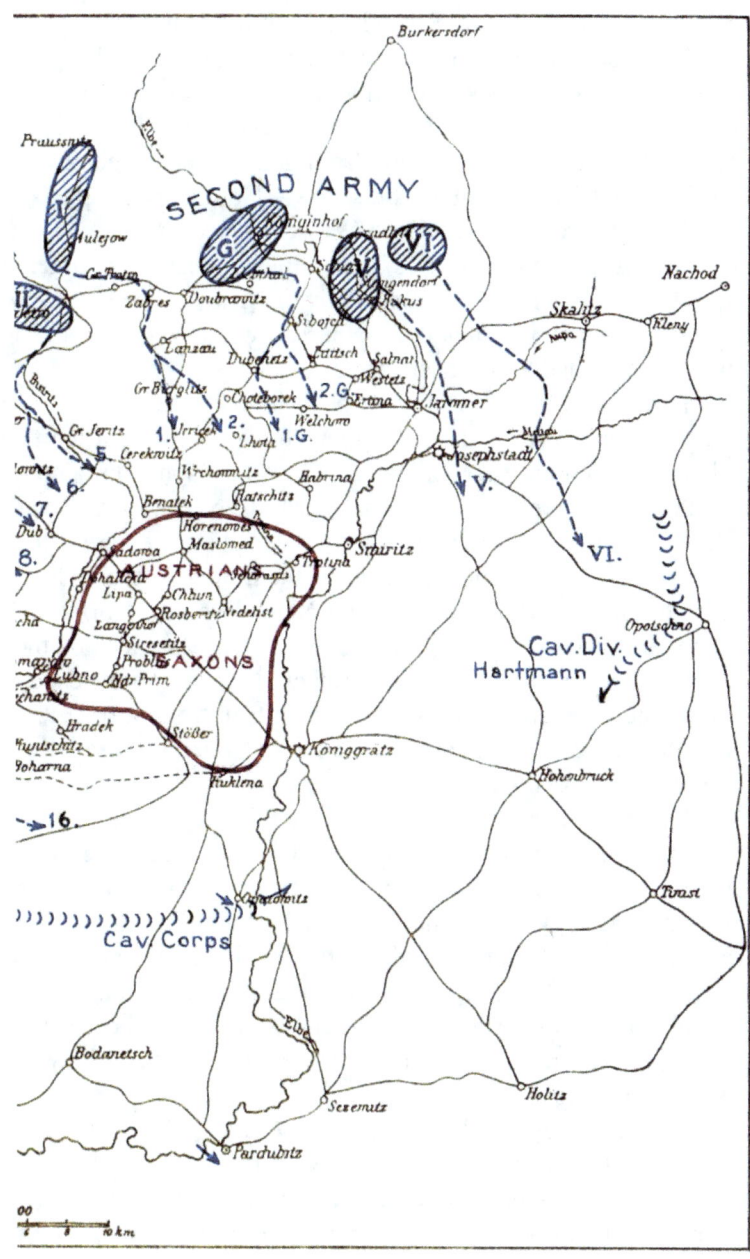

necessary to bring the First Army and the Army of the Elbe to that bank, but never to take the Second Army to the right bank.

Moltke succeeded with the greatest difficulty only in keeping three corps on the left bank on 1 July, while the I Corps went as far as Prausnitz and its advance guard as far as Aulejow. However, he could not prevent the First Army from going after the enemy to Horitz—Miletin instead of Neubidschow—Horitz, or the Army of the Elbe from turning toward Hoch-Wessely instead of going in the direction of Chlumetz. It was impossible to resist the urgent request for a day's rest on the 2nd. Only the Army of the Elbe was expected to march to Smidar. Thus pursuit was abandoned and a new campaign had to be considered.

Many believed the enemy to be behind the Elbe between Koniggratz and Josefstadt, while others thought him at Pardubitz, still others at Kolin. But Moltke wanted to know something more definite before preparing for a new attack; the Second Army was ordered to clear up the situation by a reconnaissance across the Mettau. In the meanwhile, the Army of the Elbe was to march on the 3rd to Chlumetz, the First to the line Neubidschow—Horitz, the I Corps to Gross-Burglitz and Cerekwitz, the remainder of the Second Army remaining on the left bank. Moltke's order ended "should there remain any strong hostile units in front of the Elbe, these should be immediately attacked with as great a numerical superiority as possible."

There were, in reality, strong hostile units said to be in front of the Elbe. For at the time when the order was issued, Benedek telegraphed to Vienna: "The army will remain tomorrow in its position. at Koniggratz; the day's rest and the abundant food have had a good effect. I hope no further retreat will be necessary." The Emperor's question: "Has there been a battle?" induced the general, 24 hours after he had reported his army as exposed to a catastrophe, to prepare for battle in a position in which he was absolutely sure to be surrounded.

However carefully the Prussians had avoided maintaining touch with the enemy, the immediate vicinity of the Austrians could no longer remain concealed during the day of rest. The outposts of the Prussian advance guard at Milowitz and those of the Austrian rearguard at Dub could not be more than 2 km. distant from each other. An officer from headquarters of the First Army, having boldly broken through the outposts, reported: II Corps at Sadowa, X Corps at Langenhof; in rear of these toward Koniggratz; the I and the Saxons near Problus. Another officer, who had ridden beyond Gross-Burglitz, had found Benatek occupied and a cavalry regiment advancing toward Josefstadt from Miletin had observed large bodies of infantry.

It could be concluded with a great degree of probability that the entire Austrian army or at least its greater part, was still in front of the Elbe behind the Bistritz. The right wing did not extend beyond Benatek, the left reached at least as far as Problus. The latter case, foreseen in Moltke's order, had thus happened. The enemy, still in front of the Elbe, must be immediately attacked "with as great a numerical superiority as possible," i.e., with all available forces.

The spirit of the order would have been obeyed had the First Army advanced against the supposedly 12 km. long front: Problus— Benatek, the Army of the Elbe and the Cavalry Corps prolonging the right wing and the I Corps and the Guard Corps the left. These overlapping wings would have pushed the enemy in his narrow front and deep formation, against the Elbe. For blocking the left bank, the V and VI Corps, as well as Hartmann's Cavalry Division were available which should have started the march as early as on the 2nd. Great marches had to be demanded of the left wing of the Second Army and of the Army of the Elbe. But, since the Landwehr Division of the Guard had made on that day 35 km. from Kopidino to Nechanitz, the younger and better trained troops could have fulfilled the request in the highest degree.

If not a complete, at least a partial surrounding could have been made on the 3rd. It would not have been rendered easier had the First Army stormed forward from the very beginning. It would have been more advantageous to await the coming up of the wings. Should it so happen, which was hardly to be expected, that the enemy would break through across the Bistritz, he would find himself so much the quicker and surer in the annihilating, all-encompassing surrounding movement. Such a deployment and such an attack corresponded to the ideas of Hannibal at Cannae, of Napoleon at Jena, but in no way to the views held in those days.

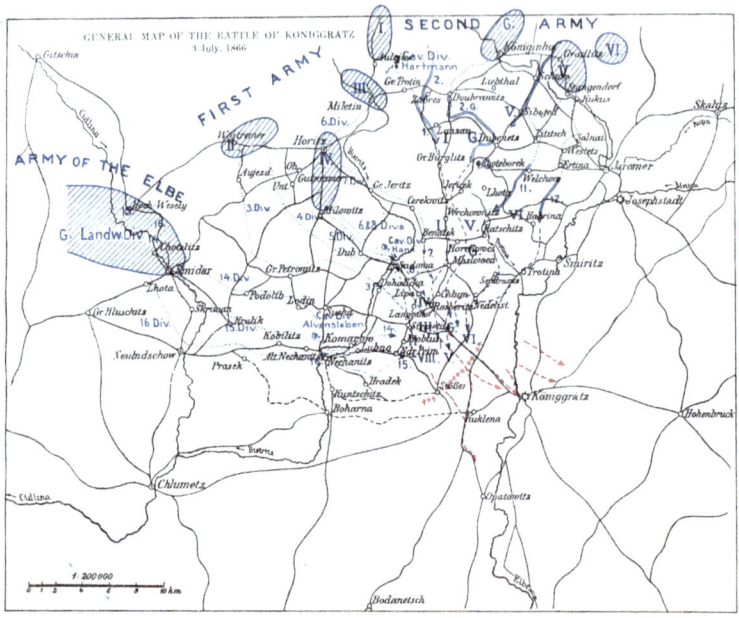

Mass attacks against the front and heaping up of reserves were considered more important than surrounding movements and flanking attacks.

Headquarters of the First Army was the first to receive the reports concerning the whereabouts of the Austrian troops on the right bank of the Elbe. Itis desired to choose independently the measures for the execution of the attack ordered. According to the picture evolved in its views, the enemy occupied "with very considerable forces," (two corps), the "position of Sadowa," and with one corps that of Problus. Against the former, five divisions of the First Army were to assemble at Milowitz, one other, the 7th to join them at Sadowa, after coming from Gross-Jeritz via Cerekwitz and Benatek; against the latter position—the Army of the Elbe was to assemble at Nechanitz.

The position of Sadowa was to be sought beyond the Bistritz on the heights of Lipa and Langenhof. A mass attack, even of 70,000 or more men, against the front of this strong position, defended by a numerous and excellent artillery, promised no success. The situation of the Army of the Elbe seemed more

The Campaign of 1866 215

favorable. The left wing of the enemy, no matter how far it extended beyond Problus, could not find a secure support. But close behind the Saxons the I Corps had been reported. Two corps should surely be able to repulse the attack of two to three divisions of the Army of the Elbe.

In spite of the disadvantage of these conditions, headquarters of the First Army was sure of success, held that its mass attack of 70,000 men would be irresistible and the "annihilation" of the enemy assured. The possibility of a flanking attack from Josefstadt alone caused concern. Headquarters of the Second Army was requested to parry such a flank attack with the Guard Corps from Koniginhof. The request was granted. The VI Corps was sent to demonstrate at Josefstadt, the V Corps and the Guard were placed beyond the Elbe in reserve, the I Corps marching via Miletin to Gross-Burglitz and Cerekwitz. Thus six divisions were held fast in front of Josefstadt, the same number at Sadowa, three at Nechanitz (facing a difficult problem), while two marched alone to an indefinite goal and an indefinite fate.

The Prussian successes were won so far through the "needle gun fire" and by "outflanking." The needle gun fire was now to be limited as much as possible by mass and deep formation and outflanking to be met by shortening the front. The strength of the Austrians lay in the long artillery lines, well and effectively posted, their weakness lay in the shock tactics. The Prussians had thus to accept these and attack. them in the front.

If the picture, evolved by the First Army, were true to reality, the 3rd would probably have brought no results either for the one or the other side. Since, however, not four but eight Austrian corps had remained this side of the Elbe, the plan of battle, issued from the common laboratory of the two army headquarters, contained dangers for the Prussian arms. Fortunately, the chief of staff of the First Army went on the evening of the 2nd to the Royal Headquarters at Gitschin to report what had been reconnoitered and ordered. As the troops of the First Army were already on the march, the orders issued for the attack against the front could no longer be directed through the suitable channels. It was necessary to rely upon the inability of the enemy to take the offensive.

On Moltke's recommendation, the King ordered that the

Second Army "advance with all its forces to support the First Army against the probably approaching enemy and attack as soon as possible." Since the question now was of hours only, it was impossible to cause part of the Second Army to advance on the left bank of the Elbe. All four corps were crowded together in the narrow strip between the Elbe and the Bistritz. This limited the hope of an attack against the rear of the enemy to the possibility of finding a bridge below Josefstadt or of restoring one. This possibility could be ascertained only during the course of the day. Moltke's next endeavor was to execute an attack against the left flank of the enemy, even if this should expose the front to a breaking through.

Considering the proximity of the enemy, Benedek expected an attack on the 3rd or on the 4th at the latest. The troops should then take position as follows: the III Corps on the heights of Lipa and Chlum; to its right the IV Corps on the heights between Chlum and Nedelist; and the II Corps in the space between Nedelist and the Elbe. To the left of the III Corps, the X Corps was to take position at Langenhof and the Saxon Corps on the heights east of Tresowitz and Ponowitz. According to the representation of the Crown Prince of Saxony that on these heights his flank was exposed from Hradek, the Saxon Corps was sent back to Problus and Nieder-Prim and the VIII Corps was kept in support in addition to the 1st Light Cavalry Division. The general reserves were: the I Corps at Rosnitz, the VI at Wsestar, the 2nd Light Cavalry Division south of Nedelist and the 1st and 3rd Reserve Cavalry Divisions at Briza.

As all others, the front of this position had its weak points and disadvantages. Thanks to the numerous and excellent Austrian, and the insufficient and badly employed Prussian artillery, these would scarcely have been noticed. So much the greater care should have been given to the flanks. The left was entirely in the air. The VIII Corps, only 3 brigades strong, defeated at Skalitz, was not able to ward off the dangers threatening through this condition. Resting the right flank on the Elbe was quite illusive. The river did not form an impassable obstacle, least of all for artillery projectiles. The river was bridged at many points and at others it was possible to construct bridges or to ford it.

The position here was untenable if even a part of the Second

Army advanced on the left bank. Should that army remain on the right bank and near Nedelist encounter serious resistance, part of the troops would have penetrated, without army orders, with elemental force to the unoccupied opposite bank and would have forced the hostile right flank to retreat. Should the Austrians remain stationary, they would be crushed, almost entirely surrounded, and annihilated. Hope of success lay in the offensive alone. Should Benedek stand firm on the right wing and in the center, and advance with four or five corps and as many cavalry divisions via Tresowitz, Nechanitz, Kuntschitz, etc., against the weak Army of the Elbe, and against the right flank of the First Army, a victory lay entirely within the scope of possibilities, provided, however, that the Austrian army was capable of such an offensive.

Above all, it was an essential condition that the right wing should maintain its position. This prerequisite was eliminated when the commander of the IV Corps, Count Festetics, found the position assigned to him, between Chlum and Nedelist, unfavorable and advanced to the heights of Maslowed which seemed better, and when the commander of the II Corps, Count Thun, in executing his order to cover the right flank of the IV Corps, followed to Maslowed-Horenowes and left only Henriquez's Brigade at Sendrasitz. The Austrian Army stood thus between Horenowes and Problus, instead of between Benatek and Problus, as reports made it appear, though it amounted almost to the same thing. The advance of the First Army and of the Army of the Elbe against this position led to three separate battles at Nechanitz, Sadowa, and Benatek.

The Army of the Elbe started at 3:00 AM, from Lhotz, Smidar, Chotelitz, and Hoch-Wesely in three columns to Prasek, Kobilitz, and Lodin. From these points it might have reached the left bank of the Bistritz, via Boharna, Kuntschitz, and Nechanitz. But on the report that Nechanitz was occupied, Herwarth assembled all three columns in order to break through, with one irresistible column, this 1000 meter defile, consisting of dams and bridges, situated in front of Nechanitz. The commander of the advance guard, General von Scholer, had already sent out two battalions via Kuntschitz, one via Komarow, and had thus opened the defile, driven off the

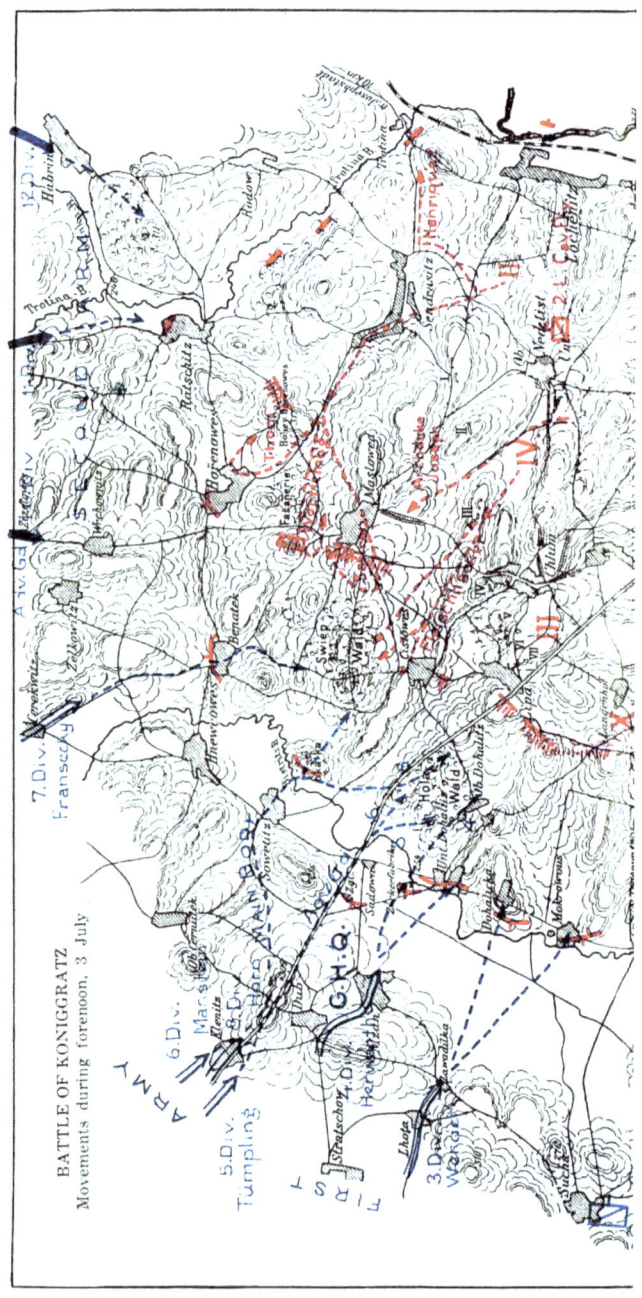

BATTLE OF KONIGGRATZ
Movements during forenoon, 3 July

The Campaign of 1866

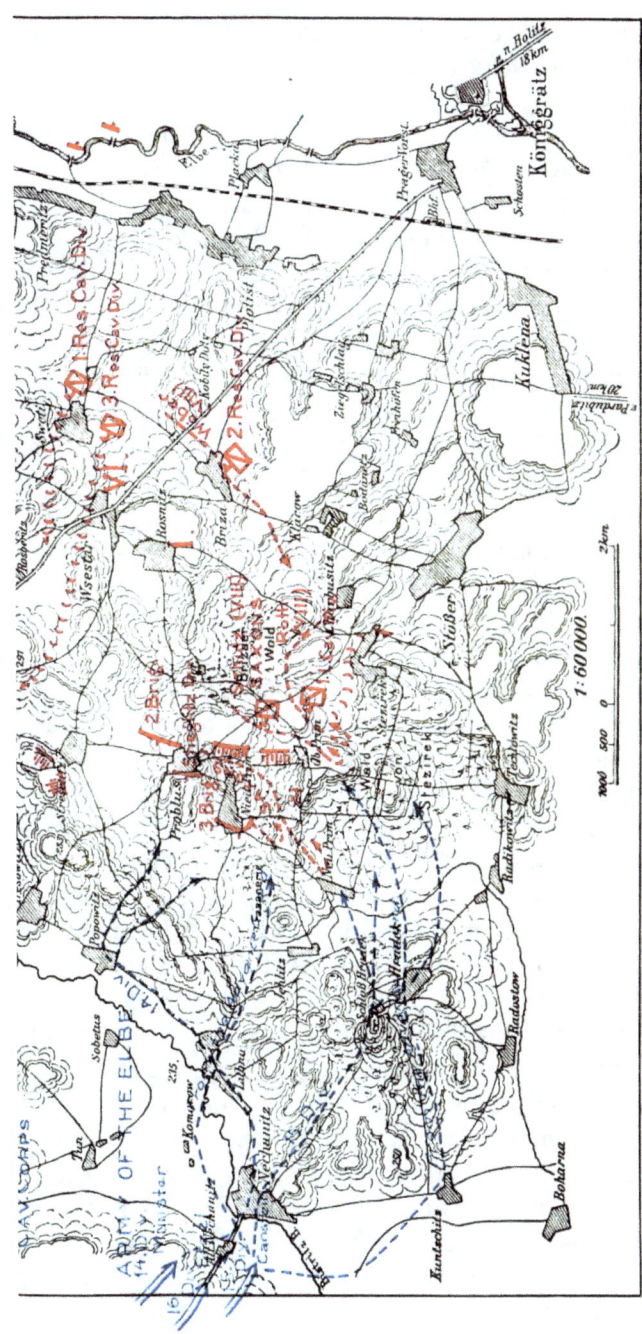

weak enemy and advanced with his seven battalions to the line: Hradek—Lubno. Covered by this position, one division could cross after the other.

The hostile position, whose left flank was believed to have been reconnoitered at Nieder-Prim, was to be attacked from the south, this appearing to be the most natural and logical plan. The advance guard, its left wing resting on the Bistritz lowland, could remain stationary for the present, the leading Division, (Canstein's), could join the attack by the right and through the wood of Stezirek via Ober-Prim, the following divisions (Munster's and Etzel's) and the Cavalry Corps gradually extending the right flank. Moltke absolutely required such a flank attack. Herwarth, on the contrary, held to an advance against the front. Canstein was to turn via Neu-Prim and the Fasauerie to Nieder-Prim, and Munster to advance from Lubno through the Popowitz wood on Problus. So much would be conceded to Moltke that one of Canstein's brigades would be directed through the wood of Stezirek to Ober-Prim. More could not be done, with the best of good will, for the old man.

Cannonading sounded warningly from Sadowa. The battle there seemed to be at a standstill if it were not receding. It was a sacred duty to go "to the rescue of the First Army." It was still more important to hold Etzel back west of Nechanitz. He should remain there in case the two other divisions were driven back through the 1000 meter defile by the numerical superiority of the enemy. Herwarth's instructions were fraught with great danger, should the enemy fall upon Canstein's right with his numerous reserves, and with his right wing and the left wing of the X Corps, attack Munster's left flank.

Of the hostile troops, the Saxon 2nd Brigade was in tcuch with Gablenz between Stresetitz and Problus. The 3rd Brigade occupied Problus and Nieder-Prim with one regiment each. Three batteries had gone into position between the two villages. In rear of Problus stood Stieglitz's Division (the Life Guard and 1st Brigades), six reserve batteries and the Cavalry Division. The left flank was covered southeast of Problus by Schulz's Austrian Brigade, which had sent its two batteries into position north of the village and finally by Roth's Brigade near the Briza wood. Consequently there were, considerable forces at hand to enable them taking a general offensive against the enemy sooner or later and to surround him on both sides.

Such movements, however, did not belong to the spirit of the times. A forcible piercing of the evening's position seemed more to the point. Scholer's advance guard was an excellent means to that end, advancing in front of the two divisions, on the right through the woods of Stezirek, in the center through Neu-Prim and the Fasauerie and on the left toward the Popowitz woods. The Life Guard Brigade with one battery was brought up. It was to advance over the meadow grounds south of Nieder-Prim against Neu-Prim, Schulz's Brigade covering its left flank. Six companies of the garrison of Nieder-Prim joined it. Two battalions were driven back, the Fasauerie and Neu-Prim were taken. At this juncture Scholer's right flank battalion arrived. It had driven the Austrian battalion from the Waldvon Stezirek and advanced against Ober-Prim opening fire against the left flank of the Life Guard Brigade.

The piercing was not continued. The flank and rear had first to be secured. The six companies from Nieder-Prim returned to their posts. The Life Guard Brigade drew closer to the village. The 2nd Brigade was sent to its support from the extreme right wing and Roth's Brigade was sent to the support of Schulz's. The cavalry divisions were to go around the woods on the south.

Schulz's Brigade drove the Austrian battalion away from Ober-Prim end pursued it south through the woods. Within the woods it encountered Canstein's right brigade. Of the left brigade only six companies continued the march to Neu-Prim, the rest entered the woods through a misunderstanding and fell unexpectedly on the flank of Schulz's Brigade engaged in combat with the right brigade. Schulz's Brigade retreated in confusion, carried Roth along, was thrown at Ober-Prim upon both Saxon brigades, which were preparing to resume the attempt to breakthrough. Rapid fire from the wood and from the six companies arriving from Neu-Prim was poured into the mass of the four brigades.

Confusion and retreat ensued under cover of a few steadfast battalions. "In order to prevent a spread of the rout," the 1st Brigade was placed behind an abatis at the edge of the wood east of Problus, three reserve batteries drove up on the east in prolongation of the southern edge of Nieder-Prim. Schulz and Roth occupied the western edge; Weber's Brigade which had just arrived, occupying the southern edge of the Briza woods. Canstein's Division had to stop its pursuit before the wide front: Nieder-Prim—Briza woods. Headquarters of the Army of the Elbe might now have had a misgiving that Moltke was not so very wrong, that Munster ought to have been on the right and not on the left of Canstein and that no more effective support of the First Army could have been given than by driving back the enemy from Problus and Nieder-Prim to Stresetitz, Langenhof, and Lipa. They must now wait until Munster should come up, and until he and Canstein, by a concentric attack, should drive the enemy to a position farther east.

The troops of the First Army, opposite Sadowa, had already been put in readiness during the night. At 6:00 AM, the advance guard of Horn's Division advanced from Klenitz in deployed front. Dub was evacuated, but the Zegelei west of Sadowa, was occupied. A combat took place at this point. An Austrian battery, in position between the Holawald and Swiepwald took part. As soon as the first shot was heard, Fransecky started his division at 7:30 AM, from Cerelkwitz towards Benatek. At about the same time the 5th and 6th Divisions deployed at Klenitz.

About 8:00 AM, Herwarth (4th Division), followed by the reserve artillery of the II Corps reached Mzan via Stratschow, WerderZawadilka via Lhcta and the Cavalry Corps, Sucha. All villages on the Bistritz from Popowitz to Sadowa inclusive of the Zuckerfabuck south of Sadowa and the Skalka woods were occupied by the enemy. Fransecky's advance guard was also under fire coming from Benatek and Horenowes.

The King arrived at Dub at 8:00 AM, and ordered the Bistritz line to be captured. Horn left his advance guard in position against Sadowa, turned with his main body and the reserve to Sowetitz and crossed the brook at the Skalka. The enemy evacuated Sadowa. Horn sent two battalions to join Fransecky and turned with the rest toward the Holawald. Herwarth had engaged early at Mzan in an artillery action, marched against the Zuckerfabuck and Unter Dohalitz and crossed the Bistritz. Both divisions, Herwarth and Horn, penetrated into the Holawald and occupied the southern edge

The Campaign of 1866

as well as Ober Dohalitz keeping twelve battalions in rear of the woods. Werder's Division succeeded in occupying Dohalitzka and Mokrowous. A success was achieved. The advanced hostile detachments on the Bistritz were driven back.

But on the heights of Lipa and Langenhof, as far as Tresowitz stood a long line of 160 guns. The smooth bore guns of the Prussians could do nothing against them and were withdrawn; the rifled guns, few in number, without room for deployment and not under united command, were at a decided disadvantage. In the lowland, guns in rear of the ridge and their effect could not be observed on account of the fog and powder smoke. Their shots, blindly fired, did not prevent the enemy from concentrating his fire on the Holawald and Upper Dohalitz.

On the southern edge of this point, on a front of 1200 meters, stood first seven, then nine and finally eleven battalions crowded into adjacent columns. They presented an impenetrable wall to all attacks, a wall which, however, was greatly damaged by ceaselessly exploding shells, broken branches and falling trees. A strong line of skirmishers, well posted, one or at the most two battalions, as had been done with the well known 2nd Battalion, 37th Regiment, at Nachod, would have afforded greater security and suffered smaller losses. But, most important of all, it would have been able to gradually work up to effective range. A larger number of battalions stood in rear of the wood and occupied Sadowa. They were not in security. For at will and according to the humor he was in, the enemy let his batteries play on them too. Finally, the 5th and 6th Divisions crossed the Bistritz and awaited, under a devastating shell fire, the order to advance.

For on both sides, the two leaders watched with eagle eyes for the favorable moment to attack. Should the Prussian columns attack, they would suffer Augereau's fate at Preussisch-Eylau, should the Austrian masses advance, the fate of Hertweck's Brigade at Nachod would surely be theirs. But of all means to attain victory, only piercing the enemy is worthy of a great general. The hour of a Wagram or an Austerlitz must strike at last.

"Not yet," said Moltke. "It will not succeed and, should it succeed, the two annihilating flanking attacks will fail in their effect."

"Not yet," said Baumbach, Benedek's chief of staff, on the other side. "Such battles last, at least, two days. Tomorrow when the combatants will have fought to utter exhaustion, it will be time to send forward Claim's and Rammig's Corps (I and VI)." He might also have said: "If we should succeed in driving back the Prussians in front of us, the flank attacks would wreak our destruction so much the quicker."

Both commanders were content. Prince Frederick Charles wanted to await the arrival of the Crown Prince. Benedek felt sure that "his old soldier's luck" would grant him the opportune moment. Thus they waited and waited.

Fransecky's Division had come under artillery fire from Horenowes and Maslowed at Benatek. The position of the hostile right wing on the line: Lipa—Maslowed—Horenowes, thus showed itself. The march of the Divisions of Horn and Fransecky was directed against this part of the position via Sowetitz and Benatek and, against this part they should have advanced, to hold the enemy at this point while Herwarth and Werder solved a similar problem on the other side of the road, Manstein and Tumpling lengthening the line at least as far as Nechanitz, six divisions attacking the long front, leaving the Army of the Elbe free for the flanking attack. But obeying the rule of assembling masses, Horn turned toward the Holawald, Fransecky wishing to reach the same goal via the Swiepwald and Cistowes.

This flank march by Fransecky along the front of two corps could not succeed. It is true that the hostile advanced troops were driven out of Benatek and further out of the Swiepwald and that even Cistowes was occupied. But when the enemy made a counterattack from the line: Chlum—Maslowed— Fasauerie, Fransecky had the greatest difficulty in escaping from being surrounded on the south and east. The southern part of the wood was lost to him, though he held out in the northern part and in the houses west of Cistowes by straining all his forces.

Lieutenant Fieldmarshal Mollinary, who had taken over the command of the IV Corps in place of the wounded Count Festetics, wanted to follow up the advantages gained. He proposed to Count Thun to advance with his right wing from Horenowes. Fransecky was to be driven off by an attack from all sides, after which the entire Prussian position on the Bistritz would be rolled up. This was splendidly planned. But 38 Austrian battalions took the longest time to overpower 14 Prussian ones. It is doubtful if five fresh battalions at Horenowes and six others in the center would have sufficed for the execution of the magnificent project. However that might have been, Benedek's order put a stop to the offensive which had hardly begun: "the IV and II Corps will return to the position Chlum, Nedelist, Elbe, to which they were assigned." Mollinary's personal representation was of no avail. A telegram from the Commandant of Josefstadt had arrived, saying: "The VI Prussian Corps apparently intends to operate against the right flank of our army from Gradlitz via Salnai, etc.; strong columns are marching past here."[*]

The Prussian Second Army which, it was hoped would remain inactive on 3 July, as it had been during previous days, had begun to move. Mollinary's proposition to attack the new enemy with the I and VI Corps, did not inspire confidence. Now that the entire Second Army was advancing, the execution of the offensive movement was impossible, even had the I and VI Corps come up in time. All that could be undertaken was the detiense either of the foremost line: Maslowed—Horenowes—Trotina—Back or the line, situated more to the rear, Chlum—Nedelist—Elbe. Both could be held a certain time, especially if the defender were reinforced. But neither could be held indefinitely.

The selection of one or the other was of no importance. It was bad in any case that the II and IV Corps had to be withdrawn. To take troops out of a serious and bloody combat, means to declare them defeated, means to tell them that they are not able to cope with the adversary. This was here so much the more critical as the Austrians had arrived, through the battles of the foregoing days, at the conviction that they were unable to cope with the better arms of the Prussians. It was doubtful if the II Corps would have been able to execute a long flank march and to form "a defensive hook" between Nedelist and the Elbe. The two corps of the right wing began to retreat and from this retreat developed naturally the

---

[*] Compare map, pages 228-229.

retreat of the entire army.

The Brigades of Saffran and Wurttemberg of the IT Corps were taken back to Maslowed from the combat at the Swiep-Wald, having to march thence toward Nedelist. To cover this march, Thom's Brigade moved from Horenowes to the hill between Maslowed and Sendrasitz, taking along 40 guns and a weak infantry detachment at Horenowes fronting north. Henriquez's Brigade was holding Ratschitz and the wooded bank of the Trotina, with two battalions, occupying later a position, Trotina village with four battalions. Of these, one kept the space between the creek and the Elbe under observation and the other secured the bridges at Lochenitz and Predmeritz. These were loose rear guards, easily surrounded and easily rolled up, who, about noon opposed the advancing Second Army.

The latter had not hurried. Moltke's order had been sent at midnight from Gitschin, reaching headquarters at Koniginhof about 4:00 AM, and only at 7:30 AM, did the 1st Division of the Guard, stationed there, receive the order to begin the march. At 8:30 AM, the advance guard of this division at Doubrawitz received orders to occupy a position there, entrench itself and await further orders. General von Alversleben did not allow this order to keep him from answering Fransecky's call for help, which reached him at the same time, and marched immediately to the rescue. One hour later the main body followed.

At 4:00 PM, the IV Army Corps had been given discretion to start before the arrival of army orders. Five and one half hours later, the advance guard started from Aulejow. At 11:00 PM it had not yet reached Gross-Burglitz. The VI Corps was instructed to start from Gradlitz, the 12th Division leaving at 6:00 AM, the 21st Brigade at 7:00 AM, and the 22nd Division at 8:00 AM, in order to make a demonstration against Josefstadt, after having crossed over to the right bank at Schurz, Stangendorf, and Kukus. The columns, already on the move, had only to be diverted to their new points of destination.

Thus marched the I Corps, followed by the Cavalry Division, via Gross-Trotin and Zabres to Gross-Burglitz, the Guard via Doubrawitz, Dubenetz, and Choteborek to Jericek and Lhota, the 11th Division followed by the V Corps, via Sibojed and Lititsch to

Welchow, the 12th Division via Salnai, Westetz, and Ertina. Continuing the march, the 1st Division of the Guard reached Choteborek, the 11th Division, on the right bank of the Trotina, the heights north of Ratschitz, the 12th Division, Habrina, all at 11:00 AM. The 1st Guard Division and the 11th Division had in front of them the great battery of Horenowes, the 11th and 12th encountered at Ratschitz and at the hill east of the Trotina detachments of Henriquez's Brigade.

At Wrchowitz, as well as northwest of Ratschitz, 48 guns were brought into action. The infantry advanced at this juncture. Ratschitz and the hill on the other bank of the Trotina fell into the hands of the Prussians. The advance guard of the 1st Guard Division finally succeeded in taking Horenowes from the west and in forcing the hostile battery to retreat. All three divisions advanced further, with some fighting: on the right to the hill of Horenowes, then to the plateau east of Maslowed, in the center to the south of Ratschitz and further to Sendrasitz, on the left via Rodow against Trotina Village.

Again they met in their front an artillery line, extending from north of Chlum to Nedelist. Under cover of 120 guns, three brigades of the Austrian II Corps retreated through the defile of Maslowed to Nedelist, left one brigade at this point, and continued their march to occupy a position to the eastward.

The Austrian IV Corps began the retreat much later than the II. The almost entirely unscathed Brigade of Archduke Joseph took up a position between Chlum and Trench III. The remnants of the Brigades of Brandenstein and Poekh sought security farther back. Fleischhacker's Brigade was still occupying Cistowes. On the Prussian side the 12th Division was held back at Trotina by Henriquez's Brigade. The 11th Division could not advance from Sendrasitz in the direction of Nedelist because of the hot artillery fire. Only the 1st Division of the Guard (about 8 battalions) succeeded, under cover of artillery which arrived at Maslowed, in descending southward to the lowland, and, covered by fog and powder smoke, possibly also by the tall wheat, in climbing the steep slope opposite.

The Austrian infantry, exhausted by march and combat, depended on the protection of their strong artillery. The latter,

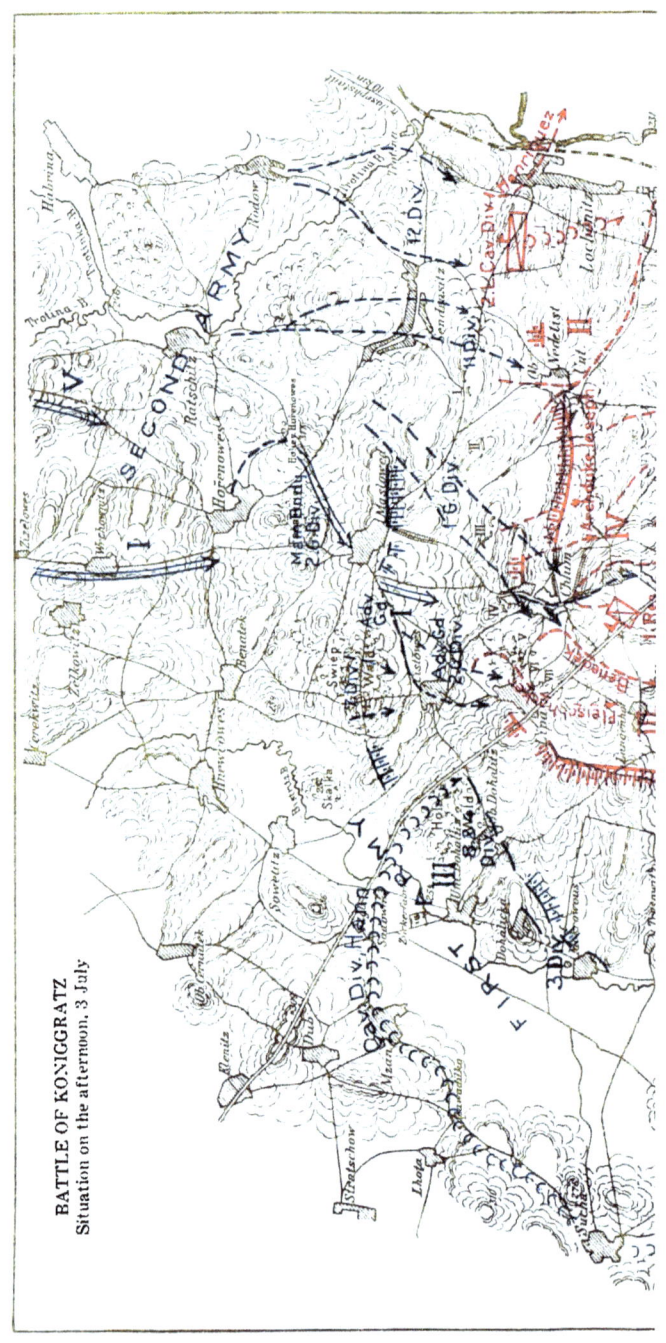

BATTLE OF KÖNIGGRATZ
Situation on the afternoon, 3 July

The Campaign of 1866

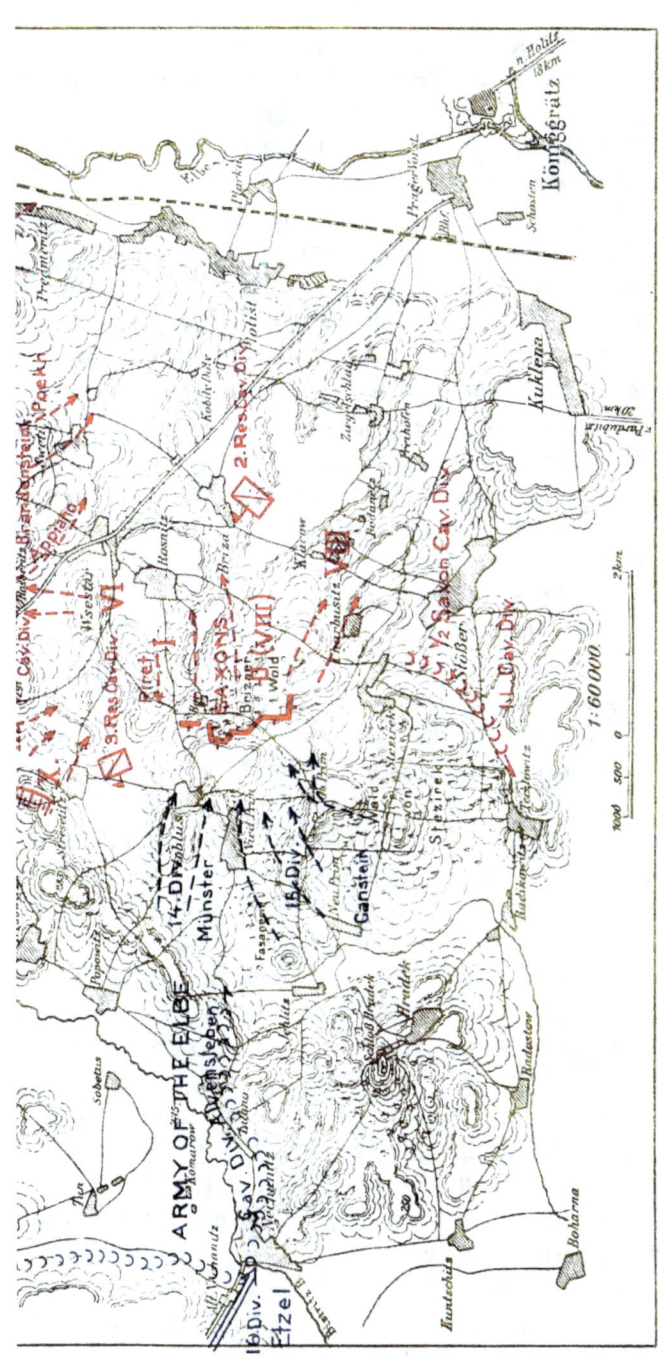

however, was kept occupied by that of the enemy. The battalions of the Guard came up unexpectedly from the lowland, swept the nearest batteries and unsuspicious battalions of Joseph's Brigade, with rapid fire, forcing them to retreat. Brandenstein's and Poekh's Brigades were carried along. The IV Corps retired in the direction of Sweti. The 11th Division advanced now also against Nedelist. Henriquez's Brigade, threatened in flank, withdrew, followed by the 12th Division, toward Lochenitz. The remaining three brigades of the II Corps had lost the cover of their left flank by the departure of the 4th Corps, and evacuated Nedelist and their position east thereof. The entire Corps attempted to cross the Elbe at Lochenitz and Predmeritz. The Guard advanced further near Chlum in an easterly direction and took likewise this weakly garrisoned point. Counterattacks of Benedek's Brigade from the south were repulsed by rapid fire. Rosberitz was occupied during the pursuit, as well as the Lipa woods and Lipa, under cover and with the support of the advance guard of the 2nd Division of the Guard.

Almost at the same time, about 3:00 PM, the concentric attack of Canstein and Munster against Nieder-Prim and Problus took place. It was not awaited. The enemy could not suppose that one division of the Army of the Elbe was holding out in rear of Nechanitz and that another was in the Popowitz woods. He was sure that both would soon prolong the right wing of Canstein. He was not strong enough against their attack. Two Saxon Brigades were defeated while still endeavoring to resume order. One of them was still greatly shaken by the affair at Gitschin. The VIII Corps, according to the report of its Chief of Staff, was destroyed. It was necessary to escape the threatening annihilating surrounding movement. The gradual retreat, under cover of the 3rd Brigade and the artillery, was now ordered. Munster and Canstein found only rear guards.

"In close formation and in truly imposing attitude," Schwarzkoppen's Brigade emerged from the Popowitz woods. Problus was taken with the first rush. Hiller's Brigade followed south of the wood as right echelon. It found Nieder-Prim already occupied by Canstein's troops, the artillery gone and it continued against the Briza wood.

The attack of the 1st Division of the Guard from the one side, of Canstein's Division from the other, shook the entire structure of the enemy. Here and there was necessary only a little assistance to make it crumble up.

The Second Army had taken Lipa, Chlum, Nedelist, the northern part of Lochenitz, an advanced detachment had occupied Rosberitz, and the Army of the Elbe occupied Problus and Nieder-Prim, while the First Army maintained its former positions. On the Austrian side, the II and IV Corps and Benedek's and Appiano's Brigades were retreating via Sweti and Wsestar. The two other brigades of the III Corps, as well as the infantry of the X Corps, felt themselves too much threatened in their positions between Lipa and Stresetitz and also started on the retreat, with the exception of a few detachments, in the general direction of Koniggratz. Fleischhacker's Brigade of the IV Corps attempted first to escape from Cistowes north of Chlum, turned back and wanted to join the stream of the retreating troops via Langenhof near Lipa. Schimpff's Brigade of the Saxon Corps had taken the direction of Rosnitz and Briza, while Stieglitz's Division followed by Schulz's Brigade of the VIII Corps held the Briza wood and the two other brigades of this corps assembled at Charbusitz.

To protect the retreat in the center and on the right wing fell to the share of the artillery. It continued to fire from the line: Lipa—Stresetitz, against the Holawald, thus holding back the First Army. Another artillery line had formed between Langenhof, Wsestar, Sweti, and beyond this village. It wished to halt any advance of the 1st Division of the Guard. In rear of it Sweti, Wsestar, and Rosnitz were still held by the infantry.

Benedek was occupied almost entirely and exclusively with the enemy at Sadowa during the first hours of the afternoon. He awaited an opportune moment to put into execution the great offensive blow. Archduke Ernest, Commauder of the III Corps, had attempted independently to attack with one brigade the Holawald, but was repulsed. Benedek, still thinking about a repetition of the attack in greater force, only learned what was taking place on his flanks and in his rear, when Chlum had already been taken. He decided to restore the battle or, at least, to cover the retreat with his reserves, the I and VI Corps, which had advanced into the space between Rosberitz and Bor. Piret's Brigade of the I Corps was sent to Problus, Rammig was ordered to retake Rosberitz and Chlum with the VI Corps, and three brigades of the I Corps were kept in reserve.

Although 24 and then 12 more Prussian guns appeared at Chlum, the 1st Division of the Guard was in a critical situation. Its eight battalions were distributed over a large extent of terrain. About 120 guns took the villages of Rosberitz and Chium, as well as the batteries of the Guard, under a devastating fire. Hard pressed, the few scattered battalions seemed unable to oppose any resistance to the attack of an entire corps. Nevertheless Benedek's intended attack had no prospect of enduring success. Such mass attacks had so far always failed and, should this one succeed in the beginning, it was bound to come against the numerous troops coming from the rear and break up of itself. The 2nd Division of the Guard and the I Corps were expected any moment from the north, while the First Army would come up from the west.

The most effective plan would have been for the VI Corps to penetrate between Sweti and the Elbe. This would have quickly forced the Austrian reserves to retreat. The V Corps, would have to follow the VI directly. With the mass of two corps, supported on the right by the 2nd Division of the Guard, it would have been possible not only to prevent the Austrians from crossing the Elbe over the bridges above Koniggratz, but also the troops could have been sent across the Elbe to invest the eastern front of the fortress. Should the army of the Elbe advance also from Ober-Prim to Charbusitz with Etzel's Division, brought up at last, toward Stosser, and the Cavalry Corps should advance to Kuklena, the retreat to Pardubitz would also have been cutoff, Only a few Austrians would have escaped, the greater part would have been hemmed in, and the attack of the reserves would only have increased the disaster.

Such a result of the day was prevented by the measures taken by the Prussian army and corps commanders. The 2nd Division of the Guard had turned left from the Horenowes—Maslowed—Chium road in order to take its place between the 1st Guard and the lith Divisions. The corps commander had sent it, however, te the other wing to fight against Fleischhacker's unfortunate Brigade which, cut off from the rest of the troops, sought only an outlet from its plight and could no longer be caught up with. The marching column of the I Corps was drawn from the right, and that of the V Corps from the left, toward the center by the army commander. They were to march straight to the "historical lindens" of Horenowes and form a strong, handsome, but entirely ineffective reserve.

Only the advance guard of the I Corps had freed itself and reached the threatened Chlum from Benatek. Of five divisions condemned to inactivity, only one could have followed the road, traced by the course of events, could have advanced between Sweti and the Elbe, and could have barred the way to the stream of fugitives, at least north of the main road. The corps commander was restrained from such decisive plan by the easily explained feeling of having to assist the hard pressed Guard. The 11th Division received orders to turn to the right, to advance against Rosberitz—Sweti, while the 12th Division was to hold Lochenitz and Predmeritz with weak forces, advancing with the rest to the right.

Thus all thought of pursuit was abandoned, the mass of the Austrian Army was allowed to continue its retreat unmolested and all available forces were employed to fight against the two reserve corps. Of these the VI Corps had advanced first. Even the narrow front of a brigade column could have executed an enveloping attack against the narrow, weakly garrisoned southern point of Rosberitz. The two to three battalions, which occupied the village, were slowly driven back to Chlum. On the southern edge of this village and near the defile leading to Nedelist and occupied by the Rifles, the attack came to a halt, then changed into a retreat. A second attack, executed by brigades of the I and detachments of the ITI Corps, had the same result, after the advance guard of the Prussian I Corps had reached Chlum, sent in support of the Guard. The retreating troops were threatened at Rosberitz on the one hand by the right wing of the 11th Division advancing from Nedelist, on the other by one brigade of the Cavalry Corps.

The Austrian artillery, between Lipa and Stresetitz. held out a long time. Enveloped by the Army of the Elbe, the left wing at last retreated. On the right, a few batteries held on, continuing their fire until the rapid fire from Lipa laid low first the horses, then the

BATTLE OF KONIGGRATZ
Situation on the evening, 3 July

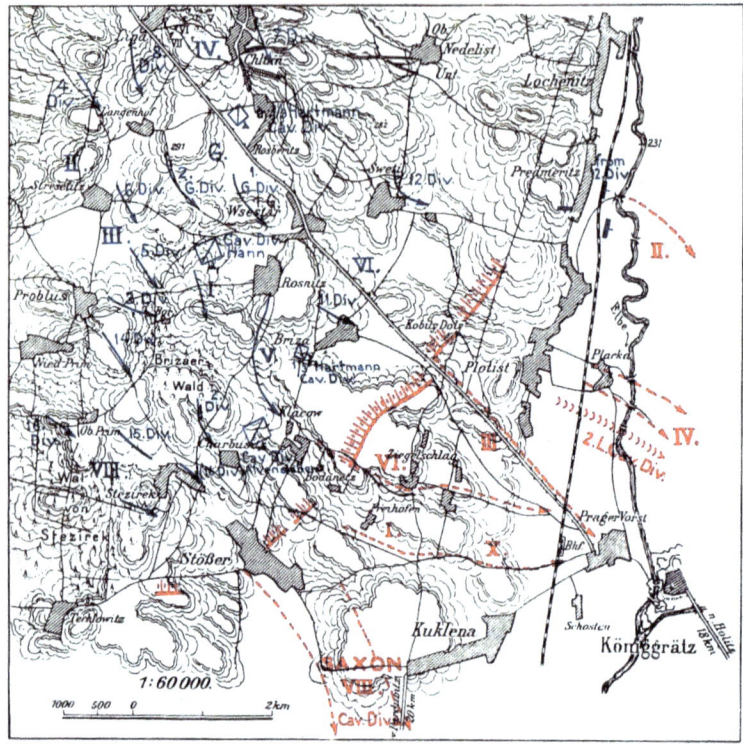

men. When the fire ceased, the First Army started, taking along at its head the two brigades of the Cavalry Corps which were at Sadowa. The foremost of these reached Rosberitz, when the retreating brigades of the Austrian I Corps were seeking to evade the attack of the 11th Division. The Reserve Cavalry Divisions of Prince Holstein (1st) and Coudenhove (3rd) advanced to cover the hard pressed infantry.

Combats ensued between this cavalry and the brigades of Hann's Division, and later, between it and the leading regiments of Alversleben's Division,* which were hurrying from Nechanitz to

---

* The Division "Alvensleben" was assigned to the Elbe Army; the Division "Hann von Sucha" was moved to the area north of Sadowa.

Stresetitz. Success hung in the balance, but rather favored the stronger and more closely formed Austrians. But, even after a successful attack, they broke under the fire of the infantry advancing from Lipa, Dohalitzka, and Mokrowous. However, they gave the last retreating infantry the urgently needed time to escape from their pursuers. The long resisting artillery did not fare so well, losing part of its horses by fire and falling helplessly into the hands of the enemy.

As soon as the cavalry combats had ceased, the infantry continued its advance. The VI Corps occupied the farm buildings on the main road south of Sweti, as well as Rosberitz and Briza. The Army of the Elbe had, in the meanwhile, repulsed the attack of Piret, had taken the Briza wood and occupied Stezirek with a brigade of Etzel's 18 infantry and 3 cavalry divisions. The dream of the commanders was realized. The three armies were assembled in one compact mass in the narrowest of space. They might advance now in close formation. But a hostile line confronted the Prussians on an equal front.

The Austrians had again placed in position their remaining, but still quite numerous artillery, with the right wing on the Koniggratz—Josefstadt road near the road to Sweti—Plotist, and the left wing in the vicinity of Stosser. This artillery apparently was resolved to oppose obstinate resistance. Yes, it might even seem that the enemy intended to execute a counterattack. For southwest of Stosser there appeared new batteries and forced, with their fire, Etzel's Brigade to retreat from Stezirek to Ober-Prim. Moltke might charge the Army of the Elbe, the commander of the Second Army might charge the V Corps and Hartmann's Cavalry Division with the pursuit, but first of all, the strong barrier, opposing all advance, would have to be broken.

The First Army had found it impossible that morning to advance straight against such a line of artillery. A flanking attack, an envelopment or a turning movement, studiously avoided, would be found unavoidable. There were abundant masses for the execution of such a movement. 200,000 men assembled on one narrow little spot, offered a wonderful sight which, however, made Prince Frederick Charles exclaim: "What wouldn't I give if I could command here and establish order!"

No one could be found to undertake this Herculean work during the remaining short hours of the evening and then to lead these masses or part of them in a flank attack. On the height of Rosnitz a council took place among all who could claim to be strategists, as to what Napoleon or Gneisenau would have done. This was quite a superfluous question as neither the one nor the other of these men would have placed himself in such a situation. This much was gleaned from the pros and cons of the views: nothing more can be done today.

This negative result was unavoidable. Moltke wanted to envelop, surround, and annihilate. For this purpose the wings should have been made strong and brought forward. The right wing of the entire army should have taken the direction of Chlumetz, Pardubitz, Holitz, the left somewhat that of Tinist across the Mettau. The essential thing was to prevent the enemy from marching to Vienna or Olmutz, i.e. in an easterly, southeasterly, or southerly direction. The commanding generals held different views: they wanted to strengthen not their wings, but their center, not send their wings, forward, but keep them away from all operations against the enemy's flank and draw them toward the center. The right wing should not go to Chlumetz, Pardubitz, Holitz against flank and rear of the enemy, but to Nechanitz against the front, the left wing should not advance to Tinist across the Mettau, but across the Elbe to the right bank.

They did not think it necessary to prevent the enemy from going to Olmutz and Vienna, but wanted to drive him there. Not the eastern and southern sides of the hostile position should be reached, but it should be attacked from the west and the north. The consequent execution of these principles had assembled the three Prussian Armies into one mass and brought it directly opposite the hostile front. The ideal, which the theorists had created was attained. It was possible to break through the enemy with 200,000 men. But the enemy did not move from the spot and continued to pour his fire into them. Thus was the Austrian army saved, at the sacrifice, it is true, of 44,000 men (24 per cent) and 188 guns. A success, even a very great success had been achieved, but not the success which the Prussians had already had in their hands. The army commanders had seen to that.

Benedek, however, could claim in the saving of his army a merit that should not be underestimated. It surely was not fortunate that the general accepted the battle with the Hibe in his rear, that he wished to gain the victory by a mass attack against the hostile front, and that he allowed in silence the right wing to wheel from the line: Chlum—Nedelist—Elbe, to the line: Chlum—Maslowed—Horenowes. But when misfortune seemed to befall him, he showed himself a true leader. By the attack of his reserves against Rosberitz and Chlum, the attacks of his cavalry and the placing of his artillery he surmounted the greatest evil as well as possible. He saved at least three fourths of his army. This success was then spoiled in the most unexpected way.

The troop units had become badly mixed, especially after the II and IV Corps, as well as the 2nd Light Cavalry Division, attempted to cross the Elbe above Koniggratz while the 8th and the Saxon Divisions together with the remaining cavalry divisions tried to cross below the fortress, The principal stream of the fleeing troops was directed towards the fortress itself. The troops held the naive belief that Koniggratz had been built for the purpose of assuring them an unmolested crossing of the Elbe.

The Commandant on the other hand, insisted that he had to hold the fortress for his Emperor against friend and foe alike and that Austria could not perish as long as Koniggratz held out. He closed the gates. The troops found themselves in front of impregnable walls, flooded ditches and flooded fields. Wedged in a labyrinth of water courses and morasses, pressed from behind, they could proceed neither forward nor sideways. A mass of vehicles and guns was thrown into the waters, mounted men, pushed to the edge of ditches, fell in and drowned. The Commandant reported to Vienna: "Entire Corps are intermingled in and around the fortress, climbing the palisades, swimming across the ditches and the Elbe, scaling the walls of the principal enceinte, and the defense is entirely crippled. I beg for orders."

Fright and confusion increased when the compressed masses began to fire their rifles to produce the impression that the enemy was already on the opposite shore. Finally at 11:00 PM, came permission to pass through the town. The stream of men pressed through the narrow streets, crowded over the bridges, and flowed ceaselessly toward Holitz.

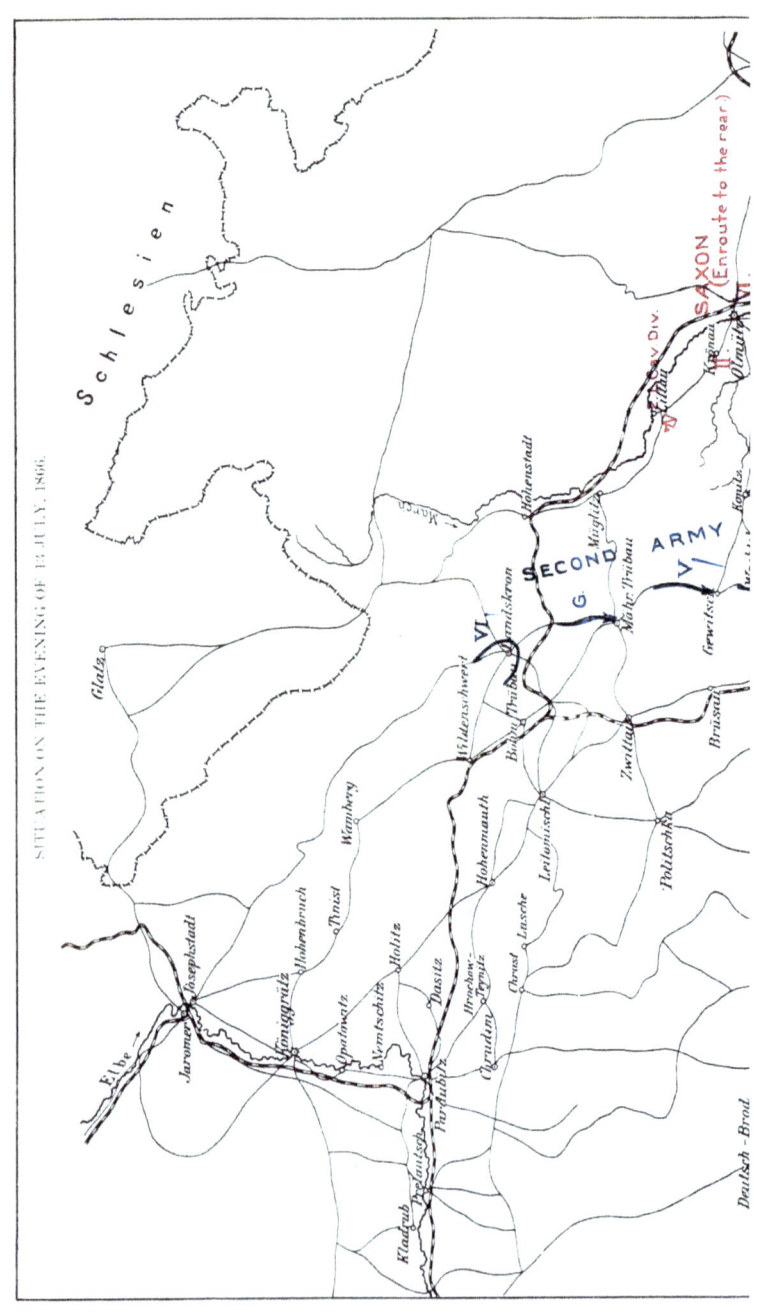

The Campaign of 1866

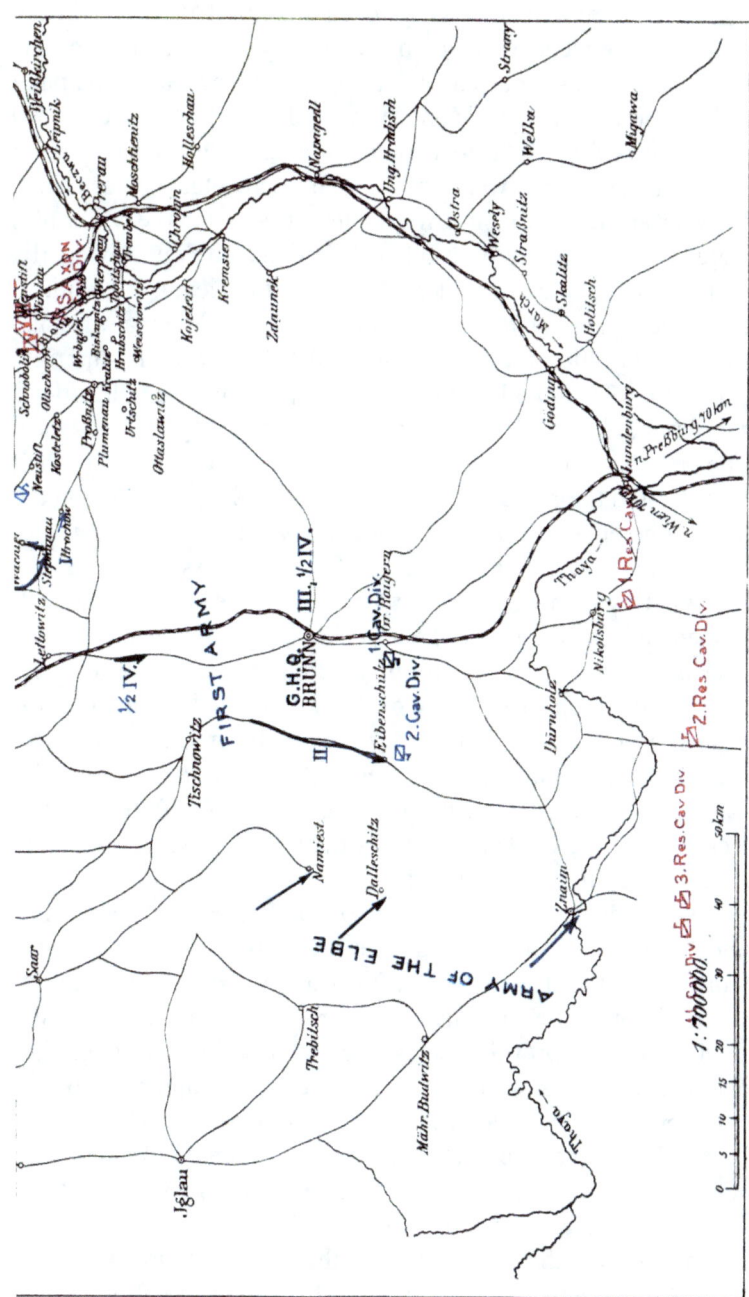

From there, Benedek telegraphed at 10:00 PM: "Catastrophe to army, apprehended day before yesterday, completely overtook it today." A catastrophe had in reality taken place, but the battle of annihilation, planned by Moltke with such promise of success, had again miscarried. A third attempt could not be made in a similar form. The Austrians were no longer in the center between three Prussian armies, advancing from different sides, but the two armies were standing facing each other. The defeated could evidently, without being greatly molested, retreat to Vienna or Olmutz. Benedek decided on the latter point. The road to Vienna was long. The army would be entirely dissolved before reaching the right bank of the Danube. In Olmutz the troops would be able, after a shorter march, to regain their strength and capacity for resistance. The capital, moreover, could be better defended from there than from behind the Danube. By taking up a flanking position on the march, the enemy would be forced to abandon all yearning after Vienna and to accommodate himself to a hopeless siege.

But this plan did not find favor with the Vienna Cabinet. Immediately upon receipt of Benedek's telegram at noon, the 1st, a decision was reached to give up the Italian possessions, to bring up the thus disengaged Army of the South and continue the war against Prussia with increased strength. In order, however, to refrain from humiliating himself as a suppliant before the vanquished of Custoza, Emperor Francis Joseph offered to cede Venice to Emperor Napoleon and demanded as compensation the extension of the armistice with Italy.

Napoleon was pleased to put the recently created sister country under a new obligation: by another gracious gift, but he was still more pleased to deal a blow at Prussia who was already sure of being victorious. France had felt every success achieved by the small despised North German power as a blow directed against her own person. She saw herself threatened in her supremacy of the continent. Napoleon was now offered the opportunity of exercising the office of arbiter. He graciously accepted Venice and courteously offered to obtain an armistice not only with Italy, but also with Prussia, to hear the demands of all the parties and then to pronounce from the magisterial seat the verdict and to levy all the dues. But an armistice would serve neither Austria nor Prussia. The one wanted to regain what had been lost, the other wished to secure what had been won.

Both, however, accepted the mediation. Austria did not wish, after Koniggratz, to refuse the only friendly hand stretched towards her, while Prussia did not want to make a new enemy. Both tried to delay the mediator. Prussia dared not conclude an armistice without the assent of allied Italy and without knowing of the peace conditions. Austria did not want to surrender Venice until Italy had expressed herself, but she needed to bring up the Army of the South and secure its junction with the Army of the North. The Minister President, Count Mensdorff, went to Imperial Headquarters and attempted in vain to make Benedelk abandon his illusions. All he accomplished was that the X Corps was designated to be transported by rail to Vienna and four cavalry divisions were directed thither by marching. Benedek continued his road to Olmutz with seven Corps and one cavalry division.

The Army had been divided for this march as early as the 4th, into three columns, within which the scattered units gradually found their own corps. The main column (I, V, VI, and X Corps, the army reserve) was to march via Holitz, Hohenmouth, Leitomischl, Zwittau, Mahrisch-Trubau, Gewitsch, and Konitz, and all to reach Olmutz on the 10th or 11th,—a right column (II, IV Corps, 2nd Light Cavalry Division) via Hohenbruch, Wamberg, Wildemschwert, Landskron, Hohenstadt, Muglitz, and Littau, a left column (VIII and Saxon Corps and four cavalry divisions) from Pardubitz via Chrudim, Chrast, Politschka, Zwittau, thence one day's march in rear of the main column, via Mahrisch-Trubau, further on following the road of the right column via Muglitz and Littau. This program was put into execution with essential changes. The following turned aside: the X Corps at Zwittau via Brusau to Lettowitz to be transported thence by rail to Vienna; the four cavalry divisions from the line: Saar—Zwittau, to march in four columns also to Vienna via Trebitsch and Brunn.

Prussian Royal Headquarters were not quite clear on the 4th as to the magnitude of the victory gained. The enemy had retreated on the preceding afternoon to Koniggratz, but had remained immobile in front of the fortress. The battle had been stopped in uncertainty in the evening. It was quite right to suppose that the enemy would evacuate 'the right bank of the Elbe by the next morning, but not that he would continue the retreat on the other side. It seemed impossible to make a frontal attack on his position behind the Elbe. A turning movement, under cover of a strong protection for the left flank, must be sought above and below Pardubitz.

Only when Gablenz arrived in the afternoon of the 4th, from Holitz, declaring with downcast mien that his Emperor no longer possessed an army and begging for an armistice, did Royal Headquarters begin to realize the scope of the success achieved. One enemy had for the time being, been eliminated. The Second Army was entrusted with his pursuit. The King wanted to advance against the new enemy, who could at any moment appear at Vienna, with the First Army and the Army of the Elbe. The following troops reached the Elbe on the 5th with their leading elements: the Second Army at Pardubitz, the First at Prelautsch, the Army of the Elbe at Kaldrub. From these points the Second Army was to turn toward Mahrisch-Trubau, the First Army and the Army of the Elbe were to go directly towards Vienna. The latter reached the line: Brunn—Mahrisch—Butwitz, on the 12th with the left wing, via Chrudim and Politschka, with the right, via Deutsch—Brod and Iglau. They had come in touch, only in small encounters, with the four retreating divisions of the Austrian cavalry.

During the first days of the march, news was received that King Victor Emmanuel had declined Venice, offered to him by Napoleon and also would not grant an armistice. Italy wanted to become free and great by her own strength, obtain the provinces belonging to her, sword in hand, and not receive ancient Italian territory as a gracious present from the hand of her protector, and maybe have to pay a shameful price even beyond Nizza and Savoy. No armistice would be granted, but the Southern Tyrol was asked for in addition to Venice, and General Cinadlini was charged to cross the Po in the night of the 7th. The Austrian Army of the South was held fast and could not march to Vienna. The Capital was entirely unprotected. Only the Army of the North could be counted upon to save it.

The situation was thus greatly changed. Moltke had supposed until then that Benedek would assume the offensive after a short rest and recovery in an entrenched camp. Therefore the Second

Army was to advance to the line: Konitz—Littau, northwest of Olmutz. Should Benedek advance against it, it was ordered to retreat toward Glat, drawing the enemy still farther away from Vienna, possibly giving an opportunity to the First Army of attacking him in the flank and rear. Should however, the Army of the North endeavor to march to Pressburg or to Vienna, the Second Army should follow it immediately, while the First should bar its way via Lundenburg in the valley of the March, the Army of the Elbe taking upon itself security against Vienna.

At the moment when the probability of a retreat to Olmutz and the impossibility of an Austrian offensive was made clear, Moltke approved the proposition of the different army commanders to march to Prossnitz, Plumenau, and Urtschitz instead of to Littau—Konitz. He, of course, presupposed that the Second Army would try to attack and cut off the retreating enemy, driving him to the north or northeast.

Nothing of the kind was in the mind of the army commander. In his judgement, the wisely selected position would keep the enemy from any retreat. Should this not be the case, it would not be expedient to attack the greatly superior Austrians "on account of complete separation from the First Army" but as soon as the retreat of the enemy to the south had been recognized, he intended to "avoid the consequences by a junction with the First Army" and thus to give the enemy a free road to the Danube. Should, however, the position at Prossnitz serve only as a means of inspiring fear, it must be reached in time.

Since the enemy had had the advantage of three marches, it was advisable to take the straightest and shortest road, bringing all the corps, if possible, on one line. There were, at least, three separate roads, if the crossing of the Elbe and Pardubitz "were not chosen for the entire army, but if the three corps (the VI remained for the time at Koniggratz and Josefstadt) were allowed to cross the Elbe over three separate bridges to the left bank. A right column could march from Pardubitz via Hrochow-Teynitz, Lusche, Leitomischl, Zwittau, Brusau, Lettowitz to Urtschitz, a central column from Nemtschitz via Holitz, Hohenmauth, Leitomisch] (separately from the right column), Mahrisch-Trubau, Gewitsch, Konitz to Prossnitz, a left column from Opatowitz via Tinist,

Wildenschwert, Landskron, Muglitz to Ollschann.

But the Second Army preferred, first in a column of three, and later of four corps, to take the road from Pardubitz via Hohenmauth, Leitomischl, Bohmisch-Trubau to Landskron and thence via Mahrisch-Trubau, Gewitsch, and Konitz. The detour was not repaid by greater celerity. On the 12th, when the First Army and the Army of the Elbe reached Brunn—Mahrisch—Budwitz, the Second Army had covered only two thirds of the distance, reaching Gewitsch with its leading elements. This march time did not correspond to the zeal shown on the opposite side. Austria wanted to disengage the Army of the South at any cost. Napoleon did not acquiesce in her urgings that a French army and fleet would render Italy more complacent, especially by the occupation of the ceded Venetian territory.

Fortunately, though energetic orders were given in Italy, they were not energetically executed, thanks it is said to French influence. The crossing of the Po by Cialdini was not very dangerous. It would be possible to hold the Italian general in check with 86,000 men, used mostly for the garrisoning of fortresses. At least 50,000 could be brought across the Alps. Archduke Albrecht was appointed commander-in-chief of all the fighting forces. He wanted to assemble a great army near Vienna. Thither should flow together all that could be assembled at the depots, sent on the march, but, first of all, the Army of the North must be drawn to that point. As early as the 9th, on his arrival at Olmutz, Benedek received orders to send first the III Corps by rail, then the Saxon Corps. The remaining corps were now also called to Vienna.

Benedek created difficulties, not being able to. abandon his beloved plan of operating against the flank of the enemy, fearing also that forced marches would completely exhaust the army. An order to go to Vienna "without further objection" by rail and on foot via Pressburg, left him no choice. The Saxon Corps continued by rail. Benedek was going to start the march to Vienna with the other five corps, the 2nd Cavalry Division and the reserve artillery on the 14th or 15th via Pressburg. This great opponent of Prussia was going to be joined by another.

Napoleon had suffered a defeat at Sadowa, a second through Victor Emmanuel's distant attitude. His position as the arbiter of

The Campaign of 1866

Europe and the Chosen of the Nation had suffered a severe blow. It was absolutely necessary for him to restore his old authority should he wish to continue to hold his court in the Tuileries. Benedetti was sent as envoy to Prussian Headquarters in order to bring about, with all necessary pressure, first an armistice, then peace. That Prussia must not be permitted to grow too powerful, was the main point. Should it not be possible to strip the victor of all advantages, the increased power obtained which was his due should be compensated for by an equivalent cession of territory to France. Napoleon was neutral only in appearance. In reality he belonged already to the belligerents. He would seek, in the beginning, to reach his aim not by force of arms, but by negotiations and more or less concealed threats. The difficulty for the diplomats lay in the fact that Prussia was very willing to conclude an armistice, provided Austria meet her demands, but that this must depend upon the approval and acquiescence of united Italy, that Austria wished to know nothing either of an armistice or of concessions, and that Italy might refuse to lay down her arms.

In order to meet this opposition, Napoleon might be forced to throw his sword into the balance. "What shall we do if France marches?" was Bismarck's question.

"We must recross the Elbe," was Moltke's answer. "This must never come to pass. We must try to hold back France, meet her demands as far as possible, and, in the meanwhile, force Austria, by a new defeat, to accept our modest requests. The army, assembling at Vienna must be defeated before Benedek has time to reach it."

Again a letter was sent to the Second Army on the 138th, reading as follows: "It is, consequently, your task to prevent, under all circumstances, the junction of the Austrian Armies of the North and South."

On the 13th, the Second Army stood as follows: the Cavalry Division at Konitz; of the I Corps, the advance guard at Wachtel; Buddenbrock's detachment (3 battalions, 2 squadrons, 1 battery) at Hrochow; the main body at Stephanau; the V Corps at Gewitsch; the Guard Corps at Marisch-Trubau; the VI at Landskron. On the same day the hostile troops were at the following points: the 2nd Light Cavalry Division at Littau, the II Corps at Kronau, the IV at

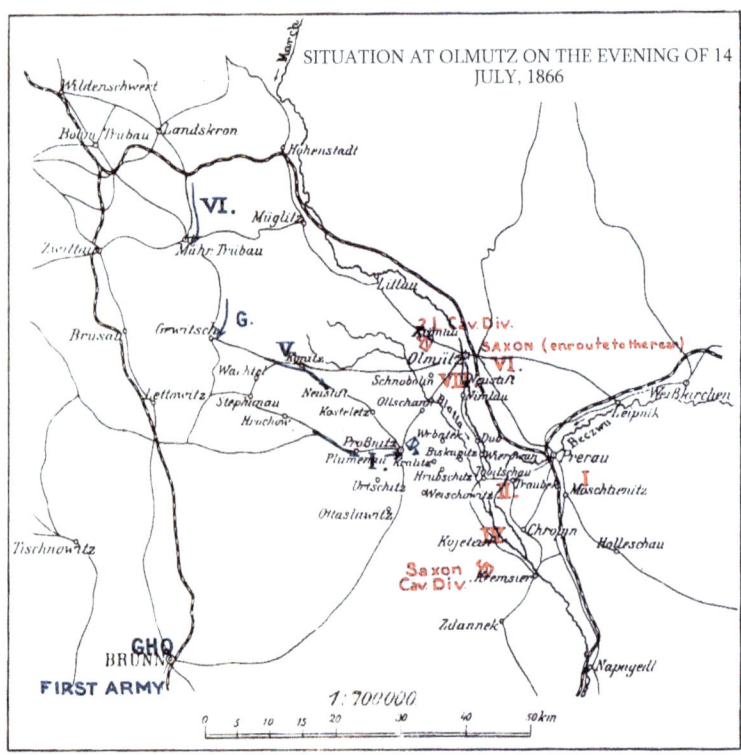

Schnobolin, the Saxon Cavalry Division at Nimlau, in rear of it the V and the not yet transported parts of the Saxon Corps at Olmutz, the VIII Corps at Neustift, the I at Prerau. On the 14th it was to march as follows: the VII Corns via Weisskirchen to the valley of the Waag, the Saxon Cavalry Division and the IV and II Corps to Kojetein and Tobitschau, the 2nd Light Cavalry Division to Kronau, the field trains via Prerau, Moschtienitz and beyond along the left bank of the March. A long column would, on the morrow, move therefore along the right bank of the March from Littau via Kronau and Schnobolin to Tobitschau and Kojetein. It was the highest time for the Second Army to commence its main task, that of cutting off the Army of the North.

Before Hartmann's Cavalry Division reached Kosteletz in the morning of the 14th, extensive clouds of dust were noticed from the heights of Hrochow arising between Littau and Olmutz and thence on the roads leading down the valley of the March. It was clear that the Austrian army was moving off. At Frossnitz, the cavalry of both sides had already clashed and, according to the inhabitants, an infantry brigade had marched in the morning through Kralitz. General Hartmann wanted to make an advance via Dub or Taubitschau in the direction of Prerau for which he requested the support of the infantry, and rode in person to the V Corps to Neustift (southeast of Konitz) in order to personally urge his demand. Steinmetz found the plan excellent, hut believed that he was too far away to be able to cooperate in it.

The I Corps was nearer and would surely be ready to give the necessary assistance. Hartmann obtained an order from the Crown Prince who happened to be there unexpectedly: "The I Corps will send this evening an infantry brigade with a battery to Tobitschau to occupy the crossings between Tobitschau and Traubeck."

It was evening before Hartmann reached Bonin at Plumenau with these orders: "It is too late today," was the answer, "but early tomorrow a brigade will start."

In the meanwhile, General von Borstel, Hartmann's second in command had started with the cavalry division to Prossnitz and sent the 1st Cuirassier Regiment to Tobitschau. This regiment encountered two outpost companies at Biskupitz and attacked them. The square formed by these companies was broken into two parts, many men being wounded. The regiment was, in the end, forced to retreat after losing 6 officers and 14 men.

In the evening, on the Austrian side the 2nd Light Cavalry Division was at Kronau, the VIII Corps at Neustift (south of Olmutz), the 2nd at Tobitschau, the IV at Kojetein, the I at Prerau. On the Prussian side the Cavalry Division and the detachment of Buddenbrock were at Prossnitz, the I Corps at Plumenau, the V at Neustift (southeast of Konitz)), the Guard Corps at Gewitsch, the VI Corps at MarischTrubau. The Second Army was widely scattered, two corps were far in the rear, but the Cavalry Division, the I and V Corps were close enough to prevent at least part of the Army of the North from marching off, to drive it back, or to pursue it. In view of the order to prevent, under any circumstances, the junction of the Armies of the North and South, it was necessary to act efficiently, straining all efforts for this purpose.

Army headquarters, however, did not deem such action

necessary. The report: "The Army of the North is retreating," was translated in view of information received "the Army of the North has retreated." The task of pursuing the enemy was, consequently, finished. The still existing, likewise ordered, task of forming a junction with the First Army remained to be solved. The Guard Corps and the VI Corps were to start immediately to reach Brunn on the 17th. The V Corps was to occupy Prossnitz first, to billet behind it at Plumenau, the I Corps to take positions at Weischowitz, Urtschitz, Ottaslawitz, the advance guard at Kralitz, to cover the road to Brunn. Both corps were charged to observe the supposedly evacuated Olmutz and "should information concerning the retreat of the enemy be confirmed," were to march to Brunn to support the First Army. The junction of the two hostile armies to be prevented, "under all circumstances," is not prevented, but allowed to take place; but the junction of the First and Second Armies was to take place, be that with or without Moltke's sanction. The plan did not succeed entirely, for the supposition that "the Army of the North has marched off," was not correct and the order "one brigade of the I Corps to march to Tobitschau," had not been countermanded.

On the 15th, the Austrian IV and II Corps were to continue their march from Kojetein and Tobitschau west of the March, the VIII following them from Neustift, the I remaining in Prerau, while the Saxon should prepare to entrain at the latter point. Count Thun considered the march on the right bank of the March as fraught with danger, decided to take the road crowded with trains on the left bank, and started, before an order to the contrary could reach him, at 2:00 AM with the II Corps via Traubeck and Chropin to Kremsier. Thus the VIII Corps started, considerably isolated, on the flank march at 4:00 AM, in the following order: three squadrons and 150 led horses, 60 vehicles, Rothkirch's Brigade, trains and vehicles, Roth's and Kirchmayer's Brigades, the 2nd Light Cavalry Division. Weber's Brigade was also to start at 4:00 AM, and as flank detachment, cover the march of the main column via Wratek and Kralitz.

Malotki's Prussian Brigade (4th and 44th Regiments) started, after agreement, at 4:00 AM, from Stichowitz and went via Prossnitz, Kralitz, Hrubschitz, Klopotowitz in the direction of

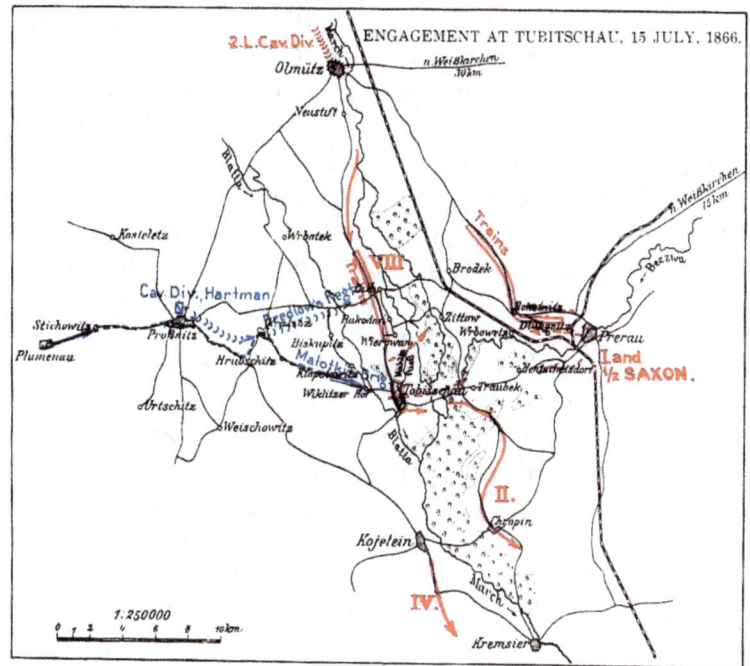

Tobitschau. The three squadrons, the led horses and the 60 vehicles had passed the town, before any contact could take place. Two companies of Rothkirch's occupied the latter, when a combat took place, between the advance guard companies on the one side and the flank detachment on the other, in the vicinity of the Wiklitzer Hof. The Fusilier battalion of the 44th Regiment, drove the enemy out of the wood northeast of the Hof and occupied it. The 44th Regiment supported at this point, deployed.

Malotki's battery, as well as the two batteries of Hartmann's Division which had just arrived, went into position at Klopotowitz, and engaged Rothkirch's battery, gradually reinforced from the artillery reserve, in the vicinity of Wierowan. The march column of the Austrian infantry turned to the right fronting along the road. As soon as the 44th Regiment had deployed, the 4th Regiment followed it on the right and Malotki gave the order to advance. The hostile left flank regiment, Toscana's, attacked by an enveloping movement, retreated partly east, partly north. Lieutenant Colonel von Bredow with the 5th Cuirassiers had found a crossing, hidden from the sight of the enemy, over the Blatta above Biskupitz and attacked unexpectedly the Austrian batteries at Wierowan.

Seventeen guns were taken, sixteen escaped via Rakodau, seven via Dub. Benedek, who had halted with his staff on the hill, was forced to ride off hurriedly. Rothkirch's Brigade threatened by Malotki from the south and by Bredow from the north, retreated to Littow. Detachments, which had returned to Tobitschau, were driven back by seven companies of the 4th Regiment over the Mulelenflies, the March and the Beczwa until they were received by detachments of the I Corps at Hentschelsdorf. Malotki went into position with the rest of his brigade at Wierowan. Archduke Leopold appeared opposite him with Roth's and Kirchmayer's Brigade at Dub. Wober's Brigade, prevented from solving its problem (covering the flank) by a small hostile detachment, and the 2nd Light Cavalry Division also came up. 22 battalions, 12 squadrons, and 40 guns did not attack, but allowed themselves to be held for 24 hours by Malotki's artillery fire, until the main body of the Prussian I Corps came up via Hrubitsch and Buddenbrock arrived via Kralitz.

The retreat was now begun via Dub and Brodek, and with one Brigade to Olmutz. Malotki remained on the March. The I Corps followed as far as the Blatta. Bonin did not wish to take further part in the combat. It was left to Hartmann with the Hussars Brigade, one squadron of Uhlans, one battery and one company in wagons, to carry out the planned attack on Prerau.

To receive the Austrian VIII Corps, the I (Austrian) Corps had sent forward from Prerau the following troops: Poschacher's Brigade north of Roketnitz, one battalion of Leiningen's Brigade into that village, two battalions to Dluhonitz, one to the southeast (between the Beczwa and the railroad), one to the west of Dluhonitz, and a battalion and a battery between the two villages. This battery and the two last named battalions were attacked by Hartmann, who crossed the Beczwa at Wrbowetz and occupied the crossing with one company. He succeeded in forcing the three Austrian units to retreat. The battalions standing in and near Diuhonitz were carried along in this retreat and the trains, marching on the Roketnitz—Prerau road were thrown into hopeless confusion. Meanwhile, an attack against the battalion which was starting from Roketnitz failed. And when Poschacher's Brigade turned to the left, advanced against the few squadrons of Hussars and brought its battery into action, Hartmann sounded the assembly and retreated via Wrbowetz. Three squadrons of the Landwehr Hussars, who had remained a little behind, were charged by Austrian Hussars, forced to retreat and to deliver their booty in captives and provisions wagons. Nevertheless, the I and VIII Corps continued their retreat toward Prerau.

Malotki and the 5th Cuirassiers had beaten back the last intact Austrian Brigade, Rothkirch's and the appearance of Bonin and Hartmann's attacks had enveloped also the VIII and I Corps in the retreat. On the same day, 15 July, the railway was destroyed at Goding by a detachment of the 8th Division. Benedek saw himself cut off from the road leading down the valley of the March and from the railway and forced to cross over bad roads through the mountains into the valley of the Waag. The VI Corps, to be followed by the Saxon Division was to continue the march from Leipnick via Weisskirchen, the I Corps and Wagner's Saxon Brigade to march via Holleschau, Wisowitz, Wlar-Pass, and Nemsowa, the VIII Corps and the 2nd Light Cavalry Division likewise via Holleschau and Wisowitz, then continuing via Boikowitz, Hrosenkau, and Kostolna, the I Corps from Kremsier via Ungarisch-Hradisch, Strany, and Neustadtl, the IV Corps and the Saxon Cavalry Division via Zdaunek, Ostra, Welka, Migawa, and Verbovce to the valley on the Waag. Benedek could still reach Vienna by a long detour via Tyrnau and Pressburg.

He should of necessity have been pursued anew, thrown back, or at least forced to retreat via Komorn. This would have destroyed his army entirely and would have given the Prussians time and opportunity to overwhelm the position at Vienna on the Danube, be it ever so strong and be the river ever so wide. On receipt of the first, though premature information early in the morning of the 15th, that Benedek had marched off, Moltke had ordered the Second Army to follow up the retreating enemy with the V and I Corps in direction of Kremsier and Napagedl. The First Army was to assemble at Lundenburg to block the valley of the March to the fugitives. The pursuit would have to be directed toward Kremsier and Napagedl and not toward Prerau.

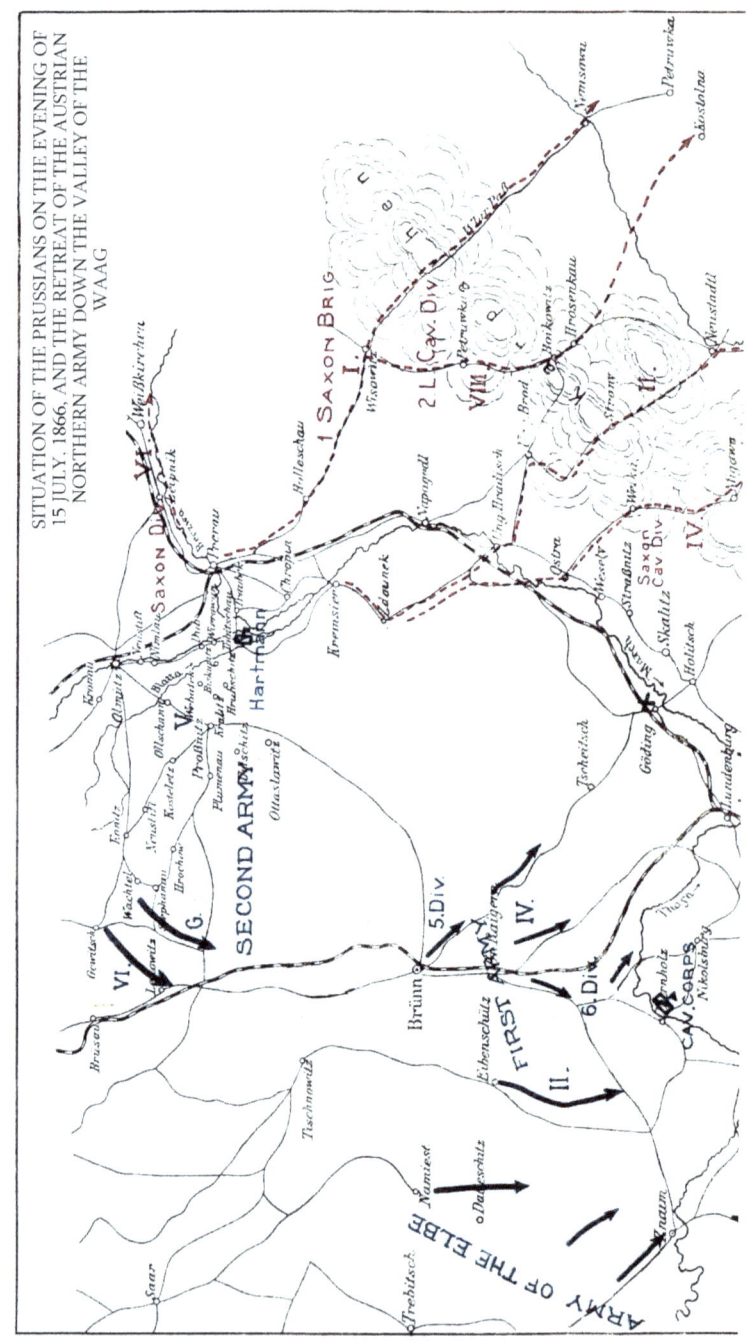

The Campaign of 1866

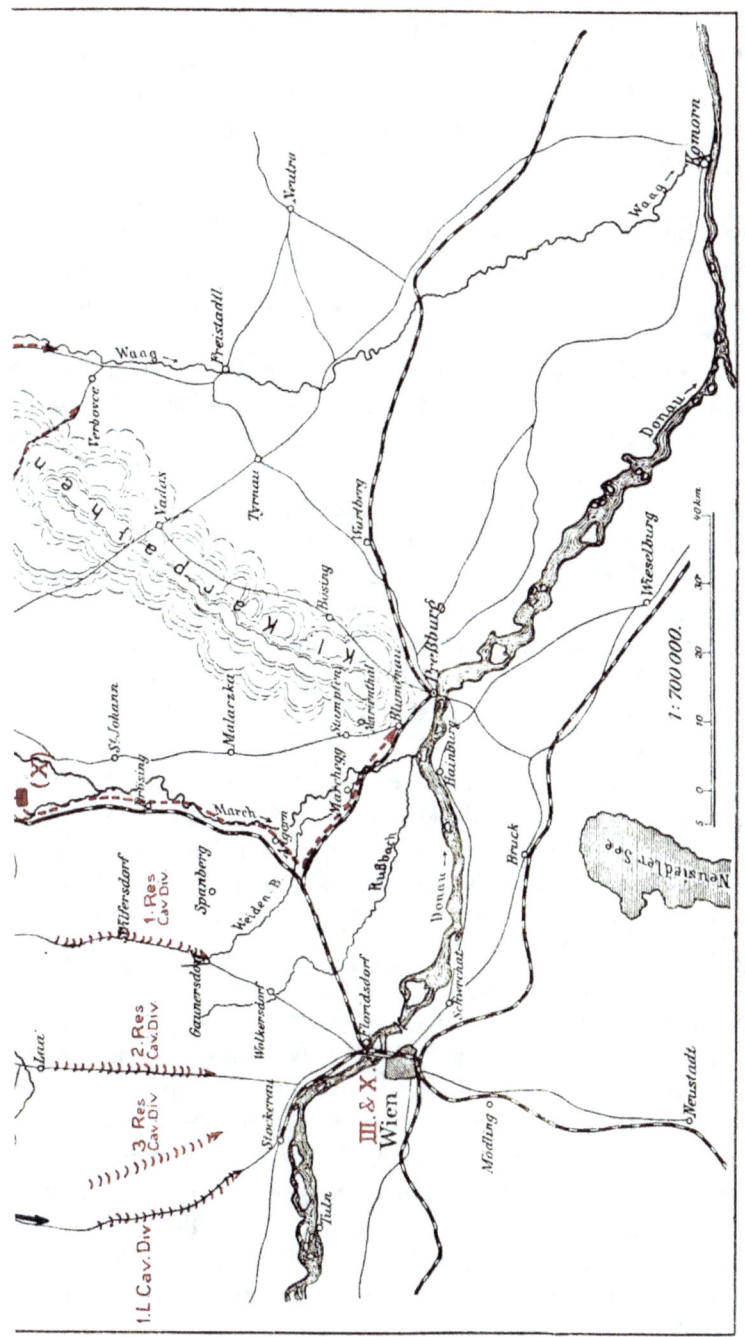

Had the Cavalry Division of the I Corps taken this road early on the 15th and the V Corps had followed them, then on the 17th one division of the former could have reached Ungarisch-Brod and another one Ostra. On the same day the 8th Division was at Holitsch, the 5th at Tscheitsch. On the 18th, one division could advance to Strany, one to Welka, one to Tyrnau and one to Pressburg, the V Corps following along the valley of the March. It is hardly doubtful but that Benedek would have been driven entirely away from Pressburg, his army entirely dispersed and the war ended.

Moltke's "incomprehensible" and "impossible" order was not transmitted by army headquarters to the lower headquarters. Instead, a proposition made by Steinmetz found approval. The evening of the 15th, Hartmann and Malotki were at Tobitschau and Wierowan, the I Corps was between Hrubschitz and Biskupitz and the V at Prossnitz. Steinmetz not acquainted with the events of the day, wanted to complete on the 16th the "advance" to Prerau, which had been planned on the 14th. He desired for this the support of one of Bonin's divisions, which he supposed to be according to the army order, at Plumenau and Urtschitz. He learned accidentally, that the I Corps was in his immediate front and found it simpler to leave the advance to Bonin.

The latter was now quite ready to do what he ought to have done the day before, but decided to cook dinner first, and started at 2:00 PM, in company with Hartmann. He reached Prerau toward evening, found there provisions and oats, but no enemy. The latter had found plenty of time, since 3:00 PM to start 40,000 men on the road to Holleschau. Bonin, in order to do at least something, directed, contrary to Moltke's orders, that the railroad bridge over the Beczwa be blown up, thus making impossible the only communication with Silesia for further operations. He then returned to bivouac for the night behind the Blatta. This put out of the question all pursuit by the Second Army, and freely permitted the junction of the enemy, which was to be prevented at all cost. By order of the commanding general, the I Corps remained at Prerau and Tobitschau to observe vacant Olmutz, while the V Corps and Hartmann's Division, after a day's rest, marched down the March, and the Guard Corps and VI Corps reached Brunn on the 17th.

The day of Tobitschau must have been felt in Vienna as a day of painful failure. Only the III and X Corps were assembled at the capital; one Saxon Brigade and four cavalry divisions would arrive, it is true, in a very short time, but the 50,000 men expected from Italy could not be there before the 22nd. Even with their support no successful resistance could be offered behind the Danube and in the Florisdorf fortifications, and still less could an attack be delivered. It was absolutely necessary to draw in the Army of the North. The nearest route, through the valley of the March, was barred. The detour via the valley of the Waag to Pressburg, demanded considerable time. The delay would be increased should this detour via Pressburg be barred and a longer one via Komorn be rendered necessary. The pass at Blumenau, leading from the valley of the March to Pressburg, was occupied by Mondel's Brigade of the X Corps. That brigade could not resist a determined attack. The II the nearest corps of the long column marching through the valley of the Waag, was ordered to reinforce it. By means of wagons and a horse tramway the corps was to hurry as fast as possible to the threatened point.

Prussian headquarters had evolved a different picture. It was not known how many corps had reached Vienna by rail from Olmutz. It appeared certain, however, that the larger part of the Army of the South had already arrived. The strength was estimated at 150,000 men ready to take the offensive. Their attack from the Florisdorf fortifications might be made simultaneously with an attack of the Army of the North from Pressburg as soon as the latter had reached that point. It is, consequently, most important to occupy Pressburg. The two hostile armies could be separated there. And from there it would be possible to attack the right flank of the Army of the South marching behind the Danube, as well as the left flank of the Army of the North marching down the valley of the Waag.

In order that the piercing might succeed, the Army of the South must be attacked behind the Danube and in the Florisdorf entrenchments, whereas the Army of the North must be attacked in the valley of the Waag. For the former problem would be available the Army of the Elbe, and that part of the First Army which was not used against Pressburg. For the latter were destined the I and

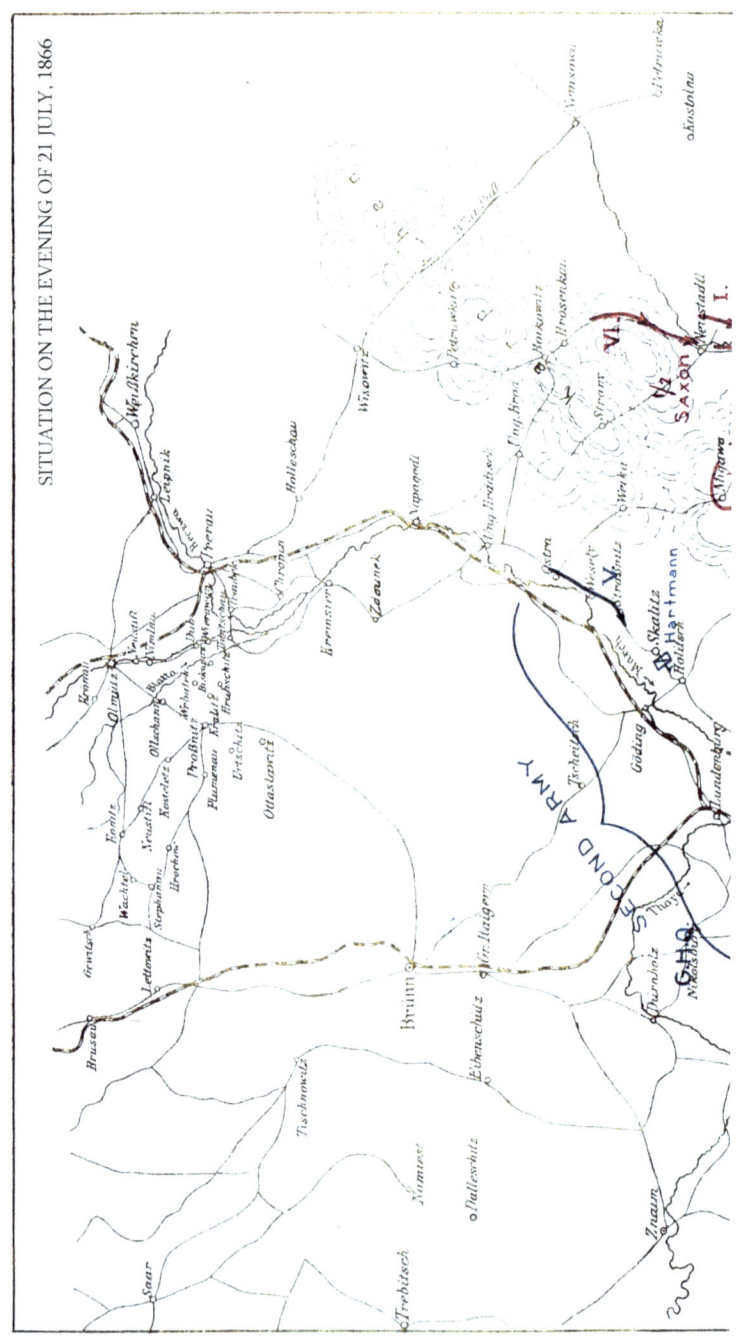

SITUATION ON THE EVENING OF 21 JULY, 1866

The Campaign of 1866

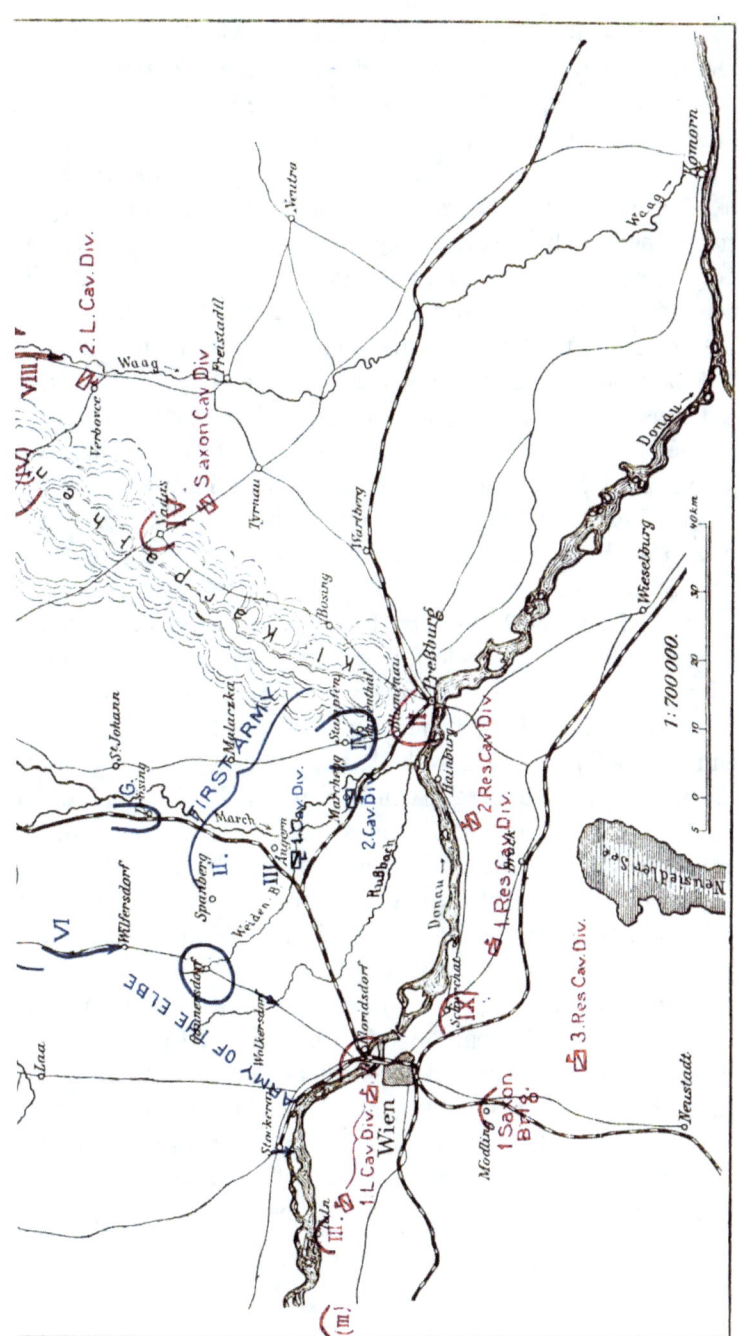

V Corps as well as Hartmann's Division, as Moltke's order gave them the direction to Kremsier and Napagedl early on the 15th.

The Second Army had disdained to take up this problem and eliminated itself from the operations. The I Corps was brought to rest in front of the empty Olmutz, the V Corps and Hartmann's Division marched to the left, the Guard Corps and the VI to the right of the March for several days behind the First Army. For the many problems; i.e., attack against the Danube front, the occupation of Pressburg, driving Benedek back, the flank attack on the left bank of the Danube, only the First Army and the Army of the Elbe were available. The Guard Corps and the VI Corps, at least, must be awaited before thinking of fighting a decisive battle. In order to prepare for the latter, the direction from Brunn, via Goding and Holitsch, down the March to Pressburg was given to the left wing of the First Army, and the direction from Znaim, via Laa and Wilmersdorf, to Vienna, was given to the right wing of the Army of the Elbe.

On the 21st, The Army of the Elbe stood near Gaunersdorf, the advance guard at Wolkersdorf, a flank detachment, two squadrons under the Prince of Hesse, at Stockerau; of the First Army, the II and III Corps as well as Alvensleben's Cavalry Division (1st) was behind the Weiden-Bach, to the left as far as Angern, and in the rear as far as Spanberg, Hann's Cavalry Division (2nd) at Marchegg, the 7th[*] and 8th Divisions under Fransecky at Stampfen and Marienthal. The Second Army was with the VI Corps (11th Division) at Wilfersdorf, the Guard Corps at Drosing, the V Corps far back in the vicinity of Strassnitz and Wesely, Hartmann's Cavalry Division as far as Skalitz.

On the Austrian side, there stood at the same time one brigade of the III Corps at Krems, two at Tuln, the X Corps and one brigade of the V, arrived from Italy on the 19th, in the fortifications of Florisdorf, the three other brigades of the latter corps in Vienna, the IX Corps, also arrived from Italy the day before, at Schwechat, one Saxon Brigade at Modling. The 1st Light Cavalry Division was divided between the IIJ and X Corps. The

---

[*] It had exchanged with the 2nd Division.

The Campaign of 1866

three Reserve Cavalry Divisions observed the Danube between Hainburg and Schwechat. Henriquez's Brigade had already joined Mondel's Brigade of the X Corps at Blumenau, and the three remaining brigades of the II Corps were expected in the morning. The IV Corps held at Nadas and Migawa, the mountain passes leading from the valley of the March to the Tyrnau and Verbovee roads. In the latter village was the 2nd Cavalry Division and in the rear of it the head of the long Benedek Column, at Neustadt].

All these troops were some three to four days' march distant from Pressburg; they are as little to be considered for the next few days as the troops behind the Danube. They were too weak for an attack against the Prussians behind the Weiden-Bach or the Russbach, yet strong enough to repulse an attack against the Florisdorf works or to prevent the crossing of the Danube. For the 22nd there was only the question whether or not Count Thun with 24 battalions, 11 squadrons, and 40 guns could hold the pass of Blumenau against Fransecky's 19 battalions, 24 squadrons, 78 guns. Everything was risked on one card.

Should it come out well, the junction of the Armies of the South and North would be assured. If it came out badly, Austria was probably lost. Fransecky would receive reinforcements the following day. Benedek would then, even if he were not pursued, decide on a retreat via Komorn and the position on the Danube could be attacked from the front and from Pressburg. Austria could not afford to have that happen. She showed herself inclined to accede to the urgings of France and to accept an armistice of 5 days beginning at noon on the 22nd. Prussia also "was willing to make this sacrifice of five days, disadvantageous from a military point of view to please Napoleon."

The forenoon hours of the 22nd were not sufficient to finish a combat begun by Fransecky with much circumspection and well conducted. At the appointed hour the combat had to be interrupted and the troops had to retreat to the assigned line of demarkation. The junction of the two Austrian armies was thus secured and Prussia placed in an unfavorable military situation. Both Austria and France wanted to utilize the success obtained, each in her own way.

Negotiations opened on that day at Nikolsburg. Austria being already outside of the German Confederation concurred in the formation of a North German and South German Confederation. Bismarck's principal demand was thus fulfilled. The King, however, insisted on the cession of territory beyond Schleswig-Holstein. The ancient demands of Frederick the Great, Austrian Silesia and part of Bohemia, moreover the losses suffered during the Napoleonic years of bitterness—the unreturned Ansbach, Bayreuth and Eastern Friesland—were demanded by him as a right, as was also part of Saxony. These demands were met by a positive refusal from Vienna. Neither Austrian nor Saxon territory should be ceded. Better by far to go under with honor than to cede one foot of territory. The King, on the other hand, would rather abdicate than return to his people without the provinces rightfully belonging to him. These could consist, besides Schleswig-Holstein, only of Hanover, Hesse, and Nassau, the implacable enemies of the North German Confederation.

Napoleon had other interests to guard than had Austria. The terrifying ghost, frightening France and the other Great Powers for centuries, was a United Germany. It was of not much importance who should be the head of this centralized power. It was equally dangerous to Europe if it were threatened by a Great Germany with 70,000,000 inhabitants under the Emperor of Austria or, without Austria, under the King of Prussia. Since the German attempts of unification by the inventor of the principle of nationality could no longer be entirely crushed, a North German Confederation seemed the lesser evil. With a South German Confederation, supported by France, perhaps with an independent German State on the Rhine, it would be possible to create a rival for the enlarged Prussian. Which of the German Kings and Princes within the North German Confederation would become the vassals of Prussia, was of no importance.

Thus all parties concerned seemed to agree to a North German Confederation under the leadership of Prussia and to the elimination of Hanover, the Electorate of Hesse and of Nassau from among the independent states. It was necessary for Prussia to come to a conclusion on this basis before any other powers could mix in, and to accept other secondary demands, such as the integrity of Saxony and the war indemnity to be paid by Austria.

France was anxious to bring the affair to a close before Prussia, becoming arrogant through a new victory, should cease to limit her demands. Austria wanted an interruption of hostilities to gain time. None of the three wanted lengthy negotiations, but a quick result in order to accept or reject the demands, to end the war or to continue it. Shortly before the expiration of the armistice, there lacked for the conclusion of the agreement only the acquiescence of the Vienna Cabinet.

The greatest delay was resorted to for the fulfillment of this formality. The armistice had done what had been expected. During the period of five days Benedek had crossed the Danube at Pressburg with his army and the II and IV Corps had followed him. Masses of reserves had arrived. An army of 276,000 men and 840 guns, as large as the world had ever seen, was assembled behind the Danube. It stood in a very inaccessible position from which it could proceed to the right or left, according to its will, against the compressed mass of 218,000 Prussians.

The victor of Custozza, who had solved the difficult problem of defeating with a small army a vastly superior one, would be able to solve the smaller problem of defeating one of numerical inferiority. A council of war was held at the Hofburg. The spirits were high as was natural after the naval victory of Lissa, which had taken place a few days ago, Lieutenant Fieldmarshal John, Archduke Albrecht's Chief of Staff, explained briefly the advantages of the situation, but arrived at the conclusion that these advantages could no longer be utilized. On 1 July, the Army of the North, was according to Benedek's judgement, immediately on the eve of its dissolution; according to Gablenz's opinion, it scarcely existed on the 4th. Since then it had been driven to Olmutz, into the valley of the March, across the Carpathians, into the valley of the Waag, through Pressburg and across the Danube to Vienna. What it had escaped in the pursuit, it had suffered from the haste of the leaders. This army was at an end. The troops were entirely exhausted, discouraged, unnerved and unavailable for an attack.

The warlike hero, drawing his sword for the wielding of a mighty blow, found that his weapon was broken. Roland's mare is the finest in the world, but she is dead. In addition to this convincing reason to desist from the continuation of the war, it was hardly necessary to point out that Hungary was awaiting a new defeat to proclaim a revolution and that the Italians were advancing, while the South Germans were retreating. The peace preliminaries between Austria and Prussia should be completed. The document was ready for signature. Benedetti then made the agreement of France to the territorial acquisitions of Prussia dependent upon a compensation, hinting at the left bank of the Rhine. Bismarck interrupted him with the words: "Do not make any official communications of this kind to me today." The document was signed. Benedetti disappeared. He will come back at a more opportune moment.

Twice could a Cannae have taken place. The idea of a complete surrounding and annihilation of the enemy was too foreign to the Prussian generals to allow Moltke's simple and grand plan to succeed. The enemy was only pushed back. It is true that he was entirely broken. But should he find some rest, he could regain strength, as was hoped, draw in reinforcements and regain capability of resistance, even of attack. The longed for rest should not have been given him. The Second Army should have pursued him. During a long period of peace nothing much was heard of pursuits. It was known, from many maneuvers, that the beaten enemy was, after a lost battle, as fresh, enterprising and dangerous as 24 hours earlier. The Austrian army must have lost almost one third of its effective strength during the series of encounters and battles. Nevertheless it was materially stronger than the Second Army and was led by a general who was considered as the personification of the idea of the offensive and to whose love of enterprise and resolution anything could be ascribed. It was, consequently, comprehensible that the Second Army, imbued with ideas prevalent in peace time, followed only cautiously an enemy who could, at any moment, face it and mete out punishment to it.

As far as Olmutz it might have been possible to maintain the fiction that the Austrians retreated to lure the enemy on so as to separate him and then to defeat the separated parts. But when Benedek, after scarcely one day of rest in the great fortress, continued hurriedly on the march, no plans of attack could be ascribed to him. He had no other thought than to escape to Pressburg or Vienna. The head of the Second Army was closer to

The Campaign of 1866

these points than the mass of the Austrians. A situation, similar to that of Jena, was established. Moltke ordered by telegraph, quite in a Napoleonic mind, that pursuit be undertaken in the decisive direction. However, 60 years had sufficed to obliterate all but the names of Jena and Prenzlau, while the sense escaped the memories. Moltke's order was simply not understood and could not be executed because it was not understood. It was due only to the initiative of one general that success was achieved with a handful of troops, a success which the entire army dared not attempt to achieve.

Under such circumstance no battle of annihilation or annihilating pursuit could be thought of. It had to be left to the enemy to gradually exhaust himself. Other generals also had to contend with the lack of understanding, training, and decision of their subordinates. They tried to eliminate these defects by the infallibility of their authority and the decision of their orders. Moltke, being no commander-in-chief, but only the Chief of the General Staff, lacked the necessary authority and was not vested with the right to speak with the assurance of a man in command. He had to content himself with polite advice, pleasant expostulations, suggestions and similar means, and only rarely could he avert the grossest mistakes by a Royal "I order." The power of his thought was sufficiently great to achieve, if not the highest, yet great things nevertheless.

Chapter IV – The Campaign of 1870-71

From the Concentration of the Armies to the Retreat of the French across the Moselle

Instead of taking home the left bank of the Rhine and Belgium from the campaign of Sadowa, Napoleon III had lost a goodly portion of his power and prestige. In order to obtain better results, the Emperor had expressed more or less hidden threats, but he dared not utilize the army which was afflicted with all the defects caused by years of neglect. Should he, however, desire to maintain his throne and France at the head of the European States, a complete unification of Germany must be prevented and Prussia must be forced back within the boundaries becoming to her.

    A war was, consequently, unavoidable and, in order to wage it, it was necessary to win allies and to reorganize the army from its very foundation, yes, even to create it anew. Zealous negotiations took place with Prussia's foes and friends of the later years. The infantry was armed with a rifle superior to the Prussian arm. All other plans of reform and improvement were still in their inception, when attempts to bring a political defeat to the opponent, brought on the war.

The Campaign of 1870-71 265

Persuaded that "he would be numerically inferior with 300,000 men," Napoleon thought "to offset the lack of numbers by the rapidity of movements." This sounded strangely from a man who was often compelled to utter immobility by fits of illness and for an army which was only to be formed and which had to be equipped with the most necessary things. Only the plan of campaign seemed to be ready.

The Rhine was to be crossed at Maxau and above, the South Germans were to rally around the ancient Rhine Confederation standard and march jointly with the French against Berlin, while the Austrians, further to the right, took the same objective, the Italians following in the wake of the greater nations and the Danes, supported by a French landing corps, invaded Hanover.

However, before the French Army could begin crossing the Rhine, it had to be assembled on the left bank. This could be effected, on account of the then existing railway net, only in two groups, one of two corps in Alsace and one of five corps in Lorraine. One corps was to be formed at Chalons in order to follow as a left echelon in the general advance. Of all the suppositions, on which the plan of campaign was based, none was realized. The South Germans decided not for the Rhine Confederation, but for the German flag. They assembled, as did the North Germans, on the Rhine between Coblenz and Karlsruhe. The French plan of campaign was thus greatly simplified. No crossing of the Rhine would be necessary. The enemy would be found already on the French side. The allied powers would not advance alone on the other side of the stream: the great coalition, which had not yet been concluded was already broken. Germany and France alone stood opposite each other.

With the knowledge of being superior to the opponent in organization, mobilization, railway transportation, and consequently in rapidity of concentration, the Germans intended to attack before the French could be assembled. The First Army (VII and VIII Corps) was to assemble on the Moselle at Wittlich, the III and X Corps of the Second Army on the railroad on the left bank of the Rhine from Bingen to Neunkirchen, the Guard Corps and the IV Corps by Mannheim to Homburg, the six corps after that to advance by Merzig-Saargemund, seek the as yet unprepared foe

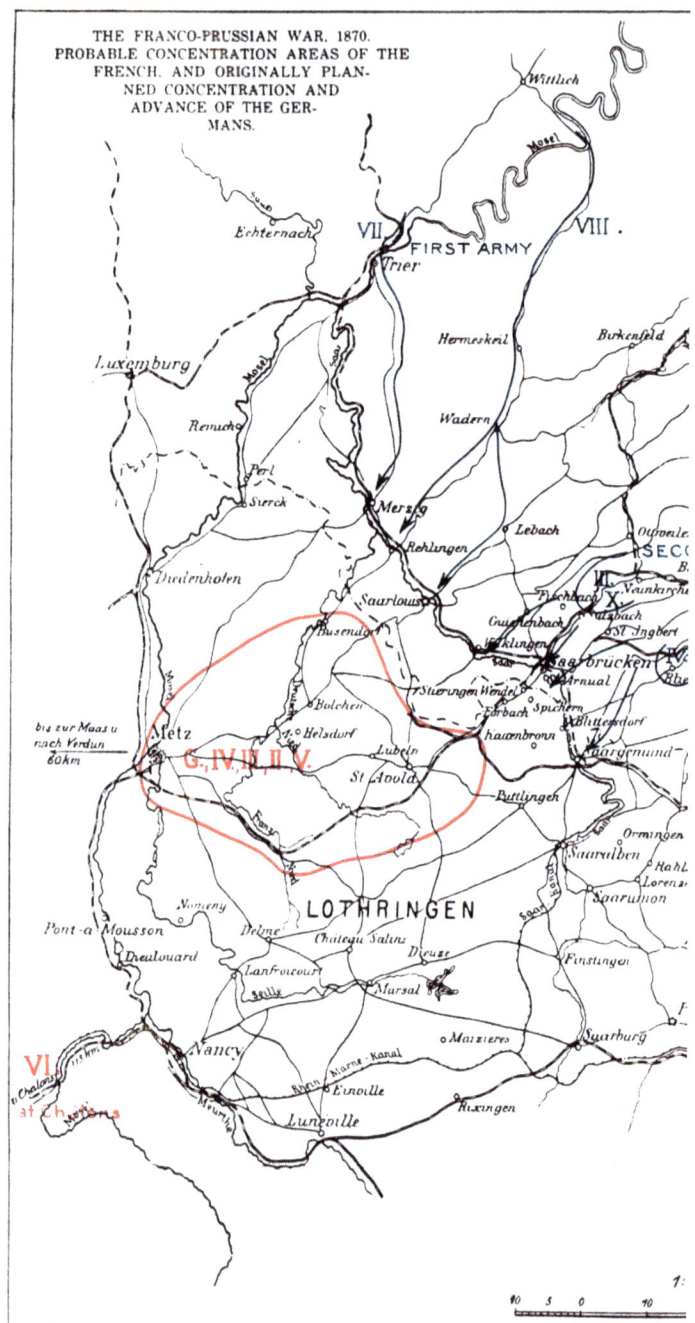

The Campaign of 1870-71

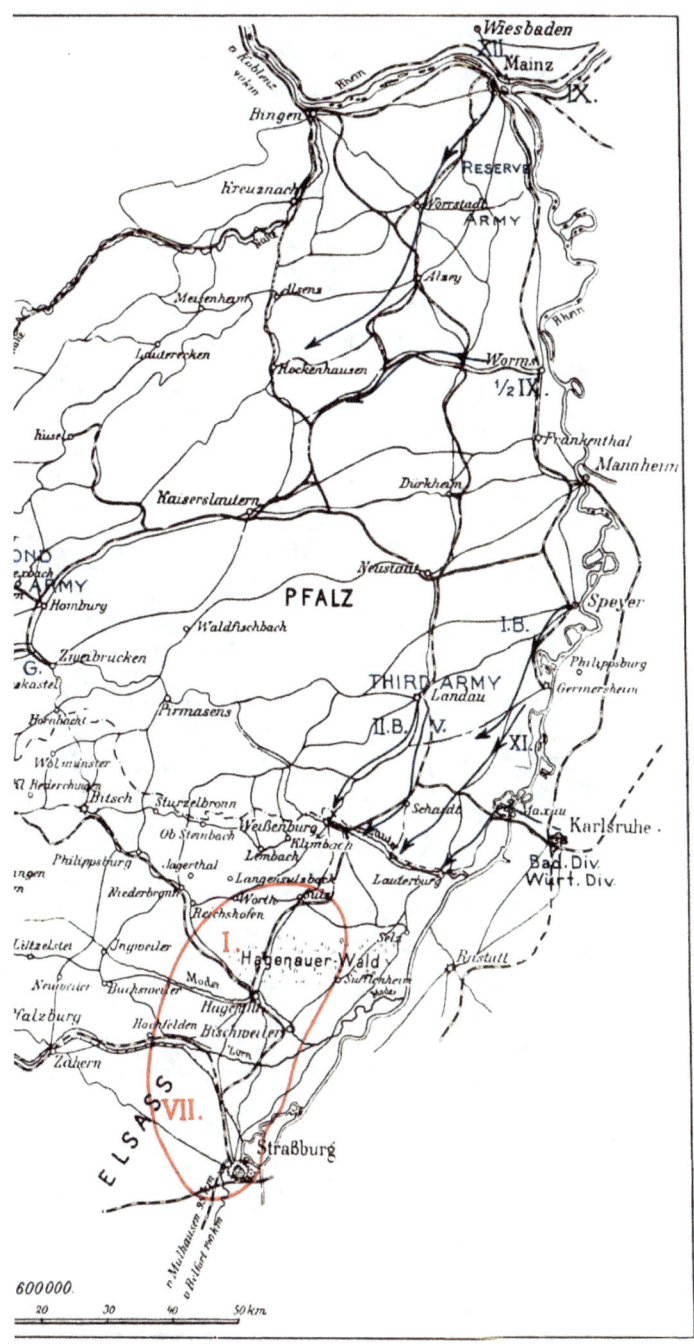

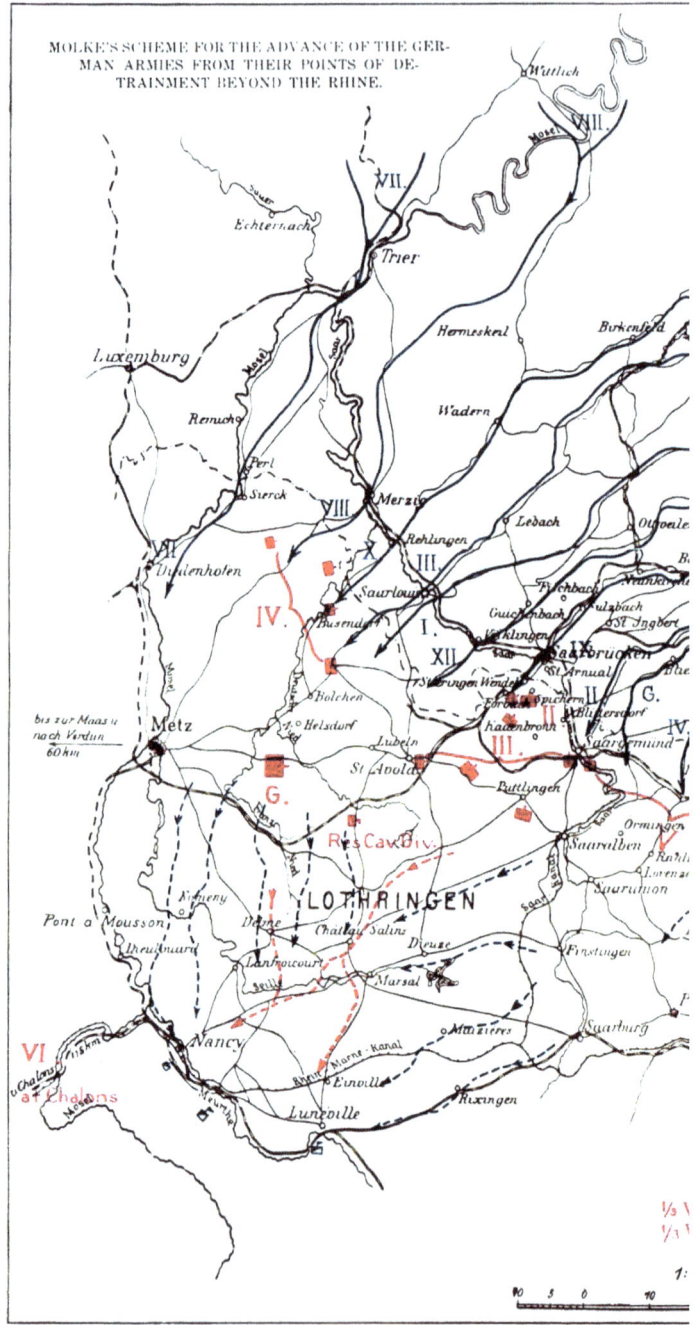

The Campaign of 1870-71

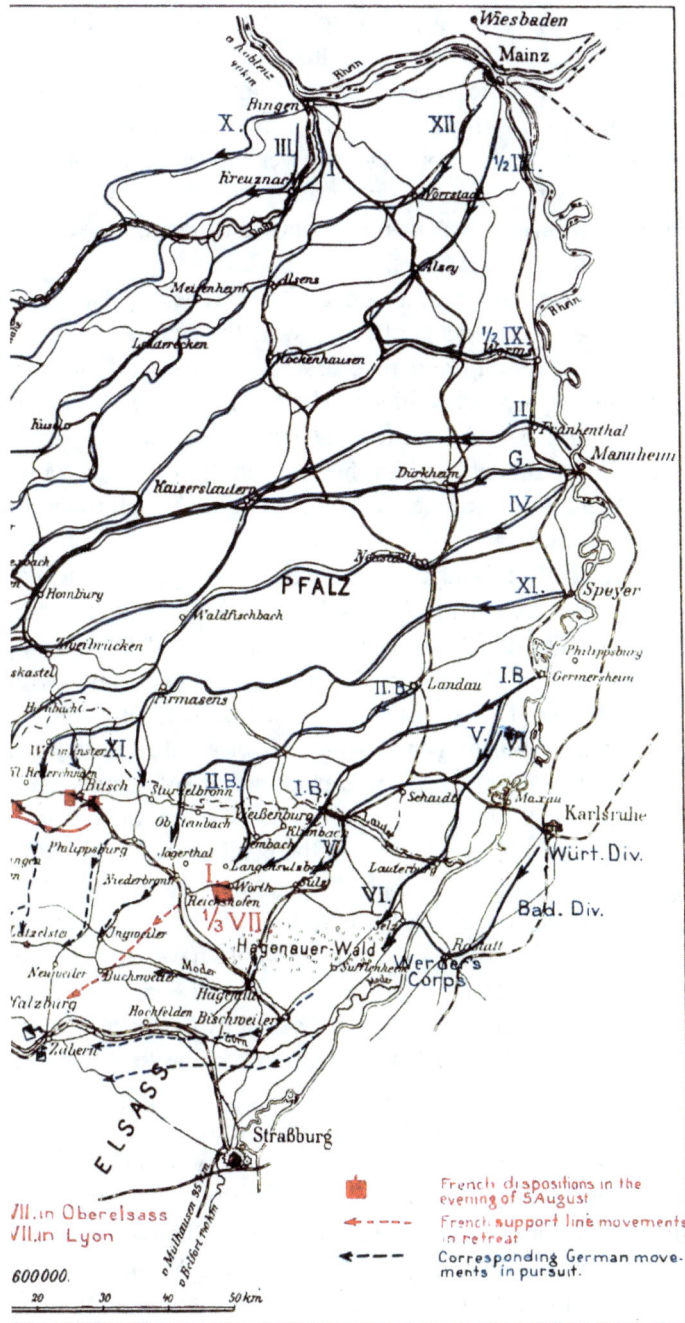

and beat him. A reserve army of which the XII and half of the IX Corps assembled north of Mayence, the other half of the IX Corps at Worms, was to follow the Second Army at a few marches interval. The Third Army (V and XI, Bavarian I and II Corps, Wurtemburg and Baden contingents) were to emerge from the Palatinate and drive the enemy, assembling in Alsace, in a southerly direction and then, turning to the right, support the attack of the First and Second Armies.

This plan had to be abandoned. The French had already commenced before the declaration of war, the transportation of troops on peace footing and thus assembled in a few days in Lorraine a fighting strength which might become dangerous, not to the First or Third Armies, but to the Corps of the Second Army which were to detrain at Neunkirchen by battalions. It was found advisable to transfer the intended detraining at Neunkirchen to Bingen and Mannheim.

Time was lost in this manner, but strength was gained. The two Corps of the Reserve Army (the XII and IX) were detrained at Mayence and Worms, almost opposite the corps of the Second Army at Bingen and Mannheim, thus being able to advance with those on one line. There was hope even that the corps, so far transported only to Berlin (I and II) might be brought early enough, after the freeing of the line of transportation of Bingen and Mannheim, to join the general advance. The two corps did not have to be awaited by the Second Army in the bend of the Rhine south of Mayence. They could have been brought in complete safety by stages, during the advance of the rest of the army, as far as Neunkirchen and Homburg. Then there would have been not six but ten corps available for the attack across the Saar. The front Merzig—Saargemund could be strengthened by one corps and be prolonged to the right as far as Sierck and to the left as far as Finstingen.

After the surprise and sudden attack against the French, who were believed to be hastily concentrating, was found to be impossible, it seemed advisable to try and attain victory by the straining of all forces even if that should be at the cost of a few days' delay. The problem, given the First and Second Armies remained the same as had been given in the beginning—to find the enemy and to defeat him. Its execution was facilitated by the greater number of corps and a broader front.

The Third Army joined the Second on the left. It was brought to the strength of six corps through the addition of the VI Corps, transported as far as Gorlitz where it had to await the departure of the V Corps. The right wing joined, via Primasens and Wolmunster, the left wing of the Second Army and sent detachments to Bitsch. Another corps went across the mountains with its right division by Sturzelbronn and Philippsburg to Neuweiler and Zabern, with the left by Ober-Steinbach, Jagerthal, and Neiderbronn to Ingweiler and Buchsweiler. Two corps crossed the Lauter between the mountains and the Hagenau forest, two others advancing south of this forest. In order to obtain a separate road for Werder's Corps, assembled at Karlsruhe (Wurttemberg and Baden Contingent) an attempt would be made to build a bridge across the Rhine between Rastatt and Selz or further upstream. In this way, the problems, entrusted to the Third Army, to drive southward the enemy reported to be assembled at Bitsch and in Lower Alsace, and to support the Second Army by an attack from the east, would be easiest of execution.

The entire German army would thus advance by all available roads between the Moselle and the Rhine, seeking the enemy. It was known about the latter, that the left group had advanced from Metz and had occupied with its advance guard (II Corps, Frossard) the heights south of Saarbrucken and the town itself, the main body (Bazaine, III Corps) standing between Saargemund and St. Avold, the reserve (Guard) advancing by the Metz road as far as the German Nied; the IV Corps (Ladmirault), divided into divisions and brigades, covered the left flank as far as Sierck, the V Corps (Failly) the right flank between Saargemund and Bitsch. The Alsatian group had been divided and assigned to the I Corps (MacMahon) and VII (Douay) along the Rhine from Belfort to Hagenau and north of the latter. One division of the latter corps was still at Lyons. Both groups, however, were in constant movement. Each day could evolve a new situation. Only four corps could be considered as sure—with their main forces between Saarbrucken and Metz, one corps in the vicinity of Bitsch, one in Upper Alsace; one, which could be reinforced at any moment by the two preceding ones, was being concentrated in Lower Alsace.

If now the German line, extending from Perl to Rastatt, was to seek the enemy, the wings of the armies finding nothing or little in front of them, were to make a turn inward. Thus they would need more time than the centers which saw the enemy directly in front of them. It was, consequently, advisable to have the wings cross the frontier earlier than the centers. On a given date, for example, on the 9th of August,* the right wing of the First Army could come from Perl to south of Diedenhofen, the left wing of the Second Army and the right of the Third Army as far as Saaralben, Ormingen, Rahlingen, and Klein Rederchingen, the left wing of the latter army to Sufflengeim and close to Bischweiler. Thus attacks were of themselves being prepared against the hostile flanks. It was true that the German wings were threatened, in their turn, on the right by Diedenhofen and Metz, on the left by Strassburg. These fortresses were, however, so weakly garrisoned that they could exert only a negligible effect on the outside and be nothing more serious than inconvenient obstacles. Much more serious would have been the movement of the army reserve (VI Corps, Canrobert) from Chalons to Nancy or Metz. One part of the turning right wing would have been occupied by it and its flank attack greatly weakened.

The question was as to what would be the decision reached at French Imperial headquarters when, in the evening of 9 August, a mass of contradictory reports and information were brought in. The decision to retreat immediately was not to be considered. For twenty days already the press had written and the crowd in Paris had shouted: "On to Berlin!" Should a retreat take place as soon as the enemy showed himself at a distance and before a shot was fired, the Emperor would lose his throne, the marshals and generals their posts, and the army its glory. Moreover, a retreat toward Metz would have brought about a battle under unfavorable conditions, one to Nancy would have exposed the scattered divisions and brigades of the IV Corps as well as those of the II to considerable

---

* The 9th of August had been designated as the date for the First and Second Armies to cross the Saar.

defeats. It could thus be taken as probable that the reinforced II Corps had gone into a position near Kadenbroon, long since reconnoitered and well known (south of Saarbrucken and west of Saargemund) and that the flanks had been covered by the remaining troops.

MacMahon, who was fully prepared for an attack from the east in an equally excellent position near Worth, would probably have acted similarly. Though a defeat was not exactly improbable, yet the battle had to be accepted as it had been accepted by Hohenlohe at Jena, Bennigsen at Friedland, and Benedek at Koniggratz. On 10 August, the Germans would have continued their march along the entire line, the right wing of the First Army east of Metz, the left of the Second Army above Saar, the right of the Third to Zabern, its left to Buchsweiler and Hochfelden. Many columns would meet with opposition, with some very obstinate resistance, by the enemy in more or less good positions. But the columns, meeting no enemy, could not be held back on this account. They could not more efficiently support the neighboring corps, whether attacking or attacked, than by continuing their march on the roads assigned them in order to fall against the flank or the rear of the enemy in case this were needed.

However the results of the fighting in Lorraine might be pictured, in the evening of 10 August, the wing corps of the German First and Second Armies would have reached on the right the vicinity of Metz, on the left west of Finstingen and then the French, however great their success or defeats might have been, would have to retreat for the purpose of escaping the threatening turning movement, the Germans starting immediately in pursuit, reaching on the right Nomeny and Delme, and on the left, Dieuze, Maizieres, and Roxingen. In order, however, to close the ring entirely, the 3rd, 5th, and 6th Divisions were attached to the First Army; the Guard and the 12th Cavalry Division to the Second, which, hurrying ahead of the right and left wings, in order to block the crossings over the Seille between Marsal and Lanfroicourt or those over the Meurthe and the Rhine—Marne Canal between Nancy and Einville, would have brought to a standstill the entire retreating mass and forced it to accept a new battle from the

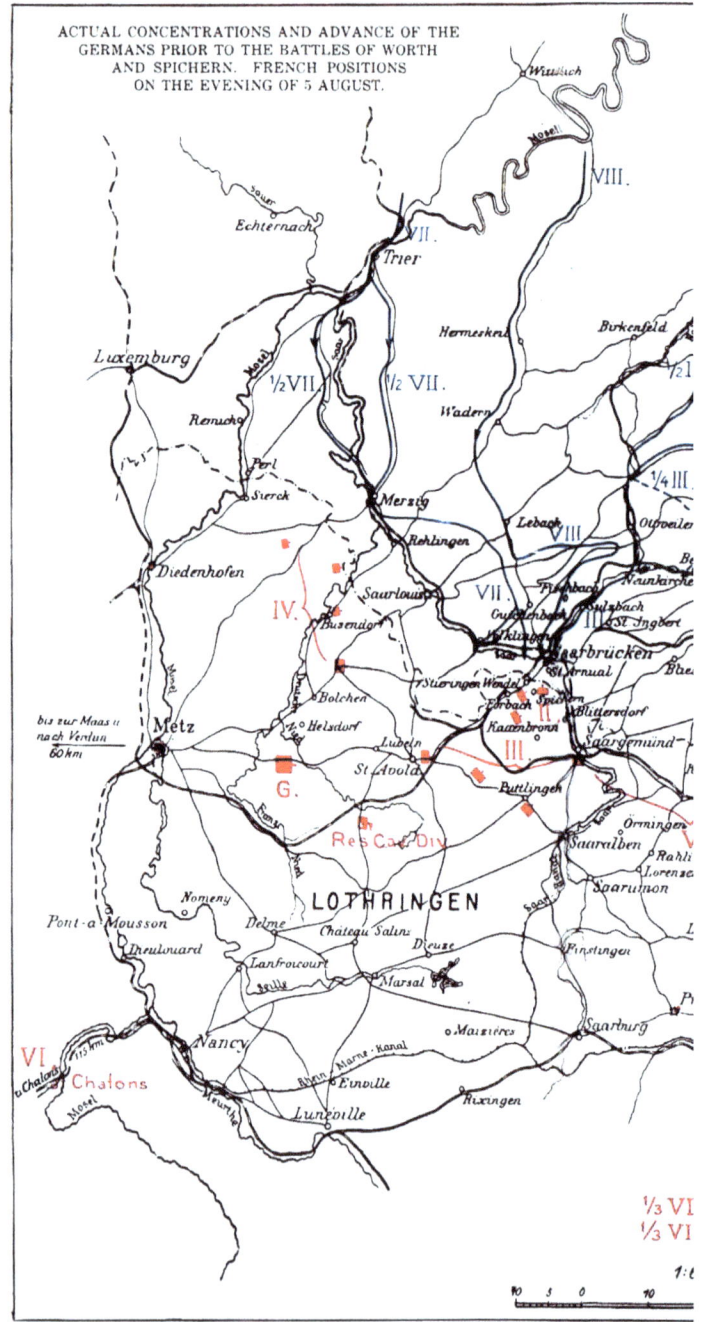

The Campaign of 1870-71

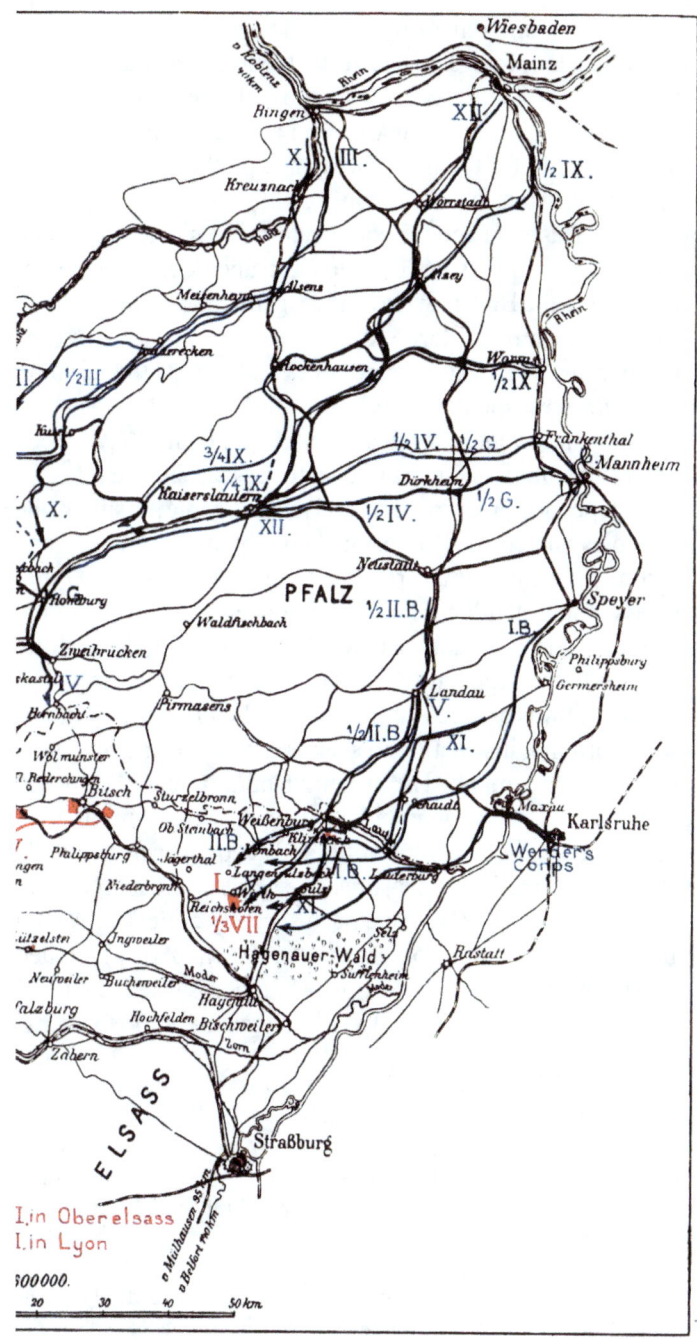

Germans, pressing upon them from all sides.*

MacMahon, too, would go back after having been attacked first from the east then from the north via Langensulzbach, Reichshofen, and Niederbronn. He might think to find an escape in a southerly direction, but would find himself threatened on the one side by the columns coming from the mountains, on the other side by those emerging from Hagenau and the south, and find his road blockaded by the 1st, 2nd, and 4th Cavalry Divisions advancing from Ingweiler and Hagenau and the Bavarian Cavalry brigades on the Moder or on the Zorn and the Rhine—Marne canal.

The V Corps, even if it were not drawn in toward the I, would find it difficult to escape being surrounded.

How far the French armies and corps could have been surrounded and annihilated need not be discussed. The greatness of the success depended on purposeful and indefatigable pursuit by the German armies and corps. But, even should many enemies escape annihilation, what might then remain of the French army would, nevertheless, not be available for any great deeds. The French field army might be considered as set aside. Only Paris and the other fortresses would then remain for the Germans to deal with.

Such a result was practically placed in the hands of the Germans by Moltke's original instruction to seek and beat the enemy on the line: Merzig—Saargemund. The execution of the plan was opposed by the ideas of the army commanders in regard to assembling the forces, massing the troops before battle, and keeping back unusually strong reserves. Benedek's measures in regard te the march from Moravia to Bohemia in 1866, have been severely criticised. As if it had to be so and could not be otherwise, the Second Army marched again in the Benedek march formation—four corps (the IV, Guard, IX,† and XII) along the main road via Kaiserslautern to Homburg,

---

* In 1870, the cavalry was so poorly equipped and armed that the problem entrusted to it could be only incompletely solved by it. After the number of batteries had been increased, machine guns introduced and the rank and file armed with carbines, the cavalry divisions were better able to fulfill more effectively the demands made on them.

† The IX Corps took advantage of the permission to use the main road only for one Brigade. It marched with the main forces along a parallel road more to the north.

The Campaign of 1870-71   277

two corps (the III and X) from Gingen by another road to Neunkirchen, although there were plenty of good roads on the right and left. From Neunkirchen, the III Corps was to continue via Sulzbach, the X from Bexbach via St. Ingbert to Saarbrucken, the Guard Corps from Homburg via Blieskastel to Blittersdorf, the IV via Zweilbrucken and Hornbach to Saargemund, the IX and XII, following the IV and the Guard Corps.

But this was not enough, however. Through misunderstood interpretation of orders from Royal Headquarters and independent ideas, the First Army started the VIII Corps from Ottweiler via Fischbach, the VII from Lebach to Saarbrucken. Thus four corps in the first line and two in the second, took this one town as their objective, while another corps was sent to the deeply cut line of the Saar, St. Arnual—Saargemund, so difficult to cross, and still another was directed against the latter town, which was easily defended. Should the plan be executed in this manner, six to seven army corps would be assembled on the narrowest strip in front of the Kadenbronn position and the enemy, after the departure of the troops necessary for the defense of the position and of Saargemund, would have had sufficient forces left to attack the west flank of the crowded German troops, left open between the Saar and Kadenbronn. As a matter of fact, such attack by the French was as improbable as was a great and decisive victory on the part of the Germans. As at Sadowa, not much more could be expected here than the confronting of two unwieldy masses.

The Third Army followed the same principles as the First and Second. For the protection of Alsace, MacMahon had selected a position near Worth, facing east. It secured for him, as he deemed, communications with the main army, and threatened in flank an advance of the Germans against Strassburg. The latter would be compelled to attack the strong position, for the defense of which the V and VII Corps could also be drawn in. In order to bar the principal crossing of the boundary stream (the Lauter), a detachment was sent to Lauterburg, Douay's Division (8 battalions) to Weissenburg, and covering detachments to Klimbach, Lembach, and Sulz.

The German Third Army had received orders from Royal Headquarters to cross the frontier on 4 August, to drive MacMahon

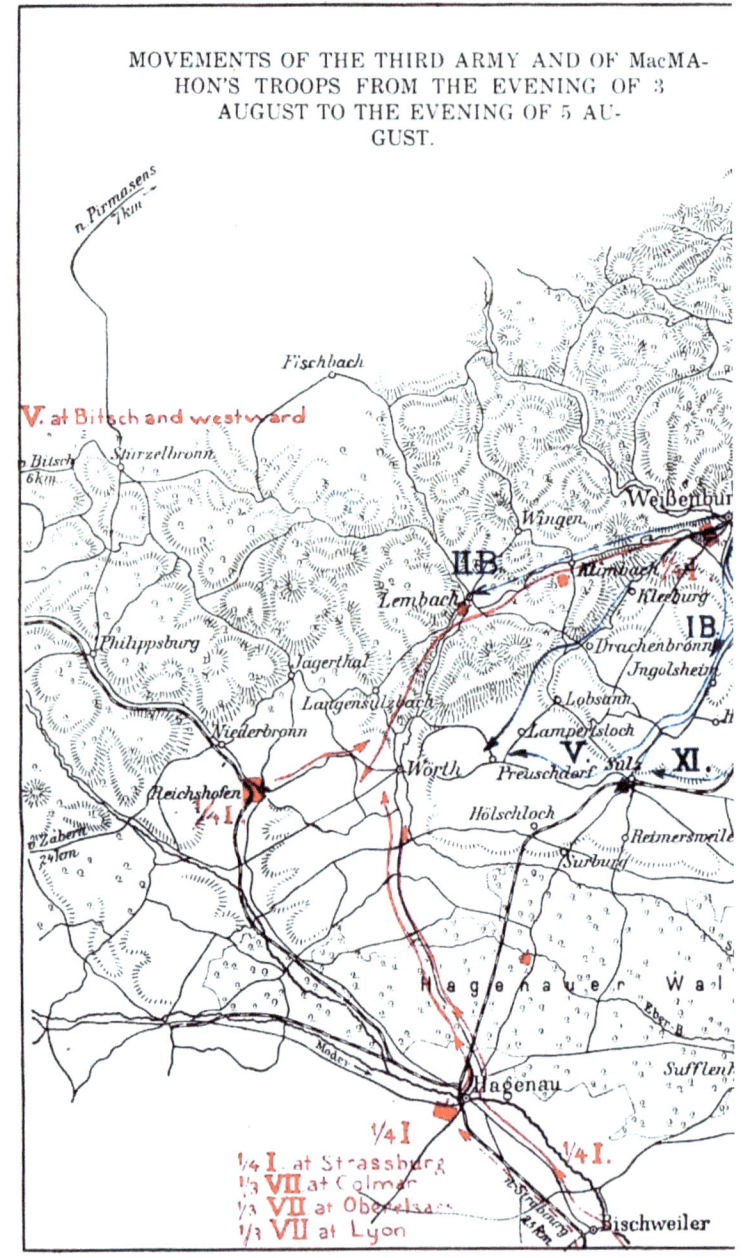

MOVEMENTS OF THE THIRD ARMY AND OF MacMAHON'S TROOPS FROM THE EVENING OF 3 AUGUST TO THE EVENING OF 5 AUGUST.

The Campaign of 1870-71

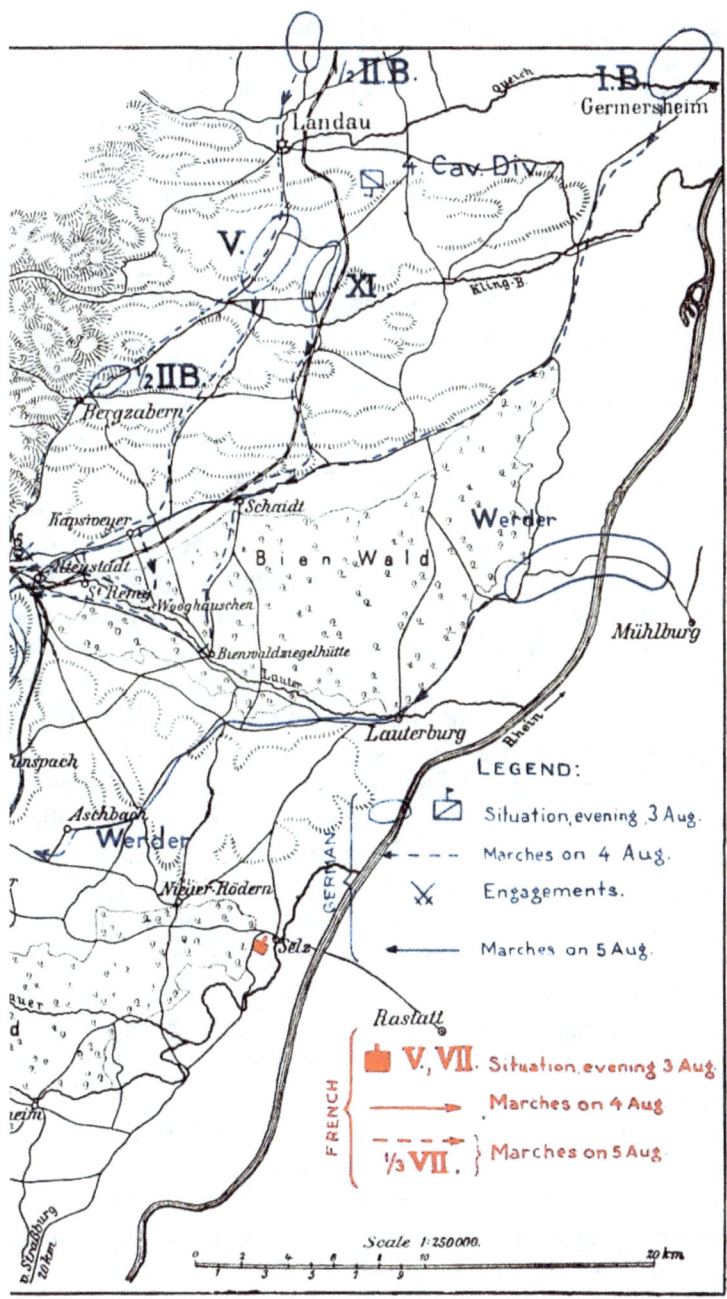

back in a southerly direction, and to advance across the Vosges Mountains toward the upper Saar, somewhere between Saaralben and Finstigen. It should reach this point in time to cooperate with the Second Army on the 9th, in an attack on the French main army along the line: Saarbrucken—Finstigen. The events of 3 July, 1866, were to be repeated. The mass of the Second Army would have stood waiting opposite the hostile position until the Third Army should bring deliverance and victory. Whether it would be successful in inducing the First Army to adopt the role of the Army of the Elbe and make an attack on the hostile left flank, appeared very doubtful, in view of General von Steinmetz's independent character. Moreover, on account of the great distance of the Lauter from the Saar, and of all the obstacles to be encountered on this road, the smooth execution of the plan was in no way assured. This was apparent as early as 4 August.

On that day the Bavarian II Corps was to reach Weissenberg from Bergzabern, the V Corps St. Remy and Wooghauschen via Kapsweiler, the XI Corps the Blenwaldziegelhutte via Schaidt, and Werder's Corps Lauterberg, while the Bavarian I Corps followed as a reserve. The objectives of the marches were reached by the three corps without much difficulty. Only the Bavarian II Corps found at Weissenberg an obsolete, but well preserved and garrisoned fortress with high walls and deep moats, and behind it Douay's Division in a strong position on the heights with excellent obstacles in front. Fortress and position were not easily to be overcome without strong artillery. Called up by the cannon thunder, the V Corps came hurrying up on the left, and the XI on the right of the Lauter. The former crossed the river at Altenstadt. Under the joint attack of the three corps in front and flank, the enemy evacuated the position, after a bloody resistance and disappeared from the sight of the victors along the road to Klimbach.

The quick and effective cooperation of the V and XI Corps in the battle of Weissenburg gave brilliant testimony as to the spirit of the leaders and troops. But had the Third Army, for the purpose of overcoming of all resistance and opposing real or phantom march columns, endeavored to assemble three corps, it would have attained small success and suffered relatively great losses, but would never have reached the Saar in good time. As shown by the war of 1866, each marching column of an advancing army should undertake, by itself alone, to take charge of each enemy it may meet. The neighboring columns should continue past the enemy in order to attack him in the flank and rear should this be necessary.

After the three corps had taken the direction of Weissenburg, the Bavarian I Corps marched also to that point. On 5 August of the four assembled corps, the Bavarian JI Corps marched via Klimbach to Lembach, the 9th Division via Kleeburg, Drachenbronn, and Lobsann to Preuschdorf, the 10th Division and the XI Corps proceeded partly by marching and partly by rail to Sulz, followed by the Bavarian I Corps to Ingolsheim; Werder's Corps was brought to Aschbach, and the 4th Cavalry Division was to proceed along the highroad to Hagenau. At Sulz, the point where the roads to the west and south intersect, stood the two divisions of the XI Corps, on the left and right one corps each at Lembach and Aschbach, and one in reserve at Ingolsheim; the V Corps was sent forward as advance guard to the west; the 4th Cavalry Division reconnoitered in a southerly direction.

The Cavalry found in that direction only a weak enemy, while near Worth beyond the Sauer the enemy was found in a strong position. On 6 August, a turning movement to the right was to be made, the Bavarian I Corps advancing to Lampersloch and Lobsann, the V Corps to Preuschdorf, the XI to Holschloch, and on the 7th the three Corps were to attack the front of the enemy almost 5 km in extent. The right flank was to be covered by the Bavarian II Corps at Lembach and Wingen, the left by Werder's Corps at Reimersweiler, the rear by the 4th Cavalry Division at Hunspach. These orders did not book the driving of the enemy to the south and an advance through the mountains in order to reach the Saar on the 8th and to take part on the 9th in a concentric attack of the entire German army against the French main army.

By an attack against the strong hostile front, with flanks well protected, hardly anything better was to be accomplished than the driving beyond the mountains against the Saar, a difficult pursuit, and a tardy arrival at the great battle. But even the most modest victory was not assured. MacMahon had for several days been given the disposition of not only of the VII Corps (Douay) but also

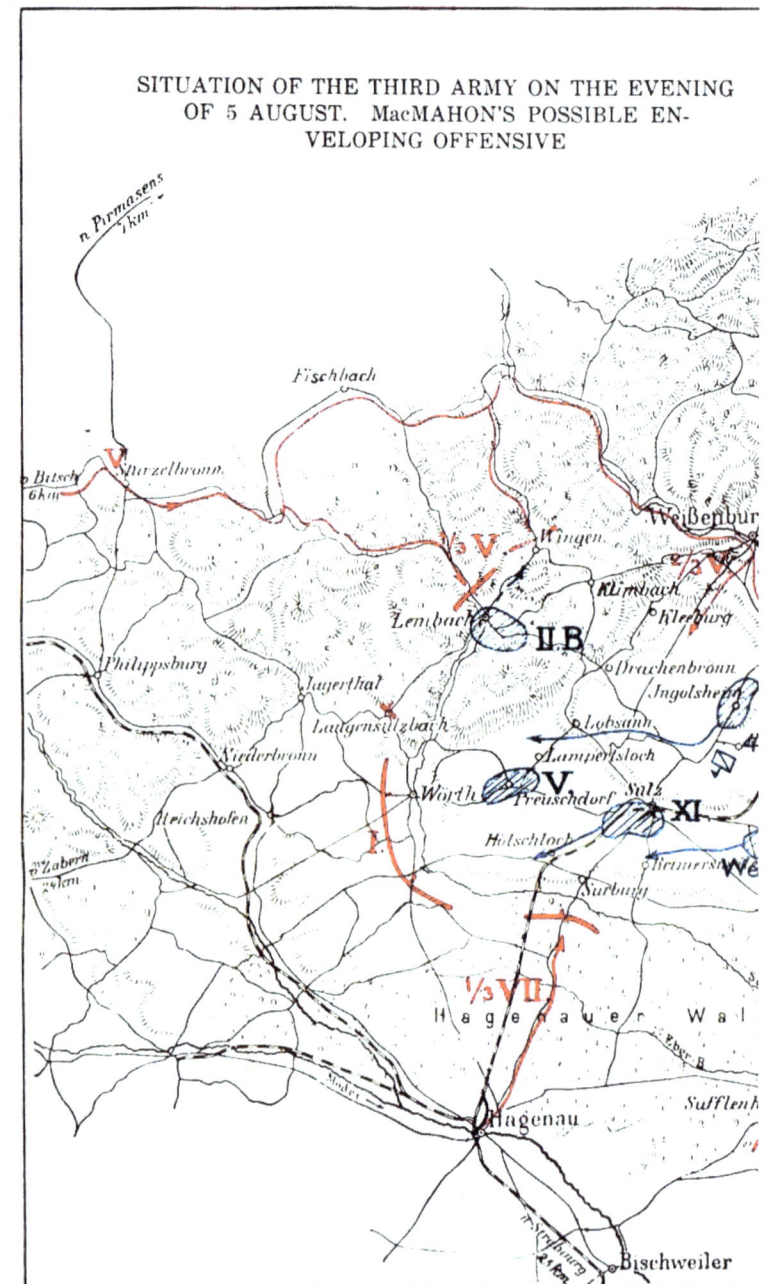

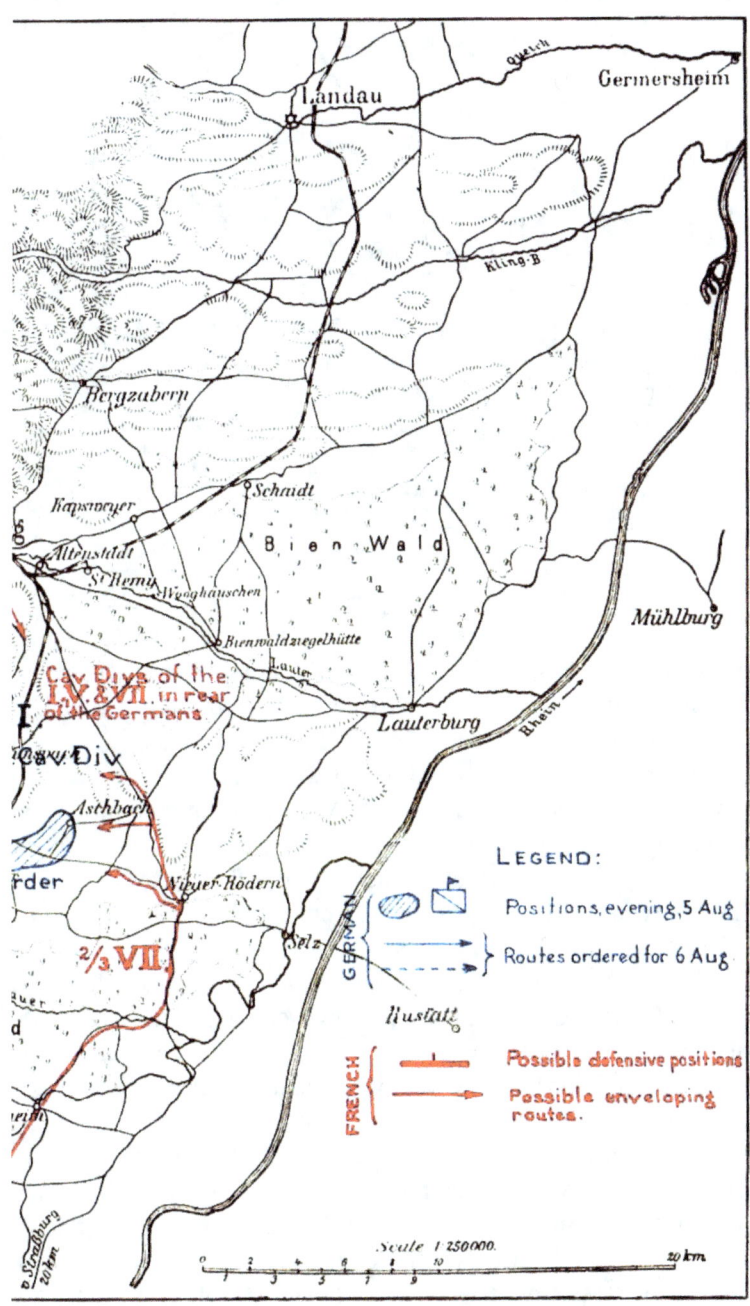

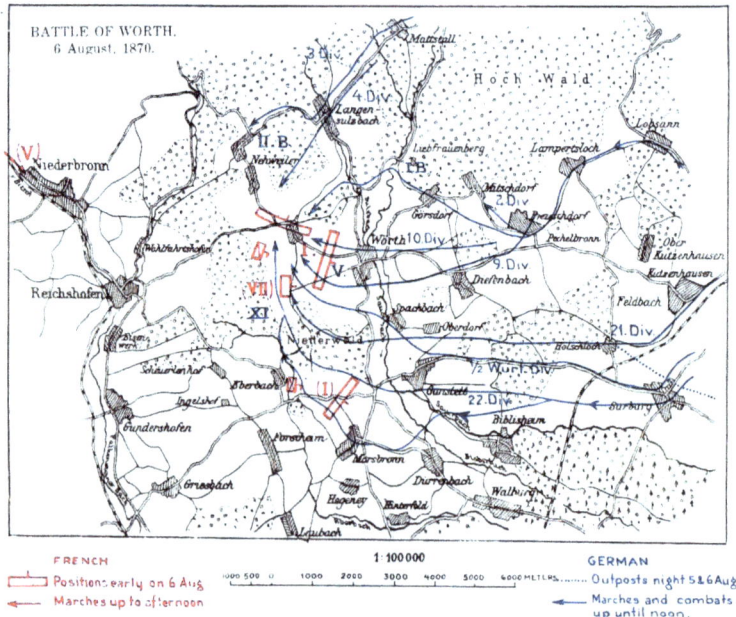

of the V (Failly). Should he have the will and should he so decide, he could have drawn up both these corps in good time to attack the hostile flanks. An advance of Failly by the main road via Stutzelbronn to Lembach and of Douay via Hagenau to Surburg would not of course, have sufficed. At each of these points, in the mountains and in the woods, it would have sufficed to hold back the enemy, with one division, which would make two divisions and three cavalry divisions available for a turning attack against Weissenburg and Nieder-Rodern.

In fact, MacMahon had considered an attack on the flanks, at least with the V Corps. He lacked, however, confidence of success and the decision necessary for its execution. By indefinite orders, only one division of the VII Corps was brought up prior to the battle on the 6th, and one division of the V Corps during its continuance. These small forces were not used for attack, but were employed as covers for the flank and as reserves. On the French side also, great importance was given to the security of the flanks. On the 6th the two armies were to face each other in two squares. Neither of the two opponents seemed to think that the best security

for his own flanks was an attack against those of the enemy.
The development of the Third Army, as planned, was not executed. The German outposts were already too close to the hostile ones, the zeal of the troops and of the subaltern commanders to go into combat was too great: the battle developed of itself. It was soon found that an attack against the strong front, be it with two divisions or three corps, would bring no decisive success. The narrow front of the French and the zeal of the Germans brought about of itself the attack against the front and of both flanks, to which MacMahon seemed to have exposed himself on purpose. A still greater success might have been achieved had the advance been made in the very start by many columns across the mountains and over the plain north and south of the Hagenau woods.

The First and Second Armies were also brought out of their difficult situation through the initiative of their subaltern commanders and the zeal of the troops. While on 6 August, the 13th Division of the VII Corps was te turn, via Volklingen to Forbach as a right flank guard, the 14th Division was to advance on the Lembach road only as far as Guichenbach, but had continued its march to Saarbrucken and beyond it and concluded from the movements of Frossard's Corps on the Spichern heights that the enemy was about to retire.

In order to hold him, the Division Commander, General von Kameke, decided to attack the strong position. The very insufficient forces were reinforced by the leading troops of the next corps, especially by the 16th and 5th Divisions. The troops succeeded, by their impetuous courage, in taking the edge of the position and advancing also on the Forbach road as far as Stieringen-Wendel. This success of the Germans would probably have induced Frossard to retire at least as far as Kadenbronn. The report, however, that the enemy had attacked Forbach,[*] settled the matter. The retreat was started in the night to Saargemund.

The French army was as good as dispersed by the victories of

---

[*] It was the 13th Division which the Commanding General of the VII Corps, von Zastrow, had sent via Volklingen as flank guard.

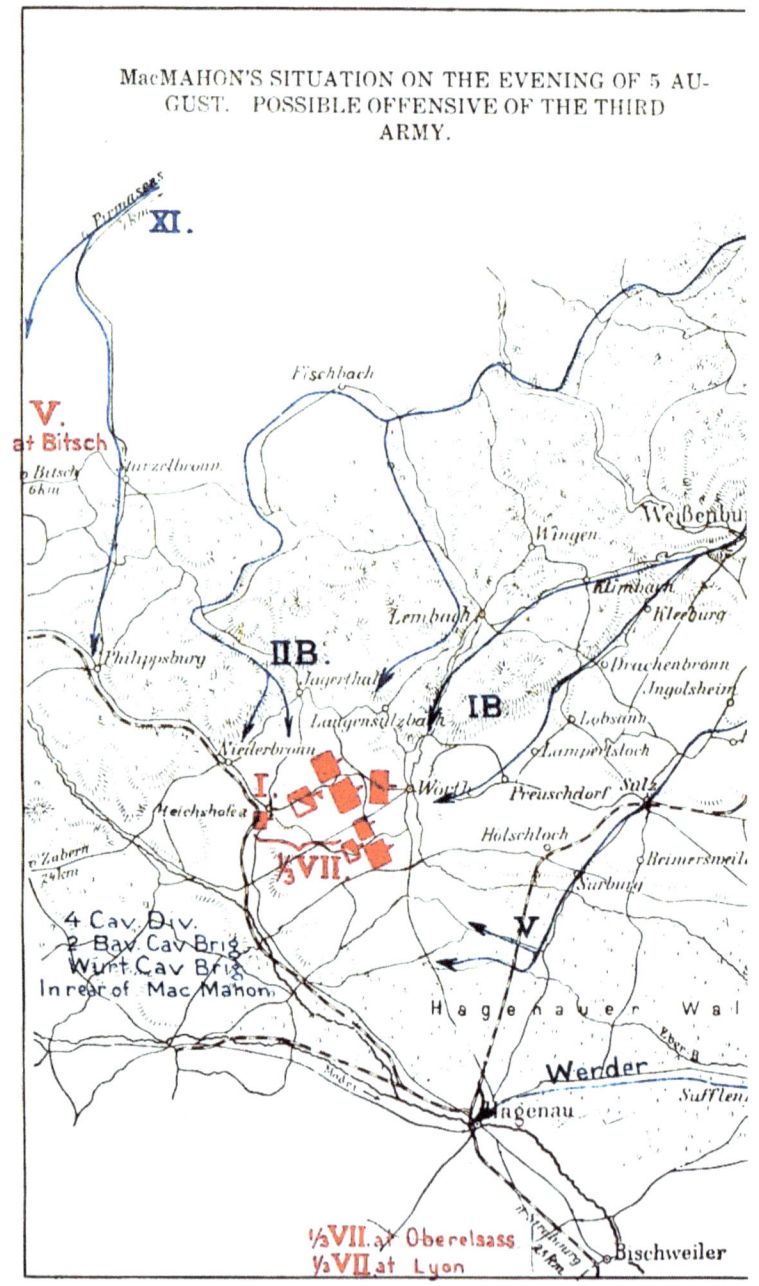

The Campaign of 1870-71

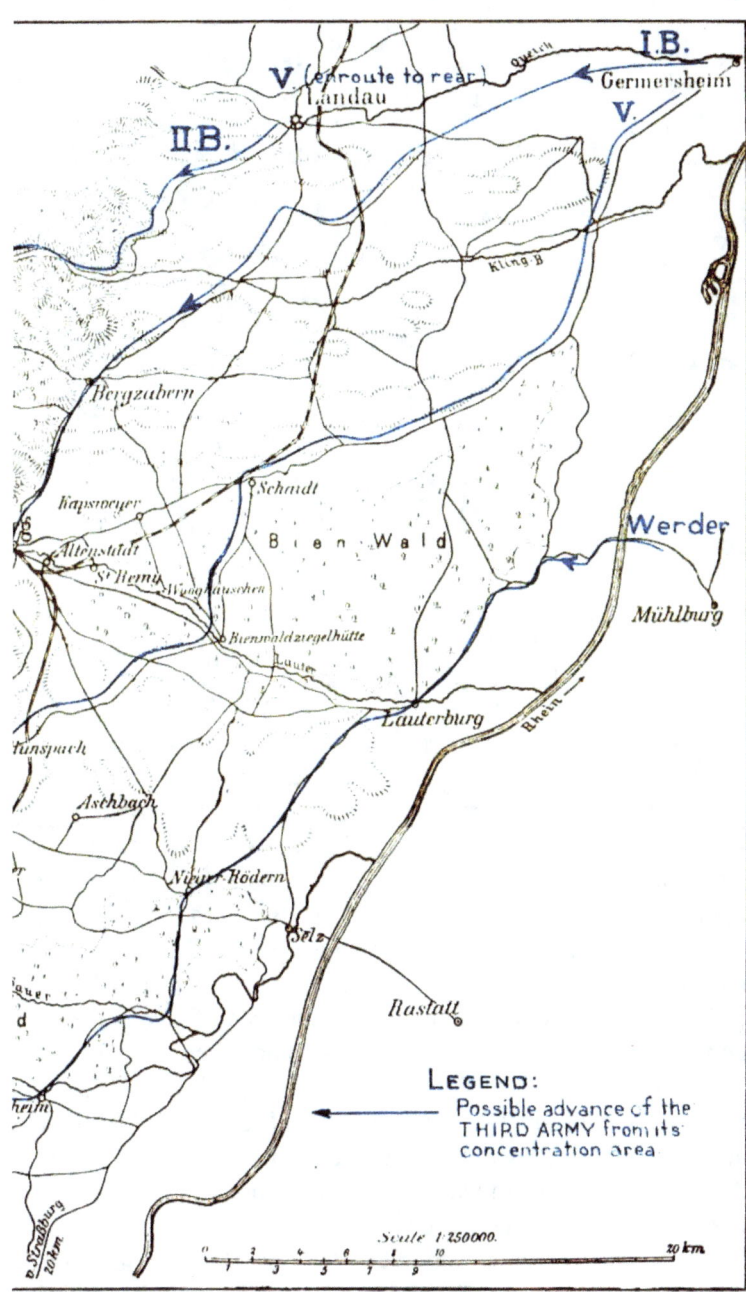

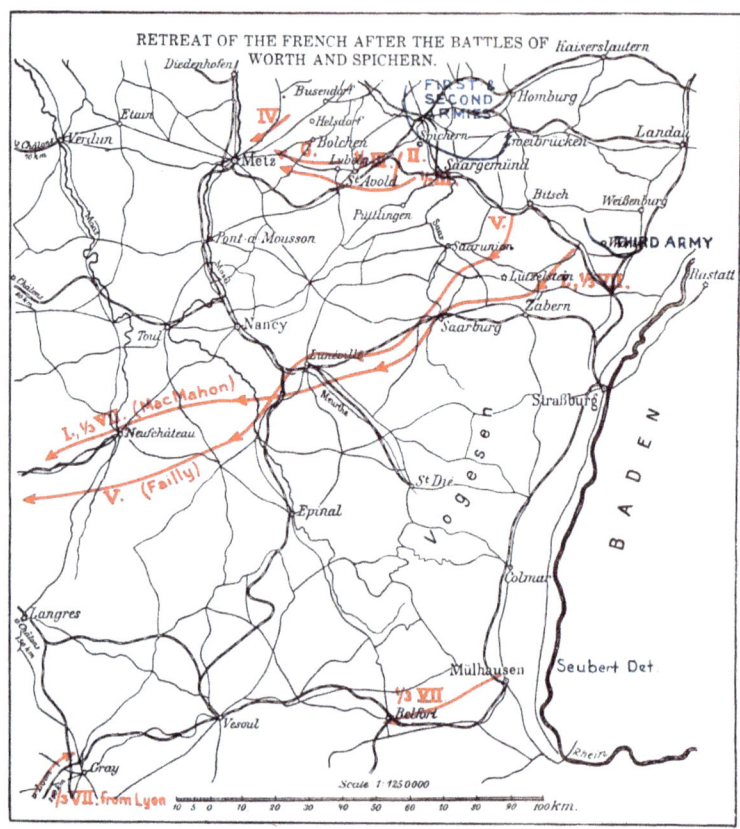

Worth and Spichern. MacMahon went with five divisions (four of the I and one of the VII Corps) via Zabern to Saarburg. One division of the VII Corps at Mulhausen thought itself threatened in rear by the detachment of the Wurttemberger, Colonel von Seubert, reported to be in South Baden, and retreated, almost in flight to Belfort, where the 3rd Division of the Corps of Lyons had also gone. Failly who had gone first to place himself under the protection of the guns of Lutze1stein, later joined MacMahon at Saarburg. On the 7th, two divisions of the III Corps joined Frossard at Purtlingen. The two other divisions of that corps were at St. Avold; in rear of them was the Guard at Lubeln, the IV Corps at Bolchen, Helsdorf, and Busendorf.

All these scattered units had to be assembled and this seemed possible only at Chalons, and no longer behind the Moselle.

The Campaign of 1870-71 289

Corresponding orders were already sent on the 7th to the corps, insofar as they could be reached. According to these, the IT, III, and [V and the Guard Corps were to assemble at Metz and thence march jointly to Chalons, MacMahon and Failly via Nancy, Douay (VII Corps) by rail to the same point. Because of false information, MacMahon believed that the road to Nancy was already blocked by the enemy and turned southward, Failly still farther southward and both reached Chalons, as well as Douay, with the help of the railway, between the 17th and 21st of August, in dissolution and demoralization, scarcely fit for service.

Only an immediate pursuit on the 6th and 7th of August could have increased the confusion and dissolution. A pursuit was attempted by the Third Army. After the enemy had disappeared from the battlefield of Worth, the 4th Cavalry Division was brought from its distant position in reserve and, since it was not known where the enemy had gone, it was sent on a false track. Nevertheless the division reached the French rear guard at Zabern on the 7th. The enemy had, in the meanwhile, come so far to his senses and had so much artillery on hand as not to allow a cavalry attack to throw him into the mountain passes. The pursuit in Alsace had thus come to an end. The Third Army followed the defeated enemy slowly and reached the Saar, not on the 8th, but on the 12th, between Saarunion and Saarburg.

The left wing of the Second Army advanced on the 7th and 8th between Bitsch and Saargemund, between the Saar and the mountains. As a matter of course, no enemy could any longer be seen. The naive hope, awakened by false information, that MacMahon would direct his retreat via Bitsch and could be thus cut off, was entirely disillusioned.

A pursuit from the battlefield of Spichern seemed simple and easy. The troops, which had fought on the 6th, were, however, quite exhausted by combats and marches and badly mixed up. The masses, more in rear had to be disentangled and brought more to the front before they could again become fit for service. At least two days of uninterrupted work were necessary to extricate the troops from the dangerous defile and much more time would be required to place the trains, which were in hopeless confusion, on the roads they had to take. Fortunately the enemy was too widely scattered. He needed time to assemble and had not yet gained any appreciable start when pursuit on the part of the Germans could be taken up.

The Advance of the Germans to and across the Moselle

The Battles of Colombey-Nouilly and Mars la Tour

After the battle of Spichern, the I Corps on the right wing of the First Army reached on 7 August, Lebach, one day's march from Rehlingen, and the IV Corps on the left wing of the Second Army reached Lorenzen, a few kilometers east of Saarunion on the 8th. Rehlingen and Saarunion were thus the extreme flank points on the line of the Saar, between which the ten corps of the 1st and 2nd Armies could be brought and formed by evening of the 9th, in order to start from there, according to Moltke's orders, "To seek the enemy and defeat him!"

This enemy did not fall back to Saarbrucken as had been supposed on the German side in the beginning. There he would have been cut off. He did not go, as had been advised on the French side, to the plateau between Toul and Nancy, surrounded by the Moselle and Meurthe rivers. He would have been surrounded there. He took, as reported by the cavalry, the natural line of retreat via Metz, Verdun, and Chalons. If the 800,000 Germans advanced from the Saar with a somewhat held back center on Metz, with somewhat advanced wings on Bertringen (south of Diedenhofen) and Dieulouard, they might count on driving the 144,000 French beyond the Moselle and into Metz. But what would have to be done after the river had been reached on about the 18th, depended on the attitude of the enemy. Should the French army march in several columns through Metz and right and left past Metz towards the Meuse, not much harm could be done to it. The pursuit would have to be continued as heretofore.

Every army on the retreat, which does not feel strong enough to face the enemy, is attracted involuntarily by a fortress in which it hopes to find rest and safety after the dangers and fatigue which it has undergone. Should the French army take the longed for rest and security in Metz only until the heads of the hostile columns appeared on the Moselle, the only road which would remain open for the continuation of the retreat would be that to Verdun, covered directly by Metz, and it would have been impossible to save the 120 km. long column of 164,090 men,* at which the French army was estimated, being surrounded by the German right wing, turning to the left on the other side of the Moselle, by the left wing, turning to the right, and by the cavalry, hurrying ahead to bar the road.

But an advance of the Germans across the Moselle on both sides of Metz could not be executed at the time. Army headquarters, which had placed on the march to the Saar four corps one behind the other on the same road and had drawn six corps into a front of a few kilometers, would not have been moved by any directions in the world to take with the ten corps as many roads on the other side of the river and a narrow front of 40 to 50 kilometers. They wanted to march in a much deeper and closer formation, but, most of all, not to be separated by Metz, not give the slightest possibility to the concentrated enemy of attacking the separated armies with united forces. Moltke was forced at the time to make allowances for such ideas and desist from his simple "seek the enemy and beat him" though the surrounding and annihilation of the enemy had. to come sooner or later through the numerical superiority of the German troops. Since the turning of both wings seemed too risky, Moltke had to be satisfied with the turning of one wing—the right. The enemy was not to be surrounded on the Moselle by an attack from both sides, but was to be driven to the north towards the frontiers of Belgium and Luxemburg.

The Second Army was to reach the left bank of the Moselle in three columns (the III, IX, and II Corps, via St. Avold, Falkenberg, and Nomeny; the X and XII, via Saargemund, Gross-Tannchen, and Delme; the Guard and IV,† via Saarbrucken and Morchingen), while

---

* The strength of the army was given by the French as 174,000 after the arrival of Canrobert. Since one division remained in Metz, the troops, led by Bazaine out of Metz on 14 August, might amount to 164,000 men.

† Since the Third Army was still far behind, the IV Corps had taken advantage of the crossing at Saarunion, assigned to it just then, and took thence a separate road, via Chateau-Salins.

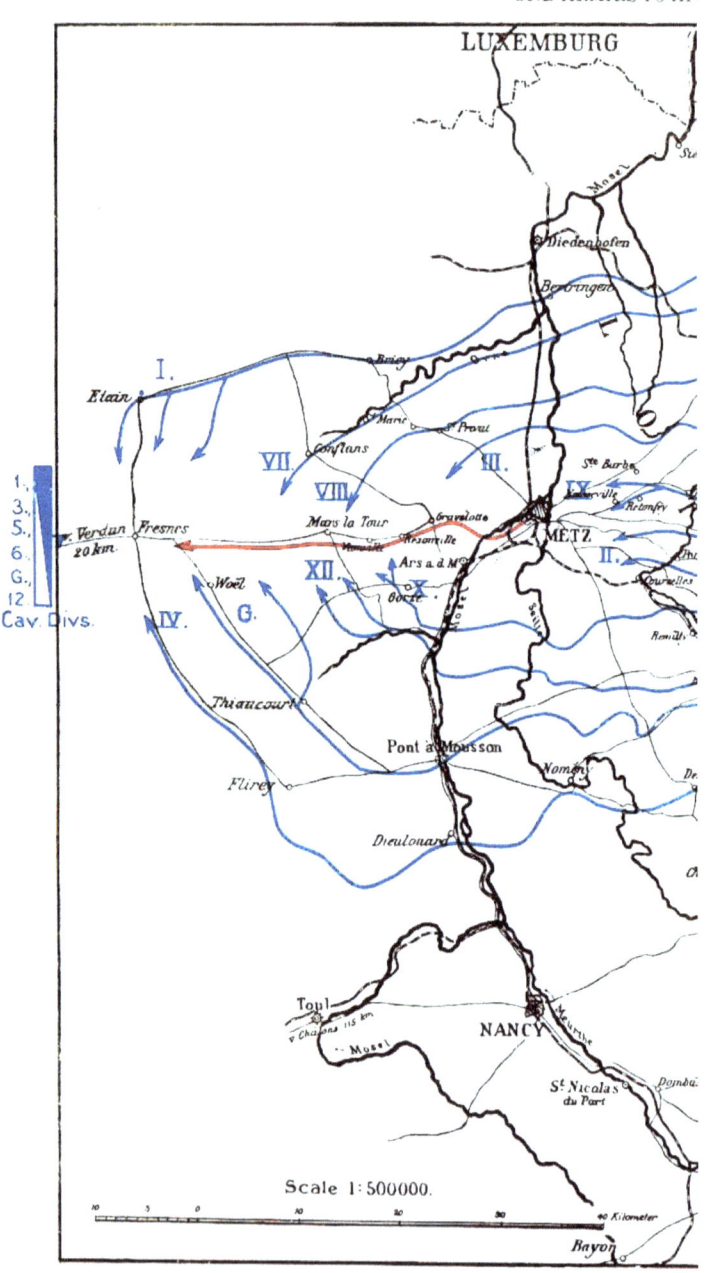

NCE OF THE FIRST AND SEC-
ID BEYOND THE MOSELLE

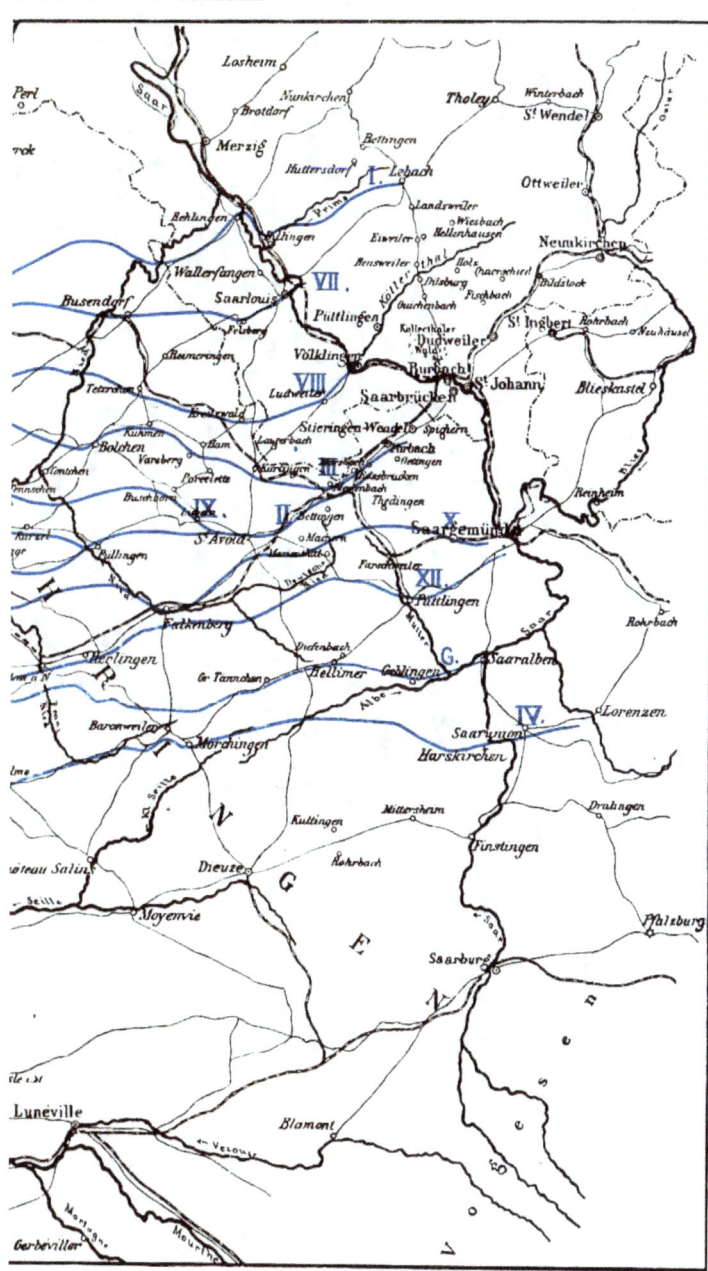

MOLKE'S PLAN FOR THE ADVANCE OF THE FIRST AND SECOND ARMIES TO THE MOSELLE.

The Campaign of 1870-71

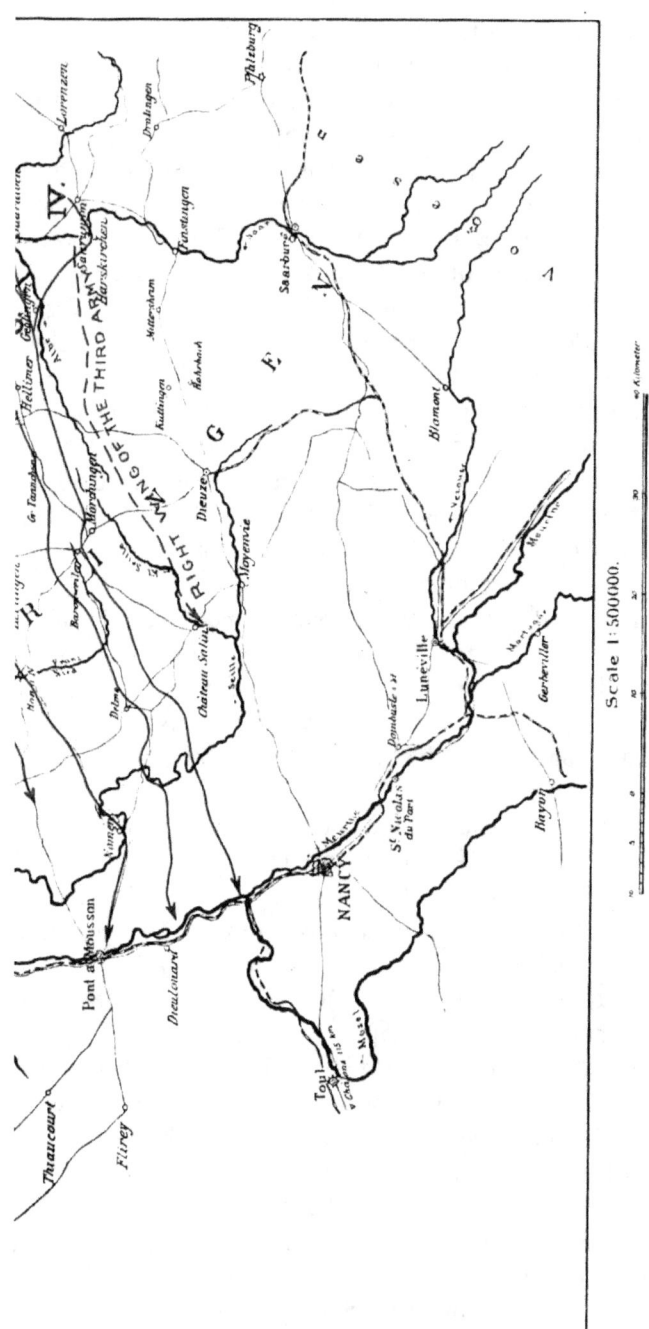

the First Army in two columns (I Corps via Kurzel and Pange, VII and VIII, via Lubeln and Remilly) was to cover the march of the Second Army against Metz, the Third Army following with its right wing via Saarunion in echelons. 450,000 men were getting ready to envelop 150,000. These 150,000 men might throw back the weak flank guard of 90,000 men (First Army), but would meet in their further advance, the Second Army and possibly, also the Third Army. The danger of a hostile attack was, consequently, not imminent, that of a hostile retreat would be greater. The success of the plan depended on the untarrying advance march of the Second Army and the longest possible stay of the enemy at Metz.

Such a stay was in no way among Napoleon's calculations. Very soon after the defeats of Worth and Spichern, he had decided on a retreat to Chalons, where he could hope to assemble all his available forces and be equal to the enemy who would have to considerably weaken his strength for the investment of fortresses and for covering his communications.

The Empress-Regent had, however, asked her husband to obey the will of the people and not give up Metz, the bulwark of the eastern frontier. Canrobert's Corps was sent thither by rail as a reinforcement. Should he have to hold Metz, Napoleon wanted to. hazard a battle on the French Nied with the fortress as a point of support in his rear.

The First Army, which on the 10th, reached with the I Corps Kreuzwald, with the VII Kalingen, with the VIII Lauterbach, had to advance against this position. It might be justified in not pressing forward at once, but remaining stationary on the 11th to await the arrival of the Second Army for a joint attack. But that the latter on the 10th, four whole days after Spichern, was still on the Saar and did not take advantage of the enemy's halt to make a great advance and reached, on the 11th, with the III Corps Falkenberg to be sure, but with the remaining corps of the first line only Hellimer, Geblingen, and Harskirchen, and with the IX and XII only Forbach and Saargemund, was in no way justified.

This army headquarters now believed that the march to the Moselle had lost its importance. Since the enemy had occupied a strong position, it entertained not so much defensive as offensive intentions, i.e., the intention of attacking an enemy of almost twice its strength. Such an attack would always have been fraught with the greatest difficulties. With the exception of the fabled feats of antiquity, of colonial wars, of Hohenlohe and Ruchel at Jena, who had adopted as an immutable principle, "always be the first to attack," only Frederick the Great had risked attacks against a twofold stronger enemy and that not always with success. And now, an old, sick man, a dilettante in generalship, with an already shaken army was to undertake a risk, which after even a possible initial success, would lead him to utter annihilation.

If Moltke saw in the taking up of the position by the enemy, only a temporary holding of it, as might be comprehensible, were his opponent not too pressing, the voice of Prince Frederick Charles, who had emerged from two campaigns a general crowned with glory, whose excellent plan of attack against the position on the Saar was crossed only by Steinmetz and who, out of ten corps commanded seven, ought not to remain unheeded.

The Prince, however, awaited or hoped for an attack and desired to prove in a brilliant manner the correctness of the principle "strategically offensive, tactically defensive." While preparing for battle, the III Corps was to seek a "defensive position," near Elkenberg, the First Army to advance with the I and VII Corps on the 12th to the German Nied between Bolchen and Mohringen, the VIII Corps to follow as far as Niederwiese and Buschborn, the IX to follow the III to Hubeln, the II to go to St. Avold. Army headquarters thought to make a turning movement to the right with the remaining corps to the line: Falkenberg—Verny, by the evening of the 15th, "straining all its forces." On the 16th, the patiently expectant Napoleon could make an attack against the Bolchen—Falkenberg position and be annihilated by a flank attack from the line: Falkenberg—Verny.

Unfortunately Napoleon knew nothing of the plans concocted against him. Otherwise he might have assembled his army behind the Seille, attacked the German left flank at Verny and rolled up the beautiful flank position,[*] while the Germans were still awaiting

---

[*] Foerster "Prince Frederick Charles of Prussia. Memorable events of his life." II, 136.

FRENCH POSITIONS ON
TERS' PLAN FOR OPE[
OND

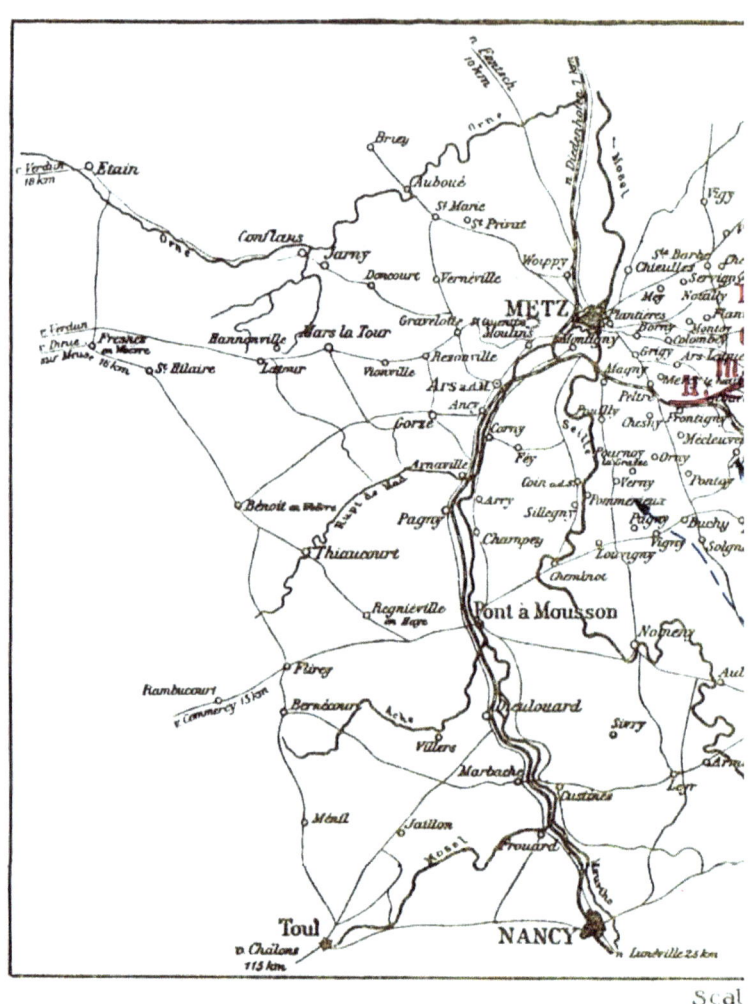

at the front the desperate attacks of a resurrected Ney and the Old Guard. Without an inkling of the heroic role, assigned him, Napoleon desisted from the defensive battle as soon as the heads of the hostile troops were seen in the distance and went on the 12th

10 AUGUST. HEADQUAR-
TATIONS BY THE SEC-
ARMY.

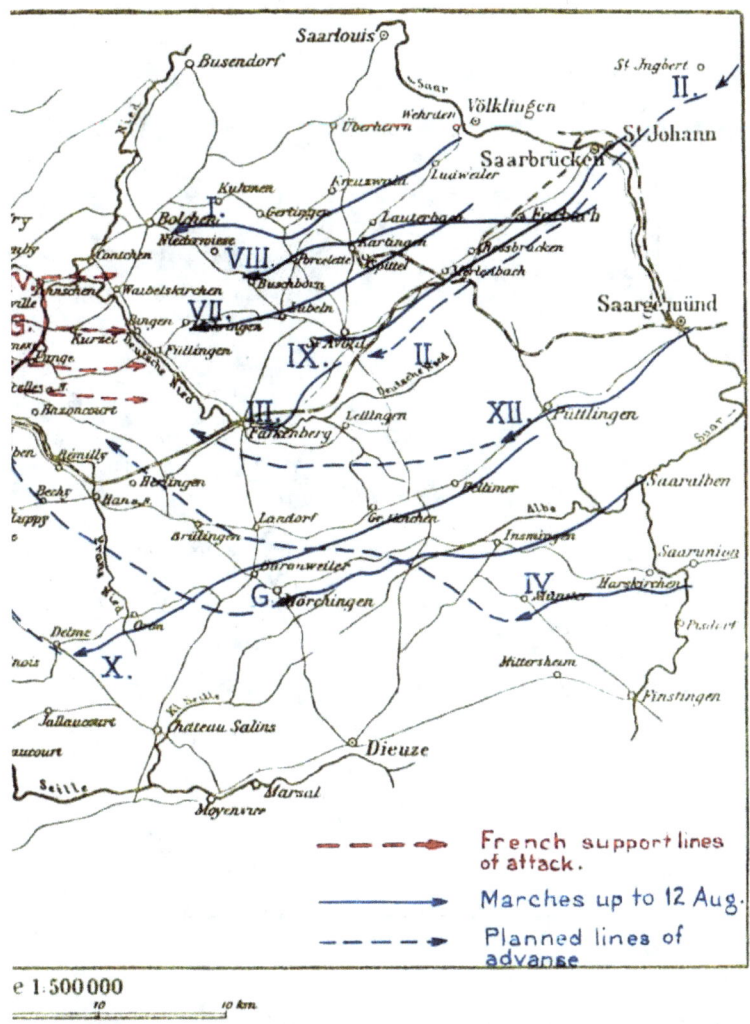

to a new position in the rear, with its right near Magny resting against the Seille and reaching the Moselle via Peltre and Colombey as far as Chieuilles.

The marches of the Germans on the 11th and 12th had been in

SITUATION ON THE EVE

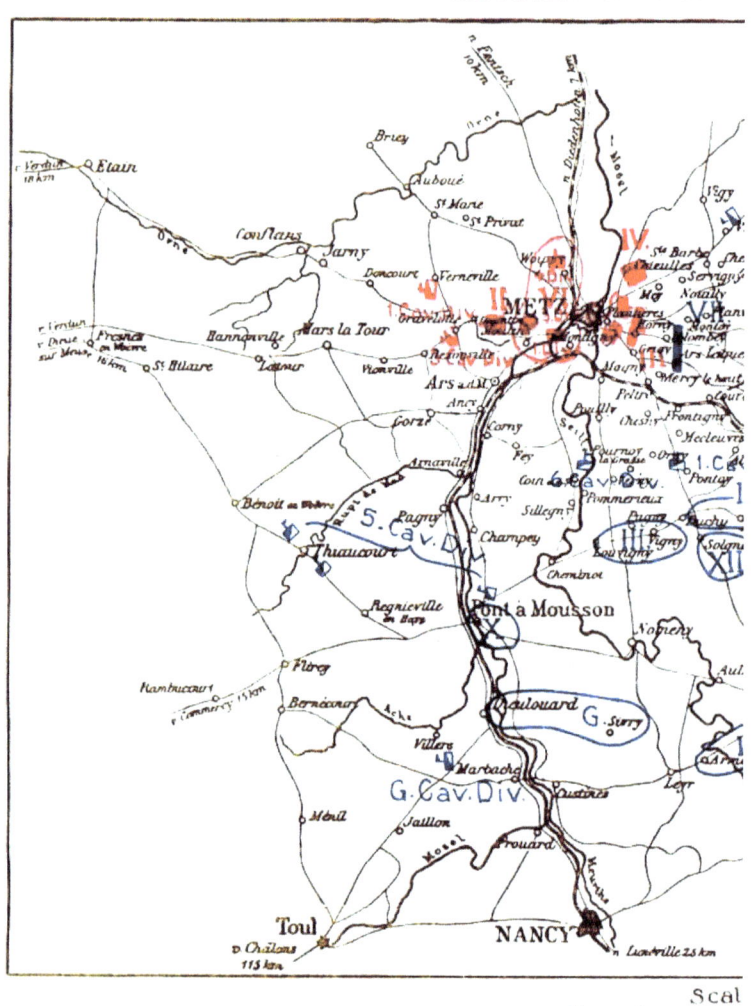

vain. In vain were the troops of the right wing assembled over bad roads under a pouring rain, concentrated in a narrow space without shelter or provisions, suffering a lack of everything. These hardships, however, disappeared and paled before the fact that the enveloping marches of the Second Army, from which the final success was expected, had been stopped. Only the X Corps had

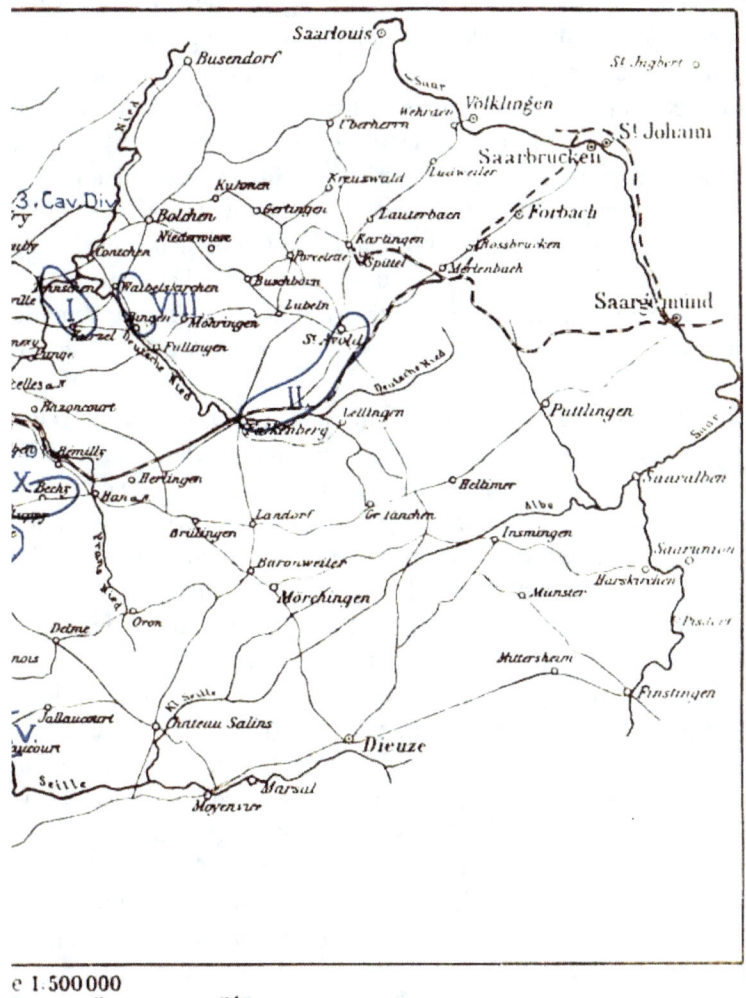

advanced one division at least to Delme. All the remaining corps were still far behind. On the 13th the march toward the Moselle was resumed. The III Corps advanced on the main road to Pont-a-Mousson as far as Buchy, the IX as far as Herlingen, but on the 14th, the former halted with its head at Louvigny, the latter at Luppy and allowed the XII Corps to come as far as Solgne to the south.

It was not so easy to abandon the hope of a hostile offensive; it was apparently believed that the enemy had retreated under the guns of Metz only in order to obtain a better run before his spring forward. Such a spring would now, it was believed, be made in a southerly direction along the road to Chateau-Salins. It would then strike at the crossroads: Saarbrucken-—Pont-a-Mousson the strongly posted III, IX, and XII Corps, which could be supported in the rear and on the sides by the II, IV, and Guard Corps, while the First Army of which the I and VII Corps had crossed the German Nied on the 18th, and the VIII had reached that stream, was to undertake Blucher's problem at Waterloo. The roles should be reversed if the enemy chose the road from Metz to Saarbrucken for his attack.

The expectation of a hostile attack did not seem quite unjustifiable. The German cavalry, which had reached the Moselle, on the 12th with its patrols, reported that along the river on the Frouard—Metz railroad there were long trains with small intervals between them supposed to contain troops of Canrobert's Corps. It was not possible to think that the army reserve, the nucleus, around which the army was to be organized at Chalons, had been brought to Metz only to be shut up with the Army of the Rhine in the fortress or, hardly detrained, would have to start the difficult retreat to Chalons, from where it had just arrived in all haste. These transports must have a special meaning. The intention of an offensive became possible; the enemy reinforced himself, while the Germans weakened themselves. Should the right wing column of the Second Army continue to march on Pont-a-Mousson, the First Army would be gradually isolated and Napoleon could easily arrive at the idea of utilizing the empty space between the Moselle and the Nied for an attack with his 174,000 men against the unprotected right wing of the First Army.

The turning movement of the Second Army could not be arrested, but the right wing column could have been given another direction. As soon as the defective system of roads south of Metz permitted, the III Corps should have turned off from the main road and moved in the direction of Champey or Arry and the IX toward Corny, in order to secure as many crossings over the Moselle as possible. To these could be added almost immediately the VII

Corps on the road to Pange; the VIII advancing via Kurzel and Teunschen; the I, via Ste. Barbe and Vry; the 1st and 3rd Cavalry Divisions, marching along the Moselle. There would then have been five corps on hand to break Napoleon's offensive no matter with how many corps it might be undertaken, or to halt the enemy as soon as he made a move to retreat further.

In other words: while the Second Army was turning the right wing of the enemy, the First Army should attempt to hold him in front, supported in this operation by the right wing of the Second Army. Had this plan of operations been adopted, since the First Army had been freed from covering the flank south of Metz and had been directed against the hostile front, ie, since the 10th, the Second Army might have reached the Moselle on the 13th and have come into contact with the enemy in the position: Magny—Chieuilles.

Long ago, at the time when the Germans were still preparing for the great battle on the Nied, Napoleon was thinking of resuming the retreat to Chalons, in spite of the Empress-Regent, the Ministry, Parliament, and public opinion. Uhlans had been seen at Pont-a-Mousson and Dieulouard which seemed to proclaim: the entire hostile army will soon cross the Moselle and to remain will mean to be surrounded. The execution of the retreat, found necessary, would cause a storm of wrath in Paris which it was urgently necessary to avoid. Therefore, the Emperor relinquished the command, transferring it to Bazaine on the evening of the 12th, with directions to start the retreat immediately. This was a very wise measure. The Emperor could feel absolutely in unison with his people, after laying down his command, and it was to be expected that Bazaine's appointment would meet with the approval of the editorial rooms of the boulevard newspapers. This however, did not remove all difficulties.

If the new commander-in-chief executed the command of his Sovereign and brought the army safely to Verdun, across the Meuse and to Chalons, he would fall under universal condemnation, would be branded as a traitor and ruined forever. For he would have left, faint-heartedly, the bulwark of the east in the lurch. A similar fate awaited him if he dreaded the difficulties of the retreat, remained in Metz, and were there surrounded. For

SITUATION ON THE EVEN[I]
FOR THE FURTHER ADV

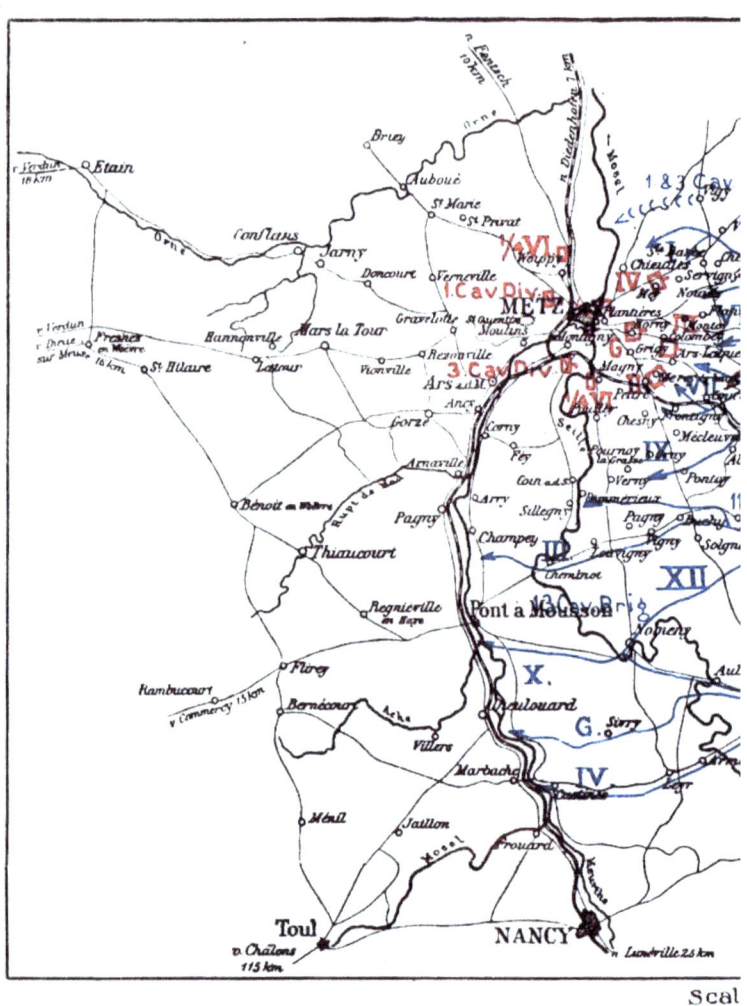

then he would have criminally neglected to unite his army with that of MacMahon into one unconquerable host. Bazaine could count only on extenuating circumstances if, after a glorious resistance, he should be forced by the numerical superiority of the enemy, to

ING OF 12 AUGUST. PLAN
ANCE TO THE MOSELLE

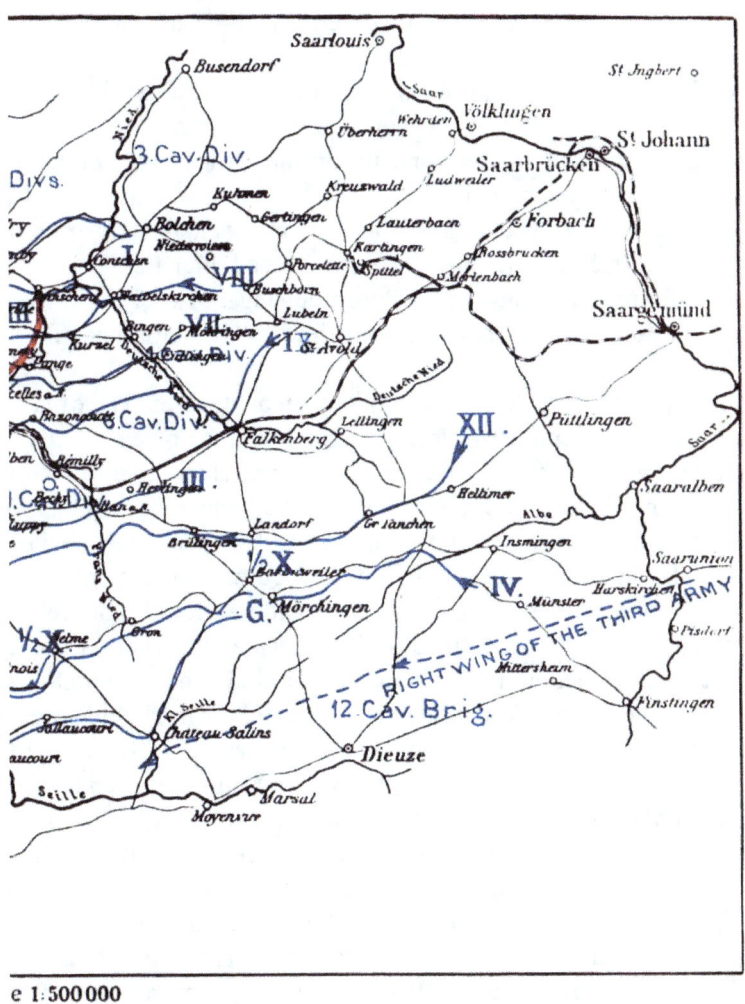

retire to Verdun or Metz. To allow himself to be invested in Metz without a battle would appear as shameful as to flee across the Meuse to Chalons. A battle was unavoidable. Bazaine needed not to worry lest it take place as soon as he started on the march to Verdun.

On the 6th, the Germans had already fought a battle south of the Saar. Between Diedenhofen and Fouard, this river is only 40 to 80 km. from the Moselle. Within seven days this space should have been crossed. At least the heads of the hostile columns must have reached the Moselle and would cross the river on the following day. The German army stood, consequently, on the Moselle above Metz, the French at Metz, mostly on the right bank. The latter might retreat by one road or be distributed over two to three roads, the columns would nevertheless be too long not to be overtaken. It was doubtful whether they would succeed in passing by the pursuer, forming front near Verdun, repulsing the closely following enemy, and gaining the necessary time for the crossing of the Meuse.

It was much more probable that an encounter would take place half way between the two fortresses and that the French would be either encircled by the overpowering numerical superiority or driven north toward the frontiers of Luxemburg or Belgium. Bazaine would then be wholly a traitor, and not he alone would be ruined, but France with him. The difficulties were great; they increased because the Marshal knew not how he could contrive the march from Metz to Verdun of 164,000 men with the horses, guns, and vehicles belonging to them. He could also not comprehend how to lead an attack with such an army, or how he should accept the battle should one be offered. In contrast with the difficulties of a retreat to Verdun, the commanding St. Quentin* enticed him to stay at Metz. Bazaine trusted that he could best oppose a victorious resistance to a superior enemy in a strong position, resting against the fortress. Should the enemy be repulsed, there would be time to take the offensive or to march to Chalons. Baizaine had to come to a decision, but at the end of each road he might take was posted the death warrant of the traitor. He was awakened from endless doubts and somber brooding by the report "Pont-a-Mousson is occupied by 100,000 men (19th Division)." The enemy was, consequently, on the point of crossing the Moselle.

That much was now certain. The French army could not

---

* Mountain 4 km. west of Metz with a fort of the same name.

remain on the right bank of the Moselle. Under all circumstances, it was necessary to cross over to the left bank to the plateau between Mars la Tour and Gravelotte. Circumstances would show, once there, if it were possible to attack the isolated hostile columns and throw then into the Moselle, if the assembled army should continue the march to Verdun or lastly, if, resting against Metz, the attack of the enemy should be awaited. The morning of the 14th was designated for the start.

Bazaine could consider unmolested how to effect the march to the left flank. A numerous staff was, it is true, at his disposal. Yet all the mistakes, committed so far, were ascribed to him personally. By his march orders, he had brought only confusion and evil. If the Marshal knew but little about the editing of march orders, still he thought that he could do it better than the strategic assistants detailed to help him.

The good advice, which was then withheld from him, was given to him later in profusion. Five roads: via Mars la Tour and Fresnes, via Conflans and Etain, via Briey, via Fentsch, and via Diedenhofen were open to him in order to disappear rapidly with his five corps. This would have been a flight, which would have brought him eternal shame and opprobrium, scattered his army to the four winds, exposed it to separate defeats and brought it to Chalons in small units, only increasing the confusion at that point.

With such advice, Bazaine was not served, since he considered a battle unavoidable and for this battle he wanted his entire army united. He decided to use for the present only the two southernmost roads via Mars la Tour and via Conflans, the one with three and the other with two corps. Unfortunately both roads formed but a single one as far as Gravelotte. All five corps with their trains and all belonging to them, had to be started over this one road in One monstrous column.

The impossibility of executing this was soon apparent. In this perplexity, there was discovered another narrow, steep deeply cut road, which could be used only to a very limited extent, leading via Plappevile—Lessy—Chatel St. Germain—Malmaison and opening into the road to Confilans. After long seeking, it was even found that it was possible to turn from the main road Woippy—Briey at St. Privat or Ananweiler toward Doncourt. With the use of these

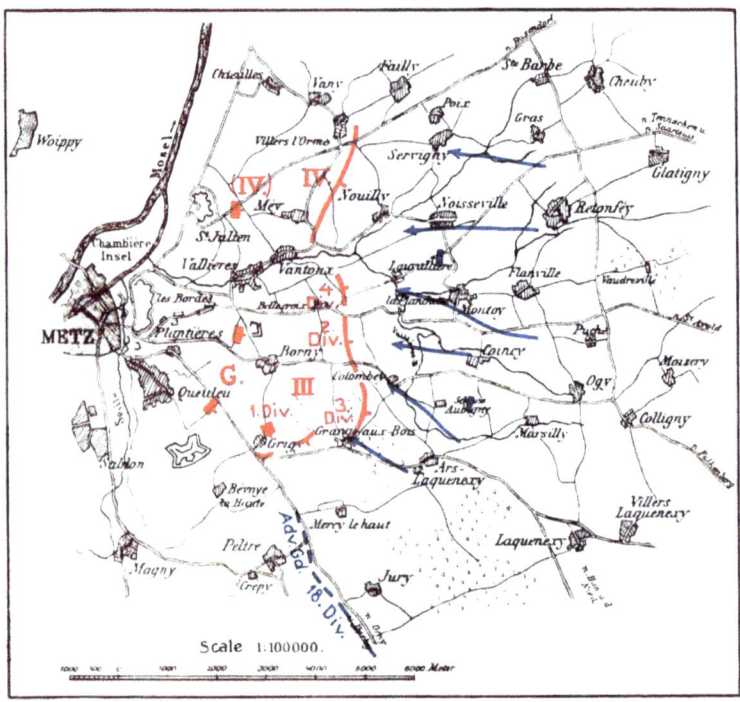

BATTLE OF COLOMBEY-NOUILLY.
14 August, 1870.

three roads, the French Army could have been assembled during the course of the 15th, though with the sacrifice of part of the trains, between Mars La Tour, Doncourt, and Gravelotte, for the purpose of attacking, retreating, or defending itself.

But on that very 15th, the Second Army, which had to reach the Moselle on the 18th, was to be expected south of the Gravelotte—Mars la Tour road. A battle must be fought at the latest, on the 16th, the First Army being able to take part in it effectively from the Moselle below Metz. However, neither the one nor the other party appeared in time at the rendezvous. The Second Army did not come because it reached the Moselle not on the 13th, but on the 15th. The French Army did not appear because it was held back on the right bank of the Moselle.

General von der Goltz had advanced with the 26th Infantry Brigade ahead of the VII Corps to Laquenexy. When he received the report of the Cavalry at noon that the French were on the point of evacuating the position: Magny—Chieuilles, and of retreating across the Moselle, he realized the necessity of detaining the enemy as long as possible to give the delayed Second Army time to come up. Not a moment was to be lost, as the II Corps, forming the right, as well as the IV Corps, forming the left flank of the French position, had already disappeared, the one south of Fort Queuleu beyond the Seille, the other across the island of Chambiere beyond the Moselle, while the center, the III Corps, as well as the Guard Corps must have already begun the march through the city had the crowding of the streets with vehicles not blocked their way.

After having reported to his division commander and informed Headquarters of the I Corps, General von der Goltz started at 3:30 PM with seven battalions, three squadrons, and two batteries on the march against the center of the hostile position at Colombey. Vallieres Creek was crossed, the village taken by the advance guard. Further advance, however, was checked by strong hostile forces deployed on the opposite plateau. The III French Corps had faced to the front at the advance of the German Brigade, Castagny's Division (2nd) had returned at a run to their old entrenchments at Colombey. On the left, Aumard's Division (4th) extended as far as the Vallieres Creek between Vantouz and Nouilly; on the right Metman's Division (3rd); the right flank was later covered by Montaudon's Division (1st), north of Grigy facing southwest. The Guard Corps took up position west of Borny. Bazaine allowed this movement to be completed, but ordered that it be limited to defense, that no advance whatever should be made, and that the troops should withdraw as soon as it were possible. .

Naturally, General von der Goltz's Brigade could not do much against the great superiority. Only gradually, hour by hour, did reinforcements come by all roads, Falkenstein's Brigade (2nd), of the I Corps from Maizery via Montoy, Memerty's half-brigade (3rd), from Retonfey via Noisseville, lengthening the front from La Planchette to Lauvalliere and thence to Nouilly. The 25th Brigade came via Coincy for the immediate reinforcement of von der Goltz's Brigade so that the entire 13th Division, supported by the corps artillery, occupied the space between La Planchette and

Colombey, while the 28th Brigade took part in the combat south of this point, the 27th south of Coincy in reserve, and only late in the evening the advance guard of the 18th Division came up from Orny via Mercy le Haut to Grigy.

This deployment, lasting several hours, was not awaited by the troops that had already arrived. Every newly arriving reinforcement gave rise to a new attack, to ever more energetic advance. The French were thus pushed back in the center as far as Borny, on the wings as far as Grigy and Bellecroix. It was impossible for the Germans to advance further. Their left wing was in the immediate vicinity of Fort Queuleu which was prevented from sweeping the front of the VII Army Corps with its guns only by the advent of darkness and by its own troops.

In the meanwhile, another combat developed more to the north. General Ladmirault, on hearing the thunder of the guns, took the IV Corps back across the Moselle, leaving one division near Fort St. Julien and occupied his former position with two others, the position reaching from the Vallieres Creek via Mey to Villiers l'Orme. To the troops of the I Corps south of the valley of Nouilly, forming the right wing of the Prussian battle line, it seemed inevitable that the overlapping French front between Mey and Villiers V'Orme would advance, turning to the right, cross over the strip between Nouilly—Servigny, crush the right Prussian wing, and roll up the entire battle line engaged in a hot combat. There was not sufficient infantry on the spot as yet to meet the threatening attack.

The protection of the flank had to be entrusted to the artillery which had hurried up. A few batteries were placed at Poix and Servigny, the greater number on the heights on each side of Noisseville, and orders were given to Memerty's Brigade, which had just come up, to hold the ground at Nouilly at all cost. Later on the 4th Brigade, brought from Tennschen, was sent to Servigny, the 1st as far as Noisseville and the batteries taken from Poix to the heights of Failly.

All these measures taken to escape a threatened surrounding movement proved unnecessary. General Ladmirault had not recrossed the Moselle to attack the enemy or wreak evil upon him. He wanted only to occupy his old position at Mey—Villiers l'Orme and to hold it for the purpose of protecting the as yet unfinished Fort St. Julien and to prevent the enemy from gaining the high right bank of the Moselle whence he could get a glimpse of the camp of the greater part of the French army between Metz and Woippy. Since the 4th and 1st Brigades of the Prussian I Corps arrived too late in the evening to undertake an attack against the French IV Corps, the combat of the two opposed north wings would have been limited to an artillery duel, if ever renewed attacks by a few companies against Mey, the key of Ladmirault's strong position, had not been made, and repulsed, as might well have been expected. The French felt elated by such cheap successes, although they withdrew in the dark, and though these feelings were hardly shared by the soldiers. Troops, obliged to retreat exhausted after a bloody battle, feel not victorious, but defeated. The courage of the Corps, which as yet was fresh, was not heightened by the battle, but depressed. The troops went forward to new encounters without confidence of victory.

The Germans had attained their object. The retreat of at least three French corps had been delayed not less than 24 hours. The French army would not be on the 15th, yes, not even on the 16th, assembled at Mars la Tour—Gravelotte.

The success might have been far greater if army headquarters, on hearing of the retreat of the enemy, had sent forward the entire First Army and had occupied towards evening the position in which the French had been posted in the morning. This would have resulted by itself in a decisive offensive across the Moselle below Metz. Army headquarters was, however, far from making such a forward movement. It had sent, on the contrary, during the battle, and finally in the evening, repeated orders to stop the engagement and to return to the previous positions. The commanding generals of the VII and I Corps (v. Zastrow and v. Manteuffel), found themselves unable to obey. They could expose their troops to the losses of a difficult attack, but not to the greater ones of a retreat. The soldiers had to be strengthened in their confidence in themselves and in their leaders, and not weakened. General von Manteuffel let himself be persuaded, however, to retreat in the night, while General von Zastrow remained, ready for combat, in the positions taken during the battle, held the battlefield alone until morning, and left only when the French had disappeared from the right bank.

Had the battle of Colombey—Nouilly brought out nothing else it would have at least clearly shown the unfitness of a position as narrow as possible, as deep as possible, and with reserves as strong as possible. Only weak advance guards could be detached from the narrow front. For support, detachments could be brought up only gradually. Absolute confidence had been placed on compressed masses and it was found that this compelled attacks of strong positions occupied by superior numbers to be made by small detachments and with the thinnest of lines. It had to be discovered that the enemy, whom it was desired to drive back, deployed on a wider front and threatened a crushing envelopment. The reserve, whose problem it was to meet such a danger and itself make such an envelopment, thought itself posted too far to the rear to be able to give any aid on the 14th. The VIII Corps thought to advance on the morrow, not to prolong its own wing and turn that of the enemy, but to reinforce a frontal attack with fresh forces, a frontal attack which had already seen its termination at the Metz fortifications.

Since the French withdrew to the west and the Germans to the east, an ever widening space formed between them. An order from Moltke was to put an end to this unwholesome state, which would have sent the First Army back to the victoriously gained positions, and then, apparently, further beyond the Moselle. In the meanwhile, the King had ridden forward with his suite. It could be seen from the heights of Flanville, that the field this side of Metz was free. On the other side, however, in the valley of the Moselle, around St. Quentin and up the plateau toward Gravelotte, clouds of dust were rising.

It was clear that the enemy was retreating by the road to Verdun. The head of the 100,000 men, who had fought the day before at Colombey, might go one day's march forward, but their rear would still be in Metz in the evening and days would go by before this column, and possibly those parts of the French Army which had gone before, would be able to shift from the Moselle to the Meuse. The enemy must be prevented from completing this march. He must be forced to stand and accept battle. The simplest and surest means. to this end was to send the First Army across the Moselle below Metz and the Second above that city and to leave the protection against the eastern side of the fortress to the II Corps. This means had to be abandoned, as the First Army could not be entrusted, at least in the beginning, with an absolutely separate and independent operation. Thus, the problem of pursuit fell to the share of the Second. Army. Its right wing was to be followed by two corps (the VII and VIII) of the First Army. The I Corps was entrusted with the observation of the eastern front.

On the French side, on the 14th, the retreat was begun. as well as was possible, in view of the general ignorance as. to what should be done, the perplexity and disorder, over roads which were overcrowded and in bad condition. Only late in the night of the 15th, did the last units of the leading corps reach the objectives assigned them. The Cavalry Divisions of Valabregue (of the II Corps), Forton (1st Reserve Cavalry Division) and du Barail (3rd Reserve Cavalry Division) were at Vionville, Gravelotte, and Malmaison, the II Corps (two and one half divisions) along the main road between Rozerieulles and Longeville, the VI Corps thence along the railroad as far as Woippy. Early on the 15th, they were to march as follows: Forton to Mars la Tour, du Barail to Doncourt, the II Corps to Rezonville, and as soon as the VI had reached the latter point, further to Mars la Tour.

The following had found their way to the evacuated camps: the Guard to Longeville and Moulins, the III Corps to Plappeville and Devant les Ponts, the IV to Woippy and east as far as the Moselle. These three corps had received orders to continue the march as soon as possible. The crowded condition of the roads as well as the utter exhaustion of the troops kept them from doing so. Only the Guard could be taken in the evening to the height of Gravelotte, in rear of the VI Corps. Two divisions of the III Corps succeeded in working through via Plappeville to Verneville and La Folie. Two other divisions, as well as the IV Corps remained in the valley of the Moselle during the night of the 16th. These five divisions had to be awaited before an offensive could be undertaken or the march to Verdun continued. The rear of the French army was thus still at Metz and its head had come to a standstill before it had been anticipated.

For days Moltke had urged the Second Army to send the mass of cavalry to the left bank of the Moselle for reconnaissance. Only Rheinbaben's Division (5th Cav. Div.) and the 3rd Cavalry Brigade of the Guard had been in response thereto, though late, utilized for this purpose. The remaining two and two thirds divisions were kept back so that they could be on hand in the ultimate attack in the hoped for battle on the Nied or in the vicinity of Metz.

The patrols ascertained that the French camps between Magny and Chieuilles had remained unchanged throughout the 13th. In confirmation of these reports, a. German brought news from Metz that, up to the evening of the 138th, no rétreat of the French in a westerly direction had taken place. About noon on the 14th, patrols found the Metz—Verdun road at Vionville free of troops in both directions. Early on the 15th, Colonel Count Groeben, who, with a few squadrons and a battery, had penetrated to the vicinity north of Augny, on the right bank of the Moselle, fired on hostile camps on the other bank between Longeville and Moulins.

Rheinbaben received orders to advance on the 15th as far as the Metz—Verdun road. After the departure of all flank detachments and of the covering detachments, six of the 36 squadrons and one battery under General von Redern reached the vicinity of Mars la Tour. The battery entered into an artillery duel with the batteries of Forton's Division. Redern gradually received reinforcements attracted by the thunder of guns. With the help of reinforcements, he was going to attack the hostile cavalry. But before the attack could be executed, the French cavalry retired to Vionville. The IZ Corps thus remained at Rezonville and joined at this point the VI, whose right wing reached as far as St. Marcel, thus forming a great mass, increased in the evening by the arrival of the Guard Corps near Gravelotte.

Naturally these particulars could not be learned by the German cavalry, but it did learn that the strong hostile forces had stopped their advance from Rezonville and east of the latter on the Metz—Verdun road. North of this road German patrols had encountered strong cavalry, not immediately followed by infantry. The picture might have been completed if the First Army had ascertained by patrols on the left bank of the Moselle below Metz or on the high right bank of the river what part of the French army had remained in the valley of the Moselle between Metz, St. Quentin, and Plappeville. But even Without such reconnaissance, it was clearly determined that the French army, in its march to Verdun, had not advanced beyond Vionville and Malmaison. Its masses stood between these points and Metz. On the 16th it would probably again advance, extending to Mars la Tour and further west; no great change, however, should be expected. Should part of the army have marched by the road to Briey, the French forces would thus only be weakened for the impending battle.

Moltke had already warned in the evening of the 14th, "advance along the left bank of the Moselle against the communicating roads: Metz—Verdun, in large force" and had telegraphed in the forenoon of the 15th: "Pursuit on the Metz—-Verdun road important." It was scarcely necessary to add in the evening of the 15th: "The fruits of the victory (on the 14th) are to be harvested by a strong offensive of the Second Army against the road from Metz to Fresnes as well as from Etain to Verdun," and further "according to the present point of view the decision of the campaign rests in driving the main forces of the enemy, escaping from Metz, in a northerly direction."

There was, consequently, no doubt as to what the Second Army must do at noon on the 15th. The French army, whose right wing stood today at Vionville, would stand on the morrow at Mars la Tour or further west and was to be driven northward. For this purpose the right, and perhaps also the so far unreconnoitered left wing, had to be turned, the one pushed away from Verdun, the other from Metz.

In order to reach this goal, all available corps had to be used, all existing or to be established crossings of the Moselle must be utilized. Of the six corps, the IX was with its head at Peltre advancing to the battlefield of the 14th, the III was at Louvigny. The 20th Division of the X was at Pont-a-Mousson, the main body of the 19th Division at Thiaucourt, Lyncker's half-brigade at Noveant. The Guard Corps, at Dieulouard, had sent an advance guard as far as Les Quatre Vents, the IV Corps was to advance on that day to Marbache, the XII to Nomey, the I to Han on the Nied. The further advance of the IX Corps was to be via Corny and Ars to Gravelotte and Rezonville, of the III via Arry to Vionville, of the

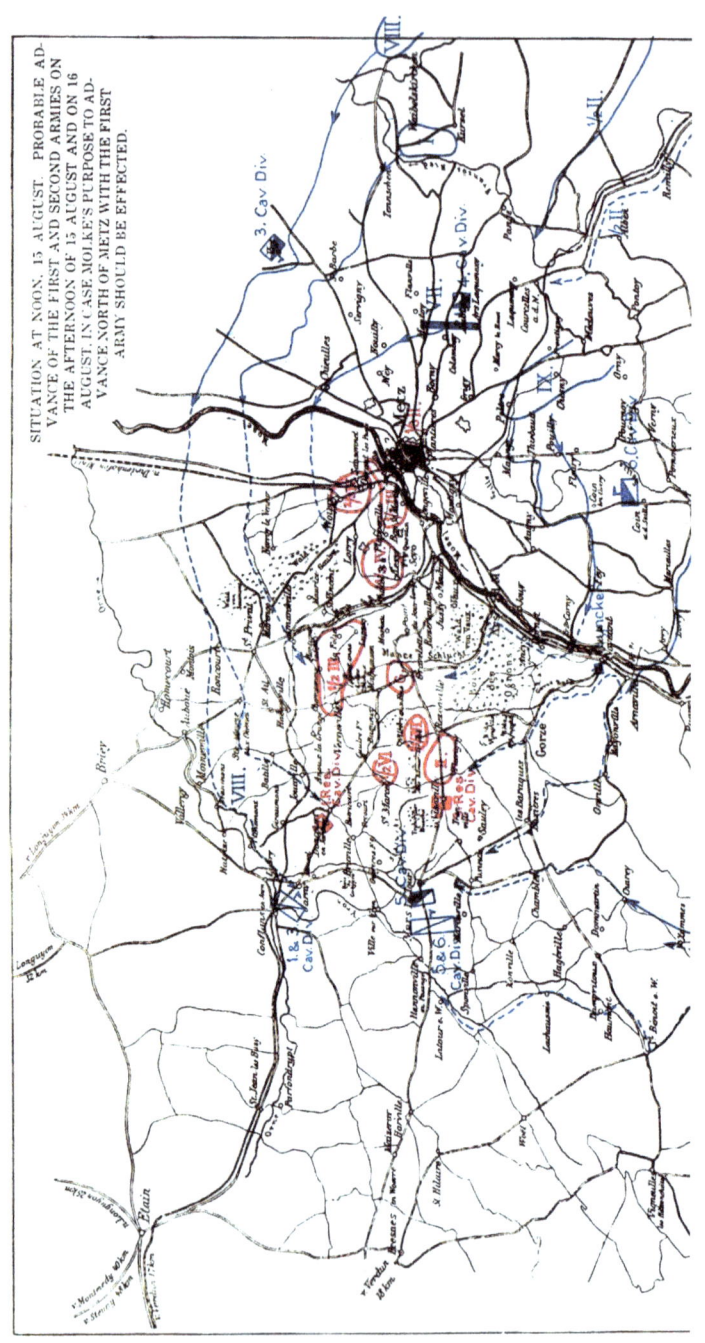

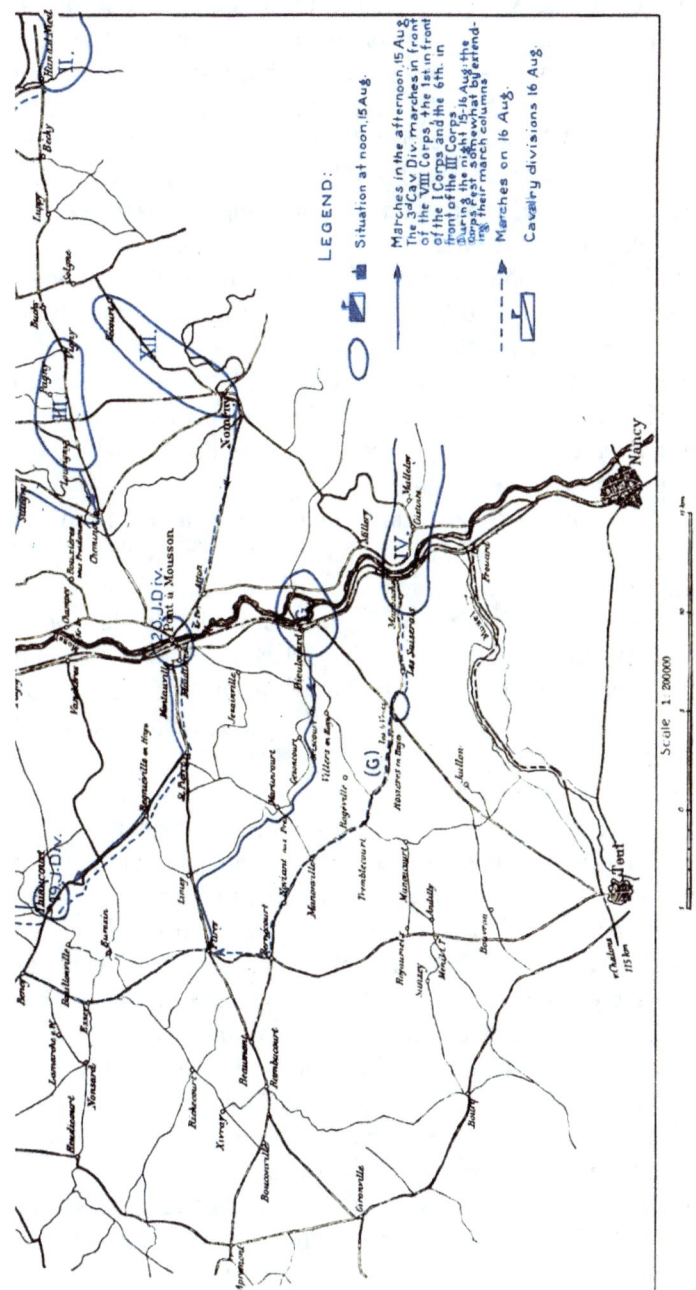

X, followed by the XII, from Thiaucourt at Mars la Tour, of the Guard Corps and the IV to Hannonville and Latour.

The corps stood at various distances from their objectives. In the afternoon of the 15th the IX Corps could march to Corny, the III across the Moselle, the X beyond Thiaucourt, the Guard Corps to Flirey. On the 16th, three Corps could surely be brought against the enemy, the VII, VIII, XII, and IV following as reserves. The reserves would not have been so strong, had the First Army gone around Metz on the north. But then there would have been not four, but seven corps available for the attack, and it would have been truly an annihilating attack.

The task of the Second Army was clear. Moltke's order was to advance by the two roads leading from Metz to Verdun. Where the enemy was on these roads had been ascertained by the cavalry as well as circumstances allowed.

It is, however, wrong to think that reports in war from the cavalry are of any importance or even desired. The higher leader generally makes himself a picture of friend and foe for whose delineation personal desires do the principal work. Should reports received coincide with these wishes, they are laid aside with complaisance. Should they contradict them, they are considered entirely false and justify the final conclusion that the cavalry had once more failed entirely.

The Second Army, in its advance from the Saar to the Moselle, regarded its task of turning the enemy only as a secondary one. Its principal aim was to prepare itself for an unlikely attack by the enemy. Now, having arrived at the Moselle, the enemy could no longer escape and had to accept battle. The Second Army paid no attention to him, taking heed only of another adversary who was said to have escaped, in the greatest hurry, from the Moselle to beyond the Meuse and who must be pursued in order to be forced into a battle on the Marne. The reports of the cavalry were considered absolutely false, resting on imagination and on pessimistic views. The battle on the 14th had not been waged by a French army, not by three corps, eight divisions, 100,000 men, but by a weak rear guard, which, after heroic resistance against superior forces has perhaps reached only Rezonville on the 15th. The task of the Second Army is, consequently, a march to the Meuse.

For this purpose, the XII Corps must go to Pont-a-Mousson on the 16th, its advance guard to Regnieville; the Guard Corps to Bernecourt, its advance to Rambaucourt, the IV Corps to Les Sezerais, its advance guard toward Toul; the II to Buchy, the III and the X Corps to strike the main Metz—Verdun road, and with this opportunity, to make short work of the weak hostile rear guard which has remained halted at Rezonville.

Sixteen German corps had invaded France, ten had caught up with the hostile army and brought it to a halt, seven could attack in the first line, two were to fight the decisive battle.

If only these two corps had at least been utilized conjointly! Each however, follows its own promptings and the misleading "orientation" given it from army headquarters. Of the X Army Corps Schwarzkoppen's half division with the 3rd Guard Cavalry Brigade (Brandenburg) was sent from Thiaucourt to St. Hilaire. Probably so that it might still catch a few stragglers. Half of Lehmann's Brigade was to advance from Thiaucourt, Lyncker's half brigade from Noveant to Mars la Tour, the former to support Rheinbaben, the latter to join Lehmann. Kraatz with the 20th Division was to march from Pont-a-Mousson to Thiaucourt and serve as a strategic reserve for the others.

All these units, led by true soldiers and brave men, though scattered to the four winds, were to find themselves united on the battlefield. But this was not yet sufficient to wage a successful combat with the French army. The greatest merit for having fought one of the most glorious battles of the century, belongs to General von Alvensleben and to the III Corps, commanded by him. Convinced of the correctness of Moltke's plan of anticipating the enemy on the left bank, the general had looked on with impatience and doubt at the attempts, on the part of army headquarters to fight and win victories on the right of the river by "strategically offensive and tactically defensive" methods,

As soon as the report of the battle of Colombey—Nouilly had arrived, he did not allow himself to be kept back any longer and marched independently toward the Moselle. Although he was again held back en route for some time by army headquarters, he still succeeded in carrying out his intention and stood in the evening of the 15th with the 6th Division at Pagny and south of it to opposite

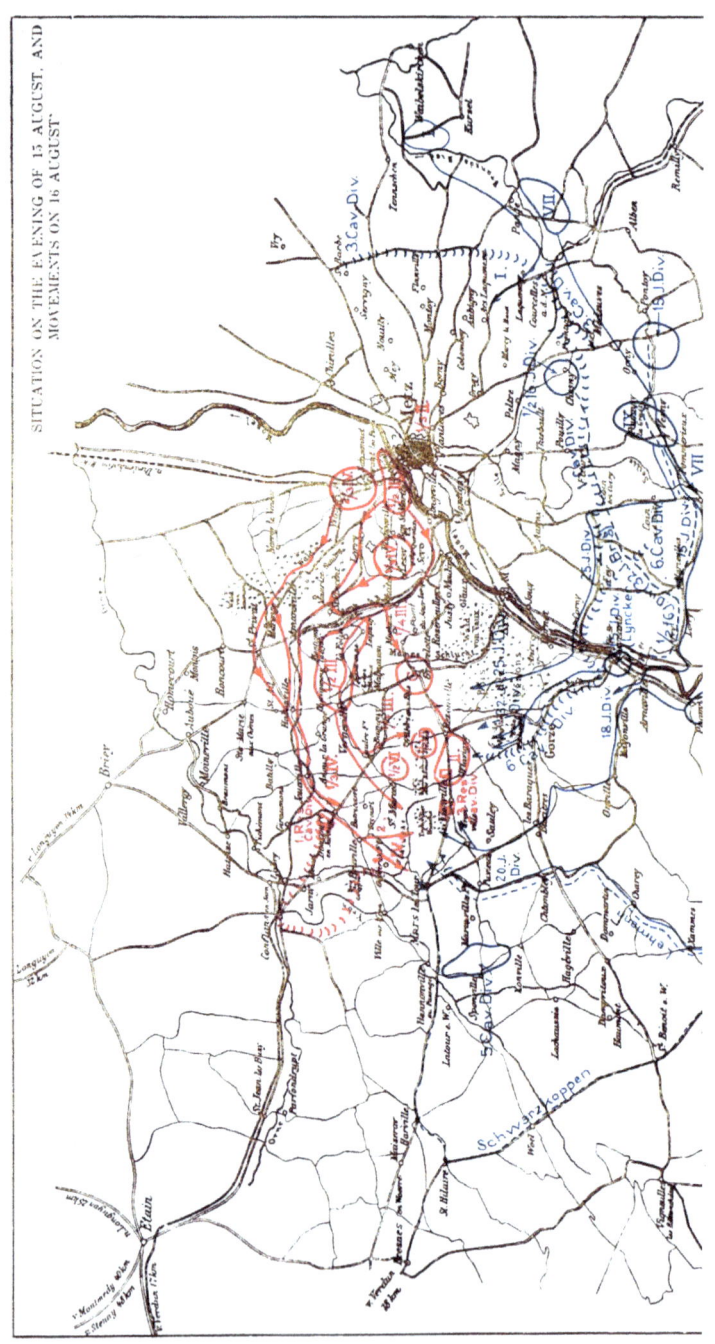

The Campaign of 1870-71

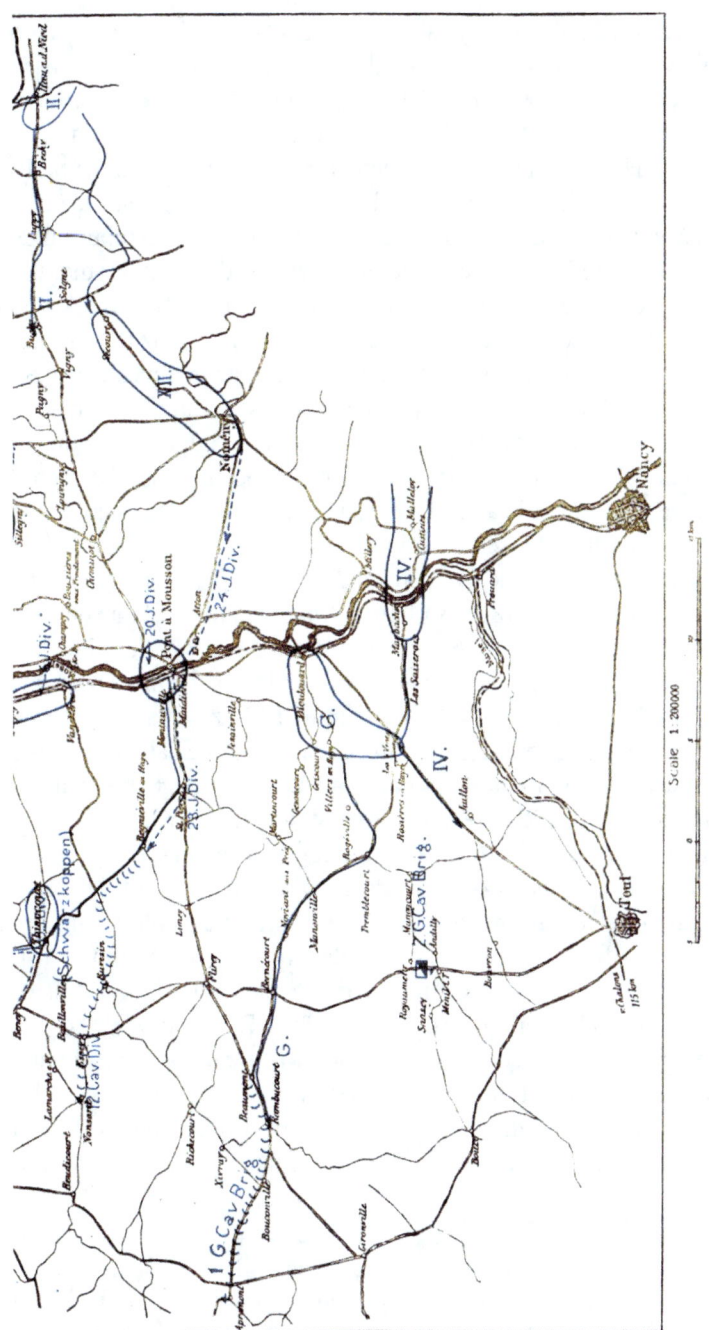

Chamrpey, with the 5th Division at Noveant on the left and with the 6th Cavalry Division at Corny on the right bank of the Moselle so as to march early on the 16th with the two latter via Gorze to Vionville, with the former via Arnaville, Onville, Chambley, and Mars la Tour to Jarny. Here he encountered the enemy. Whether the latter were weak or strong, he wanted to get ahead of him on both roads leading from Metz to Verdun, prevent him from retreating and if repulsed by superior strength, to retire in the direction Verdun, hoping that the K Army Corps and perhaps still other parts of the Second Army, might bring the enemy to a stand and force him to retreat to Metz.

The III Corps was still at the beginning of its marches when the Chief of Staff of the X Corps, Lieut. Colonel von Caprivi, arrived at Rheinbaben's Division in Xonville. "Something ought to be done to ascertain whether the cavalry was right in reporting that the enemy is between Rezonville and Metz or, as army headquarters holds, he is already on the Meuse."

The question could be answered by a simple calculation: the enemy was still at Metz early on the 14th. Since noon of that day, no Frenchman had gone in the direction from Metz to Vionville, the enemy must, consequently, at least in as much as the main road has been used, be between the latter point and Metz. This calculation, however, was not considered as sufficient. An attack alone can give the desired information. Rheinbaben advanced, brought his artillery into action against the cavalry camp at Vionville, where the men were busy cooking, feeding and watering their horses, etc.

The consequences were: disorderly retreat of Forton's Division, sudden flight of the nearby trains, but also the deployment and advance of the infantry at Rezonville. The line: St. Marcel—Vionville, was occupied by the 1st and 3rd Divisions of Canrobert (VI Corps), Frossard's 2nd Division (II Corps), lengthened the line south of the road, while the 1st Brigade and Lapasset's Brigade turned south where Hussars of the 6th Cavalry Division had shown themselves. Canrobert's 4th Division remained at Rezonville,* the Guard at Gravelotte. Thus the III Corps found an

---

* Of Canrobert's Corps only the 1st, 3rd, and 4th Divisions and one regiment of the 2nd had reached Metz. The rest were prevented from continuing the rail journey by the Germans.

already deployed army in its front. The 8th Brigade, at the head of the 5th Division, had to fight its way from Gorze in the direction of Vionville through the woods of St. Arnould and Vionville. The 10th Brigade succeeded gradually in surrounding the enemy opposing it on the road to Vionville and in driving him off in a northeasterly direction. The 5th Division was already engaged in a fierce combat, when the 6th Division deployed from Sauley with the 12th Brigade on each side of the road to Vionville and with the 11th farther south.

After hours of fighting, Vionville, the height east of it, Flavigny, and the northern edge of the woods of Vionville, and St. Arnould were taken. A weak point was found in the new French position where the front facing west joined the front facing south and where an attack was possible from two sides. This was taken advantage of by the 10th Brigade, reinforced by Lyncker's half brigade, and Valaze's Brigade, opposing it, was driven in a northerly direction on Bastoul's Brigade. As the other Prussian brigades attacked simultaneously, Frossard's entire Corps (II) had to retreat in disorder. Colin's Brigade of the VI Corps joined the retreat north of the road.

In order to protect these two brigades from pursuit, Canrobert had the other brigade of the 3rd Division, Sonnay's, turn half left and ordered the 1st Division (Tixier's), advancing from St. Marcel, to join in the extension. An annihilating flank attack threatened the 24th Regiment and one battalion of the 20th which, so far, had alone formed the weak left flank north of the road to Verdun. Bredow's Cavalry Brigade (three squadrons of the 7th Cuirassiers and three of the 16th Uhlans) was thrown against the hostile troops along the old Roman road. The first line was ridden down, the artillery line was pierced, the men and horses cut down. The second line could not stop the charging cavalry. The batteries on the heights farther in rear limbered up and fled. After a charge of 3000 paces a fresh French cavalry detachment opposed the exhausted troops. The long road had to be covered once more.

The results were: Bredow's Brigade lost half its numbers, ten French batteries left the battlefield, Canrobert's 3rd Division declined to take the offensive. It formed from now on the right wing of the position taken by Canrobert's 4th Division, by the

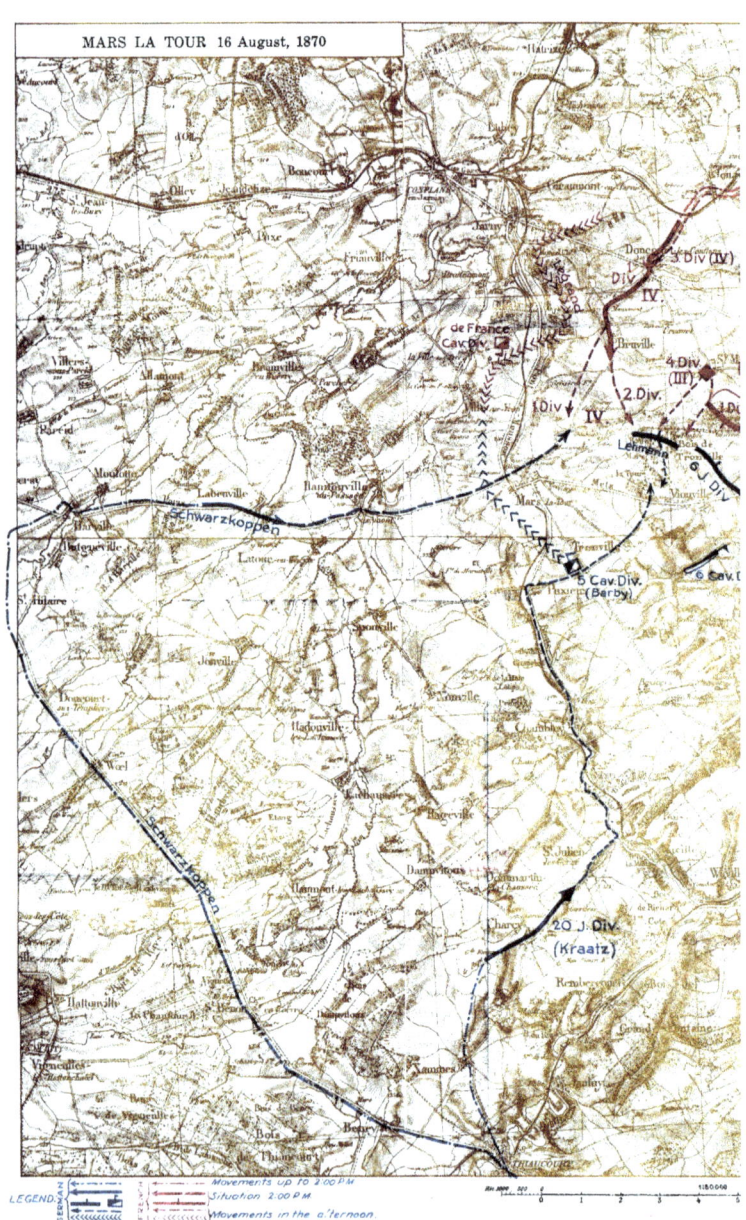

The Campaign of 1870-71

Grenadier Division of the Guard and by Lapasset's Brigade, cutting through the Roman road to the Verdun road immediately west of Rezonville and reaching to the Rezonville—Gorze road, near the Maison Blanche. Montaudon's Division of the III Corps was sent as a reserve east of Rezonville. West of Gravelotte stood Voltigeur's Division of the Guard and east of it Frossard's defeated Corps.

The front of this position, occupied by seven and one half divisions, could not be attacked with any hope of success and forces were lacking to turn it. But also an attack against the two Prussian divisions would be repulsed by infantry and artillery fire and mostly by the resolute resistance of the leaders and troops. A more or less lively combat was continued by the artillery of both sides. On the other hand the combat in the afternoon raged on the Prussian left wing north of the Verdun road. Here Tixier's Division (1st) of the VI Corps had arrived from St. Marcel at the old Roman road. To the right as far as Bruville, Leboeuf (I Corps) would come up from Verneville, as soon as he had assembled his three divisions. Further to the right, Ladmirault (IV Corps), who had been advancing since early morning with three divisions from Woippy via St. Privat and Amansvillers to Doncourt was expected. Should these seven divisions advance simply the one beside the other, the III Corps, held in front by such a strong force, would be absolutely annihilated and the X Corps would not suffice to stop for any material time the broad flank attack. The French would win a great victory on the 16th and would have the choice of pursuing this victory on the following day or, at least, of retreating unmolested across the Meuse.

However, two divisions, one of Leboeuf's (I) Corps and one of Ladmirault's (III) Corps deployed too late from their deep, compressed march columns. Thus two divisions were absent from the battle. The remaining five, however, were sufficient to carry out the overpowering flank attack.

The weak left wing of the 6th Division opposite Tixier, had to be withdrawn north of the Verdun road. The hill east of Vionville formed from then on an advanced point in the line of battle. It ran thence to the left to the Bois de Tronville, occupied by Lehmann's half brigade which had just arrived. Against these woods, occupied by only a few battalions, was now directed an attack by Tixier from the northeast, by Leboeuf from the north, and by Grenier's Division of Ladmirault's Corps from direction of Bronville. Tixier was arrested by the left wing of the 6th Division. Leboeuf with his two divisions became but slightly engaged in a fire fight. He had received orders in the morning, among others, to "hold strongly," and, he would hold to this order now where he should have quickly driven in a weak enemy. Deep formation of his forces, keeping back strong reserves, seemed to him the best means to support the powerful flanking attack and to cooperate in any undertaking which was to decide the fate of the two armies. The concentric attack of one part of Tixier's Division and of Grenier's sufficed however, to force Lehmann's half brigade to retreat. It gradually evacuated first the northern and then the southern part of the woods and retired to Tronville which was prepared for obstinate resistance. But how long could this point be held situated as it was in the rear of the II Corps position?

At this moment of danger the 20th Division (Kraatz) appeared. It had started from Pont-a-Mousson in the morning, marched from Thiacourt to the sound of the cannon, detached a few battalions to the sorely -pressed 5th Division and arrived with nine battalions at Tronville after a march of 24 miles. The advance of two battalions thence against the Bois de Tronville sufficed to bring about a change of the situation. Ladmirault saw himself threatened in the front and believed himself menaced in the right flank by an "army of infantry." Grenier's Division was taken back, Kraatz following into the Bois de Tronville. A long combat took place there. But the danger, which Tixier, Leboeuf, and Grenier had evoked with four divisions seemed averted for the time being.

In the meanwhile, Cissey's Division which had taken second place in Ladmirault's marching column had come up. It received orders to attack the enemy in rear and thus bring about the decision. The prospect of success was of the best. Should Cissey march west of the Bois de Tronville, Grenier would be freed. Kraatz's Division would retreat and should Leboeuf and Tixier join, it would be possible to attack the rear of the III Corps with five divisions while it would have to face in its front the attack of at least four and one half divisions.

Unfortunately Cissey met on his way the "army of infantry" i.e., Schwarzkoppen's half-division (Wedell's Brigade, the 16th and 57th Regiments). It had marched in the morning from Thiaucourt to St. Hilaire and thence, to the sound of the cannon, to Mars la Tour. It received orders there to attack the right flank of the enemy. What had been indicated to it as such was probably Grenier's right flank but not Cissey's, hidden from sight by the hills. Thus it came upon the latter's center.

The long march, made in the fierce heat of the August day, had completely exhausted the strength of the thirsty troops. But the cry "there is the enemy" removed all trace of fatigue from the Westphalians. With beating hearts, but resolute courage they advanced against the superior enemy who had taken position on the road to Bruville in rear of a deep ravine. The attacker disappeared for a short while in the ravine after which men climbed the steep slope. At the upper edge rapid fire at 150, 100, 50 paces met them. They answered with a like fire. Two lines, about six files deep, two immense white clouds, continually pierced by short streaks of lightning, a thundering noise and nothing to be seen until the comrade suddenly drops alongside. Impossible to halt.

"Up! Forward!" sounds the order. The voice dies. But those nearest see the leader brandishing the sabre, waving high the flag. One man calls to the next. The line storms onward. But now the overlapping wings of the enemy begin to turn inward and pour infernal fire on flank and rear of the storming Germans. Back, what is left, back into the ravine and up the hill, ever pursued by the bullets of the enemy. Artillery attempted to protect the fleeing troops. Three squadrons of the Dragoons 1st Regiment of the Guard advanced against the enemy. They found a low spot through which they could approach unseen and fell on the right flank. But it was still too broad for the small crowd. The officers and the foremost troopers broke the line of skirmishers right into the midst of bullets and bayonets.

The attacks of the infantry and cavalry were a complete failure. Wedell's Brigade and the 1st Dragoons no longer existed. The French had an open space before them for the execution of the great annihilating attack with division from the right flank. But Cissey remained on the southern edge of the ravine. The effect, produced by the attacks, was too impressive. The French were sure that new and stronger enemies would renew the attack which they had luckily repulsed. "You can not make us believe that your regiment would have attacked us with such force if it had no army corps in its rear," was said the following day to an officer of the 16th Regiment who had been wounded and taken prisoner.

Since he did not feel strong enough for the attack by another Wedell's Brigade, Ladmirault found it advisable to take Cissey's Division back to Bruville and Doncourt, being followed by Grenier and where the still absent Division of Lorencez arrived at dark.

The audacious attacks of Wedell's Brigade and of the 1st Dragoons of the Guard, though repulsed, decided Ladmirault to retreat and by this retreat, the battle was decided in favor of the Prussians.

A cavalry combat on the extreme left wing west of the Yron brook in which General von Barby with six regiments repulsed Legrand's Division and France's Brigade, as well as the occupation of the Boise de Tronville by Kraatz's Division could not increase this decision, but only confirm it. The French right wing, Ladmirault, Leboeuf, and Tixier had evacuated the battlefield or kept up, for appearances' sake, a gradually slackening rifle fire. The left wing still held the position at Rezonville. Its front. was too strong to be overpowered. But reinforcements were arriving.

At the head of the VIII Corps was the 32nd Brigade which had been joined voluntarily by the 11th Regiment of the IX Corps[*] and which had crossed the Moselle at Corny in the afternoon, still wishing to reach the battlefield. The Division Commander, General von Barnekow, had his nine battalions deploy along the road to Gorze south of the Bois des Ognons intending to strike the flank and rear of the enemy, stationed at Rezonville, through the woods. The sorely pressed 5th Division, however, demanded immediate assistance. Barnekow could do nothing else than go via Gorze along the narrow ridge along the road to Rezonville, to attack by regiments and, after initial success, to retreat, repulsed by the rapid

---

[*] The IX Corps had subsequently received the order to follow the III Corps and to cover it on the road to Metz.

fire of superior reserves. After three attempts and three failures, the Prusslans were forced to retreat to the heights immediately north of the edge of the woods while the French occupied the heights north of the Maison Blanche.

The 25th Division had likewise crossed the Moselle at Corny. At its head, General von Wittich with the 49th Brigade (4 battalions, 4 squadrons, 3 batteries) entered the Bois des Ognons, drove back a battalion of the Chasseurs of the Guard, reached the northwestern edge and directed thence his fire against the reserves retreating to Rezonville. Further advance was barred by hostile troops, still holding out in the eastern part of the woods. Only at 10:00 PM, was the battle ended at this point and a bivouack occupied in a clearing.

This much had been accomplished, that the masses, which had been assembled at Rezonville, marched to Gravelotte and beyond in by mo means an orderly way. Also the road had been shown by which great success was to be achieved and on which it might have been attained, had General von Barnekow been permitted to advance with his nine battalions through the Bois des Ognons against the enemy's line of retreat between Rezonville and Gravelotte, and had the 25th Division joined this attack via Ars east of the Mance ravine. The French would then, probably, have been driven in a northerly direction and against the frontier of Luxembourg and Belgium as demanded by Moltke.

Such aims, however, were far from Prince Frederick Charles who, on hearing that the III Corps was engaged in a serious battle, had hurried to the battlefield in the afternoon. He thought that he had an indecisive battle before him. In order to win a victory, he ordered a general attack in the evening, i.e., to do what the III Corps had been attempting for 10 hours by straining every nerve, but which met its natural end through losses, exhaustion, lack of ammunition, and the numerical superiority in that strong position. The order could be executed only in a small way, since the artillery lacked horses and the infantry ammunition. The attack of the weak infantry, which had been assembled at dark and of two cavalry brigades went to pieces in face of the rapid fire of still intact French battalions. Had it succeeded, the enemy would have been driven back in the direction which he had chosen for the retreat.

The Campaign of 1870-71 331

The order of the Prince was inspired by a high-minded feeling of proud courage, but caused the glorious day to end in a failure. That more had not been achieved in combat must be attributed to the inferior numbers of the troops and neither to the leaders nor to lack of heroism. Nothing, however, could change the result, least of all by a frontal attack with quite inadequate numbers. There was every cause to be satisfied. What 60,000 men could achieve against. 164,000, had been achieved in the highest degree. It was sufficient that the inferior numbers had forced the superior ones to abandon all offensive movement and to retire to more or less distant positions. A retreat to Verdun was thus rendered impossible and there remained only the choice of a retreat in a northern direction or back to Metz.

It can scarcely be said that the French plan of battle, whether thought out by Bazaine or imposed by circumstances themselves, would have rendered the success of the Germans easier. The intention of holding the III Corps in a strong position, of safeguarding the left flank against all envelopment, and of attacking with a very strong right wing, was very promising of success. The plan failed through the mode of execution and through the conviction of Bazaine and his corps commanders that they had before them not a small force, but a vast superiority in numbers. This was not overrating the enemy. According to not exaggerated calculations the mass of the German Army could and must be on the ground if not in the early morning, then at least during the course of the day. To have pursuaded the French to take this view and belief in the superiority of the enemy is the great feat of General von Alvensleben, and of the III Corps. The means by which the general sought to reach his aim was, as the French General Staff Account calls it, "a brutal offensive."

Had Alvensleben's Corps and Schwarzkoppen's half-division wisely and sensibly taken up a good position, they would have been annihilated without being compensated by a great success for their sacrifice. Attack and repeated attack, recklessly and without consideration, had brought unparalleled losses but had also brought victory and, it may well be said, the decision of the campaign.

For, although the last repulsed attack had given Bazaine a shadowy right to report officially: "The Prussian army, defeated at all points, retreated," he betrayed his secret thoughts by the words directed to his staff officers that "The French army must be saved."

To bring the army into safety across the Meuse was no longer possible if the Germans, as was to be expected, should follow in a northerly direction. To act according to Moltke's desire and to allow themselves to be driven to the Belgian—Luxembourg frontier, would have been courting destruction. Nothing remained to do but what Bazaine expressed in continuation of his words, "and therefore return to Metz."

This was salvation, at least for a time, during which many things might happen; possibly a better deliverance than that which might be vouchsafed by the junction at Chalons of the beaten and pursued Army of the Rhine with the remnants of MacMahon's troops and with the Guard Mobile battalions, arriving from Paris. To go to Metz immediately was not expedient since claim had just been made of a brilliant victory and since the enemy was too close to the left wing. A new battle, but one without prospect of success, must be fought.

The Battle of Gravelotte—St. Privat

The night of 16-17 August was passed by the French Army as follows: the three divisions of the IV Corps at Doncourt, two divisions of the III and the 1st Division (Tixier) of the VI Corps between St. Marcel, Villers aux Bois, and the Romer Strasse, the remaining eight and one half divisions, two of the III and two of the VI Corps, two and one half divisions of the II Corps, and two of the Guard Corps between Rezonville, Gravelotte, the northern edge of the Bois des Ognons and the height south of Rezonville.

Almost immediately opposite extended the German outposts from the Mance ravine obliquely through the Bois des Ognons along the northern edge of the Bois de Vionville, half way between Rezonville on the one side, Flavigny— Vionville on the other side toward the Bois de Tronville, which encompassed them on the north. In rear of these stood the 25th Division in the Bois des Cgnons, the 16th on the Gorze—Rezonville road, the III Corps at Vionville, the X at Tronville with a flank guard against Mars la

The Campaign of 1870-71

Tour. In the night the IX Corps started to the heights west of Gorze, the XII, via Thiaucourt, the Guard Corps via Beney, St. Benoit, and Chambley to Mars la Tour. Immediately in rear of the IX Corps the VII was to follow across the Moselle to Gravelotte, the VIII, leaving Gorze to the west, to Rezonville.

Bazaine believed that on the 17th he had been engaged with the First and the Second German Armies and was certain that on the 17th, the Third Army would join these enemies. This assumption was not based on the imaginings of a mind which saw everything through black glasses: the three German armies might have been easily assembled at that time between the Moselle and the Meuse. But, by keeping only to the undisputable facts, that the French army had retreated on the 16th, that the enemy stood close opposite, and that the reinforcements from the Moselle were advancing, Bazaine was forced to believe that he was facing a superiority, if not in numbers, at least in efficiency.

It may thus be easily understood that he did not wish to attack. This had not succeeded on the 16th and would have been a complete failure on the 17th. He did not want to remain stationary, for he had to expect that he would be surrounded on the right and left and driven back in a northwesterly direction. He could not face his army to the right in order to march in a too lengthy column along the hostile front via Conflans to Verdun or to the left via Gravelotte to Metz. He would soon have been halted and would have found himself in the same situation as before.

More favorable was the outlook for a retreat via Briey. He would go away from the enemy in a practically perpendicular direction. To the left and right of the Gravelotte—Briey road there were two other roads via Homecourt and Moineville and thus the marching columns could be considerably shortened. Nevertheless they would still be so long that, to avoid being attacked by the enemy they would have to start on the march in the evening of the 16th.

This, however, was not possible. The troops, with the exception of the IV Corps which had maintained its spirit, were almost disbanded, greatly mixed up and all in the depressed and discouraged spirits of a defeated army. To form three narrow columns in the night or even in the morning of the 17th, for the retreat over the Orne, out of the mixed up crowd, was impossible. Should this, however, take place during the day, it would result in an immediate pursuit partly via Conflans, and bring about the driving of the French to the Belgian and Luxembourg frontiers, so desired by Moltke. Even if the pursuit were begun late, repeated rearguard actions would have taken place and there would have been no sense in taking the discouraged and shaken army on a retreat, resembling a flight, thus ruining it entirely, on the long detour to Chalons in order to join there MacMahon's remnants of troops, while 450,000 Germans would have appeared at that point by a shorter road almost simultaneously, to give a decisive battle.

Such prospect was not consoling to Bazaine. It was better to take the left wing out of the threatening turning movement from Rezonville via Gravelotte to behind the Mance ravine and to execute from the front: Gravelotte—Doncourt, a face to the rear toward the Moselle. On the ridge east of the Mance and west of the ravine was an "impregnable position" where an attack could be awaited and repulsed without any fear. After this had been accomplished, it would be possible, after another face to the rear, to reach the Metz fortifications and enjoy the well deserved rest. The attempt to make the double facing at one time would have brought a complete dissolution of the army.

A halt had to be made in the strong position and a battle fought. This was the least that could be demanded from an army which had won, officially, a brilliant victory on the 16th. The short retreat was excused by the need of provisions and ammunition, and it was reported quite seriously that the ordered march to Chalons, would take place over the repulsed and annihilated enemy. Thus read the official intentions. As a matter of fact, the retreat to Metz was fully decided, if not earlier, at least in the evening of the 16th. This retreat must lead in any event to a complete downfall.

In 1757, more than one hundred years earlier, the Austrian Army under Prince Charles of Lorraine, after a . bloody battle had been thrown back to Prague and invested. The information caused great terror in Vienna. After closer investigation of the circumstances, it was recognized that this investment was of greater advantage than a retreat bordering on flight. Prince Charles was instructed to undertake attempts at breaking through the enemy without, however, allowing them to succeed. Since there were sufficient provisions, Prince Charles was to stay in Prague and keep the greater part of the Prussian army in front of this fortress. It was hoped that sufficient troops could be assembled against the rest. The battle of Kolin showed the correctness of this speculation.

The state of affairs in 1870 was somewhat different from that of 1757. The energy of a Maria Theresa was not felt in Paris, nor was there at the head of a relief army the wisely calculating Count Daun and, instead of the few Prussian battalions which bled to death at Kolin, there would still remain, after the investment of Metz, a German field army of 250,000 men. But, since a French army must be invested in a fortress, there arose therefrom conditions not very different from those of 1757, to take advantage of which there was no one to compete with Moltke.

The critique of the war was just in maintaining that it would have been best for Bazaine to beat with his 160,000 men the 450,000 of the German army. Since he, however, did not feel able to solve this problem and since he did not wish to be driven to the Belgian and Luxemburg frontiers or be received at Chalons as a completely defeated general by the likewise totally beaten MacMahon, the retreat to Metz must be considered as a tolerable expedient.

But was it still possible to use this expedient? Was the French Army, which could not be entrusted with the retreat to Briey, capable of retreating to the impregnable position? Hardly, should the enemy advance on the following morning. A panic, a sudden flight, so thought Bazaine, might occur. Fortunately, the dreaded enemy did not move throughout the entire day of the 17th and thus time remained "to save the army."

One Guard Division and the II Corps marched past the 25th German Division through Gravelotte, the other division of the Guard and the III Corps via Malmaison, the IV via Verneville to the ridge the other side of the Mance. The VI Corps was to follow as a rearguard to Verneville. Since there was no adequate position to be found there, it was sent to the right wing. The entire movement was very difficult, the regiments had first to reform, then the brigades, and lastly, the divisions. The separate march columns had to cross each other in the most varied directions.

BATTLE OF GRAVELOTTE-ST. PRIVAT
18 August, 1870
Movements and engagements from the beginning of the
battle until about 3:00 P.M.

The Campaign of 1870-71

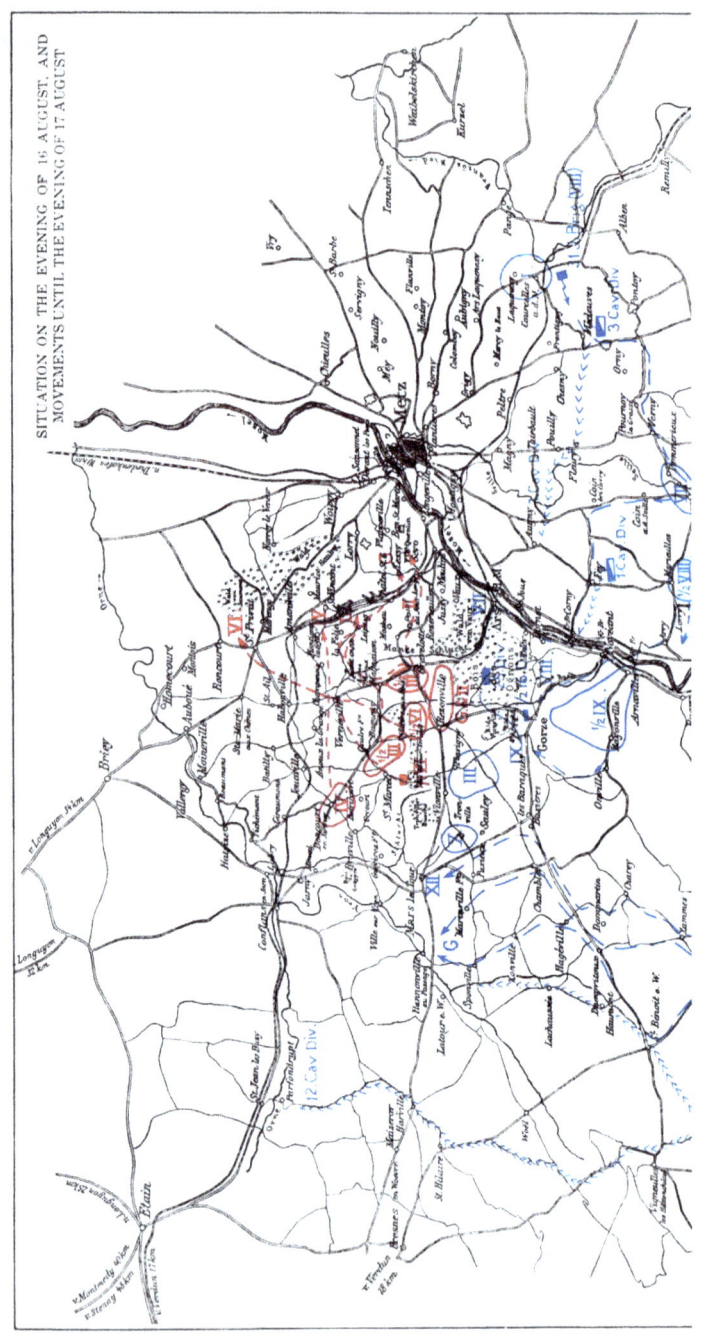

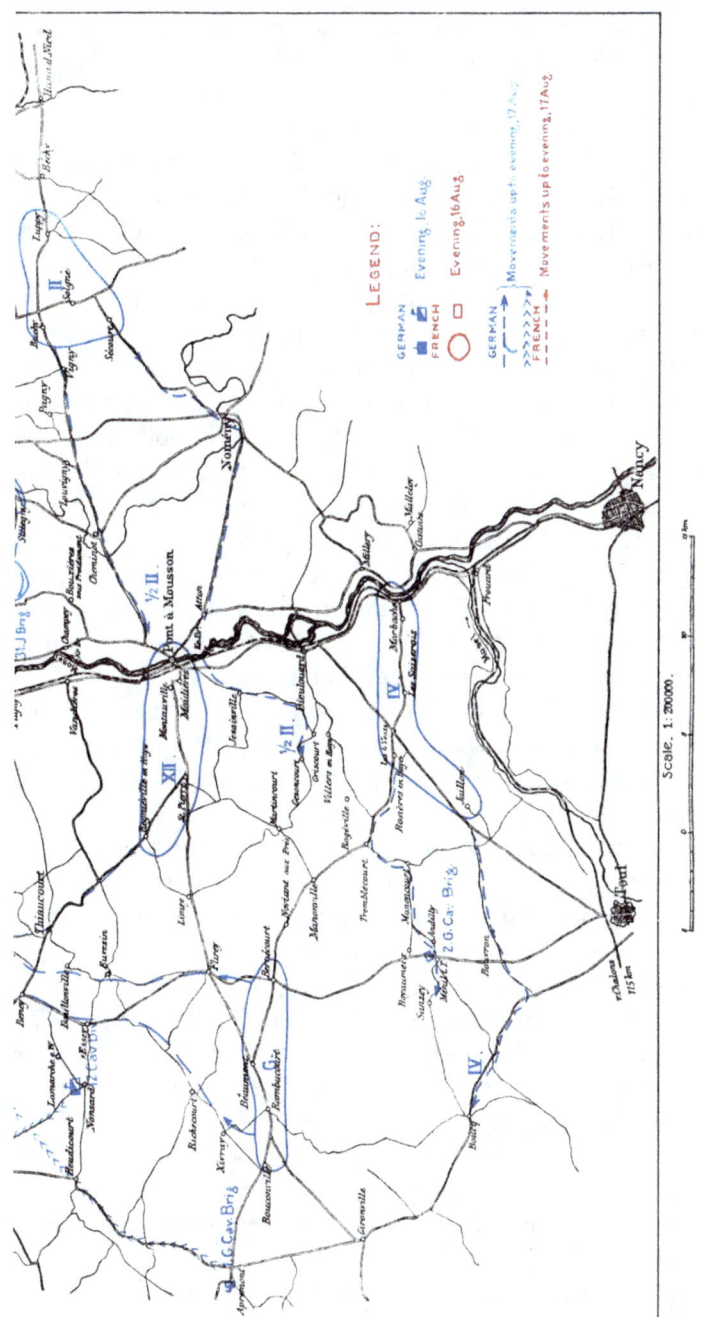

Night had come long since when the last troops reached their objective, only 10 km. distant, but without being molested in any way by the enemy. On the following day there stood: the VI Corps on a ridge between Roncourt and hill 321, some 1000 m. south of St. Privat; the FV from hill 322 north of the railway to Montigny la Grange, the III joining on the left to the bend in the road east of St. Hubert; the II thence to Rozerieulles, Lapasset's Brigade at Jussy and Ste. Ruffine, the Guard Corps at Plappeville.

Bazaine had succeeded, not only in withdrawing his army from a very serious situation, but also in placing it in position whence he could give the enemy a very difficult problem to solve.

Moltke's first thought, upon receiving information of the events of the 16th, was renewed attack and pursuit. On both wings the nearby line of retreat, via Conflans to Verdun or via Gravelotte to Metz, must be reached and the defeated enemy driven to Briey or Diedenhofen. But these intentions were decidedly opposed by headquarters of the Second Army whose reckless enterprising spirit had evidently suffered from the fatal frontal attack of the evening before. The difficult situation, the bad condition of the troops after a battle of twelve hours, was painted in the most vivid colors. The weak remnants of the III and X Corps would not dare to attack the vastly superior enemy. It would be serious enough should they be forced to defend themselves. Anything that might "entice" the enemy to an attack, should be avoided.

This could scarcely have been the view of General von Alvensleben. His aim on the 16th was to hold the enemy, whom he had attacked, until other troops came up to annihilate him. He was willing to undertake a retreat step by step, even to Verdun, should this be necessary. Even on the 17th, he would not have feared a retreat, since he knew that the Guard and XII Corps were advancing on one side and the VII, VIII, and IX Corps on the other for the purpose of transforming the pursuit into a decisive defeat.

Such reasons, however, were not considered. The fantastic ideas of the old Hotspur could not prevail against the objections of army headquarters and representations of experienced and sensible generals, like Goeben. Moltke must see that his plan would crumble if those who would have to execute it should refuse to support it and proposed to the King to delay the attack until the 18th.

The Campaign of 1870-71

At 1:45 PM, the following orders were issued:

The Second Army will start tomorrow the 18th, at 5:00 AM and advance, in echelons from the left wing between the Yron and Gorze brooks (in general between Ville sur Yron and Rezonville). The VIII Army Corps will join this movement on the left wing of the Second Army. The VII Corps will, in the beginning, secure the general movements of the Second Army against possible attacks from the direction of Metz.

The limits, set for the advance, Yron and Gorze brooks, had already been passed westward, since the left wing corps of the Second Army had been directed on Hannonville. It was found advisable to adopt this small widening of the space, much too small for the six corps, and to begin as early as the 17th, the echeloning of the troops to the left from the line: Gorze—Hannonville. Every general, intent upon victory, takes advantage of the preceding day, of the night, the morning, to place himself in the most favorable position for battle.

The Second Army, however, would not be in a favorable situation in regard to the enemy, should it remain at Gorze—Hannonville. It would not know there, for instance, whether the enemy had not started early on the 17th on a retreat with the IV Corps via Briey, and, should the cavalry bring information as to where he stood at noon, in the afternoon, or in the evening, it would still be too far off to take advantage of the situation on the 18th so as to drive the enemy toward the frontiers of Luxembourg and Belgium as desired by Moltke. It was, consequently, necessary to advance with the six corps to Confilans—Rezonville, on the 17th. Then the right wing could directly follow the enemy retreating via Briey, while the left would follow in a turning movement in the direction of Longuyon—Montmedy—Stenay.

Early on the 17th, the III and X Corps were hardly in a condition to attack. It was necessary first to restore order in the thinned units, bring up ammunition, and the horses for the batteries. But toward noon, when the retreat of the enemy could no longer be doubted, a short march might have been undertaken for the purpose of sparing the troops the view of the battlefield and to

PLAN FOR THE MOVEMENT OF THE GERMANS ON THE AFTERNOON OF 17 AUGUST, AND FOR THE ADVANCE ON 18 AUGUST

LEGEND:
- Positions to be reached by the Germans up to evening, 17 Aug
- Marches, 18 Aug.
- Continuation of march after it was known that the French right flank was at Roncourt.
- Continuation of march if the French should withdraw.

The Campaign of 1870-71

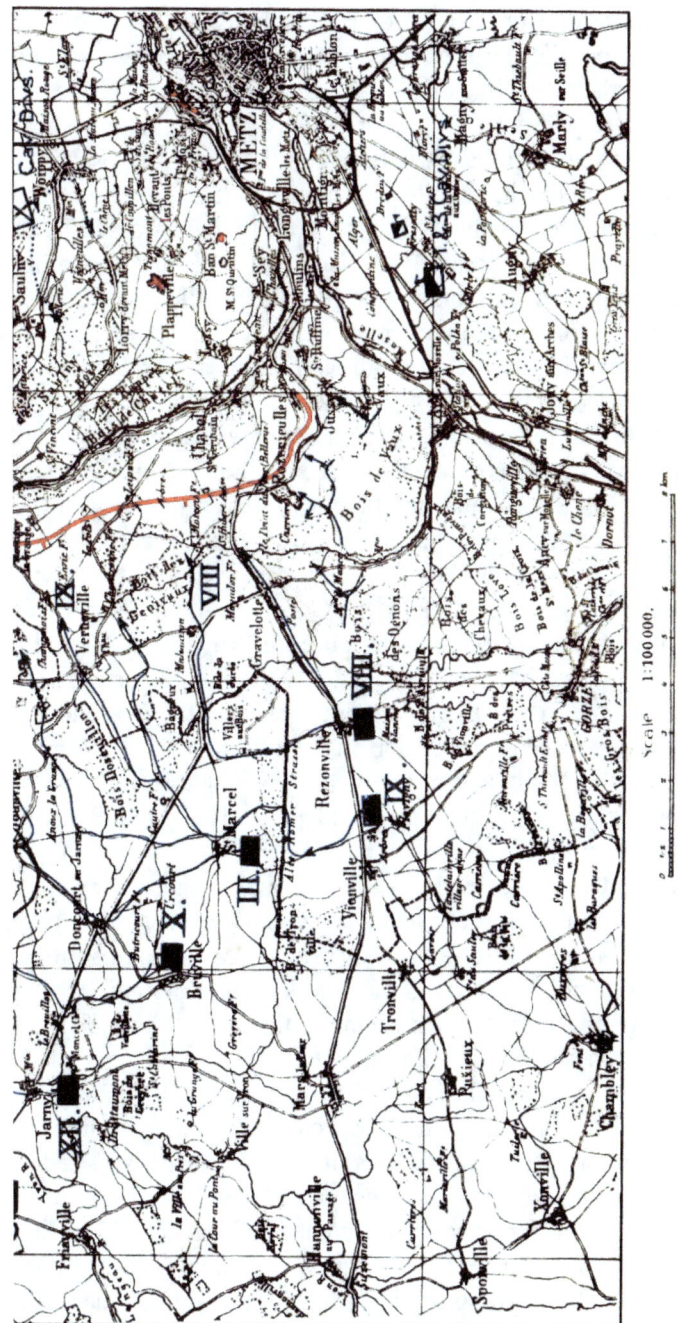

give the thirsty troops water, of which there was none on the plateau of Tronville and Vionville. It might also have been possible to give a farther objective to the corps then coming up. Indeed, all the efforts required of the troops today would benefit them tomorrow in battle. It was strictly within the limits of possibility for the troops to reach the following points on the 17th: the Guard Corps, Conflans via Hannonville; the XII, Jarny via Mars la Tour; the X, Bronville from Tronville; the III, St. Marcel from Vionville; the IX, Flavigny from Gorze; the VIII, Rezonville from east of Gorze; the VI, the northern edge of the Bois des Ognons and the Bois de Vaux via Ars; the 5th, 6th, and 12th Cavalry Divisions, past the Guard and the XII Corps, Briey and Auboue.

It would then have been learned: the enemy had not crossed the Orne, but was standing in superior force behind the Mance ravine, east of Gravelotte. Should he attempt to march to Briey in the morning, he could be found between the Gravelotte—Verneville—Ste. Marie—Auboue and Ste. Ruffine—Amanvillers—St. Privat, and Montois roads. Should he seek to march via St. Privat, Amanvillers, Chatel St. Germain, and Ste. Ruffine to Metz, he would have to pass between those roads with the entire army in his rearguards. The French Army would, consequently, if it had not already done so, occupy a position on the ridge between the Mance ravine and the Montveau ravine, whatever might have been its previous intentions. Its left wing would hold the heights at Point du Jour and Rozerieulles.

How far the right extended was not known, because by evening of the 17th not all the troops had reached the posts assigned them and because the wings of a position are very variable quantities. Whoever did not know this from military history, could have learned it on the 16th. In the morning of that day the French right wing had been ascertained to be at Rezonville. In the afternoon, it was found to be at Mars la Tour, with the cavalry still farther west beyond the Yron brook. On the 18th the French right wing stood at Roncourt. In order to ascertain this, it would not have sufficed to find St. Privat and Roncourt occupied. It had likewise to be ascertained that Montois was not occupied and that no echelon had been left at Malancourt. Had the cavalry found all this out, a rather difficult task, the morning of the 18th, still it could not guarantee that these points would not be occupied during the day.

To be prepared for all eventualities, the Germans had to assume: that the entire French Army of 150,000 men is in position on the heights east of the Mance ravine from Ste. Ruffine to the Orne near Montois and has decided to oppose obstinate resistance, Should this be overrating the opponent, all the better for the attacker. According to this supposition and in conformity with Moltke's order, the Guard Corps would advance on the 18th from Conflans to Briey and Moyeuvre la Grande, the XII Corps from Jarny along the Orne via Auboue to Montois, the X from Bruville via Graumont to Ste. Marie, the III from St. Marcel via Doncourt, Jouaville, Batilly, St. Ail, and via Habonville to St. Privat, the IX via Calure and Verneville to Amanvillers, the VIII via Malmaison and Gravelotte to Moscou and Point du Jour.

It would have been impossible for the army to march . in a closer, narrower, deeper formation. Each corps had a frontal width of hardly 3 km. and still the total front of the army was so extended, and the left wing columns could, if necessary, advance still farther to the north, that the turning and surrounding of the enemy could easily be accomplished. This turning movement had to be completed by the Guard, the 5th, 6th, and 12th Cavalry Divisions which hurried forward to the left on both banks of the Orne ahead of the infantry, and by the 1st and 3rd which were to cut off Metz, and, if necessary take under fire, the road to Verdun at Ste. Ruffine and Moulins.

Each corps, in advancing, had to march in one column. This formation had been forced upon them in the march from the Rhine to the Saar and from the Saar to the Moselle through lack of available roads. At the present moment, close to the enemy, it was necessary that not only each corps, but each division and brigade form separate columns which could march abreast of one another, even without roads, at greater or smaller intervals, over the terrain, so as to deploy into battle formation without loss of time when necessity arose. Since the enemy extended his right wing only as far as Roncourt, he could be overtaken on the right by two to three corps. These should have marched further; the X via Montois to Marengo, the XII via Bronvaux and Marengo, and the Guard to Semecourt, the cavalry to Woippy.

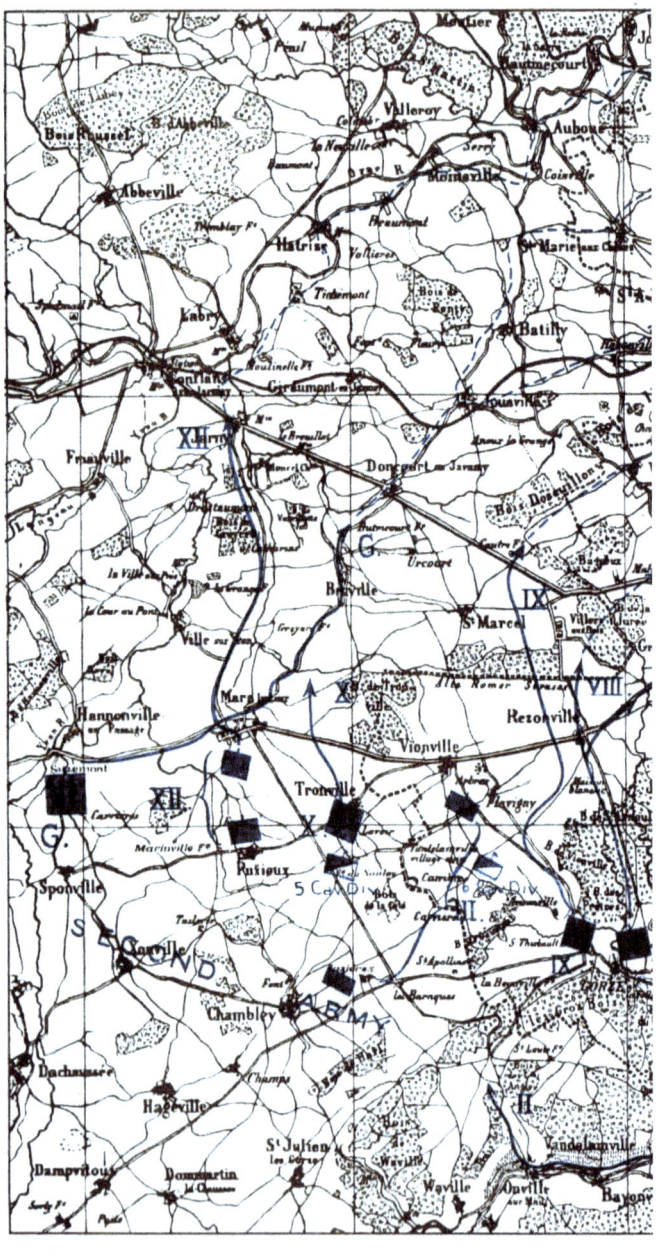

The Campaign of 1870-71

THE GERMANS

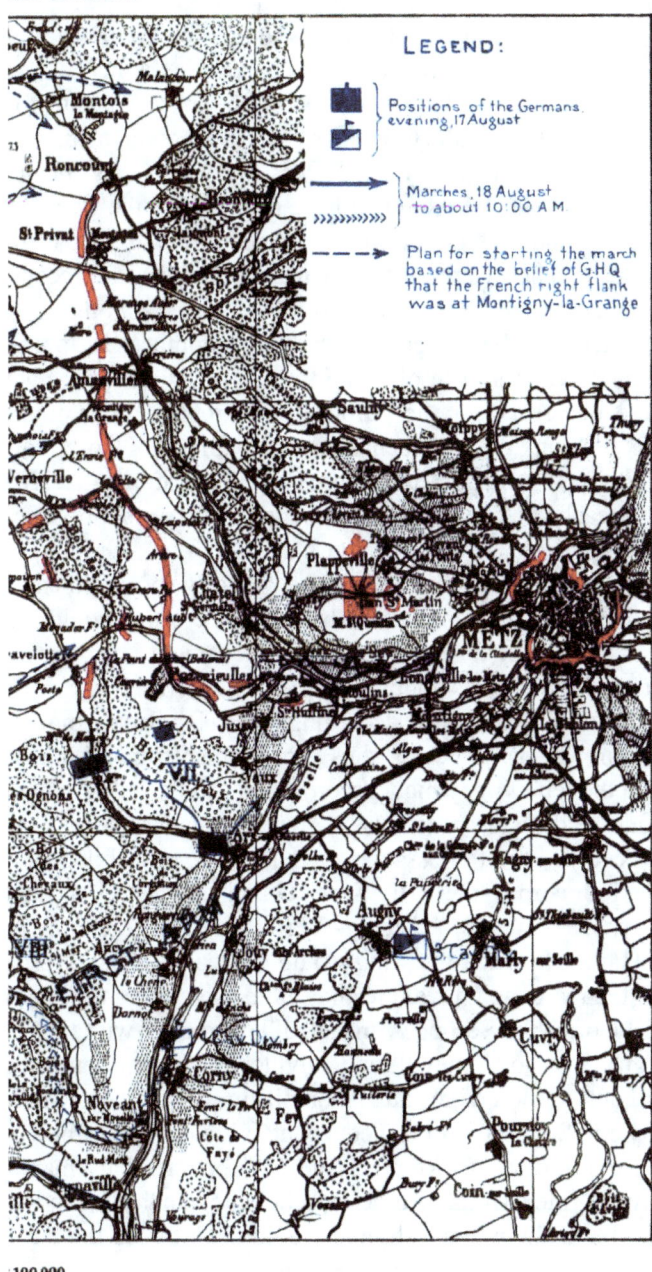

It was not probable that the enemy would defend the impregnable position up to the last man, should such a surrounding movement be developed. He would try to retreat via Saulny, Lorry, and Chatel St. Germain. This would be all the more difficult for him, should the attack of the German right wing, as well as that of the left, be violent. Considerable marches were necessary for the execution of this plan. These might have been spared the troops if the First Army had crossed the Moselle below Metz, on the 15th, 16th, and 17th. They were greatly increased because the Second Army did not advance on the 17th beyond the line: Hannonville—Gorze. Neither was anything done on the 18th to compensate for the lost time by quickness of resolve and rapidity of movement. Five hours were necessary for the purpose of marching up, halting, advancing, breaking up and reaching Caulre with the IX Corps and Jarny with the XII. And the Guard Corps, marching around the XII, had not yet reached Doncourt, in compliance with an order of army headquarters.

A decision had to be made. Certainty of victory lay until then in a strong left wing by which the hostile right wing could be overlapped, no matter how extensive it might be. Army headquarters rendered this doubtful by placing the III and X Corps, as well as the cavalry divisions, according to the Napoleonic model, as reserves in rear of the center, thus barring them from all useful action, and the left wing, which, according to Moltke's plan, must bring about the decision, was thus shortened by as many corps. In order to preserve, if not the assurance, at least the probability of a victory the four corps—the VIII, IX, the Guard, and the XII—must fill up the space between the Metz— Verdun road and the Orne in the hope that the hostile right wing would not reach to that river.

Since the march to Gravelotte and Malmaison fell to the share of the VIII Corps, the Second Army should have gone with the IX Corps from Caulre to Verneville and Anvillers, one Guard division from Doncourt via Jouaville and Habonville to St. Privat, the other via Batilly and Ste. Marie to Roncourt, the XII along the Orne via Coinville and Auboue to Montois and Malancourt. This march would have fulfilled Moltke's order of echeloning on the left and of the turn to be made by the right and would have forced the right French wing to retreat in two or three hours.

Deceived by whatsoever reports, observations or calculations, Moltke assumed the hostile right wing to be at Montigny la Grange, while Army headquarters thought it at la Folie. It was practically impossible to place an army of 150,000 men between Point du Jour and la Folie. Only a rearguard could be in this narrow space. In order to drive back the latter, the intended direction of march of the Second Army could be adhered to. Royal Headquarters and army headquarters, however, did not deem it worth while to make the great turning movement to the right with the left wing toward the Orne for a simple rearguard. The VIII Corps was, consequently, instructed to attack the front of Point du Jour—la Folie, the IX and the Guard Corps to attack the right flank and to march, for that purpose, the former from Caulre, the latter from Doncourt, to Verneville. Assembled there at one point, without the possibility of deploying, they were probably expected to achieve decision in the rearguard combat by the "weight of their mags." The XII Corps was to follow to Ste. Marie. It took that direction with one division, but wisely remained with the other on the right bank of the Orne.

The commanding general of the IX Corps, von Manstein, had marched since crossing of the Rhine in rear of other troops and ever and anon had to occupy reserve positions. As late as the 16th, he had been pushed away by the First Army from the Moselle crossing assigned to him. Only by hearsay did he know anything of victories which others won far away. At last he was at the front, full of eagerness to take his part in combat and victory. But army headquarters had said that the enemy was withdrawing partly to Metz and partly to the northwest. No time was to be lost. When he arrived breathless after a rapid ride, on the height west of Verneville and espied through his glass the white tents of a French Camp at Montigny la Grange, he exclaimed with pleasure: "All are not yet gone; the road is not yet open for them; they are cooking."

This was in fact the enemy retreating to Briey, so far as he was to be reached, if at all. Whatever was farther north had already escaped the attack unless the Guard and XII Corps had reached them in time. The IX Corps must attack, hold, and annihilate as quickly as possible the enemy who had fallen into its clutches. The two advance guard battalions of the 18th Division were left on the road to la Folie assigned them, the artillery of the division and of the corps was hastily sent to take up positions by batteries from right to left on the ridge sloping down from Amanvillers to Verneville, batteries, whose tired horses could not gallop and were rewarded with hard words.

The enemy at Montigny and south of that village did not long delay in opening fire. This might have been foreseen. But it came as a surprise that southwest of Amanvillers French batteries opened fire at a distance of 600 m. It did not help much to turn about the extreme left German batteries. "Assailed from the front, from the left, and from half rear not only by violent shell, shrapnel, and mitrailleuse fire, but by a murderous, rapid rifle fire, the artillery suffered enormous losses from the very start."

The two advance guard battalions, reinforced by three companies, were entirely occupied at Chantrenne by the right wing of the French III Corps and could give as little assistance to the hard pressed artillery as the six battalions at Verneville, still engaged in deploying, while three battalions placed in the eastern part of the Bois de la Cusse could not do much more. It seemed that only a slight pressure forward would suffice to crush the meager German forces by an all annihilating superiority.

Still the commanding general wanted to hold out and continue the artillery combat as well as could be done until the Guard should appear on his left. Then the attack would take place exactly as army headquarters had ordered, except that the extended front would be attacked not only by the VIII Corps, but by the 18th Division also, the flank by the 25th Division, called up from a position in reserve in the Bois de la Cusse, and by the Guard Corps.

It was, however, impossible to continue the artillery combat until the execution of these plans. A French skirmish line, concealed so far by a ridge, came forward. Four guns were lost. The rest of the Corps artillery was saved, in spite of losses in men and horses, through the sacrifice of one battalion. But since the French did not pursue their success and did not advance, practically nothing was changed in the general situation. The eleven advance guard companies at Chantrenne covered the right flank against the 1st Division (Montaudon) of the III Corps. West of Champenoix four batteries fought against seventeen French batteries at Montigny and Amanvillers. On the left the 25th Division and three battalions of the 18th served as an excellent bullet stop in the Bois de la Cusse. The Hessian batteries stood north of the railway line firing against the artillery of the 1st Division (Cissey), the right wing division of the IV Corps. The heights in the center were held by a few companies. About half of the infantry was deployed in the first line, the rest posted partly in the Bois de la Cusse, partly at Verneville, in readiness to advance with the Guard for the decisive attack.

The latter, upon receiving information that the hostile right wing was not at la Folie, but north of Amanvillers, had marched to Habonville instead of Verneville. When the 1st Guard Division reached that point, its commander, General von Pape, found these reports confirmed, that the hostile front was not at Amanvillers, but reached beyond St. Privat to Ste. Marie. The most natural thing for the division would have been to prolong the front of the X Corps, to deploy between the Bois de la Cusse and St. Ail and then to attack the enemy between St. Privat and Ste. Marie with artillery. Had the 2nd Guard Division then turned to the left and surrounded Ste. Marie from the west, the XII Corps could have marched not against that village, but against Coinville and Auboue, could have easily attacked the enemy's rear and thus decided the battle.

General von Pape, however, believed General von Alvensleben's assertion that the effect of the chassepot and the mitrailleuse had been materially underrated, that an attack against a French front was very difficult, and that it was necessary to maneuver. The general wished to follow this excellent advice most faithfully, turn Ste. Marie, keep marching via Montois and Malancourt and attack the French in rear.

He, therefore, led the division into the ravine, extending from north of Habonville to Auboue so as to turn later on toward Montois. The French would not have it so, however. They advanced with skirmish lines from south of St. Privat to St. Ail—Hahbonville. To cover this flank, General von Pape sent first, the divisional artillery, then the corps artillery between Habonville and St. Ail against St. Privat and his four advance guard battalions via St. Ail against the weakly occupied Ste. Marie.

The nine batteries of the Guard artillery were fully adequate to cope with the French artillery south of St. Privat. In the beginning, with no support from the infantry, then with some two battalions of the latter, they could only with difficulty defend themselves against the hostile sharpshooters, protected by the furrows of a plowed field, but nevertheless they held them at a great distance and, after hours of cannonading, achieved only the advantage of making the enemy expend his already scanty supply of ammunition.

In the meanwhile, the 1st Guard Division should have continued its turning movement, at least until it could attack Ste. Marie from the west and northwest, while the advance guard attacked it from the south. Had this succeeded, the division would have stood ready for further attack on the right wing of the French position between Roncourt and St. Privat, while the 2nd Guard Division, coming up, would have been ready to make an attack from St. Privat to the railroad north of Amanvillers. The entire hostile front between Roncourt and Montigny la Grange could have been attacked, and the XII Corps could have proceeded, unmolested with the decisive enveloping movement via Coinville and Auboue, Montois, and Malancourt.

This simple development, conforming to Moltke's order, was spoiled by army headquarters, which assigned the 3rd Guard Infantry Brigade to the IX Corps and thus greatly weakened the attack against the front south of St. Privat; also by headquarters of the Guard Corps who halted the enveloping movement of the 1st Guard Division southwest of Ste. Marie, and by General v. Pape, who, for "political considerations," begged the 47th Brigade of Nehrhoff's 2nd Saxon Division for support in the attack against Ste. Marie, although he had twelve battalions of his own. The attack undertaken from the south and the west, prepared by the Saxon batteries and two batteries of the Guard, succeeded in the first assault. But a timely deployment of the 1st Division of the Guard was prevented and the right wing of the XII Corps had gone too far south for the turning movement.

The French battalions, driven out of Ste. Marie, were reinforced by troops from the St. Privat—Roncourt line, but both were repulsed by the advance guard of the 1st Division of the

Guard (Fusiliers, Jagers) on the eastern front of Ste. Marie, by the 47th Brigade and a few Saxon batteries at the ravine sloping to Homecourt, and by the 45th Brigade in the woods east of Auboue, thus forcing them to retreat in the direction of the main position.

The 45th Brigade in the woods of Auboue formed thus the left wing, the 47th Brigade northwest of Ste. Marie, the right wing, of the XII Corps. Between these were assembled the Saxon batteries, two infantry brigades being still on the march. The infantry of the 1st Guard Division was in and around Ste. Marie, the 4th Brigade was assembled at St. Ail. The batteries of the Guard were in position between St. Ail and Habonville. They supposed that they had silenced the French batteries. In reality the latter had only ceased firing in order to keep their scarce ammunition for the decisive moment.

The deployment had shifted entirely. The Guard Corps did not stand any more before the front from Hill 321 (1 km. southwest of St. Privat) to Roncourt, the XII Corps could no longer envelop the hostile position, but three brigades of the Guard and the XII Corps assembled for attack against the strong front. The Crown Prince of Saxony saw for himself that his left wing (45th Brigade) was directed straight from the west against the seemingly strongly occupied Roncourt. He wanted to correct the mistake and sent orders to the 48th Brigade, coming up from Batilly, to advance via Auboue and Montois to Roncourt.

This was of little avail. An army of 150,000 men, occupying a defensive position, would have sufficient reserves to repulse the attack of one brigade against one of his wings. Roncourt, moreover, fronted the flank attack which was to come from Montois. Not much was needed to bar the space between the village and the quarries of Jaumont. An effective flanking attack should have extended farther, at least via Malancourt, and required more troops than one brigade. As matters stood, the Guard Corps had to attack Hill 321—St. Privat, the XII Corps to make a frontal attack on the position between that point and Roncourt. The hand of a leader was needed to restore order to the deployment which had wandered from its way.

Frederick the Great, at the battle of Prague, which was very similar to this, withdrew the second line of the left wing, added to

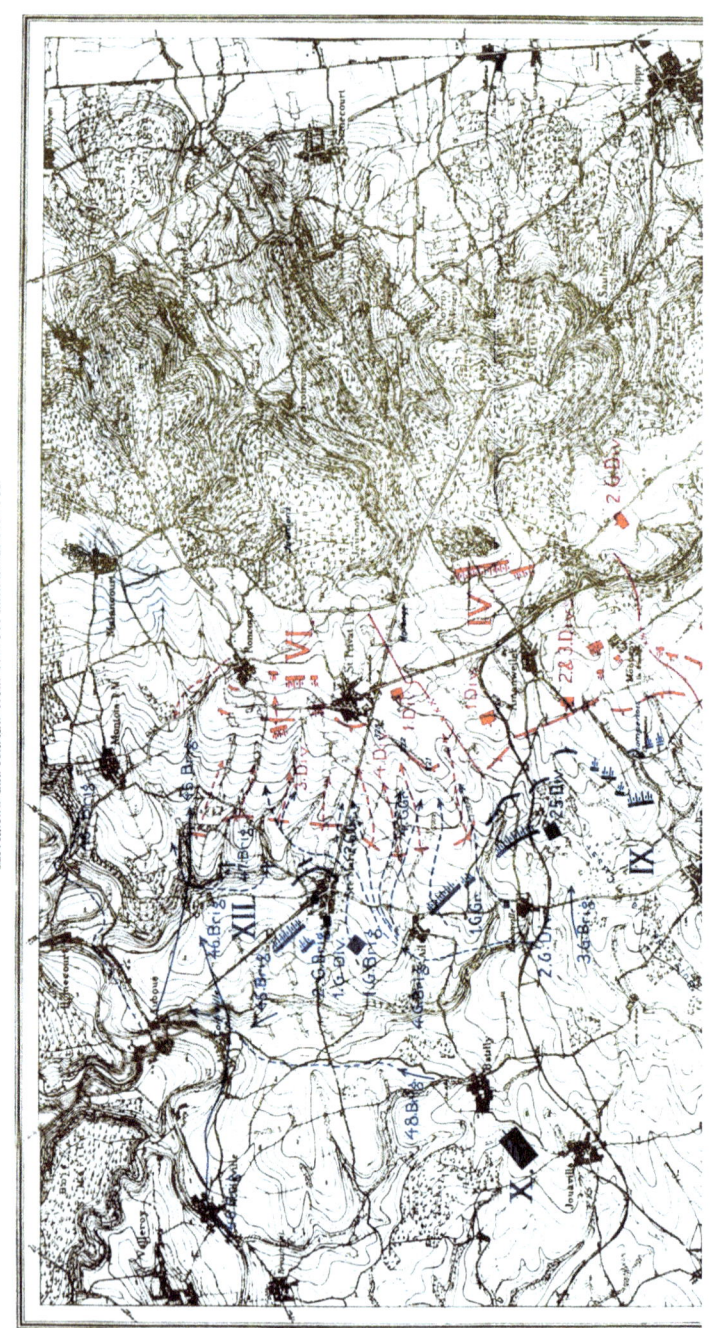

BATTLE OF GRAVELOTTE-ST. PRIVAT
Movements and combats from 3:00 PM until about 6:00 PM.

The Campaign of 1870-71

it Zieten with 50 squadrons, advanced against the enemy, enveloped his wings and won the battle. Napoleon would have made out of Ste. Marie an All Saint's point, would have assembled all available forces on right and left, and advanced with an all-encircling left wing. Moltke, had he been on the spot, would have had the Guard Corps deployed between the woods of Auboue and St. Ail, would have replaced the infantry lacking on the right and the artillery lacking on the left, by troops of the X Corps, and brought back the XII Corps to the roads of Montois and Malancourt, designated for it in the beginning. All three of these generals have conquered or wished to conquer by outflanking.

Second Army headquarters held to the end, the opinion that the enemy wanted to retreat via Briey. What had been seen of him at Amanvillers, St. Privat, and Roncourt were evidently echelons of the great retreating army, halting for a long rest in order to gather strength for the hurried march ahead of them. It would be sufficient to stop them in their march. It was scarcely necessary to drive them back to Metz in disorder and confusion, or to cut them off entirely from the fortress. Should the individual marching echelons want to remain at their halting points, a frontal attack would be sufficient to force them, in their weakness, to resume their march. Apprehension was caused only by the main forces, with which the IX Corps had apparently come in contact, as these were strong enough to attempt to break through.

This was the point where the reserves should have been sent. The 3rd Guard Infantry Brigade and the III Corps were ordered up for support or to serve as reserves. The X Corps was also to follow to the rendezvous of the great decision, but was held back. To these measures was limited the leadership of army headquarters, after the purpose of striking with a powerful attack in close order by two corps, the hostile flank at la Folie, had come to naught. What should be done on the left wing was left to the discretion of corps, division, even of brigade commanders, who, without agreement as to purpose and objective, would hinder rather than support each other.

The entire army would, consequently, be engaged in a frontal attack, the IX Corps having to await the Guard Corps and the latter the XII. Impatiently did von Manstein look for the Prince of

The Campaign of 1870-71 357

Wurttemberg, and the latter for the Crown Prince of Saxony. The latter had reported that he would start at 5:00 PM to attack Roncourt. Half an hour had passed and nothing was to be seen of the Saxons at Montois. They would march under cover and take Roncourt before the Guard had started.

It was high time to attack St. Privat. The French artillery, as reported by Prince Hohenlohe, was silenced. Infantry was thought to be seen moving from St. Privat to Amanvillers. It was evident that the weakly occupied St. Privat was being evacuated. If the Guard should not get busy to pluck the ripe fruit, the Saxons would do it and thus shame the Corps whose duty it was to undertake the most difficult problem. Permission was obtained from army headquarters to attack immediately. The 1st Guard Division was to advance north and the 2nd south of the main road straight against St. Privat.

The latter (five battalions of the 4th Brigade) deployed at St. Ail and started immediately. The tactics of the French skirmishers was to keep out of the zone of the needle gun fire, to retreat if necessary, but to shower on the approaching German infantry rapid fire from the long range chassepots. The plan was somewhat spoiled by the artillery of the 1st Guard Division which directed its fire at least partly, against the hostile skirmishers when the latter were retreating. Nevertheless, the losses of the 4th Brigade, advancing in deep formation with two battalions in the first line for prolonged combat, were great enough. The simple men with narrow minds could not understand that they somehow served King and country by letting themselves be killed in the second or third line. It could surely not harm Germany if, before being stricken with a soldier's death of honor on the field, they should strike down a few of the hereditary enemies.

They did not want to die in vain and rushed forward to form a single long line of skirmishers. There was sufficient space between the highroad and the Bois de la Cusse and the chassepots took good care that it should not be overcrowded. The two battalions of the artillery support joined on the right. North of the ravine, extending from St. Ail to St. Privat, advanced two battalions of Franz's Regiment (2nd Grenadiers of the Guard) in the ravine and south of it came half a battalion of this regiment, the Konigin Regiment (4th

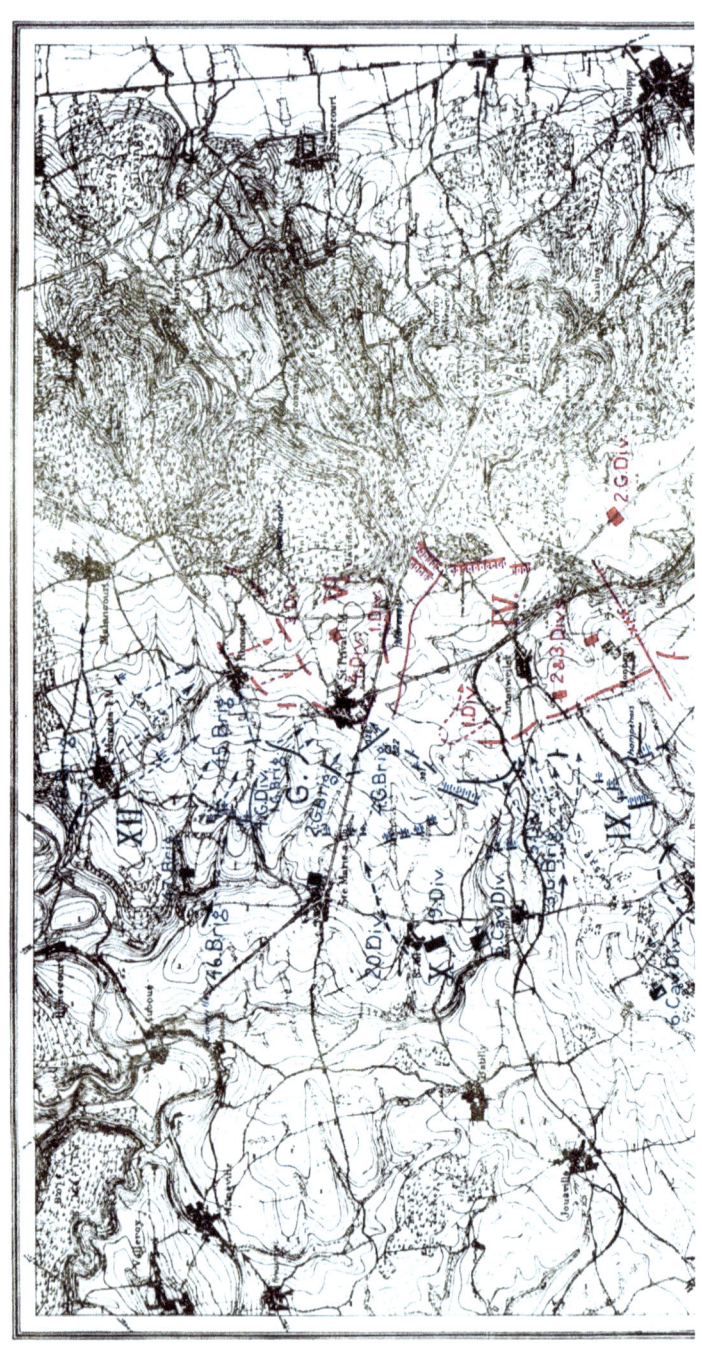

The Campaign of 1870-71

Grenadiers of the Guard) and one battalion of the Alexander (1st Grenadiers of the Guard). It was the endeavor of Count Waldersee, Commander of the Konigin Regiment, to encircle the enemy in the principal position on the ridge between St. Privat and Hill 321, from the right. The attack succeeded with the aid of the artillery. Hill 8321 was won by an assault according to regulations. The greatly superior enemy retired partly to St. Privat, partly in an easterly direction.

Soon, however, things were stirring everywhere. From the southeast another enemy approached for a counterattack. General Cissey (1st Division of the IV Corps) had left only his foremost line opposite the 25th Division and advanced with the remaining troops against Hill 321. These masses could not be withstood by the thin line of skirmishers, exhausted by the combat for the occupied position. Captain von Prittwitz climbed with his battery up the steep slope into the line of skirmishers and, though only three guns could fire at 600 meters a few well aimed shots sufficed to bring the advancing columns to a halt. The guns which had remained behind and the other batteries of the 1st Guard Division hurried up and their fire succeeded in forcing the reserves and Cissey's Division to retreat, the former to Marengo, the latter to Hill 322. The batteries and the Alexander Battalion covered the right flank from then on. The greater part of the Konigin regiment turned to St. Privat and drove the enemy from Hill 328 with the aid of the Franz half battalion. It was impossible for the weak forces to take St. Privat from the south. They surrounded in a semicircle the southwest slope and Hill 328.

The two and one half battalions of the Franz Regiment, forming the left wing of the 4th Guard Brigade, advanced straight on St. Privat and came into the hottest fire from the village which was enveloped in a white cloud of powder smoke. They sought refuge in the deep ditches and behind the trees of the highroad. There they massed in great depth. Only part of them formed a line facing southeast. This much, however, was attained: the enemy retreated behind the walls of St. Privat where he could not be reached by the infantry.

General von Pape had objected to the use of the 1st Division of the Guard. north of the highroad. The division had no artillery,

The Campaign of 1870-71   361

no shot had as yet fallen on St. Privat, and it was impossible to defeat the enemy with the short range needle gun. Colonel von der Becke, who was accidentally there, proposed to bring the artillery of the X Corps up in twenty minutes. He was told that there was no more time for this and that artillery was hardly necessary, aS the artillery of the Guard Corps had silenced an hour ago the hostile guns and the enemy was already evacuating the position. General von Pape was directed by the Prince of Wurttemberg to hurry the attack. "He is always so slow."

General von Dannenberg, chief of staff, gave him as objective the highest houses of St. Privat: exactly like the point of direction shown in brigade maneuvers—the church tower of Templehof or Britz. But here it was no brigade maneuvering, but an attack of the position: St. Privat—Roncourt, which must be attacked along its entire extent, if it were not desired to await the XII Corps. Should only the point of the left wing be attacked, the hostile right wing would turn left and sweep the attacking column with flanking fire, or, at least, with oblique fire, while there would be a sufficient frontal fire to boot.

In order to start the ordered attack, it would have been simplest to advance with the advance guard as right wing from Ste. Marie along the highroad, with the 4th and 2nd Guard Regiments, standing in and west of the village, and march to the left with the 1st Brigade of the infantry of the Guard, standing southwest of this point, letting a part of it follow in echelons, should this be necessary. Artillery (the corps artillery of the X Corps, that of the 2nd Guard Division and 47th Brigade) could still be had, not only to fire on St. Privat but also on the line of skirmishers and to help the infantry to cross the entire space in which it would be exposed to the chassepots without being able to use the needle gun. General von Pape cared to hear nothing about such a deployment. The advance guard had been designated to hold Ste. Marie in any case, the 4th and 2nd Brigades were to serve as reserves. There remained, consequently, only the 1st Brigade to cross the highroad on the shortest line and to advance quite simply against the tallest houses of St. Privat.

It had stood under cover in the ravine of Homecourt, but was taken out and sent, so that everything should be prettily put together, to the heights into the long range fire of the chassepots and guns. The men lay flat on the ground, and suffered great losses. Like salvation from an insufferable situation, after two hours of standing still, came the orders to rise, advance, and turn to the right. For an enduring attack there advanced from the depths: one thin line of skirmishers, four company columns, two half battalions, four half battalions of the second, two battalions of the third line. As soon as the eastern end of Ste. Marie had been reached, the deep ditches along the highroad were crossed facing halfway to the left, even entirely to the left and, in order not to get in rear of the 4th Brigade, some more marching was done after which they turned in battalions and companies to the right. It was soon evident that the tallest houses of St. Privat did not suffice as objectives of attack. The brigade was forced to deploy against the long line of white smoke, extending from St. Privat to Roncourt.

The losses which were comparatively small during the two hours' halt, increased as soon as the brigade started on the march and reached an awful number at the crossing of the highroad, hardly decreasing during the flank march. A monstrous cloud of dust surrounded the dense column into which a ceaseless rapid fire was poured from the right, shells smashing into it, while small white puffs hurled their contents on the parading soldiers of the Potsdam pleasaunce, marching undisturbed by the terrors hurled at them in unchanging cadence "right, left, right, left."

Were it only possible to save enough out of this fire to be able to start the combat with the needle gun. General von Kessel, the Brigade Commander called continuously "Forward, forward"; and "forward!" beat the drums; "forward" sounded the bugles, and forward went the Grenadiers. It was most fatal that the continual falling of the men required repeated halts, and closing up of the column. At last the enemy was within rifle range. Fire can be opened, the advance rushes can proceed.

Only one half, one third, one fourth of the effective strength had reached that point. The 2nd Guard Regiment had advanced to the most dangerous zone, into the space between the highroad and the right wing of the 1st Brigade. The 4th Regiment of the Guard was to prolong the left wing. One battalion of the Alexander Regiment, the Konigin and Franz Regiments, the 2nd, 3rd, 1st, and

4th Guard Regiments formed something like a swarm of skirmishers, reaching from the left wing of the 25th Division as far as Roncourt. This village also was taken by the extreme left wing (two companies of the 1st Guard Regiment, 1st Company of the Guard Pioneers, and later one half-battalion of the 3rd Guard Regiment). The entire line from hill 321 to Roncourt was in the hands of the Guard.

The troops were not formed entirely according to rule, they were very much mixed up among each other. There were great gaps here and there. Only a few reserves and echelons were in rear. The enemy was already shaken by the battle of the 16th and lost confidence in himself and in his leaders. The cleverly elaborated plan to annihilate the enemy by ceaseless rapid fire before he could approach sufficiently to make use of his inferior weapon, had failed. Needle gun and chassepot were now of equal power, the former was even superior in the hands of experienced men.

This enemy could not be opposed for any length of time. The artillery had scarcely any ammunition left. The infantry likewise began to feel the consequences of ceaseless rapid fire. One man after the other had exhausted his supply of cartridges and left the trenches. Marshal Canrobert did not think it possible to hold the position long under the circumstances: the report that new masses were advancing from Montois and the woods of Auboue, accelerated his decision. Retreat was ordered. St. Privat alone, with a prolongation to the right along the road to Chateau Jaumont, was to be held by a strong rearguard. Two battalions and a cavalry brigade, left first near Roncourt, retreated after the loss of this village, into the woods of Jaumont.

The infantry of the Guard advanced against St. Privat. Man-high stone walls, houses in rear of these with barred windows, embrasures and dormer windows, knee-high walls between gardens and fields in front of these and trenches in all the gaps, formed an impregnable fortress. The attack was brought to a halt a few hundred meters in front of it and was transformed into a fire fight between the covered and uncovered sharpshooters. But St. Privat would be invested as soon as the two German wings should advance. But the Guard was no longer able to do it after the terrible losses suffered.

However, large reinforcements were coming up. The XII Corps advanced from the left from Auboue, on the right stood the EX Corps at St. Ail. By the retreat of the one enemy to St. Privat and Marengo and of the other to Hill 322 a great gap was formed near the railway line in the French order of battle. The X Corps could penetrate here, break through, driving one enemy to the north toward the XII Corps and the other to the south. Unfortunately, the X Corps had been designated only as reserve, and as such was not to be used for the purpose of converting a doubtful victory into success, but to be kept untouched and unscathed by all the dangers and vicissitudes of battle! Thus all hope had to be placed on the XII Corps.

It had supported in the beginning with a few shots the advance of the 1st Guard Infantry Brigade. After this the 47th Brigade advanced into the woods of Auboue in rear of the 45th, and the 46th in rear of the 47th. The 48th advanced but slowly over the dusty limestone highroad from Auboue and Montois. In rear of this village deployed this brigade, joined the likewise deployed 45th Brigade and fired against Roncourt which was already occupied by the Guard.

An orderly officer of General von Pape's staff rode to the XII Corps to request the support of the batteries of the 1st Guard Brigade. Through his initiative, he had five and one half battalions of the leading brigades diverted to St. Privat. The rest continued the march to Roncourt. But the rear brigades and the mass of the artillery also gradually took the former direction. According to an ancient rule, detachments, designated for independent, but easy, flank attack, return, wherever possible, to dependence and to the difficulties of a frontal attack in mass. This was the case here. The greater part of the XII Corps crowded together with the Guard before the strong front of St. Privat. The much smaller part turned to Roncourt for a flanking attack, relieving the Guard which was garrisoning it, and saw itself, to its great surprise, opposed not only by an enemy who had advanced north of the St. Privat— Jaumont road, but also threatened on its left flank from the woods and quarries of Jaumont. Instead of outflanking, it was itself outflanked and was too weak to withstand this flank attack alone.

From the highroad to the wood of Jaumont two fronts faced

The Campaign of 1870-71 365

each other. On the right was one French flank, curved forward, on the left, the other was curved backward, holding the southern part of St. Privat. Against the latter, the few companies of the Konigin and Franz Regiments could do nothing.

St. Privat had been bombarded for some time by the artillery of the Guard and XII Corps. Fire had broken out at several points. The situation of the 14 massed battalions was growing intolerable. Many troops left the village. It would not be possible to hold out much longer and, should the enemy come up from right and left, the garrison would be lost. Canrobert ordered the gradual retreat beginning from the south and the west front.

The flames, breaking over St. Privat, seemed like a torch lighting the storm. The companies of the Konigin and Franz Regiments first followed the beacon and charged the more weakly defended south side of the village. The battalions of the Franz Regiment stationed on the highroad, would not stay behind but rushed up from the west and sent detachments up the exit leading toward Marengo. The southern part of the village fell into the hands of the Germans. The northern part, cut off from the highroad, could no longer be held alone. General von Pape had the signal for rapid advance given.

From the heaps of corpses arose the few whom the bullets had spared. All, Prussians and Saxons, stormed forward. The western front was taken almost at the first onrush. The combat, however, lasted long against the high walls, the strong houses, the cemetery on the northwest corner and on the northern front. Many an attack was repulsed. The batteries, in their laudable effort to help, hit as many of the attackers as of the defenders. Only when the last, obstinately defended houses had been surrounded on all sides, did the desperate defenders cease fighting. Numerous captives were taken. But under cover of these fights, the VI Corps succeeded in retreating almost unscathed and unmolested.

The moment seemed ripe to send in the reserves. The 20th Division had started from St. Ail. Ignorant of the condition of affairs, it wanted to advance in a northeasterly direction in order to deliver via Roncourt the decisive blow against flank and rear. But events changed the course of the division toward St. Privat. One brigade was sent through the village, and took over the outposts which had been thrown forward on the heights of Marengo against the retreated enemy.

In the meanwhile the entire artillery had come up; the Hessian batteries on the right of the Bois de la Cusse, north of the railway. They were joined by all the Guard batteries with a few of the X Corps in the "impregnable" position south of St. Privat. North of the village followed a few Prussian and all the Saxon batteries as far as the quarries of Jaumont. This was a monstrous artillery line which naught could have resisted had it been formed earlier. Now it did scarcely any harm to the enemy, and only damaged its own advanced infantry while it was most effectively answered by the French army reserve batteries, located in the quarries of Jaumont, which had found a convenient mark in the burning and illuminating St. Privat.

Almost 250 guns firing in one line form an imposing spectacle and finale for an attack which, executed by three army corps against front and flanks, should have been erushing and annihilating, but which, undertaken by two brigades (one of which had no artillery whatever) straight against the front of the strongest point of the very strong position, gave no results, in spite of all subsequent reinforcements, further than to accelerate by a few hours the retreat which the enemy had already decided upon. Such a success seems to have been bought too dearly with the enormous losses, the average of which, for each of the five regiments of the Guard engaged in the combat, amounted to 35 officers and 1000 men. The incomparable courage of the troops which, notwithstanding all the mistakes and failures of the leaders and the superiority of the enemy in numbers and arms, reached their objective, won such a victory that it placed the German army for a long time at the head of all European hosts. This was the principal success of St. Privat. The other which forced not only the VI Corps, but the entire French Army to withdraw from its "impregnable" position, is not to be so highly esteemed.

The situation of the IX Corps at 5:00 PM, though reinforced by the corps artillery of the III Corps, remained almost unchanged. On the right wing at Chantrenne, four to five battalions with four batteries, repulsed the turning attempts of Montaudon's Division (1st of the III Corps). Ten batteries with some infantry held the heights in the center against Grenier's and Lorencez's Divisions (2nd and 3rd of the IV Corps). On the left wing the 25th Division in the Bois de la Cusse was assembled for the purpose of attacking Cissey's Division (1st of the IV Corps) as soon as the Guard Corps had started. As a result of the many hours of artillery fire, the 25th Division had suffered greatly.

Nevertheless the IX Corps had nothing to fear from an enemy who had never utilized any occasion for a worthy offensive. General von Manstein requested reinforcements. These were sent to him in the form of the 3rd Guard Brigade, but at the same time the cover of his left flank was thus considerably weakened. There remained only the 4th Guard Brigade for the attack of the strong position on the heights south of St. Privat. Should it be repulsed by the one and one half divisions of the defense, and should the latter, In conjunction with Cissey's Division make a counterattack, the left flank of the IX Corps would be threatened to the utmost. It would have been advisable to leave the 3rd Guard Brigade on the left wing. As later events showed, it, in conjunction with the 25th Division, would probably have defeated Cissey's Division and rolled up the IV Corps.

However, such artificial methods were not in keeping with the ideas of the brave General von Manstein. He preferred an orderly, powerful frontal attack, regardless of whether the enemy or his position be strong or weak, to all other tactical operations, and thus the 25th Division, with the addition of six batteries, was sent to attack Cissey's Division (1st of the IV Corps); the 3rd Brigade, but without the cumbrous artillery impediment was sent to attack the two Divisions of Grenier and Lorencez in their very strong position, well reinforced by trenches, west of Amanvillers.

The attack did not take place in a line already deployed, but the deployment was made during the combat. The Guard Rifle battalion, at the head of the troops, lost all its officers and more than half of the rank and file and was led during the last phase of the combat by a luckily spared ensign. The losses of the other battalions, two of the Alexander Regiment (1st Grenadiers of the Guard) and three of the Elizabeth Regiment (3rd Grenadiers of the Guard) were, though considerable, somewhat less, and each turned to the right and entered the zone of rapid fire of the chassepots.

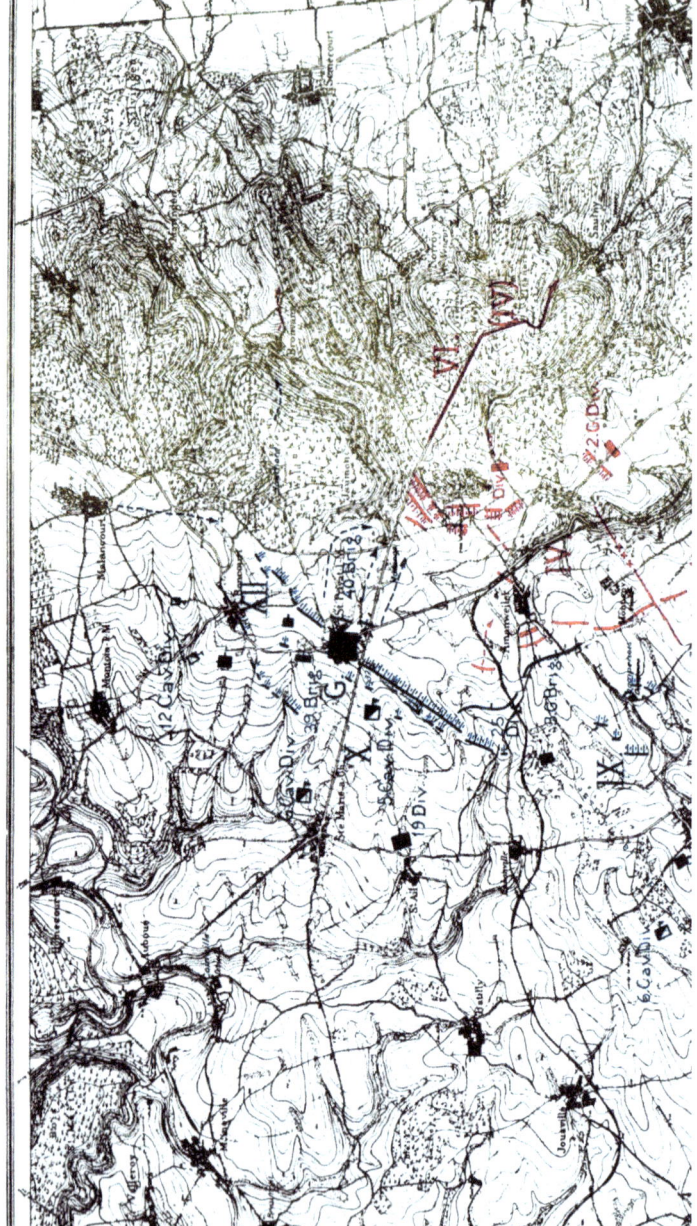

The six battalions held their own, in spite of all their losses against the hostile firing line. When they renewed the advance after nightfall, they had the satisfaction of finding the position evacuated. It had become untenable after the VI Corps had started to retreat and the right flank of the IV was threatened.

The First Army fought its battle only in loose touch with the Second. It was instructed to attack the front of the enemy between la Folie and Point du Jour with the VIII Corps, and with the VII his left flank between Point du Jour and Ste. Ruffine. The latter task was facilitated by the heights southwest of the stone quarries of Point du Jour, but was rendered more difficult by the wood of Vaux situated in front of the flank that was to be attacked. Only a few narrow and steep paths led up the hills and through the dense thickets of the wood. Infantry could go along these paths only in single file, the artillery not at all.

If the army headquarters had remembered the battle of Jena, the manner in which the Landgrafenberg had been rendered accessible and Napoleon who, torch in hand, led the work himself, it might have rendered the impossible possible. There was sufficient time even to exceed the Napoleonic feats. Had it been possible to thus bring the batteries through the wood to the height and to execute, with their help, the attack ordered against the flank simultaneously with the attack against the front, the combat on this wing would soon have come to an end. But army headquarters kept away from such venturesome enterprises.

Since the attack against the hostile left flank presented too many difficulties, the action was limited to the defense which had been recommended by Moltke only for the beginning. Six battalions, one squadron, and one battery were left at Ars to protect the German communications against an advance of the French in the valley of the Moselle, while five and one half battalions were sent to the edge of the Bois de Vaux. The rest of the VII Corps remained on the right bank of the Mance south of Gravelotte. It could cooperate from that point in the frontal attack which the VIII Corps was to undertake from Gravelotte—Malmaison through the deep ravine, the woods of the Mance and Genivaux up the slope against the French position at Point du Jour—Leipsig.

To meet such an attack, the 1st Division (Verge) of the II

Corps had strongly occupied an almost uninterrupted — trench along the main road extending from the southern bend southeast of the quarries of Point du.Jour to a point east of St. Hubert. In rear of these stood the 2nd Division (Bastoul) of the same corps, and on the right joined the Divisions of Aymard (4th), Metmann (3rd), and Nayral (2nd) of the III Corps extending as far as Leipzig. Beyond the position infantry had been posted in the woods on either side of the main road and as far as St. Hubert. There was plenty of cover, a clear field of fire, and plenty of infantry, and there would have been no lack of artillery if the principle of maintaining strong reserves of this arm had been disregarded.

It was thus quite easy for the artillery of the VII Corps south, and the VIII Corps north of Gravelotte to silence the French batteries and force them to withdraw. The combat was to be limited to an artillery duel, such were the orders from Royal Headquarters, until the IX Corps could make itself felt farther to the north. But since the French skirmishers had approached under cover and troubled the batteries with their fire, the attack had to be executed willy nilly. One, two, three battalions were sent to advance on the main road first and along side of it later. Reinforcements fed the combat and slowly extended its front. It was thus possible to penetrate, after a hot combat, into the Mance wood, to reach the eastern edge after heavy losses and to hold out there as far as the quarries of Point du Jour on the right, and 100 meters from the main road on the left. After a bloody combat, St. Hubert, situated immediately in front of the hostile position, was finally taken.

The brigade commander commanding the right wing thought that after "turning" from the Bois de Vaux, the height would be taken. Such ideas seemed absurd to General von Steinmetz. According to his opinion not only had the artillery been silenced and St. Hubert taken, but all of the enemy had been defeated and forced to retreat. All that was left was the pursuit. In order to solve this problem, one infantry brigade, the artillery of the VII Corps, and the 1st Cavalry Division, halted south of Malmaison, should advance via Gravelotte and the Mance ravine and drive the enemy into the Chatel St. Germain ravine.

Only four batteries succeeded in threading their way through the turmoil on the main road as far as the far side of the ravine.

Two of these did not succeed in unlimbering and fled. Only the batteries of Hasse and Gnugge opened fire and kept it up even against the newly appearing mitrailleuses. Hasse's Horse Battery however, suffered enormous losses. Only one gun remained in the end, for whose service the battery commander and the only surviving officer had to combine. When the ammunition boxes of the limbers had been emptied, the battery received orders from Gravelotte to return. Impossible! All the horses lay on the ground. New teams were brought up by the battalion commander, and the guns and limbers, with the wounded on the chests, were led back at a walk through the ravine. Gnugge's battery, covered by the garden walls of St. Hubert, was able to hold out a little longer.

Of the cavalry division, only the 4th Uhlan Regiment which was in the lead, succeeded in reaching the far side of the ravine and in deploying south of the road. An attack against the fire-spouting entrenchments was out of the question. After appropriate losses had been suffered in a slightly covered position, the retreat was started along a steep path through the wood, and partly in the evening, and partly in the night, it rejoined the division at Mogador.

The infantry brigade did not deploy according to regulations. The individual companies, detachments, even groups hurried to where they hoped to find room in the foremost line, stormed independently against the hostile firing line, were repulsed, but still advanced quite a bit beyond the edge of the wood and threw themselves down, mixed up among each other, at 300—400 meters in front of the hostile entrenchments. Thereupon commenced a lull in the combat.

How should the battle be renewed and continued? One brigade of the VIII Corps stood as yet in reserve in rear of Gravelotte. One regiment of the latter had to be used as a covering detachment against the French III Corps, which threatened the left flank of the VIII Corps from the Bois de Genivaux, as well as the right flank of the IX. General Goeben advanced with the last regiment close to St. Hubert. It could not be expected that this would bring a turn in the situation. Some help might come only from the flank. General von der Goltz was on the extreme right wing with the 26th Brigade, had advanced from Ars and taken Jussy, but could go no further against the strong position: Ste. Ruffine—Rozerieulles, although one brigade of the I Corps had sent out its skirmishers on the right bank of the Moselle as far as the red house opposite Moulins. Although both brigades had come quite close to the road of retreat to Metz, still they had no effect upon the events at Moscou and Point du Jour. In order to make an end here, General von Steinmetz found nothing else to do but to send in the II Corps which at 2:00 AM had left Pont-a-Mousson and at 5:00 PM reached with the 3rd Division, Rezonville.

Before this corps could start, a French counterattack was made. Batteries, taken from the reserve, initiated it, then came the infantry. The advanced German detachments were driven back, but the attack was soon checked by the fire directed from the edge of the woods and from the walls of St. Hubert. However, a panic ensued, in rear of the German front, among all the units and the rank and file who, without leaders, suddenly heard the noise of combat. The frightened mass fled in confused crowds, to Gravelotte. Hardly had they reached the protecting point and the French their trenches, when the 3rd Division started and worked its way through the seething mass of men, horses, and vehicles.

The advance guard (2nd Jagers and the 24th Regiment) upon reaching the height, penetrated somewhat beyond the former line and advanced by small detachments to the center close to the bend of the highroad east of St. Hubert, and on the right as far as quarries of Point du Jour 150 meters from the hostile entrenchments. To the left, towards Moscou, the walls of St. Hubert were crossed but not very far. Behind and into this line crowded the main body of the 3rd Division. Soon dissolved into its constituent units, it mixed up with the detachments of the VIII Corps. In the meanwhile, darkness had come. The positions of the enemy could be distinguished only by the burning buildings of Moscou and Point du Jour. The French likewise could not see their opponents, only hear them. As soon as a movement was audible on the part of the Germans, the fire of the defense flared up again, and was answered, not only by the leading troops of the attack, but also, to their serious prejudice, by their own rearmost detachments.

For the purpose of bringing some order into chaos, the troops of the VIII Corps were sent back to Gravelotte and, since this did

SITUATION ON THE NIGHT 18-19 AUGUST, AND RETREAT OF THE FRENCH

The Campaign of 1870-71

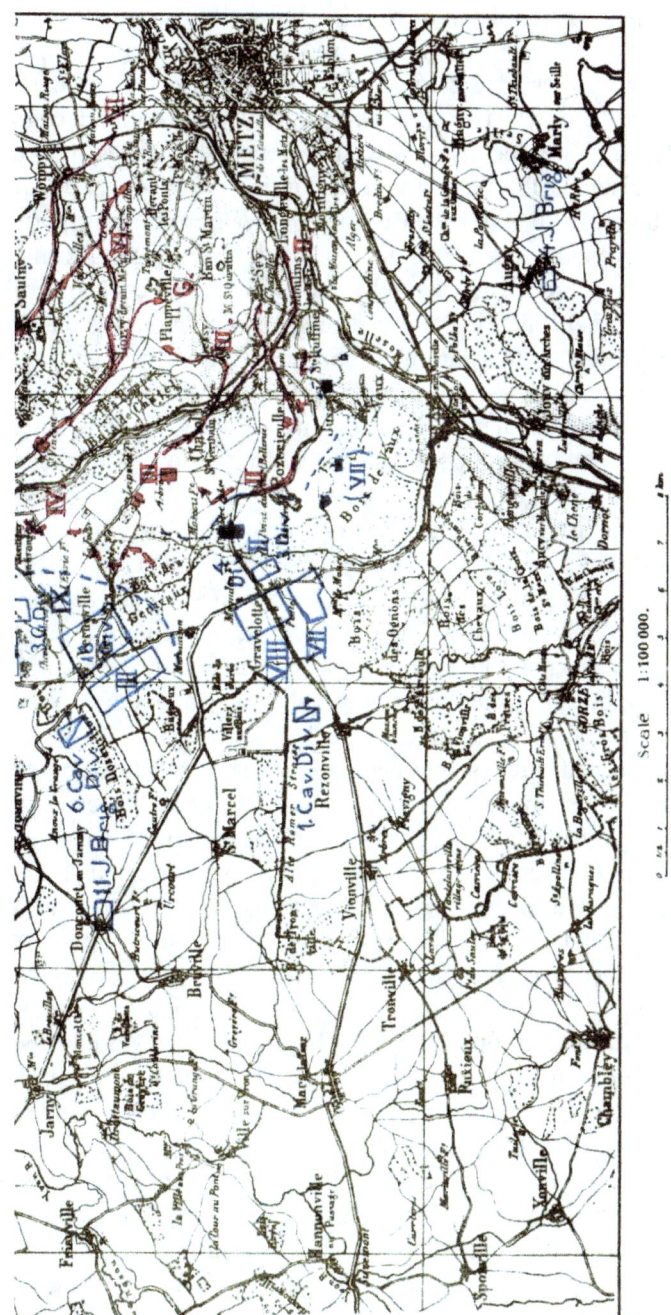

not eliminate the confusion, it was deemed well to relieve the 3rd Division by the 4th. The fire, caused by this movement, was silenced only after considerable time. Battle outposts could be placed, the line of which extended from Jussy to the northern edge of the Bois de Vaux and the southwest corner of the quarries, thence for some distance along the highroad, turning north of St. Hubert around the southern part of the Bois des Genivaux. Since no reports had come in concerning the result of the battle of the Second Army, considerable apprehension was felt at Royal Headquarters in regard to the situation of the First Army. The general opinion was that it would be necessary to await the supposed attack of the enemy on the 19th in a strong position near Gravelotte. Moltke, however, succeeded in persuading the King that it was necessary to resume the attack should a battle be found necessary. He had foreseen correctly.

A similar process to that of the Germans took place on the French side. As the VIII Corps and the 3rd Division had returned to Gravelotte, so had the men, defending the trenches at Point du Jour and Moscou, left their posts first one by one, then in groups and later in detachments. They were replaced by new troops who, like the 4th Division opposite them, awaited the renewal of the combat. They did not have long to wait.

Bazaine had already returned to his quarters, when one of Canrobert's aids reported -the retreat of the VI Corps. He consoled the despairing bringer of bad tidings by saying that the retreat of his chief had accelerated the general retreat only by twelve hours. The orders, elaborated and prepared in the morning by the General Staff, were immediately issued. They were for the purpose of taking the army to the "second position," the II Corps to Longeville between St. Quentin and the Moselle, the III to Scy, Lessy, and Lorry, the IV to Plappeville and le Sansonnet, the VI thence to Fort Moselle, the Guard, the cavalry, and the artillery reserve to the narrow space within the surrounding corps. The road to Metz was open. On the other side only the I Corps barred the road te freedom. To push this obstacle aside would not have been difficult, according to von Goeben's opinion. However, having all the German armies, including the Third, in the rear, this breaking through to freedom would have ended in being surrounded on the Rhine at the latest.

The retreat was begun in the night with the II and the III Corps. When day dawned, only weak detachments remained behind. Short fire fights took place between these and the Germans at Point du Jour and the quarries.

Through one of the bloodiest battles the only result was that a retreat which had been already decided upon, had been advanced by twelve hours. That it would have been started sooner or later was due to the conviction of Bazaine, his generals, and his army, that it was impossible to oppose permanent resistance to the "brutal offensive" of the enemy even in an "impregnable position."

The generation of 1870 lived on Napoleonic traditions. But what had been borrowed from the treasure trove of the Great War Lord's campaigns was not taken from the period of his great victories of Marengo to Friedland, but from the period subsequent to the Russian defeat. It was left unheeded that Ulm had been won by a tremendous turning movement, Jena—by wide encircling wings, Austerlitz and Friedland by attacks against one flank and Marengo by attacks on both. Imagination was excited by the gigantic attack of Leipzig on October 16th, against the center of the enemy and by the repeated attempts at Waterloo to pierce the English front. It was forgotten, through their very magnitude, that these attacks had miscarried and brought about the tragic end of the Corsican hero. Since that time an incontrovertible condition of victory was the massing of the troops before battle. Marches to be executed in deep, dense columns, the army assembled in narrow, deep masses.

What was done in this manner in 1870 is wonderful and won at the time the admiring recognition of Goeben. Eight corps of the First and Second Armies, a quarter of a million soldiers, marched on a narrow front to the Saar. It seemed that everything, coming in the way of this gigantic phalanx, would be ground to pieces under its thundering tread.

A French corps remained nevertheless on the heights of the left bank. In order to punish this temerity, the advance guard attacked. The position was too strong, the hostile rapid fire too murderous to allow the attack to succeed. Reinforcements had to be brought up. But only particles could be taken from the narrow front, led one after the other to the frontal attack, which could change nothing in the difficulties of the problem. One commanding general after the other took command, but each stood helpless before the problem. Late in the evening, there appeared, brought more by accident than by intention, one division in the flank and rear of the enemy and showed, unwittingly, to the assembled generals how strong positions have been taken since the times of Leonidas. Whoever wanted to see could see: formation of masses brings about frontal attacks with inadequate forces, brings consecutive, ever weakening, combats having almost entirely no effect.

A pursuit should have been made after the victory of Spichern. But four entire days were necessary to unravel ever so little the gigantic tangle and bring the two armies across the Saar. In the meanwhile, the defeated and scattered enemy had had time to assemble and to escape their opponent in an orderly retreat. The excess of massing was somewhat mitigated in further advance marches, but the system of narrow front, deep formations and corps following corps was maintained. To this system is due, to a large degree the monstrosity of sending, on 16 August, one single corps out of sixteen against the hostile army and on the 18th from an army of five corps, of despatching only three brigades against an impregnable position.

Such mode of warfare Moltke had opposed since 1866. He showed that compressed masses, from whom victory is being expected, can neither be quartered nor fed and, what is still worse, not even moved. He calculated the length of a division and a corps in marching column and found that the latter would need almost an entire day to reach the battlefield and deploy, that it could be sent into attack only gradually, never in its entire strength, and that it would be impossible to ever count for that day on a corps which was following another. He therefore exacted for each corps at least one road.

The corps should not follow each other over one road, but over several, over at least as many parallel roads as there are corps. The interval between the roads depends on the conformation of the network of roads, which in cultivated lands averages from 7to8km. A corps, in its present day constitution, organization, and equipment, with ammunition, can be deployed to a width of front of 6 km., and can develop fire power which would be vain to try to surpass.

The Campaign of 1870-71 379

For rapid deployment, according to Moltke's opinion, the march columns were still too long and at the present day, having been considerably increased, they would be still longer. It is impossible to shorten them on a long advance. But, on nearing the enemy, they must be divided, by divisions and brigades, into two and, whenever practicable, into four columns which can use neighboring roads or, where such cannot be found, go across the country.

Moltke wanted to open the campaign of 1870 with just such an army of six corps, cross the Saar with seven columns on a front of 50 km., between Merzig and Saargemund, seek the enemy, who was considered to be weaker, and defeat him. When it was found that the French army could assemble in Lorraine in greater strength and in a shorter time than supposed, Moltke awaited the completion of the advance before advancing with eight or ten corps to secure superiority of numbers and to surround the hostile army by the extension of the army's front. The victory he wished to win, to be annihilating, could be gained not by an attack against the front alone, but in conjunction with attacks against both flanks, as at Koniggratz. These flanking attacks are rendered more easy if the enemy forms into narrow, deep massed units for a long combat. In the end, the wider front will win, since it makes possible the outflanking of the enemy and has supposedly, the greater and more numerous army.

The first problem of the general is to obtain a greater army. It was easy for the Great Napoleon to solve it since, as the most powerful sovereign of his time, it was not difficult to form a large army. If superiority in numbers was lost to him at the end of a long campaign, he paused, as after Prussian-Eylau or Aspern, brought his forces to the normal, and continued the war against the befooled enemy. Moltke did not have such rich resources at his command, but he held together the forces at his disposition and gained his point, in spite of all advice to the contrary, that observation armies should be posted neither on the Rhine in 1866 nor in 1870 in Silesia and that the war should be limited to the actual opponent and not to possible ones. This was in itself a feat greatly contributing to bring about the decision. For Bazaine would scarcely have retired on 16 August, had he not hourly expected the attack of a larger and stronger army. It is comparatively easy to attack the enemy in front and flank with a stronger and larger army. However, all efforts to assemble this great army and bring it to the theater of war, may fail. Then the general will find himself facing a stronger opponent and must, such is the simple advice, see that he be the stronger at the decisive point.

Napoleon declared, when he found himself in the minority in the autumn of 1813, that the weakest and decisive point was the front, and assembled against it his not inconsiderable forces. An heroic, a superhuman attack, an annihilating piercing should be executed. 'The future depended on it, it had to decide if "the world was to be once more turned upside down." The monstrous attack broke as so many of those preceding it had done.

And then the inevitable occurred. The man, who did not wish to surround, was surrounded on both sides, pressed together, encircled and would have been annihilated if pale fear had not left a back door open to the terror inspiring one. This much is sure— be he the stronger or the weaker—he who does not want to turn both flanks, will or can be turned on both flanks, and he who limits himself to attacking one flank only exposes himself to the danger of being attacked on the other.* Hannibal, consequently, did not reinforce the front at Cannae, but brought its strength down to one third of that of the enemy. This caused the weak front to be driven back by the great pressure of the hostile mass. So much the easier was it for the outflanking Carthaginian wings to advance, to turn the opposing Roman Flanks and to soon stop both retreat and pursuit.

Frederick the Great saw himself facing strong oppositions and wide fronts with his small army. An attack of the latter would have brought defeat more quickly and surely to him than to Napoleon. He turned the positions to advance against a flank or even the rear of an enemy. The latter endeavored to direct his forces to the threatened point. The King saw himself facing a new position, after the execution of the turning movement, the front of which was too

---

* A hostile flank may be securely protected and be unassailable. Measures to ward off the danger of being attacked by it, must nevertheless be taken by the aggressor.

The Campaign of 1870-71 381

wide at Kolin, too strong at Kunersdorf, and whose flanks at both points were invulnerable. At Leuthen, the movement brought him likewise before a new front which, however, was so narrow and so deep, that it could be turned from both sides, though not without great difficulty. At Zorndorf, the Russians, threatened in the rear, had simply faced about and opposed the attack with as strong a front as before. It was due to the cavalry that first the front, then the one and then the other flank was attacked and the obstinate enemy could be driven back after a difficult and lengthy struggle. More decisive was the battle of Prague, where the victory was principally due to the extreme thinning of the left half of the battle line for the purpose of rendering the turning movement possible.

The example of Leuthen and Zorndorf is difficult to follow by an army counting millions of men. Not everyone can rise on a foggy December morning and turn a hostile flank with some twenty corps. But the weaker may hold to a Cannae or Prague if he will refute Napoleon's phrase "the stronger conquers" and annihilate the enemy in spite of it.

Today also, as at Cannae, can the center, with a few reinforcements—though with a large number of cartridges—be reduced and still attack as the 4th Guard had done on 18 August, with success, even today can the flanks, as at Prague, extend for an annihilating embrace and still it is possible to hope that the enemy, like Terentius Varro at Cannae, Napoleon at Leipzig, Benedek at Koniggratz, will assemble more or less in mass.

However, it should not be forgotten that the enemy will take countermeasures against such turning movements and flank attacks. Hence a modern battle will be more than ever a struggle for the flanks. At Koniggratz, the two corps of the Austrian right wing wanted to attack the left wing of the Prussian army. They encountered the resistance of Fransecky's Division. Before the latter had been vanquished, the Prussian Second Army threatened their own right flank. They went back to cover the flank of their army. This defensive flank was driven back by the 1st Guard Division which, in its turn was forced to retreat before the surrounding movement of the Austrian reserve until it was received by the advance guard of the I Corps and could put up resistance at the front, while the VI Corps turned against the right flank of the advancing Austrians. The First Army then took a hand in the retreat combats, turning to the flank from the front. The same thing took place on the southern wing.

On 16 August, the III Corps repulsed the French II Corps by an attack against the flank and front. It was received by the Guard and part of the VI Corps. The other part of the latter, two divisions of the III Corps as well as the IV, went in echelons against the left German wing. They were forced to retire one after the other by Lehmann's half brigade, the 20th Division and Schwarzkoppen's half division. 18 August would have shown a similar picture had the French taken the offensive with their reserves on the right wing. Thus the turning and counter turning movements were limited to the flanking of the extreme Saxon wing by the French detachments in the wood of Jaumont.

In the struggle for the flanks, he wins whose last reserve is not behind the front but on the extreme wing. It can not be brought thither when the eagle eye of the commander recognizes the decisive point in the midst of the turmoil raging over many square miles, but it must be brought there during the march into battle, the march from the unloading stations, directed there from the railway transports.

It could not be foreseen whether the great surrounding battle would be waged at Koniggratz. But it was already recognized that the VIII Corps on the right and the VI on the left would ensure the decision, when the former crossed the Saxon frontier and the latter demonstrated into Moravia.

It is claimed that it is quite unnecessary to resort to such envelopments and struggles for the flanks. The enemy will assemble his reserves, pierce with his masses the front which had melted, in the meanwhile, to nothing, and put an end to everything. This was the plan of Terentius Varro that served him so badly.

Let us take Koniggratz again. It was surely unnecessary there to mass the greater part of the First Army before the center of the Austrian position and offer it as a bullet stop to the hostile artillery. It was likewise unjustifiable to use part of the Army of the Elbe against that front. Two corps of the First Army would have sufficed to cover the entire front on the Bistritz and further beyond Benaek. The remainder of the Corps might have been attached to the Army of the Elbe. Should Benedek then undertake his threatening mass attack and should he have driven the two Prussian corps back, four corps brought from the north and three from the south against the flanks would have caused the inevitable catastrophe earlier and more effectively than the one that happened in reality.

The Germans marched to the Saar and to the Moselle according to Napoleon's mass tactics. They were to overwhelm the hostile position by continuous, well fed combat, shock after shock. They tried to achieve this also at Gravelotte and accomplished nothing but complete failure. At St. Privat, however, the deep columns saw long lines before them against which they could do nothing.

In the shortest time the linear tactics of infantry and artillery, condemned since Jena, were again assumed, though in a rough form. Line fought against line and in this combat the one who with greater front, could turn the hostile flank, won the victory. Instinctively did they return to the old mode of warfare, commended by Frederick the Great: "Attack them bravely with our heavy guns, fire case shot at them and then gain their flank."

The Battles of Beaumont and Sedan

The 16th and 18th of August did not bring a final result to the Germans.. Bazaine had not been driven to the Belgian and Luxembourg frontiers for annihilation as Moltke desired but had returned to Metz. The 170,000 men, saved in that city, could be considered as eliminated from a field campaign, but since it was considered that 200,000 men were needed for their investment, the calculation, as far as numbers are considered, was not in favor of the Germans.

What was left—the Third Army with five and one half corps (the V, VI, XI, Bavarian I and II Corps, and Wurttemberg Division) and two cavalry divisions (2nd and 4th) in the vicinity of Nancy, as well as the newly formed Army of the Meuse with three corps (Guard, IV, and XII) and four cavalry divisions (Guard, 5th, 6th, 12th) west of Metz, about 240,000 men—was to continue the march against Paris.

MacMahon assembled, on the road thither, an army of about 150,000 men from troops which, some 14 days ago, had suffered a severe defeat or had been shaken by the hurried retreat, and finally from all that could be gathered together. This army was not able to oppose successful resistance to the advancing German army and still less to open a road for itself through the hostile troops to the gates of Metz for the relief of Bazaine. Only a march for the relief of the capital appeared to remain. Not so well by reinforcing the garrison as by threatening the hostile flanks might MacMahon hinder, or at least for some time delay, the investment of the great fortress. Still before the beginning of his retreat, he only wanted to know whether Bazaine had succeeded in breaking through the ring which encircled him. Should the latter have succeeded in doing so, MacMahon would have gone, under any circumstances, to the assistance of his comrade.

The Germans considered it necessary, if possible, to prevent the Army of Chalons from retiring on Paris and to drive it back in a northerly direction. Thus the Army of the Meuse was to advance with its right wing (XII Corps) along the Etain—Verdun road to Chalons and reach St. Menehould on the 26th, while the Third Army should reach Vitry with its left wing. It was intended to direct the attack against the front and right flank of the hostile position from the line: St. Menehould—Vitry.

The German columns were far from this goal, when MacMahon started on the 21st for Rheims. He thought that he would be able to assist Bazaine from this point, as well as to reach Paris in time without being exposed, as at Chalons, to an overpowering attack. The Marshal and Napoleon, who happened to be at Imperial Headquarters, had lost the liberty of decision. The leadership had long since been surrendered into the power of public opinion. Its resolutions, inspired by the press and voiced by it, were simply transmitted by Parliament, the Council of Ministers and the Empress-Regent to Napoleon, MacMahon, or Bazaine. Thus the matter of the Army of the frontier had been settled some ten days before. Now the quick release of the Army of the Rhine from this bulwark was entrusted to MacMahon.

The Marshal opposed firm resistance to Rouher, the President of the Senate, who personally brought the expression of the

The Campaign of 1870-71

people's will, A march to the east would lead the army into unavoidable defeat, all the more, as nothing was known of Bazaine's intentions and plans. He would march to Paris on the 23rd, should no news come until then from Bazaine. Rouher returned to Paris with the naive intention of impressing the people favorably, through a proclamation, towards MacMahon's return. Hardly had he left when a telegram of the 19th was received from Bazaine, sent on the day of his retreat to Metz. It closed with:

> I still count on moving to the north and fighting my way via Montmedy on the road from St. Menehould to Chalons if the road is not strongly held. In the latter case I shall go to Sedan, and even Mezieres, to reach Chalons.

After this information, which should not have been taken very seriously, MacMahon believed that Bazaine was already on the road to Montmedy and resolved to meet him at Stenay, right or wrong. Soon a telegram reached him from Paris, the Minister-President, in which it was urged that the junction with the Army of the Rhine take place as soon as possible.

On the 23rd the French Army started from Rheims to the Suippe between Dontrien and St. Masmes.

The two German armies which reached on that day with the right wing the locality east of Verdun and with the left St. Dizier, found out gradually that the enemy had left the camp at Chalons, that he had marched to Rheims and taken a position there. A telegram arrived from London on the 25th announcing "MacMahon seeks junction with Bazaine," confirming current rumors, the information contained in captured letters, and newspaper reports.

In order to meet the enemy marching from Rheims via Vouziers and Stenay, Attigny, Le Chesne and, Beaumont, possibly via Rethel, Tourteron and Mouzon toward Metz, it was not possible to march in the direction hitherto followed. A turning movement to the right must be made. On the 25th, the Army of the Meuse had reached with the right wing (XII Corps) Dombasle, the Third Army with the left (XI Corps) almost Vitry. Both could have turned to the right under very favorable circumstances had they

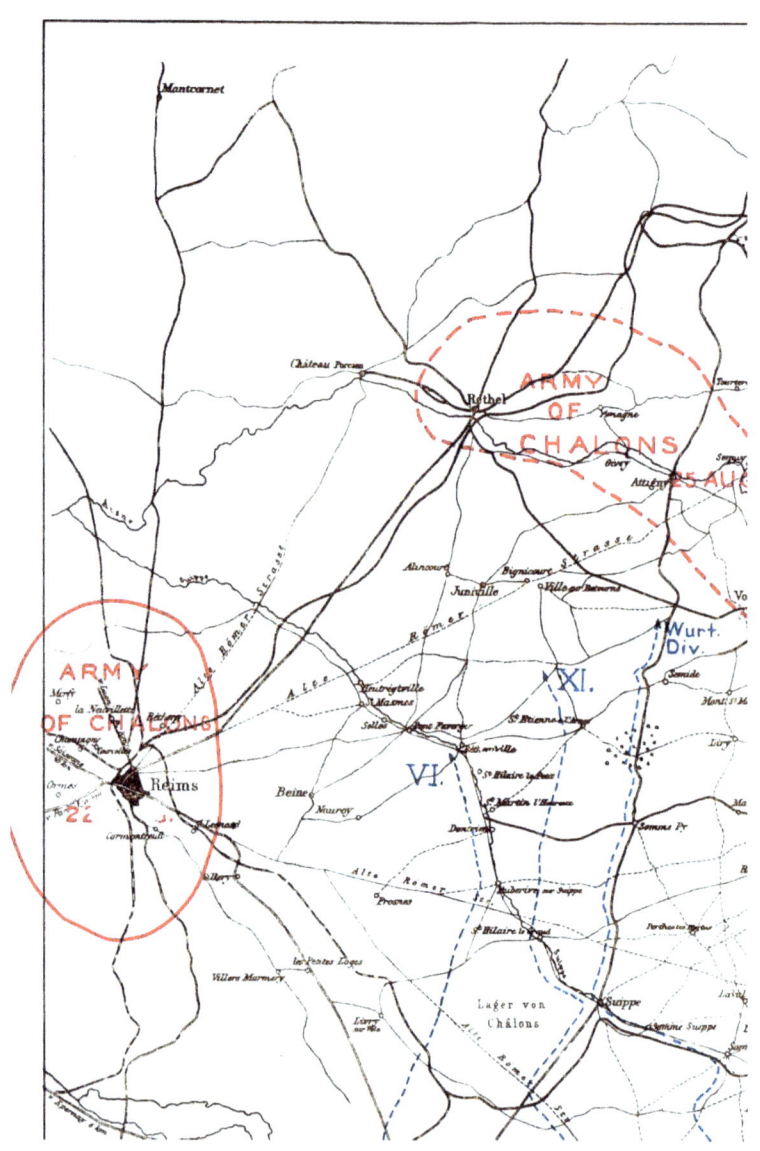

The Campaign of 1870-71 387

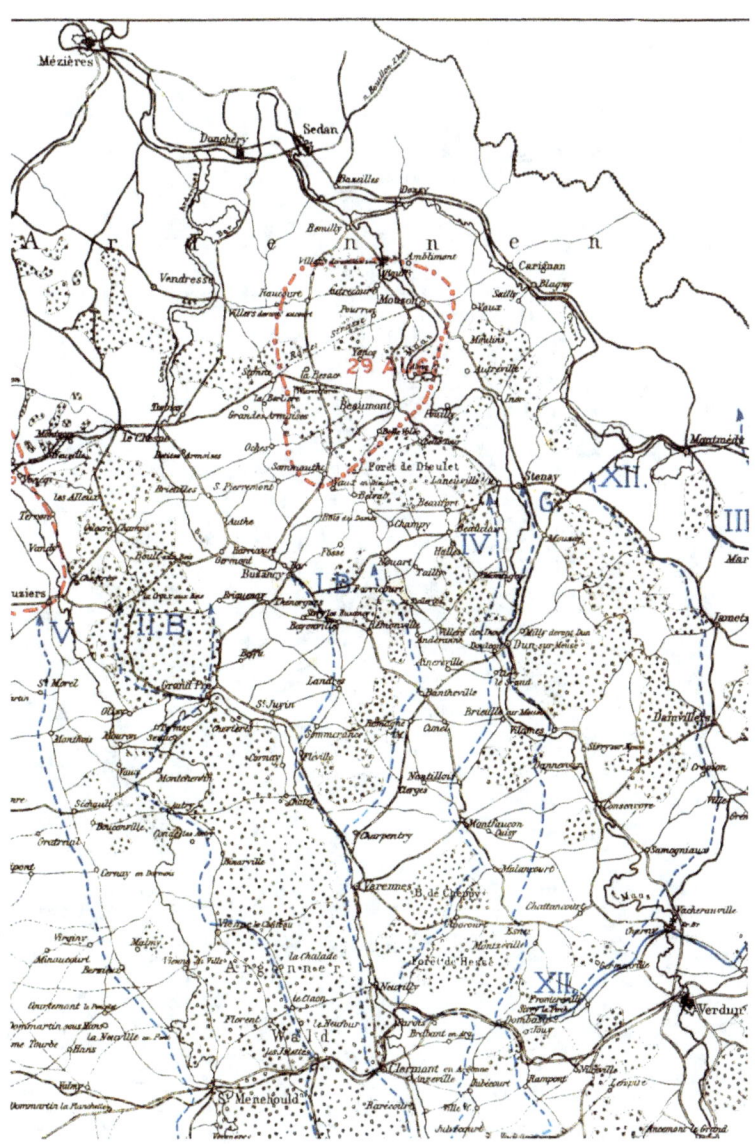

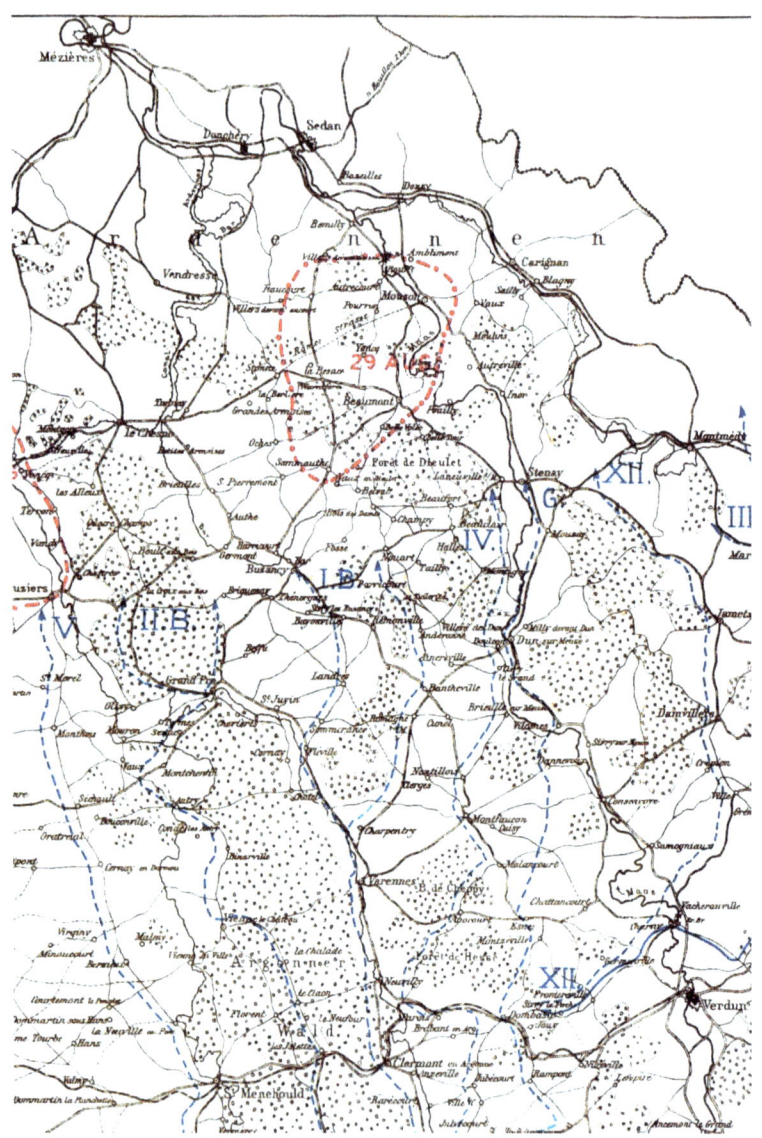

The Campaign of 1870-71

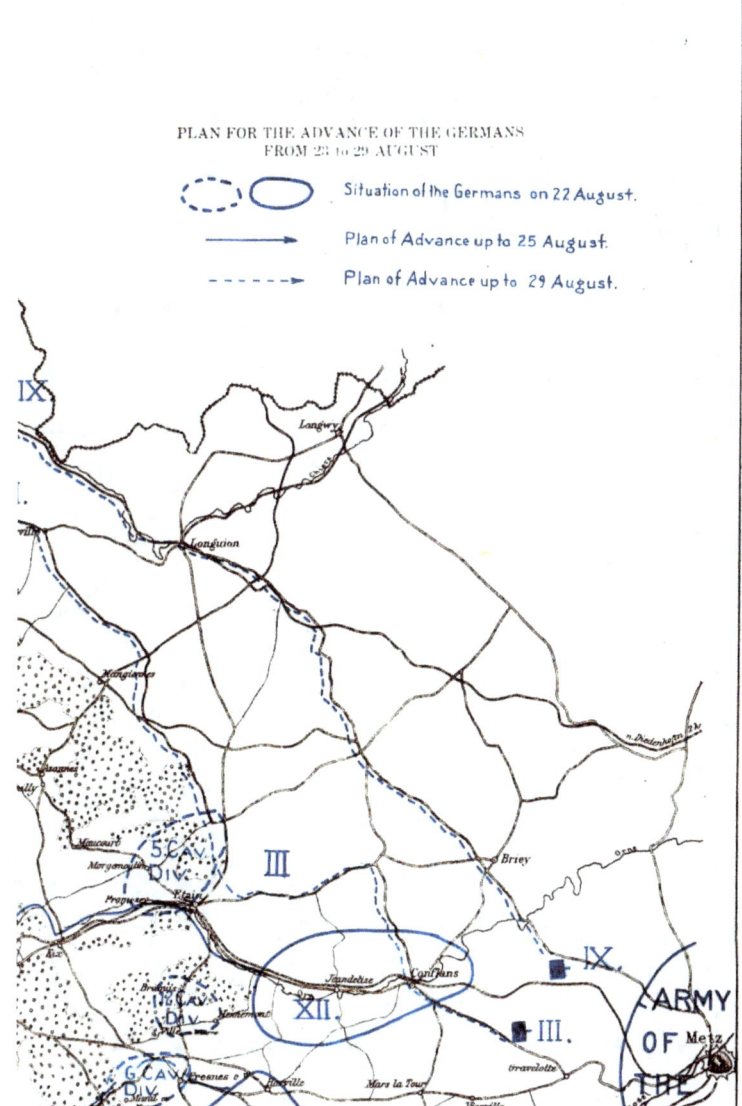

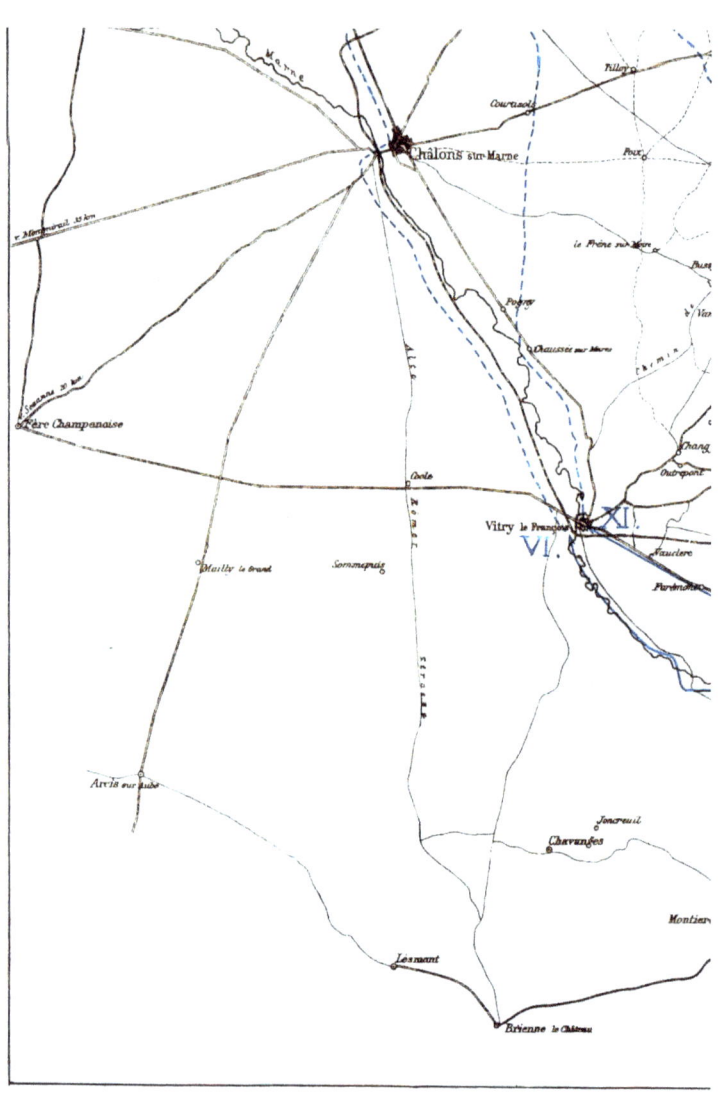

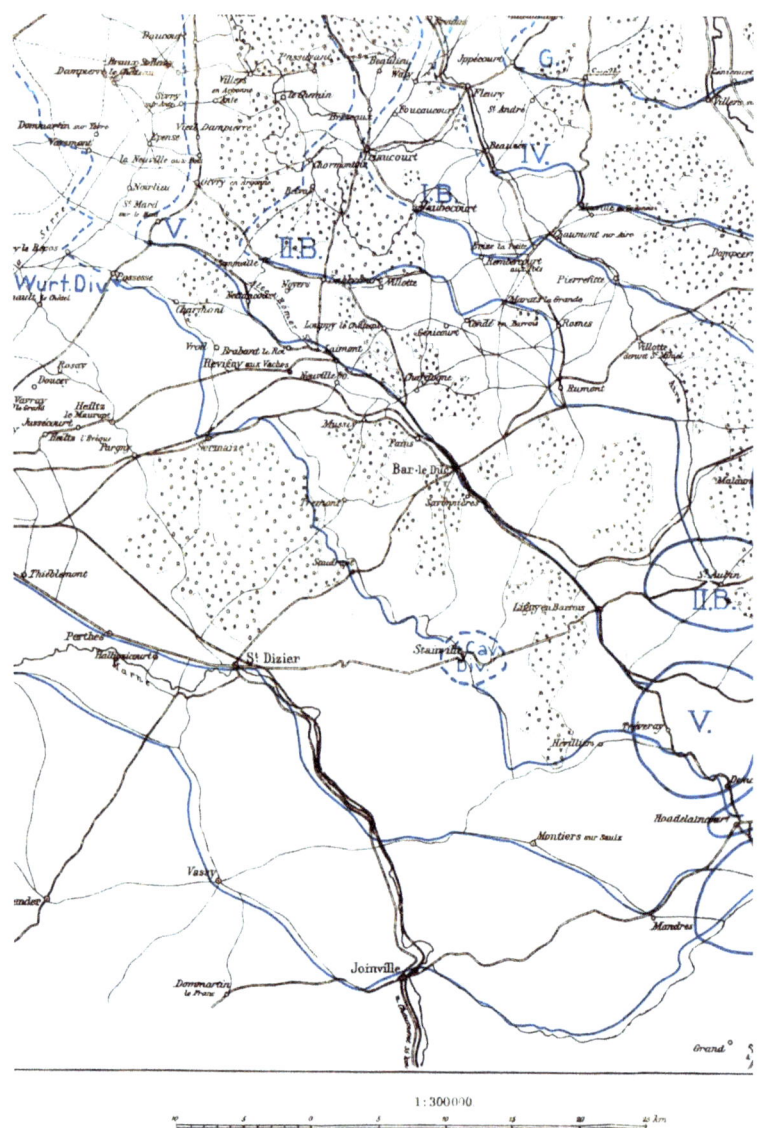

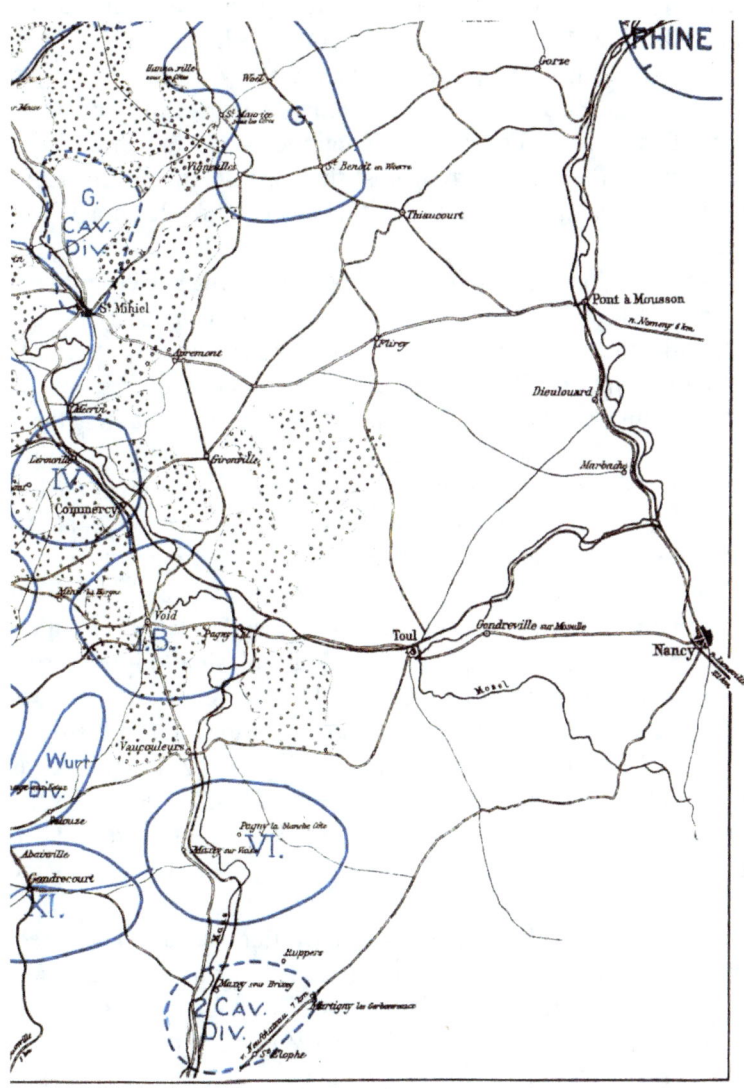

halted their leading elements on the line: Dombasle—Vitry, and given each corps a separate road. On the 26th, the XII Corps, forming the pivot, could advance to Charny, the other corps could reach the line Dombasle—St. Menehould—Chalons.

On the same day, the German cavalry reconnoitered at Vouziers and Buzancy what was seemingly the right French wing. From this point the enemy could continue, on the following days, the march to Metz or turn against the approaching Germans or, lastly, escape an encounter with the superior hostile forces by a retreat.

All these possibilities could be met by sending two corps of the investing army from Briey and Confians to Longuyon and Marville, the XII Corps from Charny to Jametz, the Guard Corps along the right bank of the Meuse, the IV and two corps of the Third Army between the Meuse and the Aisne, the remaining three and one half corps west of the latter river, cavalry divisions marching ahead of the entire front and especially in front of the left wing. Should the enemy march toward Metz or advance for attack between the Meuse and the Aisne or await there an attack in a favorable position, he still would have been attacked in the front and on one or both flanks and driven against the Belgian frontier.

Only a French retreat would be doubtful, should it be started so early that the left German wing could not reach Mezieres ahead of the enemy. The Germans would then have to seek to advance to the south by turning to the left or facing left. An advance, as pictured on pages 386-393, and as executed by 29 August, i.e., by the evening before the eve of the battle of Beaumont, corresponded to the instructions given by Moltke on another occasion "seek the enemy and defeat him."

Moltke discarded here such an operation because he wanted, more than anything else, to oppose as great a number of corps as possible to the threatened relief of Metz. To attain this, both armies had to turn from the line: Dombasle—Vitry, in a narrow front to the north. Not without many crossings and crowdings was it possible to execute this turning movement. The trains had mostly to be left behind just at the moment when advance through a mountainous terrain rendered the provisions of the supply columns most necessary.

For the security of the march and to support the Cavalry advancing to Veziers, Grand Pre, and Buzancy, the XII Corps started to Varennes on the 26th. It was followed by the Guard Corps, the IV, and the two Bavarian Corps in the direction of Dombasle, Nixeville, Verdun. The remaining corps of the Third Army prepared to advance on the following days in a northwesterly and northerly direction. Should the enemy continue his march to the east, it would hardly be possible to reach him west of the Meuse with superior numbers. He could gain the right bank of the river in two days. It was necessary to try and reach him there. According to Moltke's plan, the XII Corps, marching by way of Dun, the Guard Corps via Montfaucon and Consenvoye, the XIV via Charny should concentrate in the region of Damvillers by the 28th, two corps of the army of investment via Etain and Briey would be drawn to the right wing, the two Bavarian corps would follow to Azannes. Then no matter whether the hostile army, after crossing the Meuse, should turn to Damvillers or continue the march to Longuyon, there was still cause to hope that it would be driven to the Belgian frontier by one of the seven German Corps.

The reports, brought by the cavalry, showed that MacMahon's march to Metz had come to a halt. The seven German corps at Damvillers would have no enemy before them on the 28th. Endeavors should be made te assemble superior forces on the left bank of the Meuse for a battle of annihilation. For this purpose the corps of the first line advanced on the 27th to the line: Stenay--Dun—Montfaucon—Clermont—St. Menehould, on the 28th to the line: Stenay—Dun—Bantheville—Varennes—Vienne le Chateau—Cernay. It was very probable that the army which had advanced from Stenay to Cernay would likewise find no enemy there.

As the German army turned to the north on the 26th, against the not yet located enemy, so did the French Army instinctively turn to the south against the advancing enemy. General Douay put the VII Corps into a position east of Vouziers facing to the west and sent forward one brigade to Grand Pre and one to Buzancy. The V Corps (Failly) advanced on the 26th to Le Chesne, the I (Ducrot) to Semuy and Attigny, the XII (Lebrun) to Tourteron. The German cavalry, which showed itself during the day before

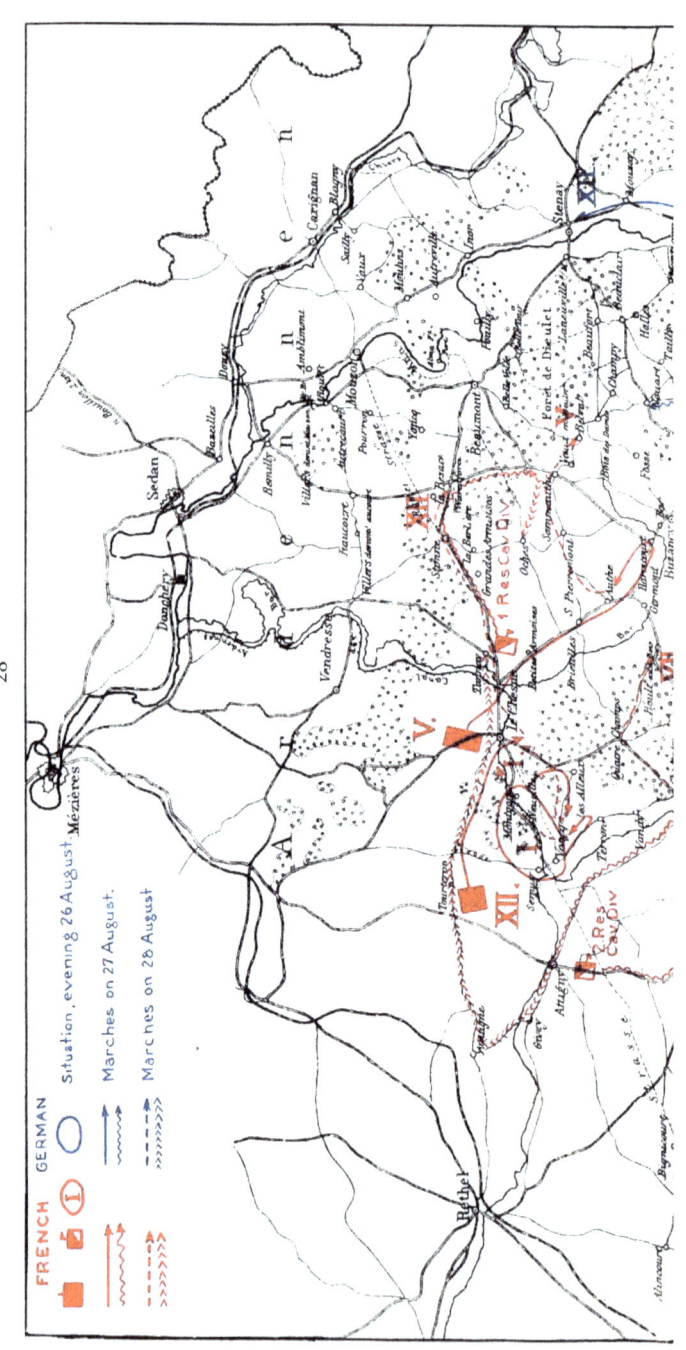

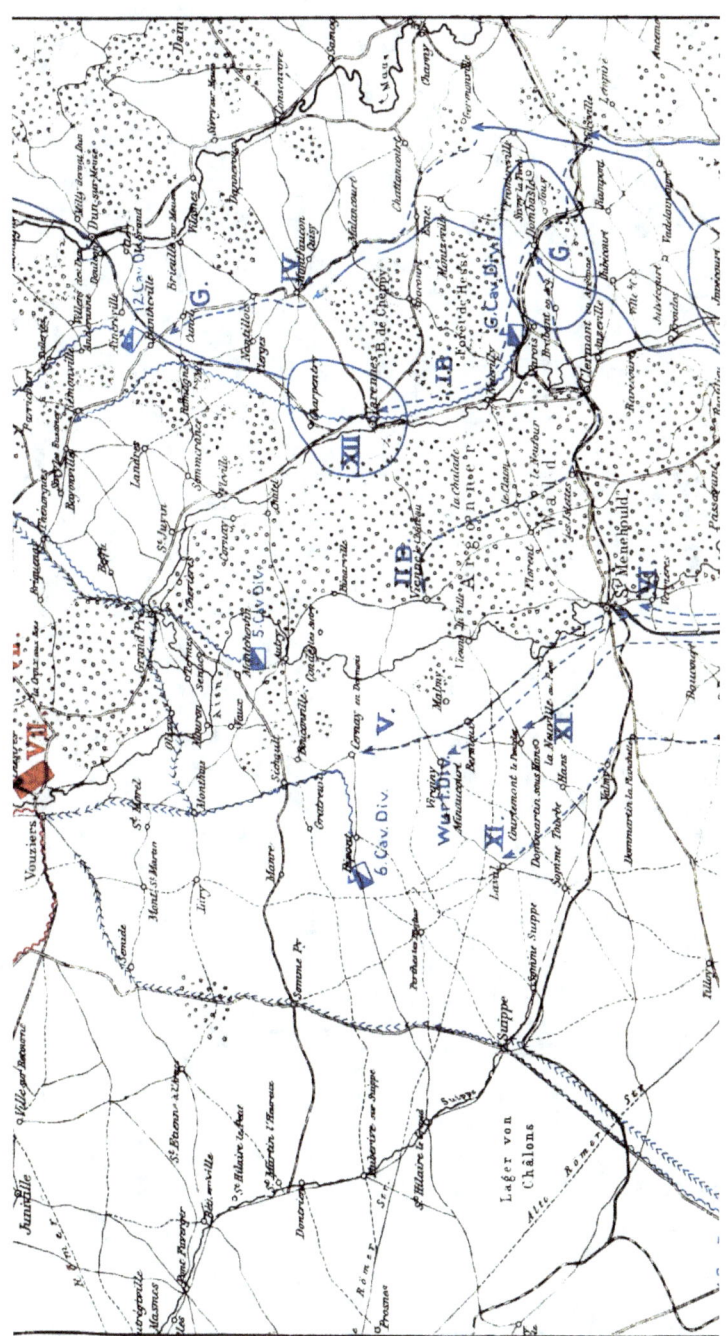

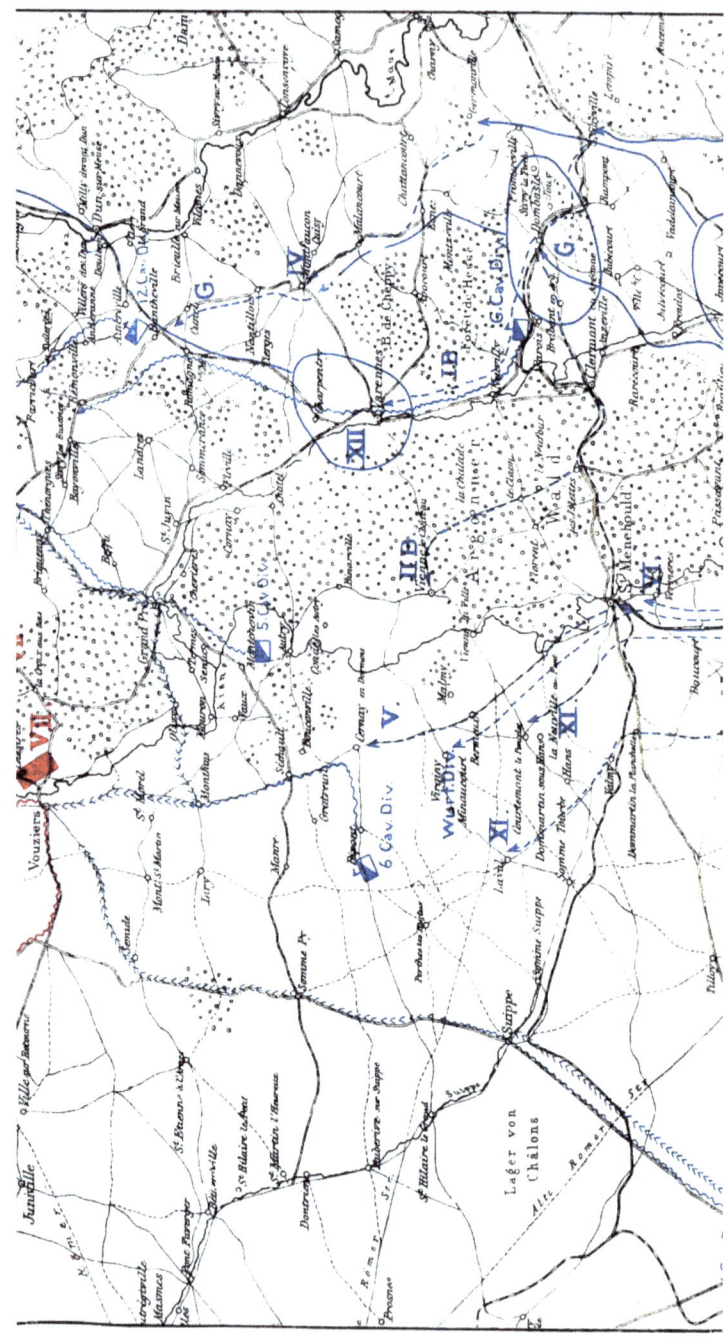

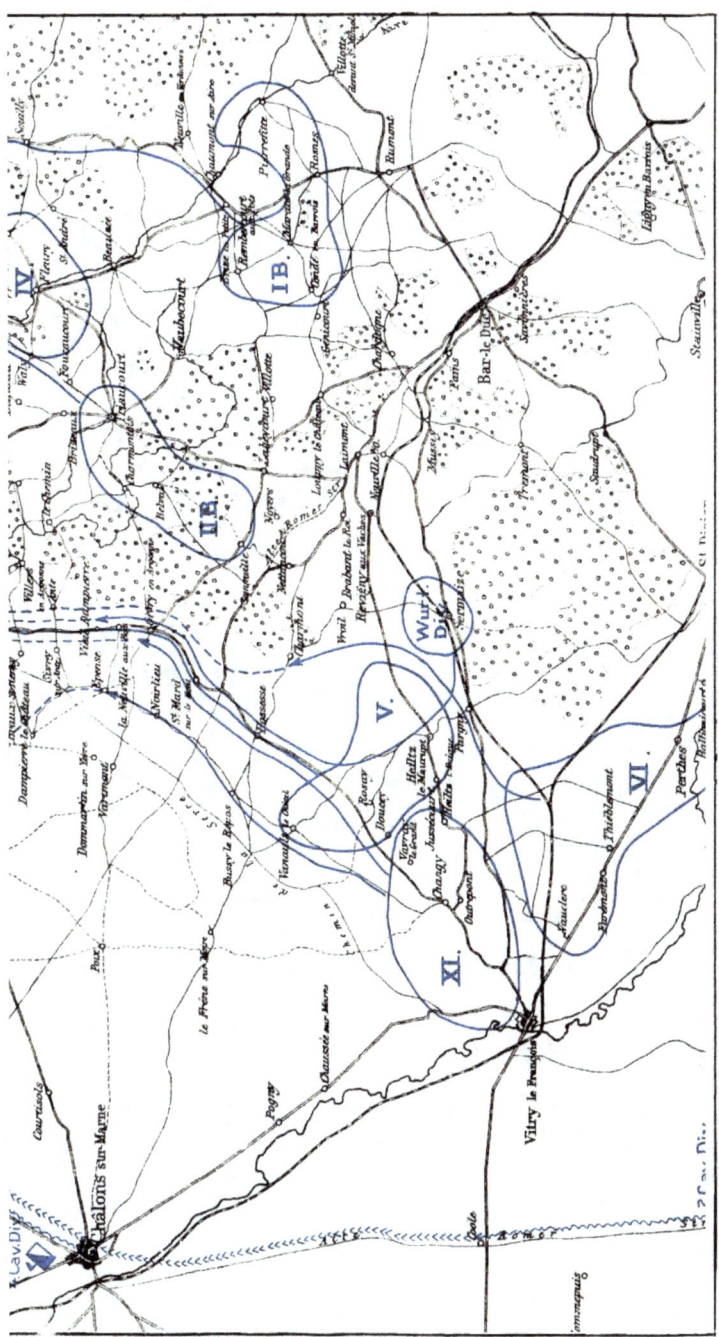

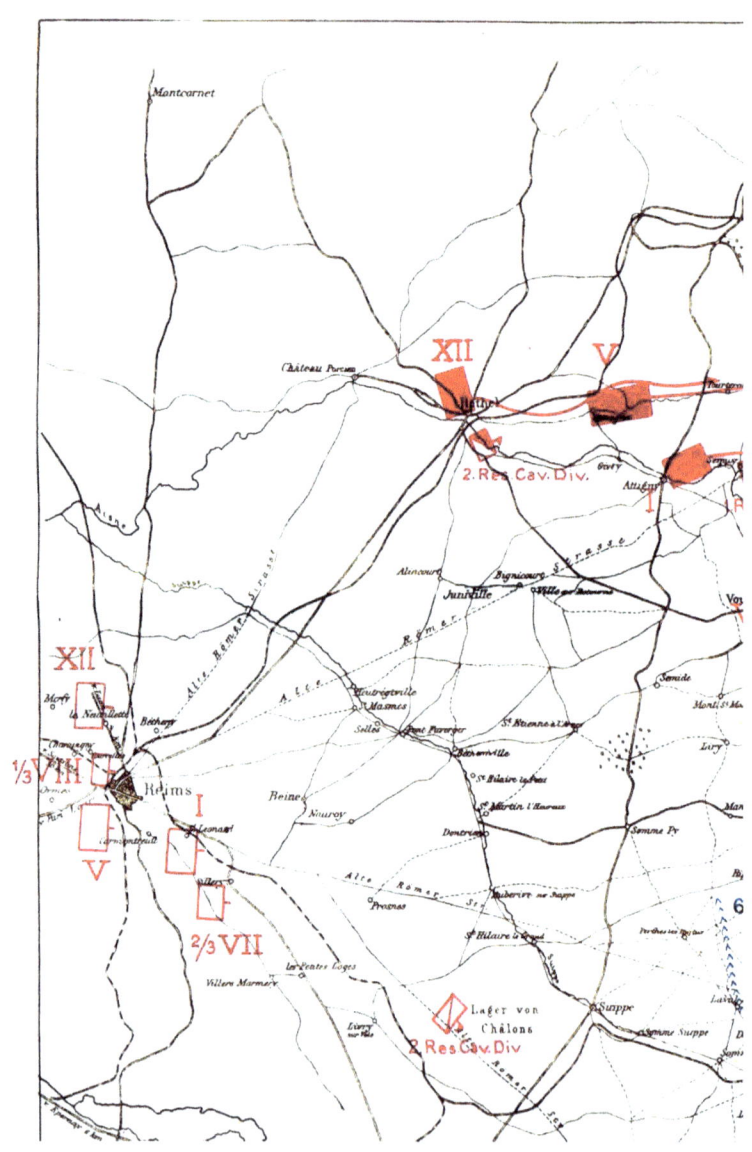

The Campaign of 1870-71

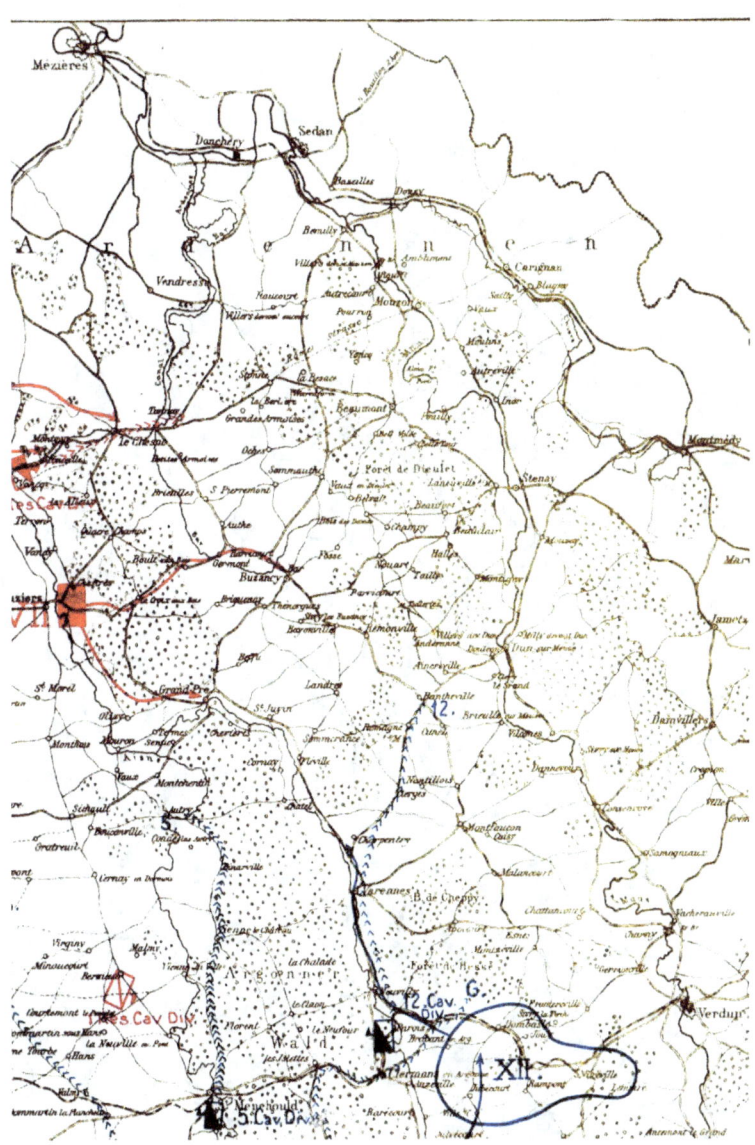

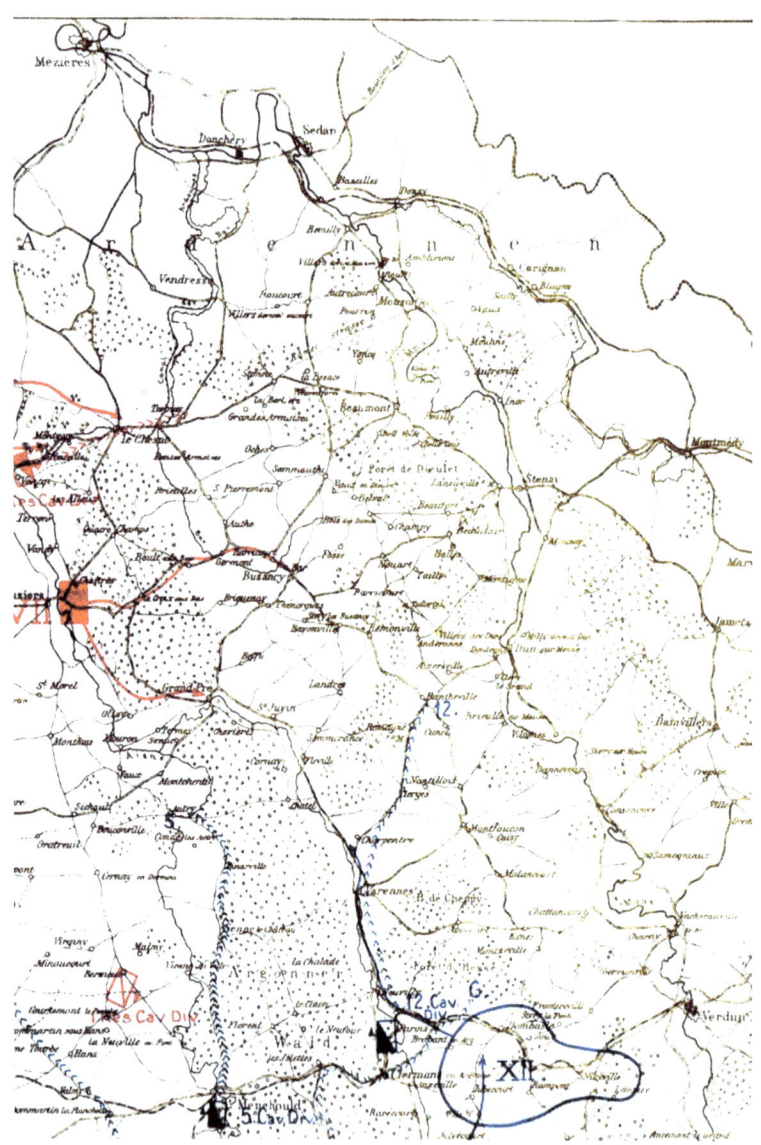

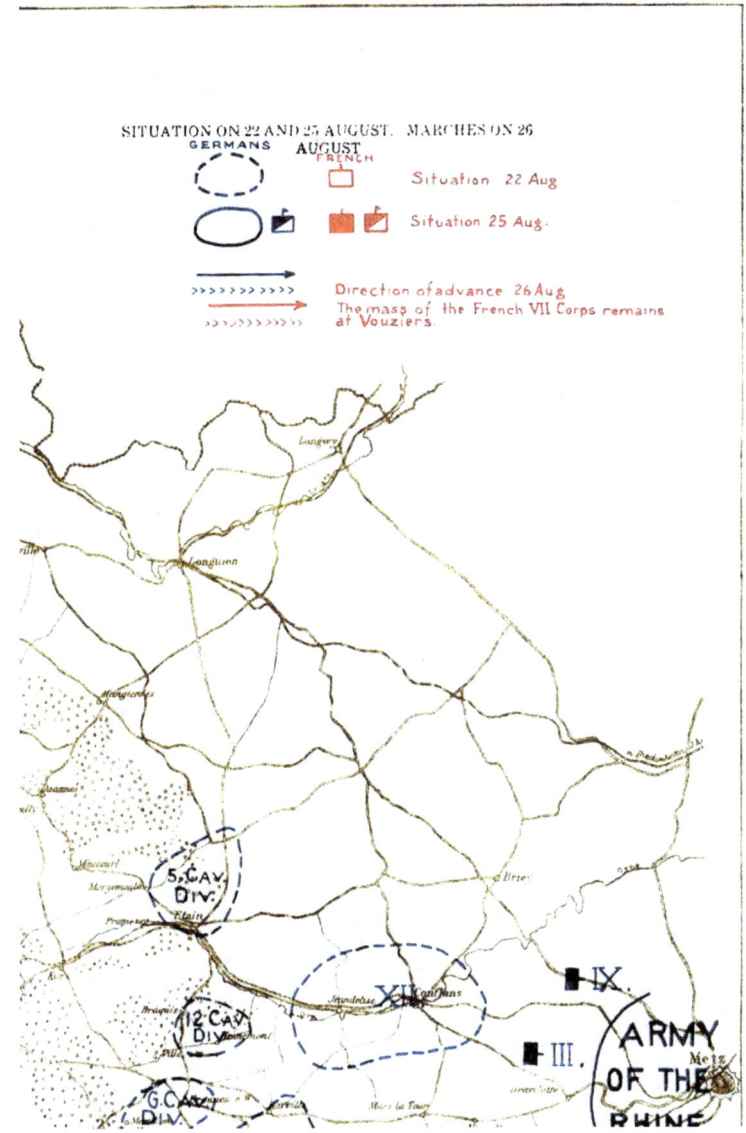

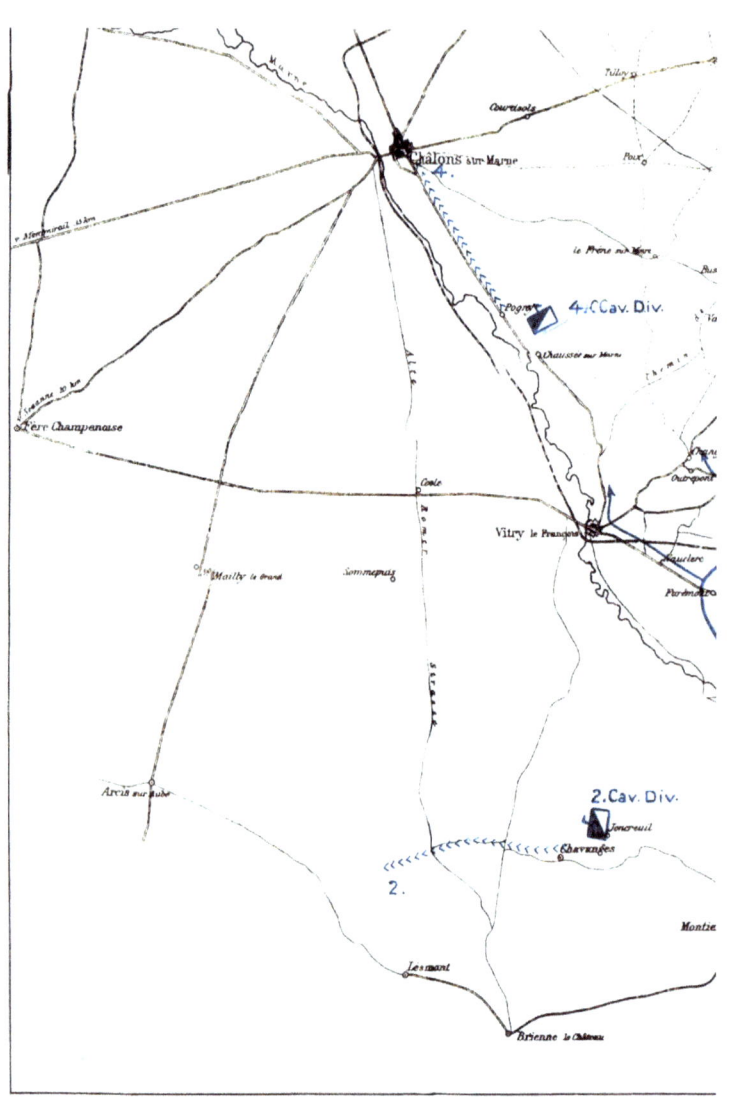

The Campaign of 1870-71

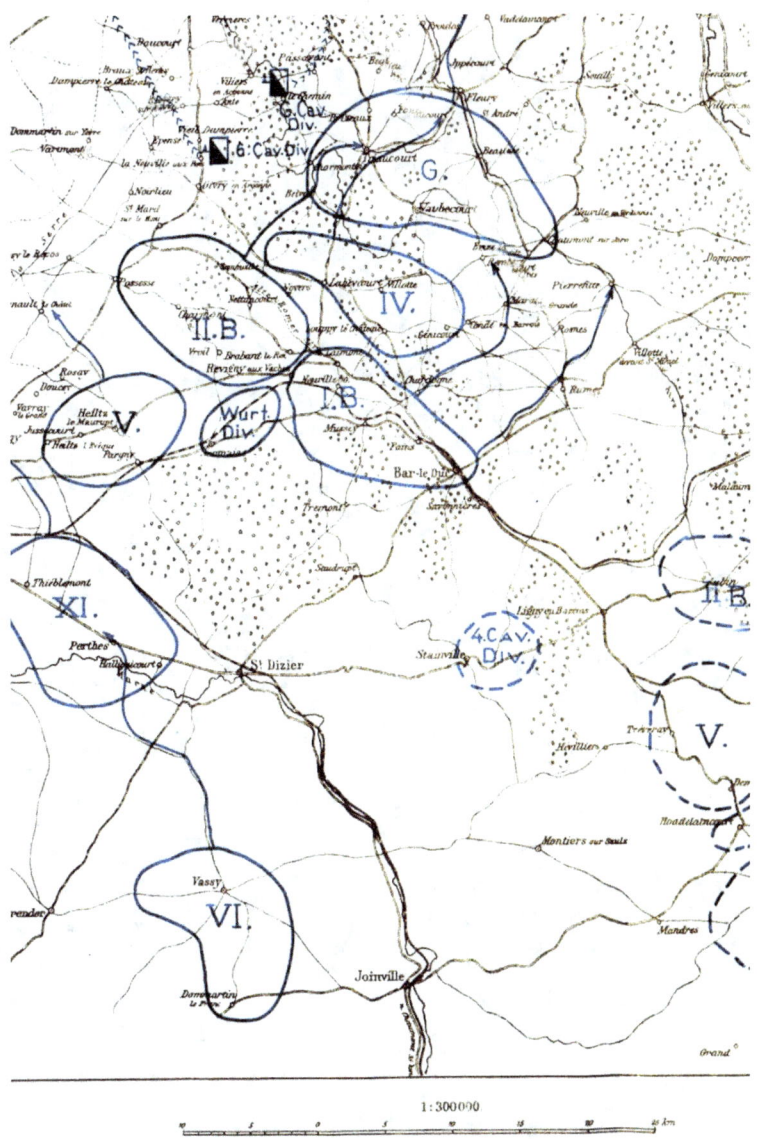

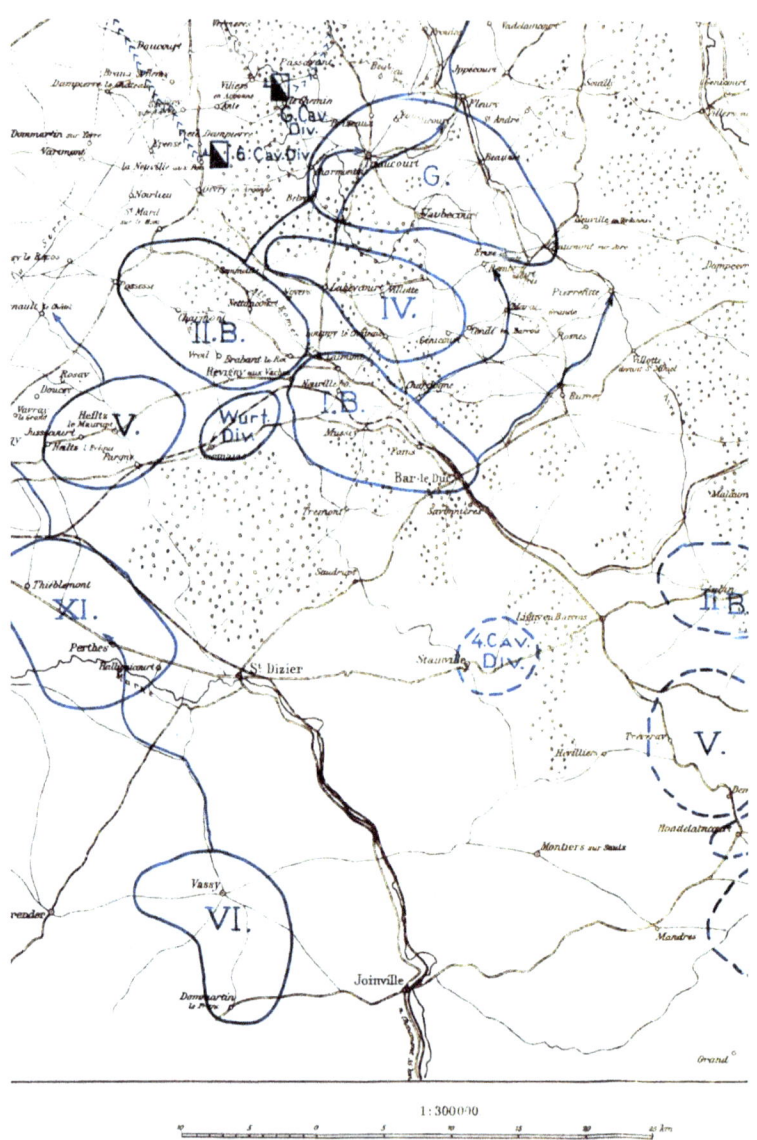

The Campaign of 1870-71

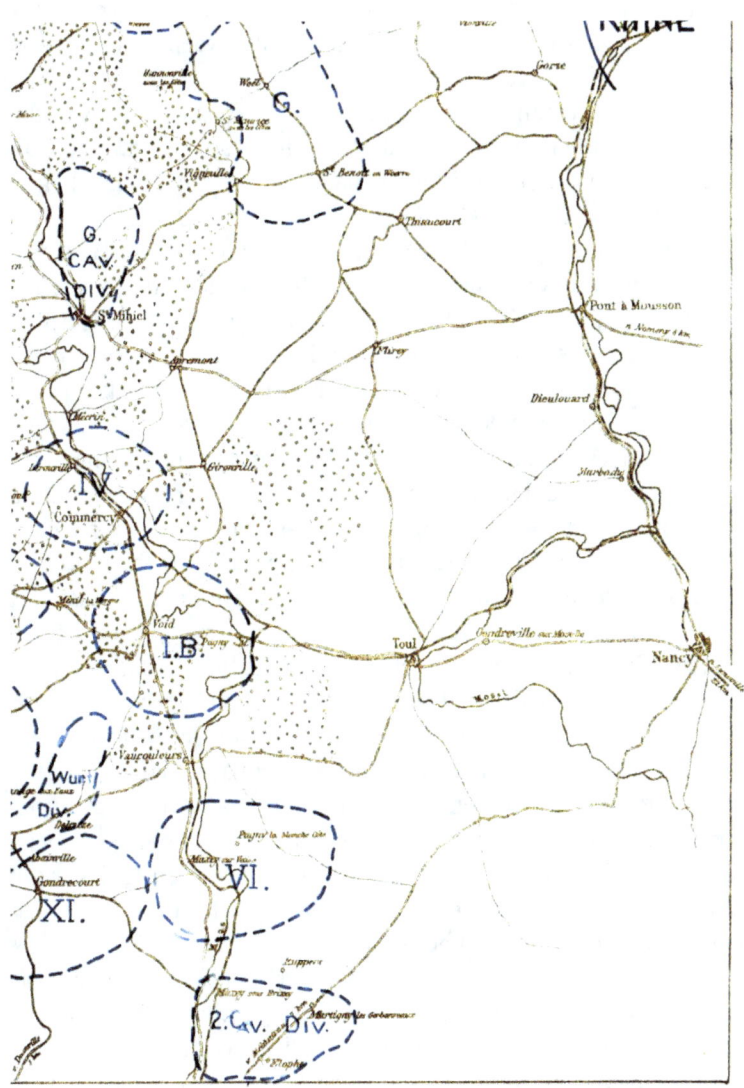

Buzancy, Grand Pre, and Vouziers, made General Douay think that an attack was impending. He decided to resist at Vouziers and Buzancy. MacMahon started on the 27th with the entire army to his assistance, but turned back when no enemy, except cavalry, was seen.

A decisive offensive, a rolling up of the advanced Army of the Meuse was afterwards recommended to MacMahon. Such an offensive could not have taken place before the 28th, when it would have met the XII Corps at Dun, the Guard Corps at Bantheville, the IV, sent from Montfaucon to Cierges, the Bavarian I Corps north of Varennes and would have found all other roads west strongly occupied. On the following day the right German wing would have halted, the left would have been sent forward. A complete surrounding of the French army would have taken place here and not at Sedan. Being unable to disregard these circumstances, good reports to the contrary notwithstanding, MacMahon found it inexpedient, in view of the German numerical superiority, either to await an attack or to venture one on his part.

He expected still less from the continuation of the march to Metz, since no news had come from Bazaine. He expected that part of the investing army would meet him, while the mass of the armies of the two Crown Princes would take him in flank and rear. If he would save his army from annihilation, all that remained for him to do was to retreat to Mezieres. Since the Germans had held back their left wing and had not sent even cavalry to the left of the Aisne and since a sufficient number of roads was at his disposition, the retreat, ordered the evening of the 27th, might have been executed without molestation. The German march to the right would have been a blow in the air and a very difficult campaign to Paris would have loomed before them.

Count Palikao, the French Minister of War, helped the Germans at this critical juncture. He telegraphed MacMahon in answer to his report concerning his decision to retire: "Should you leave Bazaine in the lurch, a revolution will break out in Paris—Your prompt junction with Bazaine seems urgently necessary." A further telegram contained the decided demand of the Council of Ministers to hurry to Bazaine's relief.

There no longer remained a choice. MacMahon decided to

resume the march he had abandoned, and to continue it as well as possible until he should be impeded by the numerical superiority of the enemy. He understood clearly that this check would coincide probably with his complete annihilation. Officers were despatched on all sides to divert toward the east the units which had received orders to go west. Many corps were reached after they had already started on the march. The turning back and facing about of the long columns, the unavoidable crossing with others caused troubles which were doubly felt in the rain and on the bad roads. Only late in the night of the 28th did the last troops come to rest. On the Attigny——-Voncq—Beaumont road, the I Corps had reached le Chesne, the XII, la Besace, its cavalry, Beaumont. On the Vouziers—Stenay road was the VII Corps turning from Quatre—Champs to Boult-aux-Bois. General Failly had not dared to continue with the V Corps the march via Bar to Buzancy on account of the hostile cavalry, but had turned via Sommauthe and bivouacked in the evening at Belval and Bois des Dames.

The reports coming in to the German Royal Headquarters during the 28th, hinted at a retreat of the enemy to the northwest. At 7:00 PM, a turn to the right between Dun and Cernay was ordered for both armies on the line: Nouart —Vouziers. New reports coming in the evening persuaded Moltke that the enemy had not abandoned his plan of relieving Metz and that he would cross the Meuse at Stenay and below. He would find Stenay occupied and would be forced to turn against the Army of the Meuse on his right flank. As long as the latter was without support it would be well for it to await in a suitable position, between Aincreville and Landres, the attack of the enemy who would soon appear on its left flank. Orders had been given to advance: the Bavarian I Corps from Varennes to St. Juvin, the II from Vienne le Chateau to Cernay, the V and the Wurttemberg Division from Cernay to Grand Pre. With these three and one half corps, which were to be followed on the left by the XI to Monthois and the VI to Vienne le Chateau, an advance was intended against the road: Buzancy—Stenay.

This calculation of Moltke would have been correct with any other enemy than MacMahon, who carried a forced pass given him by public opinion and must, under any circumstances, make an

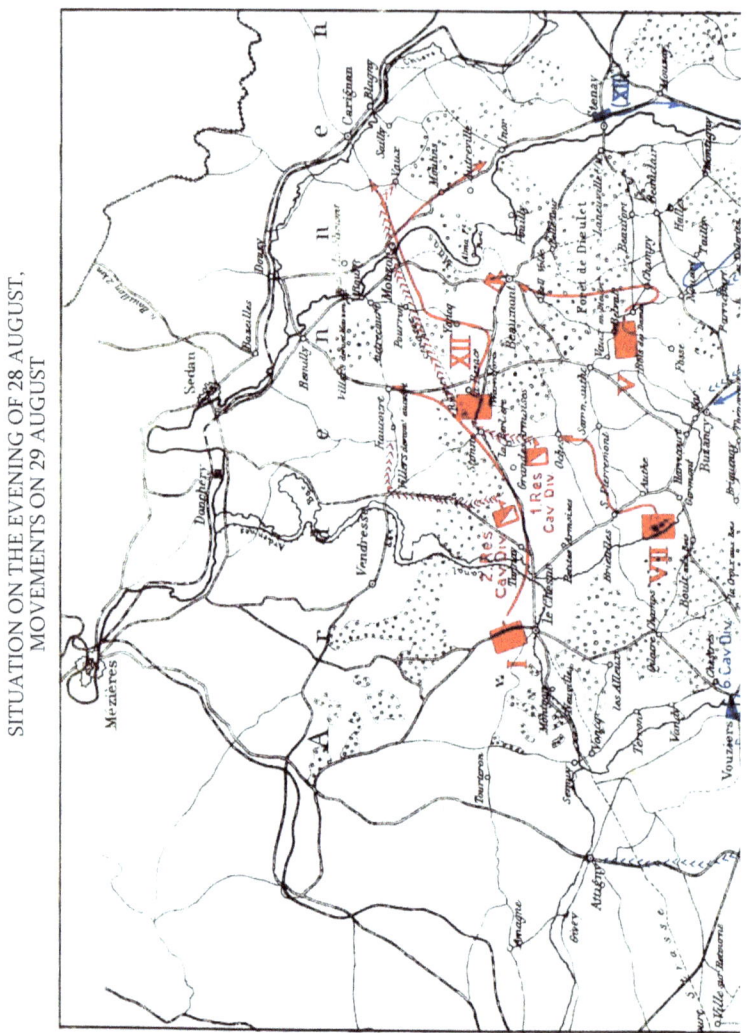

SITUATION ON THE EVENING OF 28 AUGUST, MOVEMENTS ON 29 AUGUST

effort to cross the Meuse and still avoid if possible, a combat with a superior enemy.

Upon hearing that Stenay was occupied by 15,000 Germans, MacMahon gave up crossing at that point and ordered that on the 29th the XII Corps should march to Mouzon, the I to Roncourt, the V to Beaumont, the VII to La Besace. The XII and I Corps with Margueritte's and Bonnemain's Cavalry Divisions executed this order and the former sent outposts to the roads to Carignan and

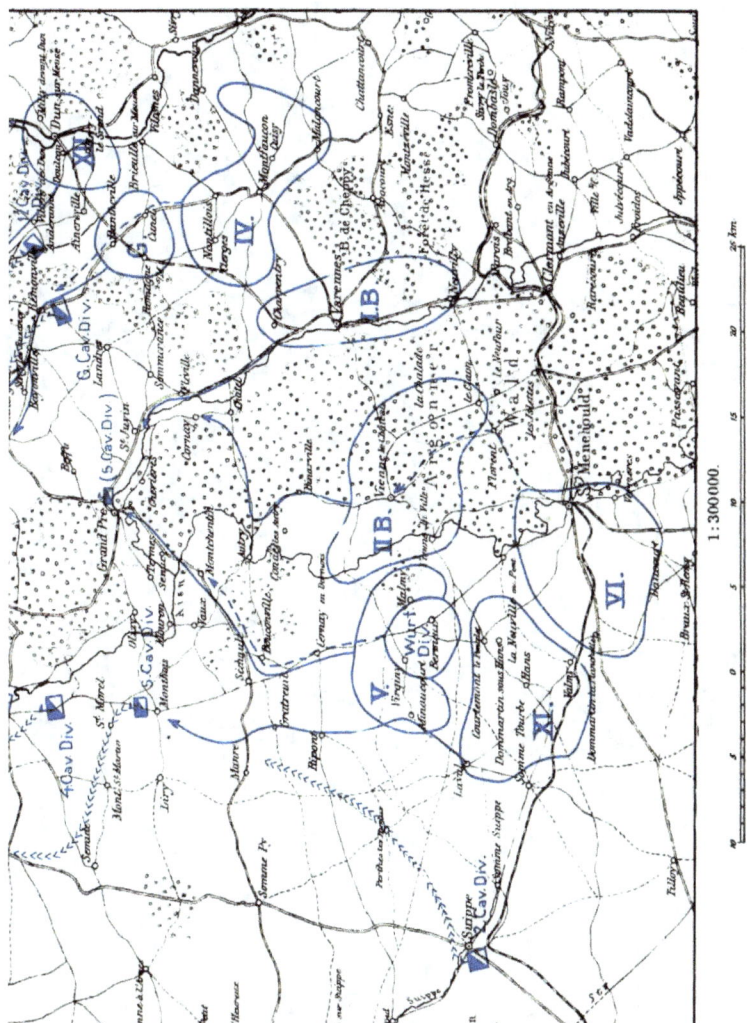

Stenay as far as Inor. The VII Corps, deceived by many false reports, reached from Boult aux Bois only as far as Oches and St. Pierremont. Since the officer carrying the order to the V Corps had been captured by a patrol of Uhlans, General Failly led his two divisions, according to a previous order, to Beaufort and Beauclair to await there MacMahon's orders for the attack on Stenay.

On the German side, the XII Corps went early on the 29th via Dun across the Meuse and occupied a position between that town

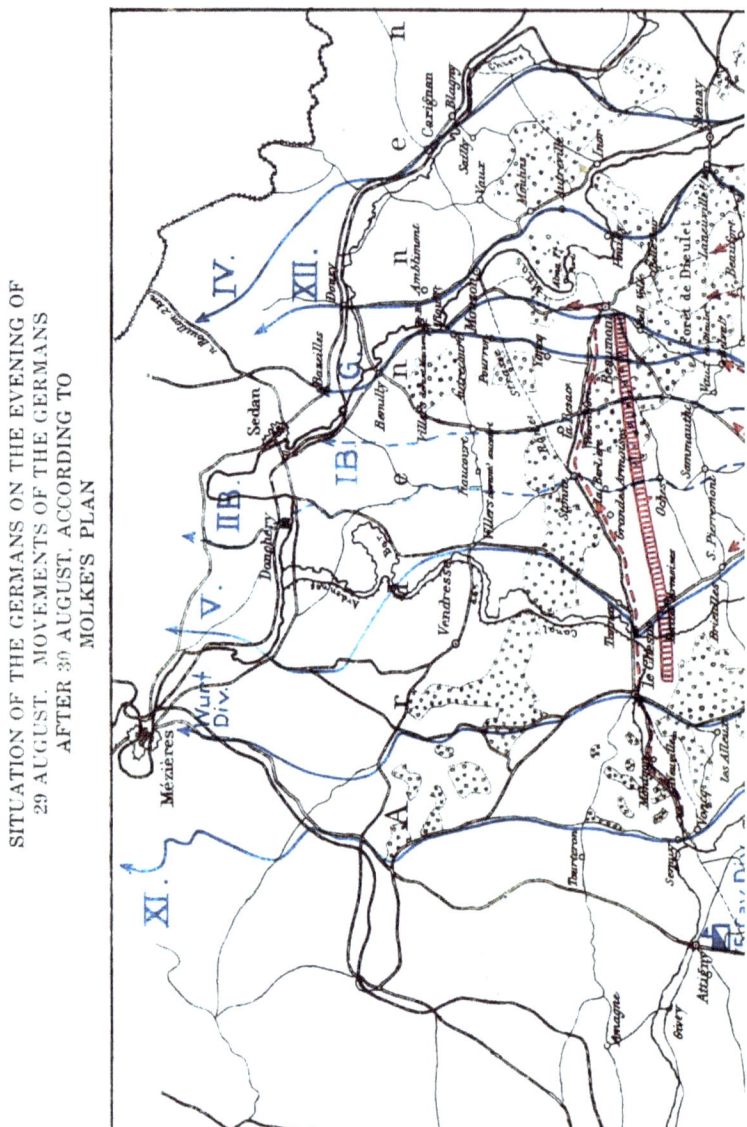

SITUATION OF THE GERMANS ON THE EVENING OF 29 AUGUST. MOVEMENTS OF THE GERMANS AFTER 29 AUGUST, ACCORDING TO MOLKE'S PLAN

and Aincreville. The reports arriving there said nothing of an impending attack, but much more of the retreat of the enemy. It seemed necessary to gain contact with the enemy, all the more since a Royal order of the evening before read—"Continue the

The Campaign of 1870-71

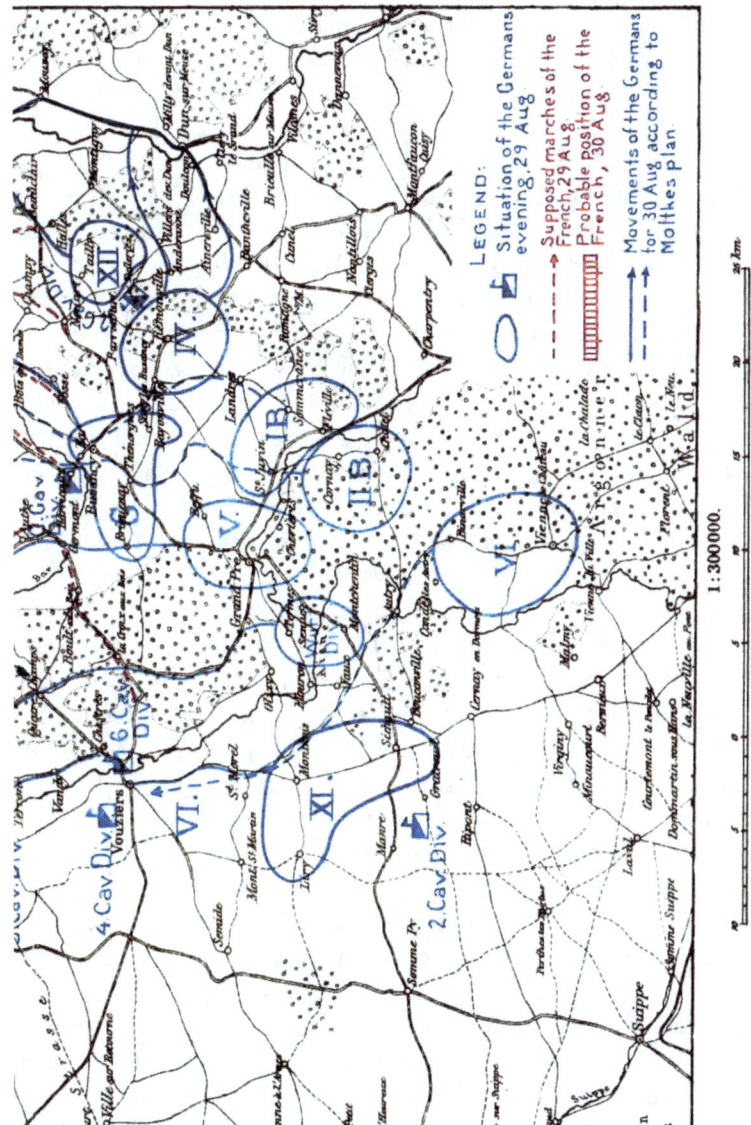

offensive against the road: Vouziers—Buzancy—Stenay. Its prompt occupation by the army of the Meuse is enjoined should it be occupied by inferior hostile forces."

Since this condition seemed to be fulfilled according to all reports received, the Crown Prince of Saxony sent the 1st Division of the Guard Corps to Buzancy, the 2nd to Thenorgues, the XII Corps from Ainereville to Nouart, the IV to Remonville. The enemy retired to St. Pierremont before the Guard, but the advance guard of the XII Corps came at Nouart upon the V French Corps. The combat which took place at this point was broken off by the Saxons in order to avoid isolated encounters, after the superiority of the French had been ascertained. When the Saxons reached the height between Nouart and Tailly on their retreat the French Corps, having at last received the army orders, marched off in an opposite direction. Two brigades, remaining as rearguard, covered this withdrawal until during the night the patrols of the 12th Cavalry Division reported the retreat of the entire corps in the direction of Beaumont. The Guard cavalry ascertained during the night that the rearguard of the VII Corps had remained at Pierremont.

Royal Headquarters had some other reports of the early morning and forenoon hours. It was not known whether they were still good or had been rendered worthless by events. Moltke assumed, in the meanwhile that the French were advancing toward the Meuse by two roads via Voncq, Le Chesne, Stonne, La Besace and Beaumont, and by Vouziers, Buzancy, and Nouart. They could not: use the southern road because the Army of the Meuse had reached Buzancy and Nouart and had been obliged to take the northern. The march would not be possible on this one either. It was, consequently, probable that the French would await a battle in a good position between Le Chesne and Beaumont reported to be the extreme points occupied by them. The part of this position east of the Buzancy—Raucourt road should be attacked by the Army of the Meuse, supported by the two Bavarian corps.

The strip west of the above road to Le Chesne fell to the share of the Third Army. It was left to army headquarters how the attack should take place. Since, however, there were scarcely more than three corps for the attack against the front: La Besace—Beaumont, including the two Bavarian units, it was expedient to send two corps of the Army of the Meuse across the river to turn the hostile left flank. Had the left flank of the Third Army been extended in the same way across the Aisne, both armies would have had to execute the movements shown on pages 412-413. There was a probability then of driving the enemy to the Belgian frontier, should he hold out between Le Chesne and Beaumont, retreat, or advance to the right or left.

Both armies, however, preferred not to surround the enemy, but to persuade him to retire by compact, separate attacks, although retreat had been his intention. Moreover they translated the information received from Royal Headquarters: "The enemy stands *between* Le Chesne and Beaumont" into "the enemy stands *at* Le Chesne and at Beaumont." According to this view, the Army of the Meuse would attack the enemy supposed to be at Beaumont with the XII, IV, and Bavarian I Corps in the first line, with the Guard and Bavarian II Corps in the second line, while the Third Army would advance against the enemy which was not at Le Chesne, with the IX Corps and the Wurttemberg Division in the first, and the VI Corps in the second line. The enemy, whose presence was ascertained to be between St. Pierremont and Oches, was taken as non-existent.

The V Corps, which had been sent via these points to Stonne, had to maintain communications between the armies only and turn, according to circumstances, against the Nothing at Le Chesne or reinforce the overstrong body of troops sent to Beaumont. The fiction that the road to Stonne was free of the enemy could not be lastingly entertained, no more than that Le Chesne was strongly occupied. It was soon found that there was not a man in Le Chesne, that the enemy, reported at Oches, had gone to Stonne and had occupied a strong position with at least a rearguard. In the meanwhile, army headquarters decided to send the XI Corps and the Wurttemberg Division to La Berliere. It might be expected in the afternoon of the 30th that three corps would attack the enemy at Beaumont and two and one half the one at Stonne. Three corps were to be kept intact as reserve.

It had been decided that for the first attack, the XII Corps should advance with one division via Laneuville on the highroad, with the other from Beauclair through the woods, the IV Corps west of it by two roads through the woods, the Bavarian I Corps on the highroad via Sommauthe—all five columns on Beaumont. The Guard Corps was to remain at Fosse, the Bavarian II Corps at Sommauthe in reserve. Of the three roads through the woods

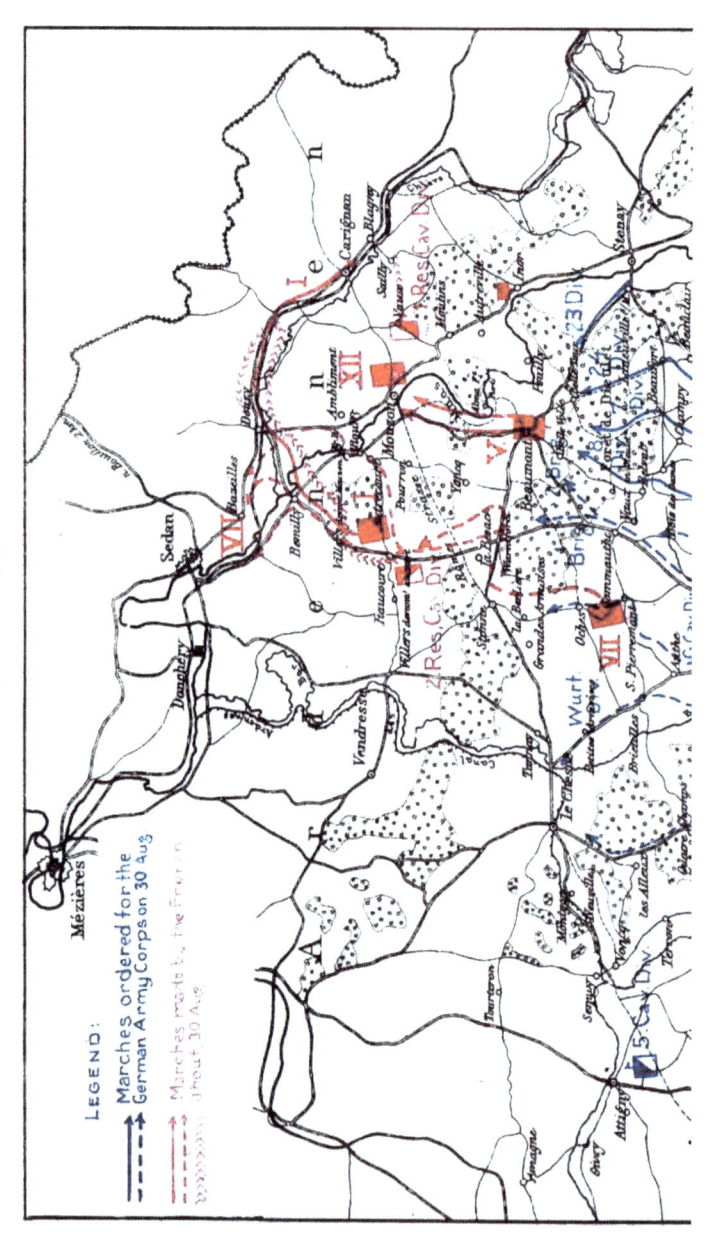

SITUATION ON THE EVENING OF 29 AUGUST. MOVEMENTS ON 30 AUGUST

The Campaign of 1870-71

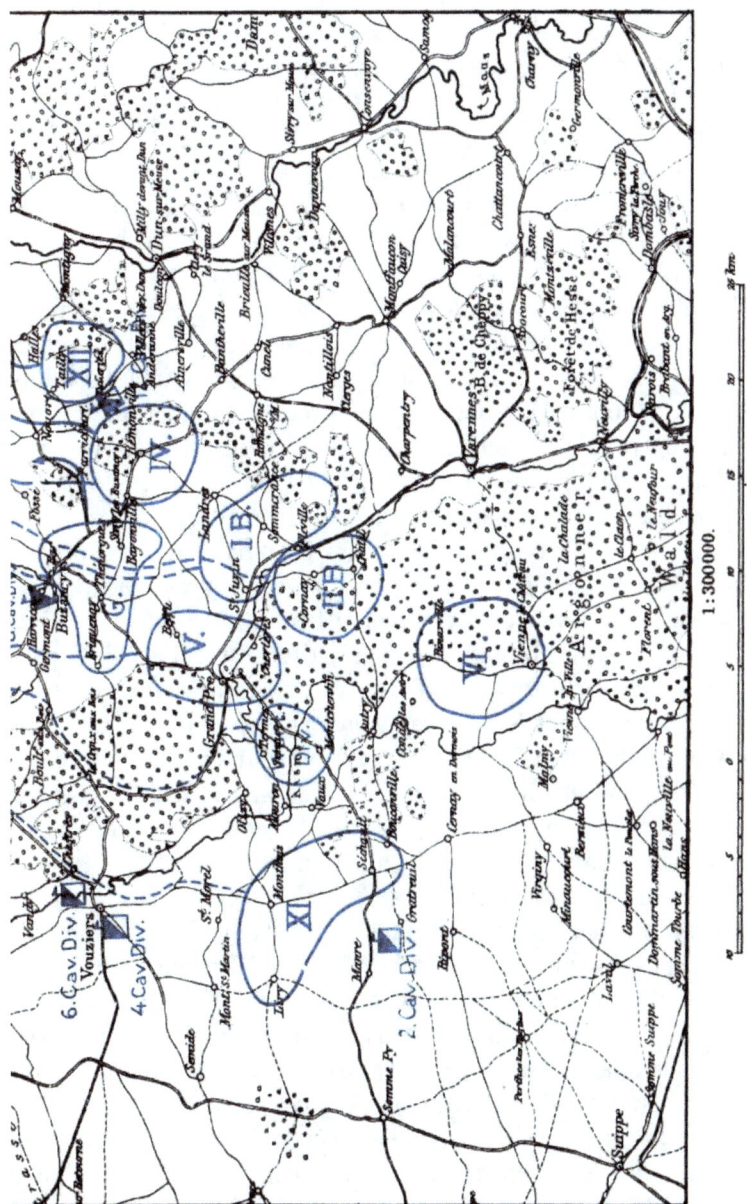

designated for the advance, the two eastern ones came close te the highroad in front of Beaument, so that only three roads opened on the city: the Stenay—Beaumont road, taken by the XII Corps and the 7th Division, the road from Sommauthe, taken by the Bavarian Corps; and between these was a path through the woods for the 8th Division.

According to the then existing views and principles, the march order, issued by the Army of the Meuse, was beyond criticism. A mass with the narrowest front and of the greatest depth could be formed by the three corps in front of Beaumont. The enemy, though much weaker, could, by deploying on a wider front, oppose as great if not greater firing strength against them. Should he retire, he could be pursued only by small detachments, so that he would be able to continue unmolested on his retreat should he have taken care to provide sufficient crossings over the Meuse. A strong reserve of two corps, which was to be held intact, could hardly compensate all the disadvantages of such an attack.

At any rate a change should have been made in these orders, when late in the evening the cavalry sent across the Meuse, reported the advance of the enemy from Mouzon to Inor, thus confirming all information which had been received through a captured French army order. It was evident that the situation, according to which Moltke had worded his order on the 30th, was no longer the same. The enemy, apparently, did not wish to accept a battle between Beaumont and Le Chesne but had crossed the Meuse with part of his forces and would follow with the rest of his troops to the other bank on the following day.

Moltke had foreseen this and also ordered a crossing of the Meuse. It was, consequently, advisable that of the surplus forces at the disposition of the Army of the Meuse, at least two corps be sent across the river in order to bar the advance of the enemy in the narrow space between the Meuse and the Belgian frontier and force him into a position where he would have to weather an attack from the west and eventually be annihilated. Army headquarters, however, did not wish to be disturbed in the measures they had ordered. The entire apparatus of 150,000 men was put in motion in the ordered formation, for the purpose of inflicting slight losses to a corps already in retreat.

Orders were given so that the surprise attack should take place against Beaumont immediately after the noon hour. That the enemy was still found there was due to the patrol, which had captured the order sent by MacMahon to the V Corps. This bad luck was the cause for that corps not starting in the morning but in the evening of the 29th, reaching Beaumont in the night and requiring the forenoon for the recuperation of the exhausted strength and not for the continuation of the march.

The officers and troops were sitting at their meal in camp south of Beaumont between the road to Stenay and the road to Beausejour, when the advance guard of the 8th Division (4th Jagers) emerged from the wood between Tuilerie and the farm of Belle Volee. It was intended not to disturb the carefree soldiers, but to have the division come up under cover. But when a peasant rushed to the French camp with the cry "the enemy is here" and the cauldrons were quickly abandoned, the division commander, General V. Scholer, believed that he had to take advantage of the advance guard batteries which had just come up.

A few shots directed into the dense mass had their effect. But the French had soon formed a swarm of skirmishers which took advantage of the far-reaching long range arm and caused such considerable losses not only to the Jager battalion, but also to the two batteries, that almost all the gunners were killed. The situation changed when the French advanced in dense skirmish lines followed by units in close order for attack and entered into the zone of effective fire of the Jagers and, showered with bullets in their turn, were forced to retreat.

A second French attack was directed against the 66th Regiment which, supported by four batteries, advanced at the head of the 7th Division via Belle Tour to Beaumont. This attack was likewise repulsed.

In the meanwhile, the deployment of the 8th Division on the height of the Ferme de Petite Foret had made but little progress. As the commander of the advance guard kept a company, each regimental commander a battalion and the brigade commander two battalions at their disposition, and since the artillery needed special covers and each building a garrison, there were only three and one half battalions and 4 batteries available, although the infantry had

BATTLE OF BEAUMONT
30 August, 1870
Movements and combats until about 3:00 PM.

The Campaign of 1870-71

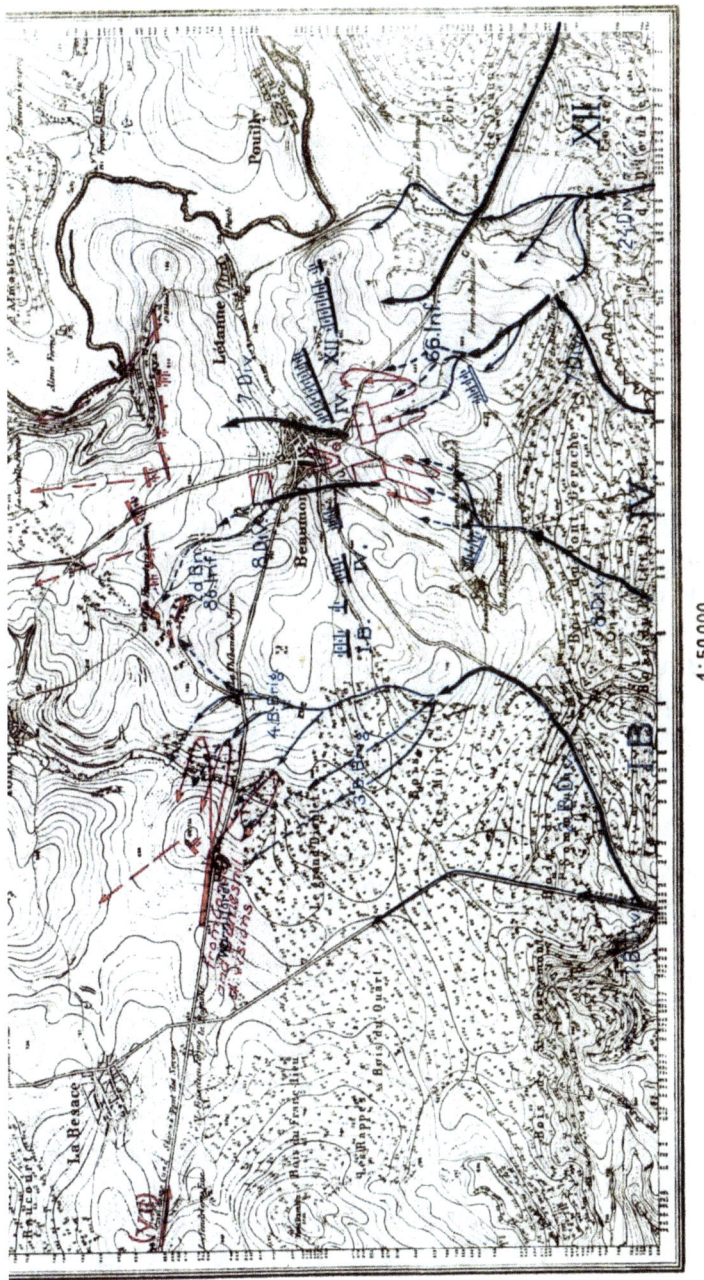

emerged from the wood in almost complete formation, with three batteries of the 7th Division from the south and southeast for the attack of the French camp, which was soon evacuated after a combat, in which great losses were inflicted by the chassepots, leaving a few prisoners and guns.

The 7th Division stood, during the fight, south of the Stenay—Beaumont road. Neither the 66th Regiment nor the 26th, following the former, had noticed the height southeast of Beaumont which dominated the camp, the city, and the route of retreat. The consequence was that the enemy who stood there or went there, nestled in the ditches behind the road embankment and fired on the right wing of the 66th. A few companies turned to the right, and after a hard fight drove the enemy out, who then retreated to Letanne, pursued by weak detachments of the Germans.

The 66th Regiment was followed from Belle Tour to Beaumont by the 26th, and the latter by the 14th Brigade. To the same point streamed the greater part of the 16th Brigade and the 7ist Regiment, via Petite Foret. Only one to two battalions of that brigade and the 71st Regiment took the direction to the height west of Beaumont. Wherever they turned, long lines of artillery confronted the Germans, extending to right and left north of Beaumont. To engage them, the 14 batteries of the IV Corps went into position, south of the city with the right wing on the hill south of Letanne, the left beyond the highroad to Sommauthe. This line was extended on the right by the 23rd Division which had advanced with six battalions and ten batteries, crossing the Wamme Creek partly at Wamme and partly at Beaulieu and came on the hill east of Beaumont.

The left wing was lengthened by the three batteries of the Bavarian I Corps which had been sent in advance. The fire of 25 batteries achieved nothing but that the hostile artillery, after covering the retreat of the infantry, withdrew from position to position, disappearing at last in the rear of the Bois de Givodeau. During this artillery duel, the battalions and 4 batteries of the IV Corps deployed in and south of Beaumont and joined the XII Corps which, with the exception of the six battalions and ten batteries, was on the hill south of Letanne left of the Wamme Creek.

The Bavarian I Corps had accelerated its march on hearing the thunder of the guns. General Schumacher, commanding the 2nd Division, the leading unit, who had hurried to the battlefield, had the proposition made him by a general staff officer of the IV Corps to take the direction of the farm La Thibaudine, as the enemy, retreating from Beaumont, could be best taken in flank from the heights at that point.

The general accepted it willingly. His advanced cavalry, however, was fired at from the woods south of the farm of La Harnoterie and in retreating, also from La Thibaudine. The former fire came from a French detachment of the V Corps which had retreated from Beaumont to La Harnoterie, the latter from the advance guard of Conseil Dumesnil's Division, marching from Oches and La Besace to Mouzon, while General Douay had cautiously taken the road leading to Remilly via Stonne and Raucourt with the two other divisions of the VII Corps.

When the 4th Brigade, at the head of the Bavarian 2nd Division, deployed and advanced to La Thibaudine, fire was directed against it from Le Grand Dieulet. It was forced to turn partly left. Another part continued its march to La Thibaudine, drove off the enemy who took position in the woods east of the Yoneq Brook north of the La Besace—Beaumont road. After a short fire fight north and south of the main road the French were driven off, by a resolute attack, to Warniforet, so quickly that the 3rd Brigade which was to make a flanking attack from the south through Le Grand Dieulet, met only a few isolated Frenchmen. A Jager battalion had, in the meanwhile, covered the right flank against La Harnoterie. Jointly with a battalion of the 86th Regiment, which had come by the ravine situated between Beaumont and La Harnoterie, and with the aid of two Prussian and one Bavarian battery, this enemy was also driven off.

The 2nd Battalion of the 86th Regiment formed on the left wing the advance guard of the IV Corps which started to Beaumont about 3:00 PM, after a rest of two hours.

The 7th Division, in deep formation with two battalions in front, advanced east, the 8th Division west of the road to Mouzon. The Bavarian I Corps was directed by Headquarters of the Third Army to advance against La Besace with as great a strength as

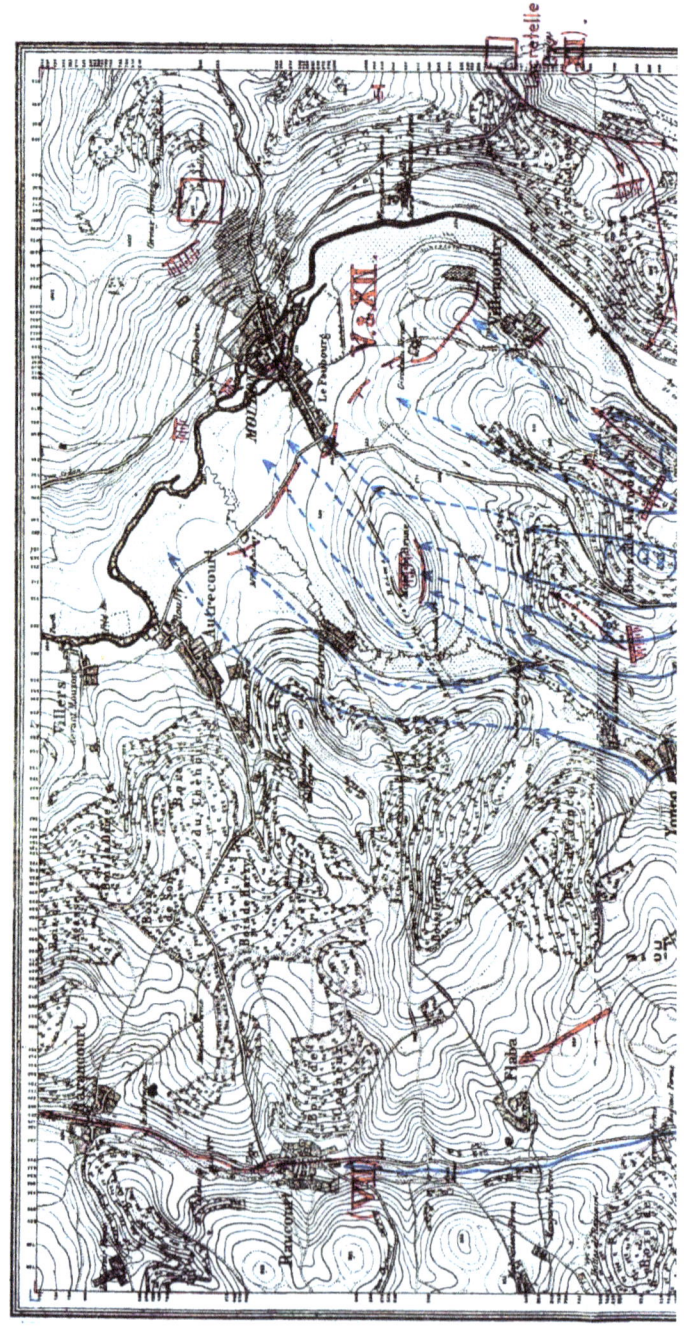

BATTLE OF BEAUMONT
Situation about 3:00 P.M. Movements and combats until evening.

The Campaign of 1870-71

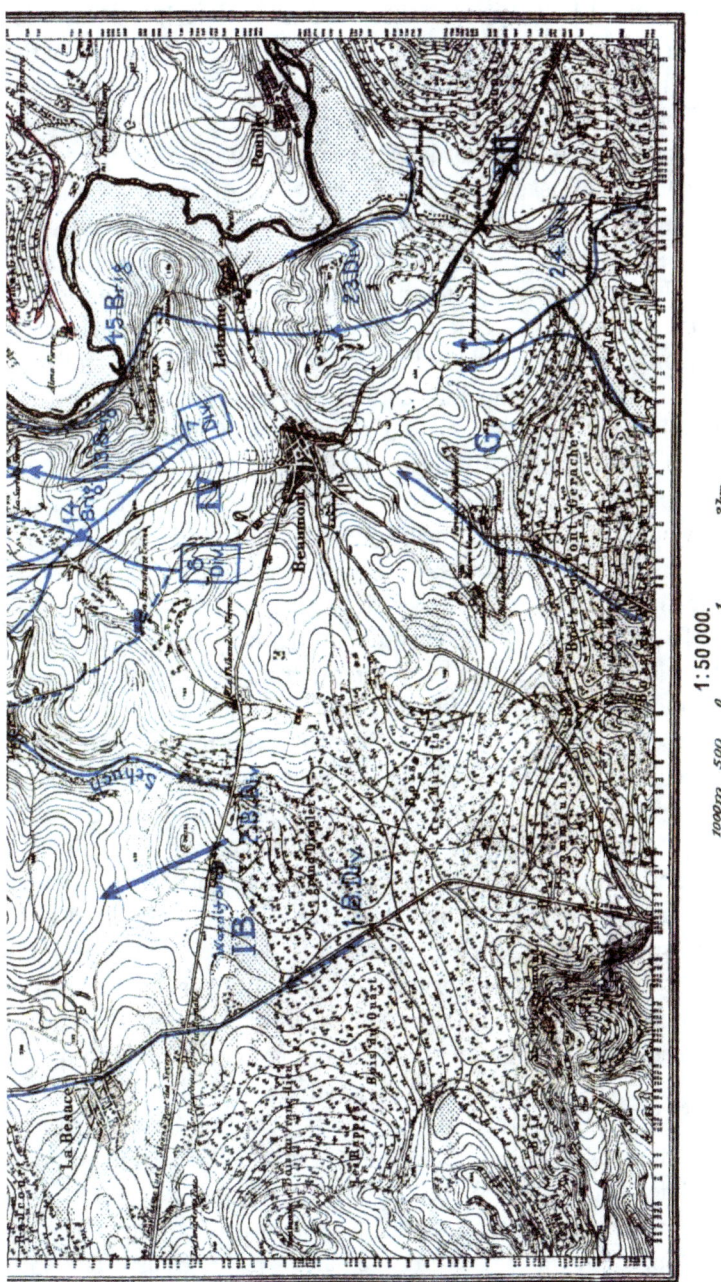

possible in order to fill "the gap existing in the line between Beaumont and Stonne." Therefore only a detachment of four battalions and two batteries under Colonel Schuch, was left on the left wing of the IV Corps.

The rest of the 2nd Division followed up from Warniforet, the enemy retreating to the north, while the 1st Division was started on the road to La Besace. Thus the advance was organized on the left wing in a more orderly manner. There might have been sufficient time also on the right wing, after the taking of Beaumont, to send the XII Corps to Pouilly and the Guard Corps to Stenay across the Meuse in order to achieve some success with the former at Mouzon. But army headquarters insisted on leaving the XII Corps in rear of the right wing and sending the Guard Corps by the paths through the woods previously used by the IV Corps.

The two battalions of the 138th Brigade at the head of the 7th Division went along the narrow ridge between the main road and the Meuse, drove out the hostile rear guard from La Sartelle and the Bois de Givodeau, but saw. themselves facing a strong position on the northern edge of the wood.

The two hours' pause ensuing during the closing up of the IV Corps, assembling it in a very narrow front in and at Beaumont, reforming the mixed units, and ordering the troops for a new advance, might have given Failly such a start that he could have crossed over several bridges to the right bank of the Meuse with but a few rear guard skirmishes. But since he could hardly count on such a pause and did not wish to be thrown across the river in disorder, he had occupied a position on the heights of Villemontry and the Mont De Brune which he must hold until nightfall, then to retire unnoticed over prepared crossings. General Lebrun sent one infantry and one cavalry brigade of the XII Corps via Mouzon to his support and had the high right bank of the Meuse occupied between Warmonterne and the Alma farm by Lacretelle's Division. The left wing of the French position was thus formidably reinforced, strengthened also by the fact that the hostile artillery could not cross the Bois de Givodeau at all and the infantry only in small detachments.

Army headquarters thought to obtain a breathing space by enveloping the left wing from the valley of the Meuse. The 45th

Brigade was ordered to advance by the road running along the bank. Pressed into the narrowest space, it was showered by Lacretelle's Division with gun, mitrailleuse, and chassepot fire. It was impossible to storm the strongly occupied heights of Villemontry, having such an enemy in the rear. The plan to envelop the enemy had to be abandoned, the brigade taken back to La Sartelle. Only two companies, which had succeeded in occupying the northeastern corner of the Bois de Givodeau. were left there.

The question now was, what should be done; should there be sent, as at Gravelotte, into a continuous combat, battalion after battalion, regiment after regiment, brigade after brigade, all mixed up in a crowd, from the wood against the French batteries, to suffer unlimited losses, the dissolution of all the units and boundless confusion, or should the numerous reserves, as at Sadowa, and the Bois de la Cusse, be used as a target for the never missing hostile shells? Neither one nor the other means seemed tempting. The idea came to some, especially to corps headquarters, that the XII Corps belonged on the right and not on the left bank of the Meuse. It might drive thence the enemy by taking his flank under fire and bar the line of retreat through Mouzon to the other enemy who had occupied an impregnable position across the German front. The road seemed too long and the day too far advanced for the execution of such splendid plans. The consequences of such a model army order, according to the lights of the time, had to be borne and it was necessary to wait for assistance to come from some other side.

At the time when the 13th Brigade advanced against the Bois de Givodeau, the commanding general of the IV Corps, von Alvensleben, had reached the conclusion that Hill 918, west of the woods, was strongly occupied. He ordered the 14th Brigade, following the 13th, to advance to the left of the main road to take, in joint action with the 8th Division, the supposed bulwark of the enemy. When the brigade had crossed the road, it filled the entire space between the latter and the Yoncq Creek and was able alone, with the batteries attached, to take the hill, occupied only by a rearguard, by an attack from the south and southwest.

The 8th Division, which had remained behind, found itself excluded and decided to go with its greater part and the detachment of Colonel Schuch into the valley of the Yoncq and the other side of the Yoneq Creek, while the smaller part pushed in between the 13th and 14th Brigades. Thus the IV Corps obtained a more extended, though still a very modest, front which permitted its forces to have some effect.

The advance continued, in about the following order: from right to left: 4 battalions of the 8th Division, the 14th Brigade, 8 battalions of the 8th Division, 4 battalions under Colonel Schuch; Mont de Brune was taken by attacks against the front and flank, the hill north of Pourron was occupied through the complete turning of the wing, the left flank was extended to Autrecourt, a descent made down the valley of the river under cover of the batteries in position on the heights, the suburb of Mouzon captured, the enemy driven into the Meuse and the columns, retiring on the opposite bank were taken under fire.

Counterattacks and cavalry charges—as customary in such situations—took place. They only increased the defeat. The enemy could no longer hold the position at Villemontry against the 18th and 45th Brigades. He was driven to the Meuse. Not all reached the opposite bank, some died in the river, others were captured, others still hid in the thickets of the bank, as darkness had already set in. Mouzon and the bridge over the Meuse remained in the hands of the French. An attempt to take the city under cover of darkness failed. The Germans had to be satisfied with the occupation of the suburb. In rear of it the IV Corps went into camp, north of Beaumont the XII, south of it the Guard Corps.

The Bavarian 1st Division had marched from Sommauthe to La Besace and further toward Raucort. This forced the French rear guard at Stonne to retire in time. It was caught up with north of Raucourt and driven back to Remilly after a fierce combat. After the long march from St. Juvin[*] to Raucourt, after many detours and fights, darkness stopped the pursuit. The 1st Division went into bivouac.

The roar of guns from Beaumont and Mouzon caused the V Corps and the 4th Cavalry Division to march to the road:

---

[*] See map on pages 416-417.

Buzancy—Raucourt, so that in the evening there stood: The Bavarian 1st Division at Raucourt, the 4th Cavalry Division at Flaba, the Bavarian 2nd Division north, the V Corps south of La Besace, the Bavarian II Corps at Sommauthe. The XI Corps had reached Stonne, the 2nd Cavalry Division, Oches, and the Wurttemberg Division, Verrieres. Quite separately from the army, as if forgotten, stood the VI Corps at Vouziers, and the 5th and 6th Cavalry Divisions at Tourteron and Le Chesne.

Casualties of 1800 dead for the French and 3500 for the Germans in the battle of Beaumont would speak not unfavorably for the former, if the loss of 3000 missing, among them 2000 unwounded prisoners, and of 42 guns, as well as the complete discouragement of the entire army already depressed, had not been added to them. Nevertheless, the French had escaped luckily enough. The battle, which MacMahon wanted to avoid as long as possible, had taken place without being, as had been feared, a battle of annihilation. It would have been such if the different army headquarters had left fewer corps in reserve and sent more to the front, if their armies were less compressed in the center and more extended on the wings and if the corps, not sent against the enemy, had not remained stationary but had rapidly advanced. The battle of the 30th, and a pursuit on the 31st would have caused a complete encircling of the French army.

Such an annihilating result had been luckily averted but it was also clearly shown that the continuation of operations for the relief of Bazaine was impossible. If annihilation beyond peradventure of a doubt were to be avoided, the retreat must commence immediately. Two roads were available in a western and two in a southerly direction for one corps each: from Remilly on the left bank of the Meuse via Donchery and Flize, from Mouzon via Sedan and Mezieres, from Stenay along the Meuse via Verdun and from Carignan via Montmedy and Fresnes.

By such a retreat directed to opposite sides, the army would have been split in two and naturally become unfit for combat. But it was desired to avoid a battle. This could be attained by retreating over as many roads as possible and in different directions. Should the movement be started in the evening of the 30th and so much attained in the night that the troops should be outside the reach of

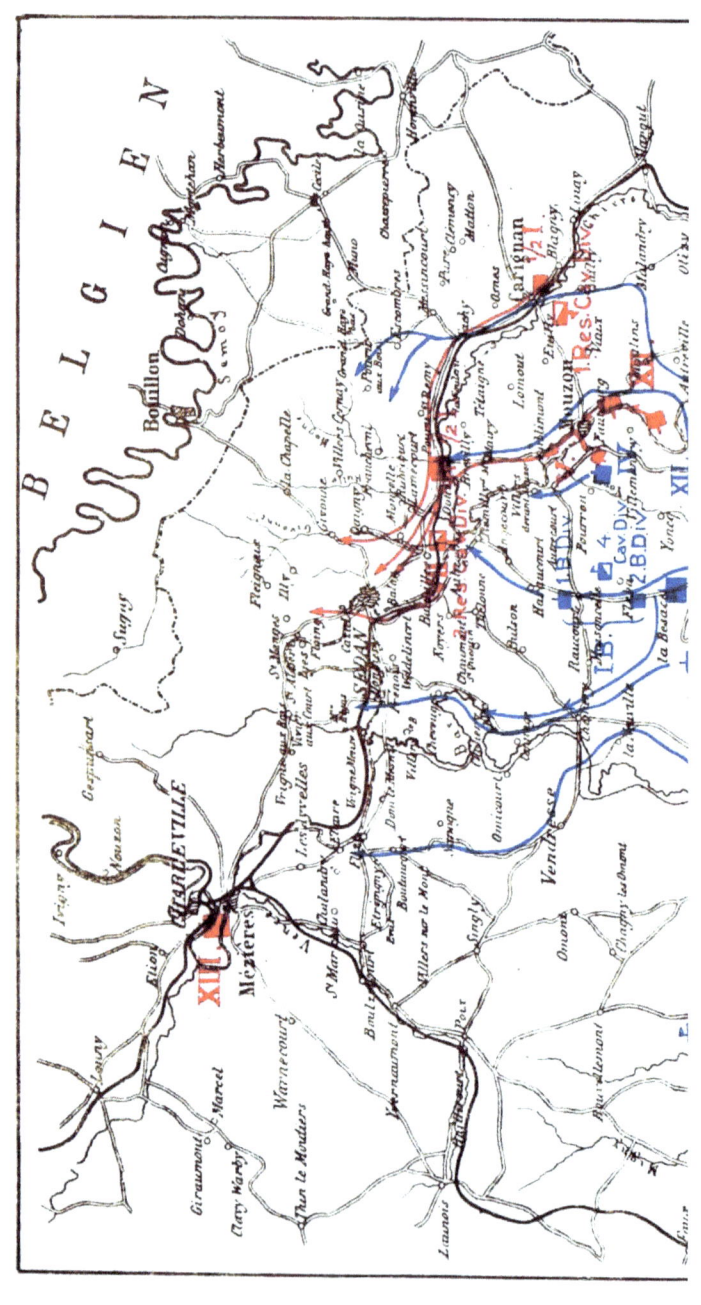

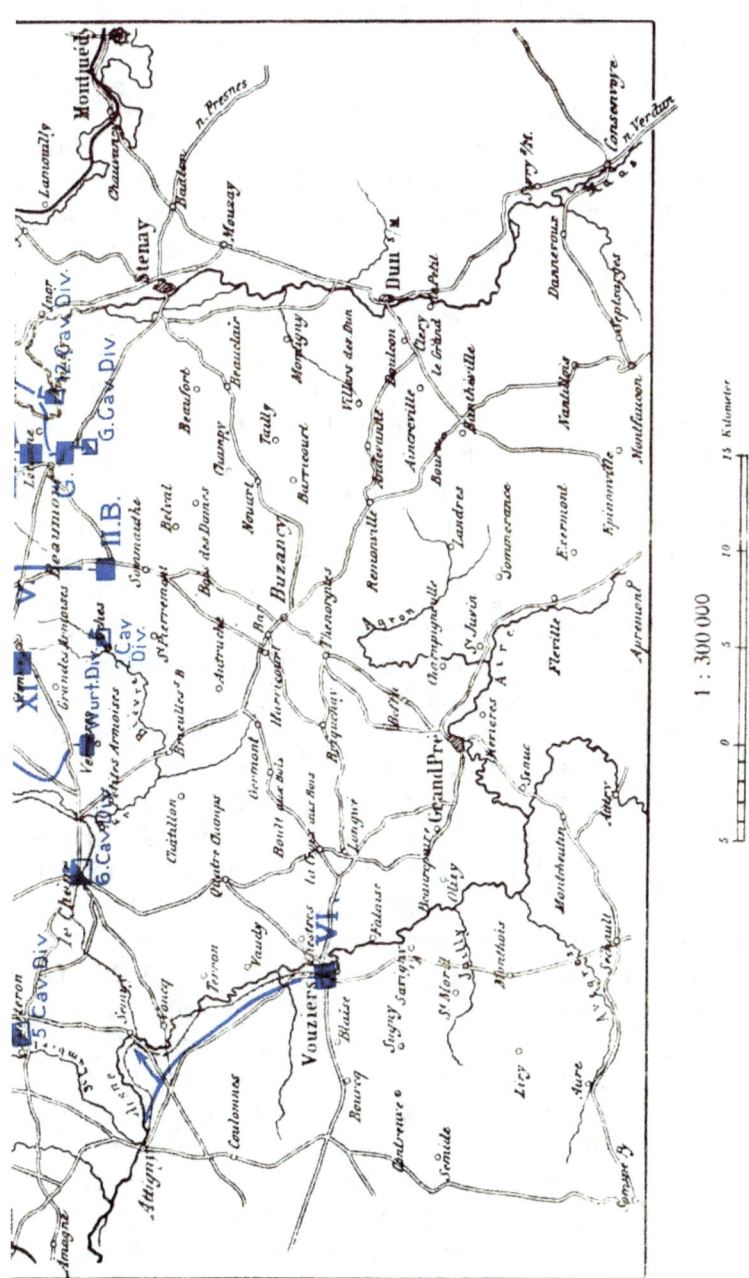

the enemy, the retreat would have succeeded as that at Worth and Spichern and, with the aid of railways, Ducrot, Failly, Lebrun, and Douay would have met in Paris as, a few days earlier, MacMahon, Failly, and Douay metin Chalons. If the army must be kept together, a retreat or the continuation of the retreat to the south offered better chances and greater freedom of movement than a march to the west. MacMahon, however, did not wish to use the road, unexpectedly opened to him but to continue the retreat to Mezieres as had been planned.

Although the troops were very much discouraged and greatly exhausted by the strain and the lack of provisions, the night march to Sedan was effected in good order. The V Corps, in front, reached Fond de Givonne, via Douzy and Bazeilles, and the northern glacis of the fortress. The three divisions of the XII Corps followed at intervals of one and one half hours and oecupied the right bank of the Givonne from Bazeilles to Daigny. The rear was formed by two divisions of the I Corps, covering the retreat east of Douzy and lengthening the left wing of the XII Corps to Givonne. The smaller portion of the VII Corps had reached Mouzon early, while the larger crossed the Meuse at Remilly in the evening and joined the march columns of the other corps.

When the reserve batteries and the last division (Liebert's) were about to cross the Meuse at Remilly, the bridge broke down. General Douay was forced to remain with this portion of his corps on the left bank. Instead of rejoicing at having a special march road and using it at least as far as Donchery, he turned at Sedan into the one road which had been assigned to the entire army. He reached Floing during the 31st where his remaining units joined his corps. Early on that day the army was assembled near Sedan. Only General Ducrot with two divisions of the I Corps and Margueritte's Cavalry Division were still southeast of Carignan at Bligny and advanced only in the afternoon to the position on the Givonne.

It was not necessary to await him for the continuation of the retreat. Had the advance guard started on the morning of the 31st, followed by one corps after the other, Ducrot would have come up early enough to join the long march column as rearguard. But the troops were too tired by the marches of the 30th until late in the night of the 31st, had been too long without nourishment to continue the retreat in the morning. A rest until noon was urgently needed and not critical.

Assembled in a narrow space, immediately in front of Sedan, the French Army could be considered secure. It was protected by the Meuse and the Givonne against the south and east, whence the enemy might be expected. Inthe north was the inviolable Belgium. No attack could be expected from that direction, those from the two other sides could be easily repulsed. Even a retreat to the west via Mezieres was considered safe.

The road leading to Mezieres was narrowed between St. Menges and Vrigne aux Bois by the bend of the Meuse from Iges on the one side and the almost inaccessible ravine east of the Bois de la Falizette on the other to a narrow dam and a narrow bridge. This defile had to be crossed by 140,000 men with horses, guns, vehicles, and baggage, in order to reach at Mezieres the other bank of the Meuse and freedom. The habit of the German army of forming a mass by placing corps in rear of corps, compressing them from right and left, was to blame that this defile was not closed to this gigantic column. They would not extend their left wing to Mezieres so as not to be forced to this extension by a surplus of strength and the IV Corps was sent back to Attigny for the security of communications in the rear. MacMahon could be fully reassured as to Mezieres even had not General Vinoy reached it in the night of the 30th with part of the XIII Corps.

He likewise did not worry much about the Meuse between Frenois and Mezieres, the strip between Donchery and Flize. He did not deem the Germans capable of so great a turning movement. He thus underrated his opponent considerably. The flank on the Meuse ought to have been secured. It was not sufficient to destroy the existing bridges. It was more important to prevent their restoration and the building of new ones, as well as their use by the enemy.

As soon as the troops had rested somewhat from the strain of the foregoing days, the VI Corps should have undertaken the defense of the strip of the Meuse between Frenois—Flize. The XIII Corps (Vinois) which had reached Mezieres in the evening of the 30th, took up a position at Boulzinecourt—Poix. North of the main road were other roads which were joined by short cuts and bridges

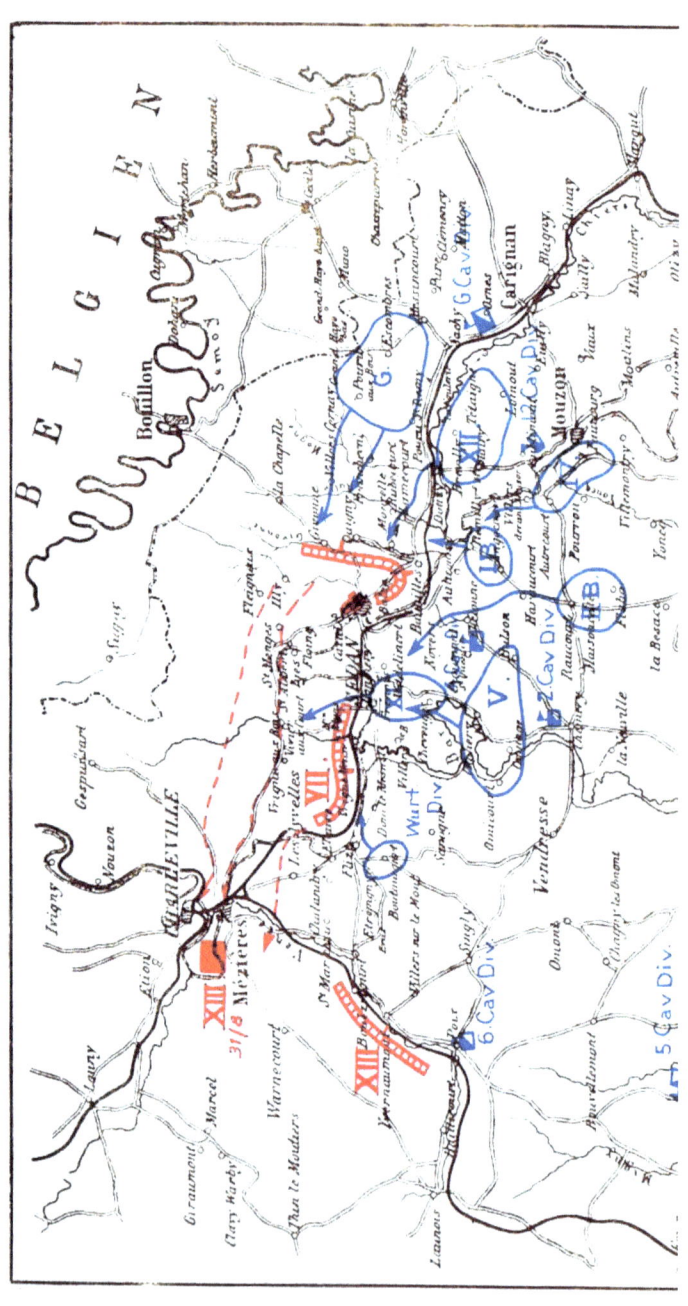

The Campaign of 1870-71

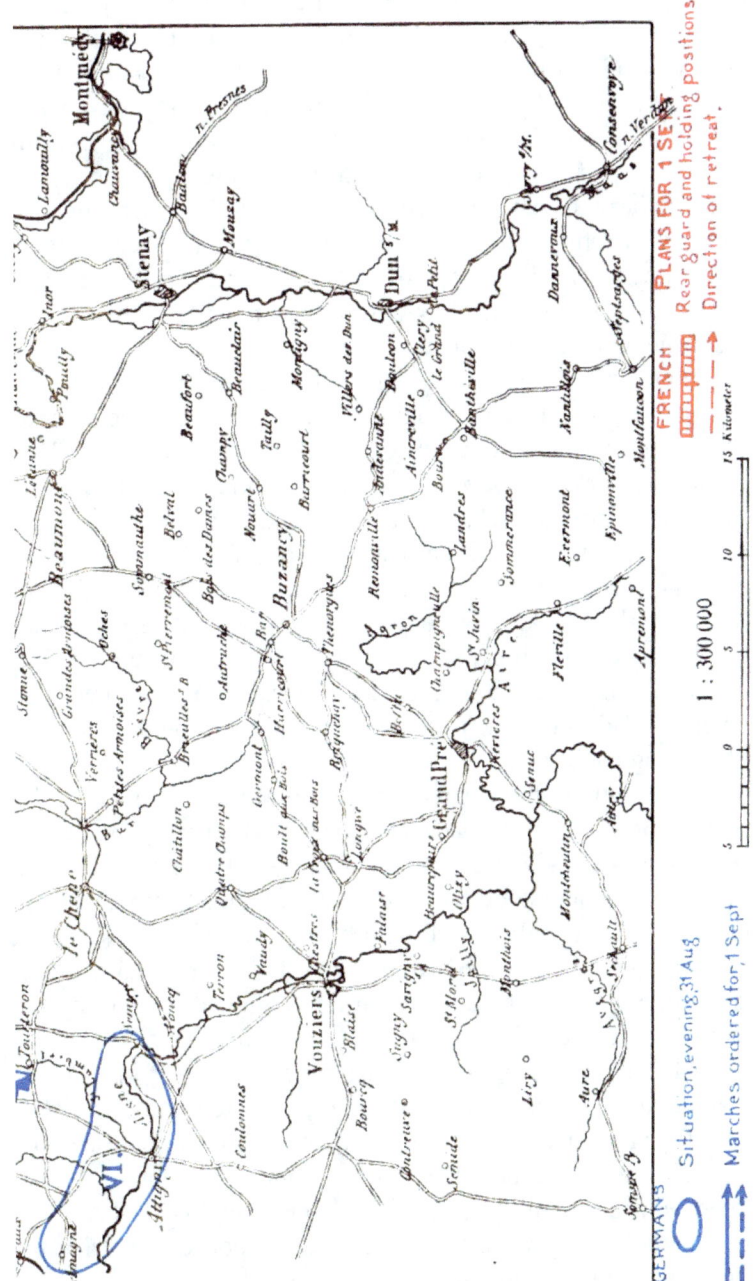

into a second marching road, debouching at Charleville. Two corps could thus start simultaneously. A third occupied a position on the Givonne and followed on both roads. On the same, parallel with the latter, the VII Corps, after destroying the bridges over the Meuse, moved from Donchery over the bridge at Les Ayvelles in the direction of Warnecourt, and lastly the XIII Corps. The retreat in a southerly or southeasterly direction could be made in four columns marching side by side over a sufficient number of roads. If the time between the noon of 31 August, and the morning of 1 September, were not much overdrawn, all molestation worthy of the name, would be excluded.

No column roads were designated. The VII Corps did not go to Donchery and the XIII remained at Mezieres. Only the order to destroy the bridges between Sedan and Mezieres was given. This order was strictly obeyed in regard to bridges situated near Mezieres, which could have been used by the French. A company of engineers was entrusted with the destruction of the most important bridge at Donchery and taken there by train from Sedan. It reached there luckily. The engineer of the locomotive, somewhat excited by the proximity of the enemy, pulled out his train before the barrels of powder and necessary tools had been unloaded. The company did not think it essential to look for other means of destroying the bridge.

Even without the destruction of the bridge at Donchery, the retreat might have been made had it been started early enough. 3 81 August passed, however, with no order issued. MacMahon could hardly have understood the seriousness of the situation, was the criticism. It was only too clear to him. It was quite clear to him when he started on — the march from Rheims on the 23rd, and it was quite clear on the 28th when he continued it again by the explicit order from Paris "to avoid a revolution."

After the battle of the 30th, he believed himself justified in abandoning the fatal plan and starting the retreat. If the self-sacrificing combat, the heroic courage of the troops and the downfall under the brutal strength of numerical superiority had been painted : in true colors, public opinion would have had some consideration, approved the retreat and postponed somewhat the outbreak of the revolution.

The Campaign of 1870-71

Unfortunately, Napoleon did not recognize the lucky gift brought him by the battle of Beaumont. Made stupid by the habit of a long reign, to beautify every misfortune, every failure, showing the blackest in a good light, he could not grasp the idea that to tell the truth in so many words would serve the purpose, and in a telegram to the Empress mentioned only a "quite insignificant combat." It was impossible for MacMahon to let himself be diverted from an important problem by an "insignificant combat," the problem which the Nation had placed in his hands, That he had gone as far as Sedan may be considered as a treachery. Only under coercion which nothing could stem, could he dare to start on the retreat. A new battle had to be fought. The situation was not desperate as yet.

It would be possible to defend oneself gloriously in rear of the Givonne, as subsequent events showed, and retreat in the end "on account of lack of munitions and provisions." It was only necessary to secure the strip of the Meuse between Mezieres and Sedan. For taking serious and adequate measures, the apathy, relaxation, and resignation to the inevitable had gone too far. MacMahon may also have thought that an extension of his position along the Givonne and the Meuse to Mezieres was too long. He wanted to keep his forces more closely together. The position, selected by him, was defensible. The front was formed by the Meuse and the fortifications of Sedan. The left flank on the deeply cut Givonne from Bazeilles to north of Givonne was covered by the XII and I Corps, the right flank and the rear by the VII Corps on the Floing Creek. The V Corps remained as a general reserve close to the fortress. Thus three fronts had been formed, all difficult to attack. Their weakness lay in that the attack against one of them would be, at the same time, an attack against the flank and rear of the other.

The Germans might have, on the 30th, outflanked, surrounded, and crushed the weak enemy. They thought to solve this problem by coming as close together as possible. _At the moment when they ought to have cut off the retreating enemy entirely by a wide front, they formed as if they had to deliver a blow into the heart or break through an iron wall in its center. Moltke tried to repair what had been spoiled. On the 31st, it was ordered to "continue the attack, enveloping both flanks." The Army of the Meuse was charged to bar the French left wing from escaping in an easterly direction and therefore advance with two corps on the right bank of the Meuse. The Third Army was ordered to go against the front and right flank of the enemy.

In compliance with this order, the Guard Corps of the Army of the Meuse went to Pouilly and the XII at Letanne across the Meuse. The former took the road via Carignan had reached Pouru-aux-Bois and Pouru St. Remy. The latter remained on the left bank of the Chiers and occupied Tetaigne, Brevilly, Douzy, Mairy, and Amblimont. The IV Corps remained at Mouzon on the left bank of the Meuse.

Of the Third Army, the Bavarian I Corps marched to Remilly, the XI, via Chemery to Donchery, the Wurttemberg Division via Vendresse to Boutaucourt; in the second line went the Bavarian II Corps to Raucourt, the V to Chemery. Moltke had supposed that the crossing over the Meuse would be destroyed and occupied and had therefore issued the order to advance only as far as the river and to take the camps and moving troops in the opposite valley under artillery fire. But when the advance guard of the XI Corps reached Donchery, it found the bridge intact, the point unoccupied and from the hill of Frenois, the 4th Cavalry Division saw the white tents of the camp north of Sedan.

The French were still at Sedan. It may be, however, surmised that they would march along the Givonne in the morning, at the latest, to Mezieres, protected by a rearguard. It did not seem necessary to cut off their way to that city. The Third Army would cross the Meuse at Donchery and over other bridges, prevent the enemy from marching further, force him to fight and throw him back on the Belgian frontier. The XI Corps occupied Donchery with an advance guard, Frenois with a flank detachment, and advanced to Cheveuges, the V Corps to Chehery and Omicourt. The Wurttemberg Division, met, coming from Vendresse, cavalry at Boutaucourt and infantry at Flize, driving them in the direction of Mezieres. Outposts were placed toward Chalandry, Flize was occupied by the advance guard and Boutaucourt by the Division.

These small encounters were without significance, but. they showed that the enemy was at Mezieres and that he could attack the left flank of the Germans, assemble forces at any rate and weaken the Third Army for the decisive battle. This army might have been stronger had not the VI Corps and the 5th Cavalry Division been left at Attigny. They might, as stated in the General Staff Account, meet all the movements of the enemy in rear of the army, from this point, and bar the way to Rheims and Paris to the French troops stationed at Mezieres. The corps did not suffice, in the least, for either of the problems. It did not meet the French XIII Corps in time, which threatened the rear of the Third Army, and it had not barred the way to Rheims and Paris to the French troops from Mezieres. But it might have solved both problems had it accompanied the advance of the Germans to Mezieres, on the left wing.

On the right wing of the Third Army, the Bavarian I Corps found the bridge at Remilly destroyed and saw French columns marching to Bazeilles on the opposite bank. An artillery duel opened across the river. The Bavarian artillery line extended gradually to le Pont Maugy, as artillery units arrived. French skirmishers, which had advanced to the Meuse and across the railway bridge, molested the gunners. One company of Jagers drove the French from the left bank, another company of Jagers drove away the workmen who were about to demolish the bridge supports. Both stormed across the bridge, in spite of the hot fire, threw the powder into the Meuse and occupied the railway embankment.

Upon the arrival of one more company the hostile sharpshooters were driven south of Bazeilles, the point was occupied and the advance continued to the northern edge. The French had in the meanwhile, broken off the artillery duel and retired north. They faced partly about to reconquer the lost village. For two hours did the five companies of Jagers under Major Raschreiter repulse the attacks of the superior French. Since, however, General von der Tann wanted to avoid isolated combats, and forbade sending for reinforcements to the other bank of the Meuse, the Major was forced to an orderly retreat. The pontoon train had arrived, in the meanwhile, and built a bridge at Aillicourt. It was protected, as well as the railway bridge, by infantry and artillery positions, on the left bank of the Meuse, in rear of which the troops bivouacked.

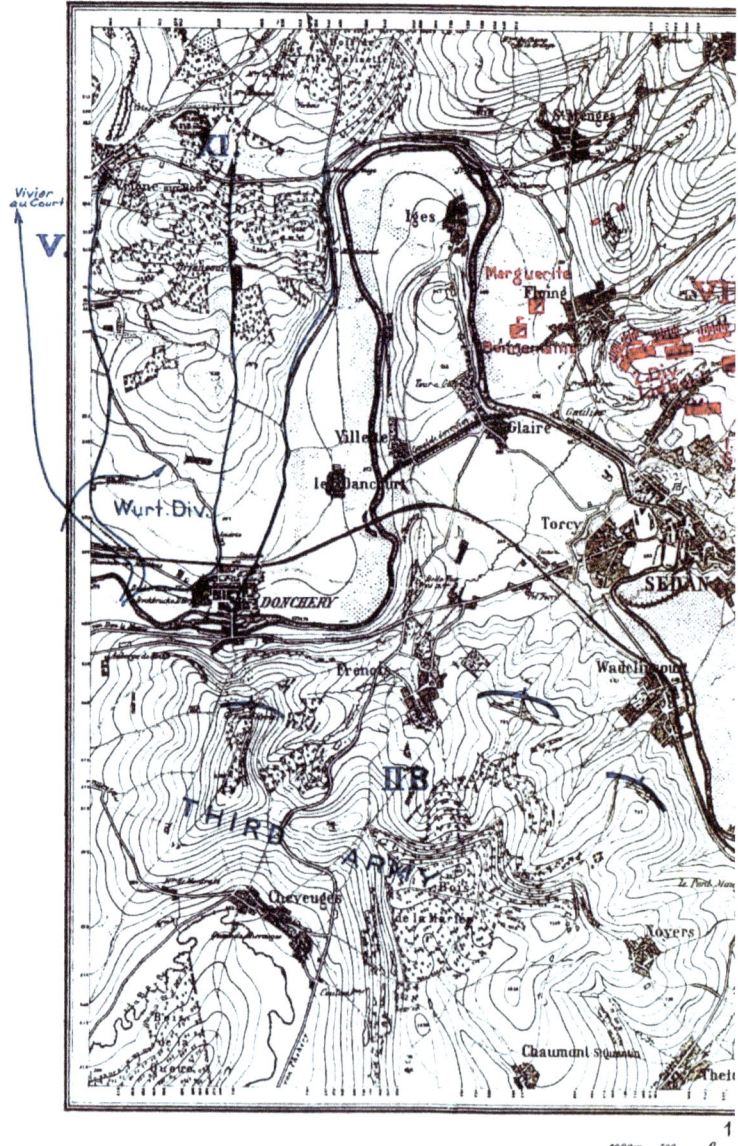

The Campaign of 1870-71

LE OF SEDAN
)tember, 1870
)n 1 September. Advance of the
the order from general head-
e's plan for the advance
Meuse Army.

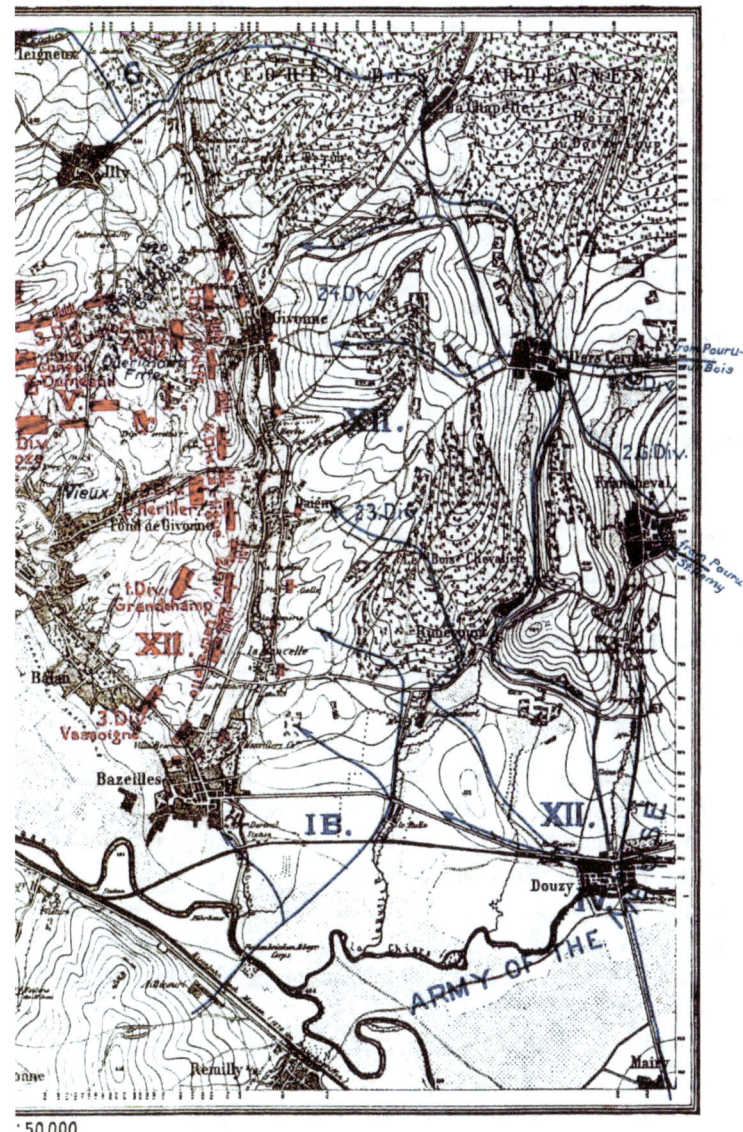

By the provisions of an order, sent out in the evening of the 31st, the XI and V Corps were to advance early on 1 September via Donchery to Vrigne-aux-Bois, the Wurttemberg Division was to cross the Meuse over a bridge not yet constructed at Dom le Mesnil and take a position so as to be able to face Mezieres or to serve as reserve to both corps. The Bavarian II Corps was to occupy with one division the heights opposite Donchery, with the other those of Frenois and Wadelincourt, the 6th Cavalry Division to hold itself ready at Flize, the 2nd at Boutaucourt, the 4th south of Frenois. The Army of the Meuse was to retain its location of the previous day "to bar the retreat of the enemy in an easterly direction." Headquarters of the Army of the Meuse thought it had already accomplished this duty by sending the Guard to Pouru-aux-Bois and Pouru St. Remy, the XII Corps to Douzy and the IV to Mouzon. A day of rest for 1 September had thus been planned, although the troops had been ordered to be ready at 7:00 AM.

Headquarters of the Third Army shared the opinion held by Royal Headquarters that the enemy would begin his retreat to Mezieres in the night. The Third Army would thus, in crossing the Meuse at Donchery and Dom le Mesnil with two and one half corps, meet considerable forces on the road: St. Menges— Mezieres, the attack of which would not be rendered easier by the terrain. It would be most desirable that the part of the enemy, left at Sedan, be kept there and prevented from reinforcing the troops already on the march. The Bavarian I Corps was, consequently, ordered to "hold that part of the enemy which opposed it."

Information was sent to the commander of the neighboring troops. concerning all the measures taken and the success expected might be considerably heightened by the assistance of the Army of the Meuse. The Crown Prince of Saxony recognized that an attack would correspond better with the holding of the enemy than a passive occupation of positions, and decided not only to hold the enemy, supposed to be in rear of the Givonne, but to prevent him from marching to Belgium. This required an attack against the front and the envelopment of the left wing.

It was known from the reports of the cavalry that Villers Cernay was occupied by a strong rearguard on the evening of the 31st. The hostile left wing was, consequently, at least at the village of Givonne if not further north.

To surround it and cut off its principal road to Belgium, the German right wing was to march to La Chapelle and further to Illy. Thus, the Bavarian I Corps was to attack the south side of Bazeilles and the front of the position at Givonne as far as La Ramorie (1 km. north of Bazeilles). The XII Corps was to move from Douzy via Rubecourt with one division against Daigny, with the other via Villers Cernay against Givonne. The Guard Corps should march from Pouru-aux-Bois direct, from Pouru St. Remy via Francheval to Villers Cernay and thence, by various roads, without crossing the XII Corps, via La Chapelle to Illy. The IV Corps was to follow the Bavarian I Corps with one division, with the other the Guard Corps.

The enemy would thus, in as much as he was north of Sedan, if not driven back, at least be held fast and kept from Belgium. A battle line of 11 km. must have appeared, in the time of mass formations, too extensive. Less than half was found sufficient. Four corps were thus placed on a width of front of 5 km. and of these three and one half corps were compressed into a front of 3 km. In spite of this small extent of the battlefield, the conduct of battle was by no means united. This was caused by the Bavarian I Corps starting at 3:00 AM, to Bazeilles, situated there in immediate vicinity, and by the distant corps of the Army of the Meuse starting at 5:00 AM, in the direction of Givonne.

General von der Tann hoped to he able to take Bazeilles, which was in his hands the day before, easily in the night and fog. The French had, in the meanwhile occupied the point with a brigade of Vassoigne's Division and prepared it for obstinate resistance. Great massive buildings, high walls, several tributaries of the Givonne facilitated the holding of a nucleus of houses and gardens, reaching in the northwesterly direction with Villa Beaurmann close to Balan, and toward the east from the railway depot via Chateau Dorival and Chateau Monvillers as far as La Monvelle was a line almost without a break. The entire energy of the enemy was directed against Bazeilles, which was comparatively harmless and farthest from the decisive point of St. Menges which remained unheeded.

Four battalions of the Bavarian 2nd Brigade crossed the railway bridge. The Jager battalion in the lead penetrated at 4:00

OF SEDAN
:agements up to noon.

AM, through dense fog from the south into Bazeilles, but was received with fire in front from a barricade, in the flanks from the two story houses lining the two sides of the street. The Jagers sought shelter in a neighboring street, but found it also barricaded. The three succeeding battalions, later 4 battalions more, advanced.

A battle raged in the streets and houses in which inhabitants also took part with all kind of alternating success and failures, counterattacks, and losses. Reinforcements arrived after a lengthy period of time for the Bavarians over the pontoon bridge and deployed gradually against Dorival and Monvillers. Three brigades were thus utilized; the fourth was kept in position as reserve south of Bazeilles. On the side of the enemy there advanced the 2nd Brigade of Vassoigne's Division, one brigade of the I Corps and parts of Goze's Division of the V Corps to Bazeilles, while Lacretelle's Division of the XII Corps, Lartigue's and Wolff's Divisions of the I Corps deployed in the first line, l'Heriller's one half Division and Pelle's Division in the second line on the heights of the right bank of the Givonne and occupied with advance detachments all the villages in the valleys of the river from La Moncelle to Laminoir.

The Army of the Meuse did not consider what might © have been already gathered from the reports of the cavalry that the attack would have for objective a front of 7 km. and that Bazeilles and La Moncelle formed only its right wing. It kept fast to the words: the enemy retreats to Mezieres and has left a rearguard at Bazeilles and La Moncelle. To win a great success against these, the XII Corps and the 7th Division were sent via Douzy and Lamecourt to La Moncelle, the 8th Division via Remilly to Bazeilles. It would be easy to crush with 8 divisions at each point the not too strong rearguard. The Guard Corps which could find no room in the valley of the Meuse was sent to Francheval and Villers Cernay. Its right was not even opposite the left wing of the enemy and far from being able to outflank it. A decision could hardly be reached here.

When the advance guard of the 24th Division (6 battalions, 1 battery) reached about 6:00 AM, La Moncelle, artillery and infantry could be recognized on the opposite hills in spite of the fog. One of the Saxon batteries opened fire and maintained it

The Campaign of 1870-71   447

throughout the great French superiority until two Bavarian batteries joined it an hour later. Two battalions took La Moncelle without encountering much resistance. The enemy retired to the heights seeking shelter in two houses on the slope. Two Saxon companies charged after them, took the houses and decided to hold them. Ten companies occupied La Moncelle and entered into communication with Bavarian troops which had extended as far as the southernmost houses of the village. Before further reinforcements could arrive, it was reported that the enemy was advancing from Daigny. General Ducrot (I Corps) was holding the bridge at Daigny believing it to be the only bridge over the Givonne which the hostile artillery could use and thought it necessary to cover it by a position on the eastern bank, charging Lartigue's Division to occupy the Bois Chevalier.

The 105th Regiment of the Saxon advance guard, was sent against it. The main body of the 24th Division had not yet arrived, but the division and corps artillery were brought up in a hurry. At 8:30 AM, south of the Lamecourt—-La Moncelle road to the Rubecourt road 10 batteries opened fire against Daigny.

On: the French side, command had been changed twice. MacMahon had been wounded on the heights east of La Moncelle by a shell splinter and had transferred the command to General Ducrot. The latter erroneously believed that the Army of the Meuse would surround Givonne from the north and render it untenable and thought just as erroneously that sufficient measures had been taken for the security of the Meuse strip of Sedan—Mezieres and decided to take a position on the Plateau of Illy resting his right against Sedan and his left against the inaccessible Foret des Ardennes.

Under cover of this very impregnable position, the army was to start on its retreat via Mezieres. The plan would have been excellent, had not the columns of the Third Army already crossed the Meuse at Donchery. This circumstance was known to General Wimpffen who, as a help in distress, had arrived on 30 August from Africa by way of Paris and carried two ministerial army orders in his pocket. The one named him commander of the V Corps instead of Failly, the other appointed him commander-in chief in case anything should befall MacMahon.

In compliance with the first, he had already taken command of the V Corps, the latter he kept secret even when he heard that MacMahon had been wounded and Ducrot had been entrusted with the command. Seeing, however, that the latter, on the basis of false suppositions, was on the point of leading the army to destruction, he made use of his right, demanded the post of commander-in-chief, which was transferred to him willingly, and decided not to go back to Mezieres, but to advance to Carignan and seek in that direction the destruction, avoided in the former. The divisions of Ducrot, which had already started on the march, received a counter order.

The situation which had just been altered, was re-established. Vassoigne's Division and Lacretelle's Division via La Moncelle were to execute the mighty stroke via Bazeilles. A powerful break through the enemy was to be made. A terrific artillery fire started the decisive battle from the heights east of Balan at 9:00 AM. Infantry advanced as far as the Givonne, drove back the 10 Saxon companies and showered rapid fire on the Saxon Corps artillery which had advanced to 300 paces from the trench. It had to retreat and occupy a position farther to the rear if it were not ta be annihilated by the fire of the advancing sharpshooters. When, however, the latter came into the open they were received by infantry and artillery fire and forced to retreat.

In the streets, houses, and gardens of Bazeilles there was still less chance of success. The fight in the streets, lulled for a while, raged more fiercely than ever. The attempt to break through the enemy had miscarried. In order to be prepared against a repetition of the danger just avoided, the march of the troops, which had remained behind, was accelerated. The 23rd Division following the 24th not via Lamecourt, but on the road to Bazecilles, took part with one brigade in the combat of the Bavarians at Monvillers and kept the other as reserve at le Rulle. The Bavarian 4th Brigade advanced to La Moneelle. The Bavarian I Corps and the XII Corps were assembled on the lower Givonne, the IV advanced with the 7th Division to the right, with the 8th to the left of the Meuse and reached at 10:00 AM, with the former Lamecourt, with the latter the railway depot of Bazeilles.

The 10th Regiment had advanced against Lartigue's Division

from the western edge of Bois Chevalier to the Rubecourt—Daigny road and took up a position with one battalion in a small wood, with the two others on the right and left of this point, in order to await the arrival of the enemy advancing on a narrow front. Several attacks were repulsed, but were always repeated by fresh troops. The right wing offered protection for some time to the artillery line. But when it was forced by hostile skirmishers to retreat somewhat to the south, the three battalions were left alone and found themselves in a very critical situation, as ammunition threatened to give out.

Distress was great, when a Jager battalion came to the rescue. But as it had to strain all its forces against the superior enemy, it soon lacked ammunition also. Only when another Jager battalion and finally an infantry regiment of the 24th Division had come up, a counterattack was launched against the enemy, superior in numbers but in deeper formation who, pressed on both sides could not reach quickly enough Daigny, the bridge, and the heights opposite, left 6 guns in the hands of the Saxons. Further combat at this point was limited to continuous firing, in which the French had the advantage, on account of the height of the right bank and of better cover.

In the meanwhile the Guard Corps had arrived partly from Pouru-aux-Bois, partly from Pouru-St.-Remy via Francheval at Villers Cernay. The 2nd Guard Division was sent to the northern point of the Bois Chevalier to the assistance of the Saxons, the 4th Brigade still farther in the direction of Daigny. The 1st Guard Division occupied Givonne and Haybes and advanced to the wood east of Givonne. The Guard Cavalry Division covered the right flank north of the wood, the regiment of Guard Hussars covered in the direction of La Chapelle. The corps in this position was outflanked by the left flank of the enemy. There could be no thought of surrounding him.

It was possible, on the other hand, that the French, by throwing in their reserves, might surround the German right wing via the wood Le petit Terme and La Chapelle. Of the two opponents the Germans were in greater danger than the French at this point. They faced each other in a continuous combat along the line of the river. It was difficult to see how the Germans could succeed in winning

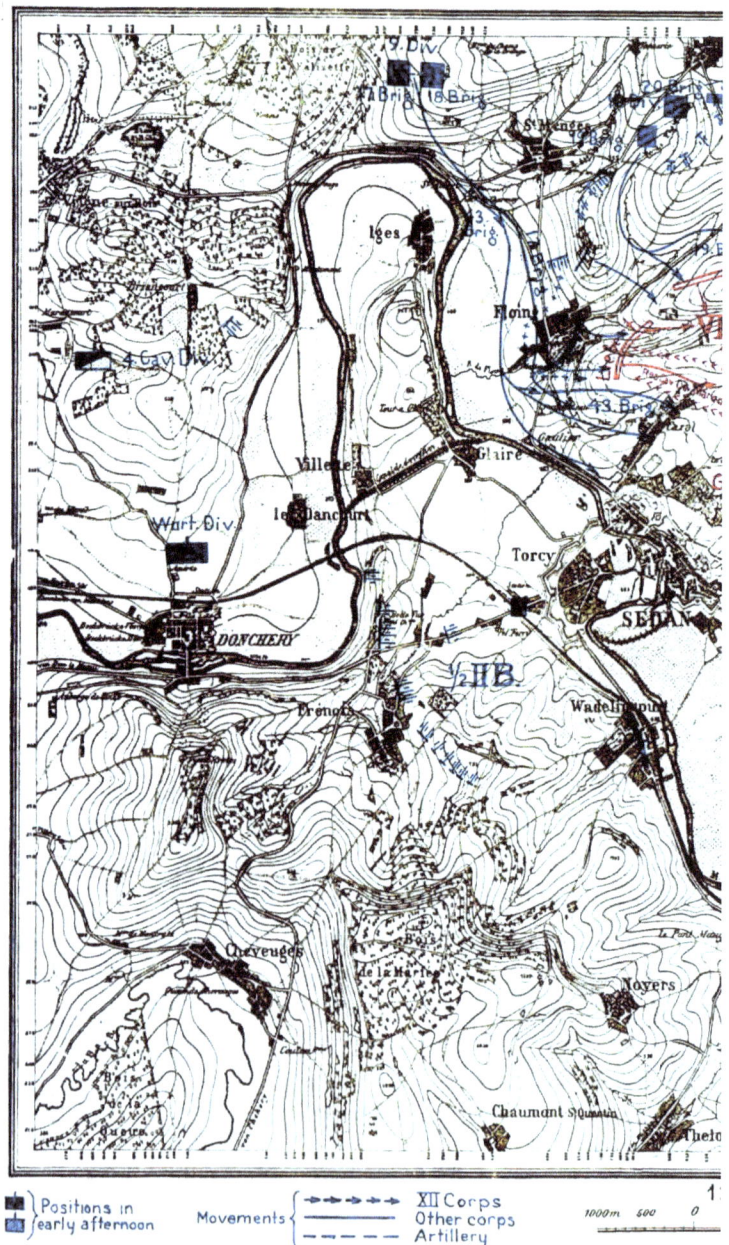

The Campaign of 1870-71

a favorable decision. The initiative of subaltern leaders then brought a quick turn of affairs.

In the two isolated houses on the road to Balan west of La Moncelle two Saxon companies had maintained their position for hours, through the changes brought by the advance and retreat of the French. In order to free them from their distress an advance was made from La Moncelle and south of it, first by Bavarian and later by Saxon troops. The garrison of the two houses was relieved. All the other troops, fighting in the valley, followed this movement. The heights were attacked also from the park of Monvillers.

All stormed forward to the defile leading from Bazeilles to Daigny via Hill 685. The French evacuated the position, not without resistance, and left three guns and numerous prisoners in the hands of the Germans.

The occupation of the ridge south of the La Moncelle— Balan road alarmed the defenders of Bazeilles, who saw their retreat threatened. Threatened, moreover, from the south and east by the 1st Brigade, from the west by the 5th Brigade of the Bavarian II Corps sent from the left bank of the Meuse, they started to retreat in the direction of Balan. After 7 hours of fierce fighting, the Bavarians remained masters of burning Bazeilles.

A general onrush of the Germans must be expected. During the long hours of fighting in the streets the troops had become mixed up. The entire Bavarian I Corps was taken back to be reformed. Only isolated companies, followed by the 5th Brigade, pursued the enemy through Balan and to the heights north of the village. The victors contented themselves, in general, with the occupation of the conquered position, on the left wing of which, close to the flooded meadowland, the 6th Brigade was advancing.

The commander of the Army of the Meuse had observed, since early morning the course of the combat from a height south of Mairy across the valley of the Meuse. He was still persuaded that there was only a rearguard of the enemy at Bazeilles and La Moncelle, the main forces having been directed against the Third Army. It was imperative to help the latter as soon as possible. Orders had been given hours before that, immediately after the taking of the Givonne entrenchments, the Guard Corps should

The Campaign of 1870-71

march to Fleigneux, and the XII Corps to the ridge east of St. Menges via Illy for junction with the Third Army. The Bavarian I Corps was charged to cover in the direction of Sedan the march of the Army of the Meuse.

General von der Tann declared that, according to existing circumstances, he could not execute this command and asked the 8th Division to undertake the task. The division, which had come quite close and some of whose companies had taken part in the latest combats, was ready to undertake, jointly with the Bavarian 3rd Division (5th and 6th Brigades) the problem set before the corps. Security against Sedan seemed thus to be established. The retreat of the Guard and XII Corps was more difficult. For not the entire entrenchment of Givonne, but only its southernmost part had been taken.

The main body of the enemy might be expected above Daigny and then Balan. The XII Corps would meet it going from La Moncelle via Illy to the heights southwest of Menges, and the Guard Corps would encounter it in marching from Givonne to Fleigneux. The latter would, consequently, first drive the enemy from the heights west of Givonne, then march further to Fleigneux and prepare the attack with its artillery, sending only the Guard Cavalry Division up the valley of the Givonne along the hostile front on the road to Fleigneux. The XII Corps could have driven off the enemy standing south of the Fond de Givonne—Haybes road and then advanced to Illy. By an attack of this corps from the south, the Guard Corps from the east, the Third Army from the north and west, the enemy would have been hopelessly driven together.

The XII Corps, however, wanted to reach Illy by a march along the Givonne and took its troops out of the position west of La Moncelle. The 8th Division took its position in a bend on both sides of the La Moncelle—Balan road on Hill 635. The right wing of the Prussian infantry reached a point opposite Petite Moncelle. In rear of the left wing south of Balan stood the Bavarian 6th Brigade, the 5th penetrated into the village and would have hard fights to wage in the park of the chateau before its skirmishers could reach the glacis of Sedan. On the right, on the heights south of Fond De Givonne stood isolated companies. Their fire and that of the Prussian artillery forced the French batteries which were covering the withdrawal, to disappear soon in rear of Hill 656.

While in the corner between Balan and Fond de Givonne the French XII Corps was retreating, the right wing of the I Corps stood on the road from Bazeilles running over Hill 635 northward, fighting against the seven battalions of the 24th Division which had occupied Daigny. In one line, side by side, separated only by Hill 705, stood the Germans, fronting west, and the French, fronting east, in a fierce conflict. This situation of utter harmlessness must be broken up, when the 23rd German Division started at about 1:00 PM, with the 45th Brigade (9 battalions, 4 batteries) on the western valley road, with the 46th Brigade (six battalions) first behind the 45th then on the eastern valley road from Monvillers past La Moncelle.

The advance guard of the 45th Brigade met with unexpected enemies in the woods west of Daigny. Six companies were sent to the left and the march was continued under their cover. The ever increasing violence of the rifle fire decided the Division Commander, General Montbe, to halt the head of the left column at Haybes, and to send 6 more companies to the hill on the left and to deploy with 6 battalions and 4 batteries on the eastern edge of the valley. The 7 battalions of the 24th Division were to hold Daigny. Thirteen battalions, and four batteries were kept in reserve, while 3 battalions only were designated for the attack.

Fortunately the latter were joined by two Grenadier battalions of the Kaiser Franz Regiment.[*] They pursued the enemy when he was driven out of the woods, and ascended by companies and battalions the western heights. Upon reaching the upper edge of the valley, they were met by battalions and batteries in close order.

General Wimpffen had decided to make another attempt to break through the enemy at 1:00 PM. He deemed it possible to drive the already exhausted Bavarians to the Meuse and thus to open a road to Carignan. Vassoigne's Division driven back and likewise exhausted, reinforced by a few regiments of infantry and battalions of Zouaves, was to march through Bazeilles. Goze's

---

[*] They were at the head of the 2nd Guard Division sent to Daigny.

Division was designated for a secondary attack in the direction of Daigny and Grandchamp's Division was sent in rear of the latter as its left echelon.

Emperor Napoleon was invited to take part in the undertaking for the purpose of being the first to ride to freedom at the head of his faithful troops. While Wimpffen was waiting on the site of the old camp at Vieux for the principal person, Goze moved to Daigny and met, close to his goal, the five Saxon-Prussian battalions which had ascended the edge. of the valley between Daigny and Haybes for the protection of Montbe's left flank. At a run, rifles at the hip, firing continually, the deep columns stormed forward. The shells of the rapidly firing German artillery tore gaps in the masses or hurled them down. Swarms only remained and stormed on still firing, but were so broken up by the calmly firing skirmishers that only a few brave men reached the German line, where they were either killed or captured.

Two companies of the 101st Regiment, one battalion of the Rifle Regiment and the two battalions of the Kaiser Franz Regiment pursued the remnants in the direction of Fond de Givonne. As soon as the ridge on either side of the Fond de Givonne—Haybes road had fallen into the hands of the Saxons, the corps artillery units of the 45th Brigade and the divisional artillery were dispatched via Givonne, the 46th Brigade was directed into that village, and the 24th Division was assembled and placed in reserve east of Daigny. Thus the Army of the Meuse and the three Bavarian divisions succeeded after 3:00 PM, in gaining a firm footing on the ridge on the right bank of the Givonne between Bazeilles and Haybes. One Bavarian Division had been sent toward Sedan via Balan. The 1st Guard Division had occupied Givonne on the right, while 10 batteries had gone into position on the heights east of the village. Army headquarters wished to limit itself so far to these results, leaving the rest to the Third Army which had, so far, contributed not a little to the success achieved.

This Army had built during the night two temporary bridges below the bridge of Donchery and had sent detachments across the Meuse for the protection of these three crossings. After crossing the river early in the morning, the XI Corps marched in three columns, in expectation of a battle, against the enemy, who had been observed in retreat between St. Menges and Mezieres, via Montimont, Briancourt, and Marancourt to Vrigne-aux-Bois, the V with one column to Vivier-au-Court.* The Wurttemberg Division threw a bridge across at Dom-le-Mesnil and accompanied the two corps as a left echelon.

As not even a patrol of the enemy was seen during the march, army headquarters ordered a turn to the right toward St. Menges. The execution of the order seemed to raise apprehension. It was to be expected that the defile of the Falizette ravine would be found hermetically closed and that Viney would advance from Mezieres against the rear of the column marching to the right. This general, however, limited himself to secondary undertakings against the crossings of the Meuse which could be easily repulsed by the Wurttemberg division, and the defile at Falizette was found unoccupied.

The leading elements encountered the enemy only at St. Menges. The village was taken and occupied and one company sent to Hill 812 south of the same and two to Floing. The latter succeeded in occupying the northern part of the village against superior hostile forces which held the southern half and the hill in rear of it, while the former occupied a small wood surrounded by walls. Reinforced by several companies, it formed the cover for the 14 batteries of the XI Corps which trotted past the marching column, gradually compressed, going into position on the hill between St. Menges and Floing and opened fire on the French artillery which was in a much more favorable position on the southern ridge between Calvaire d'Illy and Floing.

In the meanwhile, the infantry of the 21st Division had been sent beyond the artillery to Fleigneux and Ily in the upper valley of the Givonne. Under its cover, 12 batteries of the V Corps went into position on the ridge between Fleigneux and Illy. To complete the deployment, the 43rd Brigade was to turn from St. Albert to Floing, the 10th Division to take up position between St. Menges and Fleigneux, the 9th on the Champ dela Grange. The enemy was cut off on the north. Not only vehicles, but even cavalry and

---

* See map on pages 440-441.

The Campaign of 1870-71

artillery, attempting to flee at the last moment via Illy or Fleigneux, were driven back or captured. The problem now was to drive the enemy from the north back to Sedan and toward the Army of the Meuse.

General Wimpffen had thought, in the beginning, that the fights at St. Menges were only demonstrations which were to prevent him from supporting the troops on the lower Givonne. The increasing cannonade in the northwest caused him to inquire personally into the condition of the right of the VII Corps.

Since the commanding general, Douay, recommended the reinforcement of the garrisons of Calvaire d'Illy and Bois de la Carenne, General Wimpffen ordered the two divisions of the I Corps, Herriller's and Pelle's standing in reserve, to be called and himself hastened back to the XII Corps. He found that corps in full retreat and sent word to Douay to support him with all the troops he could spare. The latter sent Mousson's Brigade, attached to his command, and, on repeated request, one division of his corps was also sent in the direction of Bazeilles.

The troops of the I Corps, which were to support the VII, and troops of the VII Corps which were to support the XII, were still occupied in the Bois de la Garenne, in marching to the north and south respectively, when the 26 batteries, on the heights of St. Menges and Fleigneux, directed their full fire against the hostile position and the Calvaire d'Illy. They found a very strong support in the Guard batteries east of Givonne. Many French guns were shattered under the crossfire of these two artillery lines or silenced through the loss of their gunners, a great number of caissons were exploded and the assembled troops forced to retreat into the Bois de la Garenne.

Some isolated guns and batteries still kept their ground and, with the infantry which had remained behind, rendered a storm impossible. Only seven companies of the 82nd and 87th Regiments got as far as Illy and occupied the southern edge. Under their fire and that of the two artillery lines the defenders of the advanced bulwark melted more and more. The Guard Cavalry Division, arriving on its march up the Givonne at La Foulerie, sent two platoons of the 3rd Uhlans of the Guard, followed by one squadron, up the hill. They penetrated to the batteries, and took one gun, but had to return, driven off by the fire from Bois de la Garenne. The retreat of the defenders was, nevertheless, hastened by the bold deed and a company from Illy was able to reach, almost without losses, the Calvaire, take position there and open fire on the well defended northern edge of the wood.

General Douay quickly assembled a few battalions and charged the lost hill repeatedly. Every time he took it, he was forced to abandon it, by the infantry fire from Illy and artillery fire from front, flank, and rear. The 82nd, 87th, and 80th Regiments occupied finally the Calvaire d'Illy and the strip from Hill 920 as far as the Givonne near la Foulerie. Opposite them the enemy held the edge of the wood.

Greater trouble than the Calvaire d'Illy was caused the attacker by the other wing of the French north front. The two companies, occupying the northern part of Floing, held out for two hours without support. Gradually, in spite of the fierce artillery fire, one company after another was sent to their reinforcement from the main position in rear. When sufficient forces had been assembled, a surrounding attack was made against the southern part of the village, the enemy driven back after a bloody battle and the lower slope of the neighboring hill in front of the southeastern edge of the village occupied. The companies of the 83rd, 87th, and 46th Regiments weakened by obstinate fighting, did not feel able to take the steep hill on the southeast and Liebert's Division did not believe that the long disputed village could be torn from the victors. Being in a supposedly impregnable position, it awaited the attack.

To facilitate that attack, the 43rd Brigade had turned from St. Albert to Floing, leaving this point on the east, and deployed against the line: Gaulier—La Maladrie. The advance was made with the right on the Meuse at the south end of Cazal, the left wing straight up the slope. As soon as the Brigade had started its movement, the garrison of Floing joined in the attack of the line: la Maladrie—the cemetery.

It was not an easy thing to climb the steep ascent from point to point, from thicket to thicket, under the fire and counterattacks of the enemy. The attack was repeatedly thrown back to Floing. Lieutenant von Bardeleben succeeded in bringing eight guns into position on Hill 812 close to the slope. The artillery fire from north and west soon mowed down the defenders of the narrow plateau. The turning of Gaulier helped to shake their steadfastness. The Germans succeeded in winning the hill.

As soon as the skirmish lines climbed the steep ascents and reached the edge of the plateau, they were charged by cavalry. Margueritte's Division had come up from the Bois de la Garenne to give a new aspect to the day. The mass of troopers had already been thrown into confusion on the road to Floing by the flank fire of the Prussian batteries and the obstacles in the terrain. Still the charge was executed with impetus and utter self-sacrifice.

The thin lines of skirmishers were overridden at the first impact. Even the battery position was entered. A few detachments charged into Floing and even into St. Albert causing confusion among trains and vehicles. At many points hand to hand fights ensued. With bayonet, saber, and rammers did the Germans defend themselves against the furious attacks of the French. But the calm fire of the steadfast rifles finally broke the strength of the powerful rush. Repeated attacks only. met with stronger resistance since the advancing infantry had reached in large numbers the edge of the plateau and nestled in the abandoned entrenchments.

The 43rd Brigade pursued the retreating enemy and penetrated to the eastern edge of Cazal. Pursuit stopped here, 300 paces from the fortress. The 17th Brigade was sent as support. The former garrison of Floing went in an easterly direction along the road to the Querimont Farm, and struck there the left flank of those portions of Liebert's Division which were endeavoring to hold to the last the center of the French position.

Against these General von Kurchbach directed the 19th Brigade, from Fleigneux along Fleigneux Creek. The brigade was joined by several companies of the XI Corps, which had been employed up to that time as artillery supports, garrisons of villages, etc. They crossed the valley of Illy under severe losses, ascended the northern ridge between Calvaire d'Illy and Floing, drove off the troops at that point, and, with the help of the companies advancing from Floing, and the support of a few batteries which accompanied them, stormed the southern ridge. The enemy was driven back into the Bois de la Garenne. From the Meuse along the eastern edge of

Cazal and the western edge of the woods as far as Calvaire d'Illy, and thence to La Foulerie, the Germans cut the enemy off from the west and north.

The greater portions of the I and VII Corps, together with the reinforcements which had been sent up from the south, infantry, cavalry, and artillery, all in confusion, assembled and sought refuge in the Bois de la Garenne, which rose from the battlefield between the Meuse, Givonne, St. Menges, and Fleigneux, and commanded all the surrounding heights. Upon these masses, artillery fire was directed from the north, northwest, and east. The Guard Artillery, which had advanced closer to the Givonne, fired deliberately by battery and by piece on the woods east of the Sedan—Illy road.

When the guns seemed to have obtained sufficient effect, the advance guard and the 1st Guard Brigade entered the woods from the northeast in the direction of Querimont, while the 45th Brigade penetrated into the southeastern part. The completely disorganized French troops retreated, though not without resistance, in the direction of Sedan. They were met on the road by companies of the XI and V Corps from the west, by the 1st Battalion of the Rifle Regiment from the east, and by two battalions of the Kaiser Franz Regiment which had advanced to the quarries north of Fond de Givonne.

Since Emperor Napoleon refused his cooperation in the "useless undertaking," Wimpffen was forced to make the attempt of breaking through at Bazeilles alone. By an enveloping attack toward Balan, he succeeded, with his superior forces, in gradually driving back the weak Bavarian 5th Brigade and the reinforcements which had been brought to it from the 6th.

This attack, however, went to pieces against the troops arriving from Bazeilles and La Moncelle and under the fire of the Prussian batteries on Hill 635. Repeated orders of the Emperor to enter into negotiations with the enemy accelerated the decision to withdraw. It was high time to bring the battle to a close. The batteries of the Bavarian It Corps, which had remained on the left bank of the Meuse, and of the Wurttemberg Division had opened fire against Sedan itself and the Crown Prince of Saxony had already ordered the XII and the Guard Corps to move their batteries into effective range of the fortress.

The Campaign of 1870-71   461

The negotiations, begun late in the evening, resulted at 11:00 AM the next day in the surrender of 118,000 men, including 14,000 wounded, and 549 guns.

A battle of Cannae had at last been fought, a complete surrounding of the enemy achieved. None of the great generals of the last century had known the course of that battle on the Aufidus. Only its final results floated before their eyes as a goal to be striven for.

King Frederick, when almost sufficient forces were at his disposition at the beginning of the Seven Years' War, invested the Saxons at Pirna, the Austrians at Prague. But with this his means were at an end. His remaining forces were not strong enough to attack on all sides a second Austrian army, which was coming to the rescue. He therefore limited himself at Kolin to containing the front and striking the annihilating blow at the right flank. The Prussian left wing, designated to make this attack, struck only the extended front of the Austrians. The weak Prussian army, moreover was not strong enough for a frontal attack against the strong position; it was enveloped on both flanks and suffered a complete rout.

Taught by experience, Frederick left the front at Leuthen quite free, turned with his 35,000 men the 65,000 of Prince Charles of Lorraine and attacked his left flank. The Austrians hastily faced toward the threatened side in a deep narrow mass and could now be enveloped on their new front from right and left. They were defeated and compelled through this forced change of front, to retreat by the flank under heavy losses.

At Zorndorf the surrounding movement was continued until the Prussian army stood in rear of the Russian army, which hurriedly faced right about. The Russians were driven against the Oder by enveloping attacks, first against the right, then against the left flank. They were almost surrounded. One more attack and they would have been annihilated. But such a last attack could never have been carried through by the exhausted Prussians, even as victors against the power of resistance of the Russians. They would have been decimated and rendered unfit for the continuation of the war. The Russians had a door opened to them by which they could escape. They were not annihilated but eliminated for that campaign.

When they returned the following year, Frederick wanted to attack them from four sides at Kunersdorf and, in spite of their superior numbers, annihilate them. The attack broke against the specially strong position of the enemy and was transformed into an annihilating defeat. One thing had, however, been won by this Cannae: the Russians continued to ruin, burn, and plunder the Prussian territory, but under no circumstances would they allow themselves to be enticed into a battle with Frederick. The mere report "the King is coming" sufficed to make them flee.

Frederick abandoned perforce the attacks from four sides and at Torgau tried an attack against front and rear. The aftack was repulsed, but the fire from front and rear proved insupportable. The Austrians retreated in the night by the only flank left open to them. Only after peace had been concluded with Russia and this peace was followed by an alliance, did Frederick return to the normal attack against front, flank, and rear. The Austrians, however, were able to avoid the surrounding movement in time, since the Russians, to whom was entrusted the frontal or holding attack, limited themselves to a demonstration.

Napoleon likewise preceded his annihilating battles by turning movements which, however, were not executed, like those of Frederick, with a minority in the vicinity of the battlefield, but carrying him after days and weeks in a wide are with vastly superior numbers, into the rear of the enemy. He then attacked enveloping both his wings, or better still, allowed the weaker enemy to attack him, in order to strike the annihilating blow after the exhaustion of his opponent. From the very beginning be made Hasdrubal's decisive attack on the enemy's rear, his principal stroke, just as had been done at Zorndorf and Torgau, enveloped his opponent in rear and on both flanks, and left open to the Austrians and Prussians only the front in the direction of France. Thither they might go, followed by superior forces. This brought at Marengo and Ulm, the immediate annihilation of the enemy. At Jena it had to be attained by a lengthy pursuit. The battle which had begun at Vierzehnheiligen, was brought to a tragic conclusion at Prenzlau and Ratkau. Likewise the Beresina, in the campaign of

The Campaign of 1870-71   463

Moscow, put on the seal of a terrible Cannae, as the piercing at Hanau brought about the conclusion of the gigantic conflict of 1813. In the campaign of Prussian-Eylau the turning movement did not lead against the rear, but against the flank of the enemy, who knew how to escape through a small turning movement likewise. Napoleon stood opposite the weaker enemy. A mass attack against the front, a weak attack against one flank, strong reserves held back, were to bring the solution of the simple problem. It was brought about in a contrary sense by the opponent, who outflanked the weak flanking attack. Frederick the Great failed in many a battle of annihilation, because his forces were too small and he had nevertheless dared the utmost. Napoleon failed at Prussian-Eylau, because he had spent too much on a frontal attack, left too much in reserve and used too little on the decisive flank attack.

A risk lies in every turning and surrounding movement. The opponents of Frederick as well as of Napoleon had to learn this. They also wanted to fight a battle of annihilation, turn the enemy with superior forces and attack him in flank or rear. The plan failed at Rossbach, Liegnitz, and Austerlitz, because the enemy on his part struck the head of the turning columns with superior strength.

Once more did Napoleon fight an almost annihilating battle. The enemy placed himself at Friedland in a position exceedingly favorable for his annihilation. He had his rear against the Alle, the front against an enemy of almost double his strength and, moreover, burnt the bridge which alone could help: him to escape. The annihilation did not entirely succeed because Napoleon attacked only one flank and the front, leaving the other flank free in order to keep strong reserves in case of eventualities. These strong reserves could not decide his battle but could indeed lessen his victories.

According to the principle of Cannae a broad battle line goes forth against a narrower, but generally deeper one. The overlapping wings turn against the flanks, the cavalry preceding them, against the rear. Should the flanks be separated from the center, for some reason or other, it is not necessary to assemble them against the latter in order to continue jointly the march for a surrounding attack, as they can immediately advance, by the shorter road, against flank or rear.

This was what Moltke called "the junction of separated units on the field of battle" and declares it the highest achievement of a general. It is also the most effective and, of course, the most risky. Most generals and almost all able commanders apprehend the danger of the units being defeated before their junction and zealously endeavor to execute the junction of separate units, and on the battlefield itself, but as long as possible before the battle. In this manner they relinquish the decisive result and must be satisfied with a lesser or with no result whatever. The former was experienced by Napoleon at Regensburg, the latter at Gross-Gorschen, for the good of humanity, and Moltke would have experienced the one or the other had he listened to the advice of his contemporaries and subsequent critics and had in the beginning assembled the three armies at Koniggratz on the base line.

There exists, it is true, the danger of having one part defeated, or at least driven back. Cannae itself shows this, also Blucher in 1818 at Lowenberg, and Schwarzenberg at Dresden, and the Prussian First Army might have shown it at Koniggratz had Benedek started early in the morning of the 3rd of July to fall upon Prince Frederick Charles with his entire force. The consequences would have been that the victor would soon have had to leave the vanquished in order to turn against one of the enemies who were threatening his flanks, that the defeated opponent would again advance, and so through apparent victory the final surrounding and annihilation would be materially furthered, if it were not thus made entirely possible.

This is shown by the campaign of 1813 and the wars of 1815 and 1866. In order to defeat one of the separated enemies and destroy him with combined forces, the remainder must be so far away that no interference can be expected from them as at Prague in 1757. Should they come closer, the assembled forces must be divided for parry. Units fight units. The weaker enemy, standing in the center has no preponderance anywhere and is lost as soon as it is possible to assemble the forces of the stronger opponent on the battlefield, as at Leipzig, Waterloo, or Koniggratz. The weaker opponent Frederick, would have been lost at Bunzelwitz, if the Russians and Austrians, intimidated by previous experience, had not renounced the difficult attack.

It is desirable to have, for any kind of Cannae, the numerical

The Campaign of 1870-71

superiority in one's favor. Moltke had to create it in 1870. A large crushing coalition threatened Germany. Moltke held to the principle for which he had fought in 1866: no observation corps, no armies, where there is no enemy. All the 16 corps were destined for France. The French Army assembled in Lorraine and Alsace to cross the Rhine above Karlsruhe and invade South Germany. It was easy for the Germans to stem the stream of the invasion.

As Napoleon in 1806 turned the front of the Prussian army assembled north of the Thuringian forest, by rapid marches from the right, Moltke turned by railway transportation the French front on the upper Rhine and appeared at the central course of the river between Karlsruhe and Koblenz. Napoleon's turning movement drew the Prussians to the banks of the Saale, that of Moltke drew the French to the Saar and Lauter. Both enveloped armies wanted, after they had been completely turned, to attack the turning columns as at Rossbach. This intrepid intention, executed lamely, had a sorry end at Saalfeld in 1806, and would have in 1870 led to the attack on all sides of the French Army had it advanced in a general line: Mayence—Manheim, which would hardly have been permitted to recross the Saar.

A premonition of what might happen held Napoleon back. Thus the German armies were able to advance to the Saar and Lauter. It would have corresponded to the Napoleonic strategy of 1806, if the Germans in 1870 had crossed the Meuse with their right wing and had forced the French, did the latter accept or refuse battle, in a southerly direction to the Rhine and the Swiss frontier. The incomplete railway net of 40 years ago did not allow such an operation. The left wing, to the detriment of the right, had to be made very strong and was to bring the decision. The Third Army should have started two days earlier to throw back the enemy, who were assembling in Alsace, and to attack by turning to the right, the French main army in flank and rear, while the First and Second Armies attacked its front.

The plan failed because the First and Second Armies had started too early and the Third too late. The French Army was defeated in Alsace, but in Lorraine it could retreat to Metz, only slightly damaged. With the great numerical superiority of the Germans it would have been most simple to follow the enemy and to turn with the two overlapping wings against his flanks after a strong cavalry had stopped the retreat. The equipment and armament of the cavalry divisions did not appear to allow such operations at the time, although the 5th Cavalry Division stopped parts of the French Army on 15 and 16 August, at Vionville, from further advance and even forced them to retreat.

The cavalry might have solved the problem given by General von Alvensleben to the III Corps on 16 August, i.e., the halting of the hostile army and, if necessary the gradual retreat toward Verdun, but it also would have gained time for the German Corps to achieve a Cannae by coming up from both sides, or at least from one. Such unusual cavalry operations had not been foreseen. Moltke resolved to turn the enemy with all three armies, accompany him, if necessary in parallel pursuit, on his retreat to Metz, turn to the right at a favorable moment and drive him to the Luxemburg and Belgian frontiers, thus completing the surrounding movement.

The plan was furthered by the halt which the fortress of Metz and the battle of Colombey forced upon the French retreat, but was spoiled by the slowness and irresolution of the movements of the German armies, by the small number of bridges over the Moselle, the unfavorable network of roads on the left bank and not a little by the cautious hesitancy of Bazaine, to give up connection with the protecting fortress. The Marshal was not without reason persuaded that, if Metz were abandoned and the open reached, he would be attacked on all sides and annihilated.

Nevertheless Moltke's intention would probably have been fulfilled if General von Barnekow had been allowed on 16 August to advance through the Bois des Ognons with the 25th Division and through the Bois de Vaux against the road: Rezonville— Point du Jour. It would have been difficult for Bazaine to find a road which was not either barred by the enemy or swept by his fire. He would have gone in the northerly direction that Moltke wished him to take. But since Barnekow had been used, as customary, for fruitless frontal attacks and the 25th Division could only come up very late in his stead, the principal road of retreat was left open to the French. The Germans had to give up the annihilation of the enemy for the time and be satisfied with his investment in Metz, i.e., with hopes for the future.

MacMahon also had to be driven by frontal attacks and attacks against his right flank toward the Belgian frontier. Since, however, the position of the camp near Chalons or Rheims did not offer sufficient advantages for defense, MacMahon wanted to retire to Paris, before being seriously threatened. The difficult situation of the Germans was completely changed in their favor by MacMahon's forced march from Rheims to Stenay and Metz. The problem of the Germans was hence to attack in a turning movement an army of comparatively small strength, marching from west to east, and to drive it against the not distant frontier of Belgium.

Since two corps of the investing army in reserve could be easily brought up, the roads leading east and south could be blocked. Only the retreat west had to be left open for the present. MacMahon wanted to use this only outlet upon hearing of the advance of the Germans, but was immediately driven by Paris to inevitable destruction. Had the ten and one half German corps advanced with the right wing via Longuyon along the Belgian frontier, with the left, via Rethel, over all the existing roads in one line, the four French corps would have been gradually, but surely, driven to the Belgian frontier, whether they marched left or right, forward or back. Should they attack or oppose resistance on one or the other road, the German corps, using these same roads in an opposite direction would give them battle. The remaining corps, however, would march further in the initial direction, first to see if there were enemies in front of them, and further because they would have but one march to make to strike the enemy's flank and give effective support to the neighboring corps.

The Army of the Meuse did not wish to solve so simply the problem, laid before it on 30 August. It had three enemies before it—on the Sommauthe—La Besace road, at Beaumont, on the Mouzon—Stenay road and apparently also at Carignan. Should the two Bavarian corps be left on that road and the Army of the Meuse send the IV Corps to Beaumont, and the Guard and XII Corps to the right bank of the Meuse, it would have driven the three enemies before it and, what was still more important, would have barred their way to east and south. Army headquarters, however, did not wish to divide its forces, but wanted to assemble the five corps, three in the first line and two in the second in front of Beaumont.

This freed at least two enemies who, without evil intent, forced by the measures taken by the Germans and also by their omissions, were forced to attack the flanks of the latter and at least show them what might have happened had there been, in their place, strong, resolute and enterprising enemies. The attack against the enemy at Beaumont, being made not with the power of twenty brigades, as intended, but, through lack of space, by two, the combat of five to one was very unfavorable and might have had a sorry end, if a division commander in his zeal to get at the enemy, had not lengthened the front, forced him to retire by outflanking him and thus somewhat hastened the planned retreat of the French.

The result, bought by severe losses, amounted to just this acceleration. On the whole, the enemy, who must be pitilessly encircled, was freed from all molestation and could retire calmly and without danger in either of two directions. He fortunately, failed to use the advantage offered him by the generous enemy, and, after a short march, halted again in resignation to his fate before the annihilating blow, and, fortunately, Moltke was there to unravel the gigantic mass into which the two German armies had assembled and to render possible an attack from three sides, and later from four.

The numerical superiority of the Germans was so great that they might have executed the investment completely and yet could have given free scope to their inclination to mass troops on the narrowest space on the eastern front. It would not have been expedient to have been so extravagant, had the enemy extended his troops a little more in the strip along the Meuse between Sedan and Mezieres. A lengthening of the German wing beyond Mezieres would then have been necessary. The forces on hand would still have sufficed to send one corps by each road, so that the average length which Moltke wanted to give the marching columns, after the experience of 1870, might have been reached in order to render a timely deployment possible. Whether or not he would have retained this form after the length of a corps column, without trains, had increased from 15 to 29 km. remains unanswered.

A complete battle of Cannae is rarely met in history. For its achievement, a Hannibal is needed on the one side, and a Terentius Varro, on the other, both cooperating for the attainment of the great goal.

A Hannibal must possess, if not a superiority in numbers, the knowledge how to create one. It is desirable for this purpose that the general combine in himself something of a Scharnhorst, a Frederick William, or William I, to weld together a strong army, of a Moltke, to assemble it solely against the principal enemy, of a Frederick the Great, to bring all his guns and rifles into action, of a Frederick the Great or a Napoleon, to direct the principal attack against the flank or rear, of a Frederick the Great or a Moltke to replace the absent Hasdrubal by a natural obstacle or the frontier of a neutral state. Lastly, there are needed subordinate commanders, well trained in their profession, and able to comprehend the intentions of their chiefs.

A Terentius Varro has a great army, but does not do his best to increase and train it. He does not assemble his forces against the principal enemy. He does not wish to vanquish by fire superiority from several sides, but by the weight of masses in narrow and deep formations, selecting for attack the hostile front as being the side most capable of resistance.

All these desirable conditions will not be found combined on either side. A few of Hannibal's qualities and some of the means at his disposal were possessed by other generals. Terentius Varro, on the other side, was always the product of the school. Thus it happened, that, though no real Cannae, with the exception of Sedan, has been fought, there has been a whole series of nearly annihilating battles, and these have always been found at the turning points of history.

About the Author

Count Alfred von Schlieffen (1833-1913) was a Prussian military officer and theorist. He served as the Chief of the Great General Staff from 1891-1905, becoming famous for the Schlieffen Plan, and spent his retirement writing about military history and theory.

www.ingramcontent.com/pod-product-compliance
Lightning Source LLC
Chambersburg PA
CBHW070744020526
44116CB00032B/1927